W9-BKA-583

www.wadsworth.com

www.wadsworth.com is the World Wide Web site for Wadsworth and is your direct source to dozens of online resources.

At *www.wadsworth.com* you can find out about supplements, demonstration software, and student resources. You can also send email to many of our authors and preview new publications and exciting new technologies.

www.wadsworth.com
Changing the way the world learns®

GERALD COREY is a Professor Emeritus of Human Services at California State University at Fullerton, an Adjunct Professor of Counseling and Family Sciences at Loma Linda University, and a licensed psychologist. He received his doctorate in counseling from the University of Southern California. He is a Diplomate in Counseling Psychology, American Board of Professional Psychology; a National Certified Counselor; a Fellow of the American Psychological Association (Counseling Psychology); and a Fellow of the Association for Specialists in Group Work.

Jerry received the Outstanding Professor of the Year Award from California State University at Fullerton in 1991. He teaches both undergraduate and graduate courses in group counseling, as well as courses in experiential groups, the theory and practice of counseling, and professional ethics. He is the author or co-author of 15 textbooks in counseling currently in print, 3 student videos with workbooks, and about 60 articles in professional publications. *Theory and Practice of Counseling and Psychotherapy* has been translated into the Arabic, Indonesian, Portuguese, and Chinese languages. *Theory and Practice of Group Counseling* has been translated into Chinese and Spanish.

Along with his wife, Marianne Schneider Corey, Jerry often presents workshops in group counseling. In the past 25 years the Coreys have conducted group counseling training workshops for mental health professionals at many universities in the United States as well as in Mexico, China, Germany, Belgium, Scotland, Canada, and Ireland. The Coreys also frequently give presentations and workshops at state and national professional conferences. In his leisure time, Jerry likes to travel, hike and bicycle in the mountains, and drive his 1931 Model A Ford.

Other textbooks, student manuals and workbooks, and educational videos by Gerald Corey from Brooks/Cole–Thomson Learning include:

- *Case Approach to Counseling and Psychotherapy,* Sixth Edition (2005)
- *Theory and Practice of Group Counseling,* Sixth Edition (and *Manual*) (2004)
- *Group Techniques,* Third Edition (2004, with Marianne Schneider Corey, Patrick Callanan, and J. Michael Russell)
- *Clinical Supervision in the Helping Professions: A Practical Guide* (2003, with Robert Haynes and Patrice Moulton)
- *Issues and Ethics in the Helping Professions,* Sixth Edition (2003, with Marianne Schneider Corey and Patrick Callanan)
- *Becoming a Helper,* Fourth Edition (2003, with Marianne Schneider Corey)
- *Groups: Process and Practice,* Sixth Edition (2002, with Marianne Schneider Corey)
- *I Never Knew I Had a Choice,* Seventh Edition (2002, with Marianne Schneider Corey)
- *The Art of Integrative Counseling* (2001)

Jerry is co-author, with his daughters Cindy Corey and Heidi Jo Corey, of an orientation-to-college book entitled *Living and Learning,* published by Wadsworth. He is also co-author (with Barbara Herlihy) of *Boundary Issues in Counseling: Multiple Roles and Responsibilities* and *ACA Ethical Standards Casebook*, Fifth Edition, both published by the American Counseling Association.

He has also made three videos on various aspects of counseling practice: (1) *CD-ROM for Integrative Counseling* (2005, with Robert Haynes); (2) *Ethics in Action: CD-ROM* (2003, with Marianne Schneider Corey and Robert Haynes); and (3) *The Evolution of a Group: Student Video and Workbook* (2000, with Marianne Schneider Corey and Robert Haynes). All of these student videos and CD-ROM programs are available through Brooks/Cole–Thomson Learning.

Theories at-a-Glance

The tables in this book compare theories over a range of topics, thereby providing you with the ability to easily compare, contrast, and grasp the practical aspects of each theory. These tables also serve as invaluable resources that can be used to review the key concepts, philosophies, limitations, contributions to multicultural counseling, applications, techniques, and goals of all the theories in this text.

The following chart provides a convenient guide to the tables in this text.

Have an
INTERACTIVE,
PERSONAL
EXPERIENCE
with counseling
theories and skills!

Introducing the
Seventh Edition
of Gerald Corey's
Theory and Practice
of Counseling and Psychotherapy
and its integrated suite
of teaching and learning tools

✳ Theory and Practice of Counseling
and Psychotherapy, Seventh Edition

✳ Student Manual, Seventh Edition

✳ Case Approach to Counseling and
Psychotherapy, Sixth Edition

✳ CD-ROM for Integrative Counseling

✳ The Art of Integrative Counseling

In loving memory of my father and mother,
both of whom continue to live within my spirit:

Joseph Corey, who showed me that it is possible
to overcome adversity

Josephine Corey, who inspired me
to live a meaningful life

Theory and Practice of Counseling and Psychotherapy

SEVENTH EDITION

Gerald Corey

California State University, Fullerton

Diplomate in Counseling Psychology,

American Board of Professional Psychology

Australia • Canada • Mexico • Singapore • Spain
United Kingdom • United States

THOMSON
BROOKS/COLE

Executive Editor: Lisa Gebo
Acquisitions Editors: Julie Martinez, Marquita Flemming
Assistant Editor: Shelley Gesicki
Editorial Assistant: Amy Lam
Technology Project Manager: Barry Connolly
Marketing Manager: Caroline Concilla
Marketing Assistant: Mary Ho
Advertising Project Manager: Tami Strang
Project Manager, Editorial Production: Katy German

Print/Media Buyer: Rebecca Cross
Permissions Editor: Sarah Harkrader
Production Service: Ben Kolstad, The Cooper Company
Text and Cover Designer: Cheryl Carrington
Photo Researcher: Terri Wright
Copy Editor: Kay Mikel
Cover Image: Corbis
Printer: QuebecorWorld—Kingsport

For more information about our products, contact us at:
Thomson Learning Academic Resource Center
1-800-423-0563
For permission to use material from this text, submit a request online at www.thomsonrights.com

Library of Congress Control Number: 2003111399

Student Edition: ISBN 0-534-53605-0

Instructor's Edition: ISBN 0-534-53607-7

International Student Edition: ISBN 0-534-53662-X
(Not for sale in the United States)

Brooks/Cole—Thomson Learning
10 Davis Drive
Belmont, CA 94002
USA

Asia
Thomson Learning
5 Shenton Way #01-01
UIC Building
Singapore 068808

Australia/New Zealand
Thomson Learning
102 Dodds Street
Southbank, Victoria 3006
Australia

Canada
Nelson
1120 Birchmount Road
Toronto, Ontario M1K 5G4
Canada

Europe/Middle East/Africa
Thomson Learning
High Holborn House
50/51 Bedford Row
London WC1R 4LR
United Kingdom

Latin America
Thomson Learning
Seneca, 53
Colonia Polanco
11560 Mexico D.F.
Mexico

Spain/Portugal
Paraninfo
Calle Magallanes, 25
28015 Madrid, Spain

CONTENTS

Preface

This book is intended for counseling courses for undergraduate and graduate students in psychology, counselor education, and the human services and mental health professions. It surveys the major concepts and practices of the contemporary therapeutic systems and addresses some ethical and professional issues in counseling practice. The book aims at teaching students to select wisely from various theories and techniques, which will help them develop a personal style of counseling.

I have found that students appreciate an overview of the divergent contemporary approaches to counseling and psychotherapy. They also consistently say that the first course in counseling means more to them when it deals with them personally. Therefore, I stress the practical application of the material and encourage reflection. Using this book can be both a personal and an academic learning experience.

In this new seventh edition, every effort has been made to retain the major qualities that students and professors have found helpful in the previous editions: the succinct overview of the key concepts of each theory and their implications for practice, the straightforward and personal style, and the book's comprehensive scope. Care has been taken to present the theories in an accurate and fair way. I have also attempted to be simple, clear, and concise. Because many students want suggestions for supplementary reading as they study each therapy approach, I have included a reading list at the end of each chapter.

This edition updates the material and refines existing discussions. Part 1 deals with issues that are basic to the practice of counseling and psychotherapy. Chapter 1 puts the book into perspective, then students are introduced to the counselor—as a person and a professional—in Chapter 2. It is fitting that this material is dealt with before introducing theoretical concepts and counseling techniques because the role of the counselor as a person is highlighted throughout the text. Chapter 3 introduces students to some key ethical issues in counseling practice.

Part 2 is devoted to a consideration of 11 theories of counseling. Each of the theory chapters follows a common organizational pattern, and students can easily compare and contrast the various models. This pattern includes core topics such as key concepts, the therapeutic process, therapeutic techniques and procedures, multicultural perspectives, and summary and evaluation. In this seventh edition, six of the chapters in Part 2 have been largely rewritten to reflect recent trends. The Adlerian therapy, person-centered therapy, behavior therapy, cognitive behavior therapy, reality therapy, and family systems therapy chapters have undergone major revision. Other chapters were revised in relatively minor ways to bring the material up to date. Revisions were based on the recommendations of experts in each theory, and my thanks to them are contained in the acknowledgments. Both expert and general reviewers provided suggestions for adding and deleting material for this edition. Attention was given to current trends and recent developments in the practice of each theoretical approach.

An entirely new chapter on postmodern approaches to therapy (Chapter 13), dealing with social constructionism, solution-focused brief therapy, and narrative therapy, has been added to this edition, and Chapter 12 has been comprehensively revised. This discussion on feminist therapy provides an alternative perspective to most of the other theories covered and also illustrates how ideas and strategies from feminist therapy can be incorporated into the various theoretical approaches.

Each of the 11 theory chapters summarizes key points and evaluates the contributions, strengths, limitations, and applications of these theories. Special attention is given to evaluating each theory from a multicultural perspective as well. The consistent organization of the summary and evaluation sections makes comparing theories easier. Students are given recommendations regarding where to look for further training for all of the approaches. Updated annotated lists of reading suggestions and extensive references at the end of these chapters are offered to stimulate students to expand on the material and broaden their learning through further reading.

In Part 3 readers are helped to put the concepts together in a meaningful way through a discussion of the integrative perspective and consideration of a case study. Chapter 15 pulls together themes from all 11 theoretical orientations. This chapter develops the notion that an integrative approach to counseling practice is in keeping with meeting the needs of diverse client populations in many different settings. Numerous tables and other integrating material help students compare and contrast the 11 approaches. There is more emphasis in this edition on providing a framework for a creative synthesis among the therapeutic models, and students are given guidelines for beginning to formulate their own integration and personal philosophy of counseling.

The "Case of Stan" has been retained in Chapter 16 because it helps readers see the application of a variety of techniques at various stages in the counseling process with the same client. The focus is on an integrative approach that draws from all the therapies and uses a thinking, feeling, and behaving model. This chapter offers a good review of the various theories as applied to a case example.

This text can be used in a flexible way. Some instructors will prefer to follow my sequencing of chapters. Others will prefer to begin with the theory chapters (Part 2) and then deal later with the student's personal characteristics and ethical issues. The topics can be covered in whatever order makes the most sense. Readers are offered some suggestions for using this book in Chapter 1.

In this edition I have made every effort to incorporate those aspects that have worked best in the courses on counseling theory and practice that I regularly teach. To help readers apply theory to practice, I have also revised the Student Manual, which is designed for experiential work. The *Student Manual for Theory and Practice of Counseling and Psychotherapy* still contains open-ended questions and cases, structured exercises, self-inventories, and a variety of activities that can be done both in class and out of class. The seventh edition features a structured overview, as well as a glossary, for each of the theories and chapter quizzes for assessing the level of student mastery of basic concepts.

The newly revised and enlarged *Case Approach to Counseling and Psychotherapy* (Sixth Edition) features experts working with the case of Ruth from each of the 11 therapeutic approaches. The casebook can either supplement this book or stand alone. An additional chapter covering transactional analysis is available on WebTutor.® This material is provided in the same format as the 11 theory chapters in this book and includes experiential exercises that can be completed individually or in small groups. In addition, a case example by Dr. John Dusay, a TA therapist, demonstrates his perspective on working with the case of Ruth.

Accompanying this seventh edition of the text and Student Manual is a *CD-ROM for Integrative Counseling*, in which I demonstrate an integrative approach in counseling Ruth (the central character in the casebook). It contains mini-lectures on how I draw from key concepts and techniques from the 11 theories presented in the book. This CD-ROM has been developed for student purchase and use as a self-study program, and it makes an ideal learning package that can be used in conjunction with this text and the Student Manual. *The Art of Integrative Counseling*, which expands on the material in Chapter 15 of the textbook, also complements this book.

Some professors have found the textbook and the Student Manual to be ideal companions and realistic texts for a single course. Others like to use the textbook and the casebook as companions. With this revision it is now possible to have a complete learning package of four books, along with the *CD-ROM for Integrative Counseling*. The *Case Approach to Counseling and Psychotherapy* and the *Art of Integrative Counseling* can also be used in a case-management practicum, in fieldwork courses, or in counseling techniques courses. The integrated package affords instructors a great deal of flexibility to adapt the materials to their particular style of teaching and to the unique needs of their students.

Also available is a revised and updated *Instructor's Resource Manual*, which includes suggestions for teaching the course, class activities to stimulate interest, transparency masters, and a variety of test questions and final examinations. This instructor's manual is now geared for the following learning package: *Theory and Practice of Counseling and Psychotherapy, Student Manual for Theory and Practice of Counseling and Psychotherapy, Case Approach to Counseling and Psychotherapy, The Art of Integrative Counseling*, and *CD-ROM for Integrative Counseling*.

Acknowledgments

The suggestions I received from the many readers of prior editions who took the time to complete the survey at the end of the book have been most helpful. Many other people have contributed ideas that have found their way into this seventh edition. I especially appreciate the time and efforts of the manuscript reviewers, who offered constructive criticism and supportive commentaries, as well as those professors who have used this book and provided me with feedback that has been most useful in these revisions. Those who reviewed the manuscript of the seventh edition are: Robiner Paul Bedi, University of British Columbia; Charmayne Bohman, California State University, Dominguez Hills; David Carter, University of Nebraska–Omaha; Katheryn Dethlefsen, Amberton University; Carolyn Zerbe Enns, Cornell College; Mimi Lawson, student reviewer, California State University, Fullerton; and Beverly B. Palmer, California State University, Dominguez Hills.

Special thanks are extended to the chapter reviewers, who provided consultation and detailed critiques. Their insightful and valuable comments have generally been incorporated into this edition:

- Chapter 4 (Psychoanalytic Therapy): William Blau, Copper Mountain College and Chapman University; and J. Michael Russell of California State University, Fullerton
- Chapter 5 (Adlerian Therapy): James Bitter, East Tennessee State University; William Nicoll, Florida Atlantic University; and Richard E. Watts, Baylor University
- Chapter 6 (Existential Therapy): William Blair Gould, University of Dubuque; and J. Michael Russell, California State University, Fullerton
- Chapter 7 (Person-Centered Therapy): David Cain, United States International University, San Diego
- Chapter 8 (Gestalt Therapy): Gary Yontef, Private Practice and Gestalt Therapy Institute of the Pacific, Los Angeles
- Chapter 9 (Behavior Therapy): Sherry Cormier, West Virginia University; David C. Guevremont, Woonsocket Education Department; Arnold A. Lazarus, Rutgers University; Raymond G. Miltenberger, North Dakota State University; Patrice Moulton, Northwestern State University in Natchitoches; and Michael D. Spiegler, Providence College
- Chapter 10 (Cognitive Behavior Therapy): Albert Ellis, Albert Ellis Institute, New York; and Frank M. Dattilio, Harvard Medical School and the University of Pennsylvania School of Medicine

- Chapter 11 (Reality Therapy): William Glasser, William Glasser Institute; and Robert Wubbolding, Center for Reality Therapy, Cincinnati, Ohio
- Chapter 12 (Feminist Therapy): Dana Comstock, St. Mary's University, San Antonio; Carolyn Zerbe Enns, Cornell College; Elizabeth Kincade, Indiana University of Pennsylvania; Pam Remer, University of Kentucky; and Susan Seem, SUNY–Brockport; Barbara Herlihy co-authored Chapter 12 with me
- Chapter 13 (Postmodern Approaches): Jennifer Andrews, Loma Linda University; James Bitter, East Tennessee State University; Donald Bubenzer, Kent State University; David Clark, teacher and trainer of postmodern family therapy; Gerald Monk, San Diego State University; Stacey Sinclaire, San Diego State University; Richard E. Watts, Baylor University; and John Winslade, California State University, San Bernardino
- Chapter 14 (Family Systems Therapy): Dorothy Stroh Becvar, Washington University; Douglas Bruenlin, Northwestern University; Frank M. Dattilio, Harvard Medical School and the University of Pennsylvania School of Medicine; Herbert Goldenberg, California State University, Los Angeles; Carmen Knudsen-Martin, Loma Linda University; and Marsha Wiggins Frame, University of Colorado at Denver; James Bitter co-authored Chapter 14 with me

Appreciation goes to Art Pomponio who served as developmental editor for this project. He carefully went over all the pre-revision reviews, organized themes based on the reviews, and made suggestions that were implemented in this edition.

This book is the result of a team effort, which includes the combined talents of several people in the Brooks/Cole–Thomson Learning family. I appreciate the opportunity to work with a dedicated and talented group of professionals in the publishing business. They include Julie Martinez, editor; Amy Lam, editorial assistant, who facilitated the review process; Ben Kolstad of The Cooper Company, who coordinated the production of this book; and Kay Mikel, the manuscript editor of this edition, whose fine editorial assistance kept this book reader-friendly. I also appreciate Madeleine Clarke's work in preparing the index. Their talents, efforts, dedication, and extra time certainly have contributed to the quality of this text. With the professional assistance of these people, the ongoing task of revising this book continues to bring more joy than pain.

—Gerald Corey

Credits

PART 1

Basic Issues in Counseling Practice

Introduction and Overview

 INTRODUCTION

Counseling students can begin to acquire a counseling style tailored to their own personality by familiarizing themselves with the major approaches to therapeutic practice. This book surveys 11 approaches to counseling and psychotherapy, presenting the basic concepts of each approach and discussing features such as the therapeutic process (including goals), the client–therapist relationship, and specific procedures used in the practice of counseling. This information will help you develop a balanced view of the major ideas of various therapists and the practical techniques they employ. I encourage you to keep an open mind and to seriously consider both the unique contributions and the particular limitations of each therapeutic system presented in Part 2.

You will not gain the knowledge and experience needed to synthesize various approaches merely by completing an introductory course in counseling theory. This process will take many years of study, training, and practical counseling experience. Nevertheless, I recommend a personal synthesis as a framework for the professional education of counselors. The danger in presenting one model to which all students are expected to subscribe is that it could limit their effectiveness in working with future clients. Valuable dimensions of human behavior can be overlooked if counselors are restricted to a single theory.

An undisciplined eclectic approach, however, can be an excuse for failing to develop a sound rationale for systematically adhering to certain concepts and to the techniques that are extensions of them. It is easy to pick and choose fragments from the various therapies that merely support one's biases and preconceptions. By studying the models presented here, you will learn how to integrate concepts and techniques from different approaches when defining your own personal synthesis and framework for counseling.

Each therapeutic approach has useful dimensions. It is not a matter of a theory being "right" or "wrong," for every theory offers a unique contribution to understanding human behavior and has unique implications for counseling practice. Accepting the validity of one model does not necessarily imply rejecting seemingly divergent models. There is a clear place for theoretical pluralism, especially in a society that is becoming increasingly diverse.

 WHERE I STAND

My own philosophical orientation is strongly influenced by the existential approach. Because this approach does not prescribe a set of techniques and procedures, I draw techniques from the other models of therapy. I particularly like to use role-playing techniques. When people can reenact scenes from their lives, they often become far more involved than when they merely report anecdotes about themselves. In addition, many techniques I use are derived from cognitive behavior therapy.

I respect the psychoanalytic emphasis on early psychosexual and psychosocial development: One's past plays a crucial role in shaping one's current personality and behavior. Although I challenge the deterministic notion that humans are the product of their early conditioning and, thus, are victims of their past, an exploration of the past is essential, particularly to the degree that the past continues to influence present-day emotional or behavioral difficulties.

I value the cognitive behavioral focus on how our thinking affects the way we feel and behave. These therapies also give weight to current behavior. Although thinking and feeling are important dimensions, it can be a mistake to overemphasize them and not explore how clients are behaving. What people are doing often gives us a good clue to what they really want. I also value the emphasis on specific goals and on encouraging clients to formulate concrete aims for their own therapy sessions and in life. "Contracts" developed by clients are extremely useful, and I frequently either suggest specific "homework assignments" or ask my clients to devise their own.

More approaches have been developing methods that involve collaboration between therapist and client, making the therapeutic venture a shared responsibility. This collaborative relationship, coupled with teaching clients ways to use what they learn in therapy in their everyday lives, empowers clients to go into the world and take an active stance. Although I accept the value of increasing clients' insight and awareness, I consider it essential that they put into practice what they are learning in therapy.

A related assumption of mine is that clients can exercise increasing freedom to choose their future. Although we are surely influenced by our social environment and much of our behavior is a product of learning and conditioning, an increased awareness of these forces enables us to transcend them. Most of the contemporary models of counseling and therapy assume that clients are able to accept personal responsibility and that their failure to do so has largely resulted in their present emotional and behavioral difficulties.

This focus on acceptance of personal responsibility does not imply that we can be anything that we want. We need to recognize that social, environmental, cultural, and biological realities limit our freedom of choice. It is crucial to learn how to cope with the external and internal forces that limit our decisions and behavior. Feminist therapy has contributed an awareness of how external conditions contribute to the problems of women and men and how gender-role socialization leads to a lack of gender equality. Family therapy teaches us that it is not possible to understand the individual apart from the context of the system. Both family therapy and feminist therapy are based on the premise that to understand the individual it is essential to take into consideration the interpersonal dimensions and the sociocultural context, rather than focusing primarily on the intrapsychic domain. Thus, a comprehensive approach to counseling goes beyond focusing on our internal dynamics by addressing those environmental realities that influence us. Those therapies that focus exclusively on intrapsychic dimensions have limited utility in working with culturally diverse populations.

My philosophy of counseling does not include the assumption that therapy is exclusively for the "sick" and is aimed at "curing" psychological "ailments." Such a focus on psychopathology severely restricts therapeutic practice, mainly because it stresses deficits rather than strengths. Instead, I agree with the postmodern approaches (see Chapter 13), which are grounded on the assumption that clients have both internal and external resources to draw upon when constructing solutions to their problems. Indeed, therapists will view clients quite differently if they acknowledge that clients have competencies rather than viewing them as being passively labeled in pathological ways.

Psychotherapy is a process of engagement between two persons, both of whom are bound to change through the therapeutic venture. At its best, this is a collaborative process that involves both the therapist and the client in co-constructing solutions to concerns. Perhaps one of the most significant characteristics of an effective therapist is the quality of *presence,* which is discussed in some detail in Chapters 6, 7, and 8.

Therapists are not in business to change clients, to give them quick advice, or to solve their problems for them. Therapists are able to facilitate healing through a process of genuine dialogue with their clients. The kind of person a therapist is remains the most critical factor affecting the client and promoting change. If practitioners possess wide knowledge, both theoretical and practical, yet lack human qualities of compassion, caring, good faith, honesty, realness, and sensitivity, they are merely technicians. In my judgment those who function exclusively as technicians do not make a significant difference in the lives of their clients. It seems essential to me that counselors explore their own values, attitudes, and beliefs in depth and that they work to increase their own awareness. Throughout the book I encourage you to find ways to personally relate to each of the therapies. By applying this material to yourself personally, you can go beyond a merely academic understanding.

Therapists must be willing to remain open to their own growth and to struggle in their lives if their clients are to believe in them and the therapeutic process. Why should clients seek therapists who are "finished products" and who do not do in their own lives what they expect clients to do in theirs? In short, practitioners teach clients by the behavior they model.

With respect to mastering the techniques of counseling and applying them appropriately and effectively, it is my belief that you are your own very best technique. Your reactions to your clients, including sharing how you are affected in the relationship with them, can be the most useful catalyst in the therapeutic process. It is impossible to separate the techniques you use from your personality and the relationship you have with your clients.

Administering techniques to clients without regard for the relationship variables is ineffective. Techniques cannot substitute for the hard work it takes to develop a constructive client–therapist relationship. Although counselors can learn attitudes and skills and acquire certain knowledge about personality dynamics and the therapeutic process, much of effective therapy is the product of artistry. Counseling entails far more than becoming a skilled technician.

It implies that you are able to establish and maintain a good working relationship with your clients, that you can draw on your own experiences and reactions, and that you can identify techniques suited to the needs of your clients.

I encourage students and those with whom I consult to experience a wide variety of techniques themselves *as clients*. Reading about a technique in a book is one thing; actually experiencing it from the vantage point of a client is quite another. If you have practiced relaxation exercises, for example, you will have a much better feel for how to administer them and will know more about what to look for as you work with clients. If you have carried out real-life homework assignments as part of your own self-change program, you will have a lot more empathy for your clients and their potential problems. Your own anxiety over self-disclosing and confronting personal concerns can be a most useful anchoring point as you work with the anxieties of your clients. The courage you display in your therapy will help you appreciate how essential courage is for your clients.

The human qualities of a therapist are of primary importance, but it is not sufficient to be merely a good person with good intentions. To be effective, a therapist also must have supervised experiences in counseling and sound knowledge of counseling theory and techniques. Further, it is essential to be well grounded in the various *theories of personality* and to learn how they are related to *theories of counseling*. Your conception of the person affects the interventions you make. Another factor, of course, is the individual characteristics of the client. Some practitioners make the mistake of relying on one type of intervention (supportive, confrontational, information giving) for most clients with whom they work. In reality, different clients may respond better to one type of intervention than to another. Even during the course of an individual's therapy, he or she may need different interventions at different times. Practitioners should acquire a broad base of counseling techniques that are suitable for individual clients rather than forcing clients to fit one specialized form of intervention.

 ## SUGGESTIONS FOR USING THE BOOK

Here are some specific recommendations on how to get the fullest value from this book. The personal tone of the book invites you to relate what you are reading to your own experiences. As you read Chapter 2, "The Counselor: Person and Professional," begin the process of reflecting on your needs, motivations, values, and life experiences. Consider how you are likely to bring the person you are becoming into your professional work. You will assimilate much more knowledge about the various therapies if you make a conscious attempt to apply their key concepts and techniques to your own personal growth. Chapter 2 can also help you think about how to use yourself as your single most important therapeutic instrument, and it addresses a number of significant professional issues in counseling practice.

Before you study each therapy in depth in Part 2, I suggest that you at least skim Chapter 15, which provides a comprehensive review of the key concepts from all 11 theories presented in this textbook. I attempt to show how an integration of these perspectives can form the basis for creating your own personal synthesis to counseling. In developing an integrative perspective, it is essential to think holistically. To understand human functioning, it is imperative to account for the physical, emotional, mental, social, cultural, political, and spiritual dimensions. If any of these facets of human experience is neglected, a theory is limited in explaining how we think, feel, and act.

To provide you with a consistent framework for comparing and contrasting the various therapies, the 11 theory chapters share a common format. This format includes a few notes on the personal history of the founder or another key figure; a brief historical sketch showing how and why each theory developed at the time it did; a discussion of the approach's key concepts; an overview of the therapeutic process, including the therapist's role and client's work; therapeutic techniques and procedures; application of the theory to the case of Stan; applications of the theory from a multicultural perspective; a summary and evaluation; suggestions of how to continue your learning about each approach; and suggestions for further reading.

Refer to the Preface for a complete description of other resources that fit as a package and complement this textbook, including *Student Manual for Theory and Practice of Counseling and Psychotherapy, Case Approach to Counseling and Psychotherapy,* and the *CD-ROM for Integrative Counseling.*

 ## OVERVIEW OF THE THEORY CHAPTERS

I have selected 11 therapeutic approaches for this book. Table 1-1 presents an overview of these approaches, which are explored in depth in Chapters 4 through 14. I have grouped these approaches into four general categories.

First are the *analytic approaches. Psychoanalytic therapy* is based largely on insight, unconscious motivation, and reconstruction of the personality. The reason for including the psychoanalytic model (and placing it first) is its major influence on all of the other formal systems of psychotherapy. Some of the therapeutic models are basically extensions of psychoanalysis, others are modifications of analytic concepts and procedures, and still others are positions that emerged as a reaction against psychoanalysis. Many theories of counseling and psychotherapy have borrowed and integrated principles and techniques from psychoanalytic approaches.

Adlerian therapy differs from psychoanalytic theory in many respects, but it can broadly be considered an analytic perspective. Adlerians focus on meaning, goals, purposeful behavior, conscious action, belonging, and social interest. Although Adlerian theory accounts for present behavior by studying childhood experiences, it does not focus on unconscious dynamics.

TABLE 1-1   Overview of Contemporary Counseling Models

Psychoanalytic therapy	Key figure: Sigmund Freud. A theory of personality development, a philosophy of human nature, and a method of psychotherapy that focuses on unconscious factors that motivate behavior. Attention is given to the events of the first 6 years of life as determinants of the later development of personality.
Adlerian therapy	Key figure: Alfred Adler. Following Adler, Rudolf Dreikurs is credited with popularizing this approach in the United States. This is a growth model that stresses taking responsibility, creating one's own destiny, and finding meaning and goals to give life direction. Key concepts are used in most other current therapies.
Existential therapy	Key figures: Viktor Frankl, Rollo May, and Irvin Yalom. Reacting against the tendency to view therapy as a system of well-defined techniques, this model stresses building therapy on the basic conditions of human existence, such as choice, the freedom and responsibility to shape one's life, and self-determination. It focuses on the quality of the person-to-person therapeutic relationship.
Person-centered therapy	Founder: Carl Rogers. This approach was developed during the 1940s as a nondirective reaction against psychoanalysis. Based on a subjective view of human experiencing, it places faith in and gives responsibility to the client in dealing with problems.
Gestalt therapy	Founders: Fritz and Laura Perls. An experiential therapy stressing awareness and integration, it grew as a reaction against analytic therapy. It integrates the functioning of body and mind.
Behavior therapy	Key figures: B. F. Skinner, Arnold Lazarus, and Albert Bandura. This approach applies the principles of learning to the resolution of specific behavioral disorders. Results are subject to continual experimentation. This technique is always in the process of refinement.
Cognitive behavior therapy	Key figures: Albert Ellis founded rational emotive behavior therapy, a highly didactic, cognitive, action-oriented model of therapy that stresses the role of thinking and belief systems as the root of personal problems. A. T. Beck founded cognitive therapy.
Reality therapy	Founder: William Glasser. This short-term approach focuses on the present and stresses a person's strengths. Clients learn more realistic behavior and thus achieve success.
Feminist therapy	This approach grew out of the efforts of many women. A central concept is the concern for the psychological oppression of women. Focusing on the constraints imposed by the sociopolitical status to which women have been relegated, this approach explores women's identity development, self-concept, goals and aspirations, and emotional well-being.

TABLE 1-1   Overview of Contemporary Counseling Models (continued)

Postmodern approaches	A number of key figures are associated with the development of these various approaches to therapy. Social constructionism, solution-focused brief therapy, and narrative therapy all assume that there is no single truth; rather, it is believed that reality is socially constructed through human interaction. These approaches maintain that the client is an expert in his or her own life.
Family systems therapy	A number of significant figures have been pioneers of the family systems approach. This systemic approach is based on the assumption that the key to changing the individual is understanding and working with the family.

The second category comprises the *experiential and relationship-oriented therapies:* the existential approach, the person-centered approach, and Gestalt therapy. The *existential approach* stresses a concern for what it means to be fully human. It suggests certain themes that are part of the human condition, such as freedom and responsibility, anxiety, guilt, awareness of being finite, creating meaning in the world, and shaping one's future by making active choices. This approach is not a unified school of therapy with a clear theory and a systematic set of techniques. Rather, it is a philosophy of counseling that stresses the divergent methods of understanding the subjective world of the person. The *person-centered approach,* which is rooted in a humanistic philosophy, places emphasis on the basic attitudes of the therapist. It maintains that the quality of the client–therapist relationship is the prime determinant of the outcomes of the therapeutic process. Philosophically, this approach assumes that clients have the capacity for self-direction without active intervention and direction on the therapist's part. It is in the context of a living and authentic relationship with the therapist that this growth force within the client is released. The final experiential approach is *Gestalt therapy,* which offers a range of experiments to help clients focus on what they are experiencing now.

Third are the *action therapies,* which include reality therapy, behavior therapy, rational emotive behavior therapy, and cognitive therapy. *Reality therapy* focuses on clients' current behavior and stresses developing clear plans for new behaviors. Like reality therapy, *behavior therapy* puts a premium on doing and on taking steps to make concrete changes. A current trend in behavior therapy is toward paying increased attention to cognitive factors as an important determinant of behavior. *Rational emotive behavior therapy* and *cognitive therapy* highlight the necessity of learning how to challenge dysfunctional beliefs and automatic thoughts that lead to behavioral problems. These cognitive behavioral approaches are used to help people undermine their faulty and self-defeating assumptions and to develop new patterns of acting.

The fourth general approach is the *systems perspective,* of which feminist therapy and family therapy are a part. The systems orientation stresses the importance of understanding individuals in the context of the surroundings that influence their development. To bring about individual change, it is essential to pay attention to how the individual's personality has been affected by his or her gender-role socialization, culture, family, and other systems.

Fifth are the *postmodern approaches:* social constructionism, solution-focused brief therapy, and narrative therapy. These newer approaches challenge the basic assumptions of most of the traditional approaches described here.

In my view, practitioners need to pay attention to what their clients are *thinking, feeling,* and *doing.* Thus, a complete therapy system must address all three of these facets. Some of the therapies included here highlight the role that cognitive factors play in counseling. Others place emphasis on the experiential aspects of counseling and the role of feelings. Still others emphasize putting plans into action and learning by doing. Combining all of these dimensions provides the basis for a powerful and comprehensive therapy. If any of these dimensions is excluded, the therapy approach is incomplete.

 # INTRODUCTION TO THE CASE OF STAN

I am convinced that you will learn a lot by seeing a theory in action, preferably in a live demonstration or as part of experiential activities in which you function in the alternating roles of client and counselor. Many of my students find the case history of the hypothetical client, Stan, helpful in understanding how various techniques are applied to the same person. Stan's case, which describes his life and struggles, is presented here to give you significant background material to draw from as you study the applications of the theories. Each of the 11 theory chapters in Part 2 includes a discussion of how a therapist with the orientation under discussion is likely to proceed with Stan. We will examine the answers to questions such as these:

- What themes in Stan's life merit special attention in therapy?
- What concepts explain the nature of his problems?
- What are the general goals of his therapy?
- What possible techniques and methods would best meet these goals?
- What are some characteristics of the relationship between Stan and his therapist?
- How might the therapist proceed?
- How might the therapist evaluate the process and outcomes of therapy?

In Chapter 16 (which I recommend you read early) I present how I would work with Stan, suggesting concepts and techniques that I would draw on from many of the models (forming an integrative approach).

A single case can illustrate both contrasts and parallels among the approaches. It will also help you understand the practical applications of the 11 models and will provide some basis for integrating them. A summary of the intake interview with Stan, his autobiography, and some key themes in his life are presented here to provide context for making sense of the way therapists with various theoretical orientations might approach working with Stan. Try to sharpen your focus on certain attributes of each approach that can be incorporated into a personalized style of counseling.

Intake Interview and Stan's Autobiography

The setting is a community mental health agency where both individual and group counseling by qualified staff are available. Stan is coming to counseling because he got into trouble because of drinking. He was convicted of driving under the influence of alcohol, and the judge determined that he needed professional help. Because of a course that promoted introspection and self-awareness, Stan recognizes that he does have problems, although he is not convinced that he is addicted to alcohol. Stan arrives for an intake interview and provides the counselor with this information:

> At the present time I'm working in construction. I like building houses, but I'm pretty sure I don't want to stay in construction for the rest of my life. When it comes to my personal life, I've always had a rough time getting along with people. I suppose you could call me a "loner." I like having people in my life, but I just don't seem to know how to go about making friends or getting close to people. Probably the reason I sometimes drink a bit too much is because I'm so scared when it comes to mixing with people. Even though I hate to admit it, when I've been drinking, things don't seem quite so overwhelming. When I look at others, they seem to know the right things to say. Next to them I feel so dumb. I'm afraid that people will be bored with me and that, if they really knew me, they wouldn't want anything to do with me. Sure, I'd like to turn my life around, and I'm trying, but sometimes I just don't know where to begin. That's why I went back to school. Besides my work in construction, I'm also a part-time college student majoring in psychology. I want to better myself. In one of my classes, Psychology of Personal Adjustment, we talked about ourselves and how we wanted to change, and we also had to write an autobiographical paper. Should I bring it in?

That is the essence of Stan's introduction. The counselor says that she very much wants to read his autobiography. Stan hopes it will give her a better understanding of where he has been, where he is now, where he would like to go, and what he wants for himself. Stan brings his autobiography in, and it reads as follows:

> Where I am currently in my life? At 25 I feel that I've wasted most of my life. By now I should be finished with college and into a good job, but instead I'm only a junior. I can't afford to really commit myself to pursuing college full time because I need to work to support

myself. Even though construction work is hard, I like the satisfaction I get when I look at what I helped build.

Although I'd like to build things as a hobby, I want to get into some profession where I could work with people, if I can ever get over my fears of what people think of me. Someday, I'm hoping to get a master's degree in counseling or in social work and eventually work as a counselor with kids who are in trouble. I feel I was helped by someone who cared about me, and I would like to have a similar influence on young people.

At this time I live alone, have very few friends, and feel scared with people my own age or older. I feel good when I'm with kids, because they're so honest. But I worry a lot whether I'm smart enough to get through all the studies I'll need to do before I can become a counselor.

One of my problems is that I drink heavily and frequently get drunk. This happens mostly when I feel alone and when I'm scared that I'll always feel as lonely and isolated as I do now. At first drinking makes me feel better, but later on I really feel rotten. I used to do drugs heavily, and once in a while I still use drugs.

People really scare me, and I feel overwhelmed when I'm around strong and attractive women. I feel all cold, sweaty, and terribly nervous when I'm with a woman. Maybe I think they're judging me, and I know they'll find out that I'm not much of a man. I'm afraid I won't measure up to being a *man*—always having to be strong, tough, and perfect. I'm not any of those, so I often wonder if I'm adequate as a man. I really have trouble seeing myself as sexually adequate. When I do have sex, I get uptight and worry that I won't be able to perform, and then I really feel terrible.

I feel anxiety much of the time, particularly at night. Sometimes I get so scared that I feel like running, but I just can't move. It's awful, because I often feel as if I'm dying at times like this. Then I fantasize about committing suicide, and I wonder who would care. Sometimes I see my family coming to my funeral feeling very sorry that they didn't treat me better. I even made a weak attempt to do myself in a couple of years ago. Much of the time I feel guilty that I haven't worked up to my potential, that I've been a failure, that I've wasted much of my time, and that I let people down a lot. I can really get down on myself and wallow in my guilt, and I feel *very depressed*. At times like this I think about how rotten I am, how I'll never be able to change, and how I'd be better off dead. Then I wouldn't have to hurt anymore, and I wouldn't want anything either. It's very difficult for me to get close to anyone. I can't say that I've ever loved a person, and I know that I've never felt fully loved or wanted.

Everything is not bleak. I did have enough guts to leave a lot of my shady past behind me, and I did get into college. I like my determination—I *want* to change. I'm tired of feeling like a loser, and I know that nobody is going to change my life for me. It's up to me to get what I want. Even though I feel scared a lot, I like it that I can *feel* my feelings and that I'm willing to take risks. I hate being a quitter.

What was my past like? What are some significant events and turning points in my life? A major turning point was the confidence my supervisor had in me at the youth camp where I worked the past few summers. He helped me get my job, and he also encouraged me to go to college. He said he saw a lot of potential in me for being able to work well with young people. That was hard for me to really believe, but his faith inspired me to begin to believe in myself. Another turning point was my marriage and divorce. This "relationship" didn't last long before my wife left me. Wow, that really made me wonder about what kind of man I was! She was a strong and dominant woman who was always telling me how worthless I was and how she couldn't stand to get near me. We met in a gambling casino in Las Vegas, and we tied the knot shortly after that. We had sex only a few times, and most of the time I was impotent. That was hard to take—a real downer! I'm so afraid to get close to a woman. I'm afraid she'll control me. My parents never got a divorce, but I wish they had. They fought most of the time. I should say, my mother did most of the fighting. She was dominant and continually bitching at my father, whom I always saw as weak, passive, and mousy next to her. He would *never* stand up to her. There were four of us kids at home. My folks always compared me unfavorably with my older sister (Judy) and older brother (Frank). They were "perfect" children, successful honor students. My younger brother (Karl) and I fought a lot, and he was the one who was spoiled rotten by them. I really don't know what happened to me and how I turned out to be the failure of the bunch.

In high school I got involved with the wrong crowd and took a lot of drugs. I was thrown into a youth rehabilitation facility for stealing. Later I was expelled from regular school for fighting, and I landed in a continuation high school, where I would go to school in the mornings and have afternoons for on-the-job training. I got into auto mechanics and was fairly successful and even managed to keep myself employed for 3 years as a mechanic.

Back to my parents. I remember my father telling me: "You're really dumb. Why can't you be like your sister and brother? You'll never amount to anything! Why can't you ever do anything right?" And my mother treated me much the way she treated my father. She would say: "Why do you do so many things to hurt me? Why can't you grow up and be a man? You were a mistake. I wish I hadn't had you! Things are so much better around here when you're gone." I recall crying myself to sleep many nights, feeling so terribly alone and filled with anger and hate. And feeling so disgusted with myself. There was no talk of religion in my house, nor was there any talk about sex. In fact, I always find it hard to imagine my folks ever having sex.

Where would I like to be 5 years from now? What kind of person do I want to become, and what changes do I most want in my life? Most of all, I would just like to start feeling better about myself. I would really like to be able to stop drinking altogether and still feel good. I have an inferiority complex, and I know how to put myself down. I want to like myself much more than I do now. I hope I can learn to love at least a few other people, most of all, women. I want to lose my fear that women can destroy me. I would like to feel equal with others and not always have to feel apologetic for my existence. I don't want to suffer from this anxiety and guilt. And I hope that I can begin to think of myself as a good person. I really want to become a good counselor with kids, and to do this I know I'm going to have to change. I'm not certain how I'll change or even what all the changes are I hope for. I do know that I want to get free of my self-destructive tendencies and learn to trust people more. Maybe when I begin to like myself more, I'll be able to trust that others might find something about me that is worth liking.

Effective therapists, regardless of their theoretical orientation, would pay attention to suicidal ideation. In his autobiography Stan says, "I fantasize about committing suicide, and I wonder who would care." At times he also doubts that he will ever change and wonders if he'd be better off dead. Before embarking on the therapeutic journey, the therapist would certainly make an assessment of Stan's current ego strength, which would include a discussion of his suicidal thoughts and feelings.

Overview of Some Key Themes in Stan's Life

A number of themes appear to represent core struggles in Stan's life. Here are some of the statements we can assume that he may make at various points in his therapy and themes that will be addressed from the theoretical perspectives in Chapters 4 through 14:

- Although I'd like to have people in my life, I just don't seem to know how to go about making friends or getting close to people.
- When I'm with other people, I'm afraid of looking stupid.
- I'd like to turn my life around, but I don't know where to start.
- I'd like to find a career working with people so that I can make a difference in their lives.
- I worry about whether I'm smart enough to complete my studies and do what's needed to become a counselor.

- I know when I feel alone, scared, and overwhelmed, I drink heavily to feel better.
- When I'm around a woman, I feel nervous. I'm sure she's judging me and will think I'm not a real man.
- I'm so afraid of getting close to a woman. If I were to get close, my fear is that she would overwhelm me.
- My divorce made me wonder what kind of man I am.
- Sometimes at night I feel a terrible anxiety and feel as if I'm dying.
- There have been times when I've fantasized committing suicide, and I wondered who would care.
- I often feel guilty that I've wasted my life, that I've failed, and that I've let people down. At times like this, I get really depressed.
- I like it that I have determination and that I really want to change. I hate being a quitter.
- I remember hearing from my parents that I couldn't do much of anything right.
- My parents compared me unfavorably with my older sister and brother. I've never felt that I could measure up!
- I've never really felt loved or wanted by my parents.
- I'd like to feel equal with others and not always have to feel apologetic for my existence.
- I'd like to get rid of my self-destructive tendencies and learn to trust people more.
- Although I put myself down a lot, I'd like to feel better about myself.

In Chapters 4 through 14, you can assume that a practitioner representing each of the theories has read Stan's case and is familiar with key themes in his life. Each therapist will illustrate the concepts and techniques of the particular approach as it applies to working with Stan. In addition, in these chapters you are asked to think about how you would continue counseling him from the different perspectives. In doing so, you may find it useful to refer to the introductory material given here and to Stan's autobiography as well.

Chapter 2

The Counselor: Person and Professional

INTRODUCTION

One of the most important instruments you have to work with as a counselor is yourself as a person. In preparing for counseling, you will acquire knowledge about the theories of personality and psychotherapy, learn diagnostic and intervention techniques, and discover the dynamics of human behavior. Such knowledge and skills are essential, but by themselves they are not sufficient for establishing and maintaining effective therapeutic relationships. To every therapy session we bring our human qualities and the experiences that have influenced us. In my judgment this human dimension is one of the most powerful determinants of the therapeutic encounter.

A good way to begin your study of contemporary counseling theories is by reflecting on the personal issues raised in this chapter. Once you have studied the 11 theories of counseling, reread this chapter and reevaluate ways in which you can work on your development as a person. Your own needs, motivations, values, and personality traits can either enhance or interfere with your effectiveness as a counselor. By remaining open to self-evaluation, you not only expand your awareness of self but also build the foundation for developing your abilities as a professional. The theme of this chapter is that the *person* and the *professional* are intertwined entities that cannot be separated in reality.

THE COUNSELOR AS A THERAPEUTIC PERSON

Because counseling is an intimate form of learning, it demands a practitioner who is willing to shed stereotyped roles and be a real person in a relationship. It is precisely within the context of such a person-to-person relationship that the client experiences growth. If as counselors we hide behind the safety of our professional role, our clients will keep themselves hidden from us. If we become merely technical experts and leave our own reactions, values, and self out of our work, the result is likely to be sterile counseling. It is through our own genuineness and our aliveness that we can significantly touch our clients. If we make life-oriented choices, radiate a zest for life, and are real in our relationships with our clients, we can inspire them to develop these internal resources. This does not mean that we are self-actualized persons who have "made it" or that we are without our problems. Rather, it implies that we are willing to look at our lives and make the changes we want. Because we affirm that changing is worth the risk and the effort, we hold out hope to our clients that they can become their own person and can like the person they are becoming.

In short, as therapists we serve as models for our clients. If we model incongruent behavior, low-risk activity, and remain hidden, we can expect our clients to imitate this behavior. If we model realness by engaging in appropriate self-disclosure, our clients will tend to be honest with us in the therapeutic relationship. To be sure, counseling can be for better or for worse. Clients can become more of what they are capable of becoming, or they can become less than they might be. In my judgment the degree of aliveness and psychological health of the counselor are crucial variables that determine the outcome.

Personal Characteristics of Effective Counselors

In thinking about counselors who are therapeutic, I have identified a cluster of personal qualities and characteristics. I do not expect any therapist to fully exemplify all these traits. Rather, for me the willingness to struggle to become a more therapeutic person is the crucial quality. This list is intended to stimulate you to examine your ideas of what kind of person can make a significant difference in the lives of others.

- *Effective counselors have an identity.* They know who they are, what they are capable of becoming, what they want out of life, and what is essential.
- *They respect and appreciate themselves.* They can give help and love out of their own sense of self-worth and strength.
- *They are able to recognize and accept their own power.* They feel adequate with others and allow others to feel powerful with them.
- *They are open to change.* They exhibit a willingness and courage to leave the security of the known if they are not satisfied with what they have. They make decisions about how they would like to change, and they work toward becoming the person they would like to become.
- *They are making choices that shape their lives.* They are aware of early decisions they made about themselves, others, and the world. They are not the victims of these early decisions, for they are willing to revise them if necessary.
- *They feel alive, and their choices are life-oriented.* They are committed to living fully rather than settling for mere existence.
- *They are authentic, sincere, and honest.* They do not hide behind masks, defenses, sterile roles, and facades.
- *They have a sense of humor.* They are able to put the events of life in perspective. They have not forgotten how to laugh, especially at their own foibles and contradictions.
- *They make mistakes and are willing to admit them.* They do not dismiss their errors lightly, yet they do not choose to dwell on misery.
- *They generally live in the present.* They are not riveted to the past, nor are they fixated on the future. They are able to experience the "now" and be present with others in the now.
- *They appreciate the influence of culture.* They are aware of the ways in which their own culture affects them, and they respect the diversity of values espoused by other cultures. They are also sensitive to the unique differences arising out of social class, race, sexual orientation, and gender.

- *They have a sincere interest in the welfare of others.* This concern is based on respect, care, trust, and a real valuing of others.
- *They become deeply involved in their work and derive meaning from it.* They can accept the rewards flowing from their work, yet they are not slaves to their work.
- *They are able to maintain healthy boundaries.* Although they strive to be fully present for their clients, they don't carry the problems of their clients around with them during leisure hours. They know how to say no, which allows them to keep a balance in their lives.

This picture of the characteristics of effective counselors might appear monumental and unrealistic. Who could ever be all those things? Certainly I do not fit this bill! Do not think of these personal characteristics from an all-or-nothing perspective; rather, consider them on a continuum. A given trait may be highly characteristic of you, at one extreme, or it may be very uncharacteristic of you, at the other extreme. I have presented this picture of the therapeutic person with the hope that you will examine it and develop your own concept of what personality traits you think are essential to strive for to promote your own personal growth.

 ## PERSONAL COUNSELING FOR THE COUNSELOR

Discussion of the counselor as a therapeutic person raises another issue debated in counselor education: whether people should be required to participate in counseling or therapy before they become practitioners. My view is that counselors can benefit greatly from the experience of being clients at some time. Such self-exploration can increase your level of self-awareness. This experience can be obtained before your training, during it, or both, but I strongly support some form of personal exploration as vital preparation in learning to counsel others.

Such counseling is not to be viewed as an end in itself but as a means to help a potential counselor become a more therapeutic person who will have a greater chance of having an impact on clients. Opportunities for self-exploration can be instrumental in helping counselors-in-training assess their motivations for pursuing this profession. Examining your values, needs, attitudes, and experiences can illuminate what you are getting from helping others. It is important to know why you want to intervene in the lives of others. Self-exploration can help counselors avoid the pitfalls of continually giving to others yet finding little personal satisfaction from their efforts. There is value in continuing individual or group counseling as you begin to practice as professionals.

As therapists we are forced to confront our unexplored blocks related to loneliness, power, death, sexuality, our parents, and so on. This does not mean that we need to be free of conflicts before we can counsel others, but we should be aware of what these conflicts are and how they are likely to affect us as counselors. For example, if you have great difficulty dealing with anger, chances are that you will not be able to assist clients in dealing with their anger.

When I began counseling others, old wounds were opened and feelings I had not explored in depth came to the surface. It was difficult for me to encounter a client's depression, because I had failed to come to terms with the way I had escaped from my own depression. Thus, I did my best to cheer up depressed clients by talking them out of what they were feeling, mainly because of my own inability to deal with such feelings. In the years when I began working as a counselor in a university counseling center, I frequently wondered what I could do for my clients. I often had no idea of what, if anything, my clients were getting from our sessions. I couldn't tell if they were getting better, staying the same, or getting worse. It was very important to me to note progress and see change in my clients. Because I did not see immediate results, I had many doubts about whether I could become an effective counselor. What I did not understand at the time was that my clients needed to struggle to find their own answers. It was *my need* to see them feel better quickly, for then I would know that I was helping them. It never occurred to me that clients often feel worse as they give up their defenses and open themselves to their pain. It took me some time to appreciate the courage involved in becoming fully engaged in the therapeutic venture.

Personal therapy can be instrumental in healing the healer. If student counselors are not actively involved in the pursuit of healing their own psychological wounds, they will probably have considerable difficulty entering the world of a client. As counselors we can take our clients no further than we have been willing to go in our own lives. If we are not committed personally to the value of struggling, we will not convince clients that they should pay the price of their struggle. Through being clients ourselves, we have an experiential frame of reference to view ourselves as we are. This provides a basis for compassion for our clients, for we can draw on our own memories of reaching impasses in our therapy, of both wanting to go further and at the same time wanting to stay where we are. Our own therapy can help us develop patience with our patients! We learn what it feels like to deal with anxieties that are aroused by self-disclosure and self-exploration. We may experience transference and thus know firsthand how it is to view our therapist as a parent figure. Being willing to participate in a process of self-exploration can reduce the chances of assuming an attitude of arrogance or of being convinced that we have "arrived" as a person. Indeed, experiencing counseling as a client is very different from merely reading about the counseling process.

Yalom (2003) strongly recommends that trainees engage in their own personal therapy, contending that it is the most important part of psychotherapy training. His rationale is based on the assumption that the therapist's most valuable instrument is his or her own self. Yalom believes there is no better way for trainees to learn about psychotherapy than by entering it as clients, and he suggests a return to therapy at various phases in life: "Self-exploration is a lifelong process, and I recommend that therapy be as deep and prolonged as possible—and that the therapist enter therapy at many different stages of life" (p. 41).

The main reason for having students-in-training receive some form of psychotherapy is to help them learn to deal with countertransference (the process of seeing themselves in their clients, of overidentifying with their clients, or of meeting their needs through their clients). Recognizing the manifestations of their countertransference reactions is one of the most essential abilities of effective counselors. Unless counselors are aware of their own conflicts, needs, assets, and liabilities, they can use the therapy hour more for their own purposes than for being available for their clients, which becomes an ethical issue. Unaware counselors are in danger of being carried away on the client's emotional tidal wave, which is of no help to themselves or their client. It is unrealistic to think that counselors can completely rid themselves of any traces of countertransference or that they can ever fully resolve certain issues from the past. But they can become aware of the signs of these reactions and can deal with these feelings in their own therapy and supervision sessions.

 ## THE COUNSELOR'S VALUES AND THE THERAPEUTIC PROCESS

As alluded to in the last section, the importance of self-exploration for counselors carries over to the values and beliefs they hold. My experience in teaching and supervising students of counseling shows me how crucial it is that students be aware of their values, of where and how they acquired them, and of how their values influence their interventions with clients. An excellent focus for the process of self-searching is examining how your values are likely to affect your work as a counselor.

The Role of Values in Counseling

A core issue is the degree to which counselors' values should enter into a therapeutic relationship. As counselors we are often taught not to let our values show lest they bias the direction clients are likely to take. Yet we are simply not value-neutral, nor are we value-free; our therapeutic interventions rest on core values. It is neither possible nor desirable for counselors to be neutral with respect to values in the counseling relationship. Although our values do influence the way we practice, it is possible to maintain a sense of objectivity.

Counselors need to guard against the tendency to assume either of two extreme positions. At one extreme are counselors who hold definite and absolute beliefs and see it as their job to exert influence on clients to adopt their values. These counselors tend to direct their clients toward the attitudes and values they judge to be "right." At the other extreme are counselors who maintain that they should keep their values out of their work and that the ideal is to strive for value-free counseling. Because these counselors are so intent on not influencing their clients, they run the risk of immobilizing themselves.

From my perspective, the counselor's role is to create a climate in which clients can examine their thoughts, feelings, and actions and eventually arrive at solutions that are best for them. Your job is to assist individuals in finding answers that are most congruent with their own values. What seems critical is that you be aware of the nature of your values and how your beliefs and standards operate on the interventions you make with clients. Your function as a counselor is not to persuade or convince clients of the proper course to take but to help them assess their behavior so that they can determine the degree to which it is working for them. If clients acknowledge that what they are doing is not working, it is appropriate to challenge them to develop new ways of behaving to help them move closer to their goals. Of course, this process of challenging clients is done with full respect given to their right to decide which values they will use as a framework for living. Individuals seeking counseling are the ones who need to wrestle with clarifying their own values and goals, making informed decisions, choosing a course of action, and assuming the responsibility and accountability for the decisions they make. Because counseling is a process that involves teaching clients how to deal with their problems and find their own solutions based on their value system, it is essential that the counselor not short-circuit a client's exploration.

The question of the influence of the counselor's values on the client has ethical implications. Goals and therapeutic methods are expressions of the counselor's philosophy of life. Even though therapists should not impose specific values, therapists do implement a philosophy of counseling, which is, in effect, a philosophy of life. Counselors communicate their values by the therapeutic goals to which they subscribe and by the procedures they employ to reach these goals.

The Role of Values in Developing Therapeutic Goals

Who should establish the goals of counseling? Almost all theories are in accord that it is largely the client's responsibility to decide these objectives, collaborating with the therapist as therapy proceeds. Counselors have general goals, which are reflected in their behavior during the therapy session, in their observations of the client's behavior, and in the interventions they make. It is critical that the general goals of counselors be congruent with the personal goals of the client.

In my view therapy ought to begin with an exploration of the client's expectations and goals. Clients initially tend to have vague ideas of what they expect from therapy. They may be seeking solutions to problems, they may want to stop hurting, they may want to change others so they can live with less anxiety, or they may seek to be different so that some significant persons in their lives will be more accepting of them. In some cases clients may have no goals; they are in the therapist's office simply because they were sent for counseling by their parents, probation officer, or teacher. All they want is to be left alone.

So where can a counselor begin? The intake session can be used most productively to focus on the client's goals or lack of them. The therapist may begin by asking questions such as these: What do you expect from counseling? Why are you here? What do you want? What do you hope to leave with? How is what you are presently doing working for you? What aspects of yourself or your life situation would you most like to change?

Setting goals is inextricably related to values. The client and the counselor need to explore what they hope to obtain from the counseling relationship, whether they can work with each other, and whether their goals are compatible. Even more important, it is essential that the counselor be able to understand, respect, and work within the framework of the client's world rather than forcing the client to fit neatly into the therapist's scheme of values.

 ## BECOMING AN EFFECTIVE MULTICULTURAL COUNSELOR

Part of the process of becoming an effective counselor involves learning how to recognize diversity issues and shaping your counseling practice to fit the client's worldview. It is an ethical obligation for counselors to develop sensitivity to cultural differences if they hope to make interventions that are consistent with the values of their clients. The therapist's role is to assist clients in making decisions that are congruent with the clients' worldview, not to convince clients to live by the therapist's values.

Diversity in the therapeutic relationship is a two-way street. Counselors bring their own heritage with them to their work, so you need to recognize the ways in which cultural conditioning has influenced the directions you take with your clients. Unless the social and cultural context of clients is taken into consideration, it is most difficult to appreciate the nature of their struggles. Indeed, some clients have a difficult time in seeking and accepting professional help. Counseling students often value characteristics such as making their own choices, expressing what they are feeling, being open and self-revealing, and striving for independence. Yet some clients may not share these goals. Clients may be very slow to disclose and have different expectations about counseling than the therapist has. It is essential that counselors become aware of how clients from diverse cultures may perceive them as therapists, as well as how clients may perceive the value of formal helping. It is the task of counselors to determine whether the assumptions they have made about the nature and functioning of therapy are appropriate for culturally diverse populations.

Clearly, effective counseling must take into account the impact of culture. Culture is, quite simply, the values and behaviors shared by a group of individuals. It is important to realize that culture refers to more than ethnic or racial heritage; culture also includes factors such as age, gender, religion, sexual orientation, physical and mental ability, and socioeconomic status.

Acquiring Competencies in Multicultural Counseling

Effective counselors understand their own cultural conditioning, the conditioning of their clients, and the sociopolitical system of which they are a part. Acquiring this understanding begins with counselors' awareness of any cultural values, biases, and attitudes they may hold. A big part of becoming a diversity-competent counselor involves challenging the values we hold and how such values are likely to influence our practice with diverse clients. Furthermore, becoming a diversity-competent practitioner is not something that we arrive at once and for all; rather, it is an ongoing process.

Sue, Arredondo, and McDavis (1992) and Arredondo and her colleagues (1996) have developed a conceptual framework for competencies and standards in multicultural counseling. Their dimensions of competency involve three areas: (1) beliefs and attitudes, (2) knowledge, and (3) skill. For a more in-depth treatment of multicultural counseling and therapy competence, refer to D. W. Sue and Sue's (2003) excellent book *Counseling the Culturally Diverse: Theory and Practice*.

BELIEFS AND ATTITUDES   First, effective counselors have moved from being culturally unaware to ensuring that their personal biases, values, or problems will not interfere with their ability to work with clients who are culturally different from them. They believe cultural self-awareness and sensitivity to one's own cultural heritage are essential for any form of helping. Counselors are aware of their positive and negative emotional reactions toward other racial and ethnic groups that may prove detrimental to establishing collaborative helping relationships. They seek to examine and understand the world from the vantage point of their clients. They respect clients' religious and spiritual beliefs and values. They are comfortable with differences between themselves and others in terms of race, ethnicity, culture, and beliefs. Rather than maintaining that their cultural heritage is superior, they are able to accept and value cultural diversity. They realize that traditional theories and techniques may not be appropriate for all clients or for all problems. Culturally skilled counselors monitor their functioning through consultation, supervision, and further training or education.

KNOWLEDGE   Second, culturally effective practitioners possess certain knowledge. They know specifically about their own racial and cultural heritage and how it affects them personally and professionally. Because they understand the dynamics of oppression, racism, discrimination, and stereotyping, they are in a position to detect their own racist attitudes, beliefs, and feelings. They understand the worldview of their clients, and they learn about their clients' cultural backgrounds. They do not impose their values and expectations on their clients from differing cultural backgrounds and avoid stereotyping clients. Culturally skilled counselors understand that external sociopolitical forces influence all groups, and they know how these forces operate with respect to the treatment of minorities. These practitioners are aware of the institutional barriers that prevent minorities from utilizing the mental health services available in their communities. They possess knowledge about the historical background, traditions, and values of the client populations with whom they work. They know about minority family structures, hierarchies, values, and beliefs. Furthermore, they are knowledgeable about community characteristics and resources. Culturally skilled counselors know how to help clients make use of indigenous support systems. In areas where they are lacking in knowledge, they seek resources to assist them. The greater their depth and breadth of knowledge of culturally diverse groups, the more likely they are to be effective practitioners.

SKILLS AND INTERVENTION STRATEGIES   Third, effective counselors have acquired certain skills in working with culturally diverse populations. Counselors take responsibility for educating their clients to the way the therapeutic process works, including matters such as goals, expectations, legal rights, and the counselor's orientation. Multicultural counseling is enhanced when practitioners use methods and strategies and define goals consistent with the life experiences and cultural values of their clients. Such practitioners modify and adapt their interventions to accommodate cultural differences. They do not force their clients to fit within one counseling approach, but they recognize that counseling techniques may be culture-bound. They are able to send and receive both verbal and nonverbal messages accurately and appropriately. They become actively involved with minority individuals outside the office (community events, celebrations, and neighborhood groups). They are willing to seek out educational, consultative, and training experiences to enhance their ability to work with culturally diverse client populations. They consult regularly with other multiculturally sensitive professionals regarding issues of culture to determine whether or where referral may be necessary.

Incorporating Culture Into Counseling Practice

Although increased attention is being given to course work in multicultural issues, many practitioners remain uncertain about how and when to incorporate multicultural awareness and skills in their clinical practice (Cardemil & Battle, 2003). One way to actively incorporate a multicultural dimension is to initiate open discussions with clients regarding issues of race and ethnicity. Cardemil and Battle contend that doing so enhances the therapeutic alliance and promotes better treatment outcomes. To provoke thought and stimulate conversation about race and ethnicity, they suggest that therapists incorporate these recommendations throughout the therapeutic process:

- Suspend preconceptions about clients' race/ethnicity and that of their family members. Avoid making incorrect assumptions that could impede the development of the therapeutic relationship. Ask clients early in the therapy process how they identify their race/ethnicity.

- Engage clients in conversations about race and ethnicity to avoid stereotyping and making faulty assumptions. Clients may be quite different from other members of their racial/ethnic group.
- Address how racial/ethnic differences between therapist and client might affect the therapy process. Although it is not possible to identify every between-group difference that could surface during the course of therapy, therapists need to be willing to consider the relevance of racial/ethnic differences with clients.
- Acknowledge that power, privilege, and racism can affect interactions with clients. Having discussions in these areas is invaluable in strengthening the therapeutic relationship.
- Recognize that the more comfortable therapists are with conversations about race and ethnicity, the more easily they can respond appropriately to clients who may be uncomfortable with such discussions.
- Be open to ongoing learning about cultural factors and how they may affect therapeutic work. Be willing to identify and examine your own personal worldview, assumptions, and personal prejudices about other racial/ethnic groups. Realize that this skill does not develop quickly or without effort.

It is unrealistic to expect a counselor to know everything about the cultural background of a client, but some understanding of the client's cultural and ethnic background is essential. There is much to be said for letting clients teach counselors about relevant aspects of their culture. It is a good idea for counselors to ask clients to provide them with the information they will need to work effectively. Incorporating culture into the therapeutic process is not limited to working with clients from a certain ethnic or cultural background. Instead, it is critical that therapists take into account the worldview and background of every client. Failing to do this seriously restricts the potential impact of the therapeutic endeavor.

In the case of individuals who have the experience of living in more than one culture, it can be very useful to assess the degree of acculturation and identity development that has taken place. Clients often have allegiance to their culture of origin, and yet they may find certain characteristics of their new culture attractive. They may experience conflicts in integrating the two cultures in which they live. These core struggles can be explored productively in the therapeutic context if the counselor understands and respects this cultural conflict.

WELCOMING DIVERSITY   Counseling is by its very nature diverse in a multicultural society, so it is easy to see that there are no ideal therapeutic approaches. Instead, different theories have distinct features that have appeal for different cultural groups. Some theoretical approaches have major limitations when applied to certain populations. Effective multicultural practice demands an open stance on the part of the practitioner, flexibility, and a willingness to modify strategies to fit the needs and the situation of the individual client. Practitioners who truly respect their clients will be aware of clients' hesitations and will not be too quick to misinterpret this behavior. Instead, they will patiently attempt to enter the world of their clients as much as they can. It is not necessary for practitioners to have the same experiences as their clients, but they should be open to a similar set of feelings and struggles. It is more often by differences than by similarities that we are challenged to look at what we are doing.

MULTICULTURAL GUIDELINES   Western society is becoming increasingly diverse, yet our therapy models are based primarily on Eurocentric assumptions, which do not always consider the influence and impact of racial and cultural socialization (APA, 2003). To address the knowledge and skills needed in our changing world, the APA provides professionals with a framework for delivering services to our diverse population. Although these guidelines have been developed specifically to aid psychologists, other practitioners may also find them useful.

1. "Psychologists are encouraged to recognize that, as cultural beings, they may hold attitudes and beliefs that can detrimentally influence their perceptions of and interactions with individuals who are ethnically and racially different from themselves." (p. 382)
2. "Psychologists are encouraged to recognize the importance of multicultural sensitivity/responsiveness to, knowledge of, and understanding about ethnically and racially different individuals." (p. 385)
3. "As educators, psychologists are encouraged to employ the constructs of multiculturalism and diversity in psychological education." (p. 386)
4. "Culturally sensitive psychological researchers are encouraged to recognize the importance of conducting culture-centered and ethical psychological research among persons from ethnic, linguistic, and racial minority backgrounds." (p. 388)
5. "Psychologists are encouraged to apply culturally appropriate skills in clinical and other applied psychological practices." (p. 390)
6. "Psychologists are encouraged to use organizational change processes to support culturally informed organizational (policy) development and practices." (p. 392)

These guidelines are a working document, not a dogmatic set of prescriptions. The integration of racial and ethnic factors into psychological theory, practice, and research has only recently begun.

SOME ADDITIONAL PRACTICAL GUIDELINES   If the counseling process is to be effective it is essential that cultural issues and worldview be addressed with all clients. Here are some additional guidelines that may increase your effectiveness when working with clients from diverse backgrounds:

- Learn more about how your own cultural background has influenced your thinking and behaving. What specific steps can you take to broaden your base of understanding, both of your own culture and of other cultures?
- Identify your basic assumptions, especially as they apply to diversity in culture, ethnicity, race, gender, class, religion, and sexual orientation. Think about how your assumptions are likely to affect your professional practice.
- Examine where you obtained your knowledge about culture. Are your attitudes about diverse cultures your own? How accurate and up-to-date is your knowledge? How open are you to learning more about the ways in which cultural factors influence the therapeutic process?
- Learn to pay attention to the common ground that exists among people of diverse backgrounds. What are some of the ways in which we all share universal concerns?
- Spend time preparing clients for counseling. Teach clients how to use their therapeutic experience to meet the challenges they face in their everyday lives.
- Be flexible in applying the methods you use with clients. Don't be wedded to a specific technique if it is not appropriate for a given client.
- Remember that practicing from a multicultural perspective can make your job easier and can be rewarding for both you and your clients.

It takes time, study, and experience to become an effective multicultural counselor. Multicultural competence cannot be reduced simply to cultural awareness and sensitivity, to a body of knowledge, or to a specific set of skills. Instead, it requires a combination of all of these factors.

 ## ISSUES FACED BY BEGINNING THERAPISTS

In this section I identify some of the major issues that most of us typically face, particularly during the beginning stages of learning how to be therapists. When you complete your formal course work and begin facing clients, you will be put to the test of integrating and applying what you have learned. At that point some real concerns are likely to arise about your adequacy as a person and as a professional. Here are some useful guidelines for your reflection on dealing with the challenges of becoming an effective counselor.

Dealing With Our Anxieties

Most beginning counselors anticipate meeting their initial clients with ambivalent feelings. A certain level of anxiety demonstrates that we are aware of the uncertainties of the future with our clients and of our abilities to really be there and stay with them. Our willingness to recognize and deal with these anxieties, as opposed to denying them by pretenses, is a mark of courage. That we have self-doubts seems perfectly normal; it is how we deal with them that counts. One way is to openly discuss them with a supervisor and peers. The possibilities are rich for meaningful exchanges and for gaining support from fellow interns who probably have many of the same concerns, fears, and anxieties.

Being and Disclosing Ourselves

Because we are typically self-conscious and anxious when we begin counseling, we tend to be overconcerned with what the books say and with the mechanics of how we should proceed. Inexperienced therapists too often fail to appreciate the values inherent in simply being themselves. It is possible to err by going to extremes in two different directions. At one end are counselors who lose themselves in their fixed role and hide behind a professional facade. Here counselors are so bound up in maintaining stereotyped role expectations that little of them as a person shows through. At the other end are therapists who strive too hard to prove that they are human. They tend to make the mistake of inappropriately burdening their clients with spontaneous impressions they are having toward them. At either end of these poles we are not being ourselves.

Avoiding Perfectionism

Perhaps one of the most common self-defeating beliefs with which we burden ourselves is that we must be perfect. Although we may well know *intellectually* that humans are not perfect, *emotionally* we often feel that there is little room for error. I teach counseling students that they need not burden themselves with the idea that they must be perfect. It takes courage to admit imperfections, but there is a value in being open about being less than perfect.

To be sure, you *will* make mistakes, whether you are a beginning or a seasoned therapist. If our energies are tied up presenting an image of perfection, we will have little energy left to be present for our clients. I tell students to challenge their notions that they should know everything and should be perfectly skilled. I encourage students to share their mistakes or what they perceive as errors during their supervision. Students willing to risk making mistakes in supervised learning situations and willing to reveal their self-doubts will find a direction that leads to growth.

Being Honest About Our Limitations

We cannot realistically expect to succeed with every client. It takes honesty to admit that we cannot work successfully with everyone. However, there is a delicate balance between learning our realistic limits and challenging what we sometimes think of as being "limits." For example, we may tell ourselves that we could never work with a specific client population because we cannot identify with them. Before deciding that you do not have the life experiences or the personal qualities to work with a given population, try working in a setting with a population you do not intend to specialize in. This can be done through diversified field placements or visits to agencies.

Understanding Silence

Silent moments during a therapeutic session may seem like silent hours to a beginning therapist. Yet this silence can have many meanings. The client may be quietly thinking about some things that were discussed earlier or evaluating some insight just acquired. The client may be waiting for the therapist to take the lead and decide what to say next, or the therapist may be waiting for the client to do this. Either the client or the therapist may be bored, distracted, or preoccupied or may just not have anything to say for the moment. The client may be feeling hostile toward the therapist and thus be playing the game of "I'll just sit here like a stone and see if he [she] can get to me." The client and the therapist may be communicating without words. The silence may be refreshing, or the silence may say much more than words. Perhaps the interaction has been on a surface level, and both persons have some fear or hesitancy about getting to a deeper level. When silence occurs, acknowledge and explore with your client the meaning of the silence.

Dealing With Demands From Clients

A major issue that puzzles many beginning counselors is how to deal with clients who seem to make constant demands. Because therapists feel that they should extend themselves in being helpful, they often burden themselves with the unrealistic standard that they should give unselfishly regardless of how great the demands on them are. The demands may manifest themselves in a variety of ways. Clients may demand to see you more often or for a longer period than you can provide; want to see you socially; expect you to manipulate another person (spouse, child, parent) to see and accept their point of view; demand that you continually demonstrate how much you care; or demand that you tell them what to do and how to solve a problem. One way of heading off these demands is to make your expectations and boundaries clear during the initial counseling session or in the disclosure statement.

Dealing With Clients Who Lack Commitment

Many clients are involuntary in that they are required by a court order to obtain therapy. In these cases you may well be challenged in your attempt to establish a working relationship. But it is possible to do effective work with clients who are sent to you.

Practitioners who work with involuntary clients must begin by openly discussing the nature of the relationship. They should not promise what they cannot or will not deliver. It is good practice to make clear the limits of confidentiality as well as any other factors that may affect the course of therapy. In working with involuntary clients it is especially important to prepare them for the process, for doing so can go a long way toward dealing with resistance. Often, in fact, resistance is brought about by a counselor who omits preparation and merely assumes that all clients are open and ready to benefit from therapy.

Tolerating Ambiguity

Many beginning therapists experience the anxiety of not seeing the fruits of their labor. They ask themselves: "Am I really doing my client any good? Is the client perhaps getting worse?" I hope you will learn to tolerate the ambiguity of not knowing for sure whether your client is improving, at least during the initial sessions. It is important to realize that clients may seemingly "get worse" before they show therapeutic gains. Also, realize that the fruitful effects of the joint efforts of the therapist and the client may not be manifest for months (or even years) after the conclusion of therapy.

Avoiding Losing Ourselves in Our Clients

A common mistake for beginners is to worry too much about clients. There is a danger of incorporating clients' neuroses into our own personality. We lose sleep wondering what decisions they are making. We sometimes identify so closely with clients that we lose our own sense of identity and assume their identity. Empathy becomes distorted and militates against a therapeutic intervention. We need to learn how to "let clients go" and not carry around their problems until we see them again. The most therapeutic thing is to be as fully present as we are able to be (feeling with our clients and experiencing their struggles with them) but to let them assume the responsibility of their living and choosing outside of the session. If we become lost in clients' struggles and confusion, we cease being effective agents in helping them find their way out of the darkness. If we accept the responsibility for our clients' decisions, we are blocking rather than fostering their growth.

Because it is not appropriate for us to use clients' time to work through our reactions to them, it is all the more important that we be willing to work on ourselves in our own sessions with another therapist, supervisor, or colleague. If we do not engage in this kind of self-exploration, we increase the danger of losing ourselves in our clients and using them to meet our unfulfilled needs.

Developing a Sense of Humor

Therapy is a responsible matter, but it need not be deadly serious. Both clients and counselors can enrich a relationship by laughing. I have found that humor and tragedy are closely linked and that after allowing ourselves to feel some experiences that are painfully tragic, we can also genuinely laugh at how seriously we have taken our situation. We secretly delude ourselves into believing we are unique—that we are alone in our pain and we alone have experienced the tragic. What a welcome relief when we can admit that pain is not our exclusive domain. It is important to recognize that laughter or humor does not mean that work is not being accomplished. There are times, of course, when laughter is used to cover up anxiety or to escape from the experience of facing threatening material. The therapist needs to distinguish between humor that distracts and humor that enhances the situation.

Sharing Responsibility With the Client

You will probably struggle with finding the optimum balance in sharing responsibility with your clients. One mistake is to assume full responsibility for the direction and outcomes of therapy. This will lead to taking from your clients the rightful responsibility they need if they are to become empowered by making their own decisions. It could also increase the likelihood of your early burnout. Another mistake is for you to refuse to accept the responsibility for making accurate assessments and designing appropriate treatment plans for your clients. How responsibility will be shared should be addressed at the beginning of the therapeutic relationship. Early during the course of counseling, it is your responsibility to discuss specific matters such as length and overall duration of the sessions, confidentiality, general goals, and methods used to achieve goals. (Informed consent is discussed in Chapter 3.)

It is important to be alert to your clients' efforts to get you to assume responsibility for directing their lives. Many clients seek a "magic answer" as a way of escaping the anxiety of making their own decisions. Yet it is not your role to assume responsibility for directing your clients' lives. Collaboratively designing contracts and homework assignments with your clients can be instrumental in your clients increasingly finding direction from within themselves. Perhaps the best measure of our effectiveness as counselors is the degree to which clients are able to say to us, "I appreciate what you have been to me, and because of your faith in me, I am confident that I can go it alone." Eventually, if we are effective, we will be out of business!

Declining to Give Advice

Quite often clients who are suffering come to a therapy session seeking and even demanding advice. They want more than direction; they want a wise counselor to make a decision or resolve a problem for them. However, counseling should not be confused with dispensing information. Therapists help clients discover their own solutions and recognize their own freedom to act. Therapists do not deprive clients of the opportunity to act freely. Even if we, as therapists, were able to resolve their struggles for them, we would be fostering their dependence on us. They would continually need to seek our counsel for every new twist in their difficulties. Our job is to help clients make independent choices and accept the consequences of their choices. The habitual practice of giving advice does not work toward this end.

Defining Your Role as a Counselor

One of your challenges as a counselor will be to define and clarify your professional role. As you read about the various theoretical orientations in Part 2, you will discover the many different roles of counselors that are related to these diverse theories. As a counselor, you will likely be expected to function with a diverse range of roles.

From my perspective the central function of counseling is to help clients recognize their own strengths, discover what is preventing them from using their strengths, and clarify what kind of person they want to be. Counseling is a process by which clients are invited to look honestly at their behavior and lifestyle and make certain decisions about how they want to modify the quality of their life. In this framework counselors provide support and warmth yet care enough to challenge and confront so that clients will be able to take the actions necessary to bring about significant change.

Realize that the professional roles you assume are likely to be dependent on factors such as the client populations with whom you are working, the specific therapeutic services you are providing, the particular stage of counseling, and the setting in which you work. Your role will not be defined once and for all. You will have to reassess the nature of your professional commitments and redefine your role at various times.

Learning to Use Techniques Appropriately

When counselors are at an impasse with clients, they sometimes have a tendency to look for the "right" techniques to get the sessions moving. As you saw in Chapter 1, relying on techniques too much can lead to mechanical counseling. Ideally, therapeutic techniques should evolve from the therapeutic relationship and should enhance the client's awareness or suggest possibilities for experimenting with new behavior. It is essential to understand the theoretical rationale for each technique used and to be sure the techniques are congruent with the goals of therapy. This does not mean that counselors need to restrict themselves to drawing on accepted techniques and procedures within a single model; quite the contrary. However, effective counselors avoid using techniques in a hit-or-miss fashion, to fill time, to meet their own needs, or to get things moving. Their methods are carefully chosen as a way to help clients make therapeutic progress.

Developing Your Own Counseling Style

Counselors-in-training need to be cautioned about the tendency to mimic the style of a supervisor, therapist, or some other model. It is important to accept that there is no "right" way to conduct therapy and that wide variations in approach can be effective. You will inhibit your potential effectiveness in reaching others if you attempt to imitate another therapist's style or if you fit most of your behavior during the session into the Procrustean bed of some expert's theory. Your counseling style will be influenced by your teachers, therapists, and supervisors, but I encourage you to be watchful of blurring your potential uniqueness by trying to imitate them. I advocate borrowing from others but, at the same time, finding a way that is distinctive to you.

Staying Alive as a Person and as a Professional

Ultimately, our single most important instrument is the person we are, and our most powerful technique is our ability to model aliveness and realness. We must take care of ourselves so that we remain fully alive. We need to work at dealing with those factors that threaten to drain life from us and render us helpless. I encourage you to consider how you can apply the theories you will be studying to enhance your life from both a personal and a professional standpoint. If you are aware of the factors that sap your vitality as a person, you are in a better position to prevent the condition known as *professional burnout*.

Learn to look within yourself to determine what choices you are making (and not making) to keep yourself alive. This can go a long way toward preventing what some people consider to be an inevitable condition associated with the helping professions. You have considerable control over whether you become burned out. Although you cannot always control stressful events, you do have a great deal of control over how you interpret and react to these events. It is important to realize that you cannot continue to give and give while getting little in return. There is a price to pay for always being available and for assuming that you are able to control the lives and destinies of others. Become attuned to the subtle signs of burnout rather than waiting for a full-blown condition of emotional and physical exhaustion to set in. You will be challenged to develop your own strategy for keeping yourself alive personally and professionally.

Make periodic assessments of the direction of your own life to determine if you are living the way you want. If not, decide what you are willing to actually *do* to *make* changes occur. By being in tune with yourself, by having the experience of centeredness and solidness, and by feeling a sense of personal power, you have the basis for integrating your life experiences with your professional experiences. Such a synthesis can provide the basis for being an effective professional.

 # SUMMARY

One of the basic issues in the counseling profession concerns the significance of the counselor as a person in the therapeutic relationship. Counselors are asking people to take an honest look at themselves and to make choices concerning how they want to change, so it is critical that counselors themselves be searchers who hold their own lives open to the same kind of scrutiny. Counselors should frequently ask themselves questions such as "What do I personally have to offer others who are struggling to find their way?" and "Am I doing in my own life what I urge others to do?"

Counselors can acquire an extensive theoretical and practical knowledge and can make that knowledge available to their clients. But to every therapeutic session you also bring yourself as a person. If you are to promote growth and change in your clients, you must be willing to promote growth in your own life by exploring your own choices and decisions and by striving to become aware of the ways in which you have ignored your own potential for growth. This willingness to attempt to live in accordance with what you teach and thus to be a positive model for your clients is what makes a counselor a "therapeutic person."

Chapter 3

Ethical Issues in Counseling Practice

INTRODUCTION

This chapter introduces you to some of the ethical principles and issues that will be a basic part of your professional practice. Its purpose is to stimulate you to think further about these issues so that you can form a sound basis for making ethical decisions. Topics addressed include balancing clients' needs against your own needs, ways of making sound ethical decisions, educating clients about their rights, parameters of confidentiality, ethical concerns in counseling diverse client populations, ethical issues involving diagnosis, and dealing with dual relationships.

As you become involved in counseling, you will find that interpreting the ethical guidelines of your professional organization and applying them to particular situations demand the utmost ethical sensitivity. Even responsible practitioners differ over how to apply established ethical principles to specific situations. It is clear that therapists are challenged to deal with questions that do not always have obvious answers. You will have to struggle with yourself to decide how to act in ways that will further the best interests of your clients. To help you make these decisions, consult with colleagues, keep yourself informed about laws affecting your practice, keep up-to-date in your specialty field, stay abreast of developments in ethical practice, reflect on the impact your values have on your practice, and be willing to engage in honest self-examination.

You will need to reexamine the ethical issues raised in this chapter periodically throughout your professional life. You can benefit from both formal and informal opportunities to discuss ethical dilemmas during your training program. Even if you resolve some ethical issues while completing a graduate program, there is no guarantee that they have been settled once and for all. These issues are bound to take on new dimensions as you gain more experience. I have found that students often burden themselves unnecessarily with the expectation that they should resolve all problem issues before they are ready to practice. Ethical decision making is an evolutionary process that requires you to be continually open and self-critical.

 PUTTING CLIENTS' NEEDS BEFORE YOUR OWN

I do not think that as counselors we can keep our personal needs completely separate from our relationships with clients. Ethically, it is essential that we become aware of our own needs, areas of unfinished business, potential personal conflicts, and defenses. We need to realize how such factors could interfere with helping our clients.

Our professional relationships with our clients exist for their benefit. A useful question to frequently ask yourself is this: "Whose needs are being met in this relationship, my client's or my own?" It takes considerable professional maturity to make an honest appraisal of your behavior and its impact on clients. I do not think it is unethical for us to meet our personal needs through our professional work, yet it is essential that these needs be kept in perspective. For me, the ethical issue exists when we meet our needs, in either obvious or subtle ways, at the expense of our clients. The crux of the matter is to avoid exploiting clients.

What kind of awareness is crucial? We all have certain blind spots and distortions of reality. As helping professionals, we have responsibilities to work actively toward expanding our own self-awareness and to learn to recognize areas of prejudice and vulnerability. If we are aware of our personal problems and are willing to work them through, there is less chance that we will project them onto clients. If certain areas of struggle surface and old conflicts become reactivated, we have an ethical obligation to seek our own therapy so that we will be able to assist clients in confronting these same struggles.

We must also examine other, less obviously harmful, personal needs that can get in the way of creating growth-producing relationships. These other aspects of our personality include the need for control and power; the need to be nurturing and helpful; the need to change others in the direction of our own values; the need to persuade; the need for feeling adequate, particularly when it becomes overly important that the client confirm our competence; and the need to be respected and appreciated. I am not saying that these needs are neurotic; on the contrary, it is essential that our needs be met if we are to be involved with helping others find satisfaction in their lives. The crux of the issue is that ethically it is essential that we do not meet our needs at the expense of our clients.

 # ETHICAL DECISION MAKING

As a practitioner you will ultimately have to apply the ethics codes of your profession to the many practical problems you face. You will not be able to rely on ready-made answers or prescriptions given by professional organizations, which typically provide only broad guidelines for responsible practice.

Part of the process of making ethical decisions involves learning about the resources from which you can draw when you are struggling with an ethical question. Although you are ultimately responsible for making ethical decisions, you do not have to do so in a vacuum. You should also be aware of the consequences of practicing in ways that are not sanctioned by organizations of which you are a member or the state in which you are licensed to practice.

The Role of Ethics Codes as a Catalyst for Improving Practice

Professional codes of ethics serve a number of purposes. They educate counseling practitioners and the general public about the responsibilities of the profession. They provide a basis for accountability, and through their enforcement, clients are protected from unethical practices. Perhaps most important, codes can provide a basis for reflecting on and improving one's professional practice. Self-monitoring is a better route for professionals to take than being policed by an outside agency (Herlihy & Corey, 1996).

From my perspective, one of the unfortunate trends is for ethics codes to increasingly take on legalistic dimensions. Many practitioners are so anxious about becoming embroiled in a lawsuit that they gear their practices mainly toward fulfilling legal minimums rather than thinking of what is right for their clients. In this era of litigation it makes sense to be aware of the legal aspects of practice and to do what is possible to reduce the chances of malpractice action, but it is a mistake to confuse legal behavior with being ethical. Although following the law is part of ethical behavior, being an ethical practitioner involves far more. One of the best ways to prevent being sued for malpractice rests in demonstrating respect for clients, having their welfare as a central concern, and practicing within the framework of professional codes.

Over time, most of the ethics codes of various mental health professions have evolved into lengthy documents, setting forth what is desired behavior and proscribing behavior that may not serve the client's welfare. Even though codes are becoming more specific, they do not convey ultimate truth, nor do they provide ready-made answers for the ethical dilemmas that practitioners will encounter. Ultimately, professionals are expected to exercise prudent judgment when it comes to interpreting and applying ethical principles to specific situations. In my view, ethics codes are best used as guidelines to formulate sound reasoning and serve practitioners in making the best judgments possible. No code of ethics can delineate what would be the appropriate or best course of action in each problematic situation a professional will face.

Some Steps in Making Ethical Decisions

There are a number of different models for ethical decision making; most tend to focus on the application of principles to ethical dilemmas. After reviewing a few of these models, my colleagues and I have identified a series of procedural steps to help you think through ethical problems (see Corey, Corey, & Callanan, 2003; Corey, Corey, & Haynes, 2003):

- Identify the problem or dilemma. Gather information that will shed light on the nature of the problem. This will help you decide whether the problem is mainly ethical, legal, professional, clinical, or moral.
- Identify the potential issues. Evaluate the rights, responsibilities, and welfare of all those who are involved in the situation.
- Look at the relevant ethics codes for general guidance on the matter. Consider whether your own values and ethics are consistent with or in conflict with the relevant guidelines.
- Consider the applicable laws and regulations, and determine how they may have a bearing on an ethical dilemma.

- Seek consultation from more than one source to obtain various perspectives on the dilemma.
- Brainstorm various possible courses of action. Continue discussing options with other professionals. Include the client in this process of considering options for action.
- Enumerate the consequences of various decisions, and reflect on the implications of each course of action for your client.
- Decide on what appears to be the best possible course of action. Once the course of action has been implemented, follow up to evaluate the outcomes and to determine if further action is necessary.

In reasoning through any ethical issue, there is rarely one ideal course of action to follow; different practitioners will make a variety of decisions. The more subtle the ethical dilemma, the more difficult the decision-making process will be.

Professional maturity implies that you are open to questioning and that you are willing to discuss your quandaries with colleagues. Because ethics codes do not make decisions for you, demonstrate a willingness to struggle, to raise questions, to discuss ethical concerns with others, and to continually clarify your values and examine your motivations. To the degree that it is possible, include the client at all phases of the ethical decision-making process.

 # THE RIGHT OF INFORMED CONSENT

Regardless of the theoretical framework from which you operate, informed consent is an ethical and legal requirement and is an integral part of the therapeutic process. Providing clients with information they need to make informed choices tends to promote the active cooperation of clients in their counseling plan. By educating your clients about their rights and responsibilities, you are both empowering them and building a trusting relationship with them. Some aspects of the informed consent process include the general goals of counseling, the responsibilities of the counselor toward the client, the responsibilities of clients, limitations of and exceptions to confidentiality, legal and ethical parameters that could define the relationship, the qualifications and background of the practitioner, the fees involved, the services the client can expect, and the approximate length of the therapeutic process. Further areas might include the benefits of counseling, the risks involved, and the possibility that the client's case will be discussed with the therapist's colleagues or supervisors. This process of educating the client begins with the initial counseling session and continues for the duration of counseling.

The challenge of fulfilling the spirit of informed consent is to strike a balance between giving clients too much information and giving them too little. For example, it is too late to tell minors that you intend to consult with their parents *after* they have disclosed that they are considering an abortion. In such a case both the girl and the boy involved have a right to know about the limitations of confidentiality before they make such highly personal disclosures. Clients can be overwhelmed, however, if counselors go into too much detail initially about the interventions they are likely to make. It takes both intuition and skill for practitioners to strike a balance.

It is a good idea to have basic information about the therapy process in writing, as well as discussing with clients topics that will enable them to get the maximum benefit from their counseling experience. Clients can take this written information home and then bring up questions at the following session. For a more complete discussion of informed consent and confidentiality, see *Issues and Ethics in the Helping Professions* (Corey, Corey, and Callanan, 2003).

 ## DIMENSIONS OF CONFIDENTIALITY

Confidentiality, which is central to developing a trusting and productive client–therapist relationship, is both a legal and an ethical issue. State laws now address confidentiality in therapy, as do the ethics codes of all the mental health professions. Because no genuine therapy can occur unless clients trust in the privacy of their revelations to their therapists, professionals have the responsibility to define the degree of confidentiality that can be promised. Counselors have an ethical responsibility to discuss the nature and purpose of confidentiality with their clients early in the counseling process. In addition, clients have a right to know that their therapist may be discussing certain details of the relationship with a supervisor or a colleague.

Although most counselors agree on the essential value of confidentiality, they realize that it cannot be considered an absolute. There are times when confidential information must be divulged, and there are many instances in which whether to keep or to break confidentiality becomes a cloudy issue. In determining when to breach confidentiality, therapists must consider the requirements of the institution in which they work and the clientele they serve. Because these circumstances are frequently not clearly defined by accepted ethics codes, counselors must exercise professional judgment.

In general, confidentiality must be broken when it becomes clear that clients might do serious harm to either themselves or others. There is a legal requirement to break confidentiality in cases involving child abuse, abuse of the elderly, and of dependent adults. All mental health practitioners and interns need to be aware of their duty to report such abuse. There are other circumstances that dictate when information must legally be reported by counselors:

- When the therapist believes a client under the age of 16 is the victim of incest, rape, child abuse, or some other crime
- When the therapist determines that the client needs hospitalization
- When information is made an issue in a court action
- When clients request that their records be released to themselves or to a third party

In general, however, it is a counselor's primary obligation to protect client disclosures as a vital part of the therapeutic relationship. When assuring clients that what they reveal in sessions will generally be kept confidential, counselors should also tell them of any limitations on confidentiality. This practice does not necessarily inhibit successful counseling.

 # ETHICAL ISSUES IN A MULTICULTURAL PERSPECTIVE

Ethical practice requires that we take the client's cultural context into account in counseling practice. In this section we look at how it is possible for practitioners to practice unethically if they do not address cultural differences in counseling practice.

Are Current Theories Adequate in Working With Culturally Diverse Populations?

I believe current theories can be expanded to include a multicultural perspective. With respect to many of the traditional theories, assumptions made about mental health, optimum human development, the nature of psychopathology, and the nature of effective treatment may have little relevance for some clients. For traditional theories to be relevant in a multicultural society, they must incorporate an interactive person-in-the-environment focus. That is, individuals are best understood by taking into consideration salient cultural and environmental variables. It is essential for therapists to create therapeutic strategies that are congruent with the range of values and behaviors that are characteristic of a pluralistic society.

Is Counseling Culture-Bound?

Multicultural specialists have asserted that theories of counseling and psychotherapy represent different worldviews, each with its own values, biases, and assumptions about human behavior. Some counselors have criticized traditional therapeutic practices as irrelevant for people of color and other special populations such as the elderly. Most techniques are derived from counseling approaches developed by and for White, male, middle-class, Western clients. These approaches may not be applicable to clients from different racial, ethnic, and cultural backgrounds. Western models of counseling have major limitations when applied to special populations and minority groups such as Asian and Pacific Islanders, Latinos, Native Americans, and African Americans. Moreover, value assumptions made by culturally different counselors and clients have resulted in culturally biased counseling and have led to underuse of mental health services (Pedersen, 2000; D. W. Sue & Sue, 2003).

It cannot be denied that contemporary therapy approaches originated in Euro-American culture and are grounded on a core set of values. I think it is a myth that these approaches are value-neutral and are applicable to all human beings. For example, some of the values implicit in most traditional counseling theories include an emphasis on individualism, the separate existence of the self, individuation as the foundation for maturity, and decision making and responsibility as resting with the individual rather than the group. There is a danger of imposing these values of individual choice and autonomy as being the only "right" values and as having universal applicability. In some cultures the key values are collectivist and give primary consideration to what is good for the group. Regardless of the therapist's orientation, it is crucial to listen to clients and determine why they are seeking help and how best to deliver the help that is appropriate for them. On this point, the problem is not simply that the theories and techniques are inadequate in a multicultural context. Instead, I am convinced that the greater problem rests with unskilled clinicians and with the poor delivery of certain techniques. Competent therapists also possess at least a minimum level of development of knowledge and skills that they can bring to bear on any counseling situation. Such therapists understand what their clients need and avoid forcing clients into a preconceived mold.

Focusing on Both Individual and Environmental Factors

A theoretical orientation provides practitioners with a map to guide them in a productive direction with their clients. It is hoped that the theory orients them but does not control what they attend to in the therapeutic venture. Counselors who operate from a multicultural framework also have certain assumptions and a focus that guides their practice. They view individuals in the context of the family and the culture, and their aim is to facilitate social action that will lead to change within the client's community rather than merely increasing the individual's insight. Both multicultural practitioners and feminist therapists maintain that therapeutic practice will be effective only to the extent that interventions are tailored toward social action aimed at changing those factors that are creating the client's problem rather than blaming the client for his or her condition. These topics will be developed in more detail in later chapters.

An adequate theory of counseling *does* deal with the social and cultural factors of an individual's problems. However, there is something to be said for helping clients deal with their response to environmental realities. Counselors may well be at a loss in trying to bring about social change when they are sitting with a client who is in pain because of social injustice. By using techniques from many of the traditional therapies, counselors can help clients increase their awareness of their options in dealing with barriers and struggles. It is essential to focus on both individual and social factors if change is to occur, as the feminist, postmodern, and family systems approaches to therapy teach us. Indeed, the person-in-the-environment perspective acknowledges this interactive reality. (For a more detailed treatment of the ethical issues in multicultural counseling, see D. W. Sue and Sue, 2003; Pedersen, 2000; and Corey, Corey, and Callanan, 2003, chap. 4.)

ETHICAL ISSUES IN THE ASSESSMENT PROCESS

Both clinical and ethical issues are associated with the use of assessment and diagnostic procedures. As you will see when you study the various theories of counseling, some approaches place heavy emphasis on the role of assessment as a prelude to the treatment process. Other theories—mainly the relationship-oriented and experiential therapies—tend to view diagnosis as an external frame of reference that can remove the therapist from understanding the deeply personal and subjective world of the client.

The Role of Diagnosis in Counseling

Psychodiagnosis is the analysis and explanation of a client's problems. It may include an explanation of the causes of the client's difficulties, an account of how these problems developed over time, a classification of any disorders, a specification of preferred treatment procedure, and an estimate of the chances for a successful resolution. The purpose of diagnosis in counseling and psychotherapy is to identify disruptions in a client's present behavior and lifestyle. Once problem areas are clearly identified, the counselor and client are able to establish the goals of the therapy process, and then a treatment plan can be tailored to the unique needs of the client. A diagnosis is not a final category; rather, it provides a working hypothesis that guides the practitioner in understanding the client. The therapy sessions provide useful clues about the nature of the client's problems. Thus, diagnosis begins with the intake interview and continues throughout the duration of therapy.

The "bible" for guiding practitioners in making diagnostic assessments is the fourth edition of the American Psychiatric Association's (2000) *Diagnostic and Statistical Manual of Mental Disorders, Text Revision* (also known as the DSM-IV-TR). Clinicians who work in community mental health agencies, private practice, and other human service settings are generally expected to assess client problems within the framework of the DSM-IV-TR. This manual advises practitioners that it represents only an initial step in a comprehensive evaluation. There is also a caution about the necessity of gaining additional information about the person being evaluated beyond that required to make a DSM-IV-TR diagnosis.

Although some clinicians view diagnosis as central to the counseling process, others view it as unnecessary, as a detriment, or as discriminatory against ethnic minorities and women. Irvin Yalom (2003), who is a psychiatrist, recommends that therapists avoid diagnosis based on his belief that "diagnosis is often *counterproductive* in the everyday psychotherapy of less severely impaired patients" (p. 4). Yalom contends that diagnosis limits vision, diminishes a therapist's ability to relate to a client as a person, and may result in a self-fulfilling prophecy.

As you will see in Chapter 12, feminist therapists contend that traditional diagnostic practices are often oppressive and that such practices are based on a White, male-centered, Western notion of mental health and mental illness. Both the feminist perspective and the postmodern approaches (see Chapter 13) charge that these diagnoses ignore societal contexts. Therapists with a feminist, social constructionist, solution-focused, or narrative therapy orientation challenge many DSM-IV-TR diagnoses. However, these practitioners do make assessments and draw conclusions about client problems and strengths.

CONSIDERING ETHNIC AND CULTURAL FACTORS IN ASSESSMENT AND DIAGNOSIS

A danger of the diagnostic approach is the possible failure of counselors to consider ethnic and cultural factors in certain patterns of behavior. In assessments of clients with different backgrounds, the DSM-IV-TR emphasizes the importance of being aware of unintentional bias and keeping an open mind to the presence of distinctive ethnic and cultural patterns that could influence the diagnostic process. Unless cultural variables are considered, some clients may be subjected to erroneous diagnoses. Certain behaviors and personality styles may be labeled neurotic or deviant simply because they are not characteristic of the dominant culture. Thus, counselors who work with African Americans, Asian Americans, Latinos, and Native Americans may erroneously conclude that a client is repressed, inhibited, passive, and unmotivated, all of which are seen as undesirable by Western standards.

A COMMENTARY ON ASSESSMENT AND DIAGNOSIS

Is there a way to bridge the gap between the extreme view that diagnosis is the essential core of therapy and the extreme view that it is a detrimental factor? Most practitioners and many writers in the field consider assessment and diagnosis to be a continuing process that focuses on understanding the client. The collaborative perspective that involves the client as an active participant in the therapy process implies that both the therapist and the client are engaged in a search-and-discovery process from the first session to the last. Even though some practitioners may avoid formal diagnostic procedures and terminology, diagnosis can become a form of making tentative hypotheses. These hunches can be formed with clients and shared with them throughout the process. This perspective on assessment and diagnosis is consistent with the principles of feminist therapy, an approach that is critical of traditional diagnostic procedures.

The process of assessment and diagnosis cannot be separated from treatment, and ideally, this process helps the practitioner conceptualize a case. Ethical dilemmas are created when diagnosis is done strictly for insurance purposes, which often entails arbitrarily assigning a client to a diagnostic classification. However, it is a clinical, legal, and ethical obligation of therapists to screen clients for life-threatening problems such as organic disorders, schizophrenia, bipolar disorder, and suicidal types of depression. Students need to learn the clinical skills necessary to do this type of screening, which is a form of diagnostic thinking.

It is essential to assess the whole person, which includes assessing dimensions of mind, body, and spirit. The biological perspective can contribute to effective assessment. Therapists need to take into account the biological processes as possible underlying factors of psychological symptoms and need to work closely with a physician. A holistic perspective also includes assessing the role that clients' spiritual and religious background might play in understanding their concerns. Clients' values can be instrumental resources in the search for solutions to their problems. For an excellent discussion of the role of spiritual and religious values in the assessment and treatment process, see *Integrating Religion and Spirituality Into Counseling* (Frame, 2003).

To function in most mental health agencies, practitioners need to become skilled in understanding and utilizing assessment and diagnostic procedures. For a more detailed discussion of assessment and diagnosis in counseling practice as it is applied to a single case, consult *Case Approach to Counseling and Psychotherapy* (Corey, 2005a), in which theorists from 11 different theoretical orientations share their diagnostic perspective on the case of Ruth.

DUAL AND MULTIPLE RELATIONSHIPS IN COUNSELING PRACTICE

Dual (or multiple) relationships, either sexual or nonsexual, occur when counselors assume two (or more) roles simultaneously or sequentially with a client. Some examples of *nonsexual* dual relationships are combining the roles of teacher and therapist or of supervisor and therapist; bartering for goods or therapeutic services; borrowing money from a client; providing therapy to a friend, an employee, or a relative; engaging in a social relationship with a client; accepting an expensive gift from a client; or going into a business venture with a client. Becoming emotionally or sexually involved with a current client is clearly unethical, unprofessional, and illegal; sexual involvement with former clients is unwise and generally considered unethical.

Because nonsexual dual relationships are necessarily complex and multidimensional, there are few simple and absolute answers to neatly resolve them. It is not always possible to play a single role in your work as a counselor, nor is it always desirable. You will probably have to wrestle with managing multiple roles, regardless of the setting in which you work or the client population you serve. Thus, it is critical that you give careful thought to the complexities of multiple roles and relationships before embroiling yourself in ethically questionable situations. The revised APA (2002) ethics code pertaining to multiple relationships offers guidance to practitioners:

> (a) A multiple relationship occurs when a psychologist is in a professional role with a person and (1) at the same time is in another role with the same person, (2) at the same time is in a relationship with a person closely associated with or related to the person with whom the psychologist has the professional relationship, or (3) promises to enter into another relationship in the future with the person or a person closely associated with or related to the person.

> A psychologist refrains from entering into a multiple relation-
> ship if the multiple relationship could reasonably be expected to
> impair the psychologist's objectivity, competence, or effectiveness
> in performing his or her functions as a psychologist, or otherwise
> risks exploitation or harm to the person with whom the profes-
> sional relationship exists.
>
> Multiple relationships that would not reasonably be expected
> to cause impairment or risk exploitation or harm are not unethical.
> (Standard 3.05)

From this standard it is clear that the APA does not prohibit all forms of multiple relationships in all circumstances. Although dual relationships do carry
inherent risks, it is a mistake to conclude that nonsexual dual relationships
are always unethical and always lead to harm and exploitation. Such relationships can be beneficial to clients if they are implemented thoughtfully and
with integrity (Lazarus & Zur, 2002).

Dual relationships are rarely a clear-cut matter, for ethical reasoning and
judgment come into play when ethics codes are applied to specific situations
(Herlihy & Corey, 1997). Some dual relationships are clearly exploitative and
do serious harm both to the client and to the professional, but others may
have more potential benefits to clients than potential risks.

Perspectives on Dual and Multiple Relationships

Some of the problematic aspects of engaging in dual relationships are that
they are pervasive, they can be difficult to recognize, they are unavoidable at
times, they are potentially harmful, and they are the subject of conflicting advice from various experts. A review of the literature reveals that dual and multiple relationships are hotly debated. Except for sexual intimacy with current
clients, which is unequivocally unethical, there is not much consensus regarding the appropriate way to manage dual and multiple relationships.

Almost all of the codes of the professional organizations now advise
against forming dual and multiple relationships, mainly because of the potential for misusing power, exploiting the client, and impairing objectivity. However, the ethics codes do not mandate avoidance of all dual or multiple
relationships. The current focus of ethics codes is to remain alert to the possibilities of damaging exploitation and harm to clients rather than a universal
prohibition of all dual and multiple relationships (Lazarus & Zur, 2002).

A consensus of many writers is that dual and multiple relationships are
inevitable in some situations and that a global prohibition does not seem to
be a realistic answer. Because interpersonal boundaries are not static but undergo redefinition over time, the challenge for practitioners is to learn how to
manage boundary fluctuations and to deal effectively with overlapping roles.
One key to learning how to manage dual or multiple relationships is to think
of ways to minimize the risks involved.

WAYS OF MINIMIZING RISK   In determining whether to proceed with a dual relationship, it is critical to consider whether the potential benefit of such a relationship outweighs the potential harm. It is your responsibility to develop safeguards aimed at reducing the potential for negative consequences. Herlihy and Corey (1997) identify the following guidelines:

- Set healthy boundaries early in the therapeutic relationship. Informed consent is essential from the beginning and throughout the therapy process. Involve the client in ongoing discussions and in the decision-making process, and document your discussions.
- Consult with fellow professionals as a way to maintain objectivity and identify unanticipated difficulties. Realize that you don't need to make a decision alone.
- When dual relationships are potentially problematic, or when the risk for harm is high, it is always wise to work under supervision. Document the nature of this supervision and any actions you take in your records.
- Throughout the process, self-monitoring is critical. Ask yourself whose needs are being met and examine your motivations for considering becoming involved in a dual or multiple relationship.

In working through a dual relationship concern, it is best to begin by ascertaining whether such a relationship can be avoided. Sometimes dual relationships are avoidable, and to get involved in them may be putting the client needlessly at risk. In other cases dual relationships are unavoidable. For instance, a counselor in a rural community may have as clients the local banker, merchant, and minister. In this setting, mental health practitioners may have to blend several professional roles and functions. They may also attend the same church or belong to the same community organization as their clients. These professionals are likely to find it more difficult to maintain clear boundaries than practitioners who work in a large city.

You are likely to encounter many forms of nonsexual dual relationships. One way of dealing with any potential problems is to adopt a policy of completely avoiding such relationships. Another alternative is to deal with each dilemma as it develops, making full use of informed consent and at the same time seeking consultation and supervision in dealing with the situation. This second alternative provides a professional challenge for self-monitoring. It is one of the hallmarks of professionalism to be willing to grapple with these ethical complexities of day-to-day practice.

 SUMMARY

It is essential that you learn a process for thinking about and dealing with ethical dilemmas, keeping in mind that most ethical issues are complex and defy simple solutions. A sign of good faith is your willingness to share your struggles with colleagues. Such consultation can be of great help in clarifying issues by giving you another perspective on a situation. The task of developing a sense of professional and ethical responsibility is never really finished, and new issues are constantly surfacing. Ethical issues demand periodic reflection and an openness to change.

If there is one fundamental question that can serve to tie together all the issues discussed in this chapter, it is this: Who has the right to counsel another person? This question can be the focal point of your reflection on ethical and professional issues. It can also be the basis of your self-examination each day that you meet with clients. Continue to ask yourself: "What makes me think I have a right to counsel others?" "What do I have to offer the people I'm counseling?" "Am I doing in my own life what I'm encouraging my clients to do?" If you answer these questions honestly, you may be troubled. At times you may feel that you have no ethical right to counsel others, perhaps because your own life isn't always the model you would like it to be for your clients. More important than resolving all of life's issues is knowing what kinds of questions to ask and then remaining open to reflection.

This chapter has introduced you to a number of issues that you are bound to face at some point in your counseling practice. I hope your interest has been piqued and that you will want to learn more. For further reading on this important topic, access InfoTrac College Edition articles using the key words provided in the Ethics list at the end of the chapter and choose some of the books listed in the Recommended Supplementary Readings section for further study.

 ## InfoTrac College Edition Resources

Multicultural Perspectives and Diversity Issues   The following key words are listed in such a way as to allow the InfoTrac College Edition search engine to locate a wider range of articles in the online library. The key words should be entered exactly as shown, to include asterisks, "W1," and "AND."

ethic*	values psych*
multicult*	multicult training couns*
values couns*	multicultural counseling
values therap*	competencies

Ethics   The following key words are listed in such a way as to allow the InfoTrac College Edition search engine to locate a wider range of articles in the online library. The key words should be entered exactly as shown, to include asterisks, "W1," and "AND."

ethical decision making model*	transference
ethical community standard*	Therap* values
standard* practice psych*	values psych*
countertransference	informed W1 consent

informed consent couns*

informed consent therap*

record* couns*

record* therap*

confidentiality psych*

privileged W1 communication

privacy couns*

privacy psych*

limits W2 confidentiality

duty to warn

duty to protect

dual relationship* couns*

dual relationship* psych*

multiple relationships

Recommended Supplementary Readings for Part 1

Counseling the Culturally Diverse: Theory and Practice (D. W. Sue & Sue, 2003) is a classic in the field of multicultural counseling and therapy and is now a standard for many courses in multicultural counseling.

A Handbook for Developing Multicultural Awareness (Pedersen, 2000) is based on the assumption that all counseling is to some extent multicultural. In this useful handbook, the author deals with topics such as developing multicultural awareness, becoming aware of our culturally biased assumptions, acquiring knowledge and skills needed to deal with cultural diversity.

Overcoming Our Racism: The Journey to Liberation (Sue, 2003) is a provocative and personal book that challenges readers to look at their own racist tendencies, biases, and prejudices. This is a useful resource for counselors interested in expanding their cultural awareness and knowledge of self and others.

Caring for Ourselves: A Therapist's Guide to Personal and Professional Well-Being (Baker, 2003) is a well-written book that presents a case for the value of therapist self-care. The author develops the theme that self-care is a responsible practice for caregivers.

The Gift of Therapy: An Open Letter to a New Generation of Therapists and Their Patients (Yalom, 2003) is a highly readable, insightful, and useful resource. It includes 85 short chapters on a wide variety of topics that pertain to the counselor as a person and as a professional.

ACA Ethical Standards Casebook (Herlihy & Corey, 1996) contains a variety of useful cases that are geared to the *ACA Code of Ethics and Standards of Practice*. The examples illustrate and clarify the meaning and intent of the standards.

Boundary Issues in Counseling: Multiple Roles and Responsibilities (Herlihy & Corey, 1997) puts the multiple-relationship controversy into perspective. The book focuses on dual relationships in a variety of work settings.

Dual Relationships and Psychotherapy (Lazarus & Zur, 2002) is an excellent compilation of chapters addressing the ethics of dual relationships, the role of boundaries, and dual relationships in special populations.

Ethics in Counseling and Psychotherapy: Standards, Research, and Emerging Issues (Welfel, 2002) presents a model of ethical decision making for analyzing complex ethical problems. The author focuses on ethical issues in diverse settings, managed care, and ethics in a multicultural setting. She also addresses legal and forensic issues.

Issues and Ethics in the Helping Professions (Corey, Corey, & Callanan, 2003) is devoted entirely to the issues that were introduced briefly in Chapter 3. The book is designed to involve readers in a personal and active way, and many open-ended cases are presented to help readers formulate their thoughts on a wide range of ethical issues.

Ethics in Action: CD-ROM (Corey, Corey, & Haynes, 2003) is a self-instructional program divided into three parts: (1) ethical decision making, (2) values and the helping relationship, and (3) boundary issues and multiple relationships. The program includes video clips of vignettes demonstrating ethical situations aimed at stimulating discussion.

Case Approach to Counseling and Psychotherapy (Corey, 2005a) is structured along the same chapter lines as this textbook. This book deals with case applications of how each of the theories works in action. A hypothetical client, Ruth, experiences counseling from all of the therapeutic vantage points.

Student Manual for Theory and Practice of Counseling and Psychotherapy (Corey, 2005b) is designed to help you integrate theory with practice and to make the concepts covered in this book come alive. It consists of self-inventories, overview summaries of the theories, a glossary of key concepts, study questions, issues and questions for personal application, activities and exercises, comprehension checks and quizzes, and case examples. The manual is fully coordinated with the textbook to make it a personal study guide.

The Art of Integrative Counseling (Corey, 2001) is a presentation of concepts and techniques from the various theories of counseling. The book provides guidelines for readers in developing their own approach to counseling practice.

CD-ROM for Integrative Counseling (Corey & Haynes, 2005) is an interactive, self-study tool that contains video segments and interactive questions designed to teach students ways of working with a client (Ruth) by drawing concepts and techniques from diverse theoretical approaches. The topics in this program parallel the topics in *The Art of Integrative Counseling.*

I Never Knew I Had a Choice (Corey & Corey, 2002) is a self-help resource that counselors in training can use to explore their personal concerns. This text deals with topics such as our struggle to achieve autonomy; the roles that work, love, sexuality, intimacy, and solitude play in our lives; the meaning of loneliness, death, and loss; and the ways in which we choose our values and philosophy of life.

Becoming a Helper (M. Corey & Corey, 2003) has separate chapters that expand on issues dealing with the personal and professional lives of helpers and ethical issues in counseling practice.

References and Suggested Readings for Part 1

AMERICAN PSYCHIATRIC ASSOCIATION. (2000). *Diagnostic and statistical manual of mental disorders, text revision* (4th ed.). (DSM-IV-TR). Washington, DC: Author.

AMERICAN PSYCHOLOGICAL ASSOCIATION. (2003). Guidelines on multicultural education, training, research, practice, and organizational change for psychologists. *American Psychologist, 58*(5), 377–402.

ARREDONDO, P., TOPOREK, R., BROWN, S., JONES, J., LOCKE, D., SANCHEZ, J., & STADLER, H. (1996). Operationalization of multicultural counseling competencies. *Journal of Multicultural Counseling and Development, 24*(1), 42–78.

*Books and articles marked with an asterisk are suggested for further study.

*BAKER, E. K. (2003). *Caring for ourselves: A therapist's guide to personal and professional well-being.* Washington, DC: American Psychological Association.

CARDEMIL, E. V., & BATTLE, C. L. (2003). Guess who's coming to therapy? Getting comfortable with conversations about race and ethnicity in psychotherapy. *Professional Psychology: Research and Practice, 34*(3), 278–286.

*COREY, G. (2001). *The art of integrative counseling.* Pacific Grove, CA: Brooks/Cole.

*COREY, G. (2005a). *Case approach to counseling and psychotherapy* (6th ed.). Belmont, CA: Brooks/Cole.

*COREY, G. (2005b). *Student manual for theory and practice of counseling and psychotherapy* (7th ed.). Belmont, CA: Brooks/Cole.

*COREY, G., & COREY, M. (2002). *I never knew I had a choice* (7th ed.). Pacific Grove, CA: Brooks/Cole.

*COREY, G., COREY, M., & CALLANAN, P. (2003). *Issues and ethics in the helping professions* (6th ed.). Belmont, CA: Brooks/Cole.

*COREY, G., COREY, M., & HAYNES, R. (2003). *Ethics in action: CD-ROM.* Pacific Grove, CA: Brooks/Cole.

*COREY, G., & HAYNES, R. (2005). *CD-ROM for integrative counseling.* Belmont, CA: Brooks/Cole.

*COREY, M., & COREY, G. (2003). *Becoming a helper* (4th ed.). Pacific Grove, CA: Brooks/Cole.

*FRAME, M. W. (2003). *Integrating religion and spirituality into counseling.* Pacific Grove, CA: Brooks/Cole.

*GUY, J. D. (1987). *The personal life of the psychotherapist.* New York: Wiley.

*HERLIHY, B., & COREY, G. (1996). *ACA ethical standards casebook* (5th ed.). Alexandria, VA: American Counseling Association.

*HERLIHY, B., & COREY, G. (1997). *Boundary issues in counseling: Multiple roles and responsibilities.* Alexandria, VA: American Counseling Association.

* LAZARUS, A. A., & ZUR, O. (2002). *Dual relationships and psychotherapy.* New York: Springer.

*PEDERSEN, P. (2000). *A handbook for developing multicultural awareness* (3rd ed.). Alexandria, VA: American Counseling Association.

SUE, D. W. (2003). O*vercoming our racism: The journey to liberation.* San Francisco: Jossey-Bass.

SUE, D. W., ARREDONDO, P., & MCDAVIS, R. J. (1992). Multicultural counseling competencies and standards. A call to the profession. *Journal of Counseling and Development, 70*(4), 477–486.

*SUE, D. W., IVEY, A. E., & PEDERSEN, P. (1996). *A theory of multicultural counseling and therapy.* Pacific Grove, CA: Brooks/Cole.

*SUE, D. W., & SUE, D. (2003). *Counseling the culturally diverse: Theory and practice* (4th ed.). New York: Wiley.

*WELFEL, E. R. (2002). *Ethics in counseling and psychotherapy: Standards, research, and emerging issues* (2nd ed.). Pacific Grove, CA: Brooks/Cole.

*YALOM, I. D. (2003). *The gift of therapy: An open letter to a new generation of therapists and their patients.* New York: HarperCollins (Perennial).

Theories and Techniques of Counseling

Psychoanalytic Therapy

Sigmund *Freud*

SIGMUND FREUD (1856–1939) was the first-born in a Viennese family of three boys and five girls. His father, like many others of his time and place, was very authoritarian. Freud's family background is a factor to consider in understanding the development of his theory.

Even though Freud's family had limited finances and was forced to live in a crowded apartment, his parents made every effort to foster his obvious intellectual capacities. Freud had many interests, but his career choices were restricted because of his Jewish heritage. He finally settled on medicine. Only 4 years after earning his medical degree from the University of Vienna at the age of 26, he attained a prestigious position there as a lecturer.

Freud devoted most of his life to formulating and extending his theory of psychoanalysis. Interestingly, the most creative phase of his life corresponded to a period when he was experiencing severe emotional problems of his own. During his early 40s, Freud had numerous psychosomatic disorders, as well as exaggerated fears of dying and other phobias, and was involved in the difficult task of self-analysis. By exploring the meaning of his own dreams, he gained insights into the dynamics of personality development. He first examined his childhood memories and came to realize the intense hostility he had felt for his father. He also recalled his childhood sexual feelings for his mother, who was attractive, loving, and protective. He then clinically formulated his theory as he observed his patients work through their own problems in analysis.

Freud had little tolerance for colleagues who diverged from his psychoanalytic doctrines. He attempted to control the movement by expelling those who disagreed. Carl Jung and Alfred Adler, for example, worked closely with Freud, but each founded his own therapeutic school after repeated disagreements with Freud on theoretical and clinical issues.

Freud was highly creative and productive, frequently putting in 18-hour days. His collected works fill 24 volumes. Freud's productivity remained at this prolific level until late in his life when he contracted cancer of the jaw. During his last two decades, he underwent 33 operations and was in almost constant pain. He died in London in 1939.

As the originator of psychoanalysis, Freud distinguished himself as an intellectual giant. He pioneered new techniques for understanding human behavior, and his efforts resulted in the most comprehensive theory of personality and psychotherapy ever developed. ∎

WHERE TO GO FROM HERE

InfoTrac College Edition Resources

Recommended Supplementary Readings

References and Suggested Readings

INTRODUCTION*

Freud's views continue to influence contemporary practice. Many of his basic concepts are still part of the foundation on which other theorists build and develop. Indeed, most of the theories of counseling and psychotherapy discussed in this book have been influenced by psychoanalytic principles and techniques. Some of these therapeutic approaches extended the psychoanalytic model, others modified its concepts and procedures, and others emerged as a reaction against it.

Freud's psychoanalytic system is a model of personality development and an approach to psychotherapy. He gave psychotherapy a new look and new horizons, calling attention to psychodynamic factors that motivate behavior, focusing on the role of the unconscious, and developing the first therapeutic procedures for understanding and modifying the structure of one's basic character. Freud's theory is a benchmark against which many other theories are measured.

It is impossible to capture in one chapter the diversity of psychodynamic approaches that have arisen since Freud. The main focus of this chapter, rather, is on basic psychoanalytic concepts and practices, many of which originated with Freud. The chapter sketches therapies that apply classical psychoanalytic concepts to practice less rigorously than he did. The chapter also summarizes Erik Erikson's theory of psychosocial development, which extends Freudian theory in several ways. Brief attention is given to Carl Jung's approach and to contemporary psychoanalytic theory and practice.

 KEY CONCEPTS

View of Human Nature

The Freudian view of human nature is basically deterministic. According to Freud, our behavior is determined by irrational forces, unconscious motivations, and biological and instinctual drives as these evolve through key psychosexual stages in the first 6 years of life.

Instincts are central to the Freudian approach. Although he originally used the term *libido* to refer to sexual energy, he later broadened it to include the energy of all the *life instincts*. These instincts serve the purpose of the survival of the individual and the human race; they are oriented toward growth, development, and creativity. Libido, then, should be understood as a source of motivation that encompasses sexual energy but goes beyond it. Freud includes all pleasurable acts in his concept of the life instincts; he sees the goal of much of life as gaining pleasure and avoiding pain.

---

*I want to acknowledge the contributions of both Dr. William Blau and Dr. J. Michael Russell in updating and refining the ideas in this chapter for all the editions of this book. Recognition also goes to Dr. Art Pomponio for his suggestions and contribution to the section on the contemporary psychoanalytic approaches.

Freud also postulates *death instincts,* which account for the aggressive drive. At times, people manifest through their behavior an unconscious wish to die or to hurt themselves or others. Managing this aggressive drive is a major challenge to the human race. In Freud's view, both sexual and aggressive drives are powerful determinants of why people act as they do.

Structure of Personality

According to the psychoanalytic view, the personality consists of three systems: the id, the ego, and the superego. These are names for psychological structures and should not be thought of as manikins that separately operate the personality; one's personality functions as a whole rather than as three discrete segments. The *id* is the biological component, the *ego* is the psychological component, and the *superego* is the social component.

From the orthodox Freudian perspective, humans are viewed as energy systems. The dynamics of personality consist of the ways in which psychic energy is distributed to the id, ego, and superego. Because the amount of energy is limited, one system gains control over the available energy at the expense of the other two systems. Behavior is determined by this psychic energy.

THE ID   The id is the original system of personality; at birth a person is all id. The id is the primary source of psychic energy and the seat of the instincts. It lacks organization and is blind, demanding, and insistent. A cauldron of seething excitement, the id cannot tolerate tension, and it functions to discharge tension immediately and return to a homeostatic condition. Ruled by the *pleasure principle,* which is aimed at reducing tension, avoiding pain, and gaining pleasure, the id is illogical, amoral, and driven to satisfy instinctual needs. The id never matures, remaining the spoiled brat of personality. It does not think but only wishes or acts. The id is largely unconscious, or out of awareness.

THE EGO   The ego has contact with the external world of reality. It is the "executive" that governs, controls, and regulates the personality. As a "traffic cop," it mediates between the instincts and the surrounding environment. The ego controls consciousness and exercises censorship. Ruled by the *reality principle,* the ego does realistic and logical thinking and formulates plans of action for satisfying needs. What is the relation of the ego to the id? The ego, as the seat of intelligence and rationality, checks and controls the blind impulses of the id. Whereas the id knows only subjective reality, the ego distinguishes between mental images and things in the external world.

THE SUPEREGO   The superego is the judicial branch of personality. It includes a person's moral code, the main concern being whether an action is good or bad, right or wrong. It represents the ideal rather than the real and strives not for pleasure but for perfection. The superego represents the traditional values and ideals of society as they are handed down from parents to children. It functions to inhibit the id impulses, to persuade the ego to substitute moralistic goals for realistic ones, and to strive for perfection. The superego, then, as the internalization of the standards of parents and society, is related to psychological rewards and punishments. The rewards are feelings of pride and self-love; the punishments are feelings of guilt and inferiority.

Consciousness and the Unconscious

Perhaps Freud's greatest contributions are his concepts of the unconscious and of the levels of consciousness, which are the keys to understanding behavior and the problems of personality. The unconscious cannot be studied directly but is inferred from behavior. Clinical evidence for postulating the unconscious includes the following: (1) dreams, which are symbolic representations of unconscious needs, wishes, and conflicts; (2) slips of the tongue and forgetting, for example, a familiar name; (3) posthypnotic suggestions; (4) material derived from free-association techniques; (5) material derived from projective techniques; and (6) the symbolic content of psychotic symptoms.

For Freud, consciousness is a thin slice of the total mind. Like the greater part of the iceberg that lies below the surface of the water, the larger part of the mind exists below the surface of awareness. The unconscious stores all experiences, memories, and repressed material. Needs and motivations that are inaccessible—that is, out of awareness—are also outside the sphere of conscious control. Most psychological functioning exists in the out-of-awareness realm. The aim of psychoanalytic therapy, therefore, is to make the unconscious motives conscious, for only then can an individual exercise choice. Understanding the role of the unconscious is central to grasping the essence of the psychoanalytic model of behavior.

Unconscious processes are at the root of all forms of neurotic symptoms and behaviors. From this perspective, a "cure" is based on uncovering the meaning of symptoms, the causes of behavior, and the repressed materials that interfere with healthy functioning. It is to be noted, however, that intellectual insight alone does not resolve the symptom. The client's need to cling to old patterns (repetition) must be confronted by working through transference distortions, a process discussed later in this chapter.

Anxiety

Also essential to the psychoanalytic approach is its concept of anxiety. Anxiety is a state of tension that motivates us to do something. It develops out of a conflict among the id, ego, and superego over control of the available psychic energy. Its function is to warn of impending danger.

There are three kinds of anxiety: reality, neurotic, and moral. *Reality anxiety* is the fear of danger from the external world, and the level of such anxiety is proportionate to the degree of real threat. Neurotic and moral anxieties are evoked by threats to the "balance of power" within the person. They signal to the ego that unless appropriate measures are taken the danger may increase until the ego is overthrown. *Neurotic anxiety* is the fear that the instincts will get out of hand and cause one to do something for which one will be punished. *Moral anxiety* is the fear of one's own conscience. People with a well-developed conscience tend to feel guilty when they do something contrary to their moral code. When the ego cannot control anxiety by rational and direct methods, it relies on indirect ones—namely, ego-defense behavior.

Ego-Defense Mechanisms

Ego-defense mechanisms help the individual cope with anxiety and prevent the ego from being overwhelmed. Rather than being pathological, ego defenses are normal behaviors that can have adaptive value provided they do not become a style of life that enables the individual to avoid facing reality. The defenses employed depend on the individual's level of development and degree of anxiety. Defense mechanisms have two characteristics in common: (1) they either deny or distort reality, and (2) they operate on an unconscious level. Here are brief descriptions of some common ego defenses:

- *Repression.* Repression is one of the most important Freudian processes, and it is the basis of many other ego defenses and of neurotic disorders. It is a means of defense through which threatening or painful thoughts and feelings are excluded from awareness. Freud explained repression as an involuntary removal of something from consciousness. It is assumed that most of the painful events of the first 5 or 6 years of life are buried, yet these events do influence later behavior.
- *Denial.* Denial plays a defensive role similar to that of repression, yet it generally operates at preconscious and conscious levels. Denial of reality is perhaps the simplest of all self-defense mechanisms; it is a way of distorting what the individual thinks, feels, or perceives in a traumatic situation. It consists of defending against anxiety by "closing one's eyes" to the existence of threatening reality.
- *Reaction formation.* One defense against a threatening impulse is to actively express the opposite impulse. By developing conscious attitudes and behaviors that are diametrically opposed to disturbing desires, people do not have to face the anxiety that would result if they were to recognize these dimensions of themselves. Individuals may conceal hate with a facade of love, be extremely nice when they harbor negative reactions, or mask cruelty with excessive kindness.
- *Projection.* Another mechanism of self-deception consists of attributing to others one's own unacceptable desires and impulses. Lustful, aggressive, or other impulses are seen as being possessed by "those people out there, but not by me."

- *Displacement.* One way to cope with anxiety is to discharge impulses by shifting from a threatening object to a "safer target." Displacement consists of directing energy toward another object or person when the original object or person is inaccessible. For example, the meek man who feels intimidated by his boss comes home and unloads inappropriate hostility onto his children.

- *Rationalization.* Some people manufacture "good" reasons to explain away a bruised ego. Rationalization helps justify specific behaviors, and it aids in softening the blow connected with disappointments. When people do not get positions they have applied for in their work, they think of logical reasons they did not succeed, and they sometimes attempt to convince themselves that they really did not want the position anyway.

- *Sublimation.* From the Freudian perspective, sublimation involves diverting sexual or aggressive energy into other channels, ones that are usually socially acceptable and sometimes even admirable. For example, aggressive impulses can be channeled into athletic activities, so that the person finds a way of expressing aggressive feelings and, as an added bonus, is often praised.

- *Regression.* Regression involves going back to an earlier phase of development when there were fewer demands. In the face of severe stress or extreme challenge, individuals may attempt to cope with their anxiety by clinging to immature and inappropriate behaviors. For example, children who are frightened in school may indulge in infantile behavior such as weeping, excessive dependence, thumbsucking, hiding, or clinging to the teacher.

- *Introjection.* The mechanism of introjection consists of taking in and "swallowing" the values and standards of others. For example, in concentration camps some of the prisoners dealt with overwhelming anxiety by accepting the values of the enemy through identification with the aggressor. It should be noted that there are also positive forms of introjection, such as the incorporation of parental values or the attributes and values of the therapist (assuming that these are not merely uncritically accepted).

- *Identification.* Although identification is part of the developmental process by which children learn gender-role behaviors, it can also be a defensive reaction. Identification can enhance self-worth and protect one from a sense of being a failure. Thus, people who feel basically inferior may identify themselves with successful causes, organizations, or people in the hope that they will be perceived as worthwhile.

- *Compensation.* Compensation consists of masking perceived weaknesses or developing certain positive traits to make up for limitations. This mechanism can have direct adjustive value, and it can also be an attempt by the person to say "Don't see the ways in which I am inferior, but see me in my accomplishments."

Development of Personality

IMPORTANCE OF EARLY DEVELOPMENT   A significant contribution of the psychoanalytic model is delineation of the stages of psychosocial and psychosexual development from birth through adulthood. This provides the counselor with the conceptual tools for understanding key developmental tasks characteristic of the various stages of life.

I have found that the problems people typically bring to counseling revolve around three issues: (1) the inability to trust oneself and others, the fear of loving and forming close relationships, and low self-esteem; (2) the inability to recognize and express anger, the denial of one's own power as a person, and the lack of a sense of autonomy; and (3) the inability to fully accept one's sexuality and sexual feelings, and difficulty in accepting oneself as a man or woman. According to the Freudian psychoanalytic view, these three areas of personal and social development—love and trust, dealing with negative feelings, and developing a positive acceptance of sexuality—are all grounded in the first 6 years of life. This period is the foundation on which later personality development is built.

ERIKSON'S PSYCHOSOCIAL PERSPECTIVE   Erik Erikson (1963) built on Freud's ideas and extended his theory by stressing the psychosocial aspects of development beyond early childhood. His theory of development holds that psychosexual growth and psychosocial growth take place together, and that at each stage of life we face the task of establishing equilibrium between ourselves and our social world. He describes development in terms of the entire life span, divided by specific crises to be resolved. According to Erikson, a *crisis* is equivalent to a turning point in life, when we have the potential to move forward or to regress. At these turning points we can either resolve our conflicts or fail to master the developmental task. To a large extent, our life is the result of the choices we make at each of these stages.

Erikson is often credited with bringing an emphasis on social factors to contemporary psychoanalysis. Classical psychoanalysis is grounded on *id psychology,* and it holds that instincts and intrapsychic conflicts are the basic factors shaping personality development (both normal and abnormal). Contemporary psychoanalytic thinking tends to be based on *ego psychology,* which does not deny the role of intrapsychic conflicts but emphasizes the striving of the ego for mastery and competence throughout the human life span. Ego psychology deals with both the early and the later developmental stages, for the assumption is that current problems cannot simply be reduced to repetitions of unconscious conflicts from early childhood. The stages of adolescence, mid-adulthood, and later adulthood all involve particular crises that must be addressed. As one's past has meaning in terms of the future, there is a continuity in development, reflected by stages of growth; each stage is related to the other stages.

It can be fruitful to view an individual's development from a combined perspective that includes both psychosexual and psychosocial factors. Erikson believed Freud did not go far enough in explaining the ego's place in development and did not give enough attention to social influences throughout the life span. A comparison of Freud's psychosexual view and Erikson's psychosocial view of the stages of development is presented in Table 4-1.

TABLE 4-1   Comparison of Freud's Psychosexual Stages and Erikson's Psychosocial Stages

PERIOD OF LIFE	FREUD	ERIKSON
First year of life	*Oral stage* Sucking at mother's breasts satisfies need for food and pleasure. Infant needs to get basic nurturing, or later feelings of greediness and acquisitiveness may develop. Oral fixations result from deprivation of oral gratification in infancy. Later personality problems can include mistrust of others, rejecting others; love, and fear of or inability to form intimate relationships.	*Infancy: Trust versus mistrust* If significant others provide for basic physical and emotional needs, infant develops a sense of trust. If basic needs are not met, an attitude of mistrust toward the world, especially toward interpersonal relationships, is the result.
Ages 1–3	*Anal stage* Anal zone becomes of major significance in formation of personality. Main developmental tasks include learning independence, accepting personal power, and learning to express negative feelings such as rage and aggression. Parental discipline patterns and attitudes have significant consequences for child's later personality development.	*Early childhood: Autonomy versus shame and doubt* A time for developing autonomy. Basic struggle is between a sense of self-reliance and a sense of self-doubt. Child needs to explore and experiment, to make mistakes, and to test limits. If parents promote dependency, child's autonomy is inhibited and capacity to deal with world successfully is hampered.
Ages 3–6	*Phallic stage* Basic conflict centers on unconscious incestuous desires that child develops for parent of opposite sex and that, because of their threatening nature, are repressed. Male phallic stage, known as *Oedipus complex*, involves mother as love object for boy. Female phallic stage,	*Preschool age: Initiative versus guilt* Basic task is to achieve a sense of competence and initiative. If children are given freedom to select personally meaningful activities, they tend to develop a positive view of self and follow through with their projects. If they are not allowed to make their own deci-

TABLE 4-1   Comparison of Freud's Psychosexual Stages and Erikson's Psychosocial Stages (continued)

PERIOD OF LIFE	FREUD	ERIKSON
	known as *Electra complex,* involves girl's striving for father's love and approval. How parents respond, verbally and nonverbally, to child's emerging sexuality has an impact on sexual attitudes and feelings that child develops.	sions, they tend to develop guilt over taking initiative. They then refrain from taking an active stance and allow others to choose for them.
Ages 6–12	*Latency stage* After the torment of sexual impulses of preceding years, this period is relatively quiescent. Sexual interests are replaced by interests in school, playmates, sports, and a range of new activities. This is a time of socialization as child turns outward and forms relationships with others.	*School age: Industry versus inferiority* Child needs to expand understanding of world, continue to develop appropriate gender-role identity, and learn the basic skills required for school success Basic task is to achieve a sense of industry, which refers to setting and attaining personal goals. Failure to do so results in a sense of inadequacy.
Ages 12–18	*Genital stage* Old themes of phallic stage are revived. This stage begins with puberty and lasts until senility sets in. Even though there are societal restrictions and taboos, adolescents can deal with sexual energy by investing it in various socially acceptable activities such as forming friendships, engaging in art or in sports, and preparing for a career.	*Adolescence: Identity versus role confusion* A time of transition between childhood and adulthood. A time for testing limits, for breaking dependent ties, and for establishing a new identity. Major conflicts center on clarification of self-identity, life goals, and life's meaning. Failure to achieve a sense of identity results in role confusion.
Ages 18–35	*Genital stage continues* Core characteristic of mature adult is the freedom "to love and to work." This move toward adulthood involves freedom from parental influence and capacity to care for others.	*Young adulthood: Intimacy versus isolation.* Developmental task at this time is to form intimate relationships. Failure to achieve intimacy can lead to alienation and isolation.

(continued)

TABLE 4-1   Comparison of Freud's Psychosexual Stages and Erikson's Psychosocial Stages (continued)

PERIOD OF LIFE	FREUD	ERIKSON
Ages 35–60	*Genital stage continues*	*Middle age: Generativity versus stagnation.* There is a need to go beyond self and family and be involved in helping the next generation. This is a time of adjusting to the discrepancy between one's dream and one's actual accomplishments. Failure to achieve a sense of productivity often leads to psychological stagnation.
Ages 60+	*Genital stage continues*	*Later life: Integrity versus despair* If one looks back on life with few regrets and feels personally worthwhile, ego integrity results. Failure to achieve ego integrity can lead to feelings of despair, hopelessness, guilt, resentment, and self-rejection.

COUNSELING IMPLICATIONS   By taking a combined psychosexual and psychosocial perspective, counselors have a useful conceptual framework for understanding developmental issues as they appear in therapy. The key needs and developmental tasks, along with the challenges inherent at each stage of life, provide a model for understanding some of the core conflicts clients explore in their therapy sessions. Questions such as these can give direction to the therapeutic process:

- What are some major developmental tasks at each stage in life, and how are these tasks related to counseling?
- What themes give continuity to this individual's life?
- What are some universal concerns of people at various points in life? How can people be challenged to make life-affirming choices at these points?
- What is the relationship between an individual's current problems and significant events from earlier years?
- What choices were made at critical periods, and how did the person deal with these various crises?
- What are the sociocultural factors influencing development that need to be understood if therapy is to be comprehensive?

By attending to sociocultural factors in the therapy process, practitioners are provided with a framework for understanding the major tasks and crises of each stage of development. The principal strength of psychosocial theory is that it acknowledges that humans are biological, psychological, and social beings and that an interactive mix of these inner and outer forces shapes behavior (Hamachek, 1988). This approach gives special weight to childhood and adolescent factors that are significant in later stages of development while recognizing that the later stages also have their significant crises. Themes and threads can be found running throughout clients' lives.

 # THE THERAPEUTIC PROCESS

Therapeutic Goals

Two goals of Freudian psychoanalytic therapy are to make the unconscious conscious and to strengthen the ego so that behavior is based more on reality and less on instinctual cravings or irrational guilt. Successful analysis is believed to result in significant modification of the individual's personality and character structure. Therapeutic methods are used to bring out unconscious material. Then childhood experiences are reconstructed, discussed, interpreted, and analyzed. It is clear that the process is not limited to solving problems and learning new behaviors. Rather, there is a deeper probing into the past to develop the level of self-understanding that is assumed to be necessary for a change in character. Analytic therapy is oriented toward achieving insight, but not just an intellectual understanding; it is essential that the feelings and memories associated with this self-understanding be experienced.

Therapist's Function and Role

Classical analysts typically assume an anonymous stance, which is sometimes called the "blank-screen" approach. They engage in very little self-disclosure and maintain a sense of neutrality to foster a *transference relationship,* in which their clients will make *projections* onto them. If therapists say little about themselves and rarely share their personal reactions, they believe whatever the client feels toward them will largely be the product of feelings associated with other significant figures from the past. These projections, which have their origins in unfinished and repressed situations, are considered "grist for the mill," and their analysis is the very essence of therapeutic work.

One of the central functions of analysis is to help clients acquire the freedom to love, work, and play. Other functions include assisting clients in achieving self-awareness, honesty, and more effective personal relationships; in dealing with anxiety in a realistic way; and in gaining control over impulsive and irrational behavior. The analyst must first establish a working relationship with the client and then do a lot of listening and interpreting. Particular attention is given to the client's resistances. The analyst listens, learns, and decides when to make appropriate interpretations. A major function of interpretation is to accelerate the process of uncovering unconscious material. The analyst listens for gaps and inconsistencies in the client's story, infers the meaning of reported dreams and free associations, and remains sensitive to clues concerning the client's feelings toward the analyst.

Organizing these therapeutic processes within the context of understanding personality structure and psychodynamics enables the analyst to formulate the nature of the client's problems. One of the central functions of the analyst is to teach clients the meaning of these processes so that they are able to achieve insight into their problems, increase their awareness of ways to change, and thus gain more control over their lives.

The process of psychoanalytic therapy is somewhat like putting the pieces of a puzzle together. Whether clients change depends considerably more on their readiness to change than on the accuracy of the therapist's interpretations. If the therapist pushes the client too rapidly or offers ill-timed interpretations, therapy is likely to become counterproductive.

Client's Experience in Therapy

Clients interested in traditional psychoanalysis must be willing to commit themselves to an intensive and long-term therapy process. After some face-to-face sessions with the analyst, clients lie on a couch and free-associate; that is, they say whatever comes to mind without self-censorship. This process of free association is known as the "fundamental rule." Clients report their feelings, experiences, associations, memories, and fantasies to the analyst. Lying on the couch encourages deep, uncensored reflections and reduces the stimuli that might interfere with getting in touch with internal conflicts and productions. It also reduces clients' ability to "read" their analyst's face for reactions and, hence, fosters the projections characteristic of a regressive transference. At the same time, the analyst is freed from having to carefully monitor facial clues.

What has just been described is *classical psychoanalysis*. Many psychoanalytically oriented practitioners (as distinct from analysts) do not use all these techniques. Yet they do remain alert to transference manifestations and work with dreams and with unconscious material.

Clients in psychoanalytic therapy make a commitment with the therapist to stick with the procedures of an intensive therapeutic process. They agree to talk, because their verbal productions are the heart of psychoanalytic therapy. They are typically asked not to make any radical changes in their lifestyle during the period of analysis, such as getting a divorce or quitting their job.

Psychoanalytic clients are ready to terminate their sessions when they and their analyst mutually agree that they have resolved those symptoms and conflicts that were amenable to resolution, have clarified and accepted their remaining emotional problems, have understood the historical roots of their difficulties, and can integrate their awareness of past problems with their present relationships. Successful analysis answers a client's "why" questions regarding his or her life. Clients who emerge successfully from analytic therapy report that they have achieved such things as an understanding of their symptoms and the functions they serve, an insight into how their environment affects them and how they affect the environment, and reduced defensiveness (Saretsky, 1978).

Relationship Between Therapist and Client

The client's relationship with the analyst is conceptualized in the transference process, which is the core of the psychoanalytic approach. Transference is the client's unconscious shifting to the analyst of feelings and fantasies that are reactions to significant others in the client's past. Transference allows clients to understand and resolve "unfinished business" from these past relationships. As therapy progresses, childhood feelings and conflicts begin to surface from the depths of the unconscious. Clients regress emotionally. Some of their feelings arise from conflicts such as trust versus mistrust, love versus hate, dependence versus independence, and autonomy versus shame and guilt. Transference takes place when clients resurrect from their early years intense conflicts relating to love, sexuality, hostility, anxiety, and resentment; bring them into the present; reexperience them; and attach them to the analyst. For example, clients may transfer unresolved feelings toward a stern and unloving father to the analyst, who, in their eyes, becomes stern and unloving. Angry feelings are the product of negative transference, but clients may also develop a positive transference and, for example, fall in love with the analyst, wish to be adopted, or in many other ways seek the love, acceptance, and approval of an all-powerful therapist. In short, the analyst becomes a current substitute for significant others.

If therapy is to produce change, the transference relationship must be worked through. The *working-through* process consists of an exploration of unconscious material and defenses, most of which originated in early childhood. Working through is achieved by repeating interpretations and by exploring forms of resistance. It results in a resolution of old patterns and allows clients to make new choices. In the process of working through there is a constant going back to the raw data of the session in an attempt to gain new understandings of present experience. Effective therapy requires that the client develop a relationship in the present with the analyst that is a corrective and integrative experience.

Clients have many opportunities to see the variety of ways in which their core conflicts and core defenses are manifested in their daily life. It is assumed that for clients to become psychologically independent they must not only become aware of this unconscious material but also achieve some level of freedom from behavior motivated by infantile strivings, such as the need for total love and acceptance from parental figures. If this demanding phase of the therapeutic relationship is not properly worked through, clients simply transfer their infantile wishes for universal love and acceptance to other figures they deem powerful. It is precisely in the client–therapist relationship that the manifestation of these childhood motivations becomes apparent.

Regardless of the length of psychoanalytic therapy, traces of our child-hood needs and traumas will never be completely erased. Thus, our infantile conflicts may not be fully resolved, even though many aspects of transference are worked through with a therapist. We may need to struggle at times throughout our life with feelings that we project onto others as well as with unrealistic demands that we expect others to fulfill. In this sense we experi-ence transference with many people, and our past is always a vital part of the person we are presently becoming.

It is a mistake to assume that all feelings clients have toward their thera-pists are manifestations of transference. Many of these reactions may have a reality base, and clients' feelings may well be directed to the here-and-now style the therapist exhibits. Every positive response (such as liking the thera-pist) should not be labeled "positive transference." Conversely, a client's anger toward the therapist may be a function of the therapist's behavior; it is a mis-take to label all negative reactions as signs of "negative transference."

The notion of never becoming completely free of past experiences has sig-nificant implications for therapists who become intimately involved in the un-resolved conflicts of their clients. Even if the conflicts of therapists have surfaced to awareness, and even if therapists have dealt with these personal is-sues in their own intensive therapy, they may still project distortions onto clients. The intense therapeutic relationship is bound to ignite some of the un-conscious conflicts within therapists. Known as *countertransference*, this phe-nomenon occurs when there is inappropriate affect, when therapists respond in irrational ways, or when they lose their objectivity in a relationship because their own conflicts are triggered. Countertransference also refers to the reac-tions therapists have toward their clients that may interfere with their objectiv-ity. For example, a male client may become excessively dependent on his female therapist. The client may look to her to direct him and tell him how to live, and he may look to her for the love and acceptance that he felt he was unable to se-cure from his mother. The therapist herself may have unresolved needs to nur-ture, to foster a dependent relationship, and to be told that she is significant, and she may be meeting her own needs by in some way keeping her client de-pendent. Unless she is aware of her own needs as well as her own dynamics, it is very likely that her dynamics will interfere with the progress of therapy.

All countertransference reactions should not be considered as detrimental to therapeutic progress. Searles (1979) suggests some positive outcomes to countertransference. A growing number of psychoanalysts are maintaining that countertransference reactions can provide an important means for un-derstanding the world of the client. The relational model of psychoanalysis regards transference as being an interactive process between the client and the therapist. In this model, instead of carefully avoiding countertransference, analysts can learn a great deal about a patient's personality structure by paying attention to their reactions to the patient (Mitchell, 1988). The analyst who notes a countertransference mood of irritability, for instance, may learn something about a client's pattern of being demanding. In this light, countertransference can be seen as potentially useful if it is explored in analysis. Viewed in this more positive way, countertransference becomes a key avenue for helping the client.

What is of paramount importance is that therapists develop some level of objectivity and not react irrationally and subjectively in the face of anger, love, adulation, criticism, and other intense feelings expressed by their clients. Most psychoanalytic training programs require that trainees undergo their own extensive analysis as a client. If psychotherapists become aware of symptoms (such as strong aversion to certain types of clients, strong attraction to other types of clients, psychosomatic reactions that occur at definite times in therapeutic relationships, and the like), it behooves them to seek professional consultation or enter their own therapy for a time to work out unresolved personal issues that stand in the way of their being effective therapists.

It should be clear that the client–therapist relationship is of vital importance in psychoanalytic therapy. As a result of this relationship, particularly in working through the transference situation, clients acquire insights into their own unconscious psychodynamics. Awareness of and insights into repressed material are the bases of the analytic growth process. Clients are able to understand the association between their past experiences and their current behavior. The psychoanalytic approach assumes that without this dynamic self-understanding there can be no substantial personality change or resolution of present conflicts.

 # APPLICATION: THERAPEUTIC TECHNIQUES AND PROCEDURES

This section deals with the techniques most commonly used by psychoanalytically oriented therapists. Psychoanalytic therapy (as opposed to traditional psychoanalysis) includes these features:

- The therapy is geared more to limited objectives than to restructuring one's personality.
- The therapist is less likely to use the couch.
- There are probably fewer sessions.
- There is more frequent use of supportive interventions—such as reassurance, expressions of empathy and support, and suggestions—and more self-disclosure by the therapist.
- The focus is more on pressing practical issues than on working with fantasy material.

The techniques of psychoanalytic therapy are aimed at increasing awareness, fostering insights into the client's behavior, and understanding the meanings of symptoms. The therapy proceeds from the client's talk to catharsis to insight to working through unconscious material. This work is done to attain the goals of intellectual and emotional understanding and reeducation, which, it is hoped, lead to personality change. The six basic techniques of psychoanalytic therapy are (1) maintaining the analytic framework, (2) free association, (3) interpretation, (4) dream analysis, (5) analysis of resistance, and (6) analysis of transference. In *Case Approach to Counseling and Psychotherapy* (Corey, 2005, chap. 2), Dr. William Blau, a psychoanalytically oriented therapist, illustrates some treatment techniques in the case of Ruth.

Maintaining the Analytic Framework

The psychoanalytic process stresses maintaining a particular framework aimed at accomplishing the goals of this type of therapy. "Maintaining the analytic framework" refers to a whole range of procedural and stylistic factors, such as the analyst's relative anonymity, the regularity and consistency of meetings, and starting and ending the sessions on time. One of the most powerful features of psychoanalytically oriented therapy is that the consistent framework is itself a therapeutic factor, comparable on an emotional level to the regular feeding of an infant. Analysts attempt to minimize departures from this consistent pattern (such as vacations, changes in fees, or changes in the meeting environment).

Free Association

Free association plays a central role in the process of maintaining the analytic framework. Clients are encouraged to say whatever comes to mind, regardless of how painful, silly, trivial, illogical, or irrelevant it may be. Such *free association* is the central technique in psychoanalytic therapy. In essence, clients flow with any feelings or thoughts by reporting them immediately without censorship. As the analytic work progresses, most clients will occasionally depart from this basic rule, and these resistances will be interpreted by the therapist when it is timely to do so.

Free association is one of the basic tools used to open the doors to unconscious wishes, fantasies, conflicts, and motivations. This technique often leads to some recollection of past experiences and, at times, a release of intense feelings (catharsis) that have been blocked off. This release is not seen as crucial in itself, however. During the free-association process, the therapist's task is to identify the repressed material that is locked in the unconscious. The sequence of associations guides the therapist in understanding the connections clients make among events. Blockings or disruptions in associations serve as cues to anxiety-arousing material. The therapist interprets the material to clients, guiding them toward increased insight into the underlying dynamics.

As analytic therapists listen to their clients' free associations, they hear not only the surface content but also the hidden meaning. This awareness of the language of the unconscious has been termed "listening with the third ear" (Reik, 1948). Nothing the client says is taken at face value. For example, a slip of the tongue can suggest that an expressed affect is accompanied by a conflicting affect. Areas that clients do not talk about are as significant as the areas they do discuss. Although psychoanalytic theory offers guidelines, the individual client must determine the actual meanings of specific content through associations.

Interpretation

Interpretation consists of the analyst's pointing out, explaining, and even teaching the client the meanings of behavior that is manifested in dreams, free association, resistances, and the therapeutic relationship itself. The functions of interpretations are to enable the ego to assimilate new material and to speed up the process of uncovering further unconscious material.

Interpretation is grounded in the therapist's assessment of the client's personality and of what factors in the client's past contributed to his or her difficulties. Under contemporary definitions, interpretation includes identifying, clarifying, and translating the client's material.

In making an appropriate interpretation, the therapist must be guided by a sense of the client's readiness to consider it (Saretsky, 1978). The therapist uses the client's reactions as a gauge. It is important that interpretations be well timed; the client will reject ones that are inappropriately timed. A general rule is that interpretation should be presented when the phenomenon to be interpreted is close to conscious awareness. In other words, the analyst should interpret material that the client has not yet seen for him- or herself but is capable of tolerating and incorporating. Another general rule is that interpretation should always start from the surface and go only as deep as the client is able to go. A third general rule is that it is best to point out a resistance or defense before interpreting the emotion or conflict that lies beneath it.

Dream Analysis

Dream analysis is an important procedure for uncovering unconscious material and giving the client insight into some areas of unresolved problems. During sleep, defenses are lowered and repressed feelings surface. Freud sees dreams as the "royal road to the unconscious," for in them one's unconscious wishes, needs, and fears are expressed. Some motivations are so unacceptable to the person that they are expressed in disguised or symbolic form rather than being revealed directly.

Dreams have two levels of content: latent content and manifest content. *Latent content* consists of hidden, symbolic, and unconscious motives, wishes, and fears. Because they are so painful and threatening, the unconscious sexual and aggressive impulses that make up latent content are transformed into the more acceptable *manifest content,* which is the dream as it appears to the dreamer. The process by which the latent content of a dream is transformed into the less threatening manifest content is called *dream work.* The therapist's task is to uncover disguised meanings by studying the symbols in the manifest content of the dream.

During the session, therapists may ask clients to free-associate to some aspect of the manifest content of a dream for the purpose of uncovering the latent meanings. Therapists participate in the process by exploring clients' associations with them. Interpreting the meanings of the dream elements helps clients unlock the repression that has kept the material from consciousness and relate the new insight to their present struggles. Dreams may serve as a pathway to repressed material, but they also provide an understanding of clients' current functioning.

Analysis and Interpretation of Resistance

Resistance, a concept fundamental to the practice of psychoanalysis, is anything that works against the progress of therapy and prevents the client from producing previously unconscious material. Specifically, in analytic therapy resistance is the client's reluctance to bring to the surface of awareness unconscious material that has been repressed. Resistance refers to any idea, attitude, feeling, or action (conscious or unconscious) that fosters the status quo and gets in the way of change. During free association or association to dreams, the client may evidence an unwillingness to relate certain thoughts, feelings, and experiences. Freud views resistance as an unconscious dynamic that people use to defend against the intolerable anxiety and pain that would arise if they were to become aware of their repressed impulses and feelings.

As a defense against anxiety, resistance operates specifically in psychoanalytic therapy to prevent clients and therapists from succeeding in their joint effort to gain insights into the dynamics of the unconscious. Because resistance blocks threatening material from entering awareness, analytic therapists point it out, and clients must confront it if they hope to deal with conflicts realistically. The therapists' interpretation is aimed at helping clients become aware of the reasons for the resistance so that they can deal with them. As a general rule, therapists point out and interpret the most obvious resistances to lessen the possibility of clients' rejecting the interpretation and to increase the chance that they will begin to look at their resistive behavior.

Resistances are not just something to be overcome. Because they are representative of usual defensive approaches in daily life, they need to be recognized as devices that defend against anxiety but that interfere with the ability to accept change that could lead to experiencing a more gratifying life. It is extremely important that therapists respect the resistances of clients and assist them in working therapeutically with their defenses. When handled properly, resistance can be one of the most valuable tools in understanding the client.

Analysis and Interpretation of Transference

As was mentioned earlier, transference manifests itself in the therapeutic process at the point where clients' earlier relationships contribute to their distorting the present with the therapist. It makes sense that clients often react to their therapist as they did to a significant person. The transference situation is considered valuable because its manifestations provide clients with the opportunity to reexperience a variety of feelings that would otherwise be inaccessible. Through the relationship with the therapist, clients express feelings, beliefs, and desires that they have buried in their unconscious. Through appropriate interpretations and working through of these current expressions of early feelings, clients are able to change some of their long-standing patterns of behavior.

The analysis of transference is a central technique in psychoanalysis and psychoanalytically oriented therapy, for it allows clients to achieve here-and-now insight into the influence of the past on their present functioning. Interpretation of the transference relationship enables clients to work through old conflicts that are keeping them fixated and retarding their emotional growth. In essence, the effects of early relationships are counteracted by working through a similar emotional conflict in the therapeutic relationship. An example of utilizing transference is given in a later section on the case of Stan.

 # JUNG'S PERSPECTIVE ON THE DEVELOPMENT OF PERSONALITY

At one time Freud referred to Carl Jung as his spiritual heir, but Jung eventually developed a theory of personality that was markedly different from Freudian psychoanalysis. Jung's *analytical psychology* is an elaborate explanation of human nature that combines ideas from history, mythology, anthropology, and religion (Schultz & Schultz, 2001). Jung made monumental contributions to our deep understanding of the human personality and personal development, particularly during middle age.

Jung's pioneering work places central importance on the psychological changes that are associated with midlife. He maintains that at midlife we need to let go of many of the values and behaviors that guided the first half of our life and confront our unconscious. We can best do this by paying attention to the messages of our dreams and by engaging in creative activities such as writing or painting. The task facing us during the midlife period is to be less influenced by rational thought and to instead give expression to these unconscious forces and integrate them into our conscious life (Schultz & Schultz, 2001).

Jung himself learned a great deal from his own midlife crisis. At age 81 he wrote about his recollections in his autobiography, *Memories, Dreams, Reflections* (1961), in which he also identified some of his major contributions. Jung made a choice to focus on the unconscious realm in his personal life, which also influenced the development of his theory of personality. However, he had a very different conception of the unconscious than did Freud. Jung was a colleague of Freud's and valued many of his contributions, but Jung eventually came to the point of not being able to support some of Freud's basic concepts, especially his theory of sexuality. Jung (1961) recalls Freud's words to him: "My dear Jung, promise me never to abandon the sexual theory. This is the most essential thing of all. You see, we must make a dogma of it, an unshakable bulwark" (p. 150). Jung became convinced that he could no longer collaborate with Freud because he believed Freud placed his own authority over truth. Freud had little tolerance for other theoreticians, such as Jung and Adler, who dared to challenge his theories. Although Jung had a lot to lose professionally by withdrawing from Freud, he saw no other choice. He subsequently developed a spiritual approach that places great emphasis on being impelled to find meaning in life in contrast to being driven by the psychological and biological forces described by Freud.

Jung maintains that humans are not merely shaped by past events (Freudian determinism) but that we are influenced by our future as well as our past. Part of the nature of humans is to be constantly developing, growing, and moving toward a balanced and complete level of development. For Jung, our present personality is shaped both by who and what we have been and also by what we aspire to be in the future. His theory is based on the assumption that humans tend to move toward the fulfillment or realization of all of their capabilities. Achieving individuation—the harmonious integration of the conscious and unconscious aspects of personality—is an innate and primary goal. For Jung, we have both constructive and destructive forces, and to become integrated, it is essential to accept the dark side of our nature with its primitive impulses such as selfishness and greed. Acceptance of this dark side (or shadow) does not imply being dominated by this dimension of our being but simply recognizing that this is a part of our nature.

Jung teaches that many dreams contain messages from the deepest layer of the unconscious, which he describes as the source of creativity. Jung refers to the *collective unconscious* as "the deepest level of the psyche containing the accumulation of inherited experiences of human and prehuman species" (as cited in Schultz & Schultz, 2001, p. 100). Jung sees a connection between each person's personality and the past, not only childhood events but also the history of the species. Thus, dreams reflect both an individual's personal unconscious and the collective unconscious of all of humanity. This means that some dreams may deal with an individual's relationship to a larger whole such as the family, universal humanity, or generations over time. The contents of the collective unconscious are called *archetypes*. Among the most important archetypes are the persona, the anima and animus, and the shadow. The *persona* is a mask, or public face, that we wear to protect ourselves. The *animus* and the *anima* represent both the biological and psychological aspects of masculinity and femininity, which are thought to coexist in both sexes. The *shadow* has the deepest roots and is the most dangerous and powerful of the archetypes. It represents our dark side, the thoughts, feelings, and actions that we tend to disown by projecting them outward. In a dream all of these parts can be considered manifestations of who and what we are.

Jung agrees with Freud that dreams provide a pathway into the unconscious, but he differs from Freud on their functions. Jung writes that dreams have two purposes. They are prospective; that is, they help people prepare themselves for the experiences and events they anticipate in the near future. They also serve a compensatory function, working to bring about a balance between opposites within the person. They compensate for the overdevelopment of one facet of the individual's personality (Schultz & Schultz, 2001).

Jung views dreams more as an attempt to express than as an attempt to repress and disguise. Dreams are a creative effort of the dreamer in struggling with contradiction, complexity, and confusion. The aim of the dream is resolution and integration. According to Jung, each part of the dream can be understood as some projected quality of the dreamer. His method of interpretation draws on a series of dreams obtained from a person, during the course of which the meaning gradually unfolds. If you are interested in further reading, I suggest Jung (1961) and Harris (1996).

CONTEMPORARY TRENDS: OBJECT-RELATIONS THEORY, SELF PSYCHOLOGY, AND RELATIONAL PSYCHOANALYSIS

Psychoanalytic theory continues to evolve. Freud emphasized intrapsychic conflicts pertaining to the gratification of basic needs. Writers in the neo-Freudian school moved away from this orthodox position and contributed to the growth and expansion of the psychoanalytic movement by incorporating the cultural and social influences on personality. Then ego psychology, with its stress on psychosocial development throughout the life span, was developed, largely by Erikson. Anna Freud, with her identification of defense mechanisms, is a central figure in ego psychology. She spent most of her professional life adapting psychoanalysis to children and adolescents.

The more recent approaches are often classified under the labels of object-relations theory, self psychology, and relational psychoanalysis. *Object-relations theory* is a form of analytic treatment that involves exploration of internal unconscious identifications and internalizations of external objects (aspects of significant other people). Object relations are interpersonal relationships as they are represented intrapsychically. The term *object* was used by Freud to refer to that which satisfies a need, or to the significant person or thing that is the object, or target, of one's feelings or drives. It is used interchangeably with the term *other* to refer to an important person to whom the child, and later the adult, becomes attached. Rather than being individuals with separate identities, others are perceived by an infant as objects for gratifying needs. Object-relations theories have diverged from orthodox psychoanalysis, although some theorists, most notably Otto Kernberg, attempt to integrate the increasingly varied ideas that characterize this school of thought (St. Clair & Wigren, 2004).

As we have seen, classical psychoanalysis presents a theory of mind based on unconscious drives and defenses. Clinical psychoanalysis strives to make conscious these unconscious forces, thus reducing internal conflicts between them. Analysts identify and interpret unconscious thoughts and feelings that are expressed through avenues such as free association, slips of the tongue, and dreams. Traditional psychoanalysis assumes that the analyst can discover and name the "truth" about clients.

In time, psychoanalytic theory began to more fully consider the unconscious influence of other people. Self psychology grew out of the work of Heinz Kohut (1971). His emphasis was on how we use interpersonal relationships (self objects) to develop our own sense of self.

Contemporary psychoanalysis has challenged many of the fundamental assumptions about traditional psychoanalytic theory and treatment. Perhaps the most important single difference between contemporary and classical psychoanalysis is the reconceptualization of the nature of the analytic relationship itself. Whether called intersubjective, interpersonal, or relational, most contemporary approaches to analysis are based on the exploration of the complex conscious and unconscious dynamics at play with respect to both therapist and client.

Mitchell (2000) has written extensively about these new conceptualizations of the analytic relationship. He integrates developmental theory, attachment theory, systems theory, and interpersonal theory to demonstrate the profound ways in which we seek attachments with others, especially early caregivers. The *relational model* is based on the assumption that therapy is an interactive process between client and therapist. Interpersonal analysts believe that countertransference actually provides a rich source of information about the client's character and dynamics. Mitchell adds to this object-relations position a cultural dimension by noting that the caregiver's qualities reflect the particular culture in which the person lives. We are all deeply embedded within our cultures. Since different cultures maintain different values, there can be no objective psychic truths. Our internal (unconscious) structures are all relational and relative. This is in stark contrast to the Freudian notion of universal biological drives that could be said to function in every human.

Contemporary theorists have challenged what they consider to be the authoritarian nature of the traditional psychoanalytic relationship and replaced it with a more egalitarian model. From the time of Freud to the late 20th century, the power between analyst and patient was unequal. Contemporary approaches to analysis assume a more equal power relationship and describe the process of analysis as a mutual exploration of two subjectivities. Theoretically, this shift is seen not so much as a political statement about equality as it is a recognition that analysis consists of two individuals encountering each other in a complex interplay of emotions. The analyst is no longer cast in a detached and anonymous role but is able to be responsive and emotionally present. Today, the task of analysis is to explore each psyche in a creative way, customized to the particular analyst and patient working together in a particular culture at a particular moment in time.

SUMMARY OF STAGES OF DEVELOPMENT   The contemporary psychoanalytic theories center on predictable developmental sequences in which the early experiences of the self shift in relation to an expanding awareness of others. Once self–other patterns are established, it is assumed they influence later interpersonal relationships. Specifically, people search for relationships that match the patterns established by their earlier experiences. People who are either overly dependent or overly detached, for example, can be repeating patterns of relating they established with their mother when they were toddlers (Hedges, 1983). These newer theories provide insight into how an individual's inner world can cause difficulties in living in the actual world of people and relationships (St. Clair & Wigren, 2004).

A central influence on contemporary object-relations theory is Margaret Mahler (1968), a pediatrician who emphasized the observation of children. In her view, the resolution of the Oedipus complex is less critical than the child's progression from a symbiotic relationship with a maternal figure toward separation and individuation. Her studies focus on the interactions between the child and the mother in the first 3 years of life. Mahler conceptualizes the development of the self somewhat differently from the traditional Freudian psychosexual stages. Her belief is that the individual begins in a state of psychological fusion with the mother and progresses gradually to separation. The unfinished crises and residues of the earlier state of fusion, as well as the process of separating and individuating, have a profound influence on later relationships. Object relations of later life build on the child's search for a reconnection with the mother (St. Clair & Wigren, 2004). Psychological development can be thought of as the evolution of the way in which individuals separate and differentiate themselves from others.

Mahler calls the first 3 or 4 weeks of life *normal infantile autism*. Here the infant is presumed to be responding more to states of physiological tension than to psychological processes. Mahler believes the infant is unable to differentiate itself from its mother in many respects at this age. According to Melanie Klein (1975), another major contributor to the object-relations perspective, the infant perceives parts—breasts, face, hands, and mouth—rather than a unified self. In this undifferentiated state there is no whole self, and there are no whole objects. When adults show the most extreme forms of lack of psychological organization and sense of self, they may be thought of as returning to this most primitive infantile stage. Subsequent infant research by Daniel Stern (1985) has challenged this aspect of Mahler's theory, maintaining that infants are interested in others practically from birth.

Mahler's next phase, called *symbiosis*, is recognizable by the 3rd month and extends roughly through the 8th month. At this age the infant has a pronounced dependency on the mother. She (or the primary caregiver) is clearly a partner and not just an interchangeable part. The infant seems to expect a very high degree of emotional attunement with its mother.

The *separation–individuation* process begins in the 4th or 5th month. During this time the child moves away from symbiotic forms of relating. The child experiences separation from significant others yet still turns to them for a sense of confirmation and comfort. The child may demonstrate ambivalence, torn between enjoying separate states of independence and dependence. The toddler who proudly steps away from the parents and then runs back to be swept up in approving arms illustrates some of the main issues of this period (Hedges, 1983, p. 109). Others are looked to as approving mirrors for the child's developing sense of self; optimally, these relationships can provide a healthy self-esteem.

Children who do not experience the opportunity to differentiate, and those who lack the opportunity to idealize others while also taking pride in themselves, may later suffer from *narcissistic* character disorders and problems of self-esteem. The narcissistic personality is characterized by a grandiose and exaggerated sense of self-importance and an exploitive attitude toward others, which serve the function of masking a frail self-concept. Such individuals seek attention and admiration from others. They unrealistically exaggerate their accomplishments, and they have a tendency toward extreme self-absorption. Kernberg (1975) characterizes narcissistic people as focusing on themselves in their interactions with others, having a great need to be admired, possessing shallow affect, and being exploitive and, at times, parasitic in their relationships with others. Kohut (1971) characterizes such people as perceiving threats to their self-esteem and as having feelings of emptiness and deadness.

"Borderline" conditions are also rooted in the period of separation–individuation. People with a *borderline personality disorder* have moved into the separation process but have been thwarted by maternal rejection of their individuation. In other words, a crisis ensues when the child does develop beyond the stage of symbiosis but the mother (or the mothering figure) is unable to tolerate this beginning individuation and withdraws emotional support. Borderline people are characterized by instability, irritability, self-destructive acts, impulsive anger, and extreme mood shifts. They typically experience extended periods of disillusionment, punctuated by occasional euphoria. Kernberg describes the syndrome as including a lack of clear identity, a lack of deep understanding of other people, poor impulse control, and the inability to tolerate anxiety (1975, pp. 161–162).

Mahler's final subphase in the separation–individuation process involves a move toward constancy of self and object. This development is typically pronounced by the 36th month (Hedges, 1983). By now others are more fully seen as separate from the self. Ideally, children can begin to relate without being overwhelmed with fears of losing their sense of individuality, and they may enter into the later psychosexual and psychosocial stages with a firm foundation of selfhood.

This chapter permits only a brief treatment of the newer formulations in psychoanalytic theory. If you would like to pursue this emerging approach, an overview of this vast and growing literature can be found in Gabbard (2000), Hedges (1983), Mitchell and Black (1995), and St. Clair and Wigren (2004).

TREATING BORDERLINE AND NARCISSISTIC DISORDERS   Borderline and narcissistic disorders seem to be rooted in traumas and developmental disturbances during the separation–individuation phase. However, the full manifestations of the personality and behavioral symptoms tend to develop in early adulthood. Borderline and narcissistic symptoms such as splitting (a defensive process of keeping incompatible perceptions separate) and notions of grandiosity are behavioral manifestations of developmental tasks that were disturbed or not completed earlier (St. Clair & Wigren, 2004).

Some of the most powerful tools for understanding borderline and narcissistic personality organizations have emerged from the psychoanalytic models. Among the most significant theorists in this area are Kernberg (1975, 1976, 1997), Kohut (1971, 1977, 1984), and Masterson (1976). Although this book does not emphasize diagnostic issues, a great deal of recent psychoanalytic writing deals with the nature and treatment of borderline and narcissistic personality disorders and sheds new light on the understanding of these disorders. Kohut (1984) maintains that people are their healthiest and best when they can feel both independence and attachment, taking joy in themselves and also being able to idealize others. Mature adults feel a basic security grounded in a sense of freedom, self-sufficiency, and self-esteem; they are not compulsively dependent on others but also do not have to fear closeness.

PSYCHOANALYTIC THERAPY FROM A MULTICULTURAL PERSPECTIVE

Contributions to Multicultural Counseling

Psychoanalytically oriented therapy can be appropriate for culturally diverse populations. Comas-Diaz and Minrath (1985) recommend that the diffused sense of identity prevalent among borderline clients from ethnic minorities be examined from both a sociocultural and a developmental perspective. One aid to helping clients rebuild their identity is to emphasize strengths rather than deficiencies among ethnically different groups. Racial and ethnic minorities must simultaneously develop two sets of identity: a general overall ego identity and a cultural identity. Minority youths have a more complex adolescent experience because of this dual identity. Erikson's psychosocial approach, with its emphasis on critical issues in stages of development, has particular application to people of color. Counselors can help these clients review environmental situations at the various critical turning points in their lives to determine how certain events have affected them either positively or negatively.

Psychotherapists need to recognize and confront their own potential sources of bias and how countertransference could be conveyed unintentionally through their interventions. To the credit of the psychoanalytic approach, it stresses the value of intensive psychotherapy as part of the training of therapists. This helps therapists become aware of their own sources of countertransference, including their biases, prejudices, and racial or ethnic stereotypes.

Psychoanalytic Therapy Applied to the Case of Stan

In each of the chapters in Part 2, the case of Stan is used to demonstrate the practical applications of the theory in question. To give you a focus on Stan's central concerns, refer to the end of Chapter 1, where his biography is given. I also recommend that you at least skim Chapter 16, which deals with an integrative approach as applied to Stan.

In Chapters 4 through 14 you will notice that Stan is working with a female therapist. Given his feelings toward women, it may seem odd that he selected a woman for his therapist. However, knowing that he had difficulty with women, he deliberately made this choice as a way to challenge himself, both in his therapy and in his everyday life. As you will see, one of Stan's goals is to learn how to become less intimidated in the presence of women and to be more himself around them.

The psychoanalytic approach focuses on the unconscious psychodynamics of Stan's behavior. Considerable attention is given to material that he has repressed, such as his anxiety related to the threatened breakthrough of his sexual and aggressive impulses. In the past he had to rigidly control both these impulses, and when he did not, he got into trouble. He also developed a strong superego by introjecting parental values and standards and making them his own. These aspirations were unrealistic, for they were perfectionist goals. He could be loved only if he became perfect; yet no matter what he attempted, it never seemed adequate. He internalized his anger and guilt, which became depression.

At the extreme Stan demonstrated a self-destructive tendency, which is a way of inflicting punishment on himself. Instead of directing his hostility toward his parents and siblings, he turned it inward toward himself. Stan's preoccupation with drinking could be hypothesized as evidence of an oral fixation. Because he never received love and acceptance during his early childhood, he is still suffering from this deprivation and still desperately searching for approval and acceptance from others. Stan's gender-role identification was fraught with difficulties. He learned the basis of female–male relationships through his early experiences with his parents. What he saw was fighting, bickering, and discounting. His father was the weak one who always lost, and his mother was the strong, domineering force who could and did hurt men. Stan identified with his weak and impotent father; he generalized his fear of his mother to all women. It could be further hypothesized that he married a woman who was similar to his mother and who reinforced his feelings of impotence in her presence.

The opportunity to develop a transference relationship and work through it is the core of the therapy process. An assumption is that Stan will eventually relate to his therapist as he did to his mother and that the process will be a valuable means of gaining insight into the origin of his difficulties with women. The analytic process stresses an intensive exploration of Stan's past. The goal is to make the unconscious conscious, so that he will no longer be determined by unconscious forces. Stan devotes much therapy time to reliving and exploring his early past. As he talks, he gains increased understanding of the dynamics of his behavior. He begins to see connections between his present problems and early experiences in his childhood. Thus, Stan explores memories of relationships with his siblings and with his mother and father and also explores how he has generalized his view of women and men from his view of these family members. It is expected that he will reexperience old feelings and uncover buried feelings related to traumatic events. From another perspective, apart from whatever conscious insight Stan may acquire, the goal is for him to have a more integrated self, where feelings split off as foreign (the id) become more a part of what he is comfortable with (the ego). The relationship with his therapist, where old feelings have different outcomes from his past experiences with significant others, results in deep personality growth.

The therapist is likely to explore some of these questions with Stan: "What did you do when you felt unloved?" "As a child, what did you have to do with your negative feelings?" "Could you express your rage, hostility, hurt, and fears?" "What effects did your relationship with your mother have on you?" "What did this teach you about all women?" Brought into the here-and-now of the transference relationship, questions might include "When have you felt anything like this with me?" and "What are you learning from our relationship about how relationships with women might go?"

The analytic process focuses on key influences in Stan's developmental years, sometimes explicitly, sometimes in terms of how those earlier events are being relived in the present analytic relationship. As he comes to understand how he has been shaped by these past experiences, he is increasingly able to exert control over his present functioning. Many of Stan's fears become conscious, and then his energy does not have to remain fixed on defending himself from unconscious feelings. Instead, he can make new decisions about his current life. He can do this only if he works through the transference relationship, however, for the depth of his endeavors in therapy largely determines the depth and extent of his personality changes.

If the therapist is operating from a contemporary psychoanalytic orientation, her focus may well be on Stan's developmental sequences. Particular attention is paid to understanding his current behavior in the world as largely a repetition of one of his earlier developmental phases. Because of his dependency, it is useful in understanding his behavior to see that he is now repeating patterns that he formed with his mother during his infancy. Viewed from this perspective, Stan has not accomplished the task of separation and individuation. He is still "stuck" in the symbiotic phase on some levels. He is unable to obtain his confirmation of worth from himself, and he has not resolved the dependence–independence struggle. Looking at his behavior from the viewpoint

of self psychology can help the therapist deal with his difficulties in forming intimate relationships.

Follow-Up: You Continue as Stan's Psychoanalytic Therapist

With each of the 11 theoretical orientations, you will be encouraged to try your hand at applying the principles and techniques you have just studied in the chapter to working with Stan from that particular perspective. The information presented about Stan from each of these theory chapters will provide you with some ideas of how you might continue working with him if he were referred to you. Do your best to stay within the general spirit of each theory by identifying specific concepts you would draw from and techniques that you might use in helping him explore the struggles he identifies. Here are a series of questions to provide some structure in your thinking about his case:

- How much interest would you have in Stan's early childhood? What are some ways you'd help him see patterns between his childhood issues and his current problems?
- Consider the transference relationship that is likely to be established between you and Stan. How might you react to his making you into a significant person in his life?
- In working with Stan, what countertransference issues might arise for you?
- What resistances might you predict in your work with Stan? From a psychoanalytic perspective, how would you interpret this resistance? What might it be like for you to encounter his resistance?

Limitations for Multicultural Counseling

Traditional psychoanalytic approaches are costly, and psychoanalytic therapy is generally perceived as being based on upper- and middle-class values. Not all clients share these values, and for many the cost of treatment is prohibitive. Another limitation pertains to the ambiguity inherent in most psychoanalytic approaches. This can be problematic for clients from cultures who expect direction from a professional. For example, Hispanic and Asian American clients may prefer a more structured, problem-oriented approach to counseling and may not continue therapy if a nondirective approach is employed.

Furthermore, intrapsychic analysis may be in direct conflict with some clients' social framework and environmental perspective. This is especially true in working within the framework of long-term, in-depth analysis. Psychoanalytic therapy is more concerned with long-term personality reconstruction than with short-term problem solving.

Atkinson, Thompson, and Grant (1993) underscore the need for therapists to consider possible external sources of clients' problems, especially if clients have experienced an oppressive environment. The psychoanalytic approach can be criticized for failing to adequately address the social, cultural, and political factors that result in an individual's problems. If there is no balance between the external and internal perspectives, clients may be blamed for their condition.

There are likely to be some difficulties in applying a psychoanalytic approach with low-income clients. If these clients seek professional help, they are generally concerned with dealing with a crisis situation and with finding answers to concrete problems, or at least some direction, in addressing survival needs pertaining to housing, employment, and child care. This does not imply that low-income clients are unable to profit from analytic therapy but, rather, that this particular orientation could be more beneficial *after* more pressing issues and concerns have been resolved.

 ## SUMMARY AND EVALUATION

Summary

Some major concepts of psychoanalytic theory include the dynamics of the unconscious and its influence on behavior, the role of anxiety, and the development of personality at various stages in the life cycle.

Building on many of Freud's basic ideas, Erikson broadened the developmental perspective by including psychosocial trends. In his model, each of the eight stages of human development is characterized by a crisis, or turning point. We can either master the developmental task or fail to resolve the core struggle (Table 4-1 compares Freud's and Erikson's views on the developmental stages).

Psychoanalytic therapy consists largely of using methods to bring out unconscious material that can be worked through. It focuses primarily on childhood experiences, which are discussed, reconstructed, interpreted, and analyzed. The assumption is that this exploration of the past, which is typically accomplished by working through the transference relationship with the therapist, is necessary for character change. The most important techniques typically employed in psychoanalytic practice are maintaining the analytic framework, free association, interpretation, dream analysis, analysis of resistance, and analysis of transference.

Unlike Freudian theory, Jungian theory is not reductionist. Jung views humans positively and focuses on individuation, the capacity of humans to move toward wholeness and self-realization. To become what they are capable of becoming, individuals must explore the unconscious aspects of their personality, both the personal unconscious and the collective unconscious. In Jungian analytical therapy, the therapist assists the client in tapping his or her inner wisdom. The goal of therapy is not merely the resolution of immediate problems but the transformation of personality.

The contemporary trends in psychoanalytic theory are reflected in object-relations theory, the self psychology model, and the relational model. These approaches are based on the notion that at birth there is no differentiation between others and self and that others represent objects of need gratification for infants. Separation–individuation is achieved over time. When this process is successful, others are perceived as both separate and related.

Contributions of the Psychoanalytic Approach

I believe therapists can broaden their understanding of clients' struggles by appreciating Freud's many significant contributions. It must be emphasized that competent use of psychoanalytic techniques requires training beyond what most therapists are afforded in their training program. Regardless of theoretical orientation, however, it is well for therapists to understand such psychoanalytic phenomena as transference, countertransference, resistance, and the use of ego-defense mechanisms as reactions to anxiety. The psychoanalytic approach provides practitioners with a conceptual framework for looking at behavior and for understanding the origins and functions of symptoms. Applying the psychoanalytic point of view to therapy practice is particularly useful in (1) understanding resistances that take the form of canceling appointments, fleeing from therapy prematurely, and refusing to look at oneself; (2) understanding that unfinished business can be worked through, so that clients can provide a new ending to some of the events that have crippled them emotionally; (3) understanding the value and role of transference; and (4) understanding how the overuse of ego defenses, both in the counseling relationship and in daily life, can keep clients from functioning effectively.

Although there is little to be gained from blaming the past for the way a person is now or from dwelling on the past, considering the early history of a client is often useful in understanding and working with a client's current situation. Without completely accepting the orthodox Freudian position, we can still draw on many of the psychoanalytic concepts as a framework for understanding clients and for helping them achieve a deeper understanding of the roots of their conflicts.

If the psychoanalytic approach is considered in a broader context than its initial Freudian perspective, it becomes a more powerful and useful model for understanding human behavior. Although I find Freud's psychosexual concepts of value, I think that adding Erikson's stress on psychosocial factors gives a more complete picture of the critical turning points at each stage of development. Integrating these two perspectives is, in my view, most useful for understanding key themes in the development of personality. Erikson's developmental schema does not avoid the psychosexual issues and stages postulated by Freud; rather, Erikson extends the stages of psychosexual development throughout life. His perspective integrates psychosexual and psychosocial concepts without diminishing the import of either.

Therapists who work from a developmental perspective are able to see a continuity in life and to see certain directions their clients have taken. This perspective gives a broader picture of an individual's struggle, and clients are able to discover some significant connections among the various life stages.

Contributions of Modern Analytic Theorists

The contemporary trends in psychoanalytic thinking have contributed to the understanding of how our current behavior in the world is largely a repetition of patterns set during one of the early phases of development. Object-relations theory helps us see the ways in which clients interacted with significant others in the past and how they are superimposing these early experiences on present relationships. For the many clients in therapy who are struggling with issues such as separation and individuation, intimacy, dependence versus independence, and identity, these newer formulations can provide a framework for understanding how and where aspects of development have been fixated. They have significant implications for many areas of human interaction such as intimate relationships, the family and child rearing, and the therapeutic relationship. Some analytic therapists, such as Marmor (1997), demonstrate an openness toward integrating various methods: "I try to avoid putting every patient on a Procrustean bed of a singular therapeutic method but rather adapt my approach to the patient's own unique needs" (p. 32).

In my opinion it is possible to have an analytic framework that gives structure and direction to a counseling practice and at the same time to draw on other therapeutic techniques. I find value in the contributions of those writers who have built on the basic ideas of Freud and have added an emphasis on the social and cultural dimensions affecting personality development. In contemporary psychoanalytic practice more latitude is given to the therapist in using techniques and in developing the therapeutic relationship. The newer psychoanalytic theorists have enhanced, extended, and refocused classical analytic techniques. They are concentrating on the development of the ego and are paying attention to the social and cultural factors that influence the differentiation of an individual from others.

Although contemporary psychodynamic forms diverge considerably in many respects from the original Freudian emphasis on drives, the basic Freudian concepts of unconscious motivation, the influence of early development, transference, countertransference, and resistance are still central to the newer modifications. These concepts are of major importance in therapy and can be incorporated into therapeutic practices based on various theoretical approaches.

SOME DIRECTIONS OF CONTEMPORARY PSYCHODYNAMIC THERAPY Strupp (1992) maintains that the various contemporary modifications of psychoanalysis have infused psychodynamic psychotherapy with renewed vitality and vigor. Some of the current trends and directions in psychodynamic theory and practice that Strupp identifies are summarized here:

- Increasing attention is being given to disturbances during childhood and adolescence.
- The emphasis on treatment has shifted from the "classical" interest in curing neurotic disorders to the problems of dealing therapeutically with chronic personality disorders, borderline conditions, and narcissistic personality disorders. There is also a movement toward devising specific treatments for specific disorders.
- Increased attention is being paid to establishing a good therapeutic alliance early in therapy. A collaborative working relationship is now viewed as a key factor in a positive therapeutic outcome.
- Psychodynamic group therapy is becoming more popular. It has received widespread acceptance for a number of reasons: it is more economical, it provides clients with opportunities to learn how they function in groups, and it offers a unique perspective on understanding problems and working them through therapeutically.
- There is a renewed interest in the development of briefer forms of psychodynamic therapy, largely due to societal pressures for accountability and cost-effectiveness. The indications are that time-limited therapy will be used more in the future.

THE TREND TOWARD BRIEF PSYCHODYNAMIC THERAPY Many psychoanalytically oriented therapists are attempting to creatively meet modern challenges while retaining their original focus on depth and inner life (DeAngelis, 1996). These therapists support the move to the use of briefer therapy when this is indicated by the client's needs rather than by arbitrary limits set by a managed care system.

In keeping with the context of time-limited therapy, Messer and Warren (2001) describe *brief psychodynamic therapy* (BPT) as a promising approach. This adaptation applies the principles of psychodynamic theory and therapy to treating selective disorders within a preestablished time limit of generally 10 to 25 sessions. BPT makes use of key psychodynamic concepts such as the enduring impact of psychosexual, psychosocial, and object-relational stages of development; the existence of unconscious processes and resistance; the usefulness of interpretation; the importance of the working alliance; and the reenactment in the client's past emotional issues in relationship to the therapist. Most forms of this time-limited approach call upon the therapist to assume an active and directive role in quickly formulating a therapeutic focus that goes beneath the surface of presenting problems and symptoms and treats underlying issues. Some possible goals of this approach might include conflict resolution, greater access to feelings, increasing choice possibilities, improving interpersonal relationships, and symptom remission. Messer and Warren state that the objective of BPT is "to understand and treat people's problems in the context of their current situation and earlier life experience" (p. 83). The goals, therapeutic focus, and active role of the therapist have implications for the practice of individual therapy. Although BPT is not suitable for all clients, it meets a variety of clients' needs.

Despite the different approaches to brief psychodynamic therapy, Prochaska and Norcross (2003) believe they all share these common characteristics:

- Establish a time limitation.
- Target a specific interpersonal problem during the initial session.
- Assume a less neutral therapeutic stance than is true of traditional analytic approaches.
- Establish a strong working alliance.
- Use interpretation relatively early in the therapy relationship.

Limitations and Criticisms of the Psychoanalytic Approach

In general, considering factors such as time, expense, and availability of trained psychoanalytic therapists, the practical applications of many psychoanalytic techniques are limited. This is especially true of methods such as free association on the couch, dream analysis, and analysis of the transference relationship. A factor limiting the practical application of classical psychoanalysis is that many severely disturbed clients lack the level of ego strength needed for this treatment.

A major limitation of traditional psychoanalytic therapy is the relatively long time commitment required to accomplish analytic goals. Indeed, Alperin (1997) raises the question "Is psychoanalytically oriented psychotherapy compatible with managed care?" He persuasively argues that managed care violates many of the basic premises upon which psychoanalytic therapy rests. Alperin argues that analytic therapists who offer services under managed care cannot provide their clients with privacy and confidentiality and that the requirements and justifications for treatment under managed care plans negatively affect the therapeutic relationship and are injurious to the client. The basic principles of psychoanalytic therapy are both different from and incompatible with the philosophy of managed care. As was mentioned earlier, the emergence of brief psychodynamic therapy is a partial response to this criticism.

In a critique of long-term psychodynamic therapy, Strupp (1992) assumes that psychoanalytic therapy will remain a luxury for most people in our society. Strupp notes a decline in practices based on the classical analytic model due to reasons such as time commitment, expense, limited applications to diverse client populations, and questionable benefits. According to Strupp, the realities stemming from managed care will mean increasing emphasis on short-term treatments for specific disorders, limited goals, and containment of costs. In reaction to Strupp's position, Michael Russell (personal communication, June 22, 2003) contends that even though long-term therapy with a minimal agenda may be a luxury it remains an ideal arena from which to derive theories and techniques that can be modified to fit the realities of clinical practice. Russell suggests that, much as paramedics who practice in make-shift emergency circumstances would want to know all they could about what is available in the ideal hospital setting, therapists too will be better prepared for their work if they understand what discoveries might be available to them under more luxurious conditions.

A potential limitation of the psychoanalytic approach is the anonymous role assumed by the therapist. This stance can be justified on theoretical grounds, but in therapy situations other than classical psychoanalysis this stance is unduly restrictive. The classical technique of nondisclosure can be misused in short-term individual therapy and assessment. Therapists in these situations who adopt the blank-screen aloofness typical of the "pure" context of classical psychoanalysis may actually be keeping themselves hidden as persons in the guise of "being professional."

Yalom (2003) contends that therapist anonymity is not a good model for effective therapy. Rather than adopting a blank screen, he believes it is far better to strive to understand the past as a way of shedding light on the dynamics of the present therapist–client relationship. This is in keeping with the spirit of the relational analytic approach. Yalom encourages therapists to engage in authentic human encounters with their clients and adds, "The psychotherapy outcome literature heavily supports the view that therapist disclosure begets client disclosure" (p. 77).

From a feminist perspective there are distinct limitations to a number of Freudian concepts, especially the Oedipus and Electra complexes. In her review of feminist counseling and therapy, Enns (1993) also notes that the object-relations approach has been criticized for its emphasis on the role of the mother–child relationship in determining later interpersonal functioning. The approach gives great responsibility to mothers for deficiencies and distortions in development. Fathers are conspicuously absent from the hypothesis about patterns of early development; only mothers are blamed for inadequate parenting. Linehan's (1993a, 1993b) dialectical behavior therapy (DBT), addressed in some detail in Chapter 9, is an eclectic approach that avoids mother-bashing while accepting the notion that the borderline client experienced a childhood environment that was "invalidating" (Linehan, 1993a, pp. 49–52).

 ## WHERE TO GO FROM HERE

If this chapter has provided the impetus for you to learn more about the psychoanalytic approach or the contemporary offshoots of psychoanalysis, use the key words provided to access articles of interest from the InfoTrac College

Edition resources, or select a few books from the Recommended Supplementary Readings and References and Suggested Readings listed at the end of the chapter.

If you are using the *CD-ROM for Integrative Counseling*, refer to Session 10 ("Transference and Countertransference") and compare what I've written here with how I deal with transference and countertransference.

Various colleges and universities offer special workshops or short courses through continuing education on topics such as therapeutic considerations in working with borderline and narcissistic personalities. These workshops could give you a new perspective on the range of applications of contemporary psychoanalytic therapy. For further information about training programs, workshops, and graduate programs in various states, contact:

American Psychoanalytic Association
309 East 49th Street, New York, NY 10017
Telephone: (212) 752-0450
Fax: (212) 593–0571
Web site: http://www.apsa.org

 ## InfoTrac College Edition Resources

Psychoanalysis   The following key words are listed in such a way as to allow the InfoTrac College Edition search engine to locate a wider range of articles in the online library. The key words should be entered exactly as listed and include asterisks, "W1," and "AND."

Erik Erikson	Freud AND ego
Anna Freud	Freud AND superego
Sigmund Freud	Freud AND conscious
Otto Kernberg	Freud AND unconscious
Heinz Kohut	Psychosexual development
Margaret Mahler	Oedipus complex
Psychoanalysis	Ego-defense W1 mechanisms
Psychodynamic*	Object-relations W1 theory
Ego psychology	Transference
Object relations psych*	Carl Jung
Self psychology	Jung AND psyche
Freud AND drive	Jung AND ego
Freud AND id	Jung AND archetype*

Recommended Supplementary Readings

Psychoanalytic Theory: An Introduction (Elliott, 1994) provides thorough coverage of the psychoanalytic implications for "postmodern" theories, systems approaches, and feminist thought.

Techniques of Brief Psychotherapy (Flegenheimer, 1982) is useful in describing the processes of client selection, therapist training, and modifications of techniques used in brief psychoanalytic therapy.

Psychodynamic Psychiatry in Clinical Practice (Gabbard, 2000) offers an excellent account of various psychoanalytic perspectives on borderline and narcissistic disorders.

Object Relations and Self Psychology: An Introduction (St. Clair & Wigren, 2004) provides an overview and critical assessment of two streams of psychoanalytic theory and practice: object-relations theory and self psychology. Especially useful are the chapters discussing the approaches of Margaret Mahler, Otto Kernberg, and Heinz Kohut. This is a good place to start if you want an update on the contemporary trends in psychoanalysis.

References and Suggested Readings

*ALPERIN, R. M. (1997). Is psychoanalytically oriented psychotherapy compatible with managed care? In R. M. Alperin & D. G. Phillips (Eds.), *The impact of managed care on the practice of psychotherapy: Innovation, implementation, and controversy* (pp. 185–198). New York: Brunner/Mazel.

ATKINSON, D. R., THOMPSON, C. E., & GRANT, S. K. (1993). A three-dimensional model for counseling racial/ethnic minorities. *The Counseling Psychologist, 2*(2), 257–277.

COMAS-DIAZ, L., & MINRATH, M. (1985). Psychotherapy with ethnic minority borderline clients. *Psychotherapy, 22*(25), 418–426.

COREY, G. (2004). *Theory and practice of group counseling* (6th ed.). Belmont, CA: Brooks/Cole.

*COREY, G. (2005). *Case approach to counseling and psychotherapy* (6th ed.). Belmont, CA: Brooks/Cole.

*DeANGELIS, T. (1996). Psychoanalysis adapts to the 1990s. *APA Monitor, 27*(9), 1, 43.

*ELLIOT, A. (1994). *Psychoanalytic theory: An introduction.* Oxford UK & Cambridge USA: Blackwell.

ENNS, C. Z. (1993). Twenty years of feminist counseling and therapy: From naming biases to implementing multifaceted practice. *The Counseling Psychologist, 21*(1), 3–87.

*ERIKSON, E. H. (1963). *Childhood and society* (2nd ed.). New York: Norton.

*FLEGENHEIMER, W. V. (1982). *Techniques of brief psychotherapy.* New York: Aronson.

FREUD, S. (1949). *An outline of psychoanalysis.* New York: Norton.

*FREUD, S. (1955). *The interpretation of dreams.* London: Hogarth Press.

*GABBARD, G. (2000). *Psychodynamic psychiatry in clinical practice* (3rd ed.). Washington, DC: American Psychiatric Press.

HAMACHEK, D. F. (1988). Evaluating self-concept and ego development within Erikson's psychosocial framework: A formulation. *Journal of Counseling and Development, 66*(8), 354–360.

*HARRIS, A. S. (1996). *Living with paradox: An introduction to Jungian psychology.* Pacific Grove, CA: Brooks/Cole.

---

*Books and articles marked with an asterisk are suggested for further study.

*HEDGES, L. E. (1983). *Listening perspectives in psychotherapy*. New York: Aronson.

*JUNG, C. G. (1961). *Memories, dreams, reflections*. New York: Vintage.

KERNBERG, O. F. (1975). *Borderline conditions and pathological narcissism*. New York: Aronson.

KERNBERG, O. F. (1976). *Object-relations theory and clinical psychoanalysis*. New York: Aronson.

KERNBERG, O. F. (1997). Convergences and divergences in contemporary psychoan-alytic technique and psychoanalytic psychotherapy. In J. K. Zeig (Ed.), *The evolu-tion of psychotherapy: The third conference* (pp. 3–22). New York: Brunner/Mazel.

KLEIN, M. (1975). *The psychoanalysis of children*. New York: Dell.

KOHUT, H. (1971). *The analysis of self*. New York: International Universities Press.

KOHUT, H. (1977). *Restoration of the self*. New York: International Universities Press.

KOHUT, H. (1984). *How does psychoanalysis cure?* Chicago: University of Chicago Press.

LINEHAN, M. M. (1993a). *Cognitive-behavioral treatment of borderline personality dis-order*. New York: Guilford.

LINEHAN, M. M. (1993b). *Skills training manual for treating borderline personality dis-order*. New York: Guilford.

MAHLER, M. S. (1968). *On human symbiosis or the vicissitudes of individuation*. New York: International Universities Press.

MARMOR, J. (1997). The evolution of an analytic psychotherapist: A sixty-year search for conceptual clarity in the tower of Babel. In J. K. Zeig (Ed.), *The evolution of psychotherapy: The third conference* (pp. 23–36). New York: Brunner/Mazel.

MASTERSON, J. F. (1976). *Psychotherapy of the borderline adult: A developmental ap-proach*. New York: Brunner/Mazel.

MESSER, S. B., & WARREN, C. S. (2001). Brief psychodynamic therapy. In R. J. Corsini (Ed.), *Handbook of innovative therapies* (2nd ed., pp. 67–85). New York: Wiley.

MITCHELL, S. A. (1988). *Relational concepts in psychoanalysis: An integration*. Cam-bridge: Harvard University Press.

*MITCHELL, S. A. (2000). *Relationality: From attachment to intersubjectivity*. Hills-dale, NJ: The Analytic Press.

MITCHELL, S. A., & BLACK, M. J. (1995). *Freud and beyond: A history of modern psy-choanalytic thought*. New York: Basic Books.

PROCHASKA, J. O., & NORCROSS, J. C. (2003). *Systems of psychotherapy: A transthe-oretical analysis* (5th ed.). Pacific Grove, CA: Brooks/Cole.

REIK, T. (1948). *Listening with the third ear*. New York: Pyramid.

*ST. CLAIR, M., & WIGREN, J. (2004). *Object relations and self psychology: An intro-duction* (4th ed.). Belmont, CA: Brooks/Cole.

SARETSKY, T. (1978). The middle phase of treatment. In G. D. Goldman & D. S. Mil-man (Eds.), *Psychoanalytic psychotherapy* (pp. 91–110). Reading, MA: Addison-Wesley.

*SCHULTZ, D., & SCHULTZ, S. E. (2001). *Theories of personality* (7th ed.). Pacific Grove, CA: Brooks/Cole.

*SEARLES, H. F. (1979). *Countertransference and related subjects. Selected papers.* New York: International Universities Press.

STERN, D. N. (1985). *The interpersonal world of the infant: A view from psychoanalysis and developmental psychology.* New York: Basic Books.

STRUPP, H. H. (1992). The future of psychodynamic psychotherapy. *Psychotherapy, 29*(1), 21–27.

YALOM, I. D. (2003). *The gift of therapy: An open letter to a new generation of therapists and their patients.* New York: HarperCollins (Perennial).

Adlerian Therapy

Alfred **Adler**

ALFRED ADLER (1870–1937) Adler grew up in a Vienna family of six boys and two girls. His brother died as a very young boy in the bed next to Alfred. Adler's early childhood was not a happy time. He was sickly and very much aware of death. At age 4, he almost died of pneumonia. He heard the doctor tell his father that "Alfred is lost." Adler associated this time with his decision to become a physician. Because he was ill so much during the first few years of his life, Adler was pampered by his mother. Later he was "dethroned" by a younger brother. He developed a trusting relationship with his father but did not feel very close to his mother. He was extremely jealous of his older brother, Sigmund, which led to strained relationships between the two during childhood and adolescence. Given his early relationship with Sigmund Freud, one cannot help but suspect that patterns from his early family constellation were repeated in this relationship.

Adler's early years were characterized by struggling to overcome illnesses and feelings of inferiority. Although Adler felt inferior to his brother and his peers, he was determined to compensate for his physical limitations, and gradually he overcame many of his limitations.

It is clear that Alfred's early childhood experiences had an impact on the formation of his theory. Adler is an example of a person who shaped his own life as opposed to having it determined by fate. Adler was a poor student. His teacher advised his father to prepare Adler to be a shoemaker, but not much else. With determined effort Adler eventually rose to the top of his class. He went on to study medicine at the University of Vienna, entered private practice as an ophthalmologist, and then shifted to general medicine. He eventually specialized in neurology and psychiatry, and he had a keen interest in incurable childhood diseases.

Adler had a passionate concern for the common person and was outspoken about child-rearing practices, school reforms, and prejudices that resulted in conflict. He spoke and wrote in simple, nontechnical language so that the public could understand and apply the principles of his Individual Psychology. Adler's (1959) *Understanding Human Nature* was the first major psychology book to sell hundreds of thousands of copies in the United States. After serving in World War I as a medical officer, Adler created 32 child guidance clinics in the Vienna public schools and began training teachers, social workers, physicians, and other professionals. He pioneered the practice of teaching professionals through live demonstrations with parents and children before large audiences. The clinics he founded grew in number and in popularity, and he was indefatigable in lecturing and demonstrating his work.

Adler lived by an overcrowded work schedule most of his professional life, yet he still took some time to sing, enjoy music, and be with friends. In the mid-1920s, he began lecturing in the United States, and he later made frequent visits and tours. He ignored the warning of his friends to slow down, and on May 28, 1937, while taking a walk before a scheduled lecture in Aberdeen, Scotland, Adler collapsed and died of heart failure. ■

INTRODUCTION*

Along with Freud and Jung, Alfred Adler was a major contributor to the development of the psychodynamic approach to therapy. After 8 to 10 years of collaboration, Freud and Adler parted company, with Freud taking the position that Adler was a heretic who had deserted him. Adler resigned as president of the Vienna Psychoanalytic Society in 1911 and founded the Society for Individual Psychology in 1912. Freud then asserted that it was not possible to support Adlerian concepts and still remain in good standing as a psychoanalyst.

Later, a number of other psychoanalysts deviated from Freud's orthodox position (see Chapter 4). These Freudian revisionists, who included Karen Horney, Erich Fromm, and Harry Stack Sullivan, agreed that social and cultural factors were of great significance in shaping personality. Even though these three therapists are typically called neo-Freudians, it would be more appropriate, as Heinz Ansbacher (1979) has suggested, to refer to them as neo-Adlerians because they moved away from Freud's biological and deterministic point of view and toward Adler's social-psychological and teleological (or goal-oriented) view of human nature.

Adler stresses the unity of personality, contending that people can only be understood as integrated and complete beings. This view espouses the purposeful nature of behavior, emphasizing that where we are striving to go is more important than where we have come from. Adler saw humans as both the creators and the creations of their own lives; that is, people develop a unique style of living that is both a movement toward and an expression of their selected goals. In this sense, we create ourselves rather than merely being shaped by our childhood experiences.

After Adler's death in 1937, Rudolf Dreikurs was the most significant figure in bringing Adlerian psychology to the United States, especially as its principles applied to education, individual and group therapy, and family counseling. Dreikurs is credited with giving impetus to the idea of child guidance centers and to training professionals to work with a wide range of clients.

KEY CONCEPTS

View of Human Nature

Adler abandoned Freud's basic theories because he believed Freud was excessively narrow in his stress on biological and instinctual determination. Adler holds that the individual begins to form an approach to life somewhere in the

---

* I want to acknowledge the diligent efforts and contributions of Dr. James Bitter of East Tennessee State University in bringing this chapter up to date and for expanding the section dealing with the therapeutic process and practical applications.

first 6 years of living. Adler's focus is on how the person's perception of the past and his or her interpretation of early events has a continuing influence. On many theoretical grounds Adler was in opposition to Freud. According to Adler, for example, humans are motivated primarily by social relatedness rather than by sexual urges; behavior is purposeful and goal-directed; and consciousness, more than unconsciousness, is the focus of therapy. Unlike Freud, Adler stresses choice and responsibility, meaning in life, and the striving for success, completion, and perfection. Adler and Freud created very contrasting theories, even though both men grew up in the same city in the same era and were educated as physicians at the same university. Their individual and very different childhood experiences in their families were certainly key factors that shaped their distinctly different views of human nature (Schultz & Schultz, 2001).

Adler's theory focuses on inferiority feelings, which he sees as a normal condition of all people and as a source of all human striving. Rather than being considered a sign of weakness or abnormality, feelings of inferiority can be the wellspring of creativity. They motivate us to strive for mastery, success (superiority), and completion. We are driven to overcome our sense of inferiority and to strive for increasingly higher levels of development (Schultz & Schultz, 2001). Indeed, at around 6 years of age our fictional vision of ourselves as perfect or complete begins to form into a life goal. The life goal unifies the personality and becomes the source of human motivation; every striving and every effort to overcome inferiority is now in line with this goal.

From the Adlerian perspective, human behavior is not determined solely by heredity and environment. Instead, we have the capacity to interpret, influence, and create events. Adler asserts that *what* we were born with is not as important as what we choose to do with the abilities and limitations we possess. Adler's theory is a psychology of "use" rather than of possession. Although Adlerians reject the deterministic stance of Freud, they do not go to the other extreme and maintain that individuals can become whatever they want to be. Adlerians recognize that biological and environmental conditions limit our capacity to choose and to create.

Adlerians put the focus on reeducating individuals and reshaping society. Adler was the forerunner of a subjective approach to psychology that focuses on internal determinants of behavior such as values, beliefs, attitudes, goals, interests, and the individual perception of reality. He was a pioneer of an approach that is holistic, social, goal-oriented, systemic, and humanistic. Adler was also the first systemic therapist, in that he maintained that it is essential to understand people within the systems of which they are a part.

Subjective Perception of Reality

Adlerians attempt to view the world from the client's subjective frame of reference, an orientation described as phenomenological. The approach is phenomenological in that it pays attention to the individual way in which people perceive their world. This "subjective reality" includes the individual's perceptions, thoughts, feelings, values, beliefs, convictions, and conclusions. Behavior is understood from the vantage point of this subjective perspective. From the Adlerian perspective, objective reality is less important than how we interpret reality and the meanings we attach to what we experience.

As you will see in subsequent chapters, many contemporary theories have incorporated this notion of the client's subjective worldview as a basic factor explaining behavior. Some of the other approaches that have a phenomenological perspective are existential therapy, person-centered therapy, Gestalt therapy, the cognitive behavioral therapies, reality therapy, the postmodern approaches, and some of the systemic therapies.

Unity and Patterns of Human Personality

A basic premise of Adlerian *Individual Psychology* is that personality can only be understood holistically and systemically; that is, the individual is seen as an indivisible whole, born, reared, and living in specific familial, social, and cultural contexts. People are social, creative, decision-making beings who act with purpose and cannot be fully known outside the contexts that have meaning in their lives (Sherman & Dinkmeyer, 1987).

The human personality becomes unified through development of a life goal. An individual's thoughts, feelings, beliefs, convictions, attitudes, character, and actions are expressions of his or her uniqueness, and all reflect a plan of life that allows for movement toward a self-selected life goal. An implication of this holistic view of personality is that the client is an integral part of a social system. There is more focus on interpersonal relationships than on the individual's internal psychodynamics.

BEHAVIOR AS PURPOSEFUL AND GOAL-ORIENTED   Individual Psychology assumes that all human behavior has a purpose. Humans set goals for themselves, and behavior becomes unified in the context of these goals. The concept of the purposeful nature of behavior is perhaps the cornerstone of Adler's theory. Adler replaced deterministic explanations with teleological (purposive, goal-oriented) ones. A basic assumption of Individual Psychology is that we can only think, feel, and act in relation to our perception of our goal. Therefore, we can be fully understood only in light of knowing the purposes and goals toward which we are striving. Adlerians are interested in the future, without minimizing the importance of past influences. They assume that decisions are based on the person's experiences, on the present situation, and on the direction in which the person is moving. They look for continuity by paying attention to themes running through a person's life.

Adler was influenced by the philosopher Hans Vaihinger's (1965) view that people live by fictions (or views of how the world should be). Many Adlerians use the term *fictional finalism* to refer to an imagined central goal that guides a person's behavior. It should be noted, however, that Adler actually ceased using this term and replaced it with "guiding self-ideal" and "goal of perfection" to account for our striving toward superiority or perfection (Watts & Holden, 1994). Very early in life we begin to envision what we might be like if we were successful, complete, whole, or perfect. Applied to human motivation, a guiding self-ideal might be expressed in this way: "Only when I am perfect can I be secure" or "Only when I am important can I be accepted." The guiding self-ideal represents an individual's image of a goal of perfection, for which he or she strives in any given situation. Because of our subjective final goal, we have the creative power to choose what we will accept as truth, how we will behave, and how we will interpret events.

STRIVING FOR SIGNIFICANCE AND SUPERIORITY   Adler stresses that striving for perfection and coping with inferiority by seeking mastery are innate (Ansbacher & Ansbacher, 1979). To understand human behavior, it is essential to grasp the ideas of basic inferiority and compensation. From our earliest years, we recognize that we are helpless in many ways, which is characterized by feelings of inferiority. This inferiority is not a negative factor in life. According to Adler, the moment we experience inferiority we are pulled by the striving for superiority. He maintains that the goal of success pulls people forward toward mastery and enables them to overcome obstacles. The goal of superiority contributes to the development of human community. However, it is important to note that "superiority," as used by Adler, does not necessarily mean being superior to others. Rather, it means moving from a perceived lower position to a perceived higher position, from a felt minus to a felt plus. People cope with feelings of helplessness by striving for competence, mastery, and perfection. They can seek to change a weakness into a strength, for example, or strive to excel in one area of concentration to compensate for defects in other areas. The unique ways in which people develop a style of striving for competence is what constitutes individuality. The manner in which Adler reacted to his childhood and adolescent experiences made him a living example of this aspect of his theory.

LIFESTYLE   An individual's core beliefs and assumptions through which the person organizes his or her reality and finds meaning in life events constitutes the individual's *lifestyle*. Synonyms for this term include "plan of life," "style of life," "life movement," "strategy for living," and "road map of life." Lifestyle is the connecting theme that unifies all our actions, and our lifestyle consists of all our values and perceptions regarding self, others, and life. It is the characteristic way we move toward our life goal. Adler saw us as actors, creators, and artists. In striving for goals that have meaning to us, we develop a unique style of life (Ansbacher, 1974). This concept accounts for why all of our behaviors fit together to provide consistency to our actions. Understanding one's lifestyle is somewhat like understanding the style of a composer: "We can begin wherever we choose: every expression will lead us in the same direction—toward the one motive, the one melody, around which the personality is built" (Adler, as cited in Ansbacher & Ansbacher, 1964, p. 332). People are viewed as adopting a proactive, rather than a reactive, approach to their social environment. Although events in the environment influence the development of personality, such events are not the causes of what people become.

In striving for the goal of superiority, Adlerians believe some individuals develop their intellect; others, their artistic talent; others, athletic skills; and so on. These styles of life consist of people's views about themselves and the world and their distinctive behaviors and habits as they pursue personal goals. Everything we do is influenced by this unique lifestyle. Experiences within the family and relationships between siblings contribute to development of this self-consistent way of perceiving, thinking, feeling, and behaving.

Although our unique style is created primarily during the first 6 years of life, subsequent events may have a profound effect on the development of our personality. Experiences in themselves are not the decisive factors; rather, it is our *interpretation* of these events that shape personality. Faulty interpretations may lead to mistaken notions in our private logic, which will significantly influence present behavior. Once we become aware of the patterns and continuity of our lives, we are in a position to modify those faulty assumptions and make basic changes. We can reframe childhood experiences and *consciously* create a new style of life.

Social Interest and Community Feeling

Social interest and community feeling *(Gemeinschaftsgefühl)* are probably Adler's most significant and distinctive concepts (Ansbacher, 1992). These terms refer to individuals' awareness of being part of the human community and to individuals' attitudes in dealing with the social world.

Social interest includes striving for a better future for humanity. The socialization process, which begins in childhood, involves finding a place in society and acquiring a sense of belonging and of contributing (Kefir, 1981). Social interest is taught, learned, and used. Adler equated social interest with a sense of identification and empathy with others: "to see with the eyes of another, to hear with the ears of another, to feel with the heart of another" (as cited in Ansbacher & Ansbacher, 1979, p. 42). Social interest is the central indicator of mental health. Those with social interest tend to direct the striving toward the healthy and socially useful side of life. From the Adlerian perspective, as social interest develops, feelings of inferiority and alienation diminish. People express social interest through shared activity and mutual respect.

Individual Psychology rests on a central belief that our happiness and success are largely related to this social connectedness. Those who lack this *community feeling* become discouraged and end up on the useless side of life. Adler noted that we are socially embedded and cannot be understood in isolation from the social context. We seek a place in the family and in society to fulfill basic needs for security, acceptance, and worthiness. Many of the problems we experience are related to the fear of not being accepted by the groups we value. If our sense of belonging is not fulfilled, anxiety is the result. Only when we feel united with others are we able to act with courage in facing and dealing with our problems (Adler, 1964).

Adler taught that we must successfully master three universal life tasks: building friendships (social task), establishing intimacy (love–marriage task), and contributing to society (occupational task). All people need to address these tasks, regardless of age, gender, time in history, culture, or nationality. Dreikurs and Mosak (1967) and Mosak and Dreikurs (1967) added two other tasks of life to this list: getting along with ourselves (self-acceptance), and developing our spiritual dimension (including values, meaning, life goals, and our relationship with the universe, or cosmos). These life tasks are so fundamental to human living that dysfunction in any one of them is often an indicator of a psychological disorder (American Psychiatric Association, 2000).

Birth Order and Sibling Relationships

The Adlerian approach is unique in giving special attention to the relationships between siblings and the psychological birth position in one's family. Adler identified five psychological positions: oldest, second of only two, middle, youngest, and only. (Actual birth order itself is less important than the individual's interpretation of his or her place in the family.) Because Adlerians view most human problems as social in nature, they emphasize relationships within the family.

Adler (1958) observes that many people wonder why children in the same family often differ so widely, and he pointed out that it is a fallacy to assume that children of the same family are formed in the same environment. Although siblings share aspects in common in the family constellation, the psychological situation of each child is different from that of the others due to birth order. The following description of the influence of birth order is based on Ansbacher and Ansbacher (1964), Dreikurs (1953), and Adler (1958).

1.   The *oldest child* generally receives a good deal of attention, and during the time she is the only child, she is typically somewhat spoiled as the center of attention. She tends to be dependable and hard working and strives to keep ahead. When a new brother or sister arrives on the scene, however, she finds herself ousted from her favored position. She is no longer unique or special. She may readily believe that the newcomer (or intruder) will rob her of the love to which she is accustomed.

2.   The *second child* is in a different position. From the time she is born, she shares the attention with another child. The typical second child behaves as if she were in a race and is generally under full steam at all times. It is as though this second child were in training to surpass the older brother or sister. This competitive struggle between the first two children influences the later course of their lives. The younger child develops a knack for finding out the elder child's weak spots and proceeds to win praise from both parents and teachers

by achieving successes where the older sibling has failed. If one is talented in a given area, the other strives for recognition by developing other abilities. The second-born is often opposite to the firstborn.

3.   The *middle child* often feels squeezed out. This child may become convinced of the unfairness of life and feel cheated. This person may assume a "poor me" attitude and can become a problem child. However, especially in families characterized by conflict, the middle child may become the switchboard and the peacemaker, the person who holds things together. If there are four children in a family, the second child will often feel like a middle child and the third will be more easygoing, more social, and may align with the firstborn.

4.   The *youngest child* is always the baby of the family and tends to be the most pampered one. He has a special role to play, for all the other children are ahead of him. Youngest children tend to go their own way. They often develop in ways no others in the family have thought about.

5.   The *only child* has a problem of her own. Although she shares some of the characteristics of the oldest child (namely, high achievement drive), she may not learn to share or cooperate with other children. She will learn to deal with adults well, as they make up her original familial world. Often, the only child is pampered by her parents and may become dependently tied to one or both of them. She may want to have center stage all of the time, and if her position is challenged, she will feel it is unfair.

Birth order and the interpretation of one's position in the family have a great deal to do with how adults interact in the world. Individuals acquire a certain style of relating to others in childhood and form a definite picture of themselves that they carry into their adult interactions. In Adlerian therapy, working with family dynamics, especially relationships among siblings, assumes a key role. Although it is important to avoid stereotyping individuals, it does help to see how certain personality trends that began in childhood as a result of sibling rivalry influence individuals throughout life.

 ## THE THERAPEUTIC PROCESS

Therapeutic Goals

Adlerian counseling rests on a collaborative arrangement between the client and the counselor. In general, the therapeutic process includes forming a relationship based on mutual respect and identifying, exploring, and disclosing *mistaken goals* and *faulty assumptions* within the person's style of living. This is followed by a reeducation of the client toward the useful side of life. The main aim of therapy is to develop the client's sense of belonging and to assist in the adoption of behaviors and processes characterized by community feeling and social interest. This is accomplished by increasing the client's self-awareness and challenging and modifying his or her fundamental premises, life goals, and basic concepts (Dreikurs, 1967, 1997).

Adlerians do not see clients as being "sick" and in need of being "cured." Instead, they view clients as discouraged. Symptoms are attempted solutions. The goal is to reeducate clients so that they can live in society as equals, both giving to society and receiving from others (Mosak, 2000). Therefore, the counseling process focuses on providing information, teaching, guiding, and offering encouragement to discouraged clients. Encouragement is the most powerful method available for changing a person's beliefs. It helps clients build self-confidence and stimulates courage. Courage is the willingness to act *even when fearful* in ways that are consistent with social interest. Fear and courage go hand in hand; without fear, there would be no need for courage. The loss of courage, or discouragement, results in mistaken and dysfunctional behavior. Discouraged people do not act in line with social interest on the useful side of life.

Adlerian counselors educate clients in new ways of looking at themselves, others, and life. Through the process of providing clients with a new "cognitive map," a fundamental understanding of the purpose of their behavior, counselors assist them in changing their perceptions. Mosak (2000) lists these goals for the educational process of therapy:

- Fostering social interest
- Helping clients overcome feelings of discouragement and inferiority
- Modifying clients' views and goals—that is, changing their lifestyle
- Changing faulty motivation
- Assisting clients to feel a sense of equality with others
- Helping people to become contributing members of society

Therapist's Function and Role

Adlerian counselors realize that clients can become discouraged and function ineffectively because of mistaken beliefs, faulty values, and goals in the useless side of life. They operate on the assumption that clients will feel and behave better if they discover and correct their basic mistakes. Therapists tend to look for major mistakes in thinking and valuing such as mistrust, selfishness, unrealistic ambitions, and lack of confidence.

A major function of the therapist is to make a comprehensive assessment of the client's functioning. Therapists gather information by means of a questionnaire on the client's *family constellation*, which includes parents, siblings, and others living in the home. When summarized and interpreted, this questionnaire gives a picture of the individual's early social world. From this information the therapist is able to get a perspective on the client's major areas of success and failure and on the critical influences that have had a bearing on the role the client has decided to assume in the world.

The counselor also uses *early recollections* as a diagnostic tool. These recollections are of single incidents from childhood that we are able to reexperience. They reflect our current convictions, evaluations, attitudes, and biases

(Griffith & Powers, 1984). These memories provide a brief picture of how we see ourselves and others and what we anticipate for our future. After these early recollections are summarized and interpreted, the therapist identifies some of the major successes and mistakes in the client's life. The aim is to provide a point of departure for the therapeutic venture. This process is called a lifestyle assessment. When this process is completed, the therapist and the client have targets for therapy.

Adlerians assume a nonpathological perspective and thus do not label clients by their diagnoses. Instead of using a medical model to understand their clients, Adlerians assume a broader perspective based on a growth model. One way of looking at the role of Adlerian therapists is that they assist clients in better understanding, challenging, and changing their life story. "When individuals develop a life story that they find limiting and problem saturated, the goal is to free them from that story in favor of a preferred and equally viable alternative story" (Disque & Bitter, 1998, p. 434).

Client's Experience in Therapy

How do clients maintain their lifestyle, and why do they resist changing it? A person's style of living serves the individual by staying stable and constant. In other words, it is predictable. It is, however, also resistant to change throughout most of one's life. Generally, people fail to change because they do not recognize the errors in their thinking or the purposes of their behaviors, do not know what to do differently, and are fearful of leaving old patterns for new and unpredictable outcomes. Thus, even though their ways of thinking and behaving are not successful, they tend to cling to the familiar patterns (Sweeney, 1998). Clients in Adlerian counseling focus their work on desired outcomes and lifestyle, which will provide a blueprint for their actions.

In therapy, clients explore what Adlerians call *private logic,* the concepts about self, others, and life that constitute the philosophy on which an individual's lifestyle is based. Clients' problems arise because the conclusions based on their private logic often do not conform to the requirements of social living. The core of the therapy experience consists of clients' discovering the purposes of behavior or symptoms and the basic mistakes associated with their coping. Learning how to correct faulty assumptions and conclusions is central to therapy.

To provide a concrete example, think of a chronically depressed middle-aged man who begins therapy. After a lifestyle assessment is completed, these basic mistakes are identified:

- He has convinced himself that nobody could really care about him.
- He rejects people before they have a chance to reject him.
- He is harshly critical of himself, expecting perfection.
- He has expectations that things will rarely work out well.
- He burdens himself with guilt because he is convinced he is letting everyone down.

Even though this man may have developed these mistaken ideas about life when he was young, he is still clinging to them as rules for living. His expectations, most of which are pessimistic, tend to be fulfilled because on some level he is seeking to validate his beliefs. Indeed, his depression will eventually serve the purpose of helping him avoid contact with others, a life task at which he expects to fail. In therapy this man will learn how to challenge the structure of his private logic. In his case the syllogism goes as follows:

- "I am basically unlovable."
- "The world is filled with people who are likely to be rejecting."
- "Therefore, I must keep to myself so I won't be hurt."

This person has held onto several basic mistakes, and his private logic offers a psychological focus for treatment. Mosak (1977) might identify these central themes or convictions in this client's life: "I must get what I want in life." "I must control everything in my life." "I must know everything there is to know, and a mistake would be catastrophic." "I must be perfect in everything I do."

It is easy to see how depression might follow from this thinking, but Adlerians also know that the depression serves as an excuse for this man's retreat from life. It is important for the therapist to listen for the underlying purposes of this client's behavior. Adlerians see feelings as being aligned with thinking and as the fuel for behaving. First we think, then feel, and then act. Because emotions and cognitions serve a purpose and aim at a goal, much therapy time is spent discovering and understanding that purpose and reorienting the client in a useful way. Because the client is not perceived by the therapist to be mentally ill or emotionally disturbed, but as mainly discouraged, the therapist will offer the client encouragement so that change is possible. Through the therapeutic process, the client will discover that he or she has resources and options to draw on in dealing with significant life issues and life tasks.

Relationship Between Therapist and Client

Adlerians consider a good client–therapist relationship to be one between equals that is based on cooperation, mutual trust, respect, confidence, and alignment of goals. They place special value on the counselor's modeling of communication and acting in good faith. From the beginning of therapy the relationship is a collaborative one, characterized by two persons working equally toward specific, agreed-upon goals. Adlerian therapists strive to establish an egalitarian therapeutic alliance with their clients. Dinkmeyer and Sperry (2002) maintain that at the outset of counseling clients should begin to formulate a plan, or contract, detailing what they want, how they plan to get where they are heading, what is preventing them from successfully attaining their goals, how they can change nonproductive behavior into constructive behavior, and how they can make full use of their assets in achieving their purposes. This therapeutic contract sets forth the goals of the counseling process and specifies the responsibilities of both therapist and client. Developing a contract is not a requirement of Adlerian therapy, but it brings a tight focus to therapy.

APPLICATION: THERAPEUTIC TECHNIQUES AND PROCEDURES

Adlerian counseling is structured around four central objectives that correspond to the four phases of the therapeutic process (Dreikurs, 1967). These phases are not linear and do not progress in rigid steps; rather, they can best be understood as a weaving that leads to a tapestry. These phases are:

1. Establishing the proper therapeutic relationship
2. Exploring the psychological dynamics operating in the client (an assessment)
3. Encouraging the development of self-understanding (insight into purpose)
4. Helping the client make new choices (reorientation and reeducation)

Dreikurs (1997) incorporated these phases into what he calls *minor psychotherapy* in the context and service of holistic medicine. His approach to therapy has been elaborated in what is now called *Adlerian brief therapy* (ABT; Bitter, Christensen, Hawes, & Nicoll, 1998), and this way of working is discussed in the following sections.

Phase 1: Establishing the Relationship

The Adlerian practitioner works in a collaborative way with clients, and this relationship is based on a sense of deep caring, involvement, and friendship. Therapeutic progress is possible only when there is an alignment of clearly defined goals between therapist and client. The counseling process, to be effective, must deal with the personal issues the client recognizes as significant and is willing to explore and change. The therapeutic efficacy in the later phases of Adlerian therapy is predicated upon the development and continuation of a solid therapeutic relationship during this first phase of therapy (Watts, 2000; Watts & Pietrzak, 2000).

Adlerian therapists seek to make person-to-person contact with clients rather than starting with "the problem." Clients surface their concerns in therapy rather quickly, but the initial focus should be on the person, not the problem. One way to create effective contact is for counselors to help clients become aware of their assets and strengths, rather than dealing continually with their deficits and liabilities. During the initial phase, a positive relationship is created by listening, responding, demonstrating respect for clients' capacity to understand purpose and seek change, and exhibiting faith, hope, and caring. When clients enter therapy, they typically have a diminished sense of self-worth and self-respect. They lack faith in their ability to cope with the tasks of life. Therapists provide support, which is an antidote to despair and discouragement. For some people, therapy may be one of the few times in which they have truly experienced a caring human relationship.

Adlerians pay more attention to the subjective experiences of the client than they do to using techniques. They fit their techniques to the needs of each client. During the initial phase of counseling, the main techniques are attending and listening with empathy, following the subjective experience of the client as closely as possible, identifying and clarifying goals, and suggesting initial hunches about purpose in client symptoms, actions, and interactions. Adlerians attempt to grasp both the verbal and nonverbal messages of the client; they want to access the core patterns in the client's life. If the client feels deeply understood and accepted, the client is likely to focus on what he or she wants from therapy and thus establish goals. At this stage the counselor's function is to provide a wide-angle perspective that will eventually help the client view his or her world differently.

Phase 2: Exploring the Individual's Dynamics

The second phase of Adlerian counseling proceeds from two interview forms: the subjective interview and the objective interview (Dreikurs, 1997). In the *subjective interview* the counselor helps the client to tell his or her story as completely as possible. This process is facilitated by a generous use of empathic listening and responding. Active listening, however, is not enough. The subjective interview must follow from a sense of wonder, fascination, and interest. What the client says will spark an interest in the counselor and lead, naturally, to the next most significant question or inquiry about the client and his or her life story. Indeed, the best subjective interviews treat clients as experts in their own lives, allowing clients to feel completely heard. Throughout the subjective interview, the Adlerian counselor is listening for clues to the purposive aspects of the client's coping and approaches to life. "The subjective interview should extract patterns in the person's life, develop hypotheses about what works for the person, and determine what accounts for the various concerns in the client's life" (Bitter et al., 1998, p. 98). Toward the end of this part of the interview, Adlerian brief therapists ask: "Is there anything else you think I should know to understand you and your concerns?"

An initial assessment of the purpose symptoms, actions, or difficulties have in a person's life can be gained from what Dreikurs (1997) calls "The Question." Adlerians often end a subjective interview with this question: "How would your life be different, and what would you do differently, if you did not have this symptom or problem?" Adlerians use this question to help with differential diagnosis. If nothing would be different, especially with physical symptoms, Adlerians suspect that the problem may be organic and require medical intervention. More often the symptoms or problems experienced by the client help the client avoid something that is perceived as necessary but from which the person wishes to retreat, usually a life task: "If it weren't for this depression, I would get out more and see my friends." Such a statement betrays the client's concern about the possibility of being a good friend or being welcomed by his or her friends. "I need to get married, but how can I with these panic attacks?" indicates the person's worry about being a partner in a marriage.

The *objective interview* seeks to discover information about (a) how problems in the client's life began; (b) any precipitating events; (c) a medical history, including current and past medications; (d) a social history; (e) the reasons the client chose therapy at this time; (f) the person's coping with life tasks; and (g) a lifestyle assessment. Mozdzierz and his colleagues (1984) describe the counselor as a "lifestyle investigator" during this phase of therapy. Based on interview approaches developed by Adler and Dreikurs, the lifestyle assessment starts with an investigation of the person's family constellation and early childhood history (Powers & Griffith, 1987; Shulman & Mosak, 1988). Counselors also interpret the person's early memories, seeking to understand the whole person as he or she grew up in a social setting. They operate on the assumption that it is the interpretations people develop about themselves, others, the world, and life that govern what they do. Lifestyle assessment seeks to develop a holistic narrative of the person's life, to make sense of the way the person copes with life tasks, and to uncover the private interpretations and logic involved in that coping. For example, if Jenny has lived most of her life in a critical environment, and now she believes she must be perfect to avoid even the appearance of failure, the assessment process will highlight the restricted living that follows from this perspective.

THE FAMILY CONSTELLATION   Adler considered the family of origin as having a central impact on an individual's personality. Adler suggested that it was through the family constellation that each person forms his or her unique view of self, others, and life. Factors such as cultural and familial values, gender-role expectations, and the nature of interpersonal relationships are all influenced by a child's observation of the interactional patterns within the family. Adlerian assessment relies heavily on an exploration of the client's family constellation, including the client's evaluation of conditions that prevailed in the family when the person was a young child (family atmosphere), birth order, parental relationship and family values, and extended family and culture. Some of these questions are almost always explored:

- Who was the favorite child?
- What was your father's relationship with the children? your mother's?
- Which child was most like your father? your mother? in what respects?
- Who among the siblings was most different from you? in what ways?
- Who among the siblings was most like you? in what ways?
- What were you like as a child?
- How did your parents get along? In what did they both agree? How did they handle disagreements? How did they discipline the children?

An investigation of family constellation is far more comprehensive than these few questions, but these questions give an idea of the type of information the counselor is seeking. The questions are always tailored to the individual client with the goal of eliciting the client's perceptions of self and others, of development, and of the experiences that have affected that development.

EARLY RECOLLECTIONS   Another assessment procedure used by Adlerians is to ask the client to provide his or her earliest memories, including the age of the person at the time of the remembered events and the feelings or reactions associated with the recollections. Early recollections are one-time occurrences pictured by the client in clear detail. Adler reasoned that out of the millions of early memories we might have we select those special memories that project the essential convictions and even the basic mistakes of our lives.

Early memories cast light on the "story of our life," because they represent metaphors for our current views. From a series of early recollections, it is possible to get a clear sense of our mistaken notions, present attitudes, social interests, and possible future behavior. Exploring early recollections involves discovering how mistaken notions based on faulty goals and values continue to create problems in an individual's life.

To tap such recollections, the counselor might proceed as follows: "I would like to hear about your early memories. Think back to when you were very young, as early as you can remember, and *tell me something that happened one time.*" After receiving each memory, the counselor might also ask: "What part stands out to you? If you played the whole memory like a movie and stopped it at one frame, what would be happening? Putting yourself in that moment, what are you feeling? What's your reaction?" Three memories are usually considered a minimum to assess a pattern, and some counselors ask for as many as a dozen memories.

Adlerian therapists use early recollections for many different purposes. These include (a) assessment of the person's convictions about self, others, life, and ethics; (b) assessment of the client's stance in relation to the counseling session and the counseling relationship; (c) verification of coping patterns; and (d) assessment of individual strengths, assets, and interfering ideas (Bitter et al., 1998, p. 99).

In interpreting these early recollections, Adlerians may consider questions such as these:

- What part does the person take in the memory? Is the person an observer or a participant?
- Who else is in the memory? What position do others take in relation to the person?
- What are the dominant themes and overall patterns of the memories?
- What feelings are expressed in the memories?
- Why does the person choose to remember this event? What is the person trying to convey?

PERSONALITY PRIORITIES   For the last two decades, an assessment of personality priorities has become an important road to understanding interactional coping. An Adlerian psychologist from Israel, Nira Kefir (1981), originally designated four priorities: superiority (or significance), control, comfort, and pleasing. Personality priorities are similar to what Adler called safeguarding tendencies. Unless challenged, people rely on a number-one priority, a first line of defense that they use as an immediate response to perceived stress or difficulty. Each priority involves a dominant behavior pattern with supporting convictions that an individual uses to cope. Priorities become pathways for relating to others and for attaining a sense of significance. Kefir describes four behavioral patterns that reflect these priorities:

1. People using *superiority* (significance) strive for significance through leadership or accomplishment or through any other avenue to make them feel superior. They seek to avoid meaninglessness in life but often complain of being overworked or overburdened.
2. People who *control* look for guarantees against ridicule. They feel a need for complete mastery of situations so that they will not be humiliated. They do not want to behave in a socially unsuccessful way, and they are willing to pay the price of social distance to achieve this safety.
3. People seeking *comfort* want to avoid stress or pain at all costs. They tend to delay dealing with problems and making decisions, and they do their best to avoid anything that implies stress or pain. The price they pay is low productivity.
4. People who aim to *please* want to avoid rejection by seeking constant approval and acceptance. Out of their fear of not being liked, they go to great lengths to win approval.

It is not the therapist's job to work toward changing a client's main priority. Instead, the goal is to enable the client to recognize the feelings he or she evokes in others and the price the client pays for clinging to a number-one priority. Kefir (1981) asserts that to increase our self-awareness we must learn what our priority, or condition for feeling significant, is. We also need to find alternative ways to gain significance by using a wider range of behaviors.

INTEGRATION AND SUMMARY   Once material has been gathered from both subjective and objective interviews with the client, integrated summaries of the data are developed. Different summaries are prepared for different clients, but common ones are a narrative summary of the person's subjective experience and life story; a summary of family constellation and developmental data; a summary of early recollections, personal strengths or assets, and interfering ideas; and a summary of coping strategies. The summaries are presented to the client and discussed in the session, with the client and the counselor together refining specific points. This provides the client with the chance to discuss specific topics and to raise questions.

Mosak (2000) includes an analysis of common basic mistakes. He believes lifestyle can be conceived of as a personal mythology. People behave *as if* the myths were true because, for them, they *are true*. Mosak lists five basic mistakes:

1. *Overgeneralizations:* "There is no fairness in the world."
2. *False or impossible goals:* "I must please everyone if I am to feel loved."
3. *Misperceptions of life and life's demands:* "Life is so very difficult for me."
4. *Minimization or denial of one's basic worth:* "I'm basically stupid, so why would anyone want anything to do with me?"
5. *Faulty values:* "I must get to the top, regardless of who gets hurt in the process."

As another example of a summary of basic mistakes, consider this list of mistaken notions that are evident in Stan's autobiography (see Chapter 1):

■ "Don't get close to people, especially women, because they will suffocate and control you if they can." (overgeneralization)
■ "I was not really wanted by my parents, and therefore it is best for me to become invisible." (denial of one's basic worth)
■ "It is extremely important that people like me and approve of me; I'll bend over backwards to do what people expect." (false or impossible goals)

The Student Manual that accompanies this textbook gives a concrete example of the lifestyle assessment as it is applied to the case of Stan. In *Case Approach to Counseling and Psychotherapy* (Corey, 2005, chap. 3), Jim Bitter and Bill Nicoll present a lifestyle assessment of another hypothetical client, Ruth.

Phase 3: Encouraging Self-Understanding and Insight

Adlerians believe almost everything in human life has a purpose. Self-understanding is only possible when hidden purposes and goals of behavior are made conscious. When Adlerians speak of insight, they are referring to an understanding of the motivations that operate in a client's life. Adlerians consider insight as a special form of awareness that facilitates a meaningful understanding within the therapeutic relationship and acts as a foundation for change. Insight is a means to an end, and not an end in itself.

Disclosure and well-timed interpretations are techniques that facilitate the process of gaining insight. They are focused on here-and-now behavior and on the expectations and anticipations that arise from one's intentions. Adlerian disclosures and interpretations are concerned with creating awareness of one's direction in life, one's goals and purposes, one's private logic and how it works, and one's current behavior.

Adlerian interpretations are suggestions presented tentatively in the form of open-ended sharings that can be explored in the sessions. They are hunches or guesses, and they are often stated thusly: "It seems to me that . . . ," "Could it be that . . . ," or "This is how it appears to me. . . ." Because interpretations are presented in this manner, clients are not led to defend themselves, and they feel free to discuss and even argue with the counselor's hunches and impressions. Through this process, clients eventually come to understand their motivations, the ways in which they are now contributing to the maintenance of the problem, and what they can do to correct the situation.

Phase 4: Helping With Reorientation

The final stage of the therapeutic process is the action-oriented phase known as reorientation and reeducation: putting insights into practice. This phase focuses on helping people discover new and more functional alternatives. Clients are both encouraged and challenged to develop the courage to take risks and make changes in their life.

In some cases significant changes are needed if clients are to overcome discouragement and find a place for themselves in this life. More often, however, people merely need to be reoriented toward the useful side of life. The useful side involves a sense of belonging and being valued, having an interest in others and their welfare, courage, the acceptance of imperfection, confidence, a sense of humor, a willingness to contribute, and an outgoing friendliness. The useless side of life is characterized by self-absorption, withdrawal from life tasks, self-protection, or acts against one's fellow human beings. People on the useless side of life become less functional and are more susceptible to psychopathology. Adlerian therapy stands in opposition to self-depreciation, isolation, and retreat, and it seeks to help clients gain courage and to connect to strengths within themselves, to others, and to life. Throughout this phase, no intervention is more important than encouragement.

THE ENCOURAGEMENT PROCESS   Encouragement is the most distinctive Adlerian procedure, and it is central to all phases of counseling and therapy. It is especially important as people consider change in their lives. Encouragement literally means "to build courage" (Bitter et al., 1998). Courage develops when people become aware of their strengths, when they feel they belong and are not alone, and when they have a sense of hope and can see new possibilities for themselves and their daily living. Adlerians seize every opportunity the client provides to introduce and reinforce encouragement (Powers & Griffith, 1987). Because clients often do not recognize or accept their positive qualities, strengths, or internal resources, one of the counselor's tasks is to help them do so.

Adlerians believe discouragement is the basic condition that prevents people from functioning, and they see encouragement as the antidote. As a part of the encouragement process, Adlerians use a variety of cognitive, behavioral, and experiential techniques to help clients identify and challenge self-defeating cognitions, generate perceptional alternatives, and make use of assets, strengths, and resources (Ansbacher & Ansbacher, 1964; Dinkmeyer & Sperry, 2002; Watts & Pietrzak, 2000; Watts & Shulman, 2003).

Encouragement takes many forms, depending on the phase of the counseling process. In the relationship phase, encouragement results from the mutual respect the counselor seeks to engender. In the assessment phase, which is partially designed to illuminate personal strengths, clients are encouraged to recognize that they are in charge of their own lives and can make different choices based on new understandings. During reorientation, encouragement comes when new possibilities are generated and when people are acknowledged and affirmed for taking positive steps to change their lives for the better.

CHANGE AND THE SEARCH FOR NEW POSSIBILITIES   During the reorientation phase of counseling, clients make decisions and modify their goals. They are encouraged to act *as if* they were the people they want to be, which can serve to challenge self-limiting assumptions. Clients are asked to catch themselves in the process of repeating old patterns that have led to ineffective behavior. Commitment is an essential part of reorientation. If clients hope to change, they must be willing to set tasks for themselves and do something specific about their problems. In this way, clients translate their new insights into concrete actions.

This action-oriented phase is a time for solving problems and making decisions. The counselor and the client consider possible alternatives and their consequences, evaluate how these alternatives will meet the client's goals, and decide on a specific course of action. The best alternatives and new possibilities are those generated by the client, and the counselor must offer the client a great deal of support and encouragement during this stage of the process.

MAKING A DIFFERENCE   Adlerian counselors seek to make a difference in the lives of their clients. That difference may be manifested by a change in behavior or attitude or perception. Adlerians use many different techniques to promote change, some of which have become common interventions in other therapeutic models. Techniques that go by the names of immediacy, advice, humor, silence, paradoxical intention, acting as if, spitting in the client's soup, catching oneself, the push-button technique, externalization, re-authoring, avoiding the traps, confrontation, use of stories and fables, early recollection analysis, task setting and commitment, giving homework, and terminating and summarizing have all been used (Carlson & Slavik, 1997; Dinkmeyer & Sperry, 2000; Disque & Bitter, 1998; Mosak, 2000). Indeed, some Adlerians have attempted to associate specific techniques to given problems and concerns (Mosak & Maniacci, 1998, 1999; Sperry & Carlson, 1996). Adlerians are pragmatic when it comes to using techniques that are appropriate for a given client. In general, however, Adlerian practitioners focus on motivation modification more than behavior change and encourage clients to make holistic changes on the useful side of living. All counseling is a cooperative effort, and making a difference depends on the counselor's ability to win the client's cooperation.

Areas of Application

Adler anticipated the future direction of the helping professions by calling upon therapists to become social activists by addressing the prevention and remediation of social conditions that were contrary to social interest and resulted in human problems. Adler's pioneering efforts on prevention services in mental health led him to increasingly advocate for the role of Individual Psychology in schools and families. Because Individual Psychology is based on a growth model, not a medical model, it is applicable to such varied spheres of life as child guidance, parent–child counseling, marital counseling, family therapy, group counseling, individual counseling with children, adolescents, and adults, cultural conflicts, correctional and rehabilitation counseling, and mental health institutions. Adlerian principles have been widely applied to substance abuse programs, social problems to combat poverty and crime, problems of the aged, school systems, religion, and business.

APPLICATION TO EDUCATION   Adler advocated training both teachers and parents in effective practices that foster the child's social interests and result in a sense of competence and self-worth. Adler had a keen interest in applying his ideas to education, especially in finding ways to remedy faulty lifestyles of schoolchildren. He initiated a process to work with students in groups and to educate parents and teachers. By providing teachers with ways to prevent and correct basic mistakes of children, he sought to promote social interest and mental health. Adler was ahead of his time in advocating for schools to take an active role in developing social skills and character education as well as teaching the basics. Besides Adler, the main proponent of Individual Psychology as a foundation for the teaching–learning process was Dreikurs (1968, 1971). Major teacher education models are based on principles of Adlerian and Dreikursian psychology (see Albert, 1996).

APPLICATION TO PARENT EDUCATION   Parent education to improve the relationship between parent and child by promoting greater understanding and acceptance has been a major Adlerian contribution. Parents are taught simple Adlerian principles of behavior that can be applied in the home. Initial topics include understanding the purpose of a child's misbehavior, learning to listen, helping children accept the consequences of their behavior, applying emotion coaching, holding family meetings, and using encouragement. The two leading parent education programs in the United States are both based on Adlerian principles: they are *STEP* (Dinkmeyer, McKay, Dinkmeyer, & McKay, 1997) and *Active Parenting* (Popkin, 1993).

APPLICATION TO MARRIAGE COUNSELING   Adlerian marital therapy is designed to assess a couple's beliefs and behaviors while educating them in more effective ways of meeting their goals. Clair Hawes has developed an approach to couples counseling within the Adlerian brief therapy model. In addition to addressing the compatibility of lifestyles, Hawes looks at the early recollections of the marriage and each partner's relationship to a broad set of life tasks, including occupation, social relationships, intimate relationships, kinkeeping, spirituality, self-care, and self-worth (Bitter et al., 1998; Hawes, 1993; Hawes & Blanchard, 1993).

The full range of techniques applicable to other forms of counseling can be used in working with couples. In marriage counseling and marriage education, couples are taught specific techniques that enhance communication and co-operation. Some of these techniques are listening, paraphrasing, giving feedback, having marriage conferences, listing expectations, doing homework, and enacting problem solving.

Adlerians will sometimes see married people as a couple, sometimes individually, and then alternately as a couple and as individuals. Rather than looking for who is at fault in the relationship, the therapist considers the lifestyles of the partners and the interaction of the two lifestyles. Emphasis is given to helping them decide if they want to maintain their marriage and, if so, what changes they are willing to make.

APPLICATION TO FAMILY COUNSELING With its emphasis on the family constellation, holism, and the freedom of the therapist to improvise, Adler's approach contributed to the foundation of the family therapy perspective. Adlerians working with families focus on the family atmosphere, the family constellation, and the interactive goals of each member. The family atmosphere is the climate characterizing the relationship between the parents and their attitudes toward life, gender roles, decision making, competition, cooperation, dealing with conflict, responsibility, and so forth. This atmosphere, including the role models the parents provide, influences the children as they grow up. The therapeutic process seeks to increase awareness of the interaction of the individuals within the family system. Those who practice Adlerian family therapy strive to understand the goals, beliefs, and behaviors of each family member and the family as an entity in its own right. Adler's and Dreikurs's influence on family therapy is covered in more depth in Chapter 14.

APPLICATION TO GROUP WORK Adler and his coworkers used a group approach in their child guidance centers in Vienna as early as 1921 (Dreikurs, 1969). Dreikurs, a colleague, extended and popularized Adler's work with groups and used group psychotherapy in his private practice for more than 40 years. Although he introduced group therapy into his psychiatric practice as a way to save time, he quickly discovered some unique characteristics of groups that made them an effective way of helping people change. Inferiority feelings can be challenged and counteracted effectively in groups, and the mistaken concepts and values that are at the root of social and emotional problems can be deeply influenced because the group is a value-forming agent (Sonstegard, 1998a).

The group provides the social context in which members can develop a sense of belonging and a sense of community. Sonstegard (1998b) writes that group participants come to see that many of their problems are interpersonal in nature, that their behavior has social meaning, and that their goals can best be understood in the framework of social purposes. Adlerian brief group therapy is addressed by Sonstegard, Bitter, Pelonis-Peneros, and Nichol (2001). For more on the Adlerian approach to group counseling, refer to *Theory and Practice of Group Counseling* (Corey, 2004, chap. 7) and Corey (1999, 2003).

Adlerian Therapy Applied to the Case of Stan

The basic aims of an Adlerian therapist working with Stan are fourfold and correspond to the four stages of counseling: (1) establishing and maintaining a good working relationship with Stan, (2) exploring Stan's dynamics, (3) encouraging Stan to develop insight and understanding, and (4) helping Stan see new alternatives and make new choices.

To develop mutual trust and respect, the therapist pays close attention to Stan's subjective experience and attempts to get a sense of how he has reacted to the turning points in his life. During the initial session, Stan reacts to his counselor as the expert who has the answers. Stan is convinced he has made a mess of his life and that when he attempts to make decisions he generally ends up regretting the results. Thus, Stan approaches his counselor out of desperation and almost pleads for a prescription for coping with his problems. Because his counselor views counseling as a relationship between equals, she initially focuses on his feeling of being unequal to most other people. A good place to begin is exploring his feelings of inferiority, which he says he feels in most situations. The goals of counseling are developed mutually, and the counselor avoids deciding for Stan what his goals should be. She also resists giving Stan the simple formula he is requesting.

Stan's counselor prepares a lifestyle assessment based on a questionnaire that taps information about Stan's early years, especially his experiences in his family. (See the Student Manual for a complete description of this lifestyle assessment form as it is applied to Stan.) This assessment includes a determination of whether he poses a danger to himself because Stan did mention suicidal inclinations. During the assessment phase, which might take a few sessions, the Adlerian counselor explores Stan's social relationships, his relationships with members of his family, his work responsibilities, his role as a man, and his feelings about himself. She places considerable emphasis on Stan's goals in life and his priorities. She does not pay a great deal of attention to his past, except to show him the consistency between his past and present as he moves toward the future.

Because Stan's counselor places value on exploring early recollections as a source of understanding his goals, motivations, and values, she asks Stan to report his earliest memories. He replies as follows:

I was about 6, I went to school, and I was scared of the other kids and the teacher. When I came home, I cried and told my mother I didn't want to go back to school. She yelled at me and called me a baby. After that I felt horrible and even more scared.

Another of Stan's early recollections was at age 8:

My family was visiting my grandparents. I was playing outside, and some neighborhood kid hit me for no reason. We got in a big fight, and my mother came out and scolded me for being such a rough kid. She wouldn't believe me when I told her he had started the fight. I felt angry and hurt that she didn't believe me.

Based on these early recollections, Stan's counselor suggests that Stan sees life as frightening and unpredictably hostile and that he feels he cannot count on women; they are likely to be harsh, unbelieving, and uncaring.

Stan talks about his priorities during several therapy sessions. Initially he tentatively identifies one of his priorities as *superiority*. He tends to overstress the value of being competent, of accomplishing one feat after another, of winning, of being right at all costs, and of moving ahead in most situations. He tends to weigh himself down with the responsibility of constantly trying to prove himself, and he experiences a high level of stress in working so hard at being competent. Of course, his striving for superiority grows out of the pervasive feelings of inferiority that he has experienced for most of his life.

Eventually, Stan pinpoints *control* as his number-one priority. He often encounters situations that embarrass or humiliate him. He believes that if he can control his world he can also control his painful feelings. Some of the methods Stan uses to gain control over these feelings are escaping through alcohol, avoiding interpersonal situations that are threatening to him, keeping to himself, and deciding that he can't really count on others for psychological support. Stan begins to realize that although his style of seeking control apparently reduces his anxiety he is paying a steep price for his behavior. The feelings he evokes in others are frustration and a lack of interest; for himself, the price he pays is distance from others and diminished spontaneity and creativity.

Having gathered the data based on the lifestyle assessment about his family constellation, his early recollections, and his priorities, the therapist assists Stan in the process of summarizing and interpreting this information. Particular attention is given by the therapist to identifying basic mistakes, which are faulty conclusions about life and self-defeating perceptions. Here are some of the mistaken conclusions Stan has reached:

- "I must not get close to people, because they will surely hurt me."
- "Because my own parents didn't want me and didn't love me, I'll never be desired or loved by anybody."
- "If only I could become perfect, maybe people would acknowledge and accept me."
- "Being a man means not showing emotions."

The information the counselor summarizes and interprets leads to insight and increased self-understanding on Stan's part. He becomes more aware of how he is functioning. He learns that he is not "sick" and in need of being "cured"; rather, he is discouraged and needs to be encouraged to reorient his life. Through continued emphasis on his beliefs, goals, and intentions, Stan comes to see how his private logic is inaccurate. In his case, a syllogism for his style of life can be explained in this way: (1) "I am unloved, insignificant, and do not count;" (2) "the world is a threatening place to be, and life is unfair;" (3) "therefore, I must find ways to protect myself and keep safe." During this phase of the process, Stan's counselor makes interpretations centering on his lifestyle, his current direction, his goals and purposes, and how his private logic works. Of course, Stan is expected to carry out homework assignments that assist him in translating his insights into new behavior. In this way he is an active participant in his therapy.

In the reorientation phase of therapy, Stan and his counselor work together to consider alternative attitudes, beliefs, and actions. By now Stan sees that he does not have to be locked into past patterns, feels encouraged, and realizes that he does have the power to change his life. He accepts that he will not change merely by gaining insights and knows that he will have to make use of these insights by carrying out an action-oriented plan. Stan begins to feel that he can create a new life for himself and not remain the victim of circumstances.

Follow-Up: You Continue as Stan's Adlerian Therapist

Use these questions to help you think about how you would counsel Stan using an Adlerian approach:

- What are some ways you would attempt to establish a relationship with Stan based on trust and mutual respect? Can you imagine any difficulties you might have in developing this relationship?
- What aspects of Stan's lifestyle particularly interest you? In counseling him, how might these be explored?
- The Adlerian therapist identified four of Stan's mistaken conclusions. Can you identify with any of these basic mistakes? If so, do you think this would help or hinder your therapeutic effectiveness with him?
- Working from an Adlerian perspective, how might you assist Stan in discovering his social interest and going beyond a preoccupation with his own problems?
- What strengths and resources in Stan might you draw on to support his determination and commitment to change?

ADLERIAN THERAPY FROM A MULTICULTURAL PERSPECTIVE

Contributions to Multicultural Counseling

Adlerian theory addressed social equality issues and social embeddedness of humans long before multiculturalism assumed central importance in the profession (Watts & Pietrzak, 2000). Adler introduced notions with implications toward multiculturalism that have as much or more relevance today as they did during Adler's time (Pedersen, as cited in Nystul, 1999b). Some of these ideas include (1) the importance of the cultural context, (2) the emphasis on health as opposed to pathology, (3) a holistic perspective on life, (4) the value of understanding individuals in terms of their core goals and purposes, (5) the ability to exercise freedom within the context of societal constraints, and (6) the focus on prevention and the development of a proactive approach in dealing with problems. Adler's holistic perspective is an articulate expression of what Pedersen calls a "culture-centered" or multicultural approach to counseling.

Although the Adlerian approach is called Individual Psychology, its focus is on the person in a social context. This approach is well suited to working with culturally diverse clients. Adlerian therapists encourage clients to define themselves within their social environments. Adlerians allow broad concepts of age, ethnicity, lifestyle, and gender differences to emerge in therapy. To their credit, Adlerians practice in flexible ways from a theory that can be applied to work with ethnically diverse client populations. The therapeutic process is grounded within a client's culture and worldview rather than attempting to fit clients into preconceived models.

In their analysis of the various theoretical approaches to counseling, Arciniega and Newlon (1999) state that Adlerian theory holds the most promise for addressing multicultural issues. They note a number of characteristics of Adlerian theory that are congruent with the values of many racial, cultural, and ethnic groups, including the emphasis on understanding the individual in a familial and sociocultural context; the role of social interest and contributing to others; and the focus on belonging and the collective spirit. Cultures that stress the welfare of the social group and emphasize the role of the family will find the basic assumptions of Adlerian psychology to be consistent with their values.

Adlerian therapists tend to focus on cooperation and socially oriented values as opposed to competitive and individualistic values (Carlson & Carlson, 2000). Native American clients, for example, tend to value cooperation over competition. One such client told a story about a group of boys who were in a race. When one boy got ahead of the others, he would slow down and allow the others to catch up, and they all made it to the finish line at the same time. Although the coach tried to explain that the point of the race was for an individual to finish first, these boys were socialized to work together cooperatively as a group. Adlerian therapy is easily adaptable to cultural values that emphasize community.

Clients who enter therapy are often locked into rigid ways of perceiving, interpreting, and behaving. It is likely that they have not questioned how their culture has influenced them. Thus, they may feel resigned to "the way things are." Mozdzierz and his colleagues (1984) characterize these clients as myopic and contend that one of the therapist's functions is to provide them with another pair of glasses that will enable them to see things more clearly. The Adlerian emphasis on the subjective fashion in which people view and interpret their world leads to a respect for clients' unique values and perceptions. Adlerian counselors use interpretations as an opportunity for clients to view things from a different perspective, yet it is up to the clients to decide whether to open their eyes and use these glasses. Adlerians do not decide for clients what they should change or what their goals should be; rather, they work collaboratively with their clients in ways that enable them to reach their self-defined goals.

Not only is Adlerian theory congruent with the values of many cultural groups, but the approach offers flexibility in applying a range of cognitive and action-oriented techniques to helping clients explore their practical problems. Adlerian practitioners are not wedded to any particular set of procedures. Instead, they are conscious of the value of fitting their techniques to each client's situation. Although they utilize a diverse range of methods, most of them do conduct a lifestyle assessment. This assessment is heavily focused on the structure and dynamics within the client's family. Because of their cultural background, many clients have been conditioned to respect their family heritage and to appreciate the impact of their family on their own personal development. It is essential that counselors be sensitive to the conflicting feelings and struggles of their clients. If counselors demonstrate an understanding of these cultural values, it is likely that these clients will be receptive to an exploration of their lifestyle. Such an exploration will involve a detailed discussion of their own place within their family.

If "culture" is defined broadly (to include age, roles, lifestyle, and gender differences), cultural differences can be found even within a single family. The Adlerian approach emphasizes the value of subjectively understanding the unique world of an individual. Culture is one significant dimension for grasping the subjective and experiential perspective of an individual. Culture influences each person, but it is expressed within each individual differently, according to the perception, evaluation, and interpretation of culture that the person holds.

Adlerian counselors seek to be sensitive to cultural and gender issues. Adler was one of the first psychologists at the turn of the century to advocate equality for women. He recognized that men and women were different in many ways, but he felt that the two genders were deserving of equal value and respect. This respect and appreciation for difference extends to culture as well as gender. Adlerians find in different cultures opportunities for viewing the self, others, and the world in multidimensional ways. Indeed, the strengths of one culture can often help correct the mistakes in another culture.

Limitations for Multicultural Counseling

As is true of most Western models, the Adlerian approach tends to focus on the self as the locus of change and responsibility. Because other cultures have different conceptions, this primary emphasis on changing the autonomous self may be problematic for many clients.

Another limitation of Adlerian therapy involves its detailed explorations of one's early childhood, early memories, and dynamics within the family. Many clients who have pressing problems are likely to resent intrusions into areas of their lives that they may not see as connected to the struggles that bring them into therapy. In addition, members of some cultures may believe it is inappropriate to reveal family information. On this point Carlson and Carlson (2000) suggest that a therapist's sensitivity to and understanding of a client's culturally constructed beliefs about disclosing family information are critical. If therapists are able to demonstrate an understanding of a client's cultural values, it is likely that this client will be more open to the assessment and treatment process.

Although therapists have expertise in the problems of living, they are not experts in solving other people's problems. Instead, they view it as their function to teach people alternative methods of coping with life concerns. However, the culture of some clients may contribute to their viewing the counselor as the "expert" and expecting that the counselor will provide them with solutions to their problems. For these clients, the role of the Adlerian therapist may pose problems.

If the Adlerian approach is practiced appropriately and competently, it is difficult to identify major limitations from a multicultural perspective. The phenomenological nature of the Adlerian approach lends itself to understanding the worldview of clients. The emphasis on the subjective fashion in which people view and interpret their world leads to a respect for clients' unique values and perceptions.

It should be noted that Adlerians investigate culture in much the same way that they approach birth order and family atmosphere. Culture is a vantage point from which life is experienced and interpreted; it is also a background of values, history, convictions, beliefs, customs, and expectations that must be addressed by the individual. Adlerians do not decide for clients what they should change or what their goals should be; rather, they work cooperatively to enable clients to reach their self-defined goals.

 SUMMARY AND EVALUATION

Summary

Adler was far ahead of his time, and most contemporary therapies have incorporated at least some of his ideas. Individual Psychology assumes that people are motivated by social factors; are responsible for their own thoughts, feelings, and actions; are the creators of their own lives, as opposed to being helpless victims; and are impelled by purposes and goals, looking more toward the future than to the past.

The basic goal of the Adlerian approach is to help clients identify and change their mistaken beliefs about, self, others, and life and thus participate more fully in a social world. Clients are not viewed as mentally sick but as discouraged. The therapeutic process helps clients become aware of their patterns and make some basic changes in their style of living, which lead to changes in the way they feel and behave. The role of the family in the development of the individual is emphasized. Therapy is a cooperative venture and geared toward challenging clients to translate their insights into action in the real world. Contemporary Adlerian theory is an integrative approach, combining cognitive, constructivist, psychodynamic, and systems perspectives. Some of these common characteristics include an emphasis on establishing a respectful client–therapist relationship, an emphasis on clients' strengths and resources, and an optimistic and future orientation.

The Adlerian approach gives practitioners a great deal of freedom in working with clients. Major Adlerian contributions have been made in the following areas: elementary education, consultation groups with teachers, parent education groups, marriage and family therapy, and group counseling.

Contributions of the Adlerian Approach

A strength of the Adlerian approach is its flexibility and its integrative nature. Adlerian therapists can be both theoretically integrative and technically eclectic (Watts & Shulman, 2003). This therapeutic approach allows for the use of a variety of cognitive, behavioral, and experiential techniques. Adlerian therapists are resourceful and flexible in drawing on many methods, which can be applied to a diverse range of clients in a variety of settings and formats. Therapists are mainly concerned about doing what is in the best interests of clients rather than squeezing clients into one theoretical framework (Watts, 1999, 2000; Watts & Pietrzak, 2000; Watts & Shulman, 2003).

Another contribution of Adlerian therapy is that the approach lends itself to short-term formats. Adler was a proponent of time-limited therapy, and the techniques used by many contemporary brief therapeutic approaches are very similar to interventions created by or commonly used by Adlerian practitioners (Watts, 1999, 2000). Adlerian therapy has a psychoeducational focus, a present- and future-orientation, is brief and time-limited, and combines cognitive and systemic perspectives (Watts & Pietrzak, 2000). Bitter and Nicoll (2000) identify five characteristics that form the basis for an integrative framework in brief therapy: time limitation, focus, counselor directiveness, symptoms as solutions, and the assignment of behavioral tasks. An advantage of bringing into the therapy process a time limitation consists of conveying to clients the expectation that change will occur in a short period of time. When the number of sessions is specified, both client and therapist are motivated to stay focused on desired outcomes and to work as efficiently as possible. Bitter and Nicoll write that because there is no assurance that a future session will occur, brief therapists tend to ask themselves this question: "If I had only one session to be useful in this person's life, what would I want to accomplish?" (p. 38).

The Adlerian concepts I draw on most in my work with clients are (1) the importance of looking to one's life goals, including assessing how these goals influence an individual; (2) the focus on the individual's interpretation of early experiences in the family, with special emphasis on their current impact; (3) the clinical use of early recollections; (4) the need to understand and confront basic mistakes; (5) the cognitive emphasis, which holds that emotions and behaviors are largely influenced by one's beliefs and thinking processes; (6) the idea of working out an action plan designed to help clients make changes; (7) the collaborative relationship, whereby the client and therapist work toward mutually agreed-upon goals; and (8) the emphasis given to encouragement during the entire counseling process. Several Adlerian concepts have implications for personal development. One of these notions that has helped me to understand the direction of my life is the assumption that feelings of inferiority are linked to a striving for superiority (Corey, as cited in Nystul, 1999a).

It is difficult to overestimate the contributions of Adler to contemporary therapeutic practice. Many of his ideas were revolutionary and far ahead of his time. His influence went beyond counseling individuals, extending into the community mental health movement (Ansbacher, 1974). Abraham Maslow, Viktor Frankl, Rollo May, and Albert Ellis have all acknowledged their debt to Adler. Both Frankl and May see him as a forerunner of the existential movement because of his position that human beings are free to choose and are entirely responsible for what they make of themselves. This view also makes him a forerunner of the subjective approach to psychology, which focuses on the internal determinants of behavior: values, beliefs, attitudes, goals, interests, personal meanings, subjective perceptions of reality, and strivings toward self-realization.

In my opinion, one of Adler's most important contributions is his influence on other therapy systems. Many of his basic ideas have found their way into other psychological schools, such as family systems approaches, Gestalt therapy, learning theory, reality therapy, rational emotive behavior therapy, cognitive therapy, person-centered therapy, existential therapy, and the postmodern approaches to therapy. All of these approaches are based on a similar concept of the person as purposive, self-determining, and striving for growth. In many respects, Adler seems to have paved the way for current developments in both the cognitive and contructivist therapies (Watts, 2003). Adlerians' basic premise is that if clients can change their thinking then they can change their feelings and behavior. A study of contemporary counseling theories reveals that many of Adler's notions have reappeared in these modern approaches with different nomenclature, and often without giving Adler the credit that is due to him (Watts, 1999; Watts & Pietrzak, 2000; Watts & Shulman, 2003). It is clear that there are significant linkages of Adlerian theory with most of the present-day theories.

Limitations and Criticisms of the Adlerian Approach

Adler had to choose between devoting his time to formalizing his theory and teaching others the basic concepts of Individual Psychology. He placed practicing and teaching before organizing and presenting a well-defined and systematic theory. Thus, his written presentations are often difficult to follow, many of them coming from transcripts of lectures he gave. Initially, many people considered his ideas somewhat loose and too simplistic.

Research supporting the effectiveness of Adlerian theory is limited but has improved over the last 25 years (Watts & Shulman, 2003). However, a large part of the theory still requires empirical testing and comparative analysis. This is especially true in the conceptual areas that Adlerians accept as axiomatic: for example, the development of lifestyle; the unity of the personality and an acceptance of a singular view of self; the rejection of the prominence of heredity in determining behavior, especially pathological behavior; and the usefulness of the multiple interventions used by various Adlerians.

Adlerian theory is of limited use for clients seeking immediate solutions to their problems and for clients who have little interest in exploring early childhood experiences, early memories, and dreams. This approach also has limited effectiveness with clients who do not understand the purpose of exploring the details of a lifestyle analysis when dealing with life's current problems (Arciniega & Newlon, 1999).

 WHERE TO GO FROM HERE

If you are using the *CD-ROM for Integrative Counseling,* Session 6 ("Cognitive Focus in Counseling") illustrates Ruth's striving to live up to expectations and measure up to perfectionist standards. In this particular therapy session with Ruth, you will see how I draw upon cognitive concepts and apply them in practice.

If you find that your thinking is allied with the Adlerian approach, you might consider seeking training in Individual Psychology or becoming a member of the North American Society of Adlerian Psychology (NASAP). To obtain information on NASAP and a list of Adlerian organizations and institutes, contact:

North American Society of Adlerian Psychology (NASAP)
50 Northeast Drive
Hershey, PA 17033
Telephone: (717) 579-8795
Fax: (717) 533-8616
Email: nasap@msn.com
Web site: www.alfredadler.org

The society publishes a newsletter and a quarterly journal and maintains a list of institutes, training programs, and workshops in Adlerian psychology. *The Journal of Individual Psychology* presents current scholarly and professional research. Columns on counseling, education, and parent and family education are regular features. Information about subscriptions is available by contacting the society.

If you are interested in pursuing training, postgraduate study, continuing education, or a degree, contact NASAP for a list of Adlerian organizations and institutes. A few training institutes are listed here:

Adler School of Professional Psychology
65 East Wacker Place, Suite 2100
Chicago, IL 60601-7298
Telephone: (312) 201-5900
Fax: (312) 201-5917
Email: information@adler.edu
Web site: www.adler.edu

Adlerian Training Institute
Dr. Bill Nicoll, Coordinator
P. O. Box 276358
Boca Raton, FL 33427-6358
Telephone: (954) 757-2845

**The Alfred Adler Institutes of San Francisco
and Northwestern Washington**
The Alfred Adler Institute of Northwestern Washington
3320 Sussex Drive
Bellingham, WA 98226
Telephone: (360) 935-1661
Email: HTStein@att.net
Web site: http://ourworld.compuserv.com/homepages/hstein/

The Alfred Adler Institute of Quebec
4947 Grosvenor Avenue
Montreal, QC H3W 2M2
CANADA
Telephone: (514) 731-5675
Fax: (514) 731-9242
Email: aaiq@total.net
Web site: www.total.net/~aaiq/index.html

**The International Committee for Adlerian Summer Schools
and Institutes**
Betty Haeussler
9212 Morley Road
Lanham, MD 20706
Telephone: (301) 577-8243
Fax: (301) 595-0669
Email: PeteHMSU64@aol.com
Web site: www.icassi.org

InfoTrac College Edition Resources

Adlerian Therapy   The following key words are listed in such a way as to enable the InfoTrac College Edition search engine to locate a wider range of articles in the online library. The key words should be entered exactly as shown, to include asterisks, "W1," and "AND."

Alfred Adler

Adler AND superiority

Inferiority complex

Superiority complex

Phenomenological AND psychol*

Family W1 constellation

Birth W1 order

Recommended Supplementary Readings

Adlerian, Cognitive, and Constructivist Therapies: An Integrative Dialogue (Watts, 2003) acknowledges the important contributions of Alfred Adler and illustrates the many ways Adlerian ideas have influenced the development of the cognitive and constructivist therapies.

Primer of Adlerian Psychology (Mosak & Maniacci, 1999) offers an accessible introduction to the basic tenets of Individual Psychology geared toward readers who are not familiar with Adler's work.

Adlerian Counseling: A Practitioner's Approach (Sweeney, 1998) is the most comprehensive source on Adlerian counseling. It includes Adler's life and work, an explanation of many key Adlerian concepts, and an overview of the counseling process as it is applied to individuals, couples, families, and groups.

Techniques in Adlerian Psychology (Carlson & Slavik, 1997) is an edited volume containing techniques for individual therapy with adults, child counseling, and couples and families counseling.

Understanding Life-Style: The Psycho-Clarity Process (Powers & Griffith, 1987) is a useful source of information for doing a lifestyle assessment. Separate chapters deal with interview techniques, lifestyle assessment, early recollections, the family constellation, and methods of summarizing and interpreting information.

References and Suggested Readings

ADLER, A. (1958). *What life should mean to you.* New York: Capricorn. (Original work published 1931)

ADLER, A. (1959). *Understanding human nature.* New York: Premier Books.

ADLER, A. (1964). *Social interest. A challenge to mankind.* New York: Capricorn. (Original work published 1938)

ALBERT, L. (1996). *Cooperative discipline.* Circle Pines, MN: American Guidance Service.

AMERICAN PSYCHIATRIC ASSOCIATION. (2000). *Diagnostic and statistical manual of mental disorders, text revision,* (4th ed.). (DSM-IV-TR). Washington, DC: Author.

ANSBACHER, H. L. (1974). Goal-oriented individual psychology: Alfred Adler's theory. In A. Burton (Ed.), *Operational theories of personality* (pp. 99–142). New York: Brunner/Mazel.

*ANSBACHER, H. L. (1979). The increasing recognition of Adler. In. H. L. Ansbacher & R. R. Ansbacher (Eds.), *Superiority and social interest. Alfred Adler, A collection of his later writings* (3rd rev. ed., pp. 3–20). New York: Norton.

*ANSBACHER, H. L. (1992). Alfred Adler's concepts of community feeling and social interest and the relevance of community feeling for old age. *Individual Psychology, 48*(4), 402–412.

*ANSBACHER, H. L., & ANSBACHER, R. R. (Eds.). (1964). *The individual psychology of Alfred Adler.* New York: Harper & Row/Torchbooks. (Original work published 1956)

*ANSBACHER, H. L., & ANSBACHER, R. R. (Eds.). (1979). *Superiority and social interest. Alfred Adler, A collection of his later writings* (3rd rev. ed.). New York: Norton.

ARCINIEGA, G. M., & NEWLON, B. J. (1999). Counseling and psychotherapy: Multicultural considerations. In D. Capuzzi & D. F. Gross (Eds.), *Counseling and psychotherapy: Theories and interventions* (2nd ed., pp. 435–458). Upper Saddle River, NJ: Merrill/Prentice-Hall.

*BITTER, J. R., CHRISTENSEN, O. C., HAWES, C., & NICOLL, W. G. (1998). Adlerian brief therapy with individuals, couples, and families. *Directions in Clinical and Counseling Psychology, 8*(8), 95–111.

*BITTER, J. R., & NICOLL, W. G. (2000). Adlerian brief therapy with individuals: Process and practice. *Journal of Individual Psychology, 56*(1), 31–44.

*CARLSON, J. M., & CARLSON, J. D. (2000). The application of Adlerian psychotherapy with Asian-American clients. *Journal of Individual Psychology, 56*(2), 214–225.

*CARLSON, J., & SLAVIK, S. (Eds.). (1997). *Techniques in Adlerian psychology.* Bristol, PA: Accelerated Development.

*COREY, G. (1999). Adlerian contributions to the practice of group counseling: A personal perspective. *Journal of Individual Psychology, 55*(1), 4–14.

COREY, G. (2003). Adlerian foundations of group counseling. *Directions in Mental Health Counseling, 15*(2), 13–25.

COREY, G. (2004). *Theory and practice of group counseling* (6th ed.). Pacific Grove, CA: Brooks/Cole.

*COREY, G. (Ed.). (2005). *Case approach to counseling and psychotherapy* (6th ed.). Belmont, CA: Brooks/Cole.

---

*Books and articles marked with an asterisk are suggested for further study.

DINKMEYER, D. C., DINKMEYER, D. C., JR., & SPERRY, L. (1987). *Adlerian counseling and psychotherapy* (2nd ed.). Columbus, OH: Merrill.

DINKMEYER, D., MC KAY, G., DINKMEYER, JR., D., & MC KAY, J. (1997). *STEP: The parent handbook.* Circle Pines, MN: American Guidance Service.

DINKMEYER, D., JR., & SPERRY, L. (2002). *Counseling and psychotherapy: An integrated Individual Psychology approach* (3rd ed.). Upper Saddle River, NJ: Merrill/Prentice-Hall.

*DISQUE, J. G., & BITTER, J. R. (1998). Integrating narrative therapy with Adlerian lifestyle assessment: A case study. *Journal of Individual Psychology, 54*(4), 431–450.

*DREIKURS, R. (1953). *Fundamentals of Adlerian psychology.* Chicago: Alfred Adler Institute.

*DREIKURS, R. (1967). *Psychodynamics, psychotherapy, and counseling. Collected papers.* Chicago: Alfred Adler Institute of Chicago.

DREIKURS, R. (1968). *Psychology in the classroom* (2nd ed.). New York: Harper & Row.

DREIKURS, R. (1969). Group psychotherapy from the point of view of Adlerian psychology. In H. M. Ruitenbeck (Ed.), *Group therapy today: Styles, methods, and techniques* (pp. 37–48). New York: Aldine-Atherton. (Original work published 1957)

*DREIKURS, R. (1971). *Social equality: The challenge of today.* Chicago: Regnery.

*DREIKURS, R. (1997). Holistic medicine. *Individual Psychology, 53*(2), 127–205.

DREIKURS, R., & MOSAK, H. H. (1966). The tasks of life: I. Adler's three tasks. *The Individual Psychologist, 4,* 18–22.

DREIKURS, R., & MOSAK, H. H. (1967). The tasks of life: II. The fourth task. *The Individual Psychologist, 4,* 51–55.

GRIFFITH, J., & POWERS, R. L. (1984). *An Adlerian lexicon.* Chicago: Americas Institute of Adlerian Studies.

HAWES, E. C. (1993). Marriage counseling and enrichment. In O. C. Christensen (Ed.), *Adlerian family counseling* (Rev. ed., pp. 125–163). Minneapolis, MN: Educational Media Corp.

HAWES, C., & BLANCHARD, L. M. (1993). Life tasks as an assessment technique in marital counseling. *Individual Psychology, 49,* 306–317.

KEFIR, N. (1981). Impasse/priority therapy. In R. J. Corsini (Ed.), *Handbook of innovative psychotherapies* (pp. 401–415). New York: Wiley.

*MANASTER, G. J., & CORSINI, R. J. (1982). *Individual psychology. Theory and practice.* Itasca, IL: F. E. Peacock.

MOSAK, H. H. (1977). *On purpose.* Chicago: Alfred Adler Institute.

MOSAK, H. H. (2000). Adlerian psychotherapy. In R. J. Corsini & D. Wedding (Eds.), *Current psychotherapies* (6th ed., pp. 54–98). Itasca, IL: F. E. Peacock.

MOSAK, H. H., & DREIKURS, R. (1967). The life tasks: III. The fifth life task. *The Individual Psychologist, 5,* 16–22.

MOSAK, H. H., & MANIACCI, M. P. (1998). *Tactics in counseling and psychotherapy.* Itasca, IL: F. E. Peacock.

*MOSAK, H. H., & MANIACCI, M. P. (1999). *Primer of Adlerian psychology.* New York: Brunner/Routledge (Taylor & Francis Group).

MOSAK, H. H., & SHULMAN, B. H. (1988). *Lifestyle inventory.* Muncie, IN: Accelerated Development.

MOZDZIERZ, G. J., LISIECKI, J., BITTER, J. R., & WILLIAMS, A. L. (1984). Role-functions for Adlerian therapists. *Individual Psychology, 42*(2), 154–177.

NYSTUL, M. S. (1999a). An interview with Gerald Corey. *Journal of Individual Psychology, 55*(1), 15–25.

NYSTUL, M. S. (1999b). An interview with Paul Pedersen. *Journal of Individual Psychology, 55*(2), 216–224.

POPKIN, M. (1993). *Active parenting today.* Atlanta, GA: Active Parenting.

*POWERS, R. L., & GRIFFITH, J. (1987). *Understanding life-style. The psycho-clarity process.* Chicago: Americas Institute of Adlerian Studies.

*POWERS, R. L., & GRIFFITH, J. (1995). *IPCW: The individual psychology client workbook with supplements.* Chicago: Americas Institute of Adlerian Studies. (Original work published 1986)

SCHULTZ, D., & SCHULTZ, S. E. (2001). *Theories of personality* (7th ed.). Pacific Grove, CA: Brooks/Cole.

*SHERMAN, R., & DINKMEYER, D. (1987). *Systems of family therapy. An Adlerian integration.* New York: Brunner/Mazel.

*SHULMAN, B. H., & MOSAK, H. H. (1988). *Manual for life style assessment.* Muncie, IN: Accelerated Development.

*SONSTEGARD, M. A. (1998a). A rationale for group counseling. *Journal of Individual Psychology, 54*(2), 164–175.

*SONSTEGARD, M. A. (1998b). The theory and practice of Adlerian group counseling and psychotherapy. *Journal of Individual Psychology, 54*(2), 217–250.

*SONSTEGARD, M. A., BITTER, J. R., PELONIS-PENEROS, P. P., & NICOLL, W. G. (2001). Adlerian group psychotherapy: A brief therapy approach. *Directions in Clinical and Counseling Psychology, 11*(2), 11–12.

*SPERRY, L., & CARLSON, J. (1996). *Psychopathology and psychotherapy. From DSM-IV diagnosis to treatment.* Washington, DC: Accelerated Development.

*SWEENEY, T. J. (1998). *Adlerian counseling: A practitioner's approach* (4th ed.). Philadelphia, PA: Accelerated Development (Taylor & Francis Group).

VAIHINGER, H. (1965). *The philosophy of "as if."* London: Routledge & Kegan Paul.

*WATTS, R. E. (1999). The vision of Adler: An introduction. In R. E. Watts, & J. Carlson (Eds.), *Interventions and strategies in counseling and psychotherapy* (pp. 1–13). Philadelphia, PA: Accelerated Development (Taylor & Francis Group).

*WATTS, R. E. (2000). Entering the new millennium: Is Individual Psychology still relevant? *Journal of Individual Psychology, 56*(1), 21–30.

WATTS, R. E. (2003). *Adlerian, cognitive, and constructivist therapies: An integrative dialogue.* New York: Springer.

*WATTS, R. E., & CARLSON, J. (Eds.). (1999). *Interventions and strategies in counseling and psychotherapy.* Philadelphia, PA: Accelerated Development (Taylor & Francis Group).

WATTS, R. E., & HOLDEN, J. M. (1994). Why continue to use "fictional finalism?" *Individual Psychology, 50,* 161–163.

*WATTS, R. E., & PIETRZAK, D. (2000). Adlerian "encouragement" and the therapeutic process of solution-focused brief therapy. *Journal of Counseling and Development, 78*(4), 442–447.

*WATTS, R. E., & SHULMAN, B. H. (2003). Integrating Adlerian and constructive therapies: An Adlerian perspective. In R. E. Watts (Ed.), *Adlerian, cognitive, and constructivist therapies: An integrative dialogue* (pp. 9–37). New York: Springer.

Existential Therapy

Viktor **Frankl**

VIKTOR FRANKL (1905–1997) was born and educated in Vienna. He founded the Youth Advisement Centers there in 1928 and directed them until 1938. From 1942 to 1945 Frankl was a prisoner in the Nazi concentration camps at Auschwitz and Dachau, where his parents, brother, wife, and children died. He vividly remembered his horrible experiences in these camps, yet he was able to use them in a constructive way and did not allow them to dampen his love and enthusiasm for life. He traveled all around the world, giving lectures in Europe, Latin America, Southeast Asia, and the United States.

Frankl received his M.D. in 1930 and his Ph.D. in philosophy in 1949, both from the University of Vienna. He became an associate professor at the University of Vienna and later was a distinguished speaker at the United States International University in San Diego. He was a visiting professor at Harvard, Stanford, and Southern Methodist universities. Frankl's works have been translated into more than 20 languages, and his ideas continue to have a major impact on the development of existential therapy. His compelling book *Man's Search for Meaning* (1963), which was originally entitled *From Death Camp to Existentialism*, has been a best-seller around the world.

Although Frankl had begun to develop an existential approach to clinical practice before his grim years in the Nazi death camps, his experiences there confirmed his views. Frankl (1963) observed and personally experienced the truths expressed by existential philosophers and writers, including the view that love is the highest goal to which humans can aspire and that our salvation is through love. That we have choices in every situation is another notion confirmed by his experiences in the concentration camps. Even in terrible situations, he believed, we could preserve a vestige of spiritual freedom and independence of mind. He learned experientially that everything could be taken from a person but one thing: "the last of human freedoms—to choose one's attitude in any given set of circumstances, to choose one's own way" (p. 104). Frankl believed that the essence of being human lies in searching for meaning and purpose. We can discover this meaning through our actions and deeds, by experiencing a value (such as love or achievements through work), and by suffering.

Frankl knew and read Freud and attended some of the meetings of Freud's psychoanalytic group. Frankl acknowledged his indebtedness to Freud, although he disagreed with the rigidity of Freud's psychoanalytic system. Frankl often remarked that Freud was a *depth* psychologist and that he is a *height* psychologist who built on Freud's foundations. Reacting against most of Freud's deterministic notions, Frankl developed his theory and practice of psychotherapy emphasizing the concepts of freedom, responsibility, meaning, and the search for values. He established his international reputation as the founder of what has been called "The Third School of Viennese Psychoanalysis."

I have selected Frankl as one of the key figures of the existential approach because of the dramatic way in which his theories were tested by the tragedies of his life. His life was an illustration of his theory, for he lived what his theory espouses. ∎

Rollo *May*

ROLLO MAY (1909–1994) first lived in Ohio and then moved to Michigan as a young child along with his five brothers and a sister. He remembered his home life as being unhappy, a situation that had something to do with his interest in psychology and counseling. In his personal life May struggled with his own existential concerns and the failure of two marriages.

Despite his unhappy life experiences, he graduated from Oberlin College in 1930 and then went to Greece as a teacher. During his summers in Greece he traveled to Vienna to study with Alfred Adler. After receiving a degree in theology from Union Theological Seminary, May decided that the best way to reach out and help people was through psychology instead of theology. After completing his doctorate in clinical psychology at Columbia University, May set up private practice in New York while also becoming a supervisory and training analyst for the William Alanson Institute.

While May was pursuing his doctoral program, he came down with tuberculosis, which resulted in a 2-year stay in a sanitarium. During his recovery period, May spent much time learning firsthand about the nature of anxiety. He also spent time reading, and he studied the works of Søren Kierkegaard, which was the catalyst for his recognizing the existential dimensions of anxiety. This study resulted in his book *The Meaning of Anxiety* (1950). His popular book *Love and Will* (1969) reflects his own personal struggles with love and intimate relationships and mirrors Western society's questioning of its values pertaining to sex and marriage.

The greatest personal influence on May was the German philosopher Paul Tillich (author of *The Courage to Be,* 1952), who became his mentor and a personal friend. The two spent much time together discussing philosophical, religious, and psychological topics. Most of May's writings reflect a concern with the nature of human experience, such as recognizing and dealing with power, accepting freedom and responsibility, and discovering one's identity. He draws from his rich knowledge based on the classics and his existential perspective.

May was one of the main proponents of humanistic approaches to psychotherapy, and he was the principal American spokesman of European existential thinking as it is applied to psychotherapy. His view is that psychotherapy should be aimed at helping people discover the meaning of their lives and should be concerned with the problems of being rather than with problem solving. Questions of being include learning to deal with issues such as sex and intimacy, growing old, and facing death. According to May, the real challenge is for people to be able to live in a world where they are alone and where they will eventually have to face death. He contends that our individualism should be balanced by what Adler refers to as social interest. Therapists need to help individuals find ways to contribute to the betterment of the society in which they live. If individuals in society were grounded on these higher values, therapists might well be out of business. ■

 INTRODUCTION

Existential therapy can best be described as a *philosophical approach* that influences a counselor's therapeutic practice. As such, existential psychotherapy is neither an independent nor separate school of therapy, nor is it a neatly defined model with specific techniques. Rather, it is more appropriate to refer to *existential psychotherapies* (Walsh & McElwain, 2002). This chapter addresses some of the existential ideas and themes that have significant implications for the existentially oriented practitioner.

The existential approach rejects the deterministic view of human nature espoused by orthodox psychoanalysis and radical behaviorism. Psychoanalysis sees freedom as restricted by unconscious forces, irrational drives, and past events; behaviorists see freedom as restricted by sociocultural conditioning. In contrast, existential therapists acknowledge some of these facts about the human situation but emphasize our freedom to choose what to make of our circumstances. This approach is grounded on the assumption that we are free and therefore responsible for our choices and actions. We are the authors of our lives, and we design the signposts to follow.

A basic existential premise is that we are not victims of circumstance, because to a large extent we are what we choose to be. A major aim of therapy is to encourage clients to reflect on life, to recognize their range of alternatives, and to decide among them. Once clients begin the process of recognizing the ways in which they have passively accepted circumstances and surrendered control, they can start on a path of consciously shaping their own lives. Yalom (2003) emphasizes that the first step in the therapeutic journey is for clients to accept responsibility: "Once individuals recognize their role in creating their own life predicament, they also realize that they, and only they, have the power to change that situation" (p. 141).

E. van Deurzen-Smith (1988, 1997) writes that existential counseling is not designed to "cure" people in the tradition of the medical model. Rather, clients are viewed as being sick of life and unable to live a productive life. They need help in surveying the terrain and in deciding on the best route to take, so that they can ultimately discover their own way. Existential therapy is a process of searching for the value and meaning in life. In existential therapy attention is given to clients' immediate, ongoing experience with the aim of helping them develop a greater presence in their quest for meaning and purpose (Sharp & Bugental, 2001). The therapist's basic task is to encourage clients to explore their options for creating a meaningful existence. We can begin by recognizing that we do not have to remain passive victims of our circumstances but instead can consciously become the architects of our lives.

Historical Background in Philosophy

The existential therapy movement was not founded by any particular person or group; many streams of thought contributed to it. Drawing from a major orientation in philosophy, existential therapy arose spontaneously in different parts of Europe and among different schools of psychology and psychiatry in the 1940s and 1950s. It grew out of an effort to help people resolve the dilemmas of contemporary life, such as isolation, alienation, and meaninglessness. Early writers focused on the individual's experience of being alone in the world and facing the anxiety of this situation. The European existential perspective focused on human limitations and the tragic dimensions of life (Sharp & Bugental, 2001).

The thinking of existential psychologists and psychiatrists was influenced by a number of philosophers and writers during the 19th century. To get some flavor of the philosophical underpinnings of modern existential psychotherapy, one must have some awareness of such figures as Søren Kierkegaard, Friedrich Nietzsche, Martin Heidegger, Jean-Paul Sartre, Martin Buber, Ludwig Binswanger, and Medard Boss. These major figures of existentialism and existential phenomenology and their cultural, philosophical, and religious writings provided the basis for the formation of existential therapy.

SØREN KIERKEGAARD (1813–1855)   A Danish philosopher, Kierkegaard was particularly concerned with *angst*—a Danish and German word whose meaning lies between the English words *dread* and *anxiety*—and he addressed the role of anxiety and uncertainty in life. Without the experience of angst, we may go through life as sleepwalkers. But many of us, especially in adolescence, are awakened into real life by a terrible uneasiness. Life is one contingency after another, with no guarantees beyond the certainty of death. This is by no means a comfortable state, but it is necessary to our becoming human. Becoming human is a *project*, and our task is not so much to discover who we are as to *create* ourselves.

FRIEDRICH NIETZSCHE (1844–1900)   The German philosopher Nietzsche is the iconoclastic counterpart to Kierkegaard, expressing a revolutionary approach to the self, to ethics, and to society. Like Kierkegaard, he emphasized the importance of subjectivity. Nietzsche set out to prove that the ancient definition of humans as *rational* was entirely misleading. We are far more creatures of will than we are impersonal intellects. But where Kierkegaard emphasized the "subjective truth" of an intense concern with God, Nietzsche located values within the individual's "will to power." We give up an honest acknowledgment of this source of value when society invites us to rationalize powerlessness by advocating other worldly concerns. If, like sheep, we acquiesce in "herd morality," we will be nothing but mediocrities. But if we release ourselves by giving free rein to our will to power, we will tap our potentiality for creativity and originality. Kierkegaard and Nietzsche, with their pioneering studies of subjectivity and the emerging self, together are generally considered to be the originators of the existential perspective (Sharp & Bugental, 2001).

MARTIN HEIDEGGER (1889–1976)   The subjective experience of being human that was so dramatically expressed by Kierkegaard and Nietzsche developed into a 20th-century method of studying experience that is called phenomenology. Heidegger's phenomenological existentialism reminds us that we exist "in the world" and should not try to think of ourselves as beings apart from the world into which we are thrown. The way we fill our everyday life with superficial conversation and routine shows that we often assume we are going to live forever and can afford to waste day after day. Our moods and feelings (including anxiety about death) are a form of understanding whether we are living authentically or whether we are inauthentically constructing our life around the expectations of others. When we translate this wisdom from vague feeling to explicit awareness, we may develop more positive resolve about how we want to be. Phenomenological existentialism, as presented by Heidegger, provides a view of human history that does not focus on past events but motivates individuals to look forward to "authentic experiences" that are yet to come.

JEAN-PAUL SARTRE (1905–1980)   A philosopher and novelist, Sartre was convinced, in part by his dangerous years in the French Resistance in World War II, that humans are even more free than earlier existentialists had believed. The existence of a space—nothingness—between the whole of our past and the *now* frees us to choose what we will. Our values are what we choose. The failure to acknowledge our freedom and choices is what results in emotional problems. This freedom is hard to face up to, so we tend to invent an excuse by saying, "I can't change now because of my past conditioning." Sartre called excuses "bad faith." No matter what we *have* been, we can make choices now and thus become something quite different. But to choose is to become committed: This is the responsibility that is the other side of freedom.

MARTIN BUBER (1878–1965)   Leaving Germany to live in the new state of Israel, Buber took a less individualistic stand than most of the other existentialists. He said that we humans live in a kind of *betweenness;* that is, there is never just an *I*, but always an *other.* The *I*, the person who is the agent, changes depending on whether the other is an *it* or a *Thou.* But sometimes we make the serious mistake of reducing another person to the status of a mere object, in which case the relationship becomes *I/it.* Buber stresses the importance of *presence,* which has three functions: (1) it enables true I/Thou relationships; (2) it allows for meaning to exist in a situation; and (3) it enables an individual to be responsible in the here-and-now (Gould, 1993). In a famous dialogue with Carl Rogers, Buber argued that the therapist and client could never be on the same footing, for it is the latter who comes to the former for help. When the relationship is fully mutual, we have become "dialogic," a fully human condition.

LUDWIG BINSWANGER (1881–1966)   An existential analyst, Binswanger proposed a holistic model of self that addresses the relationship between the person and his or her environment. He used a phenomenological approach to explore significant features of the self such as choice, freedom, and caring. Binswanger accepted Heidegger's notion that we are "thrown into the world." However, this "thrown-ness" does not release us from the responsibility of our choices and for planning for the future (Gould, 1993). Existential analysis (*dasein analyse*) emphasizes the subjective and spiritual dimensions of human existence. Binswanger (1975) contended that crises in therapy were typically major choice points for the client. Although he originally looked to psychoanalytic theory to shed light on psychosis, he moved toward an existential view of his patients. This perspective enabled him to understand the worldview and immediate experience of his patients, as well as the meaning of their behavior, as opposed to superimposing his view as a therapist on their experience and behavior.

MEDARD BOSS (1903–1991)   Both Binswanger and Boss were early figures of existential psychotherapy. They made reference to *Dasein* or *being-in-the-world*, which pertains to our ability to reflect on life events and attribute meaning to these events. Humans have the capacity to make choices about many events. They believed that the therapist must enter the client's subjective world without presuppositions that would get in the way of this experiential understanding. Both Binswanger and Boss, as early existential psychoanalysts, were significantly influenced by Heidegger's seminal work, *Being and Time* (1962), which provided a broad basis for understanding the individual (May, 1958). Boss (1963) was deeply influenced by Freudian psychoanalysis, but even more so by Heidegger. Boss's major professional interest was applying Heidegger's philosophical notions to therapeutic practice, and he was especially concerned with integrating Freud's methods with Heidegger's concepts, as described in his book *Daseinanalysis and Psychoanalysis*.

Key Figures in Contemporary Existential Psychotherapy

Four prominent developers of existential psychotherapy are Viktor Frankl, Rollo May, James Bugental, and Irvin Yalom, all of whom developed their existential approaches to psychotherapy from strong backgrounds in both existential and humanistic psychology. Viktor Frankl was a central figure in developing existential therapy in Europe and also in bringing it to the United States. While Frankl, as a youth, was deeply influenced by Freud, he became a student of Adler. Later, he was influenced by the writings of existential philosophers, and he began developing his own existential philosophy and psychotherapy. He was fond of quoting Nietzsche: "He who has a *why* to live for can bear with almost any *how*" (as cited in Frankl, 1963, pp. 121, 164). Frankl contended that those words could be the motto for all psychotherapeutic practice. Another quotation from Nietzsche seems to capture the essence of his own experience and his writings: "That which does not kill me, makes me stronger" (as cited in Frankl, 1963, p. 130).

Frankl developed *logotherapy*, which means "therapy through meaning." Frankl's philosophical model sheds light on what it means to be fully alive.

"To be alive encompasses the ability to take hold of life day by day as well as to find meaning in suffering" (Gould, 1993, p. 124). The central themes running through his works are life has meaning, under all circumstances; the central motivation for living is the *will to meaning;* the freedom to find meaning in all that we think; and the integration of body, mind, and spirit. According to Frankl, the modern person has the means to live but often has no meaning to live for. The malady of our time is meaninglessness, or the "existential vacuum," which is often experienced when people do not busy themselves with routine and with work. The therapeutic process is aimed at challenging individuals to find meaning and purpose through, among other things, suffering, work, and love (Frankl, 1965).

Along with Frankl, psychologist Rollo May was deeply influenced by the existential philosophers, by the concepts of Freudian psychology, and by many aspects of Alfred Adler's Individual Psychology. Both Frankl and May welcomed flexibility and versatility in the practice of psychoanalysis (Gould, 1993). May was one of the key figures responsible for bringing existentialism from Europe to the United States and for translating key concepts into psychotherapeutic practice. His writings have had a significant impact on existentially oriented practitioners. Of primary importance in introducing existential therapy to the United States was the book *Existence: A New Dimension in Psychiatry and Psychology* (May, Angel, & Ellenberger, 1958). According to May, it takes courage to "be," and our choices determine the kind of person we become. There is a constant struggle within us. Although we want to grow toward maturity and independence, we realize that expansion is often a painful process. Hence, the struggle is between the security of dependence and the delights and pains of growth.

Along with May, two other significant existential therapists in the United States are James Bugental and Irvin Yalom. Bugental developed an approach to depth therapy based on the existential concern with an individual's immediate presence and the humanistic emphasis on the integrity of each individual (Sharp & Bugental, 2001). In *The Art of the Psychotherapist* (1987), Bugental describes a life-changing approach to therapy. He views therapy as a journey taken by the therapist and the client that delves deeply into the client's subjective world. He emphasizes that this quest demands the willingness of the therapist to be in contact with his or her own phenomenological world. According to Bugental, the central concern of therapy is to help clients examine how they have answered life's existential questions and to challenge them to revise their answers to begin living authentically. In *Psychotherapy Isn't What You Think* (1999), Bugental illustrates the here-and-now experiencing in the therapeutic relationship.

Irvin Yalom acknowledges the contributions of both European and American psychologists and psychiatrists who have influenced the development of existential thinking and practice. Drawing on his clinical experience and on empirical research, philosophy, and literature, Yalom has developed an existential approach to therapy that focuses on four ultimate human concerns:

death, freedom, existential isolation, and meaninglessness. His classic, comprehensive textbook, *Existential Psychotherapy* (1980), is considered a pioneering accomplishment. He acknowledges the influence on his own writings of several novelists and philosophers. More specifically, he draws in his book on the following themes from those philosophers discussed earlier:

- From Kierkegaard: creative anxiety, despair, fear and dread, guilt, and nothingness
- From Nietzsche: death, suicide, and will
- From Heidegger: authentic being, caring, death, guilt, individual responsibility, and isolation
- From Sartre: meaninglessness, responsibility, and choice
- From Buber: interpersonal relationships, I/Thou perspective in therapy, and self-transcendence

Yalom recognizes Frankl as an eminently pragmatic thinker who has had an impact on his writing and practice. Yalom believes the vast majority of experienced therapists, regardless of their theoretical orientation, employ many of the existential themes discussed in his book. He contends that the four "givens of existence" (the ultimate human concerns) that constitute the heart of existential psychodynamics have enormous relevance to clinical work.

 # KEY CONCEPTS

View of Human Nature

The crucial significance of the existential movement is that it reacts against the tendency to identify therapy with a set of techniques. Instead, it bases therapeutic practice on an understanding of what it means to be human. The existential movement stands for respect for the person, for exploring new aspects of human behavior, and for divergent methods of understanding people. It uses numerous approaches to therapy based on its assumptions about human nature. The current focus of the existential approach is on clients who feel alone in the world and are facing the anxiety of this isolation. Rather than trying to develop rules for therapy, existential practitioners strive to understand these deep human experiences (May & Yalom, 2000).

The existential view of human nature is captured, in part, by the notion that the significance of our existence is never fixed once and for all; rather, we continually re-create ourselves through our projects. Humans are in a constant state of transition, emerging, evolving, and becoming. Being a person implies that we are discovering and making sense of our existence. We continually question ourselves, others, and the world. Although the specific questions we raise vary in accordance with our developmental stage in life, the fundamental themes do not vary. We pose the same questions philosophers have pondered throughout Western history: "Who am I?" "What can I know?" "What ought I to do?" "What can I hope for?" "Where am I going?"

The basic dimensions of the human condition, according to the existential approach, include (1) the capacity for self-awareness; (2) freedom and responsibility; (3) creating one's identity and establishing meaningful relationships with others; (4) the search for meaning, purpose, values, and goals; (5) anxiety as a condition of living; and (6) awareness of death and nonbeing. I develop these propositions in the following sections by summarizing themes that emerge in the writings of existential philosophers and psychotherapists, and I also discuss the implications for counseling practice of each of these propositions.

Proposition 1: The Capacity for Self-Awareness

As human beings, we can reflect and make choices because we are capable of self-awareness. The greater our awareness, the greater our possibilities for freedom (see Proposition 2). Thus, we increase our capacity to live fully as we expand our awareness in the following areas:

- We are finite and do not have unlimited time to do what we want in life.
- We have the potential to take action or not to act; inaction is a decision.
- We choose our actions, and therefore we can partially create our own destiny.
- Meaning is the product of discovering how we are "thrown" or situated in the world and then, through commitment, living creatively.
- Existential anxiety, which is basically a consciousness of our own freedom, is an essential part of living; as we increase our awareness of the choices available to us, we also increase our sense of responsibility for the consequences of these choices.
- We are subject to loneliness, meaninglessness, emptiness, guilt, and isolation.
- We are basically alone, yet we have an opportunity to relate to other beings.

We can choose either to expand or to restrict our consciousness. Because self-awareness is at the root of most other human capacities, the decision to expand it is fundamental to human growth. Here are some dawning awarenesses that individuals may experience in the counseling process:

- They see how they are trading the security of dependence for the anxieties that accompany choosing for themselves.
- They begin to see that their identity is anchored in someone else's definition of them; that is, they are seeking approval and confirmation of their being in others instead of looking to themselves for affirmation.

- They learn that in many ways they are keeping themselves prisoner by some of their past decisions, and they realize that they can make new decisions.
- They learn that although they cannot change certain events in their lives they can change the way they view and react to these events.
- They learn that they are not condemned to a future similar to the past, for they can learn from their past and thereby reshape their future.
- They realize that they are so preoccupied with suffering, death, and dying that they are not appreciating living.
- They are able to accept their limitations yet still feel worthwhile, for they understand that they do not need to be perfect to feel worthy.
- They come to realize that they are failing to live in the present moment because of preoccupation with the past, planning for the future, or trying to do too many things at once.

Increasing self-awareness, which includes awareness of alternatives, motivations, factors influencing the person, and personal goals, is an aim of all counseling. It is the therapist's task to indicate to the client that a price must be paid for increased awareness. As we become more aware, it is more difficult to "go home again." Ignorance of our condition may have brought contentment along with a feeling of partial deadness, but as we open the doors in our world, we can expect more struggle as well as the potential for more fulfillment.

Proposition 2: Freedom and Responsibility

A characteristic existential theme is that people are free to choose among alternatives and therefore have a large role in shaping their destinies. Even though we have no choice about being thrust into the world, the manner in which we live and what we become are the result of our choices. Because of the reality of this essential freedom, we must accept responsibility for directing our lives. However, it is possible to avoid this reality by making excuses. In speaking about "bad faith," the existentialist philosopher Jean-Paul Sartre (1971) refers to the inauthenticity of not accepting personal responsibility. Here are two statements that reveal bad faith: "Since that's the way I'm made, I couldn't help what I did" or "Naturally I'm this way, because I grew up in an alcoholic family." Sartre claims we are constantly confronted with the choice of what kind of person we are becoming, and to exist is never to be finished with this kind of choosing.

We are responsible for our lives, for our actions, and for our failures to take action. From Sartre's perspective people are condemned to freedom. He calls for a *commitment* to choosing for ourselves. Existential guilt is being aware of having evaded a commitment, or having chosen not to choose. This is the guilt we experience when we do not live authentically. It results from allowing others to define us or to make our choices for us. Sartre said, "We are our choices." An inauthentic mode of existence consists of lacking awareness of personal responsibility for our lives and passively assuming that our existence is largely controlled by external forces. In contrast, living authentically implies being true to our own evaluation of what is a valuable existence for ourselves.

For existentialists, then, being free and being human are identical. Freedom and responsibility go hand in hand. We are the authors of our lives in the sense that we create our destiny, our life situation, and our problems (Russell, 1978). Assuming responsibility is a basic condition for change. Clients who refuse to accept responsibility by persistently blaming others for their problems will not profit from therapy.

Frankl (1978) also links freedom with responsibility. He suggested that the Statue of Liberty on the East Coast should be balanced with a Statue of Responsibility on the West Coast. His basic premise is that freedom is bound by certain limitations. We are not free from conditions, but we are free to take a stand against these restrictions. Ultimately, these conditions are subject to our decisions, which means we are responsible.

The therapist assists clients in discovering how they are avoiding freedom and encourages them to learn to risk using it. Not to do so is to cripple clients and make them neurotically dependent on the therapist. Therapists need to teach clients that they can explicitly accept that they have choices, even though they may have devoted most of their life to evading them.

People often seek psychotherapy because they feel that they have lost control of how they are living. They may look to the counselor to direct them, give them advice, or produce magical cures. They may also need to be heard and understood. Two central tasks of the therapist are inviting clients to recognize how they have allowed others to decide for them and encouraging them to take steps toward autonomy. In challenging clients to explore other ways of being that are more fulfilling than their present restricted existence, some existential counselors ask, "Although you have lived in a certain pattern, now that you recognize the price of some of your ways, are you willing to consider creating new patterns?" Others may have a vested interest in keeping the client in an old pattern, so the initiative for changing it will have to come from the client.

Proposition 3: Striving for Identity and Relationship to Others

People are concerned about preserving their uniqueness and centeredness, yet at the same time they have an interest in going outside of themselves to relate to other beings and to nature. Each of us would like to discover a self—that is, find (or create) our personal identity. This is not an automatic process, and it takes courage. As relational beings, we also strive for connectedness with others. We must give of ourselves to others and be concerned with them. Many existential writers discuss loneliness, uprootedness, and alienation, which can be seen as the failure to develop ties with others and with nature.

The trouble with so many of us is that we have sought directions, answers, values, and beliefs from the important people in our world. Rather than trusting ourselves to search within and find our own answers to the conflicts in our life, we sell out by becoming what others expect of us. Our being becomes rooted in their expectations, and we become strangers to ourselves.

THE COURAGE TO BE   Paul Tillich (1886–1965), a leading Protestant theologian of the 20th century, believes awareness of our finite nature gives us an appreciation of ultimate concerns. It takes courage to discover the true "ground of our being" and to use its power to transcend those aspects of nonbeing that would destroy us (Tillich, 1952). We struggle to discover, to create, and to maintain the core deep within our being. One of the greatest fears of clients is that they will discover that there is no core, no self, no substance, and that they are merely reflections of everyone's expectations of them. A client may say: "My fear is that I'll discover I'm nobody, that there really is nothing to me. I'll find out that I'm an empty shell, hollow inside, and nothing will exist if I shed my masks."

Existential therapists may begin by asking their clients to allow themselves to intensify the feeling that they are nothing more than the sum of others' expectations and that they are merely the introjects of parents and parent substitutes. How do they feel now? Are they condemned to stay this way forever? Is there a way out? Can they create a self if they find that they are without one? Where can they begin? Once clients have demonstrated the courage to recognize this fear, to put it into words and share it, it does not seem so overwhelming. I find that it is best to begin work by inviting clients to accept the ways in which they have lived outside themselves and to explore ways in which they are out of contact with themselves.

THE EXPERIENCE OF ALONENESS   The existentialists postulate that part of the human condition is the experience of aloneness. But they add that we can derive strength from the experience of looking to ourselves and sensing our separation. The sense of isolation comes when we recognize that we cannot depend on anyone else for our own confirmation; that is, we alone must give a sense of meaning to life, and we alone must decide how we will live. If we are unable to tolerate ourselves when we are alone, how can we expect anyone else to be enriched by our company? Before we can have any solid relationship with another, we must have a relationship with ourselves. We are challenged to learn to listen to ourselves. We have to be able to stand alone before we can truly stand beside another.

There is a paradox in the proposition that humans are existentially both alone and related, but this very paradox describes the human condition. To think that we can cure the condition, or that it should be cured, is a mistake. Ultimately we are alone.

THE EXPERIENCE OF RELATEDNESS   We humans depend on relationships with others. We want to be significant in another's world, and we want to feel that another's presence is important in our world. When we are able to stand alone and dip within ourselves for our own strength, our relationships with others are based on our fulfillment, not our deprivation. If we feel personally deprived, however, we can expect little but a clinging, parasitic, symbiotic relationship with someone else.

Perhaps one of the functions of therapy is to help clients distinguish between a neurotically dependent attachment to another and a life-affirming relationship in which both persons are enhanced. The therapist can challenge clients to examine what they get from their relationships, how they avoid intimate contact, how they prevent themselves from having equal relationships, and how they might create therapeutic, healthy, and mature human relationships.

STRUGGLING WITH OUR IDENTITY   The awareness of our ultimate aloneness can be frightening, and some clients may attempt to avoid accepting their aloneness and isolation. Because of our fear of dealing with our aloneness, Farha (1994) points out that some of us get caught up in ritualistic behavior patterns that cement us to an image or identity we acquired in early childhood. He writes that some of us become trapped in a *doing* mode to avoid the experience of *being*.

Part of the therapeutic journey consists of the therapist challenging clients to begin to examine the ways in which they have lost touch with their identity, especially by letting others design their life for them. The therapy process itself is often frightening for clients when they realize that they have surrendered their freedom to others and that in the therapy relationship they will have to assume their freedom again. By refusing to give easy solutions or answers, existential therapists confront clients with the reality that they alone must find their own answers.

Proposition 4: The Search for Meaning

A distinctly human characteristic is the struggle for a sense of significance and purpose in life. In my experience the underlying conflicts that bring people into counseling and therapy are centered in these existential questions: Why am I here? What do I want from life? What gives my life purpose? Where is the source of meaning for me in life?

Existential therapy can provide the conceptual framework for helping clients challenge the meaning in their lives. Questions that the therapist might ask are, "Do you like the direction of your life? Are you pleased with what you now are and what you are becoming? If you are confused about who you are and what you want for yourself, what are you doing to get some clarity?"

THE PROBLEM OF DISCARDING OLD VALUES   One of the problems in therapy is that clients may discard traditional (and imposed) values without finding other, suitable ones to replace them. What does the therapist do when clients no longer cling to values that they never really challenged or internalized and now experience a vacuum? Clients report that they feel like a boat without a rudder. They seek new guidelines and values that are appropriate for the newly discovered facets of themselves, and yet for a time they are without them. Perhaps the task of the therapeutic process is to help clients create a value system based on a way of living that is consistent with their way of being.

The therapist's job might well be to trust the capacity of clients to eventually discover an internally derived value system that does provide a meaningful life. They will no doubt flounder for a time and experience anxiety as a result of the absence of clear-cut values. The therapist's trust is important in teaching clients to trust their own capacity to discover a new source of values.

MEANINGLESSNESS   When the world they live in seems meaningless, clients may wonder whether it is worth it to continue struggling or even living. Faced with the prospect of our mortality, we might ask: "Is there any point to what I do now, since I will eventually die? Will what I do be forgotten once I am gone? Given the fact of mortality, why should I busy myself with anything?" A man in one of my groups captured precisely the idea of personal significance when he said, "I feel like another page in a book that has been turned quickly, and nobody bothered to read the page." For Frankl (1978) such a feeling of meaninglessness is the major existential neurosis of modern life.

Meaninglessness in life leads to emptiness and hollowness, or a condition that Frankl calls the *existential vacuum*. Because there is no preordained design for living, people are faced with the task of creating their own meaning. At times people who feel trapped by the emptiness of life withdraw from the struggle of creating a life with purpose. Experiencing meaninglessness and establishing values that are part of a meaningful life are issues that may well be taken up in counseling.

Related to the concept of meaninglessness is what existential practitioners call *existential guilt*. This is a condition that grows out of a sense of incompleteness, or a realization that we are not what we might have become. It is the awareness that our actions and choices express less than our full range as a person. This guilt is not viewed as neurotic, nor is it seen as a symptom that needs to be cured. Instead, the existential therapist explores it to see what clients can learn about the ways in which they are living their life.

CREATING NEW MEANING   Logotherapy is designed to help clients find a meaning in life. The therapist's function is not to tell clients what their particular meaning in life should be but to point out that they can discover meaning even in suffering (Frankl, 1978). This view does not share the pessimistic flavor that some people find in existential philosophy. It holds that human suffering (the tragic and negative aspects of life) can be turned into human achievement by the stand an individual takes in the face of it. Frankl also contends that people who confront pain, guilt, despair, and death can challenge their despair and thus triumph. Yet meaning is not something that we can directly search for and obtain. Paradoxically, the more rationally we seek it, the more likely we are to miss it. Yalom (2003) and Frankl are in basic agreement that, like pleasure, meaning must be pursued obliquely. Finding meaning in life is a by-product of *engagement,* which is a commitment to creating, loving, working, and building.

Proposition 5: Anxiety as a Condition of Living

Anxiety arises from one's personal strivings to survive and to maintain and assert one's being, and the feelings anxiety generates are an inevitable aspect of the human condition. Existential anxiety is conceptualized as the unavoidable result of being confronted with the "givens of existence"—death, freedom, existential isolation, and meaninglessness (Yalom, 1980).

Existential therapists differentiate between normal and neurotic anxiety, and they see anxiety as a potential source of growth. Normal anxiety is an appropriate response to an event being faced. Further, this kind of anxiety does not have to be repressed, and it can be used as a motivation to change. Neurotic anxiety, in contrast, is out of proportion to the situation. It is typically out of awareness, and it tends to immobilize the person. Because we could not survive without some anxiety, it is not a therapeutic goal to eliminate normal anxiety. Being psychologically healthy entails living with as little neurotic anxiety as possible, while accepting and struggling with the unavoidable existential anxiety (normal anxiety) that is a part of living. Life cannot be lived, nor can death be faced, without anxiety (May & Yalom, 2000).

Existential anxiety is a constructive form of normal anxiety and can be a stimulus for growth. We experience this anxiety as we become increasingly aware of our freedom and the consequences of accepting or rejecting that freedom. In fact, when we make a decision that involves reconstruction of our life, the accompanying anxiety can be a signal that we are ready for personal change. If we learn to listen to the subtle messages of anxiety, we can dare to take the steps necessary to change the direction of our lives.

Many clients who seek counseling want solutions that will enable them to eliminate anxiety. Although attempts to avoid anxiety by creating the illusion that there is security in life may help us cope with the unknown, we really know on some level that we are deceiving ourselves when we think we have found fixed security. We can blunt anxiety by constricting our life and thus reducing choices. Opening up to new life, however, means opening up to anxiety. We pay a steep price when we short-circuit anxiety.

People who have the courage to face themselves are, nonetheless, frightened. I am convinced that those who are willing to live with their anxiety for a time are the ones who profit from personal therapy. Those who flee too quickly into comfortable patterns might experience a temporary relief but in the long run seem to experience the frustration of being stuck in their old ways.

According to May (1981), freedom and anxiety are two sides of the same coin; anxiety is associated with the excitement accompanying the birth of a new idea. Thus, we experience anxiety when we use our freedom to move out of the known into the realm of the unknown. Out of fear, many of us try to avoid taking such a leap into the unknown.

Existential therapy helps clients come to terms with the paradoxes of existence—life and death, success and failure, freedom and limitations, and certainty and doubt. As people recognize the realities of their confrontation with pain and suffering, their need to struggle for survival, and their basic fallibility, anxiety surfaces. Deurzen-Smith (1991) contends that an essential aim of existential therapy is not to make life seem easier or safer but to encourage clients to recognize and deal with the sources of their insecurity and anxiety. Facing existential anxiety involves viewing life as an adventure rather than hiding behind securities that seem to offer protection. As she puts it, "We need to question and scrape away at the easy answers and expose ourselves to some of the anxiety that can bring us back to life in a real and deep way" (p. 46).

It is essential that therapists recognize existential anxiety and guide clients in finding ways of dealing with it constructively. Existential therapy does not aim at eliminating anxiety, for to do so would be to cut off a source of vitality. Counselors have the task of encouraging clients to develop the courage to face life squarely, largely by taking a stance, performing an action, or making a decision (Deurzen-Smith, 1988).

The existential therapist can help clients recognize that learning how to tolerate ambiguity and uncertainty and how to live without props can be a necessary phase in the journey from dependence to autonomy. The therapist and client can explore the possibility that although breaking away from crippling patterns and building new lifestyles will be fraught with anxiety for a while, anxiety will diminish as the client experiences more satisfaction with newer ways of being. When a client becomes more self-confident, the anxiety that results from an expectation of catastrophe will decrease.

Proposition 6: Awareness of Death and Nonbeing

The existentialist does not view death negatively but holds that awareness of death as a basic human condition gives significance to living. A distinguishing human characteristic is the ability to grasp the reality of the future and the inevitability of death. It is necessary to think about death if we are to think significantly about life. From Frankl's perspective, death should not be considered a threat. Rather, death provides the motivation for us to live our lives fully and take advantage of each opportunity to do something meaningful (Gould, 1993). If we defend ourselves against the reality of our eventual death, life becomes insipid and meaningless. But if we realize that we are mortal, we know that we do not have an eternity to complete our projects and that each present moment is crucial. Our awareness of death is the source of zest for life and creativity. Death and life are interdependent, and though physical death destroys us, the idea of death saves us (Yalom, 1980, 2003).

Yalom (2003) recommends that therapists talk directly to clients about the reality of death. He believes the fear of death percolates beneath the surface and haunts us throughout life. Death is a visitor in the therapeutic process, and Yalom believes that ignoring its presence sends the message that death is too overwhelming to explore. Confronting this fear can be the factor that helps us transform a stale mode of living into a more authentic one (Yalom, 1980).

One focus in existential therapy is on exploring the degree to which clients are doing the things they value. Without being morbidly preoccupied by the ever-present threat of nonbeing, clients can develop a healthy awareness of death as a way to evaluate how well they are living and what changes they want to make in their lives. Those who fear death also fear life. If we affirm life and live in the present as fully as possible, we will not be obsessed with the end of life.

 ## THE THERAPEUTIC PROCESS

Therapeutic Goals

A basic goal of many therapeutic systems is enabling individuals to accept the awesome freedom and responsibility to act. Existential therapy is best considered as an invitation to clients to recognize the ways in which they are not living fully authentic lives and to make choices that will lead to their becoming what they are capable of being. An aim of therapy is to assist clients in moving toward authenticity and learning to recognize when they are deceiving themselves (Deurzen-Smith, 1998). The existential orientation holds that there is no escape from freedom as we will always be held responsible. We can relinquish our freedom, however, which is the ultimate inauthenticity.

Existential therapy seeks to take clients out of their rigid grooves and to challenge the narrow and compulsive trends blocking their freedom. Although this process gives individuals a sense of release and increased autonomy, their new freedom increases their anxiety. Freedom is a venture down new pathways, and there is no certainty about where these paths will lead. The "dizziness" and dread of freedom must be confronted if growth is to occur (May, 1981). The lack of guarantees in life is precisely what generates anxiety. Thus, existential therapy aims at helping clients face this anxiety and engage in action that is based on the authentic purpose of creating a worthy existence.

May (1981) contends that people come to therapy with the self-serving illusion that they are inwardly enslaved and that someone else (the therapist) can free them. Thus, "the purpose of psychotherapy is not to 'cure' the clients in the conventional sense, but to help them become aware of what they are doing and to get them out of the victim role" (p. 210). The task of existential therapy is to teach clients to listen to what they already know about themselves, even though they may not be attending to what they know. Therapy is a process of bringing out the latent aliveness in the client (Bugental, 1986).

Bugental (1990) identifies three main tasks of therapy: (1) to assist clients in recognizing that they are not fully present in the therapy process itself and in seeing how this pattern may limit them outside of therapy; (2) to support clients in confronting the anxieties that they have so long sought to avoid; and (3) to help clients redefine themselves and their world in ways that foster greater genuineness of contact with life. Increased awareness is the central goal of existential therapy, which allows clients to discover that alternative possibilities exist where none were recognized before. Clients come to realize that they are able to make changes in their way of being in the world.

Accomplishing these tasks requires some time in existential therapy, for it is not a matter of solving problems. Sharp and Bugental (2001) state that short-term applications of existential therapy require clearly defined and less ambitious therapy goals. Time-limited therapy involves more structure of the therapeutic process. At the termination of such therapy, it is important for clients to evaluate what they have accomplished and what issues may need to be addressed later. It is essential that both therapists and clients determine if short-term work is appropriate, and if beneficial outcomes are likely.

Therapist's Function and Role

Existential therapists are primarily concerned with understanding the subjective world of clients to help them come to new understandings and options. The focus is on clients' current life situations, not on helping clients recover a personal past (May & Yalom, 2000). Typically, existential therapists show wide latitude in the methods they employ, varying not only from client to client but also with the same client at different phases of the therapeutic process. They may make use of techniques that grow from diverse theoretical orientations, yet no set of techniques is considered essential. And some existential therapists abhor techniques, seeing them as rigid, routine, and manipulative. Instead, their main interest is in the unique struggle of each client. Existential therapists assist individuals in discovering the reason for their "stuckness" (Vontress, Johnson, & Epp, 1999).

Throughout the therapeutic process, techniques are secondary to establishing a relationship that will enable the counselor to effectively understand and challenge the client. Existential therapists are especially concerned about clients avoiding responsibility; they invite clients to accept personal responsibility. When clients complain about the predicaments they are in and blame others, the therapist is likely to ask them how they contributed to their situation.

Therapists with an existential orientation usually deal with people who have what could be called a *restricted existence*. These clients have a limited awareness of themselves and are often vague about the nature of their problems. They may see few, if any, options for dealing with life situations, and they tend to feel trapped or helpless. A central task of the therapist is to confront these clients with the ways they are living a restricted existence, or how they are stuck, and to help them become aware of their own part in creating this condition. The therapist may hold up a mirror, so to speak, so that clients can gradually engage in self-confrontation. In this way clients can see how they became the way they are and how they might enlarge the way they live. Once clients are aware of factors in their past and of stifling modes of their present existence, they can begin to accept responsibility for changing their future.

Client's Experience in Therapy

Clients in existential therapy are clearly encouraged to take seriously their own subjective experience of their world. They are challenged to take responsibility for how they *now* choose to be in their world. Effective therapy does not stop with this awareness itself, for the therapist encourages clients to take action on the basis of the insights they develop through the therapeutic process. Clients are expected to go out into the world and decide *how* they will live differently. Further, they must be active in the therapeutic process, for during the sessions they must decide what fears, guilt feelings, and anxieties they will explore.

Merely deciding to enter psychotherapy is itself a scary prospect for most clients. The experience of opening the doors to oneself is often frightening, exciting, joyful, depressing, or a combination of all of these. As clients wedge open the closed doors, they also begin to loosen the deterministic shackles that have kept them psychologically bound. Gradually, they become aware of what they have been and who they are now, and they are better able to decide what kind of future they want. Through the process of their therapy, clients can explore alternatives for making their visions real.

When clients plead helplessness and attempt to convince themselves that they are powerless, May (1981) reminds them that their journey toward freedom began by putting one foot in front of the other to get to his office. As narrow as their range of freedom may be, clients can begin building and augmenting that range by taking small steps. The therapeutic journey that opens up new horizons is poetically described by Deurzen-Smith (1997):

> Embarking on our existential journey requires us to be prepared to be touched and shaken by what we find on the way and to not be afraid to discover our own limitations and weaknesses, uncertainties and doubts. It is only with such an attitude of openness and wonder that we can encounter the impenetrable everyday mysteries, which take us beyond our own preoccupations and sorrows and which by confronting us with death, make us rediscover life. (p. 5)

Another aspect of the experience of being a client in existential therapy is confronting ultimate concerns rather than coping with immediate problems. Some major themes of therapy sessions are anxiety, freedom and responsibility, isolation, alienation, death and its implications for living, and the continual search for meaning. Existential therapists assist clients in facing life with courage, hope, and a willingness to find meaning in life.

Relationship Between Therapist and Client

Existential therapists give central prominence to their relationship with the client. The relationship is important in itself because the quality of this person-to-person encounter in the therapeutic situation is the stimulus for positive change. Therapists with this orientation believe their basic attitudes toward the client and their own personal characteristics of honesty, integrity, and courage are what they have to offer. Therapy is a journey taken by therapist and client, a journey that delves deeply into the world as perceived and experienced by the client. But this type of quest demands that therapists also be in contact with their own phenomenological world. Vontress and colleagues (1999) state that existential counseling is a voyage into self-discovery for both client and therapist. In achieving the goal of assisting clients to confront ways they are experiencing "stuckness" in their lives, it is essential for the counselor to adopt a flexible style and to draw from different theoretical approaches with different clients.

Buber's (1970) conception of the I/Thou relationship has significant implications here. His understanding of the self is based on two fundamental relationships: the "I/it" and the "I/Thou." The I/it is the relation to time and space, which is a necessary starting place for the self. The I/Thou is the relationship essential for connecting the self to the spirit and, in so doing, to achieve true dialogue. This form of relationship is the paradigm of the fully human self, the achievement of which is the goal of Buber's existential philosophy. Relating in an I/Thou fashion means that there is direct, mutual, and present interaction. Rather than prizing therapeutic objectivity and professional distance, existential therapists strive to create caring and intimate relationships with clients. If counselors lack a sense of presence, it will affect the therapeutic relationship in a negative way.

Existential therapists share their reactions to clients with genuine concern and empathy as one way of deepening the therapeutic relationship. Bugental (1987) emphasizes the crucial role the *presence* of the therapist plays in this relationship. In his view many therapists and therapeutic systems overlook its fundamental importance. He contends that therapists are too often so concerned with the content of what is being said that they are not aware of the distance between themselves and their clients. "The therapeutic alliance is the powerful joining of forces which energizes and supports the long, difficult, and frequently painful work of life-changing psychotherapy. The conception of the therapist here is not of a disinterested observer-technician but of a fully alive human companion for the client" (p. 49).

The core of the therapeutic relationship is respect, which implies faith in clients' potential to cope authentically with their troubles and in their ability to discover alternative ways of being. Clients eventually come to view themselves as active and responsible for their own existence, whereas before therapy they were likely to see themselves as helpless. They develop an increased ability to accept and confront the freedom they possess.

Therapists invite clients to grow by modeling authentic behavior. If therapists keep themselves hidden during the therapeutic session or if they engage in inauthentic behavior, clients will also remain guarded and persist in their inauthentic ways. Thus, therapists can help clients become less of a stranger to themselves by selectively disclosing their own responses at appropriate times. Of course, this disclosure does not mean an uncensored sharing of every thought and reaction. Rather, it entails a willingness to share persistent reactions with clients, especially when this sharing is likely to be facilitative.

 ## APPLICATION: THERAPEUTIC TECHNIQUES AND PROCEDURES

The existential approach is unlike most other therapies in that it is not technique-oriented. The interventions existential practitioners employ are based on philosophical views about the essential nature of human existence. Existential therapists are free to draw from techniques that flow from many other orientations. However, they do not employ an array of unintegrated techniques; they have a set of assumptions and attitudes that guide their interventions with clients. See *Case Approach to Counseling and Psychotherapy* (Corey, 2005, chap. 4) for an illustration of how Dr. Donald Polkinghorne, an existential therapist, works with some key themes in the case of Ruth.

Deurzen-Smith (1997) identifies as a primary ground rule of existential work the openness to the individual creativity of the therapist and the client. She maintains that existential therapists need to adapt their interventions to their own personality and style, as well as being sensitive to what each client requires. The main guideline is that the existential practitioner's interventions are responsive to the uniqueness of each client (Deurzen-Smith, 1997; Walsh & McElwain, 2002).

In a discussion of therapeutic techniques, Deurzen-Smith (1990a) points out that the existential approach is well known for its deemphasis of techniques. She stresses the importance of therapists reaching sufficient depth and openness in their own lives to venture into clients' murky waters without getting lost. She asserts that therapists who are fully available while their clients explore their deepest issues are implying that their own being is subject to change. Deurzen-Smith (1997) reminds us that existential therapy is a collaborative adventure in which both client and therapist will be transformed if they allow themselves to be touched by life.

The use of the therapist's self is the core of therapy (Baldwin, 1987). When the deepest self of the therapist meets the deepest part of the client, the counseling process is at its best. Therapy is a creative, evolving process of discovery that can be conceptualized in three general phases.

During the initial phase, counselors assist clients in identifying and clarifying their assumptions about the world. Clients are invited to define and question the ways in which they perceive and make sense of their existence. They examine their values, beliefs, and assumptions to determine their validity. This is a difficult task for many clients because they may initially present their problems as resulting almost entirely from external causes. They may focus on what other people "make them feel" or on how others are largely responsible for their actions or inaction. The counselor teaches them how to reflect on their own existence and to examine their role in creating their problems in living.

During the middle phase of existential counseling, clients are encouraged to more fully examine the source and authority of their present value system. This process of self-exploration typically leads to new insights and some restructuring of their values and attitudes. Clients get a better idea of what kind of life they consider worthy to live and develop a clearer sense of their internal valuing process.

The final phase of existential counseling focuses on helping clients take what they are learning about themselves and put it into action. The aim of therapy is to enable clients to find ways of implementing their examined and internalized values in a concrete way. Clients typically discover their strengths and find ways to put them to the service of living a purposeful existence.

Areas of Application

What problems are most amenable to an existential approach? For which populations is existential therapy particularly useful? A strength of the perspective is its focus on available choices and pathways toward personal growth. Even for brief counseling, existential therapy can focus clients on significant areas such as assuming personal responsibility, making a commitment to deciding and acting, and expanding their awareness of their current situation. For clients who are struggling with developmental crises, doing grief work, confronting death, or facing a significant decision, existential therapy is especially appropriate (May & Yalom, 2000). Some examples of these critical turning points that mark passages from one stage of life into another are the struggle for identity in adolescence, coping with possible disappointments in middle age, adjusting to children leaving home, coping with failures in marriage and work, and dealing with increased physical limitations as one ages. These developmental challenges involve both dangers and opportunities. Uncertainty, anxiety, and struggling with decisions are all part of this process. Frankl's existential therapy has proven to be especially effective in relating to high school youths and to those who are experiencing what he calls "blows to fate" (William Gould, personal communication, February 28, 2001).

Deurzen-Smith (1990a) suggests that this form of therapy is best suited for clients who are committed to dealing with their problems about living, for people who feel alienated from the current expectations of society, or for those who are searching for meaning in their lives. It tends to work well with people who are at a crossroads and who question the state of affairs in the world and are willing to challenge the status quo. It can be useful for people

Existential Therapy Applied to the Case of Stan

The counselor with an existential orientation approaches Stan with the view that he has the capacity to increase his self-awareness and decide for himself the future direction of his life. She wants him to realize more than anything else that he does not have to be the victim of his past conditioning but can be the architect in redesigning his future. He can free himself of his deterministic shackles and accept the responsibility that comes with directing his own life. This approach does not stress techniques but emphasizes the importance of the therapist's understanding of Stan's world, primarily by establishing an authentic relationship as a means to a fuller degree of self-understanding.

Stan is demonstrating what Sartre would call "bad faith" by not accepting personal responsibility. Here are some examples of his implicit statements of bad faith: "My family never really cared for me; this is why I feel unworthy most of the time." "That's the way I am; I can't help what I do." "Naturally I'm a loser, because I've been rejected so many times." The therapist confronts Stan with the ways in which he is attempting to escape from his freedom through alcohol and drugs. Eventually, she confronts him with the passivity that is keeping him bound. She reaffirms that he is now entirely responsible for his life, for his actions, and for his failure to take action. She does this in a kind manner, but she is still firm in challenging Stan.

The counselor does not see Stan's anxiety as something that needs to be cured; rather, he needs to learn that realistic anxiety is a vital part of living with uncertainty and freedom. Because there are no guarantees and because the individual is ultimately alone, Stan can expect to experience some degree of healthy anxiety, aloneness, guilt, and even despair. These conditions are not neurotic in themselves, but the way in which Stan orients himself to these conditions and how he copes with his anxiety are critical.

Stan talks about feeling so low at times that he fantasizes about suicide. Certainly, the therapist investigates further to determine if he poses an immediate threat to himself. In addition to this assessment to determine lethality, the existential therapist may view his thoughts of "being better off dead" as symbolic. Could it be that Stan feels he is dying as a person? Is Stan using his human potential? Is he choosing a dead way of merely existing instead of affirming life? Is Stan mainly trying to elicit sympathy from his family? The existentially oriented therapist confronts Stan with the meaning and purpose in his life. Is there any reason for Stan to want to continue living? What are some of the projects that enrich his life? What can Stan do to find a sense of purpose that will make him feel more significant and more alive?

Stan needs to accept the reality that he may at times feel alone. Choosing for oneself and living from one's own center accentuates the experience of aloneness. He is not, however, condemned to a life of isolation, alienation from others, and loneliness. The therapist helps Stan discover his own centeredness and live by the values he chooses and creates for himself. By doing so, Stan can become a more substantial person and learn to appreciate himself more. When he does, the chances are lessened that he will have a clinging need to secure approval from others, particularly his parents and parental substitutes. Instead of forming a dependent relationship, Stan could choose to relate to others out of his strength. Only then would there be the possibility of overcoming his feelings of separateness and isolation.

Follow-Up: You Continue as Stan's Existential Therapist

Use these questions to help you think about how you would counsel Stan using an existential approach:

- If Stan resisted your attempts to help him see that he was responsible for the direction of his life, what interventions might you make?
- Stan experiences a great deal of anxiety. From an existential perspective, how do you view his anxiety? How might you work with his anxiety in creative ways?
- If Stan talks with you about suicide as a way out of despair and a life without meaning, how will you be inclined to work with him? Can you think of any ways Stan could find more meaning and purpose in his life?

who are on the edge of existence, such as those who are dying, who are working through a developmental or situational crisis, or who are starting a new phase of life.

Bugental and Bracke (1992) assert that the value and vitality of a psychotherapy approach depend on its ability to assist clients in dealing with the sources of pain and dissatisfaction in their lives. They contend that the existential orientation is particularly suited to individuals who are experiencing a lack of a sense of identity. The approach offers promise for individuals who are struggling to find meaning or who complain of feelings of emptiness.

 # EXISTENTIAL THERAPY FROM A MULTICULTURAL PERSPECTIVE

Contributions to Multicultural Counseling

Vontress and colleagues (1999) write about the existential foundation of cross-cultural counseling. Because the existential approach is grounded in the universal characteristics of human beings, they maintain that it is perhaps the most applicable of all approaches when working with culturally diverse clients. They write: "Existential counseling is probably the most useful approach to helping clients of all cultures find meaning and harmony in their lives, because it focuses on the sober issues each of us must inevitably face: love, anxiety, suffering, and death" (p. 32). These are the human experiences that transcend the boundaries that separate cultures. Indeed, Frankl's existential therapy has been adapted by Native Americans, Buddhists, Chinese Taoists, and Hindus (William Gould, personal communication, February 28, 2001).

Vontress (1996) points out that all people are multicultural in the sense that they are all products of many cultures. He encourages counselors in training to focus on the universal commonalities of clients first and secondarily on areas of differences. Thus, in working with cultural diversity it is essential to recognize simultaneously the commonalities and differences of human beings. He notes: "Cross-cultural counseling, in short, does not intend to teach specific interventions for each culture, but to infuse the counselor with a cultural sensitivity and tolerant philosophical outlook that will befit all cultures" (p. 164).

A strength of the existential approach is that it enables clients to examine the degree to which their behavior is being influenced by social and cultural conditioning. Clients can be challenged to look at the price they are paying for the decisions they have made. Although it is true that some clients may not feel a sense of freedom, their freedom can be increased if they recognize the social limits they are facing. Their freedom can be hindered by institutions and limited by their family. In fact, it may be difficult to separate individual freedom from the context of their family structure.

A client who is struggling with feeling limited by her family situation can be invited to look at her part in this process. For example, Meta, a Norwegian

American, is working to attain a professional identity as a social worker, but her family thinks she is being selfish and neglecting her primary duties. The family is likely to exert pressure on her to give up her personal interests in favor of what they feel is best for the welfare of the entire family. Meta may feel trapped in the situation and see no way out unless she rejects what her family wants. In cases such as this, it is useful to explore the client's underlying values and to help her determine whether her values are working for her and for her family. Clients such as Meta have the challenge of weighing values and balancing behaviors between two cultures. Ultimately, Meta must decide in what ways she might change her situation. The existential therapist will invite Meta to begin to explore what she *can* do. She can begin to reclaim her personal power by considering her own part in the difficulties she is having and in what direction she is inclined to move.

It is essential to respect the purpose that clients have in mind when they initiate therapy. If we pay careful attention to what our clients tell us about what they want, we can operate within an existential framework. We can encourage clients to weigh the alternatives and to explore the consequences of what they are doing with their lives. Even though oppressive forces may be severely limiting the quality of their lives, we can help clients see that they are not merely the victims of circumstances beyond their control. At the same time that these clients are learning how to change their external environment, they can also be challenged to look within themselves to recognize their own contributions to their plight. Through the therapy experience, they may be able to discover new courses of action that will lead to a change in their situation.

Limitations for Multicultural Counseling

There are some limitations of the existential approach as it is applied to multicultural populations. For those who hold a systemic perspective, the existentialists can be criticized on the grounds that they are excessively individualistic and that they ignore the social factors that cause human problems. Some culturally different clients may operate on the assumption that they have very little choice. They often feel that environmental circumstances severely restrict their ability to influence the direction of their lives. Even if they change internally, they see little hope that the external realities of racism, discrimination, and oppression will change. They are likely to experience a deep sense of frustration and feelings of powerlessness when it comes to making changes outside of themselves. As you will see in Chapter 12, feminist therapists maintain that therapeutic practice will be effective only to the extent that therapists intervene with some form of social action to change those factors that are creating clients' problems. In working with people of color who come from the barrio or ghetto, for example, it is important to take up their survival issues. If a counselor consistently tells these clients that they have a choice in making their lives better, they may feel patronized and misunderstood. These real-life issues can provide a good focus for counseling, assuming the therapist is willing to deal with them.

A limitation within existential theory is that it is highly focused on the philosophical assumption of self-determination, which does not take into account the complex factors that many people who have been oppressed must deal with. In many cultures it is not possible to talk about the self and self-determination apart from the context of the social network and environmental conditions.

Another problem with this approach is the lack of direction that clients may get from the counselor. Although clients may feel better if they have an opportunity to talk and to be understood, they are likely to expect the counselor to do something to bring about a change in their life situation. Many clients expect a structured and problem-oriented approach to counseling that is not found in the existential approach, which places the responsibility on the client for providing the direction of therapy. A major challenge facing the counselor is to provide enough concrete direction for these clients without taking the responsibility away from them.

SUMMARY AND EVALUATION

Summary

As humans, according to the existentialist view, we are capable of self-awareness, which is the distinctive capacity that allows us to reflect and to decide. With this awareness we become free beings who are responsible for choosing the way we live, and we thus influence our own destiny. This awareness of freedom and responsibility gives rise to existential anxiety, which is another basic human characteristic. Whether we like it or not, we are free, even though we may seek to avoid reflecting on this freedom. The knowledge that we must choose, even though the outcome is not certain, leads to anxiety. This anxiety is heightened when we reflect on the reality that we are mortal beings. Facing the inevitable prospect of eventual death gives the present moment significance, for we become aware that we do not have forever to accomplish our projects. Our task is to create a life that has meaning and purpose. As humans we are unique in that we strive toward fashioning purposes and values that give meaning to living. Whatever meaning our life has is developed through freedom and a commitment to make choices in the face of uncertainty.

Existential therapy places central prominence on the person-to-person relationship. It assumes that client growth occurs through this genuine encounter. It is not the techniques a therapist uses that make a therapeutic difference; rather, it is the quality of the client–therapist relationship that heals. It is essential that therapists reach sufficient depth and openness in their own lives to allow them to venture into their clients' subjective world without losing their own sense of identity. Because this approach is basically concerned with the goals of therapy, basic conditions of being human, and therapy as a shared journey, practitioners are not bound by specific techniques. Although existential therapists may apply techniques from other orientations, their interventions are guided by a philosophical framework about what it means to be human.

Contributions of the Existential Approach

The existential approach has helped bring the person back into central focus. It concentrates on the central facts of human existence: self-consciousness and our consequent freedom. To the existentialist goes the credit for providing a new view of death as a positive force, not a morbid prospect to fear, for death gives life meaning. Existentialists have contributed a new dimension to the understanding of anxiety, guilt, frustration, loneliness, and alienation. I particularly appreciate the way Vontress and colleagues (1999) capture the essence of an existential therapist's aim: "Ultimately, the existential counselor wishes to explore concertedly with the client all of life, not simply the random issues that emerge in session, whose transient importance may only fade into the background of the larger scheme of life that went unexplored" (p. 58).

In my own work I've found that an existential view provides a framework for understanding universal human concerns. In counseling sessions clients may wrestle with the problem of personal freedom, deal with self-alienation and estrangement from others, face the fear of death and nonbeing, find the courage to live from within their center, search for a meaningful life, discover a personal set of values, learn to deal constructively with anxiety and guilt, or make choices that lead to a fullness of personal expression.

One of the major contributions of the existential approach is its emphasis on the human quality of the therapeutic relationship. This aspect lessens the chances of dehumanizing psychotherapy by making it a mechanical process. Existential counselors reject the notions of therapeutic objectivity and professional distance, viewing them as being unhelpful. This is put quite nicely in these words: "Being an existential counselor would seem to mean having the courage to be a caring human being in an insensitive world" (Vontress et al., 1999, p. 44).

I very much value the existential emphasis on freedom and responsibility and the person's capacity to redesign his or her life by choosing with awareness. This perspective provides a sound philosophical base on which to build a personal and unique therapeutic style because it addresses itself to the core struggles of the contemporary person.

CONTRIBUTIONS TO THE INTEGRATION OF PSYCHOTHERAPIES   According to May and Yalom (2000), the founders of existential therapy hoped that the key concepts and themes they introduced would influence and become integrated into all therapeutic schools rather than existential therapy being a separate school. May and Yalom believe this integration is clearly occurring. Although Bugental and Bracke (1992) are interested in the infusion of existential notions into other therapy approaches, they have some concerns. They call for a careful examination of areas of confluence and of divergence among the theoretical perspectives. They offer these postulates for maintaining the integrity of the existential perspective as efforts toward integration proceed:

- The subjectivity of the client is a key focus in understanding significant life changes.
- A full presence and commitment of both therapist and client are essential to life-changing therapy.
- The main aim of therapy is to help clients recognize the ways in which they are constricting their awareness and action.
- A key focus of therapy is on how clients actually use the opportunities in therapy for examining and changing their lives.
- As clients become more aware of the ways in which they define themselves and their world, they can also see new alternatives for choice and action.
- In situations involving transference and countertransference, therapists have an opportunity to model taking responsibility for themselves while inviting their clients to do the same.

Bugental and Bracke see the possibility of a creative integration of the conceptual propositions of existential therapy with many other therapeutic orientations. One example of such a creative integration is provided by Dattilio (2002), who integrates cognitive behavioral techniques with the themes of an existential approach. As a cognitive behavior therapist and author, Dattilio maintains that he directs much of his efforts to "helping clients make a deep existential shift—to a new understanding of the world" (p. 75). He uses techniques such as restructuring of belief systems, relaxation methods, and a variety of cognitive and behavioral strategies, but he does so within an existential framework that can begin the process of real-life transformation. Many of his clients suffer from panic attacks or depression. Dattilio often explores with these clients existential issues of meaning, guilt, hopelessness, anxiety—and at the same time he provides them with cognitive behavioral tools to cope with the problems of daily living. In short, he grounds symptomatic treatment in an existential approach.

Limitations and Criticisms of the Existential Approach

A major criticism often aimed at this approach is that it lacks a systematic statement of the principles and practices of psychotherapy. Some practitioners have trouble with what they perceive as its mystical language and concepts. Those who prefer a counseling practice based on research contend that the concepts should be empirically sound, that definitions should be operational, that the hypotheses should be testable, and that therapeutic practice should be based on the results of research into both the process and outcomes of counseling.

Some therapists who claim adherence to an existential orientation describe their therapeutic style in vague and global terms such as *self-actualization, dialogic encounter, authenticity,* and *being in the world.* This lack of precision causes confusion at times and makes it difficult to conduct research on the process or outcomes of existential therapy.

Both beginning and advanced practitioners who are not of a philosophical turn of mind tend to find many of the existential concepts lofty and elusive. And those counselors who do find themselves close to this philosophy are often at a loss when they attempt to apply it to practice. As we have seen, this approach places primary emphasis on understanding the world of clients. It is assumed that techniques follow understanding. The fact that few techniques are generated by this approach makes it essential for practitioners to develop their own innovative procedures or to borrow from other schools of therapy.

Philosophical insight may not be appropriate for some clients. For example, the existential approach may be ineffective in working with the seriously disturbed. However, R. D. Laing (1965, 1967) has used an existential point of view in successfully treating schizophrenic patients. Laing's positive results suggest that existential practitioners may work well with all sorts of populations, treating people in humane ways that are in keeping with this approach while at the same time drawing on more active and directive intervention methods to meet the unique needs of their clients.

 # WHERE TO GO FROM HERE

Refer to the *CD-ROM for Integrative Counseling,* Session 11 ("Understanding How the Past Influences the Present") for a demonstration of ways I utilize existential notions in counseling Ruth. We engage in a role play where Ruth becomes the voice of her church and I take on a new role as Ruth—one in which I have been willing to challenge certain beliefs from church. This segment illustrates how I assist Ruth in finding new values. In Session 12 ("Working Toward Decisions and Behavioral Changes") I challenge Ruth to make new decisions, which is also an existential concept.

The Society for Existential Analysis is a professional organization devoted to exploring issues pertaining to an existential–phenomenological approach to counseling and therapy. Membership is open to anyone interested in this approach and includes students, trainees, psychotherapists, philosophers, psychiatrists, counselors, and psychologists. Members receive a regular newsletter and an annual copy of the *Journal of the Society for Existential Analysis.* The society provides a list of existentially oriented psychotherapists for referral purposes. The School of Psychotherapy and Counselling at Regent's College in London offers an advanced diploma in existential psychotherapy as well as short courses in the field. For information on any of the above, contact:

Society for Existential Analysis
BM Existential
London
WCIN 3XX
England
Web site: www.go.to/existentialanalysis
Email: info@existentialanalysis.co.uk

 InfoTrac College Edition Resources

Existential Therapy   The following key words are listed in such a way as to allow the InfoTrac College Edition search engine to locate a wider range of articles in the online library. The key words should be entered exactly as shown, to include asterisks, "W1," and "AND."

Martin Buber	Irvin Yalom
Viktor Frankl	Existential W1 phenomenology
Rollo May	Existential AND meaning
Jean-Paul Sartre	Relatedness AND psychol*

Recommended Supplementary Readings

Existential Counselling in Practice (Deurzen-Smith, 1988) develops a practical method of counseling based on the application of concepts of existential philosophy. The author puts into clear perspective topics such as anxiety, authentic living, clarifying one's worldview, determining values, discovering meaning, and coming to terms with life. She draws on her experience as an existential psychotherapist in describing numerous case illustrations.

Everyday Mysteries: Existential Dimensions of Psychotherapy (Deurzen-Smith, 1997) deals with the philosophical contributions to existential therapy and discusses the existential worldview.

Existential Psychotherapy (Yalom, 1980) is a superb treatment of ultimate human concerns of death, freedom, isolation, and meaninglessness as these issues relate to therapy. This book has depth and clarity, and it is rich with clinical examples that illustrate existential themes.

The Art of the Psychotherapist (Bugental, 1987) is an outstanding book that bridges the art and science of psychotherapy, making places for both. The author is an insightful and sensitive clinician who writes about the psychotherapist–client journey in depth from an existential perspective.

I Never Knew I Had a Choice (Corey & Corey, 2002) is a self-help book written from an existential perspective. Topics include our struggle to achieve autonomy; the meaning of loneliness, death, and loss; and how we choose our values and philosophy of life.

Cross-Cultural Counseling: A Casebook (Vontress, Johnson, & Epp, 1999) contains case studies of culturally diverse clients. These cases are explored within three frameworks: from a conceptual perspective, from an existential perspective, and from the vantage point of the DSM-IV diagnostic model. There is a marvelous chapter on the existential foundations of cross-cultural counseling.

References and Suggested Readings

BALDWIN, D. C., Jr. (1987). Some philosophical and psychological contributions to the use of self in therapy. In M. Baldwin & V. Satir (Eds.), *The use of self in therapy* (pp. 27–44). New York: Haworth Press.

BINSWANGER, L. (1975). *Being-in-the-world: Selected papers of Ludwig Binswanger.* London: Souvenir Press.

BOSS, M. (1963). *Daseinanalysis and psychoanalysis.* New York: Basic Books.

BUBER, M. (1970). *I and thou* (W. Kaufmann, Trans.). New York: Scribner's.

BUGENTAL, J. F. T. (1981). *The search for authenticity: An existential-analytic approach to psychotherapy* (rev. ed.). New York: Holt, Rinehart & Winston.

BUGENTAL, J. F. T. (1986). Existential-humanistic psychotherapy. In I. L. Kutash & A. Wolf (Eds.), *Psychotherapist's casebook* (pp. 222–236). San Francisco: Jossey-Bass.

*BUGENTAL, J. F. T. (1987). *The art of the psychotherapist.* New York: Norton.

BUGENTAL, J. F. T. (1990). Existential-humanistic psychotherapy. In J. K. Zeig & W. M. Munion (Eds.), *What is psychotherapy? Contemporary perspectives* (pp. 189–193). San Francisco: Jossey-Bass.

BUGENTAL, J. F. T. (1999). *Psychotherapy isn't what you think: Bringing the psychotherapeutic engagement into the living moment.* Phoenix, AZ: Zeig, Tucker, & Co.

BUGENTAL, J. F. T., & BRACKE, P. E. (1992). The future of existential-humanistic psychotherapy. *Psychotherapy, 29*(l), 28–33.

COREY, G. (2004). *Theory and practice of group counseling* (6th ed.). Pacific Grove, CA: Brooks/Cole.

*COREY, G. (2005). *Case approach to counseling and psychotherapy* (6th ed.). Belmont, CA: Brooks/Cole.

*COREY, G., & COREY, M. (2002). *I never knew I had a choice* (7th ed.). Pacific Grove, CA: Brooks/Cole.

DATTILIO, F. M. (2002, January-February). Cognitive-behaviorism comes of age: Grounding symptomatic treatment in an existential approach. *The Psychotherapy Networker, 26*(1), 75–78.

*DEURZEN-SMITH, E., van. (1988). *Existential counselling in practice.* London: Sage.

*DEURZEN-SMITH, E., van. (1990a). *Existential therapy.* London: Society for Existential Analysis Publications.

DEURZEN-SMITH, E., van. (1990b). What is existential analysis? *Journal of the Society for Existential Analysis, 1,* 6–14.

DEURZEN-SMITH, E., van. (1991). Ontological insecurity revisited. *Journal of the Society for Existential Analysis, 2,* 38–48.

*DEURZEN-SMITH, E., van. (1997). *Everyday mysteries: Existential dimensions of psychotherapy.* London: Routledge.

*DEURZEN-SMITH, E., van. (1998). *Paradox and passion in psychotherapy: An existential approach to therapy and counselling.* Chichester, UK: Wiley.

FARHA, B. (1994). Ontological awareness: An existential/cosmological epistemology. *The Person-Centered Periodical, 1*(I), 15–29.

---

*Books and articles marked with an asterisk are suggested for further study.

*FRANKL, V. (1963). *Man's search for meaning.* Boston: Beacon.

FRANKL, V. (1965). *The doctor and the soul.* New York: Bantam Books.

FRANKL, V. (1969). *The will to meaning: Foundations and applications of logotherapy.* New York: New American Library.

FRANKL, V. (1978). *The unheard cry for meaning.* New York: Simon & Schuster (Touchstone).

GOULD, W. B. (1993). *Viktor E. Frankl: Life with meaning.* Pacific Grove, CA: Brooks/Cole.

HEIDEGGER, M. (1962). *Being and time.* New York: Harper & Row.

LAING, R. D. (1965). *The divided self.* Baltimore: Pelican.

LAING, R. D. (1967). *The politics of experience.* New York: Ballantine.

MAY, R. (1950). *The meaning of anxiety.* New York: Ronald Press.

*MAY, R. (1953). *Man's search for himself.* New York: Dell.

MAY, R. (1958). The origins and significance of the existential movement in psychology. In R. May, E. Angel, & H. R. Ellenberger (Eds.), *Existence: A new dimension in psychiatry and psychology.* New York: Basic Books.

MAY, R. (Ed.). (1961). *Existential psychology.* New York: Random House.

MAY, R. (1969). *Love and will.* New York: Norton.

MAY, R. (1975). *The courage to create.* New York: Norton.

MAY, R. (1981). *Freedom and destiny.* New York: Norton.

*MAY, R. (1983). *The discovery of being: Writings in existential psychology.* New York: Norton.

MAY, R., ANGEL, E., & ELLENBERGER, H. F. (Eds.). (1958). *Existence: A new dimension in psychiatry and psychology.* New York: Basic Books.

*MAY, R., & YALOM, I. (2000). Existential psychotherapy. In R. J. Corsini & D. Wedding (Eds.), *Current psychotherapies* (6th ed., pp. 273–302). Itasca, IL: F. E. Peacock.

RUSSELL, J. M. (1978). Sartre, therapy, and expanding the concept of responsibility. *American Journal of Psychoanalysis, 38,* 259–269.

SARTRE, J. P. (1971). *Being and nothingness.* New York: Bantam Books.

*SCHNEIDER, K. J., & ROLLO, M. (1995). *The psychology of existence: An integrative, clinical perspective.* New York: McGraw-Hill.

SHARF, R. S. (2004). *Theories of psychotherapy and counseling: Concepts and cases* (3rd ed.). Pacific Grove, CA: Brooks/Cole.

*SHARP, J. G., & BUGENTAL, J. F. T. (2001). Existential-humanistic psychotherapy. In R. J. Corsini (Ed.), *Handbook of innovative therapies* (2nd ed., pp. 206–217). New York: Wiley.

STILES, W. B. (2002). Future directions in research on humanistic psychotherapy. In D. J. Cain & J. Seeman (Eds.), *Humanistic psychotherapies: Handbook of research and practice* (pp. 605–616). Washington, DC: American Psychological Association.

TILLICH, P. (1952). *The courage to be.* New Haven, CT: Yale University Press.

*VONTRESS, C. E. (1986). Existential anxiety: Implications for counseling. *Journal of Mental Health Counseling, 8,* 100–109.

*VONTRESS, C. E. (1996). A personal retrospective on cross-cultural counseling. *Journal of Multicultural Counseling and Development, 24*(3), 156–166.

*VONTRESS, C. E., JOHNSON, J. A., & EPP, L. R. (1999). *Cross-cultural counseling: A casebook.* Alexandria, VA: American Counseling Association.

WALSH, R. A., & McELWAIN, B. (2002). Existential psychotherapies. In D. J. Cain & J. Seeman (Eds.), *Humanistic psychotherapies: Handbook of research and practice* (pp. 253–278). Washington, DC: American Psychological Association.

*YALOM, I. D. (1980). *Existential psychotherapy.* New York: Basic Books.

YALOM, I. D. (1989). *Love's executioner: And other tales of psychotherapy.* New York: Harper Perennial.

YALOM, I. D. (1991). *When Nietzsche wept.* New York: Basic Books.

*YALOM, I. D. (2000). *Momma and the meaning of life: Tales of psychotherapy.* New York: HarperCollins (Perennial).

*YALOM, I. D. (2003). *The gift of therapy: An open letter to a new generation of therapists and their patients.* New York: HarperCollins (Perennial).

Person-Centered Therapy

Carl *Rogers*

CARL ROGERS (1902–1987), a major spokesperson for humanistic psychology, led a life that reflected the ideas he developed for half a century. He showed a questioning stance, a deep openness to change, and the courage to forge into unknown territory both as a person and as a professional. In writing about his early years, Rogers (1961) recalls his family atmosphere as characterized by close and warm relationships but also by strict religious standards. Play was discouraged, and the virtues of the Protestant ethic were extolled. His boyhood was somewhat lonely, and he pursued scholarly interests instead of social ones. Rogers was an introverted person, and he spent a lot of time reading and engaging in imaginative activity and reflection. During his college years his interests and academic major changed from agriculture to history, then to religion, and finally to clinical psychology.

In 1964 Rogers joined the staff at the Western Behavioral Sciences Institute in La Jolla, California, where he worked with groups of people who were seeking to improve their abilities in human relations. In 1968 he and his colleagues established the Center for the Studies of the Person in La Jolla.

Rogers earned recognition around the world for originating and developing the humanistic movement in psychotherapy, pioneering in psychotherapy research, and influencing all fields related to the helping professions. In an interview Rogers was asked what he would want his parents to know about his contributions if he could communicate with them. He replied that he could not imagine talking to his mother about anything of significance because he was sure she would have some negative judgment. Interestingly, a core theme in his theory is the necessity for nonjudgmental listening and acceptance if clients are to change (Heppner, Rogers, & Lee, 1984). He also encouraged clients to reflect on their experience. A theory often reflects the personal life of the theorist, and both of these ideas had their roots in Rogers's own personal life.

During the last 15 years of his life, Rogers applied the person-centered approach to world peace by training policymakers, leaders, and groups in conflict. Perhaps his greatest passion was directed toward the reduction of interracial tensions and the effort to achieve world peace, for which he was nominated for the Nobel Peace Prize. Rogers has been referred to as a "quiet revolutionary." After a fall in 1987 that resulted in a fractured hip, he successfully underwent an operation. During the night following his surgery his heart failed, and he died a few days later as he had hoped to—"with his boots on and, as always, looking forward" (Cain, 1987a).

In an assessment of Rogers's impact, Cain (1987b) writes that the therapist, author, and person were the same man. Rogers lived his life in accordance with his theory in his dealings with a wide variety of people in diverse settings. His faith in people deeply affected the development of his theories and the way that he related to all those with whom he came in contact. Rogers knew who he was, felt comfortable with his beliefs, and was without pretense. He was not afraid to take a strong position and challenge the status quo throughout his professional career. ■

INTRODUCTION

The person-centered approach is based on concepts from humanistic psychology, many of which were articulated by Rogers in the early 1940s. This approach shares many concepts and values with the existential perspective presented in Chapter 6. Rogers's basic assumptions are that people are essentially trustworthy, that they have a vast potential for understanding themselves and resolving their own problems without direct intervention on the therapist's part, and that they are capable of self-directed growth if they are involved in a specific kind of therapeutic relationship. From the beginning, Rogers emphasized the attitudes and personal characteristics of the therapist and the quality of the client–therapist relationship as the prime determinants of the outcome of the therapeutic process. He consistently relegated to a secondary position matters such as the therapist's knowledge of theory and techniques. This belief in the client's capacity for self-healing is in contrast with many theories that view the therapist's techniques as the most powerful agents that lead to change (Tallman & Bohart, 1999). Clearly, Rogers revolutionized the field of psychotherapy by proposing a theory that centered on the client as the agent for self-change (Bozarth, Zimring, & Tausch, 2002).

Contemporary person-centered therapy is the result of an evolutionary process that continues to remain open to change and refinement (see Cain & Seeman, 2002). Rogers did not present the person-centered theory as a fixed and completed approach to therapy. He hoped that others would view his theory as a set of tentative principles relating to how the therapy process develops, not as dogma. Rogers expected his model to evolve and was open and receptive to change.

Four Periods of Development of the Approach

In tracing the major turning points in Rogers's approach, Zimring and Raskin (1992) and Bozarth and colleagues (2002) have identified four periods of development. In the first period, during the 1940s, Rogers developed what was known as *nondirective counseling* as a reaction against the directive and traditional psychoanalytic approaches to individual therapy. Rogers's theory emphasized the counselor's creation of a permissive and nondirective climate. He caused a great furor when he challenged the basic assumption that "the counselor knows best." Rogers also challenged the validity of commonly accepted therapeutic procedures such as advice, suggestion, direction, persuasion, teaching, diagnosis, and interpretation. Based on his conviction that diagnostic concepts and procedures were inaccurate, prejudicial, and often misused, Rogers omitted them from his approach. Nondirective counselors avoided sharing a great deal about themselves with clients and instead focused mainly on reflecting and clarifying the clients' verbal and nonverbal communications with the aim of gaining insight into the feelings expressed by clients.

In the second period, during the 1950s, Rogers (1951) renamed his approach *client-centered therapy* to reflect its emphasis on the client rather than on nondirective methods. This period was characterized by a shift from clarification of feelings to a focus on the phenomenological world of the client. Rogers assumed that the best vantage point for understanding how people behave was from their own internal frame of reference. He focused more explicitly on the actualizing tendency as the basic motivational force that leads to client change.

The third period, which began in the late 1950s and extended into the 1970s, addressed the necessary and sufficient conditions of therapy. Rogers (1957) set forth a hypothesis that resulted in three decades of research. A significant publication was *On Becoming a Person* (Rogers, 1961), which addressed the nature of "becoming the self that one truly is." The process of "becoming one's experience" is characterized by an openness to experience, a trust in one's experience, an internal locus of evaluation, and the willingness to be in process. During the 1960s, Rogers and his associates continued to test the underlying hypotheses of the client-centered approach by conducting extensive research on both the process and the outcomes of psychotherapy. He was interested in how people best progress in psychotherapy, and he studied the qualities of the client–therapist relationship as a catalyst leading to personality change. On the basis of this research the approach was further refined and expanded (Rogers, 1961). For example, client-centered philosophy was applied to education and was called student-centered teaching. It was also applied to encounter groups, which were led by laypersons in the 1960s (Rogers, 1970).

The fourth phase, during the 1980s and the 1990s, was marked by considerable expansion to education, industry, groups, conflict resolution, and the search for world peace. Because of Rogers's ever-widening scope of influence, including his interest in how people obtain, possess, share, or surrender power and control over others and themselves, his theory became known as the *person-centered approach*. This shift in terms reflected the broadening application of the approach. Although the person-centered approach has been applied mainly to individual and group counseling, important areas of further application include education, family life, leadership and administration, organizational development, health care, cross-cultural and interracial activity, and international relations. It was during the 1980s that Rogers directed his efforts toward applying the person-centered approach to politics, especially to the achievement of world peace.

In a comprehensive review of the research on person-centered therapy over a period of 60 years, Bozarth and colleagues (2002) concluded the following:

- In the earliest years of the approach, the client rather than the therapist was in charge. This style of nondirective therapy was associated with increased understanding, greater self-exploration, and improved self-concepts.

- Later a shift from clarification of feelings to a focus on the client's frame of reference developed. Many of Rogers's hypotheses were confirmed, and there was strong evidence for the value of the therapeutic relationship and the client's resources as the crux of successful therapy.

- As person-centered therapy developed further, research centered on the core conditions assumed to be both necessary and sufficient for successful therapy. The attitude of the therapist—an empathic understanding of the client's world and the ability to communicate a nonjudgmental stance to the client—was found to be basic to a successful therapy outcome.

Existentialism and Humanism

In the 1960s and 1970s there was a growing interest among counselors in a "third force" in therapy as an alternative to the psychoanalytic and behavioral approaches. Under this heading fall existential therapy, the person-centered approach, and Gestalt therapy, developed by Fritz and Laura Perls (see Chapter 8). Both person-centered therapy and Gestalt therapy are experiential and relationship-oriented.

Partly because of this historical connection and partly because representatives of existentialist thinking and humanistic thinking have not always clearly sorted out their views, the connections between the terms *existentialism* and *humanism* have tended to be confusing for students and theorists alike. The two viewpoints have much in common, yet there are also significant philosophical differences between them. They share a respect for the client's subjective experience and a trust in the capacity of the client to make positive and constructive conscious choices. They have in common an emphasis on concepts such as freedom, choice, values, personal responsibility, autonomy, purpose, and meaning. They differ in that existentialists take the position that we are faced with the anxiety of choosing to create an identity in a world that lacks intrinsic meaning. The humanists, in contrast, take the somewhat less anxiety-evoking position that each of us has a natural potential that we can actualize and through which we can find meaning. Many contemporary existential therapists refer to themselves as *existential-humanistic* practitioners, indicating that their roots are in existential philosophy but that they have incorporated many aspects of North American humanistic psychotherapies (Cain, 2002a).

The underlying vision of humanistic philosophy is captured by the metaphor of how an acorn, if provided with the appropriate conditions, will "automatically" grow in positive ways, pushed naturally toward its actualization as an oak. In contrast, for the existentialist there is nothing that we "are," no internal "nature" we can count on. We are faced at every moment with a choice about what to make of this condition. The humanistic philosophy on which the person-centered approach rests is expressed in attitudes and behaviors that create a growth-producing climate. According to Rogers (1986b), when this philosophy is lived, it helps people develop their capacities and stimulates constructive change in others. Individuals are empowered, and they are able to use this power for personal and social transformation.

As will become evident in this chapter, the existential and person-centered approaches have parallel concepts with regard to the client–therapist relationship at the core of therapy. The phenomenology that is basic to the existentialist approach is also fundamental to person-centered theory. Both approaches focus on the client's perceptions and call for the therapist to enter the client's subjective world, and both approaches emphasize the client's capacity for self-awareness and self-healing.

 # KEY CONCEPTS

View of Human Nature

A common theme originating in Rogers's early writing and continuing to permeate all of his works is a basic sense of trust in the client's ability to move forward in a constructive manner if conditions fostering growth are present. His professional experience taught him that if one is able to get to the core of an individual, one finds a trustworthy, positive center (Rogers, 1987a). Rogers firmly maintains that people are trustworthy, resourceful, capable of self-understanding and self-direction, able to make constructive changes, and able to live effective and productive lives (Cain, 1987b). When therapists are able to experience and communicate their realness, caring, and nonjudgmental understanding, significant changes in the client are most likely to occur.

Rogers expresses little sympathy for approaches based on the assumption that the individual cannot be trusted and instead needs to be directed, motivated, instructed, punished, rewarded, controlled, and managed by others who are in a superior and "expert" position. He maintains that three therapist attributes create a growth-promoting climate in which individuals can move forward and become what they are capable of becoming: (1) congruence (genuineness, or realness), (2) unconditional positive regard (acceptance and caring), and (3) accurate empathic understanding (an ability to deeply grasp the subjective world of another person). According to Rogers, if therapists communicate these attitudes, those being helped will become less defensive and more open to themselves and their world, and they will behave in prosocial and constructive ways. The basic drive to fulfillment implies that people will move toward health if the way seems open for them to do so. Thus, the goals of counseling are to set clients free and to create those conditions that will enable them to engage in meaningful self-exploration. When people are free, they will be able to find their own way (Combs, 1989).

Broadley (1999) writes about the *actualizing tendency*, a directional process of striving toward realization, fulfillment, autonomy, self-determination, and perfection. This growth force within us provides an internal source of healing, but it does not imply a movement away from relationships, interdependence,

connection, or socialization. This positive view of human nature has significant implications for the practice of therapy. Because of the belief that the individual has an inherent capacity to move away from maladjustment and
toward psychological health, the therapist places the primary responsibility on
the client. The person-centered approach rejects the role of the therapist as the
authority who knows best and of the passive client who merely follows the dictates of the therapist. Therapy is thus rooted in the client's capacity for awareness and self-directed change in attitudes and behavior.

The person-centered therapist focuses on the constructive side of human nature, on what is right with the person, and on the assets the individual brings to
therapy. The emphasis is on how clients act in their world with others, how they
can move forward in constructive directions, and how they can successfully encounter obstacles (both from within themselves and outside of themselves) that
are blocking their growth. Practitioners with a humanistic orientation encourage their clients to make changes that will lead to living fully and authentically,
with the realization that this kind of existence demands a continuing struggle.
People never arrive at a final or a static state of being self-actualized; rather, they
are continually involved in the process of actualizing themselves.

 THE THERAPEUTIC PROCESS

Therapeutic Goals

The goals of person-centered therapy are different from those of traditional
approaches. The person-centered approach aims toward a greater degree of
independence and integration of the individual. Its focus is on the person, not
on the person's presenting problem. Rogers (1977) believed the aim of therapy is not merely to solve problems. Rather, it is to assist clients in their
growth process, so that they can better cope with problems they are now facing and with future problems.

Rogers (1961) writes that people who enter psychotherapy often ask: "How
can I discover my real self? How can I become what I deeply wish to become?
How can I get behind my facades and become myself?" The underlying aim of
therapy is to provide a climate conducive to helping the individual become a
fully functioning person. Before clients are able to work toward that goal, they
must first get behind the masks they wear, which they develop through the
process of socialization. Clients come to recognize that they have lost contact
with themselves by using facades. In a climate of safety in the therapeutic session, they also come to realize that there are other possibilities.

When the facades are worn away during the therapeutic process, what
kind of person emerges from behind the pretenses? Rogers (1961) describes
people who are becoming increasingly actualized as having (1) an openness
to experience, (2) a trust in themselves, (3) an internal source of evaluation,
and (4) a willingness to continue growing. Encouraging these characteristics
is the basic goal of person-centered therapy.

These four characteristics provide a general framework for understanding the direction of therapeutic movement. The therapist does not choose specific goals for the client. The cornerstone of person-centered theory is the view that clients in a relationship with a facilitating therapist have the capacity to define and clarify their own goals.

Therapist's Function and Role

The role of person-centered therapists is rooted in their ways of being and attitudes, not in techniques designed to get the client to "do something." Research on person-centered therapy seems to indicate that the attitude of therapists, rather than their knowledge, theories, or techniques, facilitate personality change in the client. Basically, therapists use themselves as an instrument of change. When they encounter the client on a person-to-person level, their "role" is to be without roles. It is the therapist's attitude and belief in the inner resources of the client that create the therapeutic climate for growth (Bozarth et al., 2002).

Assuming a person-centered attitude involves avoiding many of the functions carried out by directive therapists. In describing the behavioral implications of person-centered therapy, Broadley (1997) states that therapists do not aim to manage, conduct, regulate, or control the client: "In more specific terms the client-centered therapist does not intend to diagnose, create treatment plans, strategize, employ treatment techniques, or take responsibility for the client in any way" (p. 25). Person-centered therapists also avoid these functions: They generally do not take a history, they avoid asking leading and probing questions, they do not make interpretations of the client's behavior, they do not evaluate the client's ideas or plans, and they do not decide for the client about the frequency or length of the therapeutic venture (Broadley, 1997).

Person-centered theory holds that the therapist's function is to be present and accessible to clients and to focus on their immediate experience. Clients then have the necessary freedom to explore areas of their life that were either denied to awareness or distorted. First and foremost, the therapist must be willing to be real in the relationship with clients. By being congruent, accepting, and empathic, the therapist is a catalyst for change. Instead of viewing clients in preconceived diagnostic categories, the therapist meets them on a moment-to-moment experiential basis and enters their world. Through the therapist's attitude of genuine caring, respect, acceptance, and understanding, clients are able to loosen their defenses and rigid perceptions and move to a higher level of personal functioning. Clients become less defensive and more open to possibilities within themselves and in the world.

Client's Experience in Therapy

Therapeutic change depends on clients' perceptions both of their own experience in therapy and of the counselor's basic attitudes. If the counselor creates a climate conducive to self-exploration, clients have the opportunity to explore the full range of their experience, which includes their feelings, beliefs, behavior, and worldview. What follows is a general sketch of clients' experiences in therapy.

Clients come to the counselor in a state of incongruence; that is, a discrepancy exists between their self-perception and their experience in reality. For example, Leon, a college student, may see himself as a future physician, yet his below-average grades might exclude him from medical school. The discrepancy between how Leon sees himself (self-concept) or how he would *like* to view himself (ideal self-concept) and the reality of his poor academic performance may result in anxiety and personal vulnerability, which can provide the necessary motivation to enter therapy. Leon must perceive that a problem exists or, at least, that he is uncomfortable enough with his present psychological adjustment to want to explore possibilities for change.

One reason clients seek therapy is a feeling of basic helplessness, powerlessness, and an inability to make decisions or effectively direct their own lives. They may hope to find "the way" through the guidance of the therapist. Within the person-centered framework, however, clients soon learn that they can be responsible for themselves in the relationship and that they can learn to be freer by using the relationship to gain greater self-understanding.

As counseling progresses, clients are able to explore a wider range of beliefs and feelings (Rogers, 1987c). They can express their fears, anxiety, guilt, shame, hatred, anger, and other emotions that they had deemed too negative to accept and incorporate into their self-structure. With therapy, people distort less and move to a greater acceptance and integration of conflicting and confusing feelings. They increasingly discover aspects within themselves that had been kept hidden. As clients feel understood and accepted, their defensiveness is less necessary, and they become more open to their experience. Because they are not as threatened, feel safer, and are less vulnerable, they become more realistic, perceive others with greater accuracy, and become better able to understand and accept others. Individuals in therapy come to appreciate themselves more as they are, and their behavior shows more flexibility and creativity. They become less oriented to meeting others' expectations, and thus they begin to behave in ways that are truer to themselves. These individuals empower themselves to direct their own lives instead of looking outside of themselves for answers. They move in the direction of being more in contact with what they are experiencing at the present moment, less bound by the past, less determined, freer to make decisions, and increasingly trusting in themselves to manage their own lives. In short, their experience in therapy is like throwing off the self-imposed shackles that had kept them in a psychological prison. With increased freedom they tend to become more mature psychologically and more actualized.

The client is the primary agent of change, and Tallman and Bohart (1999) believe the therapy relationship provides a supportive structure within which clients' self-healing capacities are activated. "Clients then are the 'magicians' with the special healing powers. Therapists set the stage and serve as assistants who provide the conditions under which this magic can operate" (p. 95).

Relationship Between Therapist and Client

Rogers (1957) based his hypothesis of the "necessary and sufficient conditions for therapeutic personality change" on the quality of the relationship: "If I can provide a certain type of relationship, the other person will discover within himself or herself the capacity to use that relationship for growth and change, and personal development will occur" (Rogers, 1961, p. 33). Rogers (1967) hypothesized further that "significant positive personality change does not occur except in a relationship" (p. 73). Rogers's hypothesis was formulated on the basis of many years of his professional experience, and it remains basically unchanged to this day. This hypothesis (cited in Cain 2002a, p. 20) is stated thusly:

1. Two persons are in psychological contact.
2. The first, whom we shall term the client, is in a state of incongruence, being vulnerable or anxious.
3. The second person, whom we term the therapist, is congruent or integrated in the relationship.
4. The therapist experiences unconditional positive regard for the client.
5. The therapist experiences an empathic understanding of the client's internal frame of reference and endeavors to communicate this experience to the client.
6. The communication to the client of the therapist's empathic understanding and unconditional positive regard is to a minimal degree achieved.

Rogers hypothesized that no other conditions were necessary. If the core conditions exist over some period of time, constructive personality change will occur. The core conditions do not vary according to client type. Further, they are both necessary and sufficient for all approaches to therapy and apply to all personal relationships, not just to psychotherapy. The therapist need not have any specialized knowledge. Accurate psychological diagnosis is not necessary and more often than not may interfere with effective therapy.

From Rogers's perspective the client–therapist relationship is characterized by equality. Therapists do not keep their knowledge a secret or attempt to mystify the therapeutic process. The process of change in the client depends to a large degree on the quality of this equal relationship. As clients experience the therapist listening in an accepting way to them, they gradually learn how to listen acceptingly to themselves. As they find the therapist caring for and valuing them (even the aspects that have been hidden and regarded as negative), clients begin to see worth and value in themselves. As they experience the realness of the therapist, clients drop many of their pretenses and are real with both themselves and the therapist.

This approach is perhaps best characterized as a way of being and as a shared journey in which therapist and client reveal their humanness and participate in a growth experience. The therapist can be a guide on this journey because he or she is usually more experienced and more psychologically mature than the client. However, it is important to realize that the therapeutic relationship involves two people, both of whom are fallible. Both of them can get better at what they are doing, yet they have limits. It is not realistic to expect that any therapist can be real, caring, understanding, and accepting all of the time with all clients (Sanford, 1990).

Rogers admitted that his theory was striking and radical. His formulation has generated considerable controversy, for he maintained that many conditions other therapists commonly regard as necessary for effective psychotherapy were nonessential. The core therapist conditions of congruence, unconditional positive regard, and accurate empathic understanding are embraced by many therapeutic schools as helpful in facilitating therapeutic change. We now turn to a detailed discussion of how these core conditions are an integral part of the therapeutic relationship.

CONGRUENCE, OR GENUINENESS   Congruence implies that therapists are real; that is, they are genuine, integrated, and authentic during the therapy hour. They are without a false front, their inner experience and outer expression of that experience match, and they can openly express feelings, thoughts, reactions, and attitudes that are present in the relationship with the client.

Through authenticity the therapist serves as a model of a human being struggling toward greater realness. Being congruent might necessitate the expression of anger, frustration, liking, attraction, concern, boredom, annoyance, and a range of other feelings in the relationship. This does not mean that therapists should impulsively share all their reactions, for self-disclosure must also be appropriate and well timed. A pitfall is that counselors can try too hard to be genuine. Sharing because one thinks it will be good for the client, without being genuinely moved to express something regarded as personal, can be incongruent. Person-centered therapy stresses that counseling will be inhibited if the counselor feels one way about the client but acts in a different way. Hence, if the practitioner either dislikes or disapproves of the client but feigns acceptance, therapy will not work.

Rogers's concept of congruence does not imply that only a fully self-actualized therapist can be effective in counseling. Because therapists are human, they cannot be expected to be fully authentic. If therapists are congruent in their relationships with clients, however, trust will be generated and the process of therapy will get under way. Congruence exists on a continuum rather than on an all-or-nothing basis, as is true of all three characteristics.

UNCONDITIONAL POSITIVE REGARD AND ACCEPTANCE   The second attitude therapists need to communicate is deep and genuine caring for the client as a person. The caring is unconditional; it is not contaminated by evaluation or judgment of the client's feelings, thoughts, and behavior as good or bad. It is important that therapists' caring be nonpossessive. If the caring stems from their own need to be liked and appreciated, constructive change in the client is inhibited. Therapists value and warmly accept clients without placing stipulations on their acceptance. It is not an attitude of "I'll accept you when . . ."; rather, it is one of "I'll accept you as you are." Therapists communicate through their behavior that they value their clients as they are and that clients are free to have feelings and experiences without risking the loss of their therapists' acceptance. Acceptance is the recognition of clients' rights to have their own beliefs and feelings; it is not the approval of all behavior. All overt behavior need not be approved of or accepted.

According to Rogers's (1977) research, the greater the degree of caring, prizing, accepting, and valuing of the client in a nonpossessive way, the greater the chance that therapy will be successful. He also makes it clear that it is not possible for therapists to genuinely feel acceptance and unconditional caring at all times. However, if therapists have little respect for their clients, or an active dislike or disgust, it is not likely that the therapeutic work will be fruitful.

ACCURATE EMPATHIC UNDERSTANDING   One of the main tasks of the therapist is to understand clients' experience and feelings sensitively and accurately as they are revealed in the moment-to-moment interaction during the therapy session. The therapist strives to sense clients' subjective experience, particularly in the here-and-now. The aim is to encourage clients to get closer to themselves, to feel more deeply and intensely, and to recognize and resolve the incongruity that exists within them.

Empathic understanding implies that the therapist will sense clients' feelings *as if* they were his or her own without becoming lost in those feelings. It is important to understand that accurate empathy goes beyond recognition of obvious feelings to a sense of the less clearly experienced feelings of clients. Part of empathic understanding is the therapist's ability to reflect the experiencing of clients. One of the functions of therapist reflection is to encourage and enable clients to become more reflective themselves. Therapist empathy results in clients' self-understanding and clarification of their beliefs and worldviews.

Accurate empathy is the cornerstone of the person-centered approach (Bohart & Greenberg, 1997). It is a way for therapists to hear the meanings expressed by their clients that often lie at the edge of their awareness. Empathy that has depth involves more than an intellectual comprehension of what clients are saying. According to Watson (2002), full empathy entails understanding the meaning and feeling of a client's experiencing. Empathy is an active ingredient of change that facilitates clients' cognitive processes and emotional self-regulation. Watson states that 60 years of research has consistently demonstrated that empathy is the most powerful determinant of client progress in therapy. She puts the challenge to counselors this way: "Therapists need to be able to be responsively attuned to their clients and to understand them emotionally as well as cognitively. When empathy is operating on all three levels—interpersonal, cognitive, and affective—it is one of the most powerful tools therapists have at their disposal" (pp. 463–464).

Empathy is not an artificial technique that therapists routinely use. Rather, empathy is a deep and subjective understanding of the client *with* the client. Therapists are able to share the client's subjective world by tuning in to their own feelings that are like the client's feelings. Yet therapists must not lose their own separateness. Rogers asserts that when therapists can grasp the client's private world as the client sees and feels it—without losing the separateness of their own identity—constructive change is likely to occur. Empathy helps clients (1) pay attention and value their experiencing; (2) see earlier experiences in new ways; (3) modify their perceptions of themselves, others, and the world; and (4) increase their confidence in making choices and in pursuing a course of action.

 # APPLICATION: THERAPEUTIC TECHNIQUES AND PROCEDURES

Early Emphasis on Reflection of Feelings

Rogers's original emphasis was on grasping the world of the client and reflecting this understanding. As his view of psychotherapy developed, however, his focus shifted away from a nondirective stance and emphasized the therapist's relationship with the client. Many followers of Rogers simply imitated his reflective style, and client-centered therapy has often been identified primarily with the technique of reflection despite Rogers's contention that the therapist's relational attitudes and fundamental ways of being with the client constitute the heart of the change process. Rogers and other contributors to the development of the person-centered approach have been critical of the stereotypic view that this approach is basically a simple restatement of what the client just said.

Evolution of Person-Centered Methods

Contemporary person-centered therapy is best considered as the result of an evolutionary process of more than 60 years that continues to remain open to change and refinement. One of Rogers's main contributions to the counseling field is the notion that the quality of the therapeutic relationship, as opposed to administering techniques, is the primary agent of growth in the client.

Rogers believes clients have the resourcefulness for positive movement without the counselor assuming an active, directive role. What is essential for clients' progress is the therapist's presence, which refers to the therapist being completely engaged and absorbed in the relationship with the client. The therapist is empathically interested in the client and is congruent in relation to the client. Furthermore, the therapist is willing to be deeply focused on the client in order to understand the individual's inner world (Broadley, 2000). This presence is far more powerful than any techniques a therapist might use to bring about change. Interventions such as listening, accepting, respecting, understanding, and responding must be honest expressions by the therapist. As discussed in Chapter 2, counselors need to evolve as persons, not just acquire a repertoire of therapeutic strategies.

One of the main ways in which person-centered therapy has evolved is the diversity, innovation, and individualization in practice (Cain, 2002a). As this approach has developed, there has been increased latitude for therapists to share their reactions, to confront clients in a caring way, and to participate more actively in the therapeutic process (Bozarth et al., 2002). This change encourages the use of a wider variety of methods and allows for considerable diversity in personal style.

Cain (2002a) believes it is essential for therapists to modify their therapeutic approach to accommodate the specific needs of each client. Person-centered therapists have the freedom to use a variety of responses and methods to assist their clients; a guiding question therapists need to ask is, "Does it fit?" Cain contends that, ideally, therapists will continually monitor whether what they are doing "fits," especially whether their therapeutic style is compatible with their clients' way of viewing and understanding their problems. For an illustration of how Dr. David Cain would work with the case of Ruth in a person-centered style, see *Case Approach to Counseling and Psychotherapy* (Corey, 2005, chap. 5).

Today, those who practice a person-centered approach work in diverse ways that reflect both advances in theory and practice and their unique personal styles. This is appropriate and fortunate, for none of us can emulate the style of Carl Rogers and still be true to ourselves. If we strive to model our style after Rogers, and if that style does not fit for us, we are being less than fully congruent. Therapist congruence is basic to establishing trust and safety with clients, and the therapy process is likely to be adversely affected if the therapist is not fully authentic.

The Role of Assessment

Assessment is frequently viewed as a prerequisite to the treatment process. Many mental health agencies use a variety of assessment procedures, including diagnostic screening, identification of clients' strengths and liabilities, and various tests. It may seem that assessment techniques are foreign to the spirit of the person-centered approach. What matters, however, is not how the counselor assesses the client but the client's self-assessment. From a person-centered perspective, the best source of knowledge about the client is the individual client. For example, some clients may request certain tests as a part of the counseling process. It is important for the counselor to follow the client's lead in the therapeutic dance (Ward, 1994).

In the early development of nondirective therapy, Rogers (1942) recommended caution in using tests or in taking a complete case history at the outset of counseling. If a counseling relationship began with a battery of tests, he believed clients could get the impression that the counselor would be providing the solutions to their problems. Assessment seems to be gaining in importance in short-term treatments in most counseling agencies, and it is imperative that clients be involved in a collaborative process in making decisions that are central to their therapy. Thus, it may not be a question of whether to incorporate assessment into therapeutic practice but of *how* to involve clients as fully as possible in their assessment and treatment process.

Areas of Application

The person-centered approach has been applied to working with individuals, groups, and families. Bozrath, Zimring, and Tausch (2002) cite studies done in the 1990s that revealed the effectiveness of person-centered therapy with a wide range of client problems including anxiety disorders, alcoholism, psychosomatic problems, agoraphobia, interpersonal difficulties, depression, cancer, and personality disorders. Person-centered therapy has been shown to be as viable as the more goal-oriented therapies. Furthermore, outcome research conducted in the 1990s revealed that effective therapy is based on the relationship of the therapist and client in combination with the inner and external resources of the client (Hubble, Duncan, & Miller, 1999).

An area where I see the person-centered approach as being especially applicable is crisis intervention such as an unwanted pregnancy, an illness, or the loss of a loved one. People in the helping professions (nursing, medicine, education, the ministry) are often first on the scene in a variety of crises, and they can do much if the basic attitudes described in this chapter are present. When people are in crisis, one of the first steps is to give them an opportunity to fully express themselves. Sensitive listening, hearing, and understanding are essential at this point. Being heard and understood helps ground people in crises, helps to calm them in the midst of turmoil, and enables them to think more clearly and make better decisions. Although a person's crisis is not likely to be resolved by one or two contacts with a helper, such contacts can pave the way for being open to receiving help later. If the person in crisis does not feel understood and accepted, he or she may lose hope of "returning to normal" and may not seek help in the future. Genuine support, caring, and nonpossessive warmth can go a long way in building bridges that can motivate people to *do* something to work through and resolve a crisis. Communicating a deep sense of understanding should always precede other more problem-solving interventions. People in trouble do not need false reassurances that "everything will be all right." Yet the presence of and psychological contact with a caring person can do much to bring about healing.

The person-centered approach has been applied extensively in training professionals and paraprofessionals who work with people in a variety of settings. This approach emphasizes staying with clients as opposed to getting ahead of them with interpretations. Hence, it is safer than models of therapy that put the therapist in the directive position of making interpretations, forming diagnoses, probing the unconscious, analyzing dreams, and working toward more radical personality changes.

People without advanced psychological education are able to benefit by translating the therapeutic conditions of genuineness, empathic understanding, and unconditional positive regard into both their personal and professional lives. The basic concepts are straightforward and easy to comprehend, and they encourage locating power in the person rather than fostering an authoritarian structure in which control and power are denied to the person. These core skills also provide an essential foundation for virtually all of the other therapy systems covered in this book. If counselors are lacking in these relationship and communication skills, they will not be effective in carrying out a treatment program for their clients

The person-centered approach demands a great deal of the therapist. An effective person-centered therapist must be grounded, centered, present, focused, patient, and accepting in a way that involves maturity (David Cain, personal communication, July 31, 2002). Without a person-centered attitude or way of being, mere application of skills is likely to be hollow.

 ## PERSON-CENTERED THERAPY FROM A MULTICULTURAL PERSPECTIVE

Contributions to Multicultural Counseling

Person-centered therapy has made significant contributions to the field of human relations with diverse cultural groups. Rogers has had a global impact. His work has reached more than 30 countries, and his writings have been translated into 12 languages. Person-centered philosophy and practice can now be studied in several European countries, South America, and Japan. Here are some examples of ways in which this approach has been incorporated in various cultures:

- In several European countries person-centered concepts have had a significant impact on the practice of counseling as well as on education, cross-cultural communication, and reduction of racial and political tensions. In the 1980s Rogers (1987b) elaborated on a theory of reducing tension among antagonistic groups that he began developing in 1948.
- In the 1970s Rogers and his associates began conducting workshops promoting cross-cultural communication. Well into the 1980s he led large workshops in many parts of the world. International encounter groups have provided participants with multicultural experiences.
- Japan, Australia, South America, and Mexico have all been receptive to person-centered concepts and have adapted these practices to fit their cultures.

Person-Center Therapy Applied to the Case of Stan

Stan's autobiography indicates that he has a fairly clear idea of what he wants for his life. The person-centered therapist relies on his self-report of the way he views himself rather than on a formal assessment and diagnosis. She is concerned with understanding him from his internal frame of reference. Stan has stated goals that are meaningful for him. He is motivated to change and seems to have sufficient anxiety to work toward these desired changes. The person-centered counselor thus has faith in Stan's ability to find his own way and trusts that he has the necessary resources for personal growth. She encourages Stan to speak freely about the discrepancy between the person he sees himself as being and the person he would like to become; about his feelings of being a failure, being inadequate, or being unmanly; about his fears and uncertainties; and about his hopelessness at times. She strives to create an atmosphere of freedom and security that will encourage Stan to explore the threatening aspects of his self-concept. To do this, the counselor listens intently not only to Stan's words but also to the manner in which he delivers his message. She attempts to understand what it must be like to live in his world. She conveys to him the basic attitudes of understanding and accepting, and through this positive regard Stan may well be able to drop his pretenses and more fully and freely explore his personal concerns.

Stan has a low evaluation of his self-worth. Although he finds it difficult to believe that others really like him, he wants to feel loved ("I hope I can learn to love at least a few people, most of all, women"). He wants to feel equal to others and not have to apologize for his existence, yet most of the time he is keenly aware that he feels inferior. If his therapist can create a supportive, trusting, and encouraging atmosphere, Stan is likely to feel that she is genuinely interested in him. He can use the relationship to learn to be more accepting of himself, with both his strengths and limitations. He has the opportunity to openly express his fears of women, of not being able to work with people, and of feeling inadequate and stupid. He can explore how he feels judged by his parents and by authorities. He has an opportunity to express his guilt—that is, his feelings that he has not lived up to his parents' expec-

tations and that he has let them and himself down. He can also relate his feelings of hurt over not having ever felt loved and wanted. He can express the loneliness and isolation that he so often feels, as well as the need to dull these feelings with alcohol or drugs.

In relating his feelings, Stan is no longer totally alone, for he is taking the risk of letting his therapist into his private world. In doing so, how will he be helped? Through the relationship with her, Stan gradually gets a sharper focus on his experiencing and is able to clarify his own feelings and attitudes. He sees that he has the capacity to muster his own strengths and make his own decisions. In short, the therapeutic relationship tends to free him from his self-defeating ways. Because of the caring and faith he experiences from his therapist, Stan is able to increase his own faith and confidence in his ability to resolve his difficulties and discover a new way of being.

Therapy will be successful if Stan comes to view himself in a more positive light. The empathic responses of the therapist assist Stan in hearing himself and accessing himself at a deeper level. Stan will gradually become more sensitive to his own internal messages and less dependent on confirmation from others around him. As a result of the therapeutic venture, Stan will discover that there is someone in his life whom he can depend on—himself.

Follow-Up: You Continue as Stan's Person-Centered Therapist

Use these questions to help you think about how you would counsel Stan using a person-centered approach:

- Knowing what you do of Stan, how much faith do you have that he has the capacity to find his own way without active intervention on your part as a therapist? How do you imagine you would function without relying on structured techniques?
- How would you describe Stan's deeper struggles? What is his world like from his vantage point?
- To what extent do you think that the relationship you could develop with Stan would help him move forward in a positive direction? What, if anything, might get in your way—either with him or in yourself—in establishing a therapeutic relationship?

■ Shortly before his death, Rogers conducted intensive workshops with professionals in the former Soviet Union.

Cain (1987c) sums up the far-reaching extent of the person-centered approach to cultural diversity: "Our international family consists of millions of persons worldwide whose lives have been affected by Carl Rogers's writings and personal efforts as well as his many colleagues who have brought his and their own innovative thinking and programs to many corners of the earth" (p. 149).

In addition to these global contributions, the emphasis on the core conditions makes the person-centered approach useful in understanding diverse worldviews. The underlying philosophy of person-centered therapy is grounded on the importance of hearing the deeper messages of a client. Empathy, being present, and respecting the values of clients are essential attitudes and skills in counseling culturally diverse clients. Therapist empathy has moved far beyond simple "reflection," and clinicians now draw from a variety of empathic response modes (Bohart & Greenberg, 1997). This empathy may be expressed and communicated either directly or indirectly.

Glauser and Bozarth (2001) remind us to pay attention to the cultural identity that resides within the client. They caution against making assumptions about clients based on their cultural background or the specific group to which they belong. Therapists must wait for the cultural context to emerge from the client, and they caution therapists to be aware of the "specificity myth," which leads to specific treatments being assumed to be best for particular groups of people. Glauser and Bozarth's main message is that counseling in a multicultural context must embody the core conditions associated with all effective counseling. They state: "Person-centered counseling cuts to the core of what is important for therapeutic success in all counseling approaches. The counselor-client relationship and the use of the client's resources are central for multicultural counseling" (p. 146).

Limitations for Multicultural Counseling

Although the person-centered approach has made significant contributions to counseling people with diverse social, political, and cultural backgrounds, there are some limitations to practicing exclusively within this framework. Many clients who come to community mental health clinics or who are involved in outpatient treatment want more structure than is provided by this approach. Some clients seek professional help to deal with a crisis, to alleviate psychosomatic symptoms, or to learn coping skills in dealing with everyday problems. Because of certain cultural messages, when these clients do seek professional help, it may be as a last resort. They expect a directive counselor and can be put off by one who does not provide sufficient structure.

A second limitation of the person-centered approach is that it is difficult to translate the core conditions into actual practice in certain cultures. Communication of these core conditions must be consistent with the client's cultural framework. Consider, for example, the expression of therapist congruence and empathy. Clients accustomed to indirect communication may not be comfortable with direct expression of empathy or self-disclosure on the therapist's part. For some clients the most appropriate way to express empathy is for the therapist to demonstrate it indirectly through respecting their need for distance or through suggesting task-focused interventions (Bohart & Greenberg, 1997).

A third limitation in applying the person-centered approach with diverse clients pertains to the fact that this approach extols the value of an *internal* locus of evaluation. Yet some ethnic groups value collectivism more than individualism. In these cultures, clients are likely to be highly influenced by societal expectations and not simply motivated by their own personal preference. The focus on development of the individual is often at odds with the cultural value that stresses the common good. It is often viewed as being selfish to think about one's personal growth rather than being primarily concerned with what is best for the group. However, it should be noted that a competent person-centered therapist understands, accepts, and works with a client's external world as well as with the client's inner world.

Consider Lupe, a Latina client who might well consider the interests of her family over her self-interests. From a person-centered perspective she could be viewed as being in danger of "losing her own identity" by being primarily concerned with her role in taking care of others in the family. Rather than pushing her to make her personal wants a priority, the counselor will explore Lupe's cultural values and her level of commitment to these values in working with her. It would be inappropriate for the counselor to impose a vision of the kind of woman she should be. (This topic is discussed more extensively in Chapter 12.)

Although there may be distinct limitations in working exclusively within a person-centered perspective with certain clients because of their cultural background, it should not be concluded that this approach is unsuitable for these clients. There is great diversity among any group of people, and therefore, there is room for a variety of therapeutic styles. More activity and structuring may be called for than is usually the case in a person-centered framework, but the potential positive impact of a counselor who responds empathically to a culturally different client cannot be underestimated. Often, a client has never met someone like the counselor who is able to truly listen and understand. Counselors will certainly find it challenging to empathize with clients who have had vastly different life experiences.

 # SUMMARY AND EVALUATION

Summary

Person-centered therapy is based on a philosophy of human nature that postulates an innate striving for self-actualization. Further, Rogers's view of human nature is phenomenological; that is, we structure ourselves according to our perceptions of reality. We are motivated to actualize ourselves in the reality that we perceive.

Rogers's theory rests on the assumption that clients can understand the factors in their lives that are causing them to be unhappy. They also have the capacity for self-direction and constructive personal change. Change will occur if a congruent therapist makes psychological contact with a client in a state of anxiety or incongruence. It is essential for the therapist to establish a relationship the client perceives as genuine, accepting, and understanding. Therapeutic counseling is based on an I/Thou, or person-to-person, relationship in the safety and acceptance of which clients drop their defenses and come to accept and integrate aspects that they have denied or distorted. The person-centered approach emphasizes this personal relationship between client and therapist; the therapist's attitudes are more critical than are knowledge, theory, or techniques. Clients are encouraged to use this relationship to unleash their growth potential and become more of the person they choose to become.

This approach places primary responsibility for the direction of therapy on the client. Clients are confronted with the opportunity to decide for themselves and come to terms with their own personal power. The general goals of therapy are becoming more open to experience, achieving self-trust, developing an internal source of evaluation, and being willing to continue growing. Specific goals are not imposed on clients; rather, clients choose their own values and goals. Current applications of the theory emphasize more active participation by the therapist than was the case earlier. More latitude is allowed for therapists to express their values, reactions, and feelings as they are appropriate to what is occurring in therapy. Counselors can be fully involved as persons in the relationship.

Contributions of the Person-Centered Approach

When Rogers founded nondirective counseling more than 60 years ago, there were very few other therapeutic models. Cain (1990a) points out that now "there are well over 200 therapeutic approaches, [and] it is worth noting that the client-centered approach continues to have a significant place and role among the major therapeutic systems" (p. 5). The longevity of this approach is certainly a factor to consider in assessing its influence. Elsewhere Cain (2002b) contends that substantial research evidence supports the effectiveness of the client-centered approach: "Sixty years of development in theory, practice, and research have demonstrated that humanistic approaches to psychotherapy are as effective or more effective than other major therapies" (p. xxii).

Rogers had a major impact on the field of counseling and psychotherapy. When he introduced his revolutionary ideas in the 1940s, he provided a powerful and radical alternative to psychoanalysis and to the directive approaches then practiced. Rogers was a pioneer in shifting the therapeutic focus from an emphasis on technique and reliance on therapist authority to that of relationship. According to Farber (1996), Rogers's notions regarding empathy, egalitarianism, the primacy of the therapeutic relationship, and the value of research are commonly accepted by many practitioners and have been incorporated into other theoretical orientations with little acknowledgment of their origin. In spite of Rogers's enormous influence on the practice of psychotherapy, his contributions have been overlooked in clinical psychology programs. With the exception of counselor education and counseling psychology programs, Rogers's work has not been given the respect it deserves (Farber, 1996), and there are few person-centered graduate programs in the United States today.

Rogers consistently opposed the institutionalization of a client-centered "school." Likewise, he reacted negatively to the idea of founding institutes, granting certificates, and setting standards for membership. He feared this institutionalization would lead to an increasingly narrow, rigid, and dogmatic perspective. Rogers (1987a) warned that too much loyalty to a method, a school of thought, or a technique could have a counterproductive effect on the counseling process. The advice he often gave to students-in-training and followed in his own life was this: "There is one *best* school of therapy. It is the school of therapy you develop for yourself based on a continuing critical examination of the effects of your way of being in the relationship" (p. 185).

EMPHASIS ON RESEARCH   One of Rogers's contributions to the field of psychotherapy was his willingness to state his concepts as testable hypotheses and to submit them to research. He literally opened the field to research. He was truly a pioneer in his insistence on subjecting the transcripts of therapy sessions to critical examination and applying research technology to counselor–client dialogues (Combs, 1988). Rogers's basic hypothesis gave rise to a great deal of research and debate in the field of psychotherapy, perhaps more than any other school of therapy (Cain, 2002a). Even his critics give Rogers credit for having conducted and inspired others to conduct extensive studies of counseling process and outcome. Rogers presented a challenge to psychology to design new models of scientific investigation capable of dealing with the inner, subjective experiences of the person. His theories of therapy and personality change have had a tremendous heuristic effect, and though much controversy surrounds this approach, his work has challenged practitioners and theoreticians to examine their own therapeutic styles and beliefs. Based largely on research efforts of Rogers and his colleagues, "substantive advances in theory and refinements in practice have been taking place over the past 25 years" (Cain, 2002b, p. xxii).

THE IMPORTANCE OF EMPATHY   Among the major contributions of person-centered therapy are the implications of empathy for the practice of counseling. More than any other approach, person-centered therapy has demonstrated that therapist empathy plays a vital role in facilitating constructive change in the client. Watson's (2002) comprehensive review of the research literature on therapeutic empathy included these findings:

- Research consistently demonstrates that therapist empathy is the most potent predictor of client progress in therapy.
- Empathy is an essential component of successful therapy in every therapeutic modality.
- Empathy is a basic component of emotional intelligence.
- Client perception of therapist empathy, as opposed to that of external raters or therapists, is most predictive of positive client outcome.
- No study shows a negative relationship between empathy and outcome.
- Successful outcomes across different modalities are characterized by a high proportion of therapist statements expressing understanding, attentive listening, and receptive openness to the client's perspective.

Person-centered research has been conducted predominantly on the hypothesized necessary and sufficient conditions of therapeutic personality change (Cain, 1986, 1987b). Most of the other counseling approaches covered in this book have incorporated the importance of the therapist's attitude and behavior in creating a therapeutic relationship that is conducive to the use of their techniques. For instance, the cognitive behavioral approaches have developed a wide range of strategies designed to help clients deal with specific problems, and they recognize that a trusting and accepting client–therapist relationship is necessary for successful application of these procedures. In contrast to the person-centered approach, however, these practitioners contend that the working relationship is not sufficient to produce change. Active procedures are needed to bring it about.

INNOVATIONS IN PERSON-CENTERED THERAPY   One of the strengths of the person-centered approach is "the development of innovative and sophisticated methods to work with an increasingly difficult, diverse, and complex range of individuals, couples, families, and groups" (Cain, 2002b, p. xxii). A number of people have made significant advancements that are compatible with the essential values and concepts of person-centered therapy. To demonstrate some of the ways person-centered theory and practice has evolved, examine this partial list of innovators:

- Virginia Axline (1964, 1969) made seminal contributions to client-centered therapy with children and play therapy.
- Eugene Gendlin (1996) developed experiential techniques, such as focusing, as a way to enhance client experiencing.
- Laura Rice (Rice & Greenberg, 1984) taught therapists to be more evocative in re-creating crucial experiences that continue to trouble the client.
- Art Combs (1988, 1989, 1999) developed perceptual psychology.

- Several practitioners have applied the person-centered approach to working with couples and families (Gaylin, 1989; Johnson, 1996; Johnson & Greenberg, 1994; O'Leary, 1999).
- Leslie Greenberg and his colleagues (Greenberg, Korman, & Paivio, 2002; Greenberg, Rice, & Elliott, 1993) have focused on the importance of facilitating emotional change in therapy and advanced person-centered theory and methods.
- David Rennie (1998) has given us a glimpse at the inner workings of the therapeutic process.
- Art Bohart (Bohart & Greenberg, 1997) has contributed to a deeper understanding of empathy in therapeutic practice.
- Jeanne Watson (2002) has demonstrated that when empathy is operating on the cognitive, affective, and interpersonal levels, it is one of the therapist's most powerful tools.
- C. H. Patterson (1995) has shown how client-centered therapy is a universal system of psychotherapy.
- Hubble, Duncan, and Miller (1999) have shown that the client-centered relationship is essential to all therapeutic approaches.

Limitations and Criticisms of the Person-Centered Approach

Although I have applauded person-centered therapists for their willingness to subject their hypotheses and procedures to empirical scrutiny, some researchers have been critical of methodological errors contained in some of these studies. Accusations of scientific shortcomings involve using control subjects who are not candidates for therapy, failing to use an untreated control group, failing to account for placebo effects, reliance on self-reports as a major way to assess the outcomes of therapy, and using inappropriate statistical procedures.

A potential limitation of this approach is the way that some students-in-training and practitioners with a person-centered orientation have a tendency to be very supportive of clients without being challenging. Out of their misunderstanding of the basic concepts of the approach, some have limited the range of their responses and counseling styles to reflections and empathic listening. Although there is value in really hearing a client and in reflecting and communicating understanding, counseling entails more than this. I believe that the therapeutic core conditions are necessary for therapy to succeed, yet I do not see them as being sufficient conditions for change for all clients at all times. These basic attitudes are the foundation on which counselors must then build the *skills* of therapeutic intervention.

A related challenge for counselors using this approach is to truly support clients in finding their own way. Counselors sometimes experience difficulty in allowing clients to decide their own specific goals in therapy. It is easy to give lip service to the concept of clients' finding their own way, but it takes considerable respect for clients and faith on the therapist's part to encourage clients to listen to themselves and follow their own directions, particularly when they make choices that are not what the therapist hoped for.

More than any other quality, the therapist's genuineness determines the power of the therapeutic relationship. If therapists submerge their unique identity and style in a passive and nondirective way, they may not be harming many clients, but they may not be powerfully affecting clients. Therapist authenticity and congruence are so vital to this approach that those who practice within this framework must feel natural in doing so and must find a way to express their own reactions to clients. If not, a real possibility is that person-centered therapy will be reduced to a bland, safe, and ineffectual approach.

 # WHERE TO GO FROM HERE

In the *CD-ROM for Integrative Counseling* you will see a concrete illustration of how I also view the therapeutic relationship as the foundation for our work together. Refer especially to Session 1 ("Beginning of Counseling"), Session 2 ("The Therapeutic Relationship"), and Session 3 ("Establishing Therapeutic Goals") for a demonstration of how I apply principles from the person-centered approach to my work with Ruth.

The Association for Humanistic Psychology (AHP) is devoted to promoting personal integrity, creative learning, and active responsibility in embracing the challenges of being human in these times. For information, contact:

Association for Humanistic Psychology
1516 Oak St. #320A
Alameda, CA 94501-2947
Telephone: (510) 769-6495
Email: ahpoffice@aol.com
Web site: http://www.ahpweb.org/

You might consider joining the Association for the Development of the Person-Centered Approach (ADPCA), an interdisciplinary and international organization. Membership includes a subscription to the *Person-Centered Journal,* the association's newsletter, a membership directory, and information about the annual meeting. It also provides information about continuing education and supervision and training in the person-centered approach. For more information, contact:

Association for the Development of the Person-Centered Approach, Inc.
P. O. Box 3876
Chicago, IL 60690-3876
Email: adpca-web@signs.portents.com
Web site: http://adpca.org

For information about *The Person-Centered Journal,* contact Jon Rose, Editor, at jonmrose@aol.com.

The Center for Studies of the Person (CSP) in La Jolla offers workshops, experiential small groups, and sharing of learning in community meetings. The Distance Learning Project and the Carl Rogers Institute for Psychotherapy Training and Supervision provide experiential and didactic training and supervision for professionals who are interested in developing their own person-centered orientation. If you want to find out more about CSP, contact:

Center for Studies of the Person
Joachim Schwarz, Ph.D., Director
1150 Silverado, Suite 112
La Jolla, CA 92037
Telephone: (858) 459-3861
Email: Stillwell@meinet.cc
Web site: www.centerfortheperson.org

InfoTrac College Edition Resources

Person-Centered Therapy   The following key words are listed in such a way as to allow the InfoTrac College Edition search engine to locate a wider range of articles in the online library. The key words should be entered exactly as shown, to include asterisks, "W1," and "AND."

Carl Rogers

Client-centered

Person-centered

Humanistic psychology

Congruence AND psychol*

Self-actualization

Unconditional W1 positive AND regard

Internal locus

Nondirective W1 therapy

Rogers AND self-actualization

Recommended Supplementary Readings

On Becoming a Person (Rogers, 1961) is one of the best primary sources for further reading on person-centered therapy. This is a collection of Rogers's articles on the process of psychotherapy, its outcomes, the therapeutic relationship, education, family life, communication, and the nature of the healthy person.

A Way of Being (Rogers, 1980) contains a series of writings on Rogers's personal experiences and perspectives, as well as chapters on the foundations and applications of the person-centered approach.

Humanistic Psychotherapies: Handbook of Research and Practice (Cain & Seeman, 2002) provides a useful and very comprehensive discussion of person-centered therapy, Gestalt therapy, and existential therapy. This book includes research evidence for the person-centered theory.

The Psychotherapy of Carl Rogers: Cases and Commentary (Farber, Brink, & Raskin, 1996) describes the evolution of person-centered therapy, compares the views of person-centered therapists with those of other orientations, and explores the contributions that Rogers made to contemporary practice.

Facilitating Emotional Change: The Moment-by-Moment Process (Greenberg, Rice, & Elliott, 1993) is based on an experiential therapy framework and describes refinements to person-centered therapy.

References and Suggested Readings

AXLINE, V. (1964). *Dibs: In search of self.* New York: Ballantine.

AXLINE, V. (1969). *Play therapy* (Rev. ed.). New York: Ballantine.

BOHART, A. C., & GREENBERG, L. S. (Eds.). (1997). *Empathy reconsidered: New directions in psychotherapy.* Washington, DC: American Psychological Association.

*BOY, A. V., & PINE, G. J. (1999). *A person-centered foundation for counseling and psychotherapy* (2nd ed.). Springfield, IL: Charles C Thomas.

*BOZARTH, J. D., ZIMRING, F. M., & TAUSCH, R. (2002). Client-centered therapy: The evolution of a revolution. In D. J. Cain, & J. Seeman, (Eds.), *Humanistic psychotherapies: Handbook of research and practice* (pp. 147–188). Washington, DC: American Psychological Association.

BROADLEY, B. T. (1997). The nondirective attitude in client-centered therapy. *The Person-Centered Journal, 4*(1), 18–30.

BROADLEY, B. T. (1999). The actualizing tendency concept in client-centered theory. *The Person-Centered Journal, 6*(2), 108–120.

BROADLEY, B. T. (2000). Personal presence in client-centered therapy. *The Person-Centered Journal, 7*(2), 139–149.

CAIN, D. J. (1986). Editorial: A call for the "write stuff." *Person-Centered Review, 1*(2), 117–124.

CAIN, D. J. (1987a). Carl Rogers' life in review. *Person-Centered Review, 2*(4), 476–506.

CAIN, D. J. (1987b). Carl R. Rogers: The man, his vision, his impact. *Person-Centered Review, 2*(3), 283–288.

CAIN, D. J. (1987c). Our international family. *Person-Centered Review, 2*(2), 139–149.

CAIN, D. J. (1990a). Fifty years of client-centered therapy and the person-centered approach. *Person-Centered Review, 5*(1), 3–7.

CAIN, D. J. (1990b). Further thoughts about nondirectiveness and client-centered therapy. *Person-Centered Review, 5*(1), 89–99.

*CAIN, D. J. (2002a). Defining characteristics, history, and evolution of humanistic psychotherapies. In D. J. Cain, & J. Seeman (Eds.), *Humanistic psychotherapies: Handbook of research and practice* (pp. 3–54). Washington, DC: American Psychological Association.

CAIN, D. J. (2002b). Preface. In D. J. Cain, & J. Seeman (Eds.), *Humanistic psychotherapies: Handbook of research and practice* (pp. xix–xxvi). Washington, DC: American Psychological Association.

*CAIN, D. J., & SEEMAN, J. (Eds.). (2002). *Humanistic psychotherapies: Handbook of research and practice.* Washington, DC: American Psychological Association.

COMBS, A. W. (1988). Some current issues for person-centered therapy. *Person-Centered Review, 3*(3), 263–276.

---

*Books and articles marked with an asterisk are suggested for further study.

COMBS, A. W. (1989). *A theory of therapy: Guidelines for counseling practice.* Newbury Park, CA: Sage.

COMBS, A. W. (1999). *Being and becoming.* New York: Springer.

COREY, G. (2004). *Theory and practice of group counseling* (6th ed.). Pacific Grove, CA: Brooks/Cole.

COREY, G. (2005). *Case approach to counseling and psychotherapy* (6th ed.). Belmont, CA: Brooks/Cole.

FARBER, B. A. (1996). Introduction. In B. A. Farber, D. C. Brink, & P. M. Raskin (Eds.), *The psychotherapy of Carl Rogers: Cases and commentary* (pp. 1–14). New York: Guilford Press.

*FARBER, B. A., BRINK, D. C., & RASKIN, P. M. (Eds.). (1996). *The psychotherapy of Carl Rogers: Cases and commentary.* New York: Guilford Press.

GAYLIN, N. L. (1989). The necessary and sufficient conditions for change: Individual versus family therapy. *Person-Centered Review, 4*(3), 263–279.

*GENDLIN, E. T. (1996). *Focusing-oriented psychotherapy: A manual of the experiential method.* New York: Guilford Press.

*GLAUSER, A. S., & BOZARTH, J. D. (2001). Person-centered counseling: The culture within. *Journal of Counseling and Development, 79*(2), 142–147.

*GREENBERG, L. S., KORMAN, L. M., & PAIVIO, S. C. (2002). Emotion in humanistic psychotherapy. In D. J. Cain, & J. Seeman (Eds.), *Humanistic psychotherapies: Handbook of research and practice* (pp. 499–530). Washington, DC: American Psychological Association.

*GREENBERG, L. S., RICE, L. N., & ELLIOTT, R. (1993). *Facilitating emotional change: The moment-by-moment process.* New York: Guilford Press.

HEPPNER, R. R., ROGERS, M. E., & LEE, L. A. (1984). Carl Rogers: Reflections on his life. *Journal of Counseling and Development, 63*(l), 14–20.

*HUBBLE, M. A., DUNCAN, B. L., & MILLER, S. D. (Eds.). (1999). *The heart and soul of change: What works in therapy.* Washington, DC: American Psychological Association.

JOHNSON, S. M. (1996). *The practice of emotionally focused marital therapy.* New York: Brunner/Mazel.

JOHNSON, S. M, & GREENBERG, L. S. (1994). *The heart of the matter: Perspectives on emotion in marital therapy.* New York: Brunner/Mazel.

O'LEARY, C. J. (1999). *Counseling couples and families: A person-centered approach.* London: Sage.

PATTERSON, C. H. (1995). A universal system of psychotherapy. *The Person-Centered Journal, 2*(1), 54–62.

RENNIE, D. L. (1998). *Person-centered counseling: An experiential approach.* London: Sage.

RICE, L. N., & GREENBERG, L. (1984). *Patterns of change.* New York: Guilford Press.

ROGERS, C. (1942). *Counseling and psychotherapy.* Boston: Houghton Mifflin.

ROGERS, C. (1951). *Client-centered therapy.* Boston: Houghton Mifflin.

ROGERS, C. (1957). The necessary and sufficient conditions of therapeutic personality change. *Journal of Consulting Psychology, 21,* 95–103.

*ROGERS, C. (1961). *On becoming a person.* Boston: Houghton Mifflin.

ROGERS, C. (1967). The conditions of change from a client-centered viewpoint. In B. Berenson & R. Carkhuff (Eds.), *Sources of gain in counseling and psychotherapy.* New York: Holt, Rinehart & Winston.

ROGERS, C. (1970). *Carl Rogers on encounter groups.* New York: Harper & Row.

ROGERS, C. (1977). *Carl Rogers on personal power: Inner strength and its revolutionary impact.* New York: Delacorte Press.

*ROGERS, C. (1980). *A way of being.* Boston: Houghton Mifflin.

ROGERS, C. (1983). *Freedom to learn in the 80's.* Columbus, OH: Merrill.

ROGERS, C. (1986a). Carl Rogers on the development of the person-centered approach. *Person-Centered Review, 1*(3), 257–259.

ROGERS, C. (1986b). Client-centered therapy. In I. L. Kutash & A. Wolf (Eds.), *Psychotherapist's casebook* (pp. 197–208). San Francisco: Jossey-Bass.

ROGERS, C. R. (1987a). Rogers, Kohut, and Erickson: A personal perspective on some similarities and differences. In J. K. Zeig (Ed.), *The evolution of psychotherapy* (pp. 179–187). New York: Brunner/Mazel.

ROGERS, C. R. (1987b). Steps toward world peace, 1948–1986: Tension reduction in theory and practice. *Counseling and Values, 32*(1), 12–16.

ROGERS, C. R. (1987c). The underlying theory: Drawn from experiences with individuals and groups. *Counseling and Values, 32*(l), 38–45.

SANFORD, R. (1990). Client-centered psychotherapy. In J. K. Zeig & W. M. Munion (Eds.), *What is psychotherapy? Contemporary perspectives* (pp. 81–86). San Francisco: Jossey-Bass.

*TALLMAN, K., & BOHART, A. C. (1999). The client as a common factor: Clients as self-healers. In M. A. Hubble, B. L. Duncan, & S. D. Miller (Eds.), *The heart and soul of change: What works in therapy* (pp. 91–131). Washington, DC: American Psychological Association.

WARD, F. L. (1994). Client-centered assessment. *The Person-Centered Periodical, 1*(1), 31–38.

*WATSON, J. C. (2002). Re-visioning empathy. In D. J. Cain, & J. Seeman (Eds.), *Humanistic psychotherapies: Handbook of research and practice* (pp. 445–471). Washington, DC: American Psychological Association.

ZIMRING, F. M., & RASKIN, N. J. (1992). Carl Rogers and client/person-centered therapy. In D. K. Freedheim (Ed.), *History of psychotherapy: A century of change* (pp. 629–656). Washington, DC: American Psychological Association.

Gestalt Therapy

Fritz **Perls** / Laura **Perls**

FREDERICK S. ("FRITZ") PERLS (1893–1970) was the main originator and developer of Gestalt therapy. Born in Berlin into a lower-middle-class Jewish family, he later identified himself as a source of much trouble for his parents. Although he failed the seventh grade twice and was expelled from school because of difficulties with the authorities, he still managed to complete his schooling and receive an M.D. with a specialization in psychiatry. In 1916 he joined the German Army and served as a medic in World War I.

After the war Perls worked with Kurt Goldstein at the Goldstein Institute for Brain-Damaged Soldiers in Frankfurt. It was through this association that he came to see the importance of viewing humans as a whole rather than as a sum of discretely functioning parts. Later he moved to Vienna and began his psychoanalytic training. Perls was analyzed by Wilhelm Reich, a psychoanalyst who pioneered methods of self-understanding and personality change by working with the body. He was also supervised by several other key figures in the psychoanalytic movement, including Karen Horney.

Perls broke away from the psychoanalytic tradition around the time that he emigrated to the United States in 1946. He established the New York Institute for Gestalt Therapy in 1952. Eventually, he settled in Big Sur, California, and gave workshops and seminars at the Esalen Institute, carving out his reputation as an innovator in psychotherapy. Here he had a great impact on people, partly through his professional writings but mainly through personal contact in his workshops.

Personally, Perls was both vital and perplexing. People typically either responded to him in awe or found him harshly confrontive and saw him as meeting his own needs through showmanship. He was viewed variously as insightful, witty, bright, provocative, manipulative, hostile, demanding, and inspirational. Unfortunately, some of the people who attended his workshops became followers of the "guru" and went out to spread the gospel of Gestalt therapy. Even though Perls mentioned in one of his books his concerns over those who mechanically function as Gestalt therapists and promote phoniness, it appeared to many that he did little to discourage this kind of following.

For a firsthand account of the life of Fritz Perls, I recommend his autobiography, *In and Out of the Garbage Pail* (1969b).

(continued on next page)

LAURA POSNER PERLS (1905–1990) was born in Pforzheim, Germany. She began playing the piano at the age of 5 and played with professional skill by the time she was 18. From the age of 8 she was involved in modern dance, and both music and modern dance remained a vital part of her adult life. By the time Laura began her practice as a psychoanalyst, she had prepared for a career as a concert pianist, had attended law school, achieved a graduate degree in Gestalt psychology, and made an intensive study of philosophy. Clearly, Laura already had a rich background when she met Fritz in 1926 and they began their collaboration, which resulted in Gestalt therapy. Laura and Fritz were married in 1930. They founded the New York Institute for Gestalt Therapy and did a great deal of training in this approach. As a team, they made significant contributions to the development and maintenance of the Gestalt therapy movement in the United States from the late 1940s until her death in 1990. Laura Perls's own words make it clear that Fritz was a generator, not a developer or organizer. At the 25th anniversary of the New York Institute for Gestalt Therapy, Laura Perls (1990) stated: "Without the constant support from his friends, and from me, without the constant encouragement and collaboration, Fritz would never have written a line, nor founded anything" (p. 18).

Laura paid a great deal of attention to contact and support, which differed from Fritz's concern with awareness. Her emphasis on contact underscored the role of the interpersonal and of being responsive to the environment at a time when the popular notion of Gestalt therapy was that it fostered responsibility only to oneself. She corrected some of the excesses committed in the name of Gestalt therapy and adhered to the basic principles of Gestalt therapy theory. She taught that every Gestalt therapist needs to develop his or her own therapeutic style. From her perspective, whatever is integrated in our personality becomes support for what we use technically (Humphrey, 1986). ∎

 # INTRODUCTION

Gestalt therapy, developed by Fritz Perls and his wife, Laura, in the 1940s, is an existential–phenomenological approach based on the premise that individuals must be understood in the context of their ongoing relationship with the environment. The initial goal is for clients to gain *awareness* of what they are experiencing and how they are doing it. Through this awareness, change automatically occurs. The approach is phenomenological because it focuses on the client's perceptions of reality and existential because it is grounded in the notion that people are always in the process of becoming, remaking, and rediscovering themselves. As an existential approach, Gestalt therapy gives special attention to existence as individuals experience it and affirms the human capacity for growth and healing through interpersonal contact and insight (Yontef, 1995).

Gestalt therapy is lively and promotes direct experiencing rather than the abstractness of talking about situations. The approach is experiential in that clients come to grips with what and how they are thinking, feeling, and doing as they interact with the therapist. Gestalt counselors value being fully present during the therapeutic encounter, and growth occurs out of genuine contact between client and therapist.

Although Fritz Perls was influenced by psychoanalytic concepts, he took issue with Freud's theory on a number of grounds. Whereas Freud's view of human beings is basically mechanistic, Perls stresses a holistic approach to personality. Freud focused on repressed intrapsychic conflicts from early childhood, whereas Perls valued examining the present situation. This approach focuses much more on process than on content. It emphasizes what is being presently experienced rather than the content of what clients reveal. Perls asserts that *how* individuals behave in the present moment is far more crucial to self-understanding than *why* they behave as they do.

One of the therapist's main roles is to guide the phenomenological focus, or to assist clients in clarifying their awareness. Therapists devise *experiments* designed to increase clients' self-awareness of what they are doing and how they are doing it. Awareness includes insight, self-acceptance, knowledge of the environment, responsibility for choices, and the ability to make contact with others. It is based on a here-and-now experiencing that is always changing. Clients are expected to do their own seeing, feeling, sensing, and interpreting, as opposed to waiting passively for the therapist to give them insight and answers.

 ## KEY CONCEPTS

View of Human Nature

Fritz Perls (1969a) practiced Gestalt therapy paternalistically. Clients have to grow up, stand on their own two feet, and "deal with their life problems themselves" (p. 225). His style of doing therapy involved two personal agendas: moving the client from environmental support to self-support and reintegrating the disowned parts of personality. Perls's conception of human nature and agendas toward self-reliance and reintegration set the stage for a variety of techniques and for a confrontational style of conducting therapy.

In contrast to Perls's way of working, contemporary Gestalt therapy stresses dialogue between client and therapist. The therapist has no agenda, no desire to get anywhere, and understands that the essential nature of the individual's relationship with the environment is interdependence, not independence. This approach creates the ground for contact and experiments that are spontaneous and organic to the moment-to-moment experience of the therapeutic engagement.

The Gestalt view of human nature is rooted in existential philosophy, phenomenology, and field theory. Genuine knowledge is the product of what is immediately evident in the experience of the perceiver. Therapy aims not at analysis but at awareness and contact with the environment. The environment, or "field," consists of both the external and internal worlds. The quality of contact with aspects of the external world (for example, other people) and the internal world (for example, parts of the self that are disowned) is monitored. The process of "reowning" parts of oneself that have been disowned and the unification process proceed step by step until clients become strong enough to carry on with their own personal growth. By becoming aware, clients become able to make informed choices and thus to live a meaningful existence.

A basic assumption of Gestalt therapy is that individuals have the capacity to "self-regulate" in their environment if they are fully aware of what is happening in and around them. Therapy provides the setting and opportunity for that awareness and contacting process to be supported and restored.

The Gestalt theory of change posits that the more we attempt to be who or what we are not, the more we remain the same. Beisser (1970) suggests that it is not possible to change something about ourselves by trying to be different. According to his paradoxical theory of change, we change when we become aware of what we are as opposed to trying to become what we are not. It is important for clients *to be* as fully as possible in their current position, rather than striving to become what they "should be." Rather than being a change agent, Beisser sees the role of the therapist as assisting the client to increase awareness, which will allow re-identification with the part of the self from which he or she is alienated (Breshgold, 1989).

Some Principles of Gestalt Therapy Theory

Several basic principles underlying the theory of Gestalt therapy are briefly described in this section: holism, field theory, the figure-formation process, and organismic self-regulation. Other key concepts of Gestalt therapy are developed in more detail in the sections that follow.

HOLISM   According to Latner (1986), holism is one of the foundational principles of Gestalt therapy. All of nature is seen as a unified and coherent whole, and the whole is different from the sum of its parts. We can only be understood to the extent that we take into consideration all dimensions of human functioning. Because Gestalt therapists are interested in the whole person, they place no superior value on a particular aspect of the individual. Gestalt practice attends to a client's thoughts, feelings, behaviors, body, and dreams. The emphasis is on integration, how the parts fit together, and how the individual makes contact with the environment.

FIELD THEORY   Gestalt therapy is based on field theory, which is grounded on the principle that the organism must be seen in its environment, or in its context, as part of the constantly changing field. Gestalt therapy rests on the principle that everything is relational, in flux, interrelated, and in process. Gestalt therapists pay attention to and explore what is occurring at the boundary between the person and the environment.

THE FIGURE-FORMATION PROCESS   Derived from the field of visual perception by a group of Gestalt psychologists, the figure-formation process describes how the individual organizes the environment from moment to moment. In Gestalt therapy the undifferentiated field is called the background, or ground, and the emerging focus of attention is called the figure (Latner, 1986). The figure-formation process tracks how some aspect of the environmental field emerges from the background and becomes the focal point of the individual's attention and interest. The dominant needs of an individual at a given moment influence this process (Frew, 1997).

ORGANISMIC SELF-REGULATION   The figure-formation process is intertwined with the principle of "organismic self-regulation," a process by which equilibrium is "disturbed" by the emergence of a need, a sensation, or an interest. Organisms will do their best to regulate themselves, given their own capabilities and the resources of their environment (Latner, 1986). Individuals can take actions and make contacts that will restore equilibrium or contribute to growth and change. In therapeutic work what emerges for the client is associated with what is of interest or what the client needs to be able to regain a sense of equilibrium. Gestalt therapists direct the client's awareness to the figures that emerge from the background during a therapy session and use the figure-formation process as a guide for the focus of therapeutic work.

The Now

The present is the most significant tense in Gestalt therapy. One of the main contributions of the Gestalt approach is its emphasis on learning to appreciate and fully experience the present moment. Focusing on the past can be a way to avoid coming to terms with the present.

In speaking of the "now ethos," E. Polster and Polster (1973) develop the thesis that "power is in the present." Many people invest their energies in bemoaning their past mistakes and ruminating about how life could and should have been different, or they engage in endless resolutions and plans for the future. As they direct their energy toward what was or what might have been, the power of the present diminishes.

To help the client make contact with the present moment, the Gestalt therapist asks "what" and "how" questions but rarely asks "why" questions. To promote "now" awareness, the therapist encourages a dialogue in the present tense by asking questions like these: What is happening now? What is going on now? What are you experiencing as you sit there and attempt to talk? What is your awareness at this moment? How are you experiencing your fear? How are you attempting to withdraw at this moment?

Most people can stay in the present for only a short while and are inclined to find ways of interrupting the flow of the present. Instead of experiencing their feelings in the here-and-now, clients often *talk about* their feelings, almost as if their feelings were detached from their present experiencing. A

Gestalt therapist's aim is to help clients make contact with their experience with vividness and immediacy. Thus, if a client begins to talk about sadness, pain, or confusion, the therapist makes every attempt to have the client experience that sadness, pain, or confusion *now*. As the client attends to the present experience, the therapist gauges how much anxiety or discomfort is present and chooses further interventions accordingly. The therapist might choose to allow the client to flee from the present moment, only to extend another invitation several minutes later. If a feeling emerges, the therapist might suggest an experiment that would help the client to become more aware of the feeling.

Gestalt therapists recognize that the past will make regular appearances in the present moment, usually because of some lack of completion of that past experience. When the past seems to have a significant bearing on clients' present attitudes or behavior, it is dealt with by bringing it into the present as much as possible. Thus, when clients speak about their past, the therapist may ask them to reenact it as though they were living it now. The therapist directs clients to "bring the fantasy here" and strive to relive the feelings they experienced earlier. For example, rather than talking about a past childhood trauma with her father, a client becomes the hurt child and talks directly to her father in fantasy.

One way to bring vitality to the therapy sessions is to pay attention to the immediacy and the quality of the relationship between client and therapist. In a recent book, *The Gift of Therapy,* Yalom (2003) provides an extensive explanation of the here-and-now emphasis in therapy and demonstrates how clients' interpersonal problems show up in the ongoing therapeutic relationship. Yalom gives many examples of how the here-and-now focus energizes the therapy process.

Unfinished Business

When figures emerge from the background but are not completed and resolved, individuals are left with unfinished business, which can be manifest in unexpressed feelings such as resentment, rage, hatred, pain, anxiety, grief, guilt, and abandonment. Because the feelings are not fully experienced in awareness, they linger in the background and are carried into present life in ways that interfere with effective contact with oneself and others. Unfinished business persists until the individual faces and deals with the unexpressed feelings. In speaking of the effects of unfinished business, E. Polster and Polster (1973) maintain that "these incomplete directions *do seek* completion and when they get powerful enough, the individual is beset with preoccupation, compulsive behavior, wariness, oppressive energy and much self-defeating behavior" (p. 36). The effects of unfinished business often show up in some blockage within the body. Gestalt therapists emphasize paying attention to the bodily experience on the assumption that if feelings are unexpressed they tend to result in some physical symptom.

Unacknowledged feelings create unnecessary emotional debris that clutters present-centered awareness. For example, in Stan's case we have a man who never really felt loved and accepted by his mother. No matter how he sought her approval, Stan was always left feeling that he was not adequate. In an attempt to deflect the direction of this need for maternal approval in the present, Stan may look to women for his confirmation of worth as a man. In developing a variety of games to get women to approve of him, Stan reports that he is still not satisfied. The unfinished business is preventing him from authentic intimacy with women, because his need is that of a child rather than an adult. Stan needs to return to the old business and express his unacknowledged feelings of disappointment to achieve closure. He will have to tolerate the uncomfortable feelings that accompany recognizing and working through this impasse.

The impasse, or *stuck point,* is the time when external support is not available or the customary way of being does not work. The therapist's task is to accompany the client in experiencing the impasse without rescuing or frustrating the client. The counselor assists clients by providing situations that encourage them to fully experience their condition of being stuck. By completely experiencing the impasse, they are able to get into contact with their frustrations and accept whatever is, rather than wishing they were different. Gestalt therapy is based on the notion that individuals have a striving toward actualization and growth and that if they accept all aspects of themselves without judging these dimensions they can begin to think, feel, and act differently.

Contact and Resistances to Contact

In Gestalt therapy contact is necessary if change and growth are to occur. When we make contact with the environment, change is inevitable. Contact is made by seeing, hearing, smelling, touching, and moving. Effective contact means interacting with nature and with other people without losing one's sense of individuality. It is the continually renewed creative adjustment of individuals to their environment (M. Polster, 1987). Prerequisites for good contact are clear awareness, full energy, and the ability to express oneself (Zinker, 1978). Miriam Polster claims that contact is the lifeblood of growth. It entails zest, imagination, and creativity. There are only moments of this type of contact, so it is most accurate to think of levels of contact rather than a final state to achieve. After a contact experience there is typically a withdrawal to integrate what has been learned. Gestalt therapists talk about the boundary, which has two functions: to connect and to separate. Both contact and withdrawal are necessary and important to healthy functioning.

The Gestalt therapist also focuses on resistances to contact, which are defenses we develop to prevent us from experiencing the present in a full and real way. E. Polster and Polster (1973) describe five major channels of resistance that are challenged in Gestalt therapy: introjection, projection, retroflection, deflection, and confluence.

Introjection is the tendency to uncritically accept others' beliefs and standards without assimilating them to make them congruent with who we are. These introjects remain alien to us because we have not analyzed and restructured them. When we introject, we passively incorporate what the environment provides, spending little time on becoming clear about what we want or need. If we remain in this stage, our energy is bound up in taking things as we find them.

Projection is the reverse of introjection. In projection we disown certain aspects of ourselves by assigning them to the environment. When we are projecting, we have trouble distinguishing between the inside world and the outside world. Those attributes of our personality that are inconsistent with our self-image are disowned and put onto other people. By seeing in others the very qualities that we refuse to acknowledge in ourselves, we avoid taking responsibility for our own feelings and the person who we are, and this keeps us powerless to initiate change.

Retroflection consists of turning back to ourselves what we would like to do to someone else or doing to ourselves what we would like someone else to do to us. If we lash out and injure ourselves, for example, we are often directing aggression inward that we are fearful of directing toward others. This process seriously restricts engagement between the person and his or her environment. Typically, these maladaptive styles of functioning are adopted out of our awareness; part of the process of Gestalt therapy is to help us discover a self-regulatory system so that we can deal realistically with the world.

Deflection is the process of distraction so that it is difficult to maintain a sustained sense of contact. People who deflect attempt to diffuse contact through the overuse of humor, abstract generalizations, and questions rather than statements (Frew, 1986). They engage their environment on an inconsistent basis, which results in their feeling a sense of emotional depletion. Deflection involves a diminished emotional experience. People who deflect speak through and for others.

Confluence involves a blurring of the differentiation between the self and the environment. For people who are oriented toward blending in, there is no clear demarcation between internal experience and outer reality. Confluence in relationships involves an absence of conflicts, or a belief that all parties experience the same feelings and thoughts. It is a style of contact characteristic of clients who have a high need to be accepted and liked. It is a way of staying safe by going along with others and not expressing one's true feelings and opinions. This condition makes genuine contact extremely difficult. A therapist might assist clients who use this channel of resistance by asking questions such as "What are you doing now? What are you experiencing at this moment? What do you want right now?"

Introjection, projection, retroflection, deflection, and confluence represent styles of resisting contact. The concern of Gestalt therapists is the interruption of contact with the environment when the individual is unaware of this process. Terms such as *resistance to contact* or *boundary disturbance* refer to the characteristic styles people employ in their attempts to control their environment. The premise in Gestalt therapy is that contact is both normal and healthy, and clients are encouraged to become increasingly aware of their dominant style of blocking contact.

Energy and Blocks to Energy

In Gestalt therapy special attention is given to where energy is located, how it is used, and how it can be blocked. Blocked energy is another form of resistance. It can be manifested by tension in some part of the body, by posture, by keeping one's body tight and closed, by not breathing deeply, by looking away from people when speaking as a way to avoid contact, by choking off sensations, by numbing feelings, and by speaking with a restricted voice, to mention only a few.

The Gestalt therapist is especially interested in interruptions between sensation and awareness, interruptions between awareness and mobilization of energy, and interruptions between mobilization of energy and action (Zinker, 1978). Much of the therapeutic endeavor involves finding the focus of interrupted energy and bringing these sensations to the client's awareness. Clients may not be aware of their energy or where it is located, and they may experience it in a negative way. Zinker believes therapy at its best involves a dynamic relationship that awakens and nourishes the client without sapping the therapist of his or her own energy. He maintains that it is the therapist's job to help clients locate the ways in which they are blocking energy and transform this blocked energy into more adaptive behaviors. Clients can be encouraged to recognize how their resistance is being expressed in their body. Rather than trying to rid themselves of certain bodily symptoms, clients can be encouraged to delve fully into tension states. By allowing themselves to exaggerate their tight mouth and shaking legs, they can discover for themselves how they are diverting energy and keeping themselves from a full expression of aliveness.

 THE THERAPEUTIC PROCESS

Therapeutic Goals

The basic goal of Gestalt therapy is attaining awareness and, with it, greater choice. Awareness includes knowing the environment, knowing oneself, accepting oneself, and being able to make contact. Increased and enriched awareness, by itself, is seen as curative. Without awareness clients do not possess the tools for personality change. With awareness they have the capacity to face and accept denied parts as well as to fully experience their subjectivity. They can become unified and whole. When clients stay with their awareness, important unfinished business will always emerge so that it can be dealt with in therapy. The Gestalt approach helps clients note their own awareness process so that they can be responsible and can selectively and discriminatingly make choices. Awareness emerges within the context of a genuine meeting between client and therapist, or within the context of I/Thou relating (Jacobs, 1989; Yontef, 1993).

The existential view (see Chapter 6) is that we are continually engaged in a process of remaking and discovering ourselves. We do not have a static identity but discover new facets of our being as we face new challenges. Gestalt therapy is basically an existential encounter out of which clients tend to move in certain directions. Through a creative involvement in Gestalt process, Zinker (1978) expects clients will:

- Move toward increased awareness of themselves
- Gradually assume ownership of their experience (as opposed to making others responsible for what they are thinking, feeling, and doing)
- Develop skills and acquire values that will allow them to satisfy their needs without violating the rights of others
- Become more aware of all of their senses
- Learn to accept responsibility for what they do, including accepting the consequences of their actions
- Move from outside support toward increasing internal support
- Be able to ask for and get help from others and be able to give to others

Therapist's Function and Role

Through engagement with clients, Gestalt therapists assist clients in developing their own awareness and experiencing how they *are* in the present moment. According to Perls, Hefferline, and Goodman (1951), the therapist's job is to invite clients into an active partnership where they can learn about themselves by adopting an experimental attitude toward life in which they try out new behaviors and notice what happens.

Gestalt therapists notice both what is in the foreground and the background. The therapist's job is to encourage clients to attend to their sensory awareness in the present moment. According to Yontef (1993), although the therapist functions as a guide and a catalyst, presents experiments, and shares observations, the basic work of therapy is done by the client. Yontef maintains that the therapist's job is to create a climate in which clients are likely to try out new ways of being and behaving. Gestalt therapists do not force change on clients through confrontation. Instead, they work within a context of I/Thou dialogue in a here-and-now framework.

An important function of Gestalt therapists is paying attention to clients' body language. These nonverbal cues provide rich information as they often represent feelings of which the client is unaware. The therapist needs to be alert for gaps in attention and awareness and for incongruities between verbalizations and what clients are doing with their bodies. For example, therapists might direct clients to speak for and become their gestures or body parts. Gestalt therapists often ask: "What do your eyes say?" "If your hands could speak at this moment, what would they say?" "Can you carry on a conversation between your right and left hands?" Clients may verbally express anger and at the same time smile. Or they may say they are in pain and at the same time laugh. Therapists can ask clients to become aware of how they are using their laughter to mask feelings of anger or pain.

In addition to calling attention to clients' nonverbal language, the Gestalt counselor places emphasis on the relationship between language patterns and personality. Clients' speech patterns are often an expression of their feelings, thoughts, and attitudes. The Gestalt approach focuses on overt speaking habits as a way to increase clients' awareness of themselves, especially by asking them to notice whether their words are congruent with what they are experiencing or instead are distancing them from their emotions.

The Gestalt counselor gently challenges clients by interventions that help them become aware of the effects of their language patterns. Language can both describe and conceal. By focusing on language, clients are able to increase their awareness of what they are experiencing in the present moment and of how they are avoiding coming into contact with this here-and-now experience. Here are some examples of the aspects of language that Gestalt therapists might focus on:

- *"It" talk.* When clients say "it" instead of "I," they are using depersonalizing language. The counselor may ask them to substitute personal pronouns for impersonal ones so that they will assume an increased sense of responsibility. For example, a client says, "It is difficult to make friends." She could be asked to restate this by making an "I" statement—"I have trouble making friends."
- *"You" talk.* Global and impersonal language tends to keep the person hidden. The therapist often points out generalized uses of "you" and asks the client to substitute "I" when this is what is meant.
- *Questions.* Questions have a tendency to keep the questioner hidden, safe, and unknown. Gestalt counselors often ask clients to change their questions into statements. In making personal statements, clients begin to assume responsibility for what they say. They may become aware of how they are keeping themselves mysterious through a barrage of questions and how this serves to prevent them from making declarations that express themselves.
- *Language that denies power.* Some clients have a tendency to deny their personal power by adding qualifiers or disclaimers to their statements. The therapist may also point out to clients how certain qualifiers subtract from their effectiveness. Experimenting with omitting qualifiers such as "maybe," "perhaps," "sort of," "I guess," "possibly," and "I suppose" can help clients change ambivalent messages into clear and direct statements. Likewise, when clients say "I can't," they are really implying "I won't." Asking clients to substitute "won't" for "can't" often assists them in owning and accepting their power by taking responsibility for their decisions. The counselor must be careful in intervening so that clients do not feel that everything they say is subject to scrutiny. Rather than fostering a morbid kind of introspection, the counselor hopes to foster awareness of what is really being expressed through words.
- *Listening to clients' metaphors.* In his workshops, Erv Polster emphasizes the importance of a therapist learning how to listen to the metaphors of

clients. By tuning in to metaphors, the therapist gets rich clues to clients' internal struggles. Examples of metaphors that can be amplified include client statements such as "It's hard for me to spill my guts in here." "At times I feel that I don't have a leg to stand on." "I feel like I have a hole in my soul." "I need to be prepared in case someone blasts me." "I felt ripped to shreds after you confronted me last week." "After this session, I feel as though I've been put through a meat grinder." Beneath the metaphor may lie a suppressed internal dialogue that represents critical unfinished business or reactions to a present interaction. For example, to the client who says she feels that she has been put through a meat grinder, the therapist could ask: "What is your experience of being ground meat?" or "Who is doing the grinding?" It is essential to encourage this client to say more about what she is experiencing. The art of therapy consists of translating the meaning of these metaphors into manifest content so that they can be dealt with in therapy.

■   *Listening for language that uncovers a story.* Polster (1995) also teaches the value of what he calls "fleshing out a flash." He reports that clients often use language that is elusive yet gives significant clues to a story that illustrates their life struggles. Effective therapists learn to pick out a small part of what someone says and then to focus on and develop this element. Clients are likely to slide over pregnant phrases, but the alert therapist can ask questions that will help them flesh out their story line. It is essential for therapists to pay attention to what is fascinating about the person who is sitting before them and get that person to tell a story.

In a workshop I observed Erv Polster's magnificent style in challenging a person (Joe) who had volunteered for a demonstration of an individual session. Although Joe had a fascinating story to reveal about a particular facet of his life, he was presenting himself in a lifeless manner, and the energy was going flat. Eventually, Polster asked him, "Are you keeping my interest right now? Does it matter to you whether I am engaged with you?" Joe looked shocked, but he soon got the point. He accepted Polster's challenge to make sure that he not only kept the therapist interested but also presented himself in a way to keep those in the audience interested. It was clear that Polster was directing Joe's attention to a process of *how* he was expressing his feelings and life experiences rather than being concerned with *what* he was talking about.

Polster believes storytelling is not always a form of resistance. Instead, it can be the heart of the therapeutic process. He maintains that people are storytelling beings. The therapist's task is to assist clients in telling their story in a lively way. Polster has mentioned that many people come to therapy to change the titles of their stories rather than to transform their life stories.

Client's Experience in Therapy

The general orientation of Gestalt therapy is toward dialogue. Whereas Fritz Perls would have said that clients must be confronted about how they avoid accepting responsibility, the dialogic attitude carried into Gestalt therapy originally by Laura Perls creates the ground for a meeting place between client and therapist. Other issues that can become the focal point of therapy include the client–therapist relationship and the similarities in the ways clients relate to the therapist and to others in their environment.

Gestalt therapists do not make interpretations that explain the dynamics of an individual's behavior or tell clients why they are acting in a certain way. Instead, truth is the result of the shared and phenomenologically refined experience of the therapist and the client (Yontef, 1999). Clients in Gestalt therapy are active participants who make their own interpretations and meanings. It is they who increase awareness and decide what they will or will not do with their personal meaning.

Miriam Polster (1987) describes a three-stage integration sequence that characterizes client growth in therapy. The first part of this sequence consists of *discovery*. Clients are likely to reach a new realization about themselves or to acquire a novel view of an old situation, or they may take a new look at some significant person in their lives. Such discoveries often come as a surprise to them.

The second stage of the integration sequence is *accommodation*, which involves clients' recognizing that they have a choice. Clients begin by trying out new behaviors in the supportive environment of the therapy office, and then they expand their awareness of the world. Making new choices is often done awkwardly, but with support clients can gain skill in coping with difficult situations. Clients are likely to carry out homework assignments that are aimed at achieving success. If an out-of-office experiment does not go well, the client and therapist can explore what went wrong and why. The discussion can move forward into new action by asking what can be done differently next time.

The third stage of the integration sequence is *assimilation*, which involves clients' learning how to influence their environment. At this phase clients feel capable of dealing with the surprises they encounter in everyday living. They are now beginning to do more than passively accept the environment. Behavior at this stage may include taking a stand on a critical issue. Eventually, clients develop confidence in their ability to improve and improvise. Improvisation is the confidence that comes from knowledge and skills. Clients are able to make choices that will result in getting what they want. The therapist points out that something has been accomplished and acknowledges the changes that have taken place within the client. At this phase clients have learned what they can do to maximize their chances of getting what is needed from their environment.

Relationship Between Therapist and Client

As an existential brand of therapy, Gestalt practice involves a person-to-person relationship between therapist and client. Therapists are responsible for the quality of their presence, for knowing themselves and the client, and for remaining open to the client. They are also responsible for establishing and maintaining a therapeutic atmosphere that will foster a spirit of work on the client's part. The therapist's experiences, awareness, and perceptions provide the background of the therapy process, and the client's awareness and reactions constitute the foreground. It is important that therapists allow themselves to be affected by their clients and that they actively share their own present perceptions and experiences as they encounter clients in the here-and-now.

Gestalt therapists not only allow their clients to be who they are but also remain themselves and do not get lost in a role. They are willing to express their reactions and observations, they share their personal experience and stories in relevant and appropriate ways, and they do not manipulate clients. Further, they give feedback that allows clients to develop an awareness of what they are actually doing. The therapist must encounter clients with honest and immediate reactions and explore with them their fears, catastrophic expectations, blockages, and resistances.

A number of writers have given central importance to the I/Thou relationship and the quality of the therapist's presence, as opposed to technical skills. They warn of the dangers of becoming technique-bound and losing sight of their own being as they engage the client. The therapist's attitudes and behavior and the relationship that is established are what really count (Jacobs, 1989; E. Polster, 1987a, 1987b; M. Polster, 1987; Yontef, 1993, 1995; Yontef & Jacobs, 2000). These writers point out that current Gestalt therapy has moved beyond earlier therapeutic practices. Cain (2002) summarizes some major shifts in the development of Gestalt therapy:

> Since Perls's death in 1970, the practice of Gestalt therapy has softened and shifted its emphases toward the quality of the therapist– client relationship, dialogue, empathic attunement, tapping the client's wisdom and resources, an expansion of therapeutic styles, and development of theory, especially field theory and phenomenology. (p. 31)

Many contemporary Gestalt therapists place increasing emphasis on factors such as presence, authentic dialogue, gentleness, more direct self-expression by the therapist, decreased use of stereotypic exercises, and greater trust in the client's experiencing. Laura Perls (1976) expresses well this notion that the person of the therapist is more important than the techniques he or she uses:

> A Gestalt therapist does not use techniques; he applies *himself in* and *to* a situation with whatever professional skill and life experience he has accumulated and integrated. There are as many styles as there are therapists and clients who discover themselves and each other and together invent their relationship. (p. 223)

E. Polster and Polster (1973) emphasize the importance of therapists knowing themselves and being therapeutic instruments. Like artists who need to be in touch with what they are painting, therapists are artistic participants in the creation of new life. The Polsters implore therapists to use their own experiences as essential ingredients in the therapy process. According to them, therapists are more than mere responders or catalysts. If they are to function effectively, therapists must be in tune with both their clients and themselves. Therapy is a two-way engagement that changes both the client and the therapist. If therapists are not sensitively tuned to their own qualities of tenderness, toughness, and compassion and to their reactions to the client, they become technicians.

In a seminal article, "Dialogue in Gestalt Theory and Therapy," Jacobs (1989) explores the role of the therapeutic relationship as a factor in healing and the extent to which the client–therapist relationship is the focus of therapy. She shows how Martin Buber's philosophy of dialogue, which involves a genuine and loving meeting, is congruent with Gestalt concepts of contact, awareness, and the paradoxical theory of change. Jacobs asserts that a current trend in Gestalt practice is toward greater emphasis on the client–therapist relationship rather than on techniques divorced from the context of this encounter. She believes therapists who operate from this orientation establish a present-centered, nonjudgmental dialogue that allows clients to deepen their awareness and to find contact with another person.

The interventions that therapists use evolve out of this process. Experiments should be aimed at awareness, not at simple solutions to a client's problem. Jacobs maintains that if therapists use experiments when they are frustrated with a client and want to change the person, they are misusing the experiments and will probably thwart rather than foster growth and change.

 ## APPLICATION: THERAPEUTIC TECHNIQUES AND PROCEDURES

The Experiment in Gestalt Therapy

Although the Gestalt approach is concerned with the obvious, its simplicity should not be taken to mean that the therapist's job is easy. Developing a variety of interventions is simple, but employing these methods in a mechanical fashion allows clients to continue inauthentic living. If clients are to become authentic, they need contact with an authentic therapist. In *Creative Process in Gestalt Therapy,* Zinker (1978) emphasizes the role of the therapist as a creative agent of change, an inventor, and a compassionate and caring human being. Dr. John Frew, a Gestalt therapist, demonstrates Gestalt interventions applied to the case of Ruth in *Case Approach to Counseling and Psychotherapy* (Corey, 2005, chap. 6).

Before discussing the variety of Gestalt methods you could include in your repertoire of counseling procedures, it is helpful to differentiate between exercises (or techniques) and experiments. *Exercises* are ready-made techniques that are sometimes used to make something happen in a therapy session or to achieve a goal. They can be catalysts for individual work or for promoting interaction among members of a therapy group. *Experiments,* in contrast, grow out of the interaction between client and therapist. They can be considered the very cornerstone of experiential learning.

The experiment is fundamental to contemporary Gestalt therapy. Zinker (1978) sees therapy sessions as a series of experiments, which are the avenues for clients to learn experientially. What is learned from an experiment is a surprise to both the client and the counselor. Gestalt experiments are a creative adventure and a way in which clients can express themselves behaviorally. Experiments are spontaneous, one-of-a-kind, and relevant to a particular moment and a particular development of a figure-formation process. They are not designed to achieve a particular goal but occur in the context of a moment-to-moment contacting process between therapist and client. Polster (1995) indicates that experiments are designed by the therapist and evolve from the theme already developing through therapeutic engagement, such as the client's report of needs, dreams, fantasies, and body awareness. Gestalt therapists invite clients to engage in experiments that lead to fresh emotional experiencing and new insights (Strumpfel & Goldman, 2002). Experimentation is an attitude inherent in all Gestalt therapy; it is a collaborative process with full participation of the client. Clients test an experiment to determine what does and does not fit for them through their own awareness (Yontef, 1993, 1995).

Miriam Polster (1987) says that an experiment is a way to bring out some kind of internal conflict by making this struggle an actual process. It is aimed at facilitating a client's ability to work through the stuck points of his or her life. Experiments encourage spontaneity and inventiveness by bringing the possibilities for action directly into the therapy session. By dramatizing or playing out problem situations or relationships in the relative safety of the therapy context, clients increase their range of flexibility of behavior. According to Polster, Gestalt experiments can take many forms: imagining a threatening future encounter; setting up a dialogue between a client and some significant person in his or her life; dramatizing the memory of a painful event; reliving a particularly profound early experience in the present; assuming the identity of one's mother or father through role playing; focusing on gestures, posture, and other nonverbal signs of inner expression; or carrying on a dialogue between two conflicting aspects within the person. Through these experiments, clients actually experience the feelings associated with their conflicts. Experiments bring struggles to life by inviting clients to enact them in the present. It is crucial that experiments be tailored to each individual and used in a timely manner; they also need to be carried out in a context that offers a balance between support and risk. Sensitivity and careful attention on the therapist's part is essential so that clients are "neither blasted into experiences that are too threatening nor allowed to stay in safe but infertile territory" (M. Polster & Polster, 1990, p. 104).

Preparing Clients for Gestalt Experiments

If students-in-training limit their understanding of Gestalt therapy to simply reading about the approach, Gestalt methods are likely to seem abstract and the notion of experiments may seem strange. Asking clients to "become" an object in one of their dreams, for instance, may seem silly and pointless. It is important for counselors to *personally* experience the power of Gestalt experiments and to feel comfortable suggesting them to clients.

It is also essential that counselors establish a relationship with their clients, so that the clients will feel trusting enough to participate in the learning that can result from Gestalt experiments. Clients will get more from Gestalt experiments if they are oriented and prepared for them. Through a trusting relationship with the therapist, clients are likely to recognize their resistance and allow themselves to participate in these experiments.

If clients are to cooperate, counselors must avoid directing them in a commanding fashion to carry out an experiment. Typically, I ask clients if they are willing to try out an experiment to see what they might learn from it. I also tell clients that they can stop when they choose to, so the power is with them. Clients at times say that they feel silly or self-conscious or that the task feels artificial or unreal. At such times I am likely to respond: "Oh, why not go ahead and be silly? Will the roof cave in if you act foolish? Are you willing to give it a try and see what happens?"

I cannot overemphasize the power of the therapeutic relationship and the necessity for trust as the foundation for implementing any experiment. If I meet with resistance, I tend to be interested in exploring the client's reluctance. It is helpful to know the reason the client is stopping. Reluctance to become emotionally involved often is a function of the client's cultural background. Some clients have been conditioned to work hard to maintain emotional control. They may have reservations about expressing intense feelings openly, even if they are in an emotional state. This can well be due to their socialization and to cultural norms they abide by. In some cultures it is considered rude to express emotions openly, and there are certain cultural injunctions against showing one's vulnerability or psychological pain. If clients have had a long history of containing their feelings, it is understandable that they will be reluctant to participate in experiments that are likely to bring their emotions to the surface. Of course, many men have been socialized not to express intense feelings. Their reluctance to allow themselves to be emotional needs to be dealt with in a respectful manner.

Other clients may resist becoming emotionally involved because of their fear, lack of trust, concern over losing control, or some other concern. The *way* in which clients resist doing an experiment reveals a great deal about their personality and their way of being in the world. Therefore, Gestalt therapists expect and respect the emergence of resistance. The therapist's aim is not to eliminate clients' defenses but to meet clients wherever they are.

One way of conceptualizing resistance from a Gestalt perspective is to view it as a resistance to awareness of aspects of self or aspects of the environment. This may take the form of resistance to awareness of a part of the personality that was originally alienated because the painful feelings could not be tolerated. The Gestalt approach brings resistance into awareness so that more direct expression becomes possible. Through this process clients are able to re-identify with previously disowned thoughts, feelings, or impulses (Perls, Hefferline, & Goodman, 1951).

The essence of current Gestalt therapy involves honoring and respecting resistance and supporting the client to become more aware of his or her experience. This therapy approach places much less emphasis on resistance than the early version of Gestalt therapy. In fact, the current view proposes that the term "resistance" is actually incompatible with the philosophical and theoretical tenets of Gestalt therapy (Breshgold, 1989). Although it is possible to look at "resistance to awareness" and "resistance to contact," the idea of resistance is unnecessary to the Gestalt perspective. E. Polster and Polster (1976) suggest that instead of attempting to make something happen it is best for therapists to observe what is actually and presently happening. This gets away from the notion that clients are resisting and thus behaving wrongly. According to the Polsters, change occurs through contact and awareness—one does not have to try to change.

It is well to remember that Gestalt experiments are designed to expand clients' awareness and to help them try out new modes of behavior. Within the safety of the therapeutic situation, clients are given opportunities and encouraged to "try on" a new behavior. This heightens the awareness of a particular aspect of functioning, which leads to increased self-understanding (Breshgold, 1989; Yontef, 1995). Experiments are only means to the end of helping people change, not ends in themselves. The following guidelines, largely taken from Passons (1975) and Zinker (1978), are useful both in preparing clients for Gestalt experiments and in carrying them out in the course of therapy:

- It is important for the counselor to be sensitive enough to know when to leave the client alone.
- To derive maximum benefit from Gestalt experiments, the practitioner must be sensitive to introducing them at the right time and in an appropriate manner.
- The nature of the experiment depends on the individual's problems, what the person is experiencing, and the life experiences that both the client and the therapist bring to the session.
- Experiments require the client's active role in self-exploration.
- Gestalt experiments work best when the therapist is respectful of the client's cultural background and is in good contact with the person.
- If the therapist meets with hesitation, it is a good idea to explore its meaning for the client.
- It is important that the therapist be flexible in using techniques, paying particular attention to how the client is responding.
- The counselor should be ready to scale down tasks so that the client has a good chance to succeed in his or her efforts. It is not helpful to suggest experiments that are too advanced for a client.
- The therapist needs to learn which experiments can best be practiced in the session itself and which can best be performed outside.

The Role of Confrontation

Students are sometimes put off by their perception that a Gestalt counselor's style is direct and confrontational. I tell my students that it is a mistake to equate the practice of any theory with its founder. Indeed, the contemporary practice of Gestalt therapy has progressed beyond the style exhibited by Fritz Perls. Yontef (1993) refers to the Perlsian style as a "boom-boom-boom therapy" characterized by theatrics, abrasive confrontation, and intense catharsis. He implies that the charismatic style of Perls probably met more of his own narcissistic needs than the needs of his clients. Yontef (1993, 1999) is critical of the anti-intellectual, individualistic, dramatic, and confrontational flavor that characterized Gestalt therapy in the "anything goes environment" of the 1960s and 1970s. According to Yontef (1999), the newer version, which has been called "relational Gestalt therapy," has evolved to include more support and increased kindness and compassion in therapy. This approach "combines sustained empathic inquiry with crisp, clear, and relevant awareness focusing" (p. 10). Perls practiced a highly confrontational approach as a way to deal with avoidance. It is to be noted that this confrontational model is not representative of Gestalt therapy as it is currently being practiced (Yontef & Jacobs, 2000). Although there is now less emphasis on confrontation in Gestalt practice, this should not be taken to mean that confrontation is absent.

The style of the therapist and the environment that he or she creates has a great deal to do with a client's willingness to participate in experiments. Frew (1992) talks of three therapy styles—the imposing, competing, and confirming stances. He describes both the imposing stance and the competing stance as being confrontational. Using the *imposing stance,* the therapist is less concerned with understanding and respecting the client's experience than in meeting his or her own agenda for the client. The therapist is the expert who evaluates, diagnoses, confronts, interprets, and dominates the relationship. It is a position of power and control, with little attention paid to what the client wants from the therapist. Using the *competing stance,* the therapist promotes the ethos of rugged individualism. In the competing environment there is a dance of negotiation, compromise, and a process of give and take. In contrast, in the *confirming stance* the therapist is interested in acknowledging the whole being of the client. At the moment of confirmation, the client's needs and experience become the center of the relationship. Frew states that the confirming posture demands curiosity and patience, restraint and trust, and compassion and confidence. The therapist attends to the client's experience without forcing the client to be other than he or she is. By staying with the client's awareness, the therapist provides the ground for freer functioning and change.

Confrontation is used at times in the practice of Gestalt therapy, yet it does not have to be viewed as a harsh attack. Confrontation can be done in such a way that clients cooperate, especially when they are *invited* to examine their behaviors, attitudes, and thoughts. Therapists can encourage clients to look at certain incongruities, especially gaps between their verbal and nonverbal expression. Further, confrontation does not have to be aimed at weaknesses or negative traits; clients can be challenged to recognize how they are blocking their strengths and are not living as fully as they might.

An essential ingredient in effective confrontation is respect for the client. Counselors who care enough to make demands on their clients are telling them, in effect, that they could be in fuller contact with themselves and others. Ultimately, however, clients must decide for themselves if they want to accept this invitation to learn more about themselves. This caveat needs to be kept in mind with all of the experiments that are to be described.

Gestalt Therapy Interventions

Experiments can be useful tools to help the client gain fuller awareness, experience internal conflicts, resolve inconsistencies and dichotomies, and work through an impasse that is preventing completion of unfinished business.

Levitsky and Perls (1970) provide a brief description of a number of interventions used by Gestalt therapists, some of which I will describe here. I have modified this material and added suggestions for implementing these methods. As mentioned earlier, these exercises can be used to elicit emotion, produce action, or achieve a specific goal. When used at their best, these interventions fit the therapeutic situation and highlight whatever the client is experiencing.

THE INTERNAL DIALOGUE EXERCISE   One goal of Gestalt therapy is to bring about integrated functioning and acceptance of aspects of one's personality that have been disowned and denied. Gestalt therapists pay close attention to splits in personality function. A main division is between the "top dog" and the "underdog," and therapy often focuses on the war between the two.

The top dog is righteous, authoritarian, moralistic, demanding, bossy, and manipulative. This is the "critical parent" that badgers with "shoulds" and "oughts" and manipulates with threats of catastrophe. The underdog manipulates by playing the role of victim: by being defensive, apologetic, helpless, and weak and by feigning powerlessness. This is the passive side, the one without responsibility, and the one that finds excuses. The top dog and the underdog are engaged in a constant struggle for control. The struggle helps to explain why one's resolutions and promises often go unfulfilled and why one's procrastination persists. The tyrannical top dog demands that one be thus-and-so, whereas the underdog defiantly plays the role of disobedient child. As a result of this struggle for control, the individual becomes fragmented into controller and controlled. The civil war between the two sides continues, with both sides fighting for their existence.

The conflict between the two opposing poles in the personality is rooted in the mechanism of introjection, which involves incorporating aspects of others, usually parents, into one's ego system. It is essential that clients become aware of their introjects, especially the toxic introjects that poison the system and prevent personality integration.

The empty-chair technique is one way of getting the client to externalize the introject, a technique Perls used a great deal. Using two chairs, the therapist asks the client to sit in one chair and be fully the top dog and then shift to the other chair and become the underdog. The dialogue can continue between both sides of the client. Essentially, this is a role-playing technique in which all the parts are played by the client. In this way the introjects can surface, and the client can experience the conflict more fully. The conflict can be resolved by the client's acceptance and integration of both sides. This exercise helps clients get in touch with a feeling or a side of themselves that they may be denying; rather than merely talking about a conflicted feeling, they intensify the feeling and experience it fully. Further, by helping clients realize that the feeling is a very real part of themselves, the intervention discourages them from disassociating the feeling.

The goal of this exercise is to promote a higher level of integration between the polarities and conflicts that exist in everyone. The aim is not to rid oneself of certain traits but to learn to accept and live with the polarities.

MAKING THE ROUNDS   Making the rounds is a Gestalt exercise that involves asking a person in a group to go up to others in the group and either speak to or do something with each person. The purpose is to confront, to risk, to disclose the self, to experiment with new behavior, and to grow and change. I have experimented with "making the rounds" when I sensed that a participant needed to face each person in the group with some theme. For example, a group member might say: "I've been sitting here for a long time wanting to participate but holding back because I'm afraid of trusting people in here. And besides, I don't think I'm worth the time of the group anyway." I might counter with "Are you willing to do something right now to get yourself more invested and to begin to work on gaining trust and self-confidence?" If the person answers affirmatively, my suggestion could well be: "Go around to each person and finish this sentence: 'What makes it hard for me trust you is . . .'" Any number of exercises could be invented to help individuals involve themselves and choose to work on the things that keep them frozen in fear.

Some other related illustrations and examples that I find appropriate for the making-the-rounds intervention are reflected in clients' comments such as these: "I would like to reach out to people more often." "Nobody in here seems to care very much." "I'd like to make contact with you, but I'm afraid of being rejected [or accepted]." "It's hard for me to accept good stuff; I always discount good things people say to me."

THE REVERSAL EXERCISE   Certain symptoms and behaviors often represent reversals of underlying or latent impulses. Thus, the therapist could ask a person who claims to suffer from severe inhibitions and excessive timidity to play the role of an exhibitionist. I remember a client in one of our groups who had difficulty being anything but sugary sweet. I asked her to reverse her typical style and be as negative as she could be. The reversal worked well; soon she was playing her part with real gusto, and later she was able to recognize and accept her "negative side" as well as her "positive side."

The theory underlying the reversal technique is that clients take the plunge into the very thing that is fraught with anxiety and make contact with those parts of themselves that have been submerged and denied. This technique can help clients begin to accept certain personal attributes that they have tried to deny.

THE REHEARSAL EXERCISE   Oftentimes we get stuck rehearsing silently to ourselves so that we will gain acceptance. When it comes to the performance, we experience stage fright, or anxiety, because we fear that we will not play our role well. Internal rehearsal consumes much energy and frequently inhibits our spontaneity and willingness to experiment with new behavior. When clients share their rehearsals out loud with a therapist, they become more aware of the many preparatory means they use in bolstering their social roles. They also become increasingly aware of how they try to meet the expectations of others, of the degree to which they want to be approved, accepted, and liked, and of the extent to which they go to attain acceptance.

THE EXAGGERATION EXERCISE   One aim of Gestalt therapy is for clients to become more aware of the subtle signals and cues they are sending through body language. Movements, postures, and gestures may communicate significant meanings, yet the cues may be incomplete. In this exercise the person is asked to exaggerate the movement or gesture repeatedly, which usually intensifies the feeling attached to the behavior and makes the inner meaning clearer. Some examples of behaviors that lend themselves to the exaggeration technique are trembling (shaking hands, legs), slouched posture and bent shoulders, clenched fists, tight frowning, facial grimacing, crossed arms, and so forth. If a client reports that his or her legs are shaking, for instance, the therapist may ask the client to stand up and exaggerate the shaking. Then the therapist may ask the client to put words to the shaking limbs.

STAYING WITH THE FEELING   Most clients desire to escape from fearful stimuli and to avoid unpleasant feelings. At key moments when clients refer to a feeling or a mood that is unpleasant and from which they have a great urge to flee, the therapist may urge the clients to stay with their feeling. The therapist may encourage them to go deeper into the feeling or behavior they wish to avoid. Facing, confronting, and experiencing feelings not only takes courage but also is a mark of a willingness to endure the pain necessary for unblocking and making way for newer levels of growth.

THE GESTALT APPROACH TO DREAM WORK   In psychoanalysis dreams are interpreted, intellectual insight is stressed, and free association is used to explore the unconscious meanings of dreams. The Gestalt approach does not interpret and analyze dreams. Instead, the intent is to bring dreams back to life and relive them as though they were happening now. The dream is acted out in the present, and the dreamer becomes a part of his or her dream. The suggested format for working with dreams includes making a list of all the details of the dream, remembering each person, event, and mood in it, and then becoming each of these parts by transforming oneself, acting as fully as possible and inventing dialogue. Each part of the dream is assumed to be a projection of the self, and the client creates scripts for encounters between the various characters or parts. All of the different parts of a dream are expressions of the client's own contradictory and inconsistent sides, and, by engaging in a dialogue between these opposing sides, the client gradually becomes more aware of the range of his or her own feelings.

Perls's concept of projection is central in his theory of dream formation. According to him, every person and every object in the dream represents a projected aspect of the dreamer. Perls (1969a) suggests that "we start with the impossible assumption that whatever we believe we see in another person or in the world is nothing but a projection" (p. 67). He writes that the recognition of the senses and the understanding of projections go hand in hand. Clients do not think about or analyze the dream but use it as a script and experiment with the dialogue among the various parts of the dream. Because clients can act out a fight between opposing sides, eventually they can appreciate and accept their inner differences and integrate the opposing forces. Freud called the dream the royal road to the unconscious, but to Perls dreams are the "royal road to integration" (p. 66).

According to Perls, the dream is the most spontaneous expression of the existence of the human being. It represents an unfinished situation, but every dream also contains an existential message regarding oneself and one's current struggle. Everything can be found in dreams if all the parts are understood and assimilated. Perls asserts that if dreams are properly worked with, the existential message becomes clearer. According to him, dreams serve as an excellent way to discover personality voids by revealing missing parts and clients' methods of avoidance. If people do not remember dreams, they may be refusing to face what is wrong with their life. At the very least, the Gestalt counselor asks clients to talk to their missing dreams. For example, as directed by her therapist, a client reported the following dream in the present tense, as though she were still dreaming:

> I have three monkeys in a cage. One big monkey and two little ones! I feel very attached to these monkeys, although they are creating a lot of chaos in a cage that is divided into three separate spaces. They are fighting with one another—the big monkey is fighting with the little monkey. They are getting out of the cage, and they are clinging onto me. I feel like pushing them away from me. I feel totally overwhelmed by the chaos that they are creating around me. I turn

to my mother and tell her that I need help, that I can no longer handle these monkeys because they are driving me crazy. I feel very sad and very tired, and I feel discouraged. I am walking away from the cage, thinking that I really love these monkeys, yet I have to get rid of them. I am telling myself that I am like everybody else. I get pets, and then when things get rough, I want to get rid of them. I am trying very hard to find a solution to keeping these monkeys and not allowing them to have such a terrible effect on me. Before I wake up from my dream, I am making the decision to put each monkey in a separate cage, and maybe that is the way to keep them.

The therapist then asked his client, Brenda, to "become" different parts of her dream. Thus, she became the cage, and she became and had a dialogue with each monkey, and then she became her mother, and so forth. One of the most powerful aspects of this technique was Brenda's reporting her dream as though it were still happening. She quickly perceived that her dream expressed a struggle she was having with her husband and her two children. From her dialogue work, Brenda discovered that she both appreciated and resented her family. She learned that she needed to let them know about her feelings and that together they might work on improving an intensely difficult lifestyle. She did not need an interpretation from her therapist to understand the clear message of her dream.

 # GESTALT THERAPY FROM A MULTICULTURAL PERSPECTIVE

Contributions to Multicultural Counseling

There are opportunities to sensitively and creatively use Gestalt methods with culturally diverse populations if interventions are timed appropriately. One of the advantages of drawing on Gestalt experiments is that they can be tailored to fit the unique way in which an individual perceives and interprets his or her culture. Gestalt therapists approach each client in an open way and without preconceptions. This is particularly important in working with clients from other cultures.

Gestalt therapy is particularly effective in helping people integrate the polarities within themselves. Many bicultural clients experience an ongoing struggle to reconcile what appear to be diverse aspects of the two cultures in which they live. In one of my weeklong groups, a dynamic piece of work was done by a woman with European roots. Her struggle consisted of integrating her American side with her experiences in Germany as a child. I asked her to "bring her family into this group" by talking to selected members in the group as though they were members of her family. She was asked to imagine that she was 8 years old and that she could now say to her parents and siblings things that she had never expressed. I asked her to speak in German (since

Gestalt Therapy Applied to the Case of Stan

The Gestalt-oriented therapist will focus on the unfinished business that Stan has with his parents, siblings, and ex-wife. It appears that this unfinished business consists mainly of feelings of resentment, yet he turns this resentment inward toward himself. His present life situation will be spotlighted, but he may also need to reexperience past feelings that could be interfering with his present attempts to develop intimacy with others.

Although the focus is on Stan's present behavior, his therapist is likely to guide him toward becoming aware of how he is carrying old baggage around and how it interferes with his life today. Her task is to assist him in re-creating the context in which he made earlier decisions that are no longer serving him well. Essentially, Stan needs to learn that his decision about his way of being during his childhood years may no longer be appropriate. One of his cardinal decisions was: "I'm stupid, and it would be better if I were not here. I'm a loser."

Stan has been influenced by cultural messages that he has accepted. His counselor is interested in exploring his cultural background, including his values and the values characteristic of his culture. With this focus, it is likely that the counselor may help Stan identify some of the following cultural injunctions: "Don't talk about your family with strangers, and don't hang out your dirty linen in public." "Don't confront your parents, because they deserve respect." "Don't be too concerned about yourself." "Don't show your vulnerabilities; hide your feelings and weaknesses." Stan's counselor may challenge Stan to examine those injunctions that are no longer functional. Although he can decide to retain those aspects of his cultural background that he prizes, he is also in a position to modify certain cultural expectations. Of course, this will be done when these issues emerge in the foreground of his work.

Stan's therapist encourages him to attend to what becomes figural as the session begins. She may make interventions such as "What are you experiencing as we are getting started today?" As she encourages Stan to tune into his present experience and selectively makes observations, it is likely that a number of figures will emerge. The goal is to focus on a figure of interest that seems to hold the most energy or relevance for Stan. When a figure is identified, the task is to deepen Stan's awareness of this thought, feeling, body sensation, or insight through related experiments. The therapist designs these experiments to create awareness or to create contact possibilities between Stan and herself. Stan's therapist places value on practicing Gestalt therapy dialogically, which means that she aims to be as fully present as possible and is interested in understanding Stan's world. She will make decisions about how much self-disclosure to make, which will be done for Stan's benefit and to strengthen the therapeutic relationship.

In typical Gestalt fashion, Stan deals with his present struggles within the context of the relationship with his therapist, not simply by talking about his past or by analyzing his insights. She may ask him to "become" some of those individuals who told him how to think, feel, and behave as a child. He can then become the child that he was and respond to them from the place where he feels the most confusion or pain. He experiences in new ways the feelings that accompany his beliefs about himself, and he comes to a deeper appreciation of how his feelings and thoughts influence what he is doing today.

Stan has learned to hide his emotions rather than to reveal them. Understanding this about him, his counselor explores his hesitations and concerns about "getting into feelings." She recognizes that he is hesitant in expressing his emotions and helps him assess whether he would like to experience them more fully and express them more freely.

When Stan decides that he does want to experience his emotions rather than deny them, the therapist asks: "What are you aware of now having said what you did?" Stan says that he can't get his ex-wife out of his mind. He tells the therapist how he feels so much pain over that relationship and how he is frightened of getting involved again lest he be hurt another time. The therapist continues to ask Stan to focus inward and get a better sense of what is standing out for him at this very moment. Stan replies: "I'm hurt and angry over all the pain that I've allowed her to inflict on me." She asks him to imagine himself in earlier scenes with his ex-wife, as though the painful situation were occurring in

(continued on next page)

the here-and-now. He symbolically relives and reexperiences the situation, perhaps by talking "directly" to his wife. He tells her of his resentments and hurts and eventually moves toward completing his unfinished business with her. By participating in this experiment, Stan is attaining more awareness of what he is now doing and how he keeps himself locked into his past.

Once an experiment is agreed on, it is enacted and debriefed. At this point, depending on time constraints, the session ends or Stan is invited to attend to the next prominent figure that emerges. The art of practicing Gestalt therapy consists of blending the therapist's figure formation with the client's. Stan's figure should be the sovereign one, with the therapist bringing her own ideas, observations, and feelings into contact with Stan to influence his process. The therapist's disclosures can add to and deepen Stan's exploration of key issues, but to make appropriate choices, the therapist's experience, timing, and attunement are crucial.

Follow-Up: You Continue as Stan's Gestalt Therapist

Use these questions to help you think about how to counsel Stan using the Gestalt approach:

- How might you begin a session with Stan? As a Gestalt therapist, would you suggest a direction he pursue? Would you wait for him to initiate work? Would you ask him to continue from where he left off in the previous session? Would you attend to whatever theme or issue becomes figural to him?
- What unfinished business can you identify in Stan's case? Does any of his experience of being stuck remind you of aspects within yourself? As his Gestalt therapist, how might you work with Stan if he did bring up your own unfinished business?
- Stan's Gestalt therapist created an experiment to assist Stan in dealing with pain, resentment, and hurt over situations with his ex-wife. How might you have worked with the material Stan brought up? What kind of experiment might you design? How would you decide what kind of experiment to create?
- How might you work with Stan's cultural messages? Would you be able to respect his cultural values and still encourage him to make an assessment of some of the ways in which his culture is affecting him today?

---

this was her primary language as a child). The combined factors of her trust in the group, her willingness to re-create an early scene by reliving it in the present moment, and her symbolic work with fantasy helped her achieve a significant breakthrough. She was able to put a new ending to an old and unfinished situation through her participation in this Gestalt experiment.

There are many opportunities to apply Gestalt experiments in creative ways with diverse client populations. In cultures where indirect speech is the norm, nonverbal behaviors may emphasize the unspoken content of verbal communication. These clients may express themselves nonverbally more expressively than they do with words. Gestalt therapists may ask clients to focus on their gestures, facial expressions, and what they are experiencing within their own body. One of the advantages of drawing on Gestalt experiments is that they can be tailored to fit the unique way in which an individual perceives and interprets his or her culture. Gestalt therapists approach their clients with an open mind and without preconceptions. This is essential in working with clients from other cultures. Moreover, Gestalt therapists attempt to fully understand the background of their clients' culture. They are concerned about how and which aspects of this background become central or figural for their clients and what meaning clients place on these figures.

Limitations for Multicultural Counseling

To a greater extent than is true of most other approaches, there are definite hazards in too quickly utilizing some Gestalt experiments with ethnic minority clients. Gestalt methods tend to produce a high level of intense feelings. This focus on affect has some clear limitations with those clients who have been culturally conditioned to be emotionally reserved. As mentioned earlier, some clients believe expressing feelings openly is a sign of weakness and a display of one's vulnerability. Counselors who operate on the assumption that catharsis is necessary for any change to occur are likely to find certain clients becoming increasingly resistant, and such clients may prematurely terminate counseling. Other clients have strong cultural injunctions prohibiting them from directly expressing their emotions to their parents (such as "Never show your parents that you are angry at them" or "Strive for peace and harmony, and avoid conflicts"). I recall a client from India who was asked by his counselor to "bring your father into the room." The client was very reluctant to even symbolically tell his father of his disappointment with their relationship. In his culture the accepted way to deal with his father was to use his uncle as a go-between, and it was considered highly inappropriate to express any negative feelings toward one's father. The client later said that he would have felt very guilty if he had symbolically told his father what he sometimes thought and felt.

Gestalt therapists who have truly integrated their approach are sensitive enough to practice in a flexible way. They consider the client's cultural framework and are able to adapt methods that are likely to be well received. They strive to help clients experience themselves as fully as possible in the present, yet they are not rigidly bound by dictates, nor do they routinely intervene whenever clients stray from the present. Sensitively staying in contact with a client's flow of experiencing entails the ability to focus on the person and not on the mechanical use of techniques for a certain effect.

 SUMMARY AND EVALUATION

Summary

Gestalt therapy is an experiential approach that stresses present awareness and the quality of contact between the individual and the environment. The major focus is on assisting the client to become aware of how behaviors once part of creatively adjusting to past environments may be interfering with effective functioning and living in the present. The goal of the approach is, first and foremost, to gain awareness.

Another therapeutic aim is to assist clients in exploring how they make contact with elements of their environment. Change occurs through the heightened awareness of "what is." Because the Gestalt therapist has no agenda beyond assisting clients to increase their awareness, there is no need to label a client's behavior as "resistance." Instead, the therapist simply follows this new process as it emerges. The therapist has faith that self-regulation is a naturally unfolding process that does not have to be controlled (Breshgold, 1989). With awareness, clients are able to reconcile polarities and dichotomies within themselves and proceed toward the reintegration of all aspects of themselves.

The therapist works with the client to identify the "figures," or most salient aspects of the individual–environmental field, as they emerge from the background. The Gestalt therapist believes each client is capable of self-regulating if those figures are engaged and resolved so others can replace them. The role of the Gestalt therapist is to help clients identify the most pressing issues, needs, and interests and to design experiments that carry those figures into contact or that explore resistances to contact and awareness.

Contributions of Gestalt Therapy

One contribution of Gestalt therapy is the exciting way in which the past is dealt with in a lively manner by bringing relevant aspects into the present. Therapists challenge clients in creative ways to become aware of and work with issues that are obstructing current functioning. Further, paying attention to the obvious verbal and nonverbal leads provided by clients is a useful way to approach a counseling session. Through the skillful and sensitive use of Gestalt interventions, practitioners can assist clients in heightening their present-centered awareness of what they are thinking and feeling as well as what they are doing. Cain (2002) identifies the most significant contributions of the Gestalt approach:

- The critical importance of contact with oneself, others, and the environment
- The central role of authentic relationship and dialogue in therapy
- The emphasis on field theory, phenomenology, and awareness
- The therapeutic focus on the present, the here-and-now experiencing of the client
- The creative and spontaneous use of active experiments as a pathway to experiential learning

Gestalt methods bring conflicts and human struggles to life. With this approach, people actually experience their struggles, as opposed to merely talking about problems endlessly in a detached manner. Gestalt therapy is a creative approach that uses experiments to move clients from talk to action and experience. The focus is on growth and enhancement rather than being a system of techniques to treat disorders. Clients are provided with a wide range of tools—in the form of Gestalt experiments—for discovering new facets of themselves and making decisions about changing their course of living.

The Gestalt approach to working with dreams is a unique pathway for people to increase their awareness of key themes in their lives. By seeing each aspect of a dream as a projection of themselves, clients are able to bring the dream to life, to interpret its personal meaning, and to assume responsibility for it.

Gestalt therapy is a holistic approach that values each aspect of the individual's experience equally. Therapists allow the figure-formation process to guide them. They do not approach clients with a preconceived set of biases or a set agenda. Instead, they place emphasis on what occurs at the boundary between the individual and the environment.

Gestalt therapy operates with a unique notion about change. The therapist does not try to move the client anywhere. The main goal is to increase the client's awareness of "what is." Instead of trying to make something happen, the therapist's role is assisting the client to increase awareness that will allow re-identification with the part of the self from which he or she is alienated.

A key strength of Gestalt therapy is the attempt to integrate theory, practice, and research. Strumpfel and Goldman (2002) note that both process and outcome studies have advanced the theory and practice of Gestalt therapy, and they summarize a number of significant findings based on outcome research:

- Outcome studies have demonstrated Gestalt therapy to be equal to or greater than other therapies for various disorders.
- More recent studies have shown that Gestalt therapy has a beneficial impact with personality disturbances, psychosomatic problems, and substance addictions.
- The effects of therapy tend to be stable in follow-up studies 1 to 3 years after the termination of treatment.
- Gestalt therapy has demonstrated effectiveness in treating a variety of psychological disorders.

Strumpfel and Goldman conclude: "Within the field of humanistic psychotherapy, research and development in Gestalt therapy have shown how powerful and effective therapy can be in helping people lead healthier and more fulfilling lives" (pp. 212–213).

Limitations and Criticisms of Gestalt Therapy

Most of my criticisms of Gestalt therapy pertain to the older version, or the style of Fritz Perls, which emphasized confrontation and deemphasized the cognitive factors of personality. This style of Gestalt therapy placed more attention on using techniques to confront clients and getting them to experience their feelings. Contemporary Gestalt therapy has come a long way, and more attention is being given to theoretical instruction, theoretical exposition, and cognitive factors in general (Yontef, 1993, 1995).

In Gestalt therapy clients clarify their thinking, explore beliefs, and put meaning to experiences they are reliving in therapy. However, the Gestalt approach does not place a premium on the role of the therapist as a teacher. The emphasis is on *facilitating* the clients' own process of self-discovery and learning. This experiential and self-directed learning process is based on the fundamental belief in organismic self-regulation, which implies that clients arrive at their own truths through awareness and improved contact with the environment. It seems to me, however, that clients can engage in self-discovery and at the same time benefit from appropriate teaching by the therapist. As you will see, I favor blending the emotional and experiential work of Gestalt therapy with concepts and techniques of the cognitive and behavioral approaches (especially behavior therapy, rational emotive behavior therapy, and reality therapy).

Current Gestalt practice places a high value on the contact and dialogue between therapist and client. For Gestalt therapy to be effective, the therapist must have a high level of personal development. Being aware of one's own needs and seeing that they do not interfere with the client's process, being present in the moment, and being willing to be nondefensive and self-revealing all demand a lot of the therapist. There is a danger that therapists who are inadequately trained will be primarily concerned with impressing clients.

SOME CAUTIONS   A major concern I have about Gestalt therapy is the potential danger for abusing power. Typically, Gestalt therapists are highly active and directive, and if they do not have the characteristics mentioned by Zinker (1978)—sensitivity, timing, inventiveness, empathy, and respect for the client—their experiments can easily boomerang.

The techniques employed by Fritz Perls have been incorporated by many therapists who do not have a solid grounding in the theory and practice of Gestalt therapy. Therapists who rely on ready-made techniques, rather than experiments that grow out of dialogue in the therapeutic relationship, can actually damage this relationship. Inept therapists may use powerful techniques to stir up feelings and open up problems clients have kept from full awareness only to abandon the clients once they have managed to have a dramatic catharsis. Such a failure to stay with clients, helping them work through what they have experienced and bring some closure to the experience, can be detrimental and is certainly unethical practice.

Ethical practice depends on adequate training and supervision of therapists, and the most immediate limitation of Gestalt or any other therapy is the skill, training, experience, and judgment of the therapist. Proper training in Gestalt therapy involves reading and learning the theory, hours of supervised practice, observing Gestalt therapists at work, and experiencing one's own personal therapy. Therapists who are trained in the theory and method of Gestalt therapy are likely to do effective work. Such therapists have learned to blend a phenomenological and dialogic approach, which is inherently respectful to the client, with well-timed experiments.

WHERE TO GO FROM HERE

In the *CD-ROM for Integrative Counseling,* Session 7 ("Emotive Focus in Counseling"), I demonstrate how I create experiments to heighten Ruth's awareness. In my version of Gestalt work with Ruth, I watch for cues from Ruth about what she is experiencing in the here-and-now. By attending to what she is expressing both verbally and nonverbally, I am able to suggest experiments during our sessions. In this particular session I employ a Gestalt experiment, asking Ruth to talk to me as if I were her husband, John. During this experiment, Ruth becomes quite emotional. You will see ways of exploring emotional material and integrating this work into a cognitive framework as well.

If you are interested in furthering your knowledge and skill in the area of Gestalt therapy, you might consider pursuing Gestalt training, which would include attending workshops, seeking out personal therapy from a Gestalt therapist, and enrolling in a Gestalt training program that would involve reading, practice, and supervision. Here are few resources for training in Gestalt therapy:

Gestalt Institute of Cleveland. Inc.
1588 Hazel Drive
Cleveland, OH 44106-1791
Telephone: (216) 421-0468
Fax: (216) 421-1729
Email: gestaltclv@aol.com
Web site: www.gestaltcleveland.org

Pacific Gestalt Institute
1626 Westwood Blvd., Suite 104
Los Angeles, CA 90024
Telephone: (310) 446-9720
Fax: (310) 475-4704
Email: info@gestalttherapy.org
Web site: www.gestalttherapy.org

Gestalt Center for Psychotherapy and Training
26 West 9th Street, Suite 8E
New York, NY 10011
Telephone: (212) 387-9429
Email: info@gestaltnyc.org
Web site: www.gestaltnyc.org

The New York Institute for Gestalt Therapy
P.O. Box 238, Old Chelsea Station
New York, NY 10011
Telephone: (212) 864-8277
Email: info@newyorkgestalt.org
Web site: www.newyorkgestalt.org

The International Gestalt Therapy Association
P. O. Box 1045
Highland, NY 12528-1045
Web site: www.gestalt.org/igta.htm

The Center for Gestalt Development, Inc.
P.O. Box 990
Highland, NY 12528-0990
Telephone: (845) 691-7192
Fax: (775) 254-1855
Email: tgjournal@gestalt.org
Web site: http://www.gestalt.org

The Center for Gestalt Development, Inc., publishes *The Gestalt Directory,* which includes information about Gestalt practitioners and training programs throughout the world. The training center's program is described in detail, including admission requirements, costs, length of the program, certifications, and other pertinent data. Single copies of *The Gestalt Directory* are free of charge. Requests for a copy must be in writing. Also available are books, audiotapes, and videotapes dealing with Gestalt practice.

The Gestalt Journal, which is devoted to the theory and practice of Gestalt therapy, is available from The Center for Gestalt Development, Inc. Published twice yearly, it offers articles, reviews, and commentaries of interest to the practitioner, theoretician, academician, and student; the current subscription fee is $35.

InfoTrac College Edition Resources

Gestalt Therapy   The following key words are listed in such a way as to allow the InfoTrac College Edition search engine to locate a wider range of articles in the online library. The key words should be entered exactly as shown, to include asterisks, "W1," and "AND."

Gestalt psychology	Introjection
Gestalt therapy	Awareness AND psychol*
Projection AND psychol*	Awareness AND therap*

Recommended Supplementary Readings

Gestalt Therapy Verbatim (Perls, 1969a) is one of the best places to get a firsthand account of the style in which Perls worked. There are many verbatim transcripts of workshop demonstrations.

Gestalt Therapy Integrated: Contours of Theory and Practice (E. Polster & Polster, 1973) is an excellent source for those who want a more advanced and theoretical treatment of this model.

Creative Process in Gestalt Therapy (Zinker, 1978) is a beautifully written book that is a delight to read. Zinker shows how the therapist functions much like an artist in creating experiments that encourage clients to expand their boundaries.

Awareness, Dialogue and Process: Essays on Gestalt Therapy (Yontef, 1993) is an excellent collection that develops the message that much of Gestalt therapy theory and practice consists of dialogue.

The Healing Relationship in Gestalt Therapy: A Dialogic Self Psychology Approach (Hycner & Jacobs, 1995) is a useful source for understanding contemporary Gestalt therapy based on a meaningful dialogic relationship between client and therapist.

From the Radical Center: The Heart of Gestalt Therapy (E. Polster & Polster, 1999) is an edited collection of central themes in the work of Erving and Miriam Polster. The 20 chapters in this book are taken from the various writings of the Polsters.

References and Suggested Readings

BEISSER, A. R. (1970). The paradoxical theory of change. In J. Fagan & I. L. Shepherd (Eds.), *Gestalt therapy now* (pp. 77–80). New York: Harper & Row (Colophon).

BRESHGOLD, E. (1989). Resistance in Gestalt therapy: An historical theoretical perspective. *The Gestalt Journal, 12*(2), 73–102.

*CAIN, D. J. (2002). Defining characteristics, history, and evolution of humanistic psychotherapies. In D. J. Cain & J. Seeman (Eds.), *Humanistic psychotherapies: Handbook of research and practice* (pp. 3–54). Washington, DC: American Psychological Association.

COREY, G. (2004). *Theory and practice of group counseling* (6th ed.). Belmont, CA: Brooks/Cole.

*COREY, G. (2005). *Case approach to counseling and psychotherapy* (6th ed.). Belmont, CA: Brooks/Cole.

FREW, J. E. (1986). The functions and patterns of occurrence of individual contact styles during the development phase of the Gestalt group. *The Gestalt Journal, 9*(1), 55–70.

FREW, J. E. (1992). From the perspective of the environment. *The Gestalt Journal, 15*(1), 39–60.

FREW, J. E. (1997). A Gestalt therapy theory application to the practice of group leadership. *Gestalt Review, 1*(2), 131–149.

HUMPHREY, K. (1986). Laura Perls: A biographical sketch. *The Gestalt Journal, 9*(1), 5–11.

*HYCNER, R., & JACOBS, L. (1995). *The healing relationship in Gestalt therapy*. Highland, NY: Gestalt Journal Press.

JACOBS, L. (1989). Dialogue in Gestalt theory and therapy. *The Gestalt Journal, 12*(1), 25–67.

---

*Books and articles marked with an asterisk are suggested for further study.

*LATNER, J. (1986). *The Gestalt therapy book.* Highland, NY: Center for Gestalt Development.

LEVITSKY, A., & PERLS, F. (1970). The rules and games of Gestalt therapy. In J. Fagan & I. Shepherd (Eds.), *Gestalt therapy now* (pp. 140–149). New York: Harper & Row (Colophon).

PASSONS, W. R. (1975). *Gestalt approaches in counseling.* New York: Holt, Rinehart & Winston.

*PERLS, F. (1969a). *Gestalt therapy verbatim.* Moab, UT: Real People Press.

PERLS, F. (1969b). *In and out of the garbage pail.* Moab, UT: Real People Press.

PERLS, F., HEFFERLINE, R., & GOODMAN, R. (1951). *Gestalt therapy integrated: Excitement and growth in the human personality.* New York: Dell.

PERLS, L. (1976). Comments on new directions. In E. W. L. Smith (Ed.), *The growing edge of Gestalt therapy* (pp. 221–226). New York: Brunner/Mazel.

PERLS, L. (1986). Opening address: 8th annual conference on the theory and practice of Gestalt therapy—May 17, 1985. *The Gestalt Journal, 9*(1), 12–15.

PERLS, L. (1990). A talk for the 25th anniversary. *The Gestalt Journal, 13*(2), 15–22.

POLSTER, E. (1987a). Escape from the present: Transition and storyline. In J. K. Zeig (Ed.), *The evolution of psychotherapy* (pp. 326–340). New York: Brunner/Mazel.

POLSTER, E. (1987b). *Every person's life is worth a novel.* New York: Norton.

*POLSTER, E. (1995). *A population of selves: A therapeutic exploration of personality diversity.* San Francisco: Jossey-Bass.

*POLSTER, E., & POLSTER, M. (1973). *Gestalt therapy integrated: Contours of theory and practice.* New York: Brunner/Mazel.

POLSTER, E., & POLSTER, M. (1976). Therapy without resistance: Gestalt therapy. In A. Burton (Ed.), *What makes behavior change possible?* (pp. 259–277). New York: Brunner/Mazel.

POLSTER, E., & POLSTER, M. (1999). *From the radical center: The heart of Gestalt therapy.* Cambridge, MA: Gestalt Institute of Cleveland Press.

POLSTER, M. (1987). Gestalt therapy: Evolution and application. In J. K. Zeig (Ed.), *The evolution of psychotherapy* (pp. 312–325). New York: Brunner/Mazel.

POLSTER, M., & POLSTER, E. (1990). Gestalt therapy. In J. K. Zeig & W. M. Munion (Eds.), *What is psychotherapy? Contemporary perspectives* (pp. 103–107). San Francisco: Jossey-Bass.

*STRUMPFEL, U., & GOLDMAN, R. (2002). Contacting Gestalt therapy. In D. J. Cain & J. Seeman (Eds.), *Humanistic psychotherapies: Handbook of research and practice* (pp. 189–219). Washington, DC: American Psychological Association.

YALOM, I. D. (2003). *The gift of therapy: An open letter to a new generation of therapists and their patients.* New York: HarperCollins (Perennial).

*YONTEF, G. M. (1993). *Awareness, dialogue and process: Essays on Gestalt therapy.* Highland, NY: Gestalt Journal Press.

*YONTEF, G. (1995). Gestalt therapy. In A. S. Gurman & S. B. Messer (Eds.), *Essential psychotherapies: Theory and practice* (pp. 261–303). New York: Guilford Press.

YONTEF, G. (1999). Awareness, dialogue and process: Preface to the 1998 German edition. *The Gestalt Journal, 22*(1), 9–20.

*YONTEF, G., & JACOBS, L. (2000). Gestalt therapy. In R. Corsini & D. Wedding (Eds.), *Current psychotherapies* (6th ed., pp. 303–339). Itasca, IL: F. E. Peacock.

*ZINKER, J. (1978). *Creative process in Gestalt therapy.* New York: Random House (Vintage).

Behavior Therapy

B. F. Skinner

B. F. SKINNER (1904–1990) reported that he was brought up in a warm, stable family environment.* As he was growing up, Skinner was greatly interested in building all sorts of things, an interest that followed him throughout his professional life. He received his Ph.D. in psychology from Harvard University in 1931 and eventually returned to Harvard after teaching in several universities. He had two daughters, one of whom is an educational psychologist and the other an artist.

Skinner was a prominent spokesperson for behaviorism and can be considered the father of the behavioral approach to psychology. Skinner championed radical behaviorism, which places primary emphasis on the effects of environment on behavior. Skinner was also a determinist; he did not believe that humans had free choice. He acknowledged that feelings and thoughts exist, but he denied that they *caused* our actions. Instead, he stressed the cause-and-effect links between objective, observable environmental conditions and behavior. Skinner maintained that too much attention had been given to internal states of mind and motives, which cannot be observed and changed directly, and that too little focus had been given to environmental factors that can be directly observed and changed.

Most of Skinner's work was of an experimental nature in the laboratory, but others have applied his ideas to teaching, managing human problems, and social planning. *Science and Human Behavior* (Skinner, 1953) best illustrates how Skinner thought behavioral concepts could be applied to every domain of human behavior. In *Walden Two* (1948) Skinner describes a utopian community in which his ideas, derived from the laboratory, are applied to social issues. His 1971 book, *Beyond Freedom and Dignity*, addresses the need for drastic changes if our society is to survive. Skinner believed that science and technology held the promise for a better future. ■

—

*This biography is based largely on Nye's (2000) discussion of B. F. Skinner's radical behaviorism.

WHERE TO GO FROM HERE

InfoTrac College Edition Resources

Recommended Supplementary Readings

References and Suggested Readings

INTRODUCTION

The terms *behavior modification* and *behavior therapy* are often used interchangeably, but they have slightly different meanings. Behavior modification is an approach to assessment, evaluation, and behavior change that focuses on the development of adaptive, prosocial behaviors and the decrease of maladaptive behavior in daily living (Kazdin, 2001). Behavior modification is used by therapists and paraprofessional workers to help individuals improve some aspect of daily life (Miltenberger, 2004).

Behavior therapy is a clinical approach that can be used to treat a variety of disorders, in various types of settings, and with a wide range of special population groups. Anxiety disorders, depression, substance abuse, eating disorders, domestic violence, sexual deviance, pain management, and hypertension have all been successfully treated using this approach. Some areas where behavioral procedures are used include developmental disabilities, mental illness, education and special education, community psychology, clinical psychology, rehabilitation, business, self-management, sports psychology, health-related behaviors, and gerontology (Miltenberger, 2004).

Historical Background

The behavioral approach had its origin in the 1950s and early 1960s, and it was a radical departure from the dominant psychoanalytic perspective. The behavior therapy movement differed from other therapeutic approaches in its application of principles of classical and operant conditioning (which will be explained shortly) to the treatment of a variety of problem behaviors. Today, it is difficult to find a consensus on the definition of behavior therapy because the field has grown and become more complex (Wilson, 2000). The discussion presented here is based on Spiegler and Guevremont's (2003) historical sketch of behavior therapy.

Contemporary behavior therapy arose simultaneously in the United States, South Africa, and Great Britain in the 1950s. In spite of harsh criticism and resistance from traditional psychotherapists, the approach survived. Its focus was on demonstrating that behavioral conditioning techniques were effective and were a viable alternative to traditional psychotherapy.

In the 1960s Albert Bandura developed social learning theory, which combined classical and operant conditioning with observational learning. He made cognition a legitimate focus for behavior therapy. During the 1960s a number of cognitive behavioral approaches sprang up, and they still have a significant impact on therapeutic practice (see Chapter 10).

It was during the 1970s that behavior therapy emerged as a major force in psychology and made a significant impact on education, psychology, psychotherapy, psychiatry, and social work. Behavioral techniques were developed and expanded, and they were also applied to fields such as business, industry, and child rearing. This approach was now viewed as the treatment of choice for many psychological problems.

The 1980s were characterized by a search for new horizons in concepts and methods that went beyond traditional learning theory. Behavior therapists continued to subject their methods to empirical scrutiny and to consider the impact of the practice of therapy on both their clients and the larger society. Increased attention was given to the role of emotions in therapeutic change, as well as to the role of biological factors in psychological disorders. Two of the most significant developments in the field were (1) the continued emergence of cognitive behavior therapy as a major force and (2) the application of behavioral techniques to the prevention and treatment of medical disorders.

By the late 1990s the Association for Advancement of Behavior Therapy claimed a membership of about 4,300. Today, scores of behavior therapy societies and at least 50 journals devoted to behavior therapy and its many off-shoots are found around the world (Fishman & Franks, 1997). Behavior therapy is marked by a diversity of views and procedures, but all practitioners focus on observable behavior, current determinants of behavior, learning experiences to promote change, and rigorous assessment and evaluation (Kazdin, 2001).

Four Areas of Development

Contemporary behavior therapy can be understood by considering four major areas of development: (1) classical conditioning, (2) operant conditioning, (3) social learning theory, and (4) cognitive behavior therapy.

In *classical conditioning* certain respondent behaviors, such as knee jerks and salivation, are elicited from a passive organism. In the 1950s Joseph Wolpe and Arnold Lazarus of South Africa and Hans Eysenck of England began using the findings of experimental research with animals to help treat phobias in clinical settings. They based their work on Hullian learning theory and Pavlovian (or classical) conditioning. An underlying characteristic of the work of these pioneers was the focus on experimental analysis and evaluation of therapeutic procedures.

Classical conditioning (respondent conditioning) refers to what happens prior to learning that creates a response through pairing. A key figure in this area is Ivan Pavlov who illustrated classical conditioning through experiments with dogs. Placing food in a dog's mouth leads to salivation, which is respondent behavior. When food is repeatedly presented with some originally neutral stimulus, such as the sound of a bell, the dog will eventually salivate to the sound of the bell alone. However, if a bell is sounded repeatedly, but not paired again with food, the salivation response will eventually diminish and become extinct. An example of a procedure that is based on the classical conditioning model is Joseph Wolpe's systematic desensitization, which is described later in this chapter. This technique illustrates how principles of learning derived from the experimental laboratory can be applied clinically.

Most of the significant responses we make in everyday life are examples of operant behaviors, such as reading, writing, driving a car, and eating with utensils. *Operant conditioning* involves a type of learning in which behaviors are influenced mainly by the consequences that follow them. If the environmental changes brought about by the behavior are reinforcing—that is, if they provide some reward to the organism or eliminate aversive stimuli—the chances are increased that the behavior will occur again. If the environmental changes produce no reinforcement or produce aversive stimuli, the chances are lessened that the behavior will recur. Positive and negative reinforcement, punishment, and extinction techniques, described later in this chapter, illustrate how operant conditioning in applied settings can be instrumental in developing prosocial and adaptive behaviors.

Skinner contends that learning cannot occur in the absence of some kind of *reinforcement*, either positive or negative. Reinforcement involves some kind of reward or the removal of an aversive stimulus following a response. Reinforcement takes place when the consequences of a behavior increase the likelihood that the behavior will be repeated. For Skinner, actions that are reinforced tend to be repeated, and those that are not reinforced tend to be extinguished. His general writings apply concepts of operant conditioning to society. His model is based on reinforcement principles and has the goal of identifying and controlling environmental factors that lead to behavioral change.

The behaviorists of both the classical and operant conditioning models excluded any reference to mediational concepts (such as the role of thinking processes, attitudes, and values), perhaps as a reaction against the insight-oriented psychodynamic approaches. The *social learning approach,* developed by Albert Bandura and Richard Walters (1963), is interactional, interdisciplinary, and multimodal (Bandura, 1977, 1982). Behavior is influenced by stimulus events, by external reinforcement, and by cognitive mediational processes. Social learning and cognitive theory involves a triadic reciprocal interaction among the environment, personal factors (beliefs, preferences, expectations, self-perceptions, and so forth), and individual behavior. A basic assumption is that people are capable of self-directed behavior change. For Bandura (1982, 1997) self-efficacy is the individual's belief or expectation that he or she can master a situation and bring about desired change. The theory of self-efficacy represents one of the first major attempts to provide a unified theoretical explanation of how behavior therapy and other psychotherapy procedures work (Fishman & Franks, 1997).

Cognitive behavior therapy, along with social learning theory, now represent the mainstream of contemporary behavior therapy. Since the early 1970s, the behavioral movement has conceded a legitimate place to thinking, even to the extent of giving cognitive factors a central role in understanding and treating emotional and behavioral problems. Many techniques, particularly those developed within the last three decades, emphasize cognitive processes that involve private events such as the client's self-talk as mediators of behavior change (see Bandura, 1969, 1986; Beck, 1976; Beck & Weishaar, 2000). This approach offers various action-oriented methods to help people change what they are doing and thinking.

In a broad sense, behavior therapy "refers to practice based primarily on social-cognitive theory and encompassing a range of cognitive principles and procedures" (Wilson, 2000, p. 207). Current behavior therapy tends to be integrated with cognitive therapy and is often referred to as cognitive behavior therapy. Today there are relatively few traditional behavioral practitioners. This chapter goes beyond the pure or traditional behavioral perspective and deals mainly with the applied aspects of this model. Chapter 10 is devoted to the cognitive behavioral approaches, which focus on changing clients' cognitions (thoughts and beliefs) that maintain psychological problems.

 # KEY CONCEPTS

View of Human Nature

Modern behavior therapy is grounded on a scientific view of human behavior that implies a systematic and structured approach to counseling. This view does not rest on a deterministic assumption that humans are a mere product of their sociocultural conditioning. Rather, the current view is that the person is the producer *and* the product of his or her environment.

The current trend in behavior therapy is toward developing procedures that actually give control to clients and thus increase their range of freedom. Behavior therapy aims to increase people's skills so that they have more options for responding. By overcoming debilitating behaviors that restrict choices, people are freer to select from possibilities that were not available earlier. Thus, as behavior therapy is typically applied, it will increase individual freedom (Kazdin, 1978, 2001).

Philosophically, the behavioral and humanistic approaches have often been viewed as polar opposites. The writings of contemporary behavior therapists suggest that bridges are being built, allowing the possibility of a fruitful synthesis. The strict environmental view of human nature based on a stimulus–response or response–consequence model of behavior has been criticized by Bandura (1974, 1977, 1986), the pioneer of social learning theory. He rejects this mechanistic and deterministic model because of its exclusive reliance on environmental determinants, which fails to take into account our capacity to actually affect our environment.

Other writers have made a case for using behavioral methods to attain humanistic ends (Kazdin, 2001; Meichenbaum, 1977; Thoresen & Coates, 1980; Watson & Tharp, 2002). According to Thoresen and Coates (1980), greater attention is being given to the emerging similarities among theories, and they identify three interrelated themes that characterize this convergence. First is the focus on therapy as an action-oriented approach. Clients are being asked to act rather than to reflect passively and introspect at length on their problems. They are being helped to take specific actions to change their lives. Second is the increasing concern of behavior therapists with how stimulus events are mediated by cognitive processes and private or subjective meanings. Third is the increasing emphasis on the role of responsibility for one's behavior. Given the techniques and skills of self-change, people have the capacity to improve their lives by altering one or more of the various factors influencing their behavior. These three converging themes provide a conceptual framework for a bridge between the behavioral and humanistic approaches.

Basic Characteristics and Assumptions

The 10 key characteristics of behavior therapy discussed here are based on descriptions provided by Kazdin (2001), Miltenberger (2004), and Spiegler and Guevremont (2003).

1. Behavior therapy is based on the principles and procedures of the scientific method. Experimentally derived principles of learning are systematically applied to help people change their maladaptive behaviors. The distinguishing characteristic of behavioral practitioners is their systematic adherence to precision and to empirical evaluation. Behavior therapists state treatment goals in concrete objective terms to make replication of their interventions possible. Treatment goals are agreed upon by the client and the therapist. Throughout the course of therapy, the therapist assesses problem behaviors and the conditions that are maintaining them. Research methods are used to evaluate the effectiveness of both assessment and treatment procedures. Therapeutic techniques employed must have demonstrated effectiveness. In short, behavioral concepts and procedures are stated explicitly, tested empirically, and revised continually.

2. Behavior therapy deals with the client's current problems and the factors influencing them, as opposed to an analysis of possible historical determinants. Emphasis is on specific factors that influence present functioning and what factors can be used to modify performance. At times understanding of the past may offer useful information about environmental events related to present behavior. Behavior therapists look to the current environmental events that maintain problem behaviors and help clients produce behavior change by changing environmental events. Therapists use behavioral techniques to change the relevant current factors that are influencing the client's behaviors.

3. Clients involved in behavior therapy are expected to assume an active role by engaging in specific actions to deal with their problems. Rather than simply talking about their condition, they are required to *do* something to bring about change. Clients monitor their behaviors both during and outside the therapy sessions, learn and practice coping skills, and role-play new behavior. Behavior therapy is an action-oriented approach, and learning is viewed as being at the core of therapy. Therapeutic tasks that clients carry out in daily life, or homework assignments, are a basic part of this approach. Although referred to as "therapy," this is an educational approach in which clients participate in a teaching–learning process.

4. The behavioral approach emphasizes teaching clients skills of self-management, with the expectation that they will be responsible for transferring what they learn in the therapist's office to their everyday lives. Behavior therapy is generally carried out in the client's natural environment as much as possible.

5. The focus is on assessing overt and covert behavior directly, identifying the problem, and evaluating change. There is direct assessment of the target problem through observation or self-monitoring. Therapists also assess their clients' cultures as part of their social environments, including social support networks relating to target behaviors (Tanaka-Matsumi, Higginbotham, & Chang, 2002). Critical to behavioral approaches is the careful assessment and evaluation of the interventions used to determine whether the behavior change resulted from the procedure.

6. Behavior therapy emphasizes a self-control approach in which clients learn self-management strategies. Therapists frequently train clients to initiate, conduct, and evaluate their own therapy. Clients are empowered through this process of being responsible for their changes.

7. Behavioral treatment interventions are individually tailored to specific problems experienced by clients. Several therapy techniques may be used to treat an individual client's problems. An important question that serves as a guide for this choice is *"What* treatment, by *whom,* is the most effective for *this* individual with *that* specific problem and under *which* set of circumstances?" (Paul, 1967, p. 111).

8. The practice of behavior therapy is based on a collaborative partnership between therapist and client, and every attempt is made to inform clients about the nature and course of treatment.

9. The emphasis is on practical applications. Interventions are applied to all facets of daily life in which maladaptive behaviors are to be decreased and adaptive behaviors are to be increased.

10. Therapists strive to develop culture-specific procedures and obtain their clients' adherence and cooperation (Tanaka-Matsumi et al., 2002).

THE THERAPEUTIC PROCESS

Therapeutic Goals

Goals occupy a place of central importance in behavior therapy. The general goals of behavior therapy are to increase personal choice and to create new conditions for learning. The client, with the help of the therapist, defines specific goals at the outset of the therapeutic process. Although assessment and treatment occur together, a formal assessment takes place prior to treatment to determine behaviors that are targets of change. Continual assessment throughout therapy determines the degree to which identified goals are being met. It is important to devise a way to measure progress toward goals based on empirical validation.

Contemporary behavior therapy stresses clients' active role in deciding about their treatment. The therapist assists clients in formulating specific measurable goals. Goals must be clear, concrete, understood, and agreed on by the client and the counselor. This process of determining therapeutic goals entails a negotiation between client and counselor that results in a contract that guides the course of therapy. Behavior therapists and clients alter goals throughout the therapeutic process as needed.

The sequence of selecting goals is described by Cormier and Nurius (2003, pp. 262–267). This process demonstrates the essential nature of a collaborative relationship:

- The counselor provides a rationale for goals, explaining the role of goals in therapy, the purpose of goals, and the client's participation in the goal-setting process.
- The client identifies desired outcomes by specifying the positive changes he or she wants from counseling. Focus is on what the client wants to do rather than on what the client does not want to do.
- The client is the person seeking help, and only he or she can make a change. The counselor helps the client accept the responsibility for change rather than trying to get someone else to change.
- The cost-benefit effect of all identified goals are explored, and counselor and client discuss the possible advantages and disadvantages of these goals.
- The client and counselor then decide to continue pursuing the selected goals, to reconsider the client's initial goals, or to seek the services of another practitioner.

Once goals have been agreed upon, a process of defining them begins. The counselor and client discuss the behaviors associated with the goals, the circumstances required for change, the nature of subgoals, and a plan of action to work toward these goals.

Therapist's Function and Role

Behavior therapists tend to be active and directive and to function as consultants and problem solvers. Practitioners pay attention to the clues given by clients, and they are willing to follow their clinical hunches. They use some techniques common to other approaches, such as summarizing, reflection, clarification, and open-ended questioning. However, behavioral clinicians perform these other functions as well (Miltenberger, 2004; Spiegler & Guevremont, 2003):

- Conduct a thorough functional assessment to identify the maintaining conditions by systematically gathering information about situational antecedents, the dimensions of the problem behavior, and the consequences of the problem.
- Formulate initial treatment goals, and design and implement a treatment plan to accomplish these goals.

- Use strategies to promote generalization and maintenance of behavior change.
- Evaluate the success of the change plan by measuring progress toward the goals throughout the duration of treatment.
- Conduct follow-up assessments.

Let's examine how a behavior therapist might perform these functions. A client comes to therapy to reduce her anxiety, which is preventing her from leaving the house. The therapist is likely to begin with a specific analysis of the nature of her anxiety. The therapist will ask how she experiences the anxiety of leaving her house, including what she actually *does* in these situations. Systematically, the therapist gathers information about this anxiety. When did the problem begin? In what situations does it arise? What does she do at these times? What are her feelings and thoughts in these situations? Who is present when she experiences anxiety? How do her present fears interfere with living effectively? After this assessment, specific behavioral goals will be developed, and strategies will be designed to help the client reduce her anxiety to a manageable level. The therapist will get a commitment from her to work toward the specified goals, and the two of them will evaluate her progress toward meeting these goals throughout the duration of therapy.

Another important function of the therapist is role modeling for the client. Bandura (1969, 1971a, 1971b, 1977, 1986) maintains that most of the learning that occurs through direct experiences can also be acquired through observation of others' behavior. One of the fundamental processes by which clients learn new behavior is through imitation. The therapist, as a person, becomes a significant model. Because clients often view the therapist as worthy of emulation, clients pattern attitudes, values, beliefs, and behavior after the therapist. It is essential that therapists be aware of the crucial role they play in the therapeutic process.

Client's Experience in Therapy

One of the unique contributions of behavior therapy is that it provides the therapist with a well-defined system of procedures to employ. Both therapist and client have clearly defined roles, and the importance of client awareness and participation in the therapeutic process is stressed. Behavior therapy is characterized by an active role for both therapist and client. A large part of the therapist's role is to teach concrete skills through the provision of instructions, modeling, and performance feedback. The client engages in behavioral rehearsal with feedback until skills are well learned and generally receives active homework assignments (such as self-monitoring of problem behaviors) to complete between therapy sessions. Clients must be motivated to change and are expected to cooperate in carrying out therapeutic activities, both during therapy sessions and in everyday life. If clients are not involved in this way, the chances are slim that therapy will be successful.

Clients are encouraged to experiment for the purpose of enlarging their repertoire of adaptive behaviors. They are helped to generalize and to transfer the learning acquired within the therapeutic situation to situations outside therapy. Counseling is not complete unless actions follow verbalizations. Indeed, it is only when the transfer of changes is made from the sessions to everyday life and when the effects of therapy are extended beyond termination that treatment can be considered successful (Granvold & Wodarski, 1994). It is clear that clients are expected to do more than merely gather insights; they need to be willing to make changes and to continue implementing new behavior once formal treatment has ended.

Because treatment goals are stated in measurable terms, clients have a frame of reference for assessing their progress in accomplishing their goals. Clients are as aware as the therapist is regarding when the goals have been accomplished and it is appropriate to terminate treatment. After successful behavior therapy, clients experience an increase of options for behaving, which broadens their range of personal freedom (Spiegler & Guevremont, 2003).

Relationship Between Therapist and Client

Some clinical and research evidence suggests that a therapeutic relationship, even in the context of a behavioral orientation, can contribute significantly to the process of behavior change (Granvold & Wodarski, 1994). A good therapeutic relationship increases the chances that the client will be receptive to therapy. Not only is it important that the client cooperate with the therapeutic procedures, but the client's positive expectations and hope for success about the effectiveness of therapy often contribute to successful outcomes. The skilled behavior therapist conceptualizes problems behaviorally and makes use of the client–therapist relationship in facilitating change.

As you will recall, the experiential therapies (existential therapy, person-centered therapy, and Gestalt therapy) place primary emphasis on the nature of the engagement between counselor and client. In contrast, most behavioral practitioners contend that factors such as warmth, empathy, authenticity, permissiveness, and acceptance are necessary, but not sufficient, for behavior change to occur. The client–therapist relationship is a foundation on which therapeutic strategies are built to help clients change in the direction they wish. However, behavior therapists assume that clients make progress primarily because of the specific behavioral techniques used rather than because of the relationship with the therapist.

 APPLICATION: THERAPEUTIC TECHNIQUES AND PROCEDURES

Behavioral assessment, which begins with a description of the client's complaint, is central to behavior therapy. The client keeps a record of the frequency and intensity of occurrences, and this becomes the tool in devising a therapeutic plan and in deciding whether the therapy is working. There are numerous practical and easy-to-use assessment instruments, including countless self-report inventories, behavior rating scales, self-monitoring forms, and simple observational techniques for collecting useful information on clients' problems. Behavioral assessment methods can be usefully applied to working with clients with a diverse range of problems.

A strength of the behavioral approach is the development of specific therapeutic procedures that must be shown to be effective through objective means. Behavior therapists have hypotheses that they operate from in applying therapeutic procedures, which can be tested for confirmation. Thus, the results of their interventions become clear because they receive continual direct feedback from their clients.

The main finding produced by research in the behavioral therapies is that treatment outcomes are multifaceted. Changes are not all or nothing. Improvements are likely to occur in some areas but not in others. All improvements do not emerge at one time, and gains in some areas may be associated with problems emerging in other areas (Kazdin, 1982; Voltz & Evans, 1982).

According to Arnold Lazarus (1989, 1992b, 1996b, 1997a, 2000b), a pioneer in contemporary clinical behavior therapy, behavioral practitioners can incorporate into their treatment plans any technique that can be demonstrated to effectively change behavior. Lazarus advocates the use of diverse techniques, regardless of their theoretical origin. In his view, the more extensive the range of therapy techniques, the more potentially effective the therapist is. It is clear that behavior therapists do not have to restrict themselves strictly to methods derived from learning theory. Likewise, behavioral techniques can be incorporated into other approaches.

The therapeutic procedures used by behavior therapists are specifically designed for a particular client rather than being randomly selected from a "bag of techniques." Therapists are often quite creative in their interventions. In the following sections I will describe a range of behavioral techniques available to the practitioner: applied behavioral analysis, a functional assessment model, relaxation training, systematic desensitization, exposure therapies, eye movement desensitization and reprocessing, assertion training, self-management programs and self-directed behavior, and multimodal therapy. These techniques do not encompass the full spectrum of behavioral procedures, but they do represent a sample of the approaches used in behavior therapy.

Applied Behavioral Analysis: Operant Conditioning Techniques

This section describes a few key principles of operant conditioning: positive reinforcement, negative reinforcement, extinction, positive punishment, and negative punishment. For a detailed treatment of the wide range of operant conditioning methods that are part of contemporary behavior modification, I highly recommend Kazdin (2001) and Miltenberger (2004).

In applied behavior analysis, operant conditioning techniques and methods of assessment and evaluation are applied to a wide range of problems in many different settings (Kazdin, 2001). The most important contribution of applied behavior analysis is that it offers a functional approach to understanding clients' problems and addresses these problems by changing antecedents and consequences.

Behaviorists believe we respond in predictable ways because of the gains we experience (positive reinforcement) or because of the need to escape or avoid unpleasant consequences (negative reinforcement). Once clients' goals have been assessed, specific behaviors are targeted. The goal of reinforcement, whether positive or negative, is to increase the target behavior. *Positive reinforcement* involves the addition of something of value to the individual (such as praise, attention, money, or food) as a consequence of certain behavior. The stimulus that follows the behavior is the positive reinforcer. For example, a child earns excellent grades and is praised by her parents. If she values this praise, it is likely that she will have an investment in striving for good grades in the future. When the goal of a program is to decrease or eliminate undesirable behaviors, positive reinforcement is often used to increase the frequency of more desirable behaviors, which replace undesirable behaviors.

Negative reinforcement involves the escape from or the avoidance of aversive (unpleasant) stimuli. The individual is motivated to exhibit a desired behavior to avoid the unpleasant condition. For example, a friend of mine does not appreciate waking up to the shrill sound of an alarm clock. She has trained herself to wake up a few minutes before the alarm sounds to avoid the aversive stimulus of the alarm buzzer.

Another operant method of changing behavior is *extinction*, which refers to withholding reinforcement from a previously reinforced response. In applied settings, extinction can be used for behaviors that have been maintained by positive reinforcement or negative reinforcement. For example, children who display temper tantrums are often reinforced by the attention parents give to such behavior. An approach to dealing with problematic behavior is to eliminate the connection between a certain behavior (tantrums) and positive reinforcement (attention). Doing so can decrease or eliminate such behaviors. It should be noted that extinction might well have negative side effects, such as anger and aggression. Extinction can reduce or eliminate certain behaviors, but extinction does not replace those responses that have been extinguished. For this reason, extinction is most often used in behavior modification programs in conjunction with various reinforcement strategies (Kazdin, 2001).

Another way behavior is controlled is through *punishment*, sometimes referred to as aversive control, in which the consequences of a certain behavior result in a decrease of that behavior. The goal of reinforcement is to increase target behavior, but the goal of punishment is to decrease target behavior. Miltenberger (2004) describes two kinds of punishment that may occur as a consequence of behavior: positive punishment and negative punishment. In *positive punishment* an aversive stimulus is added after the behavior to decrease the frequency of a behavior (such as spanking a child for misbehavior or reprimanding a student for acting out in class). In *negative punishment* a reinforcing stimulus is removed following the behavior to decrease the frequency of a target behavior (such as deducting money from a worker's salary for missing time at work, or taking television time away from a child for misbehavior). In both kinds of punishment, the behavior is less likely to occur in the future.

Skinner (1948) believed punishment had limited value in changing behavior and was often an undesirable way to modify behavior. He opposed using aversive control or punishment, and recommended substituting positive reinforcement. The key principle is to use the least aversive means possible to change behavior, and positive reinforcement is known to be the most powerful change agent. Skinner believed in the value of analyzing environmental factors for both the causes and remedies for behavior problems and contended that the greatest benefits to the individual and to society occur by using systematic positive reinforcement as a route to behavior control (Nye, 2000).

Other writers have also addressed the side effects of punishment and concluded that even though punishment may eliminate the target behavior aversive techniques frequently result in undesirable side effects and are often difficult to administer (Kazdin, 2001; Miltenberger, 2004). Some of these side effects are emotional reactions to punishment, the development of escape and avoidance behaviors, negative reinforcement for the use of punishment, modeling of the use of punishment, and ethical issues. Punishment should be used only after nonaversive approaches have been implemented and found to be ineffective in changing problematic behavior (Kazdin, 2001; Miltenberger, 2004).

In everyday life, punishment is often used as a means of getting revenge or expressing frustration. However, as Kazdin (2001) has noted, "punishment in everyday life is not likely to teach lessons or suppress intolerable behavior because of the specific punishments that are used and how they are applied" (p. 231). Even in those cases when punishment suppresses undesirable responses, punishment does not result in teaching desirable behaviors. It is essential that reinforcement be used as a way to develop appropriate behaviors that replace the behaviors that are suppressed. There is a place for punishment in behavior modification programs, but punishment should generally be used only to supplement reinforcement strategies aimed at developing other appropriate behaviors (Kazdin, 2001).

The Functional Assessment Model

The functional assessment model offers a blueprint for therapists in the selection of operant interventions that are based on prior assessment information and conceptualization of a client's problem. Miltenberger (2004) describes how to deal with problem behaviors through a step-by-step functional assessment and treatment program:

1. The first step is to conduct a functional assessment to gather data about the antecedents and consequences that are functionally related to the occurrence of problematic behaviors.

2. To conduct a functional assessment, both indirect methods (behavioral interviews or questionnaires to gather information about the problem behavior) and direct observation methods are used. A functional assessment yields information about antecedent events, including the time and place of the behavior and the people present when the behavior occurs.
3. Based on the information gathered from the functional assessment, the therapist develops hypotheses about the nature of the problem behavior and the conditions contributing to this behavior.
4. Once the different functions of problem behaviors are identified, functional treatments are devised to address the antecedents and consequences hypothesized to be maintaining the problem behaviors. Functional treatments include the following techniques:

   ■ Differential reinforcement of desirable behaviors to replace problem behaviors, which may include both positive and negative reinforcement procedures
   ■ Extinction of problem behaviors by withholding the reinforcers (identified in the functional assessment process) found to be maintaining the problem
   ■ Antecedent control procedures in which antecedents are manipulated in an attempt to prevent the occurrence of problem behaviors and to promote desirable alternative behaviors to replace the problem behaviors

5. Negative punishment procedures may be used to decrease problem behaviors, but only after the functional approaches have been tried.
6. After these treatment methods have been used, it is very important to develop strategies to promote the generalization and maintenance of behavioral changes that have occurred.

Substantial research supports the functional model of assessment and treatment using operant procedures, and this model can be applied to a variety of problem behaviors (Miltenberger, 2004).

Relaxation Training and Related Methods

Relaxation training has become increasingly popular as a method of teaching people to cope with the stresses produced by daily living. It is aimed at achieving muscle and mental relaxation and is easily learned. After clients learn the basics of relaxation procedures, it is essential that they practice these exercises daily to obtain maximum results.

Jacobson (1938) is credited with initially developing the progressive relaxation procedure. It has since been refined and modified, and relaxation procedures are frequently used in combination with a number of other behavioral techniques. These include systematic desensitization, assertion training, self-management programs, audiotape recordings of guided relaxation procedures, computer simulation programs, biofeedback-induced relaxation, hypnosis, meditation, and autogenic training (teaching control of bodily and imaginal functions through autosuggestion).

Relaxation training involves several components that typically require from 4 to 8 hours of instruction. Clients are given a set of instructions that asks them to relax. They assume a passive and relaxed position in a quiet environment while alternately contracting and relaxing muscles. Deep and regular breathing is also associated with producing relaxation. At the same time clients learn to mentally "let go," perhaps by focusing on pleasant thoughts or images. Clients are encouraged to actually feel and experience the tension building up, to notice their muscles getting tighter and study this tension, and to hold and fully experience the tension. Also, it is useful for clients to experience the difference between a tense and a relaxed state. Relaxation becomes a well-learned response, which can become a habitual pattern if practiced daily for 20 or 25 minutes.

Relaxation procedures have been applied to a variety of clinical problems, either as a separate technique or in conjunction with related methods. The most common use has been with problems related to stress and anxiety, which are often manifested in psychosomatic symptoms. Some other ailments for which relaxation training is helpful include asthma, headache, hypertension, insomnia, irritable bowel syndrome, and panic disorder (Cormier & Nurius, 2003).

Systematic Desensitization

Systematic desensitization, which is based on the principle of classical conditioning, is a basic behavioral procedure developed by Joseph Wolpe, one of the pioneers of behavior therapy. Clients imagine successively more anxiety-arousing situations at the same time that they engage in a behavior that competes with anxiety. Gradually, or systematically, clients become less sensitive (desensitized) to the anxiety-arousing situation. This procedure can be considered a form of exposure therapy because clients are required to expose themselves to anxiety-arousing images as a way to reduce anxiety.

Systematic desensitization is one of the most widely employed and empirically researched behavior therapy procedures. Although desensitization is a time-consuming procedure, it is clearly an effective and efficient treatment of anxiety-related disorders (Cormier & Nurius, 2003; Spiegler & Guevremont, 2003).

Before implementing the desensitization procedure, the therapist conducts an initial interview to identify specific information about the anxiety and to gather relevant background information about the client. This interview, which may last several sessions, gives the therapist a good understanding of who the client is. The therapist questions the client about the particular circumstances that elicit the conditioned fears. For instance, under what circumstances does the client feel anxious? If the client is anxious in social situations, does the anxiety vary with the number of people present? Is the client more anxious with women or men? The client is asked to begin a self-monitoring process consisting of observing and recording situations during the week that elicit anxiety responses. Some therapists also administer a questionnaire to gather additional data about situations leading to anxiety.

If the decision is made to use the desensitization procedure, the therapist gives the client a rationale for the procedure and briefly describes what is involved. Cormier and Nurius (2003) describe several steps in the use of systematic desensitization: (1) relaxation training, (2) development of the anxiety hierarchy, and (3) systematic desensitization proper.

The steps in *relaxation training* are described in detail by Wolpe (1990). The therapist uses a very quiet, soft, and pleasant voice to teach progressive muscular relaxation. The client is asked to create imagery of previously relaxing situations, such as sitting by a lake or wandering through a beautiful field. It is important that the client reach a state of calm and peacefulness. The client is then taught how to relax all the muscles while visualizing the various parts of the body, with emphasis on the facial muscles. The arm muscles are relaxed first, followed by the head, the neck and shoulders, the back, abdomen, and thorax, and then the lower limbs. The client is instructed to practice relaxation outside the session for about 30 minutes each day.

The therapist then works with the client to develop an *anxiety hierarchy* for each of the identified areas. Stimuli that elicit anxiety in a particular area, such as rejection, jealousy, criticism, disapproval, or any phobia, are analyzed. The therapist constructs a ranked list of situations that elicit increasing degrees of anxiety or avoidance. The hierarchy is arranged in order from the worst situation the client can imagine down to the situation that evokes the least anxiety. If it has been determined that the client has anxiety related to fear of rejection, for example, the highest anxiety-producing situation might be rejection by the spouse, next, rejection by a close friend, and then rejection by a coworker. The least disturbing situation might be a stranger's indifference toward the client at a party.

Desensitization does not begin until several sessions after the initial interview has been completed. Enough time is allowed for clients to learn relaxation in therapy sessions, to practice it at home, and to construct their anxiety hierarchy. The desensitization process begins with the client reaching complete relaxation with eyes closed. A neutral scene is presented, and the client is asked to imagine it. If the client remains relaxed, he or she is asked to imagine the least anxiety-arousing scene on the hierarchy of situations that has been developed. The therapist moves progressively up the hierarchy until the client signals that he or she is experiencing anxiety, at which time the scene is terminated. Relaxation is then induced again, and the scene is reintroduced again until little anxiety is experienced to it. Treatment ends when the client is able to remain in a relaxed state while imagining the scene that was formerly the most disturbing and anxiety-producing. The core of systematic desensitization is repeated exposure in the imagination to anxiety-evoking situations without experiencing any negative consequences.

Homework and follow-up are essential components of successful desensitization. Clients can practice selected relaxation procedures daily, at which time they visualize scenes completed in the previous session. Gradually, they also expose themselves to daily-life situations as a further way to manage their anxieties. Clients tend to benefit the most when they have a variety of ways to cope with anxiety-arousing situations that they can continue to use once therapy has ended (Cormier & Nurius, 2003).

Systematic desensitization is an appropriate technique for treating phobias, but it is a misconception that it can be applied only to the treatment of anxiety. It has also been used effectively in dealing with nightmares, anorexia nervosa, obsessions, compulsions, stuttering, body image disturbances, and depression. Historically, desensitization probably has the longest track record of any behavioral technique in dealing with fears, and its positive results have been documented repeatedly (Cormier & Nurius, 2003). Systematic desensitization is often acceptable to clients because they are gradually and symbolically exposed to anxiety-evoking situations. A safeguard is that clients are in control of the process by going at their own pace and terminating exposure when they begin to experience more anxiety than they want to tolerate (Spiegler & Guevremont, 2003).

Exposure Therapies

Exposure therapies are designed to treat fears and other negative emotional responses by introducing clients, under carefully controlled conditions, to the situations that contributed to such problems. Desensitization is one type of exposure therapy, but there are others. Two variations of traditional systematic desensitization are *in vivo* desensitization and flooding.

IN VIVO DESENSITIZATION   *In vivo* desensitization involves client exposure to the actual feared situations in the hierarchy in real life rather than simply imagining situations. Clients engage in brief and graduated series of exposures to feared events. Clients can terminate exposure if they experience a high level of anxiety. As is the case with systematic desensitization, clients learn competing responses involving muscular relaxation. In some cases the therapist may accompany clients as they encounter feared situations. For example, a therapist could go with clients in an elevator if they had phobias of using elevators. People who have extreme fears of certain animals could be exposed to these animals in real life in a safe setting with a therapist. Self-managed *in vivo* desensitization—a procedure in which clients expose themselves to anxiety-evoking events on their own—is an alternative when it is not practical for a therapist to be with clients in real-life situations.

FLOODING   Another form of exposure therapy is flooding, which refers to either *in vivo* or imaginal exposure to anxiety-evoking stimuli for a prolonged period of time. As is characteristic of all exposure therapies, even though the client experiences anxiety during the exposure, the feared consequences do not occur.

In vivo flooding consists of intense and prolonged exposure to the actual anxiety-producing stimuli. Remaining exposed to feared stimuli for a prolonged period without engaging in any anxiety-reducing behaviors allows the anxiety to decrease on its own. Generally, highly fearful clients tend to curb their anxiety through the use of maladaptive behaviors. In flooding, clients are prevented from engaging in their usual maladaptive responses to anxiety-arousing situations. *In vivo* flooding tends to reduce anxiety rapidly.

Imaginal flooding is based on similar principles and follows the same procedures except the exposure occurs in the client's imagination instead of in daily life. An advantage of using imaginal flooding over *in vivo* flooding is that there are no restrictions on the nature of the anxiety-arousing situations that can be treated. *In vivo* exposure to actual traumatic events (airplane crash, rape, fire, flood) is often not possible nor is it appropriate for both ethical and practical reasons. Imaginal flooding can re-create the circumstances of the trauma in a way that does not bring about adverse consequences to the client. Survivors of an airplane crash, for example, may suffer from a range of debilitating symptoms. They are likely to have nightmares and flashbacks to the disaster, they may avoid travel by air or have anxiety about travel by any means, and they probably have a variety of distressing symptoms such as guilt, anxiety, and depression.

The exposure technique of flooding can be fruitfully applied to a range of intense fears, such as fears of flying, riding in a subway or a train, fears of riding on escalators or elevators, and phobic reactions to certain animals. Flooding is frequently used in the behavioral treatment for anxiety-related disorders, phobias, obsessive-compulsive disorder, post-traumatic stress disorder, and agoraphobia.

Prolonged and intense exposure can be both an effective and efficient way to reduce clients' anxiety. However, because of the discomfort associated with prolonged and intense exposure, some clients may not elect these exposure treatments. From an ethical perspective, clients should have adequate information about prolonged and intense exposure therapy before agreeing to participate. It is important that they understand that anxiety will be induced as a way to reduce it. Clients need to make informed decisions after considering the pros and cons of subjecting themselves to temporarily stressful aspects of treatment.

Spiegler and Guevremont (2003) conclude that exposure therapies are the single most potent behavioral procedures available for anxiety-related disorders, and they can have long-lasting effects. However, they add, using exposure as a sole treatment procedure is not always sufficient. In cases involving severe and multifaceted disorders, more than one behavioral intervention is often required. Increasingly, imaginal and *in vivo* exposure are being used in combination, which fits with the trend in behavior therapy to use treatment packages as a way to enhance the effectiveness of therapy.

Eye Movement Desensitization and Reprocessing

Eye movement desensitization and reprocessing (EMDR) is a form of exposure therapy that involves imaginal flooding, cognitive restructuring, and the use of rapid, rhythmic eye movements and other bilateral stimulation to treat clients who have experienced traumatic stress. Developed by Francine Shapiro (2001), this therapeutic procedure draws from a wide range of behavioral interventions. Designed to assist clients in dealing with posttraumatic stress disorders, EMDR has been applied to a variety of populations including children, couples, sexual abuse victims, combat veterans, victims of crime, rape survivors, accident victims, and individuals dealing with anxiety, panic, depression, grief, addictions, and phobias.

EMDR consists of eight essential phases, and it draws from many of the procedures used in behavior therapy. A more complete discussion of these phases can be found in Shapiro (2001); only a brief explanation is provided here.

1. EMDR is used to help clients restructure their cognitions or to reprocess information. The first phase of treatment involves obtaining a client's history. Once the practitioner has completed a full evaluation of the client, a detailed treatment plan is designed. As is typical of behavior therapy, this initial phase involves conceptualizing and defining the client's problem and identifying and evaluating specific outcome goals. Additionally, specific targets are selected, such as (1) dysfunctional memories that set the groundwork for the pathology, (2) present situations that trigger the disturbance, and (3) specific skills and behaviors necessary for adaptive future action.

2. The preparation phase involves establishing a therapeutic alliance. The therapist explains the EMDR process and its effects, discusses any concerns or expectations the client may have, initiates relaxation procedures, and creates a safe climate where the client is able to engage in emotive imagery.

3. The assessment phase includes identifying a traumatic memory that results in anxiety, identifying the emotion and physical sensations associated with the traumatic event, evaluating the subjective unit of disturbance (SUD) scale of images, identifying a negative cognition that is associated with the disturbing event, and finding an adaptive belief (or positive cognition) that would lessen the anxiety surrounding the traumatic event.

4. In the desensitization phase, the client visualizes the traumatic image, verbalizes the maladaptive belief (or negative cognition), and pays attention to the physical sensations. Exposure is limited, and the client may have direct exposure to the most disturbing element for less than one minute per session. During this process, the client is instructed to visually track the therapist's index finger as it is moved rapidly and rhythmically back and forth across the client's line of vision from 12 to 24 times. The client is instructed (1) to block out the negative experience momentarily and breathe deeply and (2) to report what he or she is imagining, feeling, and thinking.

5.   The installation phase consists of installing and increasing the strength of the positive cognition the client has identified as the replacement for the original negative cognition. The objective is to associate the traumatic event with an adaptive belief so that the memory no longer has the power to result in anxiety and negative thinking. The focus is on the strength of the client's positive self-assessment, which is pivotal for therapeutic gains to be maintained.

6.   After the positive cognition has been installed, the client is asked to visualize the traumatic event and the positive cognition and to scan his or her body mentally from top to bottom and identify any bodily tension states. The body scan is completed when the client is able to visualize the target event and, at the same time, experience little bodily tension and be able to experience the positive cognition.

7.   It is essential that adequate closure be brought to the end of each session. The therapist reminds the client that he or she may experience disturbing images, emotions, and thoughts between the sessions. The client is asked to keep a log or journal and record any disturbing material. Instructions are typically given to the client in the form of homework to be completed. Some interventions clients are expected to make use of during this phase of treatment include relaxation, guided imagery, meditation, self-monitoring, and breathing exercises.

8.   Reevaluation is the last phase of treatment, which should be implemented at the beginning of each new session. The clinician using EMDR assists the client in reaccessing previously reprocessed targets and reviews the client's responses to determine if the treatment is progressing. This last phase of EMDR includes several behavioral processes: reconceptualization of the client's problems, establishing new therapeutic goals, engaging in further desensitization, continuing the work of cognitive restructuring, continuing the self-monitoring process, and collaboratively evaluating the outcome of treatment.

Current research on EMDR is mixed, and EMDR has become both popular and controversial in the United States, Canada, Europe, and Australia since the mid-1990s. Shapiro and her associates claim that EMDR is an effective treatment of trauma. In her review of 13 controlled studies of EMDR, Shapiro (2002b) points out that since the introduction of EMDR 12 years ago, this approach has been subjected to more controlled research than any other method to treat trauma. She adds that EMDR is clearly better than no treatment and that it is an effective approach to treatment of PTSD. Alberti and Emmons (2001a) note that the EMDR method appears to be effective in dealing with anxieties associated with assertive behavior. They state: "EMDR is showing excellent results in helping overcome the guilt, fear, upset, faulty thinking, and anxiety that often result from traumatic experiences" (p. 98).

The critics claim that EMDR is of questionable value and that practitioners should proceed with caution. In their summary of the literature on EMDR, Cormier and Nurius (2003) state that concern has been raised about using a technique before it has met rigorous empirical testing to demonstrate its effectiveness. Cautions have been raised about the clinical, ethical, and legal issues involved in using EMDR without proper training and supervision.

Several writers have noted that the effectiveness of EMDR has been shrouded in controversy and uncertainty (Cormier & Nurius, 2003; Prochaska & Norcross, 2003; Spiegler & Guevremont, 2003). In their summary of research on EMDR, Spiegler and Guevremont contend that the claims of success are misleading because most of the sources of evidence for the effectiveness of EMDR have serious methodological flaws. The evidence in favor of EMDR is mainly based on case studies, on self-report measures, and on the subjective evaluations of success by therapists. Spiegler and Guevremont (2003) state: "At present the effectiveness of EMDR has not been demonstrated according to the standards of empirical validation typically required of behavior therapy procedures" (p. 249). In writing about the future of EMDR, Prochaska and Norcross (2003) make several predictions: increasing numbers of practitioners will receive training in EMDR; outcome research will shed light on EMDR's effectiveness compared to other current therapies for trauma; and further research and practice will provide a sense of its effectiveness with disorders besides PTSD.

Shapiro (2001) emphasizes the ethical parameters of using this approach, stressing the importance of the safety and welfare of the client. Shapiro points out that EMDR may appear simple to some, yet the ethical use of the procedure demands training and clinical supervision. Because of the powerful reactions from clients, it is essential that practitioners know how to safely and effectively manage these occurrences. Therapists should not use this procedure unless they receive proper training and supervision from an EMDR-authorized instructor.

Assertion Training

Many people have difficulty feeling that it is appropriate or right to assert themselves. People who lack social skills frequently experience interpersonal difficulties at home, at work, at school, and during leisure time. Assertion training can be useful for those (1) who cannot express anger or irritation, (2) who have difficulty saying no, (3) who are overly polite and allow others to take advantage of them, (4) who find it difficult to express affection and other positive responses, (5) who feel they do not have a right to express their thoughts, beliefs, and feelings, or (6) who have social phobias.

The basic assumption underlying assertion training is that people have the right (but not the obligation) to express themselves. One goal of assertion training is to increase people's behavioral repertoire so that they can make the *choice* of whether to behave assertively in certain situations. Another goal is teaching people to express themselves in ways that reflect sensitivity to the feelings and rights of others. Assertion does not mean aggression. Thus, truly assertive people do not stand up for their rights at all costs, ignoring the feelings of others.

Many assertion training methods are based on principles of the cognitive behavioral therapies (Chapter 10). Generally, the therapist both teaches and models desired behaviors the client wants to acquire. These behaviors are practiced in the therapy office and then enacted in everyday life. Most assertion training programs focus on clients' negative self-statements, self-defeating beliefs, and faulty thinking. People often behave in unassertive ways because they don't think they have a right to state a viewpoint or ask for what they want or deserve. Thus, their thinking leads to passive behavior. Effective assertion training programs do more than give people skills and techniques for dealing with difficult situations. These programs challenge people's beliefs that accompany their lack of assertiveness and teach them to make constructive self-statements and to adopt a new set of beliefs that will result in assertive behavior.

Assertion training is often conducted in groups. When a group format is used, the modeling and instructions are presented to the entire group. The members then rehearse behavioral skills in role-playing situations. After the rehearsal, the member is given feedback that consists of reinforcing the correct aspects of the behavior and instructions on how to improve the behavior. Each member engages in further rehearsals of assertive behaviors until the skills are performed adequately in a variety of simulated situations (Miltenberger, 2004).

Assertion training is not a panacea, but it can be an effective treatment for many clients who have skill deficits in assertive behavior or for individuals who experience difficulties in their interpersonal relationships. Assertion training attempts to equip clients with the skills and attitudes necessary to deal effectively with a wide range of interpersonal situations. Although counselors can adapt assertion training procedures to suit their own style, it is important to include behavioral rehearsal and continual assessment as basic aspects of the program. If you are interested in learning more assertion training, consult *Your Perfect Right: A Guide to Assertive Behavior* (Alberti & Emmons, 2001a).

Self-Management Programs and Self-Directed Behavior

For some time there has been a trend toward "giving psychology away." This involves psychologists being willing to share their knowledge so that "consumers" can increasingly lead self-directed lives and not be dependent on experts to deal with their problems. Psychologists who share this perspective are primarily concerned with teaching people the skills they will need to manage their own lives effectively. An advantage of self-management techniques is that treatment can be extended to the public in ways that cannot be done with traditional approaches to therapy. Another advantage is that costs are minimal. Because clients have a direct role in their own treatment, techniques aimed at self-change tend to increase involvement and commitment to their treatment.

Self-management strategies include, but are not limited to, self-monitoring, self-reward, self-contracting, stimulus control, and self-as-model. The basic idea of self-management assessments and interventions is that change can be brought about by teaching people to use coping skills in problematic situations. Generalization and maintenance of the outcomes are enhanced by encouraging clients to accept the responsibility for carrying out these strategies in daily life.

In self-management programs people make decisions concerning specific behaviors they want to control or change. Some common examples are control of smoking, drinking, or drugs; learning study and time-management skills; and dealing with obesity and overeating. People frequently discover that a major reason that they do not attain their goals is the lack of certain skills or unrealistic expectations of change. It is in such areas that a self-directed approach can provide the guidelines for change and a plan that will lead to change.

Five characteristics of an effective self-management program are identified by Cormier and Nurius (2003, pp. 586–589):

1. A combination of self-management strategies is usually more useful than a single strategy.
2. Self-management efforts need to be employed regularly over a sustained period or their effectiveness may be too limited to produce any significant change.
3. It is essential that clients make a self-evaluation and set goals that are personally meaningful to them.
4. The use of self-reinforcement is an important component of self-management programs.
5. Some degree of environmental support is necessary to maintain changes that result from a self-management program.

Although hope can be a therapeutic factor that leads to change, unrealistic hope can pave the way for a pattern of failures in a self-change program. For people to succeed in such a program, a careful analysis of the context of the behavior pattern is essential, and these basic steps of a self-management program provided by Watson and Tharp (2002) must be followed:

1. *Selecting goals.* The initial stage begins with specifying what changes are desired. Goals should be established one at a time, and they should be measurable, attainable, positive, and significant for the person. It is essential that expectations be realistic.

2. *Translating goals into target behaviors.* Next, the goals selected are translated into target behaviors. A key question is, "What specific behaviors do I want to increase or decrease?"

3. *Self-monitoring.* A major first step in self-directed change is the process of self-monitoring, in which clients deliberately and systematically observe their own behavior. One of the simplest methods for observing behavior is keeping a *behavioral diary.* The occurrence of a particular behavior is recorded by the client, along with comments about the relevant antecedent cues and consequences.

4. *Working out a plan for change.* This stage begins with a comparison between the information obtained from self-monitoring and clients' standards for a specific behavior. After clients make the evaluation of behavioral changes they want to acquire, they devise an action program to bring about actual change that may include methods such as punishment, stimulus control, behavioral contracts, and social support. Some type of self-reinforcement system is necessary in this plan because reinforcement is the cornerstone of modern behavior therapy. Self-reinforcement is a temporary strategy clients use until they successfully implement the new behaviors in everyday life. It is essential that clients take steps to ensure that they maintain the gains they have made.

5. *Evaluating an action plan.* To determine the degree to which clients are achieving their goals, it is essential to evaluate the plan for change. The plan is continually adjusted and revised as clients learn other ways to meet their goals. Evaluation is an ongoing process rather than a one-time occurrence, and self-change is a lifelong practice.

Many people who develop some kind of self-management program encounter repeated failure, a situation Polivy and Herman (2002) refer to as the "false hope syndrome," which is characterized by unrealistic expectations regarding the likely speed, amount, ease, and consequences of self-change attempts. Self-change efforts are frequently doomed to failure from the outset by these unrealistic expectations, but individuals often continue to try and try in the hope that they will eventually succeed in changing a behavioral pattern. Many people interpret their failures to change as the result of inadequate effort or getting involved in the wrong program.

Successful self-change efforts begin with setting realistic goals and providing a concrete plan for achieving behavioral change. Self-management strategies have been applied to many populations and to problems such as anxiety, depression, and pain. Research on self-management has been conducted in a wide variety of health problems, a few of which include arthritis, asthma, cancer, cardiac disease, substance abuse, diabetes, headaches, vision loss, nutrition, and self-health care (Cormier & Nurius, 2003).

Multimodal Therapy: Clinical Behavior Therapy

Multimodal therapy is a comprehensive, systematic, holistic approach to behavior therapy developed by Arnold Lazarus (1976, 1986, 1987b, 1989, 1992a, 1992b, 1997a, 2000b). It is grounded in social learning and cognitive theory and applies diverse behavioral techniques to a wide range of problems. This model implies that we are social beings who move, feel, sense, imagine, and think. Cyril Franks (1997) contends that "multimodal therapy is best regarded as behavior therapy in one of its most methodologically sophisticated expressions to date" (p. xii). Franks states that although Lazarus practices outstanding behavior therapy, he refers to his approach simply as "multimodal therapy." This contemporary approach is particularly important as it serves as a major link between some behavioral principles and the cognitive behavioral approach that has largely replaced traditional behavioral psychology.

Multimodal therapy is an open system that encourages *technical eclecticism.* New techniques are constantly being introduced and existing techniques refined, but they are never used in a shotgun manner. Multimodal therapists take great pains to determine precisely what relationship and what treatment strategies will work best with each client and under which particular circumstances. The underlying assumption of this approach is that because individuals are troubled by a variety of specific problems it is appropriate that a multitude of treatment strategies be used in bringing about change. Therapeutic flexibility and versatility, along with breadth over depth, are highly valued, and multimodal therapists are constantly adjusting their procedures to achieve the client's goals (Lazarus, 1997a, 2000b).

TECHNICAL ECLECTICISM   Multimodal therapists borrow techniques from many other therapy systems. Some techniques they employ in individual therapy are anxiety-management training, behavior rehearsal, bibliotherapy, biofeedback, communication training, contingency contracting, meditation, modeling, positive imagery, positive reinforcement, relaxation training, self-instruction training, sensate-focus training, social skills and assertiveness training, time projection, and thought stopping. (See Lazarus, 1987a, for a detailed description of these methods.) Most of these techniques are standard behavioral methods drawn from the four major branches of the behavioral approach: classical, operant, social learning, and cognitive behavioral.

Multimodal therapists recognize that many clients come to therapy needing to learn skills, and therapists are willing to teach, coach, train, model, and direct their clients. They typically function directively by providing information, instruction, and reactions. They challenge self-defeating beliefs, offer constructive feedback, provide positive reinforcement, and are appropriately self-disclosing. It is essential that therapists start where the client is and then move into other productive areas for exploration. Failure to apprehend the client's situation can easily leave the client feeling alienated and misunderstood (Lazarus, 2000b).

THE BASIC I.D.   The essence of Lazarus's multimodal approach is the premise that the complex personality of human beings can be divided into seven major areas of functioning: B = behavior; A = affective responses; S = sensations; I = images; C = cognitions; I = interpersonal relationships; and D = drugs, biological functions, nutrition, and exercise (Lazarus, 1989, 1992a, 1992b, 1997a, 1997b, 2000a). Although these modalities are interactive, they can be considered discrete functions.

Multimodal therapy begins with a comprehensive assessment of the seven modalities of human functioning and the interaction among them. A complete assessment and treatment program must account for each modality of the BASIC I.D., which is the cognitive map linking each aspect of personality.

Clients are asked questions pertaining to the BASIC I.D. What follows is a modification of this assessment process based on questions Lazarus typically asks (1989, 1997a, 2000a):

1. *Behavior.* This modality refers primarily to overt behaviors, including acts, habits, and reactions that are observable and measurable. Some questions asked are: "What would you like to change?" "How active are you?" "What would you like to start doing?" "What would you like to stop doing?" "What are some of your main strengths?" "What specific behaviors keep you from getting what you want?"

2. *Affect.* This modality refers to emotions, moods, and strong feelings. Questions sometimes asked include: "What emotions do you experience most often?" "What makes you laugh?" "What makes you cry?" "What makes you sad, mad, glad, scared?" "What emotions are problematic for you?"

3. *Sensation.* This area refers to the five basic senses of touch, taste, smell, sight, and hearing. Examples of questions asked are: "Do you suffer from unpleasant sensations, such as pains, aches, dizziness, and so forth?" "What do you particularly like or dislike in the way of seeing, smelling, hearing, touching, and tasting?"

4. *Imagery.* This modality pertains to ways in which we picture ourselves, and it includes memories, dreams, and fantasies. Some questions asked are: "What are some bothersome recurring dreams and vivid memories?" "Do you have a vivid imagination?" "How do you view your body?" "How do you see yourself now?" "How would you like to be able to see yourself in the future?"

5. *Cognition.* This modality refers to insights, philosophies, ideas, opinions, self-talk, and judgments that constitute one's fundamental values, attitudes, and beliefs. Questions include: "What are some ways in which you meet your intellectual needs?" "How do your thoughts affect your emotions?" "What are the values and beliefs you most cherish?" "What are some negative things you say to yourself?" "What are some of your central faulty beliefs?" "What are the main 'shoulds,' 'oughts,' and 'musts' in your life? How do they get in the way of effective living?"

6. *Interpersonal relationships.* This modality refers to interactions with other people. Examples of questions include: "How much of a social being are you?" "To what degree do you desire intimacy with others?" "What do you expect from the significant people in your life?" "What do they expect from you?" "Are there any relationships with others that you would hope to change?" "If so, what kinds of changes do you want?"

7. *Drugs/biology.* This modality includes more than drugs, encompassing consideration of clients' nutritional habits and exercise patterns as well. Some questions asked are: "Are you healthy and health conscious?" "Do you have any concerns about your health?" "Do you take any prescribed drugs?" "What are your habits pertaining to diet, exercise, and physical fitness?"

This preliminary investigation brings out some central and significant themes that can then be productively explored using a detailed life-history questionnaire.

(See Lazarus and Lazarus, 1991, for the multimodal life-history inventory.) Once the main profile of a person's BASIC I.D. has been established, the next step consists of an examination of the interactions among the different modalities. For an illustration of how Dr. Lazarus applies the BASIC I.D. assessment model to the case of Ruth, along with examples of various techniques he uses, see *Case Approach to Counseling and Psychotherapy* (Corey, 2005, chap. 7).

BRIEF AND COMPREHENSIVE THERAPY Comprehensive brief therapy involves correcting faulty beliefs, deviant behaviors, unpleasant feelings, bothersome images, stressful relationships, negative sensations, and possible biochemical imbalances. Multimodal therapists believe that the more clients learn in therapy the less likely it is that old problems will reoccur. They view enduring change as a function of combined strategies and modalities.

Lazarus (1997a, 1997b) advocates for short-term and comprehensive treatment but cautions: "Virtually anyone can be brief, but can they also be effective and achieve durable results?" (1997b, p. 85). Franks (1997) asserts that brief multimodal therapy fits well with the goals and aspirations of managed care. He states: "brief multimodal therapy is behavior therapy in one of its most advanced forms. It is efficient, effective, teachable, demonstrably valid, and comprehensive without being rigid" (p. xii).

A major premise of multimodal therapy is that *breadth* is often more important than *depth*. The more coping responses a client learns in therapy, the less are the chances for a relapse (Lazarus, 1996a; Lazarus & Lazarus, 2002). Therapists identify one specific issue from each aspect of the BASIC I.D. framework as a target for change and teach clients a range of techniques they can use to combat faulty thinking, to learn to relax in stressful situations, and to acquire effective interpersonal skills. Clients can then apply these skills to a broad range of problems in their everyday lives.

ROLE OF THE MULTIMODAL THERAPIST Multimodal therapists tend to be very active during therapy sessions, functioning as trainers, educators, consultants, and role models. They provide information, instruction, and feedback as well as modeling assertive behaviors, challenging self-defeating beliefs, offering constructive criticism and suggestions, offering positive reinforcements, and being appropriately self-disclosing.

Effective therapy calls for counselors to be "authentic chameleons" (Lazarus, 1993), meaning that a flexible repertoire of relationship styles is as important as a wide range of techniques in enhancing treatment outcomes. Therapists need to make choices regarding different styles of relating to clients. They will have to decide when and how to be directive or supportive, cold or warm, formal or informal, and tough or tender. Lazarus (1996a) states that one of his major accomplishments as a therapist over the years has been learning to blend appropriate and effective techniques with the most suitable relationship style.

Integrating Behavioral Techniques With Contemporary Psychoanalytic Approaches

Certain aspects of behavior therapy can be combined with a number of other therapeutic approaches. For example, behavioral and cognitive behavioral techniques can be combined with the conceptual framework of contemporary psychoanalytic therapies (see Chapter 4). Morgan and MacMillan (1999) developed a three-phase integrated counseling model based on theoretical constructs of object-relations and attachment theory that incorporates behavioral techniques.

In the first phase, object-relations theory serves as the conceptual basis for the assessment and relationship-building process. What children learn from early interactions with parents clearly affects personality development and may result in problematic adult relationships. For meaningful assessment to occur, it is essential that the counselor is able to hear the stories of their clients, to grasp their phenomenological world, and to establish rapport with them. During this phase, therapists provide a supportive holding environment that offers a safe place for clients to recall and explore painful earlier memories. At this phase counseling includes an exploration of clients' feelings regarding past and present circumstances and thought patterns that influence the clients' interpretation of the world.

In the second phase, the aim is to link insights gleaned from the initial assessment phase to the present to create an understanding of how early relational patterns are related to present difficulties. This insight often enables clients to acknowledge and express painful memories, feelings, and thoughts. As clients are able to process previously repressed and dissociated memories and feelings in counseling, cognitive changes in perception of self and others often occur. Both experiential and cognitive techniques are utilized in the second phase. As clients engage in the process of cognitively restructuring life situations, they acquire new and adaptive ways of thinking, feeling, and coping. They become increasingly able to take active steps to improve their present existence.

In the third and final phase of treatment, behavioral techniques with goal setting and homework assignments are emphasized to maximize change. This is the action phase, a time for clients to attempt new behaviors based on the insight, understanding, and cognitive restructuring achieved in the prior phases of counseling. Clients take action, which leads to empowerment. Termination of counseling is a joint decision based on qualitative changes in clients' relationships and lifestyle.

According to Morgan and MacMillan (1999), there is increasing support in the literature that integrating contemporary psychodynamic theory with behavioral and cognitive behavioral techniques can lead to observable, constructive client changes. Establishing clear goals for each of the three phases of their integrative model provides an efficient framework within which to structure the counseling interventions. Morgan and MacMillan claim that if these treatment goals are well defined it is possible to work through all three phases in a reasonable amount of time. Adapting the conceptual foundation of psychoanalytic thinking to relatively brief therapy makes this approach useful in time-limited therapy.

Another promising blend of behavioral and psychoanalytic techniques is dialectical behavior therapy (DBT). Linehan (1993a, 1993b) formulated DBT for treating borderline personality disorders. Like analytic therapy, DBT emphasizes the importance of the psychotherapeutic relationship, validation of the client, the etiologic importance of the client having experienced an "invalidating environment" as a child, and confrontation of resistance. DBT employs behavioral techniques, including a form of exposure therapy in which the client learns to tolerate painful emotions. DBT integrates its cognitive behaviorism not only with analytic concepts but also with the mindfulness training of "Eastern psychological and spiritual practices (primarily Zen practice)" (Linehan, 1993b, p. 6). DBT skills training is not a "quick fix" approach. It generally involves a minimum of one year of treatment and includes both individual therapy and skills training. This therapeutic approach attempts to accept and validate the client's behavior "as it is in the moment" (p. 5), while also demanding change. The tension between these seemingly incompatible stances is one of the "dialectical" aspects of the treatment. To competently practice DBT, it is essential to get training in this approach.

 # BEHAVIOR THERAPY FROM A MULTICULTURAL PERSPECTIVE

Contributions to Multicultural Counseling

Behavior therapy has some clear advantages over many other theories in working with multicultural populations. Because of their cultural and ethnic backgrounds, some clients hold values that are contrary to the free expression of feelings and the sharing of personal concerns. Behavioral counseling does not place emphasis on experiencing catharsis. Rather, it stresses changing specific behaviors and developing problem-solving skills. Clients who are looking for action plans and behavioral change are likely to cooperate with this approach because they can see that it offers them concrete methods for dealing with their problems of living.

Behavior therapy focuses on environmental conditions that contribute to a client's problems. Social and political influences can play a significant role in the lives of people of color through discriminatory practices and economic problems. A strength of behavioral procedures is that they take into consideration the social and cultural dimensions of the client's life. Tanaka-Matsumi and colleagues (2002) point out that behavior therapy is based on an experimental analysis of behavior in the client's own social environment. These authors state that the behavioral approach gives special attention to a number of specific conditions: the client's cultural conception of problem behaviors, establishing specific therapeutic goals, arranging conditions to increase the client's expectation of successful therapeutic outcomes, and employing appropriate social influence agents. The foundation of ethical practice involves a therapist's familiarity with the client's culture, as well as the competent application of this knowledge in formulating assessment, diagnostic, and treatment strategies.

Behavior Therapy Applied to the Case of Stan

Working with Stan from a behavioral approach, the therapist is interested in understanding his problem behaviors through a functional assessment. In Stan's case many specific and interrelated problems can be identified. *Behaviorally*, he is defensive, avoids eye contact, speaks hesitantly, uses alcohol excessively, has a poor sleep pattern, and displays various avoidance behaviors. In the *emotional* area, Stan has a number of specific problems, some of which include anxiety, panic attacks, depression, fear of criticism and rejection, feeling worthless and stupid, and feeling isolated and alienated. He experiences a range of physiological complaints such as dizziness, heart palpitations, and headaches. *Cognitively,* he worries about death and dying, has many self-defeating thoughts and beliefs, is governed by categorical imperatives ("shoulds," "oughts," "musts"), engages in fatalistic thinking, and compares himself negatively with others. In the *interpersonal* area, Stan is unassertive, has an unsatisfactory relationship with his parents, has few friends, is afraid of contact with women and fears intimacy, and feels socially inferior.

After completing this assessment, Stan's therapist focuses on helping him define the specific areas where he would like to make changes. Before developing a treatment plan, the therapist helps Stan understand the purposes of his behavior. The therapist then educates Stan about how the therapy sessions (and his work outside of the sessions) can help him reach his goals. Early during treatment the therapist helps Stan translate some of his general goals into concrete and measurable ones. Thus, when he says "I want to feel better about myself," she helps him define more specific goals. When he says "I want to get rid of my inferiority complex," she replies: "What are some situations in which you feel inferior?" "What do you actually do that leads to feelings of inferiority?" Stan's concrete aims include his desire to function without drugs or alcohol. She asks him to keep a record of when he drinks and what events lead to drinking.

Stan indicates that he does not want to feel apologetic for his existence. The therapist introduces behavioral skills training because he has trouble talking with his boss and coworkers. She demonstrates specific skills that he can use in approaching them more directly and confidently. This procedure includes modeling, role playing, and behavior rehearsal. He then tries more effective behaviors with his therapist, who plays the role of the boss and then gives feedback on how strong or apologetic he seemed.

Stan's anxiety about women can also be explored using behavior rehearsal. The therapist plays the role of a woman Stan wants to date. He practices being the way he would like to be with his date and says the things to his therapist that he might be afraid to say to his date. During this rehearsal, Stan can explore his fears, get feedback on the effects of his behavior, and experiment with more assertive behavior.

Systematic desensitization is appropriate in working with Stan's fear of failing. He first learns relaxation procedures during the sessions and then practices them daily at home. Next, he lists his specific fears relating to failure. Stan identifies his greatest fear as sexual impotence with a woman. The least fearful situation he identifies is being with a female student for whom he does not feel an attraction. He then imagines a pleasant scene and begins a desensitization process focusing first on his lesser fears and working up to the anxiety associated with his greatest fear.

The goal of therapy is to help Stan modify the behavior that results in his feelings of guilt and anxiety. This approach does not place importance on his past except to the extent necessary to modify his faulty learning. The therapist does not explore his childhood experiences but works directly with the present behaviors that are causing his difficulties. Insight is not seen as important, nor is having Stan experience or reexperience his feelings. By learning more appropriate coping behaviors, eliminating unrealistic anxiety and guilt, and acquiring more adaptive responses, Stan's presenting symptoms will decrease, and he will report a greater degree of satisfaction.

Follow-Up: You Continue as Stan's Behavior Therapist

Use these questions to help you think about how you would work with Stan using a behavioral approach:

- How would you collaboratively work with Stan in identifying specific behavioral goals to give a direction to your therapy?

- What behavioral techniques might be most appropriate in helping Stan with his problems?
- Stan indicates that he does not want to feel apologetic for his existence. How might you help him translate this wish into a specific behavioral goal? What behavioral techniques might you draw on in helping him in this area?
- What homework assignments are you likely to suggest for Stan?

The behavioral approach has moved beyond treating clients for a specific symptom or behavioral problem. Instead, it stresses a thorough assessment of the person's life circumstances to ascertain not only what conditions give rise to the client's problems but also whether the target behavior is amenable to change and whether such a change is likely to lead to a significant improvement in the client's total life situation.

In designing a change program for clients from diverse backgrounds, effective behavioral practitioners conduct a functional analysis of the problem situation. This assessment includes the cultural context in which the problem behavior occurs, the consequences both to the client and to the client's sociocultural environment, the resources within the environment that can promote change, and the impact that change is likely to have on others in the client's surroundings. Assessment methods should be chosen with the client's cultural background in mind (Spiegler & Guevremont, 2003; Tanaka-Matsumi et al., 2002). Counselors must be knowledgeable as well as open and sensitive to issues such as these: What is considered normal and abnormal behavior in the client's culture? What are the client's culturally based conceptions of his or her problems? What kind of information about the client is essential in making an accurate assessment?

Limitations for Multicultural Counseling

According to Spiegler and Guevremont (2003), a future challenge for behavior therapists is to develop empirically based recommendations for how behavior therapy can optimally serve culturally diverse clients. Although behavior therapy is sensitive to differences among clients in a broad sense, behavior therapists need to become more responsive to *specific* issues pertaining to all forms of diversity. Because race, gender, ethnicity, and sexual orientation are critical variables that influence the process and outcome of therapy, it is essential that behavior therapists pay greater attention to such factors than they often do. For example, some African American clients are slow to trust a European American therapist, which may be a healthy response to racism. However, a culturally insensitive therapist may misinterpret this "cultural paranoia" as clinical paranoia (Ridley, 1995).

Some behavioral counselors may focus on using a variety of techniques in narrowly treating specific behavioral problems. Instead of viewing clients in the context of their sociocultural environment, these practitioners concentrate too much on problems within the individual. In doing so they may overlook significant issues in the lives of clients. Such practitioners are not likely to bring about beneficial changes for ethnically diverse clients.

The fact that behavioral interventions often work well raises an interesting issue in multicultural counseling. When clients make significant personal changes, it is very likely that others in their environment will react to these people differently. Before deciding too quickly on goals for therapy, the counselor and client need to discuss the advantages and disadvantages of change. It is essential for therapists to conduct a thorough assessment of the interpersonal and cultural dimensions of the problem. Clients should be helped in assessing the possible consequences of some of their newly acquired social skills. Once goals are determined and therapy is under way, clients should have opportunities to talk about the problems they encounter as they become different people in their home and work settings. For example, a client may want to become more assertive with her husband and children and may strive for increased independence. It is conceivable that as she becomes more assertive and independent divorce may result. Her culture may place a premium on compliance with tradition, and being assertive can lead to problems if she decides to stay within that culture. As a divorced woman, she could find herself without any support from relatives and friends, and she might eventually regret having made the changes she did.

 ## SUMMARY AND EVALUATION

Summary

Behavior therapy is diverse with respect not only to basic concepts but also to techniques that can be applied in coping with specific problems. The behavioral movement includes four major areas of development: classical conditioning, operant conditioning, social learning theory, and increasing attention to the cognitive factors influencing behavior (see Chapter 10). A unique characteristic of behavior therapy is its strict reliance on the principles of the scientific method. Concepts and procedures are stated explicitly, tested empirically, and revised continually. Treatment and assessment are interrelated and occur simultaneously. Research is considered to be a basic aspect of the approach, and therapeutic techniques are continually refined.

A hallmark of behavior therapy is identifying specific goals at the outset of the therapeutic process. In helping clients achieve their goals, behavior therapists typically assume an active and directive role. Although the client generally determines *what* behavior will be changed, the therapist typically determines *how* this behavior can best be modified. In designing a treatment plan, behavior therapists employ techniques and procedures from a wide variety of therapeutic systems and apply them to the unique needs of each client.

Contemporary behavior therapy places emphasis on the interplay between the individual and the environment. Because cognitive factors have a place in the practice of behavior therapy, techniques from this approach can be used to attain humanistic ends. It is clear that bridges can connect humanistic and behavioral therapies, especially with the current focus of attention on self-directed approaches. Behavioral strategies can be used to attain both individual goals and societal goals.

Contributions of Behavior Therapy

Behavior therapy challenges us to reconsider our global approach to counseling. Some may assume they know what a client means by the statement, "I feel unloved; life has no meaning." A humanist might nod in acceptance to such a statement, but the behaviorist will retort: "Who specifically do you feel is not loving you?" "What is going on in your life to make you think it has no meaning?" "What are some specific things you might be doing that contribute to the state you are in?" "What would you most like to change?" Behavior therapy focuses on specifics.

An advantage behavior therapists have is the wide variety of specific behavioral techniques at their disposal. Because behavior therapy stresses *doing,* as opposed to merely talking about problems and gathering insights, practitioners use many behavioral strategies to assist clients in formulating a plan of action for changing behavior. The basic therapeutic conditions stressed by person-centered therapists—active listening, accurate empathy, positive regard, genuineness, respect, and immediacy—need to be integrated in a behavioral framework.

Behavioral techniques have been extended to more areas of human functioning than have any of the other therapeutic approaches (Kazdin, 2001). Behavior therapy is deeply enmeshed in medicine, geriatrics, pediatrics, rehabilitation programs, and stress management. This approach has made significant contributions to health psychology, especially in helping people maintain a healthy lifestyle. In fact, behavioral medicine, the wellness movement, and approaches to holistic health incorporate behavioral strategies as part of their practice. Behavior modification techniques are often used in preventing illness, altering diet and exercise habits, helping individuals cope with pain, improving parenting skills, and addressing a variety of clinical problems (Kazdin, 2001).

A major contribution of behavior therapy is its emphasis on research into and assessment of treatment outcomes. It is up to practitioners to demonstrate that therapy is working. If progress is not being made, therapists look carefully at the original analysis and treatment plan. Of all the therapies presented in this book, this approach and its techniques have been subjected to the most empirical research. Behavioral practitioners are put to the test of identifying specific interventions that have been demonstrated to be effective.

Behavior therapists use empirically tested techniques, assuring that clients are receiving both effective and relatively brief treatment. Evidence-based therapies (EBT) are a hallmark of both behavior therapy and cognitive behavior therapy. Cummings (2002) believes evidenced-based therapies will be mandatory for third party reimbursement in the future: "EBT's are defensible both legally and morally. The court often looks to research studies to find its answers. This emphasis on the use of empirically tested procedures fits well with the requirements of managed care mental health programs. Restricting payments to EBT's would reduce much of what managed care regards as run-away, questionable or needlessly long-term psychotherapy" (p. 4).

To their credit, behavior therapists are willing to examine the effectiveness of their procedures in terms of the generalizability, meaningfulness, and durability of change. Most studies show that behavior therapy methods are more effective than no treatment. Moreover, a number of behavioral procedures are currently the best treatment strategies available for a range of specific problems. Compared with alternative approaches, behavioral techniques have generally been shown to be at least as effective and frequently more effective in changing target behaviors (Kazdin, 2001; Spiegler & Guevremont, 2003).

A strength of the behavioral approach is the emphasis on ethical accountability. Behavior therapy is ethically neutral in that it does not dictate whose behavior or what behavior should be changed. At least in cases of voluntary counseling, the behavioral practitioner only specifies *how* to change those behaviors the client targets for change. Clients have a good deal of control and freedom in deciding *what* the goals of therapy will be.

Behavior therapists address ethical issues by stating that therapy is basically an education process (Tanaka-Matsumi et al., 2002). At the outset of behavior therapy clients learn about the nature of counseling, the procedures that may be employed, and the benefits and risks. Clients are given information about the specific therapy procedures appropriate for their particular problems. An essential feature of behavior therapy involves the collaboration between therapist and client. Not only do clients decide on the therapy goals, but they also participate in the choice of techniques that will be used in dealing with their problems. With this information clients become informed, fully enfranchised partners in the therapeutic venture.

Limitations and Criticisms of Behavior Therapy

Behavior therapy has been criticized for a variety of reasons. Let's examine five common criticisms and misconceptions people often have about behavior therapy, together with my reactions.

1. *Behavior therapy may change behaviors, but it does not change feelings.* Some critics argue that feelings must change before behavior can change. Behavioral practitioners hold that empirical evidence has not shown that feelings must be changed first, and behavioral clinicians do in actual practice deal with

feelings as an overall part of the treatment process. A general criticism of both the behavioral and the cognitive approaches is that clients are not encouraged to experience their emotions. In concentrating on how clients are behaving or thinking, some behavior therapists tend to play down the working through of emotional issues. Generally, I favor initially focusing on what clients are feeling and then working with the behavioral and cognitive dimensions.

   2. *Behavior therapy ignores the important relational factors in therapy.* The charge is often made that the importance of the relationship between client and therapist is discounted in behavior therapy. Although behavior therapists do not place primary weight on the relationship variable, they do acknowledge that a good working relationship with clients is a basic foundation necessary for the effective use of techniques. They work on establishing rapport with their clients, and Lazarus (1996b) states, "The relationship is the soil that enables the techniques to take root" (p. 61).

   3. *Behavior therapy does not provide insight.* If this assertion is indeed true, behavior therapists would probably respond that insight is not necessary. They do not focus on insight because of the absence of clear evidence that insight is critical to outcome. Behavior is changed directly. A change in behavior often leads to a change in understanding; it is a two-way street.

   4. *Behavior therapy treats symptoms rather than causes.* The psychoanalytic assumption is that early traumatic events are at the root of present dysfunction. Behavior therapists may acknowledge that deviant responses have historical origins, but they contend that history is seldom important in the maintenance of current problems. However, behavior therapists emphasize changing current environmental circumstances to change behavior.

   Related to this criticism is the notion that, unless historical causes of present behavior are therapeutically explored, new symptoms will soon take the place of those that were "cured." Behaviorists rebut this assertion on both theoretical and empirical grounds. They do not accept the assumption that symptoms are manifestations of underlying intrapsychic conflicts. Instead, they contend that behavior therapy directly changes the maintaining conditions, which are the causes of problem behaviors (symptoms). Furthermore, they assert that there is no empirical evidence that symptom substitution occurs after behavior therapy has successfully eliminated unwanted behavior because they have changed the conditions that give rise to those behaviors (Kazdin & Wilson, 1978; Sloane et al., 1975; Spiegler & Guevremont, 2003).

   5. *Behavior therapy involves control and manipulation by the therapist.* All therapists have a power relationship with the client and thus have control. Behavior therapists are just clearer with their clients about this role (Miltenberger, 2004). Kazdin (2001) believes no issues of control and manipulation are associated with behavioral strategies that are not also raised by other therapeutic approaches. Kazdin maintains that behavior therapy does not embrace particular goals or argue for a particular lifestyle, nor does it have an agenda for changing society.

   Surely, in all therapeutic approaches there is control by the therapist, who hopes to change behavior in some way. This does not mean, however, that clients are helpless victims at the mercy of the whims and values of the therapist. Contemporary behavior therapists employ techniques aimed at increased self-direction and self-control, which are skills clients actually learn in the therapy process.

 ## WHERE TO GO FROM HERE

In the *CD-ROM for Integrative Counseling,* Session 8 ("Behavioral Focus in Counseling"), I demonstrate a behavioral way to assist Ruth in developing an exercise program. It is crucial that Ruth makes her own decisions about specific behavioral goals she wants to pursue. This applies to my attempts to work with her in developing methods of relaxation, increasing her self-efficacy, and designing an exercise plan.

Because the literature in this field is so extensive and diverse, it is not possible in one brief survey chapter to present a comprehensive, in-depth discussion of behavioral techniques. I hope you will be challenged to examine any misconceptions you may hold about behavior therapy and be stimulated to do some further reading of selected sources.

If you have an interest in further training in behavior therapy, the Association for Advancement of Behavior Therapy (AABT) is an excellent source. AABT is a membership organization of more than 4,300 mental health professionals and students who are interested in behavior therapy, cognitive behavior therapy, behavioral assessment, and applied behavioral analysis. If you are interested in becoming a member of this organization, contact:

> **Association for Advancement of Behavior Therapy**
> 305 Seventh Avenue, 16th Floor
> New York, NY 10001-6008
> Telephone: (212) 647-1890 or (800) 685-AABT
> Fax: (212) 647-1865
> Email: membership@aabt.org
> Web site: www.aabt.org

Full and associate memberships are $205 and include one journal subscription (to either *Behavior Therapy* or *Cognitive and Behavioral Practice*), and a subscription to the *Behavior Therapist* (a newsletter with feature articles, training updates, and association news). Membership also includes reduced registration and continuing education course fees for AABT's annual convention held every November, which features workshops, master clinician programs, symposia, and other educational presentations. Student memberships are $55. Members receive discounts on all AABT publications, some of which are:

- *Directory of Graduate Training in Behavior Therapy and Experimental-Clinical Psychology.* An excellent source for students and job seekers who want information on programs with an emphasis on behavioral training.

- *Directory of Psychology Internships: Programs Offering Behavioral Training*. Describes training programs having a behavioral component.
- *Behavior Therapy*. An international quarterly journal focusing on original experimental and clinical research, theory, and practice.
- *Cognitive and Behavioral Practice*. A quarterly journal that features clinically oriented articles.

Francine Shapiro is the executive director of the EMDR Institute, which trains and credentials EMDR practitioners. For information regarding EMDR training, contact:

EMDR Institute
P.O. Box 51010
Pacific Grove, CA 93950
Telephone: (831) 372-3900
Fax: (831) 647-9881
Email: Inst@EMDR.com
Web site: www.EMDR.com

 ## InfoTrac College Edition Resources

Behavior Therapy   The following key words are listed in such a way as to allow the InfoTrac College Edition search engine to locate a wider range of articles in the online library. The key words should be entered exactly as shown, to include asterisks, "W1," and "AND."

Albert Bandura	Positive reinforcement
Donald Meichenbaum	Observational learning
Ivan Pavlov	Covert behavior
B. F. Skinner	Cognitive W1 process*
Classical conditioning	Systematic desensitization
Operant conditioning	Exposure W1 therapy
Social Cognitive Theory	Exposure and response prevention
Social Learning Theory	Eye movement desensitization and reprocessing
Overt behavior	

Recommended Supplementary Readings

Contemporary Behavior Therapy (Spiegler & Guevremont, 2003) is a comprehensive and up-to-date treatment of basic principles and applications of the behavior therapies, as well as a fine discussion of ethical issues. Specific chapters deal with procedures that can be usefully applied to a range of client populations: behavioral assessment, modeling therapy, systematic desensitization, exposure therapies, cognitive restructuring, and cognitive coping skills.

Interviewing and Change Strategies for Helpers: Fundamental Skills and Cognitive Behavioral Interventions (Cormier & Nurius, 2003) is a comprehensive and clearly written textbook dealing with training experiences and skill development. Its excellent documentation offers practitioners a wealth of material on a variety of topics, such as assessment procedures, selection of goals, development of appropriate treatment programs, and methods of evaluating outcomes.

Behavior Modification: Principles and Procedures (Miltenberger, 2004) is an excellent resource for learning more about basic principles such as reinforcement, extinction, punishment, and procedures to establish new behavior.

Behavior Modification in Applied Settings (Kazdin, 2001) offers a contemporary look at behavior modification principles that are derived from operant conditioning and describes how techniques can be applied in clinical, home, school, and work settings.

Self-Directed Behavior: Self-Modification for Personal Adjustment (Watson & Tharp, 2002) provides readers with specific steps for carrying out self-modification programs. The authors deal with selecting a goal, developing a plan, keeping progress notes, and recognizing and coping with obstacles to following through with a self-directed program.

Brief But Comprehensive Psychotherapy: The Multimodal Way (Lazarus, 1997a) is an excellent source of techniques and procedures for brief interventions that can be applied with diverse client populations in various settings.

Clinical Behavior Therapy (Goldfried & Davison, 1994) is a classic text that covers the theoretical underpinnings of behavior therapy as well as approaches to behavioral assessment and therapeutic techniques.

References and Suggested Readings

*ALBERTI, R. E., & EMMONS, M. L. (2001a). *Your perfect right: A guide to assertive behavior* (8th ed.). Atascadero, CA: Impact.

ALBERTI, R. E., & EMMONS, M. L. (2001b). *Your perfect right: A manual for assertiveness trainers*. Atascadero, CA: Impact.

BANDURA, A. (1969). *Principles of behavior modification*. New York: Holt, Rinehart & Winston.

BANDURA, A. (Ed.). (1971a). *Psychological modeling: Conflicting theories*. Chicago: Aldine-Atherton.

BANDURA, A. (1971b). Psychotherapy based upon modeling principles. In A. E. Bergin & S. L. Garfield (Eds.), *Handbook of psychotherapy and behavior change*. New York: Wiley.

BANDURA, A. (1974). Behavior therapy and the models of man. *American Psychologist, 29*, 859–869.

BANDURA, A. (1977). *Social learning theory*. Englewood Cliffs, NJ: Prentice-Hall.

BANDURA, A. (1982). Self-efficacy mechanisms in human agency. *American Psychologist, 37*, 122–147.

BANDURA, A. (1986). *Social foundations of thought and action: A social cognitive theory*. Englewood Cliffs, NJ: Prentice-Hall.

---

*Books and articles marked with an asterisk are suggested for further study.

BANDURA, A. (1997). *Self-efficacy: The exercise of self-control.* New York: Freeman.

BANDURA, A., & WALTERS, R. H. (1963). *Social learning and personality development.* New York: Holt, Rinehart & Winston.

BARKER, S. B., & HAWES, E. C. (1999). Eye movement desensitization and reprocessing in Individual Psychology. *Journal of Individual Psychology, 55*(2), 146–161.

*BARLOW, D. H. (Ed.). (2001). *Clinical handbook of psychological disorders: A step-by-step manual* (3rd ed.). New York: Guilford Press.

*BECK, A. T. (1976). *Cognitive therapy and emotional disorders.* New York: New American Library.

BECK, A. T., & WEISHAAR, M. E. (2000). Cognitive therapy. In R. J. Corsini & D. Wedding (Eds.), *Current psychotherapies* (6th ed., pp. 241–272). Itasca, IL: F. E. Peacock.

COREY, G. (2004). *Theory and practice of group counseling* (6th ed.). Pacific Grove, CA: Brooks/Cole.

*COREY, G. (2005). *Case approach to counseling and psychotherapy* (6th ed.). Belmont, CA: Brooks/Cole.

*CORMIER, S., & NURIUS, P. S. (2003). *Interviewing and change strategies for helpers: Fundamental skills and cognitive behavioral interventions* (5th ed.). Pacific Grove, CA: Brooks/Cole.

CUMMINGS, N. (2002). Evidence based therapies and the future of mental health care. *The Milton H. Erickson Foundation Newsletter, 22*(2), 4.

*FISHMAN, D. B., & FRANKS, C. M. (1997). The conceptual evolution of behavior therapy. In P. L. Wachtel & S. B. Messer (Eds.), *Theories of psychotherapy: Origins and evolution* (pp. 131–180). Washington, DC: American Psychological Association.

FRANKS, C. M. (1997). Foreword to A. A. Lazarus, *Brief but comprehensive psychotherapy: The multimodal way* (pp. ix–xii). New York: Springer.

GOLDFRIED, M. R., & DAVISON, G. C. (1994). *Clinical behavior therapy* (expanded ed.). New York: Wiley.

GRANVOLD, D. K., & WODARSKI, J. S. (1994). Cognitive and behavioral treatment: Clinical issues, transfer of training, and relapse prevention. In D. K. Granvold (Ed.), *Cognitive and behavioral treatment: Method and applications* (pp. 353–375). Pacific Grove, CA: Brooks/Cole.

JACOBSON, E. (1938). *Progressive relaxation.* Chicago: University of Chicago Press.

KAZDIN, A. E. (1978). *History of behavior modification: Experimental foundations of contemporary research.* Baltimore: University Park Press.

KAZDIN, A. E. (1982). Symptom substitution, generalization, and response covariation: Implications for psychotherapy outcome. *Psychological Bulletin, 91,* 349–365.

*KAZDIN, A. E. (2001). *Behavior modification in applied settings* (6th ed.). Pacific Grove, CA: Brooks/Cole.

KAZDIN, A. E., & WILSON, G. T. (1978). *Evaluation of behavior therapy: Issues, evidence, and research strategies.* Cambridge, MA: Ballinger.

LAZARUS, A. A. (1976). *Multimodal behavior therapy.* New York:Springer.

LAZARUS, A. A. (1986). Multimodal therapy. In J. C. Norcross (Ed.), *Handbook of eclectic psychotherapy* (pp. 65–93). New York: Brunner/Mazel.

LAZARUS, A. A. (1987a). The multimodal approach with adult outpatients. In N. S. Jacobson (Ed.), *Psychotherapists in clinical practice.* New York: Guilford Press.

LAZARUS, A. A. (1987b). The need for technical eclecticism: Science, breadth, depth, and specificity In J. K. Zeig (Ed.), *The evolution of psychotherapy* (pp. 164–178). New York: Brunner/Mazel.

*LAZARUS, A. A. (1989). *The practice of multimodal therapy.* Baltimore: Johns Hopkins University Press.

LAZARUS, A. A. (1992a). The multimodal approach to the treatment of minor depression. *American Journal of Psychotherapy, 46*(l), 50–57.

LAZARUS, A. A. (1992b). Multimodal therapy: Technical eclecticism with minimal integration. In J. C. Norcross & M. R. Goldfried (Eds.), *Handbook of psychotherapy integration* (pp. 231–263). New York: Basic Books.

*LAZARUS, A. A. (1993). Tailoring the therapeutic relationship, or being an authentic chameleon. *Psychotherapy, 30,* 404–407.

*LAZARUS, A. A. (1996a). Some reflections after 40 years of trying to be an effective psychotherapist. *Psychotherapy, 33*(1), 142–145.

*LAZARUS, A. A. (1996b). The utility and futility of combining treatments in psychotherapy. *Clinical Psychology: Science and Practice, 3*(1), 59–68.

*LAZARUS, A. A. (1997a). *Brief but comprehensive psychotherapy: The multimodal way.* New York: Springer.

*LAZARUS, A. A. (1997b). Can psychotherapy be brief, focused, solution-oriented, and yet comprehensive? A personal evolutionary perspective. In J. K. Zeig (Ed.), *The evolution of psychotherapy: The third conference* (pp. 83–94). New York: Brunner/Mazel.

LAZARUS, A. A. (2000a). Multimodal strategies with adults. In J. Carlson & L. Sperry (Eds.), *Brief therapy with individuals and couples* (pp. 106–124). Phoenix: Zeig & Tucker.

LAZARUS, A. A. (2000b). Multimodal therapy. In R. Corsini & D. Wedding (Eds.), *Current psychotherapies* (6th ed., pp. 340–374). Itasca, IL: F. E. Peacock.

LAZARUS, A. A., & LAZARUS, C. N. (1991). *Multimodal life-history inventory.* Champaign, IL: Research Press.

LAZARUS, C. N., & LAZARUS, A. A. (2002). EMDR: An elegantly concentrated multimodal procedure? In F. Shapiro (Ed.), *EMDR as an integrative psychotherapy approach* (pp. 209–223). Washington, DC: American Psychological Association.

LINEHAN, M. M. (1993a). *Cognitive-behavioral treatment of borderline personality disorder.* New York: Guilford Press.

LINEHAN, M. M. (1993b). *Skills training manual for treating borderline personality disorder.* New York: Guilford Press.

*MEICHENBAUM, D. (1977). *Cognitive behavior modification: An integrative approach.* New York: Plenum.

MEICHENBAUM, D. (1985). *Stress inoculation training.* New York: Pergamon Press.

*MILTENBERGER, R. G. (2004). *Behavior modification: Principles and procedures* (3rd ed.). Pacific Grove, CA: Brooks/Cole.

MORGAN, B., & MACMILLAN, P. (1999). Helping clients move toward constructive change: A three-phase integrative counseling model. *Journal of Counseling and Development, 77*(2), 153–159.

NYE, R. D. (2000). *Three psychologies: Perspectives from Freud, Skinner, and Rogers* (6th ed.). Pacific Grove, CA: Brooks/Cole.

PAUL, G. L. (1967). Outcome research in psychotherapy. *Journal of Consulting Psychology, 31,* 109–188.

POLIVY, J., & HERMAN, C. P. (2002). If at first you don't succeed: False hopes of self-change. *American Psychologist, 57*(9), 677–689.

PROCHASKA, J. O., & NORCROSS, J. C. (2003). *Systems of psychotherapy: A transtheoretical analysis* (5th ed.). Pacific Grove, CA: Brooks/Cole.

RIDLEY, C. R. (1995). *Overcoming unintentional racism in counseling and therapy: A practitioner's guide to intentional intervention.* Thousand Oaks, CA: Sage.

*SHAPIRO, F. (2001). *Eye movement desensitization and reprocessing: Basic principles, protocols, and procedures* (2nd ed.). New York: Guilford Press.

*SHAPIRO, F. (2002a). *EMDR as an integrative psychotherapy approach.* Washington, DC: American Psychological Association.

*SHAPIRO, F. (2002b). EMDR twelve years after its introduction: Past and future research. *Journal of Clinical Psychology, 58,* 1–22.

SHAPIRO, F., & FORREST, M. S. (1997). *EMDR: The breakthrough therapy for overcoming anxiety, stress, and trauma.* New York: Basic Books.

SKINNER, B. F. (1948). *Walden two.* New York: Macmillan.

SKINNER, B. F. (1953). *Science and human behavior.* New York: Macmillan.

SKINNER, B. F. (1971). *Beyond freedom and dignity.* New York: Knopf.

SKINNER, B. F. (1974). *About behaviorism.* New York: Knopf.

SLOANE, R. B., STAPLES, E. R., CRISTOL, A. H., YORKSTON, N. J., & WHIPPLE, K. (1975). *Psychotherapy versus behavior therapy.* Cambridge, MA: Harvard University Press.

*SPIEGLER, M. D., & GUEVREMONT, D. C. (2003). *Contemporary behavior therapy* (4th ed.). Pacific Grove, CA: Brooks/Cole.

TANAKA-MATSUMI, J., HIGGINBOTHAM, H. N., & CHANG, R. (2002). Cognitive-behavioral approaches to counseling across cultures: A functional analytic approach for clinical applications. In P. B. Pedersen, J. G. Draguns, W. J. Lonner, & J. E. Trimble (Eds.), *Counseling across cultures* (5th ed., pp. 337–379). Thousand Oaks, CA: Sage.

THORESEN, C. E., & COATES, T. J. (1980). What does it mean to be a behavior therapist? In C. E. Thoresen (Ed.), *The behavior therapist.* Pacific Grove, CA: Brooks/Cole.

VOLTZ, L. M., & EVANS, I. M. (1982). The assessment of behavioral interrelationships in child behavior therapy. *Behavioral Assessment, 4,* 131–165.

*WATSON, D. L., & THARP, R. G. (2002). *Self-directed behavior: Self-modification for personal adjustment* (8th ed.). Pacific Grove, CA: Brooks/Cole.

WILSON, G. T. (2000). Behavior therapy. In R. Corsini & D. Wedding (Eds.), *Current psychotherapies* (6th ed., pp. 205–240). Itasca, IL: F. E. Peacock.

WOLPE, J. (1990). *The practice of behavior therapy* (4th ed.). Elmsford, NY: Pergamon Press.

Cognitive Behavior Therapy

Albert *Ellis*

ALBERT ELLIS (b. 1913) was born in Pittsburgh but escaped to the wilds of New York at the age of 4 and has lived there (except for a year in New Jersey) ever since. He was hospitalized nine times as a child, mainly with nephritis, and developed renal glycosuria at the age of 19 and diabetes at the age of 40. By rigorously taking care of his health and stubbornly refusing to make himself miserable about it, he has lived an unusually robust and energetic life.

Realizing that he could counsel people skillfully and that he greatly enjoyed doing so, Ellis decided to become a psychologist. Believing psychoanalysis to be the deepest form of psychotherapy, Ellis was analyzed and supervised by a training analyst. From 1947 to 1953 he practiced classical analysis and analytically oriented psychotherapy.

After coming to the conclusion that psychoanalysis was a relatively superficial and unscientific form of treatment, he experimented with several other systems. Early in 1955 he combined humanistic, philosophical, and behavioral therapy to form rational-emotive therapy (now known as rational emotive behavior therapy, or REBT). Ellis is rightly known as the grandfather of cognitive behavior therapy.

To some extent Ellis developed his approach as a method of dealing with his own problems during his youth. At one point in his life, for example, he had exaggerated fears of speaking in public. During his adolescence he was extremely shy around young women. At age 19 he forced himself to talk to 100 women in the Bronx Botanical Gardens over a period of one month. Although he never managed to get a date from these brief encounters, he does report that he desensitized himself to his fear of rejection by women. By applying cognitive behavioral methods, he has managed to conquer some of his worst blocks (Ellis, 1994, 1997). Moreover, he has learned to actually enjoy public speaking and other activities about which he was once highly anxious.

People who hear Ellis lecture often comment on his abrasive, humorous, and flamboyant style (Dryden, 1989). He does see himself as more abrasive than most in his workshops, and he also considers himself humorous and startling in some ways. In his workshops it seems that he takes delight in giving vent to his eccentric side. He enjoys his work, which is his primary commitment in life.

At age 90, Ellis is highly energetic and productive. He continues to work 7 days a week and is surely one of the most prolific writers in the field of counseling and psychotherapy. He has practiced psychotherapy, group therapy, marriage and family counseling, and sex therapy for more than 60 years. In his busy professional life he sees as many as 60 clients a week for individual sessions, conducts 4 group therapy sessions weekly, and gives about 200 talks and workshops to professionals and the public each year.

Ellis has published over 70 books and more than 800 articles, mostly on the theory and applications of REBT. He is a Diplomate in Clinical Psychology of the American Board of Professional Psychology; in Clinical Hypnosis of the American Board of Psychological Hypnosis; of the American Board of Medical Psychotherapists; and of the American Board of Sexology. ■

Aaron T. Beck

AARON TEMKIN BECK (b. 1921) was born in Providence, Rhode Island. His childhood was characterized by adversity, and his early schooling was interrupted by a life-threatening illness, yet he overcame this problem and ended up a year ahead of his peer group (Weishaar, 1993). Throughout his life he struggled with a variety of fears: blood injury fears, fear of suffocation, tunnel phobia, anxiety about his health, and public speaking anxiety. Beck used his personal problems as a basis for understanding others and developing his theory.

A graduate of Brown University and Yale School of Medicine, Beck was initially attracted to neurology but switched to psychiatry during his residency. Beck is the pioneering figure in cognitive therapy, one of the most influential and empirically validated approaches to psychotherapy. Cognitive therapy is also the most comprehensive theory of depression in the world.

Beck attempted to validate Freud's theory of depression, but his research resulted in his parting company with Freud's motivational model and the explanation of depression as self-directed anger. As a result of this decision, Beck endured isolation and rejection from many in the psychiatric community for many years. Through his research, Beck developed a cognitive theory of depression. He found the cognitions of depressed persons to be characterized by errors in logic that he called "cognitive distortions." For Beck, negative thoughts reflect underlying dysfunctional beliefs and assumptions. When these beliefs are triggered by situational events, a depressive pattern is put in motion. Beck believes clients can assume an active role in modifying their dysfunctional thinking and thereby gain relief from a range of psychiatric conditions. His continuous research in the areas of psychopathology and the utility of cognitive therapy has earned him a place of prominence in the scientific community in the United States.

Beck joined the Department of Psychiatry of the University of Pennsylvania in 1954, where he currently holds the position of Professor (Emeritus) of Psychiatry. Beck's pioneering research established the efficacy of cognitive therapy for depression. He has successfully applied cognitive therapy to depression, generalized anxiety and panic disorders, alcoholism and drug abuse, eating disorders, marital and relationship problems, and personality disorders. He has developed assessment scales for depression, suicide risk, anxiety, self-concept, and personality.

He is the founder of the Beck Institute, which is a research and training center directed by one of his four children, Dr. Judith Beck. He has eight grandchildren and has been married for 50 years. To his credit, Aaron Beck has focused on developing the cognitive therapy skills of hundreds of clinicians. In turn, they have established their own cognitive therapy centers. ∎

INTRODUCTION

This chapter is an extension of the previous chapter on behavior therapy. As you saw in Chapter 9, traditional behavior therapy has broadened and largely moved in the direction of cognitive behavior therapy. Several of the more prominent cognitive behavioral approaches are featured in this chapter, including Albert Ellis's rational emotive behavior therapy (REBT), Aaron T. Beck's cognitive therapy (CT), and Donald Meichenbaum's cognitive behavior therapy (CBT). More than 20 different therapies have been labeled "cognitive" or "cognitive behavioral" (Dattilio & Padesky, 1990; Mahoney & Lyddon, 1988). Cognitive behavior therapy, which combines both cognitive and behavioral principles and methods in a short-term treatment approach, has generated more empirical research than any other psychotherapy model (Dattilio, 2000a).

As is true of behavior therapy, the cognitive behavioral approaches are quite diverse, but they do share these attributes: (1) a collaborative relationship between client and therapist, (2) the premise that psychological distress is largely a function of disturbances in cognitive processes, (3) a focus on changing cognitions to produce desired changes in affect and behavior, and (4) a generally time-limited and educational treatment focusing on specific and structured target problems (Arnkoff & Glass, 1992; Dobson & Block, 1988; Weishaar, 1993). All of the cognitive behavioral approaches are based on a structured psychoeducational model, and they all emphasize the role of homework, place responsibility on the client to assume an active role both during and outside of the therapy sessions, and draw from a variety of cognitive and behavioral strategies to bring about change.

To a large degree cognitive behavior therapy is based on the assumption that a reorganization of one's self-statements will result in a corresponding reorganization of one's behavior. Meichenbaum (1977) writes that within a learning theory framework clients' cognitions are explicit behaviors that can be modified in their own right, just as are overt behaviors that can be directly observed. Thus, behavioral techniques such as operant conditioning, modeling, and behavioral rehearsal can also be applied to the more covert and subjective processes of thinking and internal dialogue. The cognitive behavioral approaches discussed in this chapter include a variety of behavioral strategies as a part of their integrative repertoire.

 ALBERT ELLIS'S RATIONAL EMOTIVE BEHAVIOR THERAPY

Rational emotive behavior therapy (REBT) has a great deal in common with the therapies that are oriented toward cognition and behavior in that the approach stresses thinking, judging, deciding, analyzing, and doing. The basic assumption of REBT is that people contribute to their own psychological problems, as well as to specific symptoms, by the way they interpret events and situations. REBT is based on the assumption that cognitions, emotions, and behaviors interact significantly and have a reciprocal cause-and-effect relationship. REBT has consistently emphasized all three of these modalities and their interactions, thus qualifying it as an integrative approach (Ellis, 1994, 1999, 2000b, 2001a, 2001b, 2002; Ellis & Dryden, 1997).

Ellis argued that the psychoanalytic approach is sometimes very inefficient because people often seem to get worse instead of better (Ellis,1999, 2000a, 2001b, 2002). He began to persuade and encourage his clients to do the very things they were most afraid of doing, such as risking rejection by significant others. Gradually, he became much more eclectic and more active and directive as a therapist, and REBT became a general school of psychotherapy aimed at providing clients with the tools to restructure their philosophical and behavioral styles (Ellis, 2001b; Ellis & Blau, 1998).

Although REBT is generally conceded to be the parent of today's cognitive behavioral approaches, it was preceded by earlier schools of thought. Ellis acknowledges his debt to the ancient Greeks, especially the Stoic philosopher Epictetus, who said, in the first century A.D., "People are disturbed not by things, but by the view which they take of them" (as cited in Ellis, 2001a, p. 16). Ellis contends that how people disturb themselves is more comprehensive and precise than that: "People disturb themselves by the things that happen to them, and by their views, feelings, and actions" (p. 16). Horney's (1950) ideas on the "tyranny of the shoulds" are also apparent in the conceptual framework of REBT.

Ellis also gives credit to Adler as an influential precursor. As you will recall, Adler writes that our emotional reactions and lifestyle are associated with our basic beliefs and are therefore cognitively created. Like the Adlerian approach, REBT emphasizes the role of social interest in determining psychological health. There are other Adlerian influences on REBT, such as the importance of goals, purposes, values, and meanings in human existence; the focus on active teaching; the use of persuasive methods; and the giving of live demonstrations before an audience (Ellis, Gordon, Neenan, & Palmer, 1997; Yankura & Dryden, 1994).

REBT's basic hypothesis is that our emotions stem mainly from our beliefs, evaluations, interpretations, and reactions to life situations. Through the therapeutic process, clients learn skills that give them the tools to identify and dispute irrational beliefs that have been acquired and self-constructed and are now maintained by self-indoctrination. They learn how to replace such ineffective ways of thinking with effective and rational cognitions, and as a result they change their emotional reactions to situations. The therapeutic process allows clients to apply REBT principles of change not only to a particular presenting problem but also to many other problems in life or future problems they might encounter (Ellis, 1999).

Several therapeutic implications flow from these assumptions: The focus is on working with *thinking* and *acting* rather than primarily with expressing feelings. Therapy is seen as an *educational process*. The therapist functions in many ways like a teacher, especially in collaborating with a client on homework assignments and in teaching strategies for straight thinking; and the client is a learner, who practices the skills discussed in therapy in everyday life.

REBT differs from many other therapeutic approaches in that it does not place much value on free association, working with dreams, focusing on the client's past history, endlessly expressing feelings, or dealing with transference phenomena. Ellis (2000b) refers to devoting any length of time to these factors "indulgence therapy." Such work may result in clients feeling better, but it will rarely aid them in getting better.

 ## KEY CONCEPTS

View of Human Nature

Rational emotive behavior therapy is based on the assumption that human beings are born with a potential for both rational, or "straight," thinking and irrational, or "crooked," thinking. People have predispositions for self-preservation, happiness, thinking and verbalizing, loving, communion with others, and growth and self-actualization. They also have propensities for self-destruction, avoidance of thought, procrastination, endless repetition of mistakes, superstition, intolerance, perfectionism and self-blame, and avoidance of actualizing growth potentials. Taking for granted that humans are fallible, REBT attempts to help them accept themselves as creatures who will continue to make mistakes yet at the same time learn to live more at peace with themselves.

Ellis assumes that we are *self-talking, self-evaluating,* and *self-sustaining.* We develop emotional and behavioral difficulties when we mistake *simple preferences* (desires for love, approval, success) for dire needs. Ellis also affirms that we have an inborn tendency toward growth and actualization, yet we often sabotage our movement toward growth due to self-defeating patterns we have learned (Ellis, 1999, 2000a; Ellis & Blau, 1998; Ellis & Dryden, 1997; Ellis & Tafrate, 1997).

View of Emotional Disturbance

We originally learn irrational beliefs from significant others during childhood. Additionally, we create irrational dogmas and superstitions by ourselves. Then we actively reinforce self-defeating beliefs by the processes of autosuggestion and self-repetition and by behaving as if they are useful. Hence, it is largely our own repetition of early-indoctrinated irrational thoughts, rather than a parent's repetition, that keeps dysfunctional attitudes alive and operative within us.

Ellis contends that people do not *need* to be accepted and loved, even though this may be highly desirable. The therapist teaches clients how to feel undepressed even when they are unaccepted and unloved by significant others. Although REBT encourages people to experience healthy feelings of sadness over being unaccepted, it attempts to help them find ways of overcoming unhealthy feelings of depression, anxiety, hurt, loss of self-worth, and hatred.

Ellis insists that blame is at the core of most emotional disturbances. Therefore, to recover from a neurosis or a personality disorder, we had better stop blaming ourselves and others. Instead, it is important that we learn to accept ourselves despite our imperfections. Ellis (Ellis & Blau, 1998; Ellis & Harper, 1997) hypothesizes that we have strong tendencies to escalate our desires and preferences into dogmatic "shoulds," "musts," "oughts," demands, and commands. When we are upset, it is a good idea to look to our hidden dogmatic "musts" and absolutist "shoulds." Such demands create disruptive feelings and dysfunctional behaviors (Ellis, 2001a; Ellis & Dryden, 1997).

Here are some irrational ideas that we internalize and that inevitably lead to self-defeat (Ellis, 1994, 1997, 1999; Ellis & Dryden, 1997; Ellis & Harper, 1997):

- "I *must* have love or approval from all the significant people in my life."
- "I *must* perform important tasks competently and perfectly well."
- "Because I strongly desire that people treat me considerately and fairly, they *absolutely must* do so!"
- "If I don't get what I want, it's terrible, and I can't stand it."
- "It's easier to avoid facing life's difficulties and responsibilities than to undertake more rewarding forms of self-discipline."

We have a strong tendency to make and keep ourselves emotionally disturbed by internalizing self-defeating beliefs such as these, which is why it is a real challenge to achieve and maintain good psychological health (Ellis, 2001a, 2001b).

A-B-C Theory of Personality

The A-B-C theory of personality is central to REBT theory and practice. A is the existence of a fact, an event, or the behavior or attitude of an individual. C is the emotional and behavioral consequence or reaction of the individual; the reaction can be either healthy or unhealthy. A (the activating event) does not cause C (the emotional consequence). Instead, B, which is the person's belief about A, largely causes C, the emotional reaction.

The interaction of the various components can be diagrammed like this:

$$A \text{ (activating event)} \leftarrow B \text{ (belief)} \rightarrow C \text{ (emotional and behavioral consequence)}$$
$$\uparrow$$
$$D \text{ (disputing intervention)} \rightarrow E \text{ (effect)} \rightarrow F \text{ (new feeling)}$$

If a person experiences depression after a divorce, for example, it may not be the divorce itself that causes the depressive reaction but the person's *beliefs* about being a failure, being rejected, or losing a mate. Ellis would maintain that the beliefs about the rejection and failure (at point B) are what mainly cause the depression (at point C)—not the actual event of the divorce (at point A). Thus, human beings are largely responsible for creating their own emotional reactions and disturbances. Showing people how they can change the irrational beliefs that directly "cause" their disturbed emotional consequences is the heart of REBT (Ellis, 1999; Ellis & Dryden, 1997; Ellis et al., 1997; Ellis & Harper, 1997).

How is an emotional disturbance fostered? It is fed by the self-defeating sentences clients continually repeat to themselves, such as "I am totally to blame for the divorce," "I am a miserable failure, and everything I did was wrong," "I am a worthless person." Ellis repeatedly makes the point that "you mainly feel the way you think." Disturbed emotional reactions such as depression and anxiety are initiated and perpetuated by clients' self-defeating belief systems, which are based on irrational ideas clients have incorporated and invented. The revised A-B-Cs of REBT now define B as believing, emoting, and behaving. Because belief involves strong emotional and behavioral elements, Ellis (2001a) added these latter two components to the A-B-C framework.

After A, B, and C comes D (disputing). Essentially, D is the application of methods to help clients challenge their irrational beliefs. There are three components of this disputing process: *detecting*, *debating*, and *discriminating*. First, clients learn how to *detect* their irrational beliefs, particularly their absolutist "shoulds" and "musts," their "awfulizing," and their "self-downing." Then clients *debate* their dysfunctional beliefs by learning how to logically and empirically question them and to vigorously argue themselves out of and act against believing them. Finally, clients learn to *discriminate* irrational (self-defeating) beliefs from rational (self-helping) beliefs (Ellis, 1994, 1996).

Although REBT uses many other cognitive, emotive, and behavioral methods to help clients minimize their irrational beliefs, it stresses this process of disputing both during therapy sessions and in everyday life. Eventually clients arrive at E, an effective philosophy, which has a practical side. A new and effective belief system consists of replacing unhealthy thoughts with healthy ones. If we are successful in doing this, we also create F, a new set of feelings. Instead of feeling seriously anxious and depressed, we feel healthily sorry and disappointed in accord with a situation.

In sum, philosophical restructuring to change our dysfunctional personality involves these steps: (1) fully acknowledging that we are largely responsible for creating our own emotional problems; (2) accepting the notion that we have the ability to change these disturbances significantly; (3) recognizing that our emotional problems largely stem from irrational beliefs; (4) clearly perceiving these beliefs; (5) seeing the value of disputing such self-defeating beliefs; (6) accepting the fact that if we expect to change we had better work hard in emotive and behavioral ways to counteract our beliefs and the dysfunctional feelings and actions that follow; and (7) practicing REBT methods of uprooting or changing disturbed consequences for the rest of our life (Ellis, 1999, 2001b, 2002).

 # THE THERAPEUTIC PROCESS

Therapeutic Goals

According to Ellis (2001b; Ellis & Harper, 1997), we have a strong tendency not only to rate our acts and behaviors as "good" or "bad," "worthy" or "unworthy," but also to rate ourselves as a total person on the basis of our performances.

These ratings constitute one of the main sources of our emotional distur-bances. Therefore, most cognitive behavior therapists have the general goal of teaching clients how to separate the evaluation of their behaviors from the evaluation of themselves—their essence and their totality—and how to accept themselves in spite of their imperfections.

The many roads taken in rational emotive behavior therapy lead toward the destination of clients minimizing their emotional disturbances and self-defeating behaviors by acquiring a more realistic and workable philosophy of life. A basic goal is to teach clients how to change their dysfunctional emo-tions and behaviors into healthy ones. Ellis (2001b) states that two of the main goals of REBT are to assist clients in the process of achieving unconditional self-acceptance (USA) and unconditional other acceptance (UOA), and to see how these are interrelated. As clients become more able to accept themselves, they are more likely to unconditionally accept others.

Therapist's Function and Role

The therapist has specific tasks, and the first step is to show clients that they have incorporated many irrational "shoulds," "oughts," and "musts." Clients learn to change their rigid "musts" into preferences. The therapist encourages and often persuades clients to engage in activities that will counter their self-defeating beliefs.

A second step in the therapeutic process is to demonstrate that clients are keeping their emotional disturbances active by continuing to think illogically and unrealistically. In other words, because clients keep reindoctrinating themselves, they are largely responsible for their own neuroses.

Merely showing clients that they have illogical processes is not enough, how-ever, for a client is likely to say, "Now I understand that I have fears of failing and that these fears are exaggerated and unrealistic. But I'm still afraid of fail-ing!" To get beyond client's mere recognition of irrational thoughts, the therapist takes a third step—helping clients modify their thinking and abandon their irra-tional ideas. The therapist assists clients in understanding the vicious circle of the self-blaming process, which also changes their self-defeating behaviors.

The fourth step in the therapeutic process is to challenge clients to develop a rational philosophy of life so that in the future they can avoid becoming the vic-tim of other irrational beliefs. Tackling only specific problems or symptoms can give no assurance that new illogical fears will not emerge. What is desirable, then, is for the therapist to dispute the core of the irrational thinking and to teach clients how to substitute rational beliefs and behaviors for irrational ones.

The therapist mainly employs a persuasive methodology that emphasizes education. Ellis outlines some of the functions the REBT practitioner per-forms (1994, 1999, 2000a; Ellis & Dryden, 1997; Ellis & MacLaren, 1998; Ellis & Velten, 1998):

- Encourages clients to discover a few basic irrational ideas that motivate much disturbed behavior
- Shows how these beliefs are inoperative and how they will lead to future emotional and behavioral disturbances
- Challenges clients to change their self-sabotaging beliefs
- Uses several cognitive, emotive, and behavioral methods to help clients work directly on their feelings and to act against their disturbances

The therapist takes the mystery out of the therapeutic process, teaching clients about the cognitive hypothesis of disturbance and showing how faulty beliefs lead to negative consequences. Insight alone does not typically lead to personality change, but it can help clients see how they are continuing to sabotage themselves and what they can do to change.

Client's Experience in Therapy

Once clients begin to accept that their beliefs are the primary cause of their emotions and behaviors, they are able to participate effectively in the cognitive restructuring process (Ellis et al., 1997; Ellis & MacLaren, 1998). In large measure, the client's role in REBT is that of a learner and doer. Psychotherapy is viewed as a reeducative process whereby the client learns how to apply logical thought, experiential exercises, and behavioral homework to problem solving and emotional change.

The therapeutic process focuses on clients' experiences in the present. Like the person-centered and existential approaches to therapy, REBT mainly emphasizes here-and-now experiences and clients' present ability to change the patterns of thinking and emoting that they constructed earlier. The therapist does not devote much time to exploring clients' early history and making connections between their past and present behavior. Nor does the therapist usually explore in depth clients' early relationships with their parents or siblings. Instead, the therapeutic process stresses to clients that they are presently disturbed because they still believe in and act upon their self-defeating view of themselves and their world.

Clients are expected to actively work outside the therapy sessions. Clients learn that by working hard and carrying out behavioral homework assignments they can minimize faulty thinking, which leads to disturbances in feeling and behaving. Homework is carefully designed and agreed upon and is aimed at getting clients to carry out positive actions that induce emotional and attitudinal change. These assignments are checked in later sessions, and clients learn effective ways to dispute self-defeating thinking. Toward the end of therapy, clients review their progress, make plans, and identify strategies for dealing with continuing or potential problems.

Relationship Between Therapist and Client

Because REBT is essentially a cognitive and directive behavioral process, an intense relationship between therapist and client is not required. As with the person-centered therapy of Rogers, REBT practitioners unconditionally accept all clients and also teach them to unconditionally accept others and themselves. Therapists show their full acceptance by refusing to evaluate their clients as persons while at the same time being willing to honestly confront clients' faulty thinking and self-destructive behaviors.

Ellis believes that too much warmth and understanding can be counterproductive, fostering a sense of dependence for approval from the therapist. REBT practitioners accept their clients as imperfect beings who can be helped by showing that their therapist cares for them without babying them and by also using a variety of techniques such as teaching, bibliotherapy, and behavior modification (Ellis, 2000b; Ellis & Blau, 1998; Ellis & Harper, 1997), but always modeling as well as teaching unconditional full acceptance. Ellis builds rapport with his clients by showing them that he has great faith in their ability to change themselves and that he has the tools to help them do this.

Rational emotive behavior therapists are often open and direct in disclosing their own beliefs and values. Some are willing to share their own imperfections as a way of disputing clients' unrealistic notions that therapists are "completely put together" persons. Transference is not encouraged, and when it does occur, the therapist is likely to confront it. The therapist wants to show that a transference relationship is based on the irrational belief that the client must be liked and loved by the therapist, or parent figure (Ellis, 2002).

 APPLICATION: THERAPEUTIC TECHNIQUES AND PROCEDURES

The Practice of Rational Emotive Behavior Therapy

Rational emotive behavior therapists are multimodal and integrative. REBT generally starts with clients' disturbed feelings and intensely explores these feelings in connection with thoughts and behaviors. Therapists use a variety of cognitive, affective, and behavioral techniques, tailoring them to individual clients (Kwee & Ellis, 1997). These techniques are applied to the treatment of a range of common clinical problems such as anxiety, depression, anger, marital difficulties, poor interpersonal skills, parenting failures, personality disorders, obsessive-compulsive disorders, eating disorders, psychosomatic disorders, addictions, and psychotic disorders (Warren & McLellarn, 1987). For a concrete illustration of how Dr. Ellis works with the client Ruth drawing from cognitive, emotive, and behavioral techniques, see *Case Approach to Counseling and Psychotherapy* (Corey, 2005, chap. 8). What follows is a brief summary of the major cognitive, emotive, and behavioral techniques Ellis describes (Ellis, 1994, 1999; Ellis & Crawford, 2000; Ellis & Dryden, 1997; Ellis & MacLaren, 1998; Ellis & Velten, 1998).

COGNITIVE METHODS REBT practitioners usually incorporate a forceful cognitive methodology in the therapeutic process. They demonstrate to clients in a quick and direct manner what it is that they are continuing to tell themselves. Then they teach clients how to deal with these self-statements so that they no longer believe them, encouraging them to acquire a philosophy based on reality. REBT relies heavily on thinking, disputing, debating, challenging, interpreting, explaining, and teaching. Here are some cognitive techniques available to the therapist.

- *Disputing irrational beliefs.* The most common cognitive method of REBT consists of the therapist actively disputing clients' irrational beliefs and teaching them how to do this challenging on their own. Clients go over a particular "must," "should," or "ought" until they no longer hold that irrational belief, or at least until it is diminished in strength. Here are some examples of questions or statements clients learn to tell themselves: "Why *must* people treat me fairly?" "How do I become a total flop if I don't succeed at important tasks I try?" "If I don't get the job I want, it may be disappointing, but I can certainly stand it." "If life doesn't always go the way I would like it to, it isn't *awful*, just inconvenient."

- *Doing cognitive homework.* REBT clients are expected to make lists of their problems, look for their absolutist beliefs, and dispute these beliefs. They often fill out the REBT Self-Help Form (which is reproduced in the Student Manual). Homework assignments are a way of tracking down the absolutist "shoulds" and "musts" that are part of their internalized self-messages. Part of homework consists of applying the A-B-C theory to many of the problems clients encounter in daily life. The REBT therapist actually teaches the client how to think differently, or models for them, as opposed to the other forms of cognitive behavior therapy.

In carrying out homework, clients are encouraged to put themselves in risk-taking situations that will allow them to challenge their self-limiting beliefs. For example, a client with a talent for acting who is afraid to act in front of an audience because of fear of failure may be asked to take a small part in a stage play. The client is instructed to replace negative self-statements such as "I will fail," "I will look foolish," or "No one will like me" with more positive messages such as "Even if I do behave foolishly at times, this does not make me a foolish *person*. I can act. I will do the best I can. It's nice to be liked, but not everybody will like me, and that isn't the end of the world."

The theory behind this and similar assignments is that clients often create a negative, self-fulfilling prophecy and actually fail because they told themselves in advance that they would. Clients are encouraged to carry out specific assignments during the sessions and, especially, in everyday situations between sessions. In this way clients gradually learn to deal with anxiety and challenge basic irrational thinking. Because therapy is seen as an educational process, clients are also encouraged to read REBT self-help books, such as Ellis's *How to Make Yourself Happy and Remarkably Less Disturbable* (1999). They also listen to and evaluate tapes of their own therapy sessions. Making changes is hard work, and doing work outside the sessions is of real value in revising clients' thinking, feeling, and behaving.

- *Changing one's language.* REBT contends that imprecise language is one of the causes of distorted thinking processes. Clients learn that "musts," "oughts," and "shoulds" can be replaced by *preferences*. Instead of saying "It would be absolutely awful if . . . ," they learn to say "It would be inconvenient if . . .". Clients who use language patterns that reflect helplessness and self-condemnation can learn to employ new self-statements, which help them think and behave differently. As a consequence, they also begin to feel differently.

- *Using humor.* REBT contends that emotional disturbances often result from taking oneself too seriously and losing one's sense of perspective and humor over the events of life. Humor shows the absurdity of certain ideas that clients steadfastly maintain, and it can be of value in helping clients take themselves much less seriously. Ellis (2001a) himself tends to use a good deal of humor to combat exaggerated thinking that leads clients into trouble. In his workshops and therapy sessions Ellis typically uses humorous songs, and he encourages people to sing to themselves or in groups when they feel depressed or anxious (Ellis, 1999, 2001a, 2001b).

EMOTIVE TECHNIQUES   REBT practitioners use a variety of emotive procedures, including unconditional acceptance, rational-emotive role playing, modeling, rational-emotive imagery, and shame-attacking exercises. Clients are taught the value of unconditional self-acceptance. Even though their behavior may be difficult to accept, they can decide to see themselves as worthwhile persons. Clients are taught how destructive it is to engage in "putting oneself down" for perceived deficiencies.

Although REBT employs a variety of emotive and forceful therapeutic strategies, it does so in a selective and discriminating manner. These strategies are used both during the therapy sessions and as homework assignments in daily life. Their purpose is not simply to provide a cathartic experience but to help clients *change* some of their thoughts, emotions, and behaviors (Ellis, 1996, 1999, 2000b, 2001b; Ellis & Dryden, 1997). Let's look at some of these evocative and emotive therapeutic techniques in more detail.

- *Rational-emotive imagery.* This technique is a form of intense mental practice designed to establish new emotional patterns. Clients imagine themselves thinking, feeling, and behaving exactly the way they would like to think, feel, and behave in real life (Maultsby, 1984). They can also be shown how to imagine one of the worst things that could happen to them, how to feel unhealthily upset about this situation, how to intensely experience their feelings, and then how to change the experience to a healthy negative feeling (Ellis, 1999, 2000a). As clients change their feelings about adversities, they stand a better chance of changing their behavior in the situation. Such a technique can be usefully applied to interpersonal and other situations that are problematic for the individual. Ellis (2001a, 2001b) maintains that if we keep practicing rational-emotive imagery several times a week for a few weeks, we can reach the point that we no longer feel upset over negative events. (If you are interested in an illustration of rational-emotive imagery, see Ellis, 2001a, 2001b).

■ *Role playing.* There are both emotional and behavioral components in role playing. The therapist often interrupts to show clients what they are telling themselves to create their disturbances and what they can do to change their unhealthy feelings to healthy ones. Clients can rehearse certain behaviors to bring out what they feel in a situation. The focus is on working through the underlying irrational beliefs that are related to unpleasant feelings. For example, a woman may put off applying to a graduate school because of her fears of not being accepted. Just the thought of not being accepted to the school of her choice brings out her feelings of "being stupid." She role-plays an interview with the dean of graduate students, notes her anxiety and the specific beliefs leading to it, and challenges her conviction that she absolutely must be accepted and that not gaining such acceptance means that she is a stupid and incompetent person.

■ *Shame-attacking exercises.* Ellis (1999, 2000a, 2001a, 2001b) has developed exercises to help people reduce shame over behaving in certain ways. He thinks that we can stubbornly refuse to feel ashamed by telling ourselves that it is not catastrophic if someone thinks we are foolish. The main point of these exercises, which typically involve both emotive and behavioral components, is that clients work to feel unashamed even when others clearly disapprove of them. The exercises are aimed at increasing self-acceptance and mature responsibility, as well as helping clients see that much of what they think of as being shameful has to do with the way they define reality for themselves. Clients may accept a homework assignment to take the risk of doing something that they are ordinarily afraid to do because of what others might think. Minor infractions of social conventions often serve as useful catalysts. For example, clients may shout out the stops on a bus or a train, wear "loud" clothes designed to attract attention, sing at the top of their lungs, ask a silly question at a lecture, or ask for a left-handed monkey wrench in a grocery store. By carrying out such assignments, clients are likely to find out that other people are not really that interested in their behavior. They work on themselves so that they do not feel ashamed or humiliated, even when they acknowledge that some of their acts will lead to judgments by others. They continue practicing these exercises until they realize that their feelings of shame are self-created and until they are able to behave in less inhibited ways. Clients eventually learn that they often have no reason for continuing to let others' reactions or possible disapproval stop them from doing the things they would like to do.

■ *Use of force and vigor.* Ellis has suggested the use of force and energy as a way to help clients go from intellectual to emotional insight. Clients are also shown how to conduct forceful dialogues with themselves in which they express their unsubstantiated beliefs and then powerfully dispute them. Sometimes the therapist will engage in reverse role playing by strongly clinging to the client's self-defeating philosophy. Then, the client is asked to vigorously debate with the therapist in an attempt to persuade him or her to give up these dysfunctional ideas. Force and energy are a basic part of shame-attacking exercises.

BEHAVIORAL TECHNIQUES   REBT practitioners use most of the standard behavior therapy procedures, especially operant conditioning, self-management principles, systematic desensitization, relaxation techniques, and modeling. Behavioral homework assignments to be carried out in real-life situations are particularly important. These assignments are done systematically and are recorded and analyzed on a form. Many involve desensitization, skill training, and assertiveness training. REBT clients may be encouraged to desensitize themselves gradually but also, at times, to perform the very things they dread doing implosively. For example, a person with a fear of elevators may decrease this fear by going up and down in an elevator 20 or 30 times in a day. Clients actually do new and difficult things, and in this way they put their insights to use in the form of concrete action. By acting differently, they also tend to incorporate functional beliefs.

RESEARCH EFFORTS   REBT is characterized by a growing collection of therapeutic strategies for assisting people in changing their maladaptive cognitions. Therapists typically use a combination of cognitive, emotive, and behavioral methods within a single session with a given client. If a particular technique does not seem to be producing results, the therapist is likely to switch to another. This technical eclecticism and therapeutic flexibility make controlled research difficult. As enthusiastic as he is about cognitive behavior therapy, Ellis admits that practically all therapy outcome studies are flawed. According to him, these studies mainly test how people *feel better* but not how they have made a profound philosophical-behavioral change and thereby *get better* (Ellis, 1999, 2001a). Most studies focus only on cognitive methods and do not consider emotive and behavioral methods, yet the studies would be improved if they focused on all three REBT methods.

Applications of REBT to Client Populations

REBT has been widely applied to the treatment of anxiety, hostility, character disorders, psychotic disorders, and depression; to problems of sex, love, and marriage (Ellis & Blau, 1998); to child rearing and adolescence (Ellis & Wilde, 2001); and to social skills training and self-management (Ellis, 2001b; Ellis et al., 1997). However, Ellis does not assert that all clients can be helped through logical analysis and philosophical reconstruction. Therefore, REBT includes many emotive-experiential and behavioral methods.

In one-to-one work REBT tends to be focused on a specific problem. Ellis (1994) writes that most clients who are seen for individual therapy have 1 session weekly for anywhere from 5 to 50 sessions. REBT is also suitable for group therapy, because the members are taught to apply its principles to one another in the group setting. Ellis recommends that most clients experience group therapy as well as individual therapy at some point.

REBT is also applied to couples counseling and family therapy. In working with couples the partners are taught the principles of REBT so that they can work out their differences or at least become less disturbed about them. In family therapy, individual family members are encouraged to consider letting go of the demand that others in the family behave in ways they would like them to. Instead, REBT teaches family members that they are primarily responsible for their own actions and for changing their own reactions to the family situation.

REBT is well suited as a brief form of therapy, whether it is applied to individuals, groups, couples, or families. Ellis originally developed REBT to try to make psychotherapy shorter and more efficient than most other systems of therapy; hence, it is often a brief therapy. The A-B-C approach to changing basic disturbance-creating attitudes can be learned in 1 to 10 sessions. Ellis has used REBT successfully in 1- and 2-day marathons and in 9-hour REBT intensives (Ellis, 1996; Ellis & Dryden, 1997). People with specific problems, such as coping with the loss of a job or dealing with retirement, are taught how to apply REBT principles to treat themselves, often with supplementary didactic materials (books, tapes, self-help forms, and the like). REBT is also a useful perspective for helping people who are experiencing a crisis. In most crises our cognitive perspective has a lot to do with how a particular event affects us. REBT can help people understand their dysfunctional cognitions and also show them how their emotions and behaviors influence the way that they think about events.

AARON BECK'S COGNITIVE THERAPY

Introduction

Aaron T. Beck developed an approach known as *cognitive therapy* (CT) as a result of his research on depression (Beck 1963,1967). His observations of depressed clients revealed that they had a negative bias in their interpretation of certain life events, which contributed to their cognitive distortions (Dattilio, 2000a). Cognitive therapy has a number of similarities to rational emotive behavior therapy. Both are active, directive, time-limited, present-centered, collaborative, structured approaches (Beck, Rush, Shaw, & Emery, 1979).

Like REBT, CT is an insight-focused therapy that emphasizes recognizing and changing negative thoughts and maladaptive beliefs. Thus, it is a psychological education model of therapy. Beck's approach is based on the theoretical rationale that the way people feel and behave is determined by how they perceive and structure their experience. The theoretical assumptions of cognitive therapy are (1) that people's internal communication is accessible to introspection, (2) that clients' beliefs have highly personal meanings, and (3) that these meanings can be discovered by the client rather than being taught or interpreted by the therapist (Weishaar, 1993).

Beck developed his theory independently of Ellis, but they exchanged ideas. Beck credits Ellis with introducing the fundamental concept of focusing on cognitive factors as a route to changing feelings and behaviors. Ellis views Beck as an extremely clear thinker who has made major contributions to psychotherapy through his research (Weishaar, 1993).

The basic theory of CT holds that to understand the nature of an emotional episode or disturbance it is essential to focus on the cognitive content of an individual's reaction to the upsetting event or stream of thoughts (DeRubeis & Beck, 1988). The goal is to change the way clients think by using their automatic thoughts to reach the core schemata and begin to introduce the idea of schema restructuring. This is done by encouraging clients to gather and weigh the evidence in support of their beliefs.

Basic Principles of Cognitive Therapy

Beck, a practicing psychoanalytic therapist for many years, grew interested in his clients' "automatic thoughts" (personalized notions that are triggered by particular stimuli that lead to emotional responses). As a part of his psychoanalytic study, he was examining the dream content of depressed clients for anger that they were turning back on themselves. He began to notice that more than retroflected anger, as Freud theorized with depression, there was a bias in their interpretation or thinking. Beck asked clients to observe negative automatic thoughts that persisted even though they were contrary to objective evidence, and from this he developed the most comprehensive theory on depression in the world.

Beck contends that people with emotional difficulties tend to commit characteristic "logical errors" that tilt objective reality in the direction of self-deprecation. Cognitive therapy perceives psychological problems as stemming from commonplace processes such as faulty thinking, making incorrect inferences on the basis of inadequate or incorrect information, and failing to distinguish between fantasy and reality. Let's examine some of the systematic errors in reasoning that lead to faulty assumptions and misconceptions, which are termed *cognitive distortions* (Beck et al., 1979; Beck & Weishaar, 2000; Dattilio & Freeman, 1992).

■ *Arbitrary inferences* refer to making conclusions without supporting and relevant evidence. This includes "catastrophizing," or thinking of the absolute worst scenario and outcomes for most situations. You might begin your first job as a counselor with the conviction that you will not be liked or valued by either your colleagues or your clients. You are convinced that you fooled your professors and somehow just managed to get your degree, but now people will certainly see through you!

■ *Selective abstraction* consists of forming conclusions based on an isolated detail of an event. In this process other information is ignored, and the significance of the total context is missed. The assumption is that the events that matter are those dealing with failure and deprivation. As a counselor, you might measure your worth by your errors and weaknesses, not by your successes.

■ *Overgeneralization* is a process of holding extreme beliefs on the basis of a single incident and applying them inappropriately to dissimilar events or settings. If you have difficulty working with one adolescent, for example, you might conclude that you will not be effective counseling any adolescents. You might also conclude that you will not be effective working with *any* clients!

■ *Magnification and minimization* consist of perceiving a case or situation in a greater or lesser light than it truly deserves. You might make this cognitive error by assuming that even minor mistakes in counseling a client could easily create a crisis for the individual and might result in psychological damage.

■ *Personalization* is a tendency for individuals to relate external events to themselves, even when there is no basis for making this connection. If a client does not return for a second counseling session, you might be absolutely convinced that this absence is due to your terrible performance during the initial session. You might tell yourself, "This situation proves that I really let that client down, and now she may never seek help again."

■ *Labeling and mislabeling* involve portraying one's identity on the basis of imperfections and mistakes made in the past and allowing them to define one's true identity. Thus, if you are not able to live up to all of a client's expectations, you might say to yourself, "I'm totally worthless and should turn my professional license in right away."

■ *Polarized thinking* involves thinking and interpreting in all-or-nothing terms, or categorizing experiences in either-or extremes. With such dichotomous thinking, events are labeled in black or white terms. You might give yourself no latitude for being an imperfect person and imperfect counselor. You might view yourself as either being the perfectly competent counselor (which means you always succeed with all clients) or as a total flop if you are not fully competent (which means there is no room for any mistakes).

Beck (1976) writes that, in the broadest sense, "cognitive therapy consists of all of the approaches that alleviate psychological distress through the medium of correcting faulty conceptions and self-signals" (p. 214). For him the most direct way to change dysfunctional emotions and behaviors is to modify inaccurate and dysfunctional thinking. The cognitive therapist teaches clients how to identify these distorted and dysfunctional cognitions through a process of evaluation. Through a collaborative effort, clients learn to discriminate between their own thoughts and events that occur in reality. They learn the influence that cognition has on their feelings and behaviors and even on environmental events. Clients are taught to recognize, observe, and monitor their own thoughts and assumptions, especially their negative automatic thoughts.

After they have gained insight into how their unrealistically negative thoughts are affecting them, clients are trained to test these automatic thoughts against reality by examining and weighing the evidence for and against them. This process involves empirically testing their beliefs by actively engaging in a Socratic dialogue with the therapist, carrying out homework assignments, gathering data on assumptions they make, keeping a record of activities, and forming alternative interpretations (Dattilio, 2000a; Freeman & Dattilio, 1994). Clients form hypotheses about their behavior and eventually learn to employ specific problem-solving and coping skills. Through a process of guided discovery, clients acquire insight about the connection between their thinking and the ways they act and feel.

Cognitive therapy emphasizes the present and aims to be time limited. Therapy is focused on current problems, regardless of diagnosis, although the past may be brought into therapy under certain circumstances, such as when the client expresses a strong desire to talk about a past situation; when work on current problems results in little or no cognitive, behavioral, and emotional change; or when the therapist considers it essential to understand how and when certain dysfunctional beliefs originated and how these ideas have a current impact on the client's specific schema (Dattilio, 2002a). With this present-centered focus, cognitive therapy tends to be brief. The therapy goals include providing symptom relief, assisting clients in resolving their most pressing problems, and teaching clients relapse prevention strategies. More recently, increasing attention has been placed on the unconscious, affective, and even existential components of CT treatment (Dattilio, 2002a; Safran, 1998).

SOME DIFFERENCES BETWEEN CT AND REBT   In both Beck's cognitive therapy and REBT, reality testing is highly organized. Clients come to realize on an experiential level that they have misconstrued situations. Yet there are some important differences between REBT and CT, especially with respect to therapeutic methods and style.

REBT is often highly directive, persuasive, and confrontive; it also focuses on the teaching role of the therapist. In contrast, Beck uses a Socratic dialogue by posing open-ended questions to clients with the aim of getting clients to reflect on personal issues and arrive at their own conclusions. CT places more emphasis on helping clients discover their misconceptions for themselves and generally applies more structure than REBT. Through this reflective questioning process, the cognitive therapist attempts to collaborate with clients in testing the validity of their cognitions (a process termed *collaborative empiricism*). Therapeutic change is the result of clients confronting faulty beliefs with contradictory evidence that they have gathered and evaluated.

Through a process of rational disputation, the REBT therapist works to persuade clients that certain of their beliefs are irrational and nonfunctional. Beck (1976) takes exception to REBT's concept of irrational beliefs, asserting that telling clients they are "thinking irrationally" can be detrimental because many clients believe they are "seeing things as they really are" (p. 246). Cognitive therapists view dysfunctional beliefs as being problematic because they interfere with normal cognitive processing, not because they are irrational (Beck & Weishaar, 2000). Instead of irrational beliefs, Beck maintains that some ideas are too absolute, broad, and extreme. For him, people live by *rules* (premises or formulas); they get into trouble when they label, interpret, and evaluate by a set of rules that are unrealistic or when they use the rules inappropriately or excessively. If clients make the determination that they are living by rules that are likely to lead to misery, the therapist may suggest alternative rules for them to consider, without indoctrinating them. Although cognitive therapy often begins by recognizing the client's frame of reference, the therapist continues to ask for evidence for a belief system.

The Client–Therapist Relationship

One of the main ways the practice of cognitive therapy differs from the practice of rational emotive behavior therapy is its emphasis on the therapeutic relationship. As you will recall, Ellis views the therapist largely as a teacher and does *not* think that a warm personal relationship with clients is essential. In contrast, Beck (1987) emphasizes that the quality of the therapeutic relationship is basic to the application of cognitive therapy. Successful counseling rests on a number of desirable characteristics of therapists, such as genuine warmth, accurate empathy, nonjudgmental acceptance, and the ability to establish trust and rapport with clients. The core therapeutic conditions described by Rogers in his person-centered approach are viewed by cognitive therapists as being necessary, but not sufficient, to produce optimum therapeutic effect. Therapists must also have a cognitive conceptualization of cases, be creative and active, be able to engage clients through a process of Socratic questioning, and be knowledgeable and skilled in the use of cognitive and behavioral strategies aimed at guiding clients in significant self-discoveries that will lead to change (Weishaar, 1993). The therapist functions as a catalyst and a guide who helps clients understand how their beliefs and attitudes influence the way they feel and act. In agreement with Ellis's assumption about cognitive change, Beck also assumes that therapists promote corrective experiences that lead to cognitive change and acquiring new skills (Beck et al., 1979; Beck & Weishaar, 2000).

Cognitive therapists encourage clients to take an active role in the therapy process. Clients are expected to bring up topics to explore, identify the distortions in their thinking, summarize important points in the session, and collaboratively devise homework assignments that they agree to carry out (J. Beck, 1995; Dattilio, 2002b; Meichenbaum, 1997).

Cognitive therapists are continuously active and deliberately interactive with clients; they also strive to engage clients' active participation and collaboration throughout all phases of therapy. The therapist and client work together to frame the client's conclusions in the form of a testable hypothesis. Beck conceptualizes a partnership to devise personally meaningful evaluations of the client's negative assumptions, as opposed to the therapist directly suggesting alternative cognitions (Beck & Haaga, 1992; J. Beck, 1995). Just as Ellis teaches clients about self-reflective thinking, so does the cognitive therapist. Rather than emphasizing the therapist's role in teaching, however, Beck places more weight on the client's role in self-discovery. Beck's assumption is that lasting changes in the client's thinking and behavior will be most likely to occur with the client's initiative, understanding, awareness, and effort (Beck et al., 1979; Weishaar, 1993). This makes cognitive therapy, like REBT, an integrative form of psychotherapy.

Cognitive therapists aim to teach clients how to be their own therapist. Typically, a therapist will educate clients about the nature and course of their problem, about the process of cognitive therapy, and how thoughts influence their emotions and behaviors. The educative process includes providing clients with information about their presenting problems and about relapse prevention.

Homework and bibliotherapy are often used as a part of cognitive therapy. The homework is tailored to the client's specific problem and arises out of the collaborative therapeutic relationship. The purpose of homework in cognitive therapy is not merely to teach clients new skills but also to enable them to test their beliefs in daily-life situations. Homework is generally presented to clients as an experiment, which increases the openness of clients to get involved in an assignment. Emphasis is placed on self-help assignments that serve as a continuation of issues addressed in a therapy session (Dattilio, 2002b).

Clients may be asked to complete readings dealing with the philosophy of cognitive therapy. According to Dattilio and Freeman (1992, 2000), these readings are assigned as an adjunct to therapy and are designed to enhance the therapeutic process by providing an educational focus. Some popular books often recommended are *Love Is Never Enough* (Beck, 1988); *Feeling Good* (Burns, 1988); *The Feeling Good Handbook* (Burns, 1989); *Woulda, Coulda, Shoulda* (Freeman & DeWolf, 1990); and *Mind Over Mood* (Greenberger & Padesky, 1995). Through self-help books such as these, cognitive therapy has become known to the general public.

Applications of Cognitive Therapy

Cognitive therapy initially gained recognition as an approach to treating depression, but extensive research has also been devoted to the study and treatment of anxiety disorders. These two clinical problems have been the most extensively researched using cognitive therapy (Beck, 1991; Dattilio, 2000a) but cognitive therapy has been successfully used in a wide variety of other disorders. Some of these areas include treating phobias, anxiety disorders, psychosomatic disorders, eating disorders, anger, panic attacks (Dattilio & Salas-Auvert, 2000), posttraumatic stress disorder, suicidal behavior, borderline personality disorders, narcissistic personality disorders, and schizophrenic disorders (Dattilio & Freeman, 2000), substance abuse (Beck, Wright, Newman, & Liese, 1993), chronic pain (Beck, 1987), and medical illness (Dattilio & Castaldo, 2001). Cognitive therapy has been used in crisis intervention (Dattilio & Freeman, 2000) and also with couples and families (Dattilio, 1993, 1998, 2001; Dattilio & Padesky, 1990), child abusers, divorce counseling, skills training, and stress management (Dattilio, 1998; Granvold, 1994; Reinecke, Dattilio, & Freeman, 2002). Clearly, cognitive behavioral programs have been designed for all ages and for a variety of client populations.

APPLYING COGNITIVE TECHNIQUES   Regardless of the nature of the specific problem, the cognitive therapist is mainly interested in applying procedures that will assist individuals in making alternative interpretations of events in their daily living. Think about how you might apply the principles of CT to yourself in the classroom situation outlined here, thus changing your feelings surrounding the situation (Beck, 1976; J. Beck, 1995):

> Your professor does not call on you during a particular class session. You *feel* depressed. *Cognitively,* you are telling yourself: "My professor thinks I'm stupid and that I really don't have much of value to offer the class. Furthermore, she's right, because everyone else is brighter and more articulate than I am. It's been this way most of my life!"

Some possible *alternative interpretations* are that the professor wants to include others in the discussion, that she is short on time and wants to move ahead, that she already knows your views, or that you are self-conscious about being singled out or called on.

The therapist would have you become aware of the distortions in your thinking patterns by examining your automatic thoughts. The therapist would ask you to look at your inferences, which may be faulty, and then trace them back to earlier experiences in your life. Then the therapist would help you see how you sometimes come to a conclusion (your decision that you are stupid, with little of value to offer) when evidence for such a conclusion is either lacking or based on distorted information from the past.

As a client in cognitive therapy, you would also learn about the process of magnification or minimization of thinking, which involves either exaggerating the meaning of an event (you believe the professor thinks you are stupid because she did not acknowledge you on this one occasion) or minimizing it (you belittle your value as a student in the class). The therapist would assist you in learning about how you disregard important aspects of a situation, engage in overly simplified and rigid thinking, and generalize from a single incident of failure. Can you think of other situations where you could apply CT procedures?

TREATMENT OF DEPRESSION   Beck challenged the notion that depression results from anger turned inward. Instead, he focuses on the content of the depressive's negative thinking and biased interpretation of events (DeRubeis & Beck, 1988). In an earlier study that provided much of the backbone of his theory, Beck (1963) even found cognitive errors in the dream content of depressed clients.

Beck (1987) writes about the *cognitive triad* as a pattern that triggers depression. In the first component of the triad, clients hold a negative view of themselves. They blame their setbacks on personal inadequacies without considering circumstantial explanations. They are convinced that they lack the qualities essential to bring them happiness. The second component of the triad consists of the tendency to interpret experiences in a negative manner. It almost seems as if depressed people select certain facts that conform to their negative conclusions, a process Beck refers to as selective abstraction. The third component of the triad pertains to depressed clients' gloomy vision and projections about the future. They expect their present difficulties to continue, and they anticipate only failure in the future.

Depression-prone people often set rigid, perfectionist goals for themselves that are impossible to attain. Their negative expectations are so strong that even if they experience success in specific tasks they anticipate failure the next time. They screen out successful experiences that are not consistent with their negative self-concept. The thought content of depressed individuals centers on a sense of irreversible loss, which results in emotional states of sadness, disappointment, and apathy.

The Beck Depression Inventory (BDI) was designed as a standardized device to assess the depth of depression. The items are based on observations of the symptoms and basic beliefs of depressed people. The inventory contains 21 symptoms and attitudes: (1) sadness, (2) pessimism, (3) sense of failure, (4) dissatisfaction, (5) guilt, (6) sense of punishment, (7) self-dislike, (8) self-accusations, (9) suicidal ideation, (10) crying spells, (11) irritability, (12) social withdrawal, (13) indecision, (14) distorted body image, (15) work inhibition, (16) sleep disturbance, (17) tendency to become fatigued, (18) loss of appetite, (19) weight loss, (20) somatic preoccupations, and (21) loss of libido (Beck, 1967).

Beck's therapeutic approach to treating depressed clients focuses on specific problem areas and the reasons clients give for their symptoms. Some of the behavioral symptoms of depression are inactivity, withdrawal, and avoidance. Clients report that they are too tired to do anything, that they will feel even worse if they become active, and that they will fail at anything they try. The therapist is likely to probe with Socratic questioning such as this: "What would be lost by trying? Will you feel worse if you are passive? How do you know that it is pointless to try?" Therapy procedures include setting up an activity schedule with graded tasks to be completed. Clients are asked to complete easy tasks first, so that they will meet with some success and become slightly more optimistic. The point is to enlist the client's cooperation with the therapist on the assumption that *doing something* is more likely to lead to feeling better than *doing nothing*.

Some depressed clients may harbor suicidal wishes. Cognitive therapy strategies may include exposing the client's ambivalence, generating alternatives, and reducing problems to manageable proportions. For example, the therapist may ask the client to list the reasons for living and for dying. Further, if the client can develop alternative views of a problem, then alternative courses of action can be developed. This can result not only in a client feeling better but also behaving in more effective ways (Freeman & Reinecke, 1993).

A central characteristic of most depressive people is self-criticism. Underneath the person's self-hate are attitudes of weakness, inadequacy, and lack of responsibility. A number of therapeutic strategies can be used. Clients can be asked to identify and provide reasons for their excessively self-critical behavior. The therapist may ask the client, "If I were to make a mistake the way you do, would you despise me as much as you do yourself?" A skillful therapist may play the role of the depressed client, portraying the client as inadequate, inept, and weak. This technique can be effective in demonstrating the client's cognitive distortions and arbitrary inferences. The therapist can then discuss with the client how the "tyranny of shoulds" can lead to self-hate and depression.

Depressed clients typically experience painful emotions. They may say that they cannot stand the pain or that nothing can make them feel better. One procedure to counteract painful affect is humor. A therapist can demonstrate the ironic aspects of a situation. If clients can even briefly experience some light-heartedness, it can serve as an antidote to their sadness. Such a shift in their cognitive set is simply not compatible with their self-critical attitude.

Another specific characteristic of depressed people is an exaggeration of external demands, problems, and pressures. Such people often exclaim that they feel overwhelmed and that there is so much to accomplish that they can never do it. A cognitive therapist might ask clients to list things that need to be done, set priorities, check off tasks that have been accomplished, and break down an external problem into manageable units. When problems are discussed, clients often become aware of how they are magnifying the importance of these difficulties. Through rational exploration, clients are able to regain a perspective on defining and accomplishing tasks.

The therapist typically has to take the lead in helping clients make a list of their responsibilities, set priorities, and develop a realistic plan of action. Because carrying out such a plan is often inhibited by self-defeating thoughts, it is well for therapists to use cognitive rehearsal techniques in both identifying and changing negative thoughts. If clients can learn to combat their self-doubts in the therapy session, they may be able to apply their newly acquired cognitive and behavioral skills in real-life situations.

APPLICATION TO FAMILY THERAPY   The cognitive behavioral approach focuses on family interaction patterns, and family relationships, cognitions, emotions, and behavior are viewed as exerting a mutual influence on one another. A cognitive inference can evoke emotion and behavior, and emotion and behavior can likewise influence cognition in a reciprocal process that sometimes serves to maintain the dysfunction of the family unit.

Cognitive therapy, as set forth by Beck (1976), places a heavy emphasis on *schema*, or what have otherwise been defined as core beliefs. A key aspect of the therapeutic process involves restructuring distorted beliefs (or schema), which has a pivotal impact on changing dysfunctional behaviors. Some cognitive behavior therapists place a heavy emphasis on examining cognitions among individual family members as well as on what may be termed the "family schemata" (Dattilio, 1993, 1998, 2001). These are jointly held beliefs about the family that have formed as a result of years of integrated interaction among members of the family unit. It is the experiences and perceptions from the family of origin that shape the schema about both the immediate family and families in general. These schemata have a major impact on how the individual thinks, feels, and behaves in the family system (Dattilio, 2001).

For a concrete illustration of how Dr. Dattilio applies cognitive principles and works with family schemata, see his cognitive behavioral approach with Ruth in *Case Approach to Counseling and Psychotherapy* (Corey, 2005, chap. 8). For a discussion of myths and misconceptions of cognitive behavior family therapy, see Dattilio (2001). Also, for an expanded treatment of applications of cognitive behavioral approaches to working with couples and families, see Dattilio (1998). This seminal work allows practitioners and theorists to appreciate the integrative nature that is characteristic of cognitive behavior therapy.

DONALD MEICHENBAUM'S COGNITIVE BEHAVIOR MODIFICATION

Introduction

Another major alternative to rational emotive behavior therapy is Donald Meichenbaum's *cognitive behavior modification* (CBM), which focuses on changing the client's self-verbalizations. According to Meichenbaum (1977), self-statements affect a person's behavior in much the same way as statements made by another person. A basic premise of CBM is that clients, as a prerequisite to behavior change, must notice how they think, feel, and behave and the impact they have on others. For change to occur, clients need to interrupt the scripted nature of their behavior so that they can evaluate their behavior in various situations (Meichenbaum, 1986).

This approach shares with REBT and Beck's cognitive therapy the assumption that distressing emotions are typically the result of maladaptive thoughts. There are differences, however. Whereas REBT is more direct and confrontational in uncovering and disputing irrational thoughts, Meichenbaum's *self-instructional training* focuses more on helping clients become aware of their self-talk. The therapeutic process consists of teaching clients to make self-statements and training clients to modify the instructions they give to themselves so that they can cope more effectively with the problems they encounter. Together, the therapist and client practice the self-instructions and the desirable behaviors in role-play situations that simulate problem situations in the client's daily life. The emphasis is on acquiring practical coping skills for problematic situations such as impulsive and aggressive behavior, fear of taking tests, and fear of public speaking.

Cognitive restructuring plays a central role in Meichenbaum's (1977) approach. He describes cognitive structure as the organizing aspect of thinking, which seems to monitor and direct the choice of thoughts. Cognitive structure implies an "executive processor," which "holds the blueprints of thinking" that determine when to continue, interrupt, or change thinking.

How Behavior Changes

Meichenbaum (1977) proposes that "behavior change occurs through a sequence of mediating processes involving the interaction of inner speech, cognitive structures, and behaviors and their resultant outcomes" (p. 218). He describes a three-phase process of change in which those three aspects are interwoven. According to him, focusing on only one aspect will probably prove insufficient.

Phase 1: self-observation. The beginning step in the change process consists of clients learning how to observe their own behavior. When they begin therapy, their internal dialogue is characterized by negative self-statements and imagery. A critical factor is their willingness and ability to *listen* to themselves. This process involves an increased sensitivity to their thoughts, feelings, actions, physiological reactions, and ways of reacting to others. If depressed clients hope to make constructive changes, for example, they must first realize that they are not "victims" of negative thoughts and feelings. Rather, they are actually contributing to their depression through the things they tell themselves. Although self-observation is seen as a necessary process if change is to occur, it is not sufficient, per se, for change. As therapy progresses, clients acquire new cognitive structures that enable them to view their problems in a new light. This reconceptualization process comes about through a collaborative effort between client and therapist.

Phase 2: starting a new internal dialogue. As a result of the early client–therapist contacts, clients learn to notice their maladaptive behaviors, and they begin to see opportunities for adaptive behavioral alternatives. If clients hope to change, what they say to themselves must initiate a new behavioral chain, one that is incompatible with their maladaptive behaviors. Clients learn to change their internal dialogue through therapy. Their new internal dialogue serves as a guide to new behavior. In turn, this process has an impact on clients' cognitive structures.

Phase 3: learning new skills. The third phase of the modification process consists of teaching clients more effective coping skills, which are practiced in real-life situations. (For example, clients who can't cope with failure may avoid appealing activities for fear of not succeeding at them. Cognitive restructuring can help them change their negative view, thus making them more willing to engage in desired activities.) At the same time, clients continue to focus on telling themselves new sentences and observing and assessing the outcomes. As they behave differently in situations, they typically get different reactions from others. The stability of what they learn is greatly influenced by what they say to themselves about their newly acquired behavior and its consequences.

Coping Skills Programs

The rationale for coping skills programs is that we can acquire more effective strategies in dealing with stressful situations by learning how to modify our cognitive "set." The following procedures are designed to teach coping skills:

- Exposing clients to anxiety-provoking situations by means of role playing and imagery
- Requiring clients to evaluate their anxiety level
- Teaching clients to become aware of the anxiety-provoking cognitions they experience in stressful situations
- Helping clients examine these thoughts by reevaluating their self-statements
- Having clients note the level of anxiety following this reevaluation

Research studies have demonstrated the success of coping skills programs when applied to problems such as speech anxiety, test anxiety, phobias, anger, social incompetence, addictions, alcoholism, sexual dysfunctions, posttraumatic stress disorders, and social withdrawal in children (Meichenbaum, 1977, 1986, 1994).

A particular application of a coping skills program is teaching clients stress management techniques by way of a strategy known as *stress inoculation.* Using cognitive techniques, Meichenbaum (1985) has developed stress inoculation procedures that are a psychological and behavioral analog to immunization on a biological level. Individuals are given opportunities to deal with relatively mild stress stimuli in successful ways, so that they gradually develop a tolerance for stronger stimuli. This training is based on the assumption that we can affect our ability to cope with stress by modifying our beliefs and self-statements about our performance in stressful situations. Meichenbaum's stress inoculation training is concerned with more than merely teaching people specific coping skills. His program is designed to prepare clients for intervention and motivate them to change, and it deals with issues such as resistance and relapse. Stress inoculation training (SIT) consists of a combination of information giving, Socratic discussion, cognitive restructuring, problem solving, relaxation training, behavioral rehearsals, self-monitoring, self-instruction, self-reinforcement, and modifying environmental situations. This approach is designed to teach coping skills that can be applied to both present problems and future difficulties.

Meichenbaum (1985) has designed a three-stage model for stress inoculation training: (1) the conceptual phase, (2) the skills acquisition and rehearsal phase, and (3) the application and follow-through phase.

During the *conceptual phase,* the primary focus is on creating a working relationship with clients. This is mainly done by helping them gain a better understanding of the nature of stress and reconceptualizing it in social-interactive terms. The therapist enlists client collaboration during this early phase. Together they rethink the nature of the problem(s). Initially, clients are provided with a conceptual framework in simple terms designed to help them understand how they are responding to a variety of stressful situations. They learn about the role that cognitions and emotions play in creating and maintaining stress. They are taught this by didactic presentations, through Socratic questioning, and by a process of guided self-discovery.

Clients often begin treatment feeling that they are the victims of external circumstances, thoughts, feelings, and behaviors over which they have no control. Training includes teaching clients to become aware of their own role in creating their stress. They acquire this awareness by systematically observing the statements they make internally as well as by monitoring the maladaptive behaviors that flow from this inner dialogue. Such self-monitoring continues throughout all the phases. As is true in cognitive therapy, clients typically keep an open-ended diary in which they systematically record their specific thoughts, feelings, and behaviors. In teaching these coping skills, therapists strive to be flexible in their use of techniques and to be sensitive to the individual, cultural, and situational circumstances of their clients.

During the *skills acquisition and rehearsal phase*, the focus is on giving clients a variety of behavioral and cognitive coping techniques to apply to stressful situations. This phase involves direct actions, such as gathering information about their fears, learning specifically what situations bring about stress, arranging for ways to lessen the stress by doing something different, and learning methods of physical and psychological relaxation. The training involves cognitive coping; clients are taught that adaptive and maladaptive behaviors are linked to their inner dialogue. They acquire and rehearse a new set of self-statements. Meichenbaum (1986) provides some examples of coping statements that are rehearsed in this phase of SIT:

- "How can I prepare for a stressor?" ("What do I have to do? Can I develop a plan to deal with the stress?")
- "How can I confront and deal with what is stressing me?" ("What are some ways I can handle a stressor? How can I meet this challenge?")
- "How can I cope with feeling overwhelmed?" ("What can I do right now? How can I keep my fears in check?")
- "How can I make reinforcing self-statements?" ("How can I give myself credit?")

As a part of the stress management program, clients are also exposed to various behavioral interventions, some of which are relaxation training, social skills training, time-management instruction, and self-instructional training. They are helped to make lifestyle changes such as reevaluating priorities, developing support systems, and taking direct action to alter stressful situations. Clients are introduced to a variety of methods of relaxation and are taught to use these skills to decrease arousal due to stress. Through teaching, demonstration, and guided practice, clients learn the skills of progressive relaxation, which are to be practiced regularly. Other approaches that are recommended for learning to relax include meditation, yoga, tensing and relaxing muscle groups, and breath-control techniques. Relaxation also includes activities such as walking, jogging, gardening, knitting, or other physical activities. Meichenbaum stresses that relaxation is as much a state of mind as it is a physical state.

During the *application and follow-through phase*, the focus is on carefully arranging for transfer and maintenance of change from the therapeutic situation to the real world. It is clear that teaching coping skills is a complex procedure that relies on varied treatment programs. For clients to merely say new things to themselves is generally not sufficient to produce change. They need to practice these self-statements and apply their new skills in real-life situations. Once they have become proficient in cognitive and behavioral coping skills, clients practice behavioral assignments, which become increasingly demanding. Clients are asked to write down the homework assignments they are willing to complete. The outcomes of these assignments are carefully checked at subsequent meetings, and if clients do not follow through with them, the therapist and the client collaboratively consider the reasons for the failure. Follow-up and booster sessions typically take place at 3-, 6-, and 12-month periods as an incentive for clients to continue practicing and refining their coping skills. SIT can be considered part of an ongoing stress management program that extends the benefits of training into the future.

Stress management training has potentially useful applications for a wide variety of problems and clients, both for remediation and prevention. Some of these applications include anger control, anxiety management, assertion training, improving creative thinking, treating depression, and dealing with health problems. The approach has also been used in treating obese people, hyperactive children, social isolates, posttraumatic stress victims, and people with schizophrenia (Meichenbaum, 1977, 1985, 1994).

Recent Developments: Constructivist Approach

For the past several years, Meichenbaum (1997) has been immersed in the constructivist narrative perspective (CNP), which focuses on the stories people tell about themselves and others about significant events in their lives. This approach begins with the assumption that there are multiple realities. One of the therapeutic tasks is to help clients appreciate how they construct their realities and how they author their own stories (see Chapter 13).

Meichenbaum describes the constructivist approach to cognitive behavior therapy as less structured and more discovery-oriented than standard cognitive therapy. The constructivist approach gives more emphasis to past development, tends to target deeper core beliefs, and explores the behavioral impact and emotional toll a client pays for clinging to certain root metaphors. Meichenbaum uses these questions to evaluate the outcomes of therapy:

- Are clients now able to tell a new story about themselves and the world?
- Do clients now use more positive metaphors to describe themselves?
- Are clients able to predict high-risk situations and employ coping skills in dealing with emerging problems?
- Are clients able to take credit for the changes they have been able to bring about?

In successful therapy clients develop their own voices, take pride in what they have accomplished, and take ownership of the changes they are bringing about.

Cognitive Behavior Therapy Applied to the Case of Stan

The cognitive behavior therapist has as her broad objective minimizing Stan's self-defeating attitudes and helping him acquire a more realistic outlook on life. Stan's therapist is goal-oriented and problem-focused. The therapist will ask Stan, from the initial session, to identify his problems and formulate specific goals. Furthermore, she will help him reconceptualize his problems in a way that will increase his chances of finding solutions.

Stan's therapist will follow a clear structure for every session. The basic procedural sequence of Stan's therapy includes (1) preparing Stan by providing a cognitive rationale for treatment and demystifying treatment; (2) encouraging Stan to monitor his thoughts that accompany his distress; (3) implementing behavioral and cognitive techniques; (4) working with Stan to assist him in identifying and challenging some basic beliefs and ideas; (5) teaching Stan ways to examine his beliefs and assumptions by testing them in reality; and (6) teaching Stan basic coping skills that will enable him to avoid relapsing into old patterns.

As a part of the structure of Stan's therapy sessions, the therapist will ask Stan for a brief review of the week, elicit feedback from the previous session, review homework assignments, collaboratively create an agenda for the session, discuss topics on the agenda, and set new homework for the week. Stan will be encouraged to perform personal experiments and practice coping skills *in vivo*. It is not enough to learn about his problems in the therapy sessions; Stan will be expected to apply what he is learning in his everyday life.

Although the role of insight is not a central concept in cognitive behavior therapy, three levels of awareness can contribute to Stan's improvement, provided he is willing to put his insights into action. He tells his therapist that he would like to work on his fear of women and would hope to feel far less intimidated by them. He reports that he feels threatened by most women, but especially by women he perceives as powerful.

In the first level of insight, he becomes aware that there is some antecedent cause of his fear of women. This cause is not that his mother tried, for example, to dominate him. Rather, it is his self-defeating beliefs that she should not have tried to dominate him and that it was, and still is, awful that she did try and that other women may dominate him too.

On the second level of insight, Stan recognizes that he is still threatened by women and feels uncomfortable in their presence because he still believes in, and keeps repeating endlessly to himself, the faulty beliefs he once accepted. He sees that he keeps himself in a state of panic with women because he continues to tell himself "Women can castrate me!" or "They'll expect me to be a superman!" or some other dysfunctional notion.

The third level of insight consists of Stan's acceptance that he will not improve unless he works diligently and practices changing his self-defeating beliefs by actively examining them and engaging in behavior that allows him to confront his fears. Once he clearly identifies some of his faulty or distorted beliefs, he can examine them in his therapy sessions.

First, Stan's therapist educates him about the importance of examining his automatic thoughts, his self-talk, and the many "shoulds," "oughts," and "musts" he has accepted without questioning. Working with Stan as a collaborative partner in his therapy, the therapist guides Stan in discovering some basic cognitions that influence what he tells himself and how he feels and acts. This is some of Stan's self-talk:

- "I always have to be strong, tough, and perfect."
- "I'm not a man if I show any signs of weakness."
- "If everyone didn't love me and approve of me, things would be catastrophic."
- "If a woman rejected me, I really would be diminished to a 'nothing.'"
- "If I fail, I am then a failure as a person."
- "I'm apologetic for my existence, because I don't feel equal to others."

Second, the therapist assists Stan in monitoring and evaluating the ways in which he keeps telling himself these self-defeating sentences. She challenges specific problems and confronts the core of his faulty thinking:

(continued on next page)

You're not your father. I wonder why you continue telling yourself that you're just like him? Do you think you need to continue accepting without question your parents' value judgments about your worth? Where is the evidence that they were right in their assessment of you? You say you're such a failure and that you feel inferior. Do your present activities support this? If you were not so hard on yourself, how might your life be different? Does having been the scapegoat in your family mean that you need to continue making yourself the scapegoat?

Third, once Stan comes to more fully understand the nature of his cognitive distortions and his self-defeating beliefs, his therapist will draw on a variety of cognitive, emotive, and behavioral techniques to help Stan make the changes he is most interested in making. Stan learns to identify, evaluate, and respond to his dysfunctional beliefs. The therapist uses both didactic and Socratic educational methods to assist him in examining the evidence that seems to support or contradict his core beliefs. Through this process Stan will be able to unfreeze his beliefs about himself and the world. The therapist works with Stan so he will view his basic beliefs and automatic thinking as hypotheses to be tested. In a way, Stan will become a personal scientist by checking out the validity of many of the conclusions and basic assumptions that contribute to his personal difficulties. By the use of guided discovery, Stan learns to evaluate the validity and functionality of his beliefs and conclusions.

Stan's counselor gives him specific homework assignments to help him deal with his fears. At one point, for instance, she asks him to explore his fears of powerful women and his reasons for continuing to tell himself: "They can castrate me. They expect me to be strong and perfect. If I'm not careful, they'll dominate me." His homework includes approaching a woman for a date. If he succeeds in getting the date, he can challenge his catastrophic expectations of what might happen. What would be so terrible if she did not like him or if she refused the date? Why does he have to get all his confirmation from one woman? Stan tells himself over and over that he must be *approved of* by women and that if any woman rebuffs him the consequences are more than he can bear. With practice, Stan learns to label distortions

and is able to automatically identify his dysfunctional thoughts and monitor his cognitive patterns. Through a variety of cognitive behavioral strategies, Stan acquires new information and changes his basic beliefs or schemata.

In addition to homework assignments, the therapist may employ many other behavioral techniques, such as role playing, humor, modeling, behavior rehearsal, and desensitization. She asks Stan to read some cognitive behavioral self-help books. He can use the ideas he learns from them as he practices changing. Basically, she works in an active manner and focuses on cognitive and behavioral dimensions. She pays little attention to Stan's past. Instead, she highlights his present functioning and his faulty thinking and teaches him to rethink and reverbalize in a more constructive way. Thus, he can learn how to be different by telling himself a new set of statements such as these:

- "I can be lovable."
- "I'm able to succeed as well as fail at times."
- "I need not make all women into my mother."
- "I don't have to punish myself by making myself feel guilty over past failures, because it is not essential to always be perfect."

Stan can benefit from the range of cognitive behavioral procedures aimed at helping him learn to make constructive self-statements. He can profit from cognitive restructuring, which proceeds as follows: First, the therapist assists him in learning ways to observe his own behavior in various situations. During the week he can take a particular situation that is problematic for him, paying particular attention to his automatic thoughts and internal dialogue. What is he telling himself as he approaches a difficult situation? How is he setting himself up for failure with his self-talk? Second, as he learns to attend to his maladaptive behaviors, he begins to see that what he tells himself has as much impact as others' statements about him. He also sees the connections between his thinking and his behavioral problems. With this awareness he is in an ideal place to begin to learn a new, more functional internal dialogue. Third, he can also learn new coping skills, which he can practice first in the sessions and then in daily-life situations. It will not be enough for him to merely say new things to himself, for to become proficient in new cognitive and behavioral coping skills he needs to apply them in various daily situations. As he experiences success with his assignments, these tasks can become increasingly demanding.

Follow-Up: You Continue as Stan's Cognitive Behavior Therapist

Use these questions to help you think about how to counsel Stan using a cognitive behavior approach:

- Stan's therapist's style is characterized as an integrative form of cognitive behavioral therapy. She borrows concepts and techniques from the approaches of Ellis, Beck, and Meichenbaum. In your work with Stan, what specific concepts would you borrow from each of these approaches? What techniques would you draw from each of the cognitive behavioral approaches? What possible advantages do you see, if any, in applying an integrative cognitive behavioral approach in your work with Stan?

- What are some things you would most want to teach Stan about how cognitive behavior therapy works? What would you tell him about the therapeutic alliance and the collaborative therapeutic relationship?
- What are some of Stan's most prominent faulty beliefs that are getting in the way of his living fully? What cognitive, emotive, and behavioral techniques might you use in helping him examine his core beliefs?
- Stan lives by many "shoulds" and "oughts." His automatic thoughts seem to get in his way of getting what he wants. What techniques would you use to encourage guided discovery on his part?
- What are some homework assignments that might be useful for Stan to carry out? In what ways could you collaboratively design homework with Stan? How would you encourage him to develop action plans whereby he could test the validity of his thinking and his conclusions?

 # COGNITIVE BEHAVIOR THERAPY FROM A MULTICULTURAL PERSPECTIVE

Contributions to Multicultural Counseling

The cognitive behavioral approaches have certain advantages in multicultural counseling situations. If therapists understand the core values of their culturally diverse clients, they can help clients explore these values and gain a full awareness of their conflicting feelings. Then client and therapist can work together to modify selected beliefs and practices.

Because counselors with a cognitive behavioral orientation function as teachers, clients' focus on learning skills to deal with the problems of living. In speaking with colleagues who work with culturally diverse populations, I have learned that their clients tend to appreciate the emphasis on cognition and action, as well as the stress on relationship issues. Beck's collaborative approach offers clients the structure they often feel they need, yet the therapist still makes every effort to enlist their active cooperation and participation.

In his workshops, Ellis describes REBT as intrinsically multicultural in its principles and practices because it does not question the goals and values of clients but only challenges their rigid, inflexible demands and their absolutist "shoulds," "oughts," and "musts." Ellis explains that it is not the strict rules of their original culture that makes them disturbed but their view of these rules. When clients surrender their absolutist beliefs about following rules, they are in a position to decide to follow the rules, give them up, or make some kind of compromise with them. Clients decide which values to adopt; the therapist's role is to help clients become more flexible in their thinking, feeling, and behaving.

Ellis (2001b) believes that an essential part of people's lives is group living and that their happiness depends largely on the quality of their functioning within their community. Thus, individuals can make the mistake of being too self-centered and self-indulgent. REBT stresses the relationship of individuals to the family, community, and other systems. This orientation is consistent with valuing diversity and the interdependence of being an individual and a productive member of the community.

Limitations for Multicultural Counseling

Exploring values and core beliefs plays an important role in all of the cognitive behavioral approaches, and it is crucial for therapists to have some understanding of the cultural background of clients and to be sensitive to their struggles. Therapists would do well to use caution in challenging clients about their beliefs and behaviors until they clearly understand their cultural context.

Consider an Asian American client, Sung, from a culture that stresses values such as doing one's best, cooperation, interdependence, and working hard. It is likely that Sung is struggling with feelings of shame and guilt if she perceives that she is not living up to the expectations and standards set for her by her family and her community. She may feel that she is bringing shame to her family if she is going through a divorce. The counselor needs to understand the ways gender interacts with culture. The rules for Sung are likely to be different than are the rules for a male member of her culture. The counselor could assist Sung in understanding and exploring how both her gender and her culture are factors to consider in her situation. If Sung is confronted too quickly on living by the expectations or rules of others, the results are likely to be counterproductive. Sung might even leave counseling because of feeling misunderstood.

One of the shortcomings of applying cognitive behavior therapy to diverse cultures pertains to the hesitation of some clients to question their basic cultural values. Dattilio (1995) notes that some Mediterranean and Middle Eastern cultures have strict rules with regard to religion, marriage and family, and child-rearing practices. These rules are often in conflict with the cognitive behavioral suggestions of disputation. For example, a therapist might suggest to a woman that she question her husband's motive. Clearly, in some Middle Eastern or other Asian cultures, such questioning is forbidden.

One limitation of REBT in multicultural settings stems from its negative view of dependency. Many cultures view interdependence as necessary to good mental health. According to Ellis (1994), REBT is aimed at inducing people to examine and change some of their most basic values. Clients with certain long-cherished cultural values pertaining to interdependence are not likely to respond favorably to forceful methods of persuasion toward independence. Thus, modifications in a therapist's style need to be made depending on the client's culture.

A potential limitation of the cognitive behavioral approaches is that culturally diverse clients could become dependent on the counselor to make decisions about what constitutes rationality and about the appropriate ways to solve problems. Cognitive behavior therapists walk a fine line between being directive and promoting dependence. Such practitioners may be directive, yet it is important that they teach their clients to question and to assume an active role in the therapeutic process.

 # SUMMARY AND EVALUATION

Summary

REBT has evolved into a comprehensive and integrative approach that emphasizes thinking, judging, deciding, and doing. Therapy begins with clients' problematic behaviors and emotions and disputes the thoughts that directly create them. To block the self-defeating beliefs that are reinforced by a process of self-indoctrination, REBT therapists employ active and directive techniques such as teaching, suggestion, persuasion, and homework assignments, and they challenge clients to substitute a rational belief system for an irrational one. Therapists demonstrate how and why dysfunctional beliefs lead to negative emotional and behavioral results. They teach clients how to dispute self-defeating beliefs and behaviors that might occur in the future. REBT stresses action—doing something about the insights one gains in therapy. Change comes about mainly by a commitment to consistently practice new behaviors that replace old and ineffective ones.

Rational emotive behavior therapists are typically eclectic in selecting therapeutic strategies. They have the latitude to develop their own personal style and to exercise creativity; they are not bound by fixed techniques for particular problems.

REBT is the forerunner of other cognitive behavioral approaches, especially Beck's cognitive therapy and Meichenbaum's cognitive behavior modification. All of these approaches stress the importance of cognitive processes as determinants of behavior. They maintain that how people feel and what they actually do is largely influenced by their subjective assessment of situations. Because this appraisal of life situations is influenced by beliefs, attitudes, assumptions, and internal dialogue, such cognitions become the major focus of therapy.

Contributions of the Cognitive Behavioral Approaches

Most of the therapies discussed in this book can be considered "cognitive," in a general sense, because they have the aim of changing clients' subjective views of themselves and the world. But the cognitive behavioral approaches focus on undermining faulty assumptions and beliefs and teaching clients the coping skills needed to deal with their problems.

ELLIS'S REBT   I find aspects of REBT very valuable in my work because I believe we are responsible for maintaining self-destructive ideas and attitudes that influence our daily transactions. I see value in confronting clients with questions such as "What are your assumptions and basic beliefs?" and "Have you really examined the core ideas you live by to determine if they are your own values or merely introjects?" REBT has built on the Adlerian notion that events themselves do not have the power to determine us; rather, it is our interpretation of these events that is crucial. The A-B-C model simply and clearly illustrates how human disturbances occur and the ways in which problematic behavior can be changed. Rather than focusing on events themselves, therapy stresses how clients interpret and react to what happens to them.

Another contribution of the cognitive behavioral approaches is the emphasis on putting newly acquired insights into action. Homework assignments are well suited to enabling clients to practice new behaviors and assisting them in the process of their reconditioning. Adlerian therapy, reality therapy, and behavior therapy all share with the cognitive behavioral approaches this action orientation. It is important that homework be a natural outgrowth of what is taking place in the therapy session. Clients are more likely to carry out their homework if the assignments are collaboratively created.

One of the strengths of REBT is the focus on teaching clients ways to carry on their own therapy without the direct intervention of a therapist. I particularly like the emphasis that REBT puts on supplementary and psychoeducational approaches such as listening to tapes, reading self-help books, keeping a record of what they are doing and thinking, and attending workshops. In this way clients can further the process of change in themselves without becoming excessively dependent on a therapist.

A major contribution of REBT is its emphasis on a comprehensive and eclectic therapeutic practice. Numerous cognitive, emotive, and behavioral techniques can be employed in changing one's emotions and behaviors by changing the structure of one's cognitions.

BECK'S COGNITIVE THERAPY   Beck's key concepts share similarities with REBT but differ in underlying philosophy and the process by which therapy proceeds. Beck made pioneering efforts in the treatment of anxiety, phobias, and depression. Today, empirically validated treatments for both anxiety and depression have revolutionized therapeutic practice (Leahy, 2002). Beck developed specific cognitive procedures that are useful in challenging a depressive client's assumptions and beliefs and in providing a new cognitive perspective that can lead to optimism and changed behavior. His approach has received a great deal of attention from clinical researchers, and a number of experiments support its efficacy for depressed clients (Haaga & Davison, 1986). The effects of cognitive therapy on depression and hopelessness seem to be maintained for at least one year after treatment. Cognitive therapy has been applied to a wide range of clinical populations Beck did not originally believe were appropriate for this model, including treatment for schizophrenia, delusional disorders, bipolar disorder, and various personality disorders (Leahy, 2002).

According to Weishaar (1993), Beck demonstrated that a structured therapy that is present-centered and problem-oriented can be very effective in treating depression and anxiety in a relatively short time. In fact, Beck considers cognitive therapy to be *the* integrative psychotherapy because it draws from so many different modalities of psychotherapy (Alford & Beck, 1997).

One of the contributions of cognitive therapy is that it focuses on developing a detailed case conceptualization as a way to understand how clients view their world. Thus, cognitive therapy shares the phenomenological perspective with the Adlerian, existential, person-centered, and Gestalt approaches. Cognitive therapy provides a structured, focused, active approach that focuses on the client's inner world. According to Weishaar (1993), one of Beck's major theoretical contributions has been bringing private experience back into the realm of legitimate scientific inquiry.

A key strength of cognitive behavior therapy is that it is an eclectic psychotherapy. Dattilio (2002a) advocates using cognitive behavioral techniques within an existential framework. Thus, a client with panic disorder might well be encouraged to explore existential concerns such as the meaning of life, guilt, despair, and hope. Clients can be provided with cognitive behavioral tools to deal with events of everyday living and at the same time explore critical existential issues that confront them. Grounding symptomatic treatment within the context of an existential approach can be most fruitful.

The credibility of the cognitive model grows out of the fact that many of its propositions have been empirically tested. According to Leahy (2002), "Over the past 20 years, the cognitive model has gained wide appeal and appears to be influencing the development of the field more than any other model" (p. 419). Leahy identifies several reasons this approach has found such wide appeal:

- It works.
- It is an effective, focused, and practical treatment for specific problems.
- It is not mysterious or complicated, which facilitates transfer of knowledge from therapist to client.
- It is a cost-effective form of treatment.

MEICHENBAUM'S COGNITIVE BEHAVIOR MODIFICATION

Meichenbaum's work in self-instruction training and stress inoculation training has been applied successfully to a variety of client populations and specific problems. Of special note is his contribution to understanding how stress is largely self-induced through inner dialogue. He has gone beyond simply adding a few cognitive techniques to behavior therapy and has actually broadened its theoretical base through his demonstration of the importance of self-talk (Patterson & Watkins, 1996). Meichenbaum (1986) cautions cognitive behavioral practitioners against the tendency to become overly preoccupied with techniques. If progress is to be made, he suggests that cognitive behavior therapy must develop a testable theory of behavior change. He reports that some attempts have been made to formulate a cognitive social learning theory that will explain behavior change and specify the best methods of intervention.

A major contribution made by both Beck and Meichenbaum is the demystification of the therapy process. Both of these cognitive behavioral approaches are based on an educational model that stresses a working alliance between therapist and client. The models encourage self-help, provide for continuous feedback from the client on how well treatment strategies are working, and provide a structure and direction to the therapy process that allows for evaluation of outcomes. Clients are active, informed, and responsible for the direction of therapy because they are partners in the enterprise. The cognitive behavioral approaches may well be the treatment of choice in the current managed care environment.

Limitations and Criticisms of the Cognitive Behavioral Approaches

ELLIS'S REBT   REBT is a confrontational therapy, which provides both advantages and disadvantages. Some clients will have trouble with a confrontive therapist before he or she has earned their respect and trust. If clients feel they are not being listened to and cared about, there is a good chance they will terminate therapy.

I value paying attention to a client's past without getting lost in this past and without assuming a fatalistic stance about earlier traumatic experiences. I question the view of most cognitive behavioral therapists that exploring the past is ineffective in helping clients change faulty thinking and behavior. In some cases not enough emphasis is given to encouraging clients to express and explore their feelings. I believe the cognitive behavioral approaches can work best once clients have expressed their current feelings, which often occurs when they relive and work through earlier emotional issues in the here-and-now. Past unfinished business and childhood experiences can have a great deal of therapeutic power if they are connected to our present functioning. From my perspective, some painful early experiences need to be recognized, felt fully, reexperienced, and worked through in therapy before people can free themselves of restrictive influences.

REBT therapists can misuse their power by imposing their ideas of what constitutes rational thinking. Ellis (2001b) acknowledges that clients may feel pressured to adopt goals and values the therapist sells rather than acting within the framework of their own value system. Due to the directive nature of this approach, it is particularly important for practitioners to know themselves well and to take care not to impose their own philosophy of life on their clients. Because the therapist has a large amount of power by virtue of persuasion, psychological harm is more possible in REBT than in less directive approaches.

Furthermore, this power imbalance may disrupt the collaborative and cooperative client–therapist relationship essential to a successful outcome.

The therapist's level of training, knowledge, skill, perceptiveness, and judgment is particularly important. It is essential that the therapist be aware of when and how much to confront clients. An untrained therapist who uses REBT might view therapy as wearing down a client's resistance with persuasion, indoctrination, logic, and advice. Thus, a practitioner can misuse REBT by reducing it to dispensing quick-cure procedures—that is, by telling clients what is wrong with them and how they can best change.

It is well to underscore that REBT can be effective when practiced in a style different from Ellis's. Because Ellis has so much visibility, it is worth distinguishing between the principles and techniques of REBT and his very confrontational tactics. Indeed, a therapist can be soft-spoken and gentle and still use REBT concepts and methods. At times inexperienced REBT practitioners may assume that they must follow the fast pace of Ellis. Therapists who employ REBT techniques can use different degrees of directiveness, can vary the amount of activity, and can be themselves by developing a style that is consistent with their own personality.

BECK'S COGNITIVE THERAPY Cognitive therapy has been criticized for focusing too much on the power of positive thinking; being too superficial and simplistic; denying the importance of the client's past; being too technique-oriented; failing to use the therapeutic relationship; working only on eliminating symptoms, but failing to explore the underlying causes of difficulties; ignoring the role of unconscious factors; and neglecting the role of feelings (Freeman & Dattilio, 1992; Weishaar, 1993).

Freeman and Dattilio (1992, 1994; Dattilio, 2001) do a good job of debunking the myths and misconceptions about cognitive therapy. Weishaar (1993) concisely addresses a number of criticisms leveled at the approach. Although the cognitive therapist is straightforward and looks for simple rather than complex solutions, this does not imply that the practice of cognitive therapy is simple. Cognitive therapists do not explore the unconscious or underlying conflicts but work with clients in the present to bring about schematic changes. However, they do recognize that clients' current problems are often a product of earlier life experiences, and they do not ignore unconscious content such as dreams (Frank Dattilio, personal communication, June 25, 2002).

A criticism of cognitive therapy, like REBT, is that emotions tend to be played down in treatment. Both approaches draw on emotional techniques, along with cognitive and behavioral strategies, to bring about client change, but neither encourages emotional ventilation or emotionally reexperiencing painful events. Although Dattilio (2001) admits that CBT places central emphasis on cognition and behavior, he adds that emotion is not ignored in the therapy process; rather, he maintains that emotion is a byproduct of cognition and behavior and is addressed in a different fashion. In fact, in his discussion of the case of Celeste, Dattilio (2002a) shows how he worked with this client to identify and express her emotions fully. Dattilio does not assume that problematic emotions are simply the result of faulty thinking; rather, he contends that emotions have independent, adaptive, and healing functions of their own. Dattilio (2000a) puts the limitations of this approach nicely into perspective: "While CBT does have its limitations, it remains one of the most efficacious and well-researched modalities in existence" (p. 65). Leahy (2002) cautions against the tendency to pontificate rather than test out new ideas, and he endorses an openness to ideas advocated by other therapists: "It may be that 'true-believers' in cognitive therapy find themselves starting out with a devotion to a formulaic model but will move toward integrating cognitive therapy with more awareness of the complexities and limitations of the model" (p. 432).

MEICHENBAUM'S COGNITIVE BEHAVIOR MODIFICATION   In their critique of Meichenbaum's approach, Patterson and Watkins (1996) raise some excellent questions that can be asked of most cognitive behavioral approaches. The basic issue is discovering the best way to change a client's internal dialogue. Is directly teaching the client the most effective approach? Is the client's failure to think rationally or logically always due to a lack of understanding of reasoning or problem solving? Is learning by self-discovery more effective and longer lasting than being taught by a therapist? Although we don't have definitive answers to these questions yet, we cannot assume that learning occurs *only* by teaching. It is a mistake to conclude that therapy is mainly a cognitive process. Experiential therapies stress that learning also involves emotions and self-discovery.

 # WHERE TO GO FROM HERE

In the *CD-ROM for Integrative Counseling,* I work with Ruth from a cognitive behavioral perspective in a number of therapy sessions. Refer to the three sessions where I demonstrate my way of working with Ruth from a cognitive, emotive, and behavioral focus (Sessions 6, 7, and 8). See also Session 9 ("Integrative Perspective"), which illustrates the interactive nature of working with Ruth on thinking, feeling, and doing levels.

The *Journal of Rational-Emotive and Cognitive-Behavior Therapy* is published by Kluwer Academic/Human Sciences Press. This quarterly journal is an excellent way to keep informed of a wide variety of cognitive behavioral specialists. Subscriptions can be obtained from the Albert Ellis Institute for $70 a year.

The Albert Ellis Institute in New York City offers a variety of professional training involving a primary (3-day) certificate, an advanced (4-day) certificate, an associate fellowship, and a fellowship program. The institute also offers a "home-study" primary certificate program. Students get direct hands-on training supervision in REBT disputing and assessment techniques. Each of these programs has requirements in the areas of clinical experience, supervision, and personal experience in therapy. Therapists who wish to practice REBT are encouraged to participate in some form of directly supervised training.

For a catalog describing REBT training programs, workshops, books, cassette tapes, films, self-help forms, software items, and an order form for publications, contact:

Albert Ellis Institute
45 East 65th Street
New York, NY 10021-6593
Telephone: (212) 535-0822 or (800) 323-4738
Fax: (212) 249-3582
Email: info@rebt.org
Web site: http://www.rebt.org

The institute and many affiliated centers throughout the country provide official training programs that qualify for the Primary Training Certificate in REBT for professionals. Some of the places where this training is available are Chicago, Illinois; Tampa, Florida; Jamesville, Iowa; Lake Oswego, Oregon; Wilkes-Barre, Pennsylvania; and Salt Lake City, Utah. For information regarding both international affiliated training centers and for a list of training institutes in the United States, contact the Albert Ellis Institute. Training outside the United States is available through centers in Argentina, Australia, Canada, England, France, Germany, Greece, Israel, Italy, Mexico, the Netherlands, Peru, Romania, and Yugoslavia.

The *Journal of Cognitive Psychotherapy: An International Quarterly,* edited by John Riskind, also provides information on theory, practice, and research in cognitive behavior therapy. Information about the journal is available from the International Association of Cognitive Psychotherapy or by contacting John Riskind directly:

Dr. John Riskind
George Mason University
Department of Psychology, MSN 3F5
Fairfax, VA 22030-4444
Telephone: (703) 993-4094
Private Practice Telephone: (703) 280-8060
Fax: (703) 993-1359
Email: jriskind@gmu.edu
Web site: http://iacp.asu.edu

The Center for Cognitive Therapy, Newport Beach, California, maintains a Web site for mental health professionals. They list cognitive therapy books, audio and video training tapes, current advanced training workshops, and other cognitive therapy resources and information.

Email: mooney@padesky.com
Web site: http://www.padesky.com

For more information about a one-year, full-time postdoctoral fellowship and for shorter term clinical institutes, contact:

Beck Institute for Cognitive Therapy and Research
GSB Building
City Line and Belmont Avenues, Suite 700
Bala Cynwyd, PA 19004-1610
Telephone: (610) 664-3020
Fax: (610) 664-4437
Email: beckinst@gim.net
Web site: http://www.beckinstitute.org

For information regarding ongoing training and supervision in cognitive therapy, contact:

Department of Clinical Psychology
Philadelphia College of Osteopathic Medicine
4190 City Avenue
Philadelphia, PA 19131-1693
Web site: www.pcom.edu/academicprograms/psyd/index.html

InfoTrac College Edition Resources

Cognitive Behavior Therapy   The following key words are listed in such a way as to allow the InfoTrac College Edition search engine to locate a wider range of articles in the online library. The key words should be entered exactly as shown, to include asterisks, "W1," and "AND."

Albert Ellis	Cognitive distortions
Rational emotive behavior therapy	Catastrophizing
Rational W1 emotive	Reattribution
Aaron Beck	Cognitive W1 restructuring
Cognitive therapy	Beck AND depression
Automatic thoughts	

Recommended Supplementary Readings

Rational Emotive Behavior Therapy: A Therapist's Guide (Ellis & MacLaren, 1998) is an excellent comprehensive guidebook that gives clear descriptions of cognitive, emotive–experiential, and behavioral techniques. A useful chapter describes the integration of REBT with other therapeutic approaches.

How to Make Yourself Happy and Remarkably Less Disturbable (Ellis, 1999) presents a wide range of techniques for challenging self-defeating beliefs and trying on new behaviors. It is a user-friendly self-help book that is fun to read.

Feeling Better, Getting Better, and Staying Better (Ellis, 2001a) is a self-help book that describes a wide range of cognitive, emotive, and behavioral approaches to not only feeling better but getting better.

Overcoming Destructive Beliefs, Feelings, and Behaviors (Ellis, 2001b) brings REBT up to date and shows how it helps neurotic clients and those suffering from severe personality disorders.

Cognitive Therapy: Basics and Beyond (J. Beck, 1995) covers the nuts and bolts of cognitive therapy with all populations and cites important research on cognitive therapy since its inception.

Cognitive Therapy of Depression (Beck et al., 1979) is a classic text describing techniques used with depressed clients. The wide range of cognitive techniques is a useful handbook for practitioners.

Mind Over Mood: Change How You Feel by Changing the Way You Think (Greenberger & Padesky, 1995) provides step-by-step worksheets to identify moods, solve problems, and test thoughts related to depression, anxiety, anger, guilt, and shame. This is a popular self-help workbook and a valuable tool for therapists and clients learning cognitive therapy skills.

Clinician's Guide to Mind Over Mood (Padesky & Greenberger, 1995) shows therapists how to integrate *Mind Over Mood* in therapy and use cognitive therapy treatment protocols for specific diagnoses. This succinct overview of cognitive therapy has troubleshooting guides, reviews cultural issues, and offers guidelines for individual, couples, and group therapy.

References and Suggested Readings

*ALFORD, B. A., & BECK, A. T. (1997). *The integrative power of cognitive therapy.* New York: Guilford Press.

ARNKOFF, D. B., & GLASS, C. R. (1992). Cognitive therapy and psychotherapy integration. In D. K. Freedheim (Ed.), *History of psychotherapy: A century of change* (pp. 657–694). Washington, DC: American Psychological Association.

BECK, A. T. (1963). Thinking and depression: Idiosyncratic content and cognitive distortions. *Archives of General Psychiatry, 9,* 324–333.

BECK, A. T. (1967). *Depression: Clinical, experimental, and theoretical aspects.* New York: Harper & Row. (Republished as *Depression: Causes and treatment.* Philadelphia: University of Pennsylvania Press, 1972)

*BECK, A. T. (1976). *Cognitive therapy and emotional disorders.* New York: International Universities Press.

BECK, A. T. (1987). Cognitive therapy. In J. K. Zeig (Ed.), *The evolution of psychotherapy* (pp. 149–178). New York: Brunner/Mazel.

*BECK, A. T. (1988). *Love is never enough.* New York: Harper & Row.

BECK, A. T. (1991). Cognitive therapy: A 30-year retrospective. *American Psychologist, 46*(4), 368–375.

BECK, A. T., & HAAGA, D. A. F. (1992). The future of cognitive therapy. *Psychotherapy, 29*(1), 34–38.

*BECK, A. T., RUSH, A., SHAW, B., & EMERY, G. (1979). *Cognitive therapy of depression.* New York: Guilford Press.

---

*Books and articles marked with an asterisk are suggested for further study.

BECK, A. T., & WEISHAAR, M. E. (2000). In R. J. Corsini & D. Wedding (Eds.), *Current psychotherapies* (6th ed., pp. 241–272). Itasca, IL: F. E. Peacock.

BECK, A., WRIGHT, E. D., NEWMAN, C. E., & LIESE, B. (1993). *Cognitive therapy of substance abuse.* New York: Guilford Press.

*BECK, J. S. (1995). *Cognitive therapy: Basics and beyond.* New York: Guilford Press.

BERNARD, M. E., & WOLFE, J. L. (Eds.). (2000). *The RET sourcebook for practitioners.* New York: Albert Ellis Institute.

*BURNS, D. (1988). *Feeling good: The new mood therapy.* New York: Signet.

BURNS, D. (1989). *The feeling good handbook.* New York: Morrow.

COREY, G. (2004). *Theory and practice of group counseling* (6th ed.). Pacific Grove, CA: Brooks/Cole.

*COREY, G. (2005). *Case approach to counseling and psychotherapy* (6th ed.). Belmont, CA: Brooks/Cole.

*DATTILIO, F. M. (1993). Cognitive techniques with couples and families. *The Family Journal, 1*(1), 51–65.

DATTILIO, F. M. (1995). Cognitive therapy in Egypt. *Journal of Cognitive Psychotherapy, 9*(4), Winter, 285–286.

*DATTILIO, F. M. (Ed.). (1998). *Case studies in couple and family therapy: Systemic and cognitive perspectives.* New York: Guilford Press.

DATTILIO, F. M. (2000a). Cognitive-behavioral strategies. In J. Carlson & L. Sperry (Eds.), *Brief therapy with individuals and couples* (pp. 33–70). Phoenix, AZ: Zeig, Tucker & Theisen.

DATTILIO, F. M. (2000b). Families in crisis. In F. M. Dattilio & A. Freeman (Eds.), *Cognitive-behavioral strategies in crisis intervention* (2nd ed., pp. 316–338). New York: Guilford Press.

DATTILIO, F. M. (2001). Cognitive-behavior family therapy: Contemporary myths and misconceptions. *Contemporary Family Therapy, 23*(1), 3–18.

DATTILIO, F. M. (2002a, January–February). Cognitive-behaviorism comes of age: Grounding symptomatic treatment in an existential approach. *The Psychotherapy Networker, 26*(1), 75–78.

DATTILIO, F. M. (2002b). Homework assignments in couple and family therapy. *Journal of Clinical Psychology, 58*(5), 535–547.

DATTILIO, F. M., & CASTALDO, J. E. (2001). Differentiating symptoms of anxiety from relapse of Guillain-Barre-syndrome. *Harvard Review of Psychiatry, 9*(5), 260–265.

*DATTILIO, F. M., & FREEMAN, A. (1992). Introduction to cognitive therapy. In A. Freeman & E. M. Dattilio (Eds.), *Comprehensive casebook of cognitive therapy* (pp. 3–11). New York: Plenum.

*DATTILIO, F. M., & FREEMAN, A. (Eds.). (2000). *Cognitive-behavioral strategies in crisis intervention* (2nd ed.). New York: Guilford Press.

*DATTILIO, F. M., & PADESKY, C. A. (1990). *Cognitive therapy with couples.* Sarasota, FL: Professional Resources Exchange.

DATTILIO, F. M., & SALAS-AUVERT, J. A. (2000). *Panic disorders: Assessment and treatment through a wide angle lens.* Phoenix, AZ: Zeig, Tucker & Company.

DeRUBEIS, R. J., & BECK, A. T. (1988). Cognitive therapy. In K. S. Dobson (Ed.), *Handbook of cognitive-behavioral therapies* (pp. 273–306). New York: Guilford Press.

DOBSON, K. S., & BLOCK, L. (1988). Historical and philosophical bases of the cognitive-behavioral therapies. In K. S. Dobson (Ed.), *Handbook of cognitive-behavioral therapies* (pp. 3–38). New York: Guilford Press.

DRYDEN, W. (1989). Albert Ellis: An efficient and passionate life. *Journal of Counseling and Development, 67*(10), 539–546.

*ELLIS, A. (1994). *Reason and emotion in psychotherapy revised.* New York: Kensington.

*ELLIS, A. (1996). *Better, deeper, and more enduring brief therapy: The rational emotive behavior therapy approach.* New York: Brunner/Mazel.

*ELLIS, A. (1997). The evolution of Albert Ellis and rational emotive behavior therapy. In J. K. Zeig (Ed.), *The evolution of psychotherapy: The third conference* (pp. 69–82). New York: Brunner/Mazel.

*ELLIS, A. (1999). *How to make yourself happy and remarkably less disturbable.* Atascadero, CA: Impact.

*ELLIS, A. (2000a). *How to control your anxiety before it controls you.* New York: Citadel Press.

ELLIS, A. (2000b). Rational emotive behavior therapy. In R. Corsini & D. Wedding (Eds.), *Current psychotherapies* (6th ed., pp. 168–204). Itasca, IL: F. E. Peacock.

*ELLIS, A. (2001a). *Feeling better, getting better, and staying better.* Atascadero, CA: Impact.

*ELLIS, A. (2001b). *Overcoming destructive beliefs, feelings, and behaviors.* Amherst, NY: Prometheus Books.

*ELLIS, A. (2002). *Overcoming resistance: A rational emotive behavior therapy integrated approach* (2nd ed.). New York: Springer.

*ELLIS, A., & BLAU, S. (Eds.). (1998). *The Albert Ellis reader.* New York: Kensington.

*ELLIS, A., & CRAWFORD, T. (2000). *Making intimate connections: Seven guidelines for great relationships and better communication.* Atascadero, CA: Impact.

*ELLIS, A., & DRYDEN, W. (1997). *The practice of rational-emotive therapy* (Rev. ed.). New York: Springer.

ELLIS, A., GORDON, J., NEENAN, M., & PALMER, S. (1997). *Stress counseling: A rational emotive behavior approach.* New York: Springer.

*ELLIS, A., & HARPER, R. A. (1997). *A guide to rational living* (3rd ed.). North Hollywood, CA: Melvin Powers (Wilshire Books).

*ELLIS, A., & MACLAREN, C. (1998). *Rational emotive behavior therapy: A therapist's guide.* Atascadero, CA: Impact.

ELLIS, A., & TAFRATE, R. C. (1997). *How to control your anger—before it controls you.* New York: Citadel Press.

*ELLIS, A., & VELTEN, E. (1998). *Optimal aging: How to get over growing older.* Chicago: Open Court.

ELLIS, A., & WILDE, J. (2001). *Case studies in rational emotive behavior therapy with children and adolescents.* Upper Saddle River, NJ: Merrill, Prentice-Hall.

FREEMAN, A., & DATTILIO, R. M. (Eds.). (1992). *Comprehensive casebook of cognitive therapy.* New York: Plenum.

FREEMAN, A., & DATTILIO, R. M. (1994). Cognitive therapy. In J. L. Ronch, W. Van Ornum, & N. C. Stilwell (Eds.), *The counseling sourcebook: A practical reference on contemporary issues* (pp. 60–71). New York: Continuum Press.

FREEMAN, A., & DeWOLF, R. (1990). *Woulda, coulda, shoulda.* New York: Morrow.

FREEMAN, A., & REINECKE, M. A. (1993). *Cognitive therapy of suicidal behavior: A manual for treatment.* New York: Springer.

GRANVOLD, D. K. (Ed.). (1994). *Cognitive and behavioral treatment: Method and applications.* Pacific Grove, CA: Brooks/Cole.

GREENBERGER, D., & PADESKY, C. A. (1995). *Mind over mood: Change how you feel by changing the way you think.* New York: Guilford Press.

HAAGA, D. A., & DAVISON, G. C. (1986). Cognitive change methods. In F. H. Kanfer & A. P. Goldstein (Eds.), *Helping people change: A textbook of methods* (3rd ed., pp. 236–282). New York: Pergamon Press.

HORNEY, K. (1950). *Neurosis and human growth.* New York: Norton.

KWEE, M. G. T., & ELLIS, A. (1997). Can multimodal and rational emotive behavioral therapy be reconciled? *Journal of Rational-Emotive and Cognitive-Behavior Therapy, 15,* 95–132.

*LEAHY, R. L. (2002). Cognitive therapy: Current problems and future directions. In R. L. Leahy & E. T. Dowd (Eds.), *Clinical advances in cognitive psychotherapy: Theory and application* (pp. 418–434). New York: Springer.

MAHONEY, M. J., & LYDDON, W. (1988). Recent developments in cognitive approaches to counseling and psychotherapy. *Counseling Psychology, 16,* 190–234.

MAULTSBY, M. C. (1984). *Rational behavior therapy.* Englewood Cliffs, NJ: Prentice-Hall.

*MEICHENBAUM, D. (1977). *Cognitive behavior modification: An integrative approach.* New York: Plenum.

*MEICHENBAUM, D. (1985). *Stress inoculation training.* New York: Pergamon Press.

MEICHENBAUM, D. (1986). Cognitive behavior modification. In F. H. Kanfer & A. P. Goldstein (Eds.), *Helping people change: A textbook of methods* (pp. 346–380). New York: Pergamon Press.

MEICHENBAUM, D. (1994). *A clinical handbook/practical therapist manual: For assessing and treating adults with post-traumatic stress disorder (PTSD).* Waterloo, Ontario: Institute Press.

*MEICHENBAUM, D. (1997). The evolution of a cognitive-behavior therapist. In J. K. Zeig (Ed.), *The evolution of psychotherapy: The third conference* (pp. 96–104). New York: Brunner/Mazel.

PADESKY, C. A., & GREENBERGER, D. (1995). *Clinician's guide to mind over mood.* New York: Guilford Press.

PATTERSON, C. H., & WATKINS, C. E. (1996). *Theories of psychotherapy* (5th ed.). New York: Harper/Collins.

REINECKE, M., DATTILIO, F. M., & FREEMAN, A. (Eds.). (2002). *Casebook of cognitive behavior therapy with children and adolescents* (2nd ed.). New York: Guilford Press.

SAFRAN, J. D. (1998). *Widening the scope of cognitive therapy*. Northvale, NJ: Jason Aronson.

WARREN, R., & MCLELLARN, R. W. (1987). What do RET therapists think they are doing? An international survey. *Journal of Rational-Emotive Therapy, 5*(2), 92–107.

WEISHAAR, M. E. (1993). *Aaron T. Beck*. London: Sage.

YANKURA, J., & DRYDEN, W. (1994). *Albert Ellis*. Thousand Oaks, CA: Sage.

Reality Therapy

William *Glasser*

WILLIAM GLASSER (B. 1925) was educated at Case Western Reserve University in Cleveland, Ohio. Initially a chemical engineer, he turned to psychology (M.A., Clinical Psychology, 1948) and then to psychiatry, attending medical school (M.D., 1953) with the intention of becoming a psychiatrist. By 1957 he had completed his psychiatric training at the Veterans Administration and UCLA in Los Angeles and in 1961 was board certified in psychiatry.

Very early he rejected the Freudian model, and by the end of his residency he began to put together what by 1962 became known as reality therapy. The essence of reality therapy, now taught all over the world, is that we are all responsible for what we choose to do. The basic assumption is that all any of us can control is our present lives.

By the late 1970s Glasser was looking for a theory that could explain all his work. Glasser learned about *control theory* from William Powers, and he believed this theory had great potential. He spent the next 20 years expanding, revising, and clarifying what he was initially taught. By 1996 Glasser had become convinced that these revisions had so changed the theory that it was misleading to continue to call it control theory, and he changed the name to *choice theory* to reflect all that he had developed. In some of his more recent books, Glasser (1998, 2000, 2003) outlines the basics on his updated theory, which he calls the "new reality therapy." ■

INTRODUCTION

Reality therapy is based on choice theory as it is explained in Glasser's (1998, 2000, 2003) most recent books.* (This discussion of Glasser's ideas pertains to these three books unless otherwise specified.) Reality therapists believe the underlying problem of most clients is the same: They are either involved in a present unsatisfying relationship or lack what could even be called a relationship. Many of the problems of clients are caused by their inability to connect, to get close to others, or to have a satisfying or successful relationship with at least one of the significant people in their lives. The therapist guides clients toward a satisfying relationship and teaches them to behave in more effective ways than they are presently behaving. The more clients are able to connect with people, the greater chance they have to experience happiness.

Few clients have any clear understanding that their problem is the way they are choosing to behave. What they do know is that they feel a great deal of pain or that they are unhappy because they have been sent for counseling by someone with authority who is not satisfied with their behavior—typically a court official, a school administrator, or a spouse or parent. Reality therapists recognize that clients choose their behaviors as a way to deal with the frustration caused by the unsatisfying relationship. All of these behavioral choices—ranging from profound psychosis to mild depression—are described in detail in the DSM-IV-TR (APA, 2000).

Glasser contends that clients should not be labeled with a diagnosis except when it is necessary for insurance purposes. From Glasser's perspective, all diagnoses are descriptions of the behaviors people choose in their attempt to deal with the pain and frustration that is endemic to unsatisfying present relationships. Therefore, labeling ineffective behavior as mental illness is not accurate. He believes mental illnesses are conditions such as Alzheimer's disease, epilepsy, head trauma, and brain infections—conditions associated with tangible brain damage. Because these people are suffering from a brain abnormality, they should be treated primarily by neurologists. As Glasser (2003) forcefully states, using drugs to treat symptoms of unhappiness is counterproductive and rarely helps anyone who is suffering.

Therapy consists mainly of teaching clients to make more effective choices as they deal with the people they need in their lives. Because choice theory explains how to choose to behave in ways that improve relationships, teaching choice theory to clients is part of reality therapy. Glasser maintains that it is essential for the therapist to establish a satisfying relationship with clients.

---

* I asked William Glasser to review this chapter for this seventh edition. Along with this review, Glasser provided a great deal of new material that reflects his current thinking. This extensively revised chapter explains how choice theory has been integrated into what Glasser calls the "new reality therapy."

Once this relationship is developed, the skill of the therapist as a teacher becomes paramount.

Reality therapy has been used in a variety of settings. The approach is applicable to counseling, social work, education, crisis intervention, corrections and rehabilitation, institutional management, and community development. Reality therapy is popular in schools, correctional institutions, general hospitals, state mental hospitals, halfway houses, and substance abuse centers. Most of the military clinics that treat drug and alcohol abusers use reality therapy as their preferred therapeutic approach.

 ## KEY CONCEPTS

View of Human Nature

Choice theory posits that we are not born blank slates waiting to be *externally motivated* by forces in the world around us. Rather, we are born with five genetically encoded needs—*survival, love and belonging, power or achievement, freedom or independence,* and *fun*—that drive us all our lives. Each of us has all five needs, but they vary in strength. For example, we all have a need for love and belonging, but some of us need more love than others. Choice theory is based on the premise that because we are by nature social creatures we need to both receive and give love. Glasser (2000) believes the need to *love and to belong* is the primary need because we need people to satisfy the other needs. It is also the most difficult need to satisfy because we must have a cooperative person to help us meet it.

Our brain functions as a control system. It continually monitors our feelings to determine how well we are doing in our lifelong effort to satisfy these needs. Whenever we feel bad, one or more of these five needs is unsatisfied. Although we may not be aware of our needs, we know that we want to feel better. Driven by pain, we try to figure out how to feel better. Reality therapists teach clients choice theory so clients can identify the frustrated need and try to satisfy it. When clients succeed, they are rewarded with good feelings.

Choice theory explains that we do not satisfy our needs directly. What we do, beginning shortly after birth and continuing all our lives, is to keep close track of anything we do that feels very good. We store this knowledge in a special place in our brain called our *quality world.* The quality world is at the core of our lives. It is our personal Shangri-la—the world we would like to live in if we could. It is completely based on our needs, but unlike the needs, which are general, it is very specific. Our quality world is like a picture album. Some pictures may be blurred, however, and the therapist helps the client clarify them. Pictures exist in priority for most people, yet clients may have difficulty identifying their priorities. The therapist's job is to assist clients in prioritizing their wants and deciding what is most important to them.

People are the most important component of our quality world, and these are the people we most want to connect with. It contains the people we are closest to and most enjoy being with. Those who enter therapy generally have no one in their quality world or, more often, someone in their quality world that they are unable to relate to in a satisfying way. For therapy to have a chance of success, a therapist must be the kind of person that clients would consider putting in their quality world. Getting into the clients' quality world is the art of therapy. It is from this relationship with the therapist that clients begin to learn how to get close to the people they need.

Choice Theory Explanation of Behavior

Choice theory explains that all we ever do from birth to death is behave and, with rare exceptions, everything we do is chosen. Every total behavior is always our best attempt to get what we want to satisfy our needs. *Total behavior* teaches that all behavior is made up of four inseparable but distinct components—*acting, thinking, feeling,* and *physiology*—that necessarily accompany all of our actions, thoughts, and feelings. Behavior is purposeful because it is designed to close the gap between what we want and what we perceive we are getting. Specific behaviors are always generated from this discrepancy. Our behaviors come from the inside, and thus we choose our destiny.

Glasser says that to speak of being depressed, having a headache, being angry, or being anxious implies passivity and lack of personal responsibility, and it is inaccurate. It is more accurate to think of these as parts of total behaviors and to use the verb forms *depressing, headaching, angering,* and *anxietying* to describe them. It is more accurate to think of people depressing or angering themselves rather than being depressed or being angry. When people choose misery by developing a range of "paining" behaviors, it is because these are the best behaviors they are able to devise at the time, and these behaviors often get them what they want.

When a reality therapist starts teaching choice theory, the client will often protest and say, "I'm suffering, don't tell me I'm choosing to suffer like this." The therapist can explain, as painful as depressing is, people do not choose pain and suffering directly. Rather, it is an unchosen part of one's total behavior. The behavior of the person is the best effort, ineffective as it is, to satisfy needs.

Characteristics of Reality Therapy

Contemporary reality therapy focuses quickly on the unsatisfying relationship or the lack of a relationship, which is often the cause of clients' problems. Clients may complain of a problem in which they are failing to succeed such as not being able to keep a job, not doing well in school, or not having a meaningful relationship. When clients complain about how other people are causing them pain, the therapist does not get involved with finding fault. Reality therapy focuses on what clients *can* control in the relationship. Choice theory teaches that there is no sense talking about what clients can't control. The basic axiom of choice theory, which is crucial for clients to understand, is this:

The only person you can control is yourself. When clients point out correctly that this is unfair, the therapist may agree and say, "There is no guarantee that life is fair. You are the only person who can change. Complaining may feel good for a short time, but it is a completely ineffective behavior."

Reality therapists do not listen very long to complaining, blaming, and criticizing, because these are the most ineffective behaviors in our behavioral repertoire. Because reality therapists give little attention to these self-defeating total behaviors, they tend to disappear from therapy. What do reality therapists focus on? Here are some underlying characteristics of reality therapy.

EMPHASIZE CHOICE AND RESPONSIBILITY If we choose all we do, we must be responsible for what we choose. This does not mean we should be blamed or punished, unless we break the law, but it does mean the therapist should never lose sight of the fact that clients are responsible for what they do. Choice theory changes the focus on responsibility to choice and choosing.

Reality therapists deal with people "as if" they have choices. Therapists should focus on those areas where clients have choice, for doing so gets them closer to the people they need. For example, being involved in meaningful activities, such as work, is a good way to gain the respect of other people, and work can help them fulfill their need for power. It is very difficult for adults to feel good about themselves if they don't engage in some form of meaningful activity. As clients begin to feel good about themselves, it is less necessary for them to continue to choose ineffective and self-destructive behaviors.

REJECT TRANSFERENCE Reality therapists strive to be themselves in their professional work. By being themselves, therapists can use the relationship to teach clients how to relate to others in their lives. Glasser contends that transference is a way that both therapist and client avoid being who they are and owning what they are doing right now. It is unrealistic for therapists to go along with the idea that they are anyone but themselves. Assume the client claims, "I see you as my father or mother and this is why I'm behaving the way I am." In such a situation a reality therapist is likely to say clearly and firmly, "I am not your mother, father, or anyone but myself."

KEEP THE THERAPY IN THE PRESENT Some clients come to counseling convinced that their problems started in the past and that they must revisit the past if they are to be helped. Glasser (2000) grants that we are products of our past but argues that we are not victims of our past unless we choose to be. Still, many therapeutic models continue to teach that to function well in the present we must understand and revisit our past. Glasser disagrees with this belief and contends that whatever mistakes were made in the past are not pertinent now. We can only satisfy our needs in the present.

The reality therapist does not totally reject the past. If the client wants to talk about past successes or good relationships in the past, the therapist will listen because these may be repeated in the present. Reality therapists will devote only enough time to past failures to assure clients that they are not rejecting them. As soon as possible, therapists tell clients: "What has happened is over; it can't be changed. The more time we spend looking back, the more we avoid looking forward."

AVOID FOCUSING ON SYMPTOMS   In traditional therapy a great deal of time is spent focusing on symptoms by asking clients how they feel and why they are obsessing or phobicking. Focusing on the past "protects" clients from facing the reality of unsatisfying present relationships, and focusing on symptoms does the same thing. Glasser (2003) contends that people who have symptoms believe that if they could only be symptom-free they would find happiness. Whether people are depressing or paining, they tend to think that what they are experiencing is happening to them. They are reluctant to accept the reality that their suffering is due to the total behavior they are choosing. Their symptoms can be viewed as the body's way of warning them that the behavior they are choosing is not satisfying their basic needs. The reality therapist spends as little time as he or she can on the symptoms, because they will last only as long as they are needed to deal with an unsatisfying relationship or the frustration of basic needs.

According to Glasser, if clients believe that the therapist wants to hear about their symptoms or spend time talking about the past, they are more than willing to comply. Engaging in long journeys into the past or exploring symptoms results in lengthy therapy. Getting rid of these two impediments to therapy and focusing on present problems can shorten most therapy considerably.

CHALLENGE TRADITIONAL VIEWS OF MENTAL ILLNESS   Choice theory rejects the traditional notion that people with problematic physical and psychological symptoms are mentally ill. Glasser (2003) has warned people to be cautious of psychiatry, which can be hazardous to both one's physical and mental health. He criticizes the psychiatric establishment for relying heavily on the DSM-IV-TR for both diagnosis and treatment. Glasser paints a picture of biological psychiatrists who diagnose individuals with a wide range of mental illnesses and who attempt to convince their patients that brain pathology is the cause of their problems. People who exhibit symptoms of anxiety and depression are often told that their condition is due to an imbalance in their brain chemistry. These psychiatrists treat individuals they view as having some form of mental illness by prescribing psychiatric drugs. Glasser is critical of traditional psychiatry that tends to discourage psychotherapy or the idea that there is anything that people with symptoms can do for themselves to alleviate their disabling symptoms. Glasser admits that he has never prescribed a brain drug, no matter how severe the symptoms of the psychological problem. He asserts that psychiatric drugs have negative side effects both physically and psychologically. Reality therapy has challenged the traditionally accepted views of mental illness and treatment by the use of medication.

THE THERAPEUTIC PROCESS

Therapeutic Goals

A primary goal of contemporary reality therapy is to help clients get connected or reconnected with the people they have chosen to put in their quality world. In addition to fulfilling this need for love and belonging, a basic goal of reality therapy is to help clients learn better ways of fulfilling all of their needs, including power or achievement, freedom or independence, and fun.

In most instances clients come voluntarily for therapy, and these clients are the easiest to help. However, another goal entails working with the large group of people who are so resistant to psychotherapy that it seems impossible to get them involved. For the most part, these people do not want to see the therapist and actively resist therapy. They often engage in violent behavior, addictions, and other kinds of antisocial behaviors. If they once had responsible people in their quality world, they have removed them.

As soon as a counselor recognizes that he or she is dealing with a disconnected, pleasure-seeking person, it is best to give up all the usual goals of counseling and focus on just one thing—doing whatever is possible to get connected with this person. If the counselor can't make a connection, there is no possibility of providing significant help. If the counselor *can* make a connection with this client, then the goal of teaching the client how to fulfill his or her needs can slowly begin.

Therapist's Function and Role

The first function of therapists is to create a good relationship with their clients. From this relationship, they can help clients move toward people and activities that are satisfying to them. Another key function of reality therapists is to teach clients how to engage in self-evaluation. This is done by raising the question, "Are your behaviors getting you what you want and need?" The role of the therapist is not to make the evaluation for clients, but to challenge them to evaluate themselves.

It is the job of therapists to convey the idea that no matter how bad things are there is hope. If therapists are able to instill this sense of hope, clients feel that they are no longer alone and that change is possible. The therapist functions as an advocate, or someone who is on the client's side. Together they can creatively address a range of concerns.

Client's Experience in Therapy

Clients are not expected to backtrack into the past or get sidetracked into talking about symptoms. Neither will much time be spent talking about feelings separate from the acting and thinking that are part of the total behaviors over which clients have direct control.

Clients will most likely find therapists to be gently, but firmly, confronting. Reality therapists will often ask clients questions such as these: "Is what you are choosing to do bringing you closer to the people you want to be closer to right now?" "Is what you are doing getting you closer to a new person if you are presently disconnected from everyone?" These questions are part of the self-evaluation process, which is the cornerstone of reality therapy.

Clients can expect to experience some urgency in therapy. Time is important, as each session may be the last. This need not be a long, drawn-out process. Clients should be able to think, "I can begin to use what we talked about today in my life. I am able to bring my present experiences to the therapy as my problems are in the present and my therapist will not let me escape from that fact."

Relationship Between Therapist and Client

Reality therapy emphasizes an understanding and supportive relationship. An important factor is the willingness of counselors to develop their own individual therapeutic style. Sincerity and being comfortable with one's style are crucial traits in being able to carry out therapeutic functions.

For involvement between the therapist and the client to occur, the counselor must have certain personal qualities, including warmth, congruence, understanding, acceptance, concern, respect for the client, openness, and the willingness to be challenged by others. One of the best ways to develop this goodwill and therapeutic friendship is simply by listening to clients. Involvement is also promoted by talking about a wide range of topics that have relevance for clients. Once involvement has been established, the counselor assists clients in gaining a deeper understanding of the consequences of their current behavior.

Choice theory takes all the mystery and uncertainty out of what the therapist is trying to do. From this theory, the therapist will develop the procedures and techniques required for effective counseling. Therapy is always a mentoring process in which the therapist is the teacher and the client is the student.

 # APPLICATION: THERAPEUTIC TECHNIQUES AND PROCEDURES

The Practice of Reality Therapy

The practice of reality therapy can best be conceptualized as the *cycle of counseling*, which consists of two major components: (1) creating the counseling environment and (2) implementing specific procedures that lead to changes in behavior. The art of counseling is to weave these components together in ways that lead clients to evaluate their lives and decide to move in more effective directions.

How do these components blend in the counseling process? The cycle of counseling begins with establishing a working relationship with clients. The process proceeds through an exploration of clients' wants, needs, and perceptions. Clients explore their total behavior and make their own evalua-tion of how effective they are in getting what they want. If clients decide to try new behavior, they make plans that will lead to change, and they commit themselves to their plan. The cycle of counseling includes following up on how well clients are doing and offering further consultation as needed.

It is important to keep in mind that although the concepts may seem sim-ple as they are presented here, being able to translate them into actual thera-peutic practice takes considerable skill and creativity. Although the principles will be the same when used by any counselor who is certified in reality ther-apy, the manner in which they are applied does vary depending on the coun-selor's style and personal characteristics. Just because the principles are applied in a progressive manner, they should not be thought of as discrete and rigid categories. The art of practicing reality therapy involves far more than following procedures in a step-by-step fashion. Counseling is not a simplistic method that is applied in the same way with every client. With choice theory in the background of practice, the counselor tailors the counseling to what the client presents. Although the counselor is prepared to work in a way that is meaningful to the client, the move toward satisfying relationships remains in the foreground.

In this section I draw heavily from the writings of Robert Wubbolding, a reality therapist who has extended the practice of reality therapy (WDEP sys-tem) for both implementing and teaching reality therapy. I especially value Wubbolding's contributions to teaching reality therapy and to conceptualiz-ing therapeutic procedures. This material renders choice theory practical and useable by counselors, and it provides a basis for conceptualizing and apply-ing the theory. As is true of all the theories presented in this book, there are various ways of putting these theories into actual practice. Although reality therapists operate within the spirit of choice theory, they practice in their own unique ways. The discussion that follows is best considered as an aid for teaching reality therapy, but it should not be thought of as a replacement for the extensive training that is needed to counsel effectively. This section is based on an integrated summary and adaptation of material from various sources (Glasser, 1992, 1998, 2000; Wubbolding, 1988, 1991, 1996, 2000, 2001; Wubbolding & Associates, 1998). The Student Manual that accompanies this textbook contains a chart by Wubbolding that highlights issues and tasks to be accomplished throughout the cycle of counseling.

The Counseling Environment

The practice of reality therapy begins with the counselor's efforts to create a supportive environment within which clients can begin to make life changes. In a short period of time, clients generally begin to appreciate the caring, accept-ing, noncoercive choice theory environment. It is from this mildly confrontive yet always noncriticizing, nonblaming, noncomplaining, caring environment that clients learn to create the satisfying environment that leads to successful relationships. In this coercion-free atmosphere, clients feel free to be creative and to begin to try new behaviors.

Counselor involvement, or investment, with clients is a basic part of creating working relationships. In his description of the cycle of counseling, Wubbolding (2000, 2002) identifies specific ways for counselors to create a climate that leads to involvement with clients. Some of the approaches to establishing a therapeutic environment include using attending behavior, suspending judgment of clients, doing the unexpected, using humor appropriately, being oneself as a counselor, engaging in facilitative self-disclosure, listening for metaphors in the client's mode of self-expression, listening for themes, summarizing and focusing, and being an ethical practitioner. The basis for therapeutic interventions to work rests on a fair, firm, friendly, and trusting environment.

Procedures That Lead to Change

Change is always a choice. Reality therapists begin by asking clients what they want from therapy. They also inquire about the choices clients are making in their relationships. In most instances, there is a major unsatisfied relationship and usually clients do not believe they have any choice in what is going on in this relationship. In the beginning the client may deny this is the case. For example, the client might say, "I'm depressed. My depression is the problem. Why are you talking about my relationships?" The client often does not want to talk about the real problem, which is the unsatisfying relationship or lack thereof.

In the first session a skilled therapist looks for and defines the wants of the client. The therapist also looks for a key unsatisfying present relationship—usually with a spouse, a child, a parent, or an employer. The therapist might ask, "Whose behavior can you control?" This question may need to be asked several times during the next few sessions to deal with the client's resistance to looking at his or her own behavior.

When clients begin to realize that they can control only their own behavior, therapy is under way. The rest of therapy focuses on how clients can make better choices. There are more choices available than clients realize, and the therapist explores these possible choices. Clients may be stuck in misery, blaming, and the past, but they can choose to change—even if the other person in the relationship does not change.

Reality therapists explore the tenets of choice theory with clients, helping clients identify basic needs, discovering clients' quality world, and finally, helping clients understand that they are choosing the total behaviors that are their symptoms. In every instance when clients make a change, it is their choice. With the therapist's help, clients learn to make better choices than they did when they were on their own.

Through this process, clients learn that things don't just happen. With planning, clients are able to take much more effective control of their lives.

We are not at the mercy of others, and we are not victims. Using choice theory to gain and maintain successful relationships is a skill that can be learned. According to Glasser (1992), the procedures that lead to change are based on the assumption that human beings are motivated to change (1) when they are convinced that their present behavior is not getting them what they want and (2) when they believe they can choose other behaviors that will get them closer to what they want.

The "WDEP" System

Wubbolding (2000, 2001, 2002; Wubbolding & Associates, 1998) uses an acronym, WDEP, to describe key procedures that can be used in the practice of reality therapy. Each of the letters refers to a cluster of strategies: W = wants and needs; D = direction and doing; E = self-evaluation; and P = planning. These strategies are designed to promote change. Let's look at each one in more detail.

WANTS (EXPLORING WANTS, NEEDS, AND PERCEPTIONS)   Reality therapists ask, "What do you want?" Through the therapist's skillful questioning, clients are encouraged to recognize, define, and refine how they wish to meet their needs. Part of counseling consists of exploring the "picture album," or quality world, of clients and how their behavior is aimed at moving their perception of the external world closer to their inner world of wants.

The skilled reality therapist counsels in a noncritical and accepting way so that clients will reveal what is in their special world. Clients are given the opportunity to explore every facet of their lives, including what they want from their family, friends, and work. Furthermore, it is useful for clients to define what they expect and want from the counselor and from themselves (Wubbolding, 2000; Wubbolding & Associates, 1998). This exploration of wants, needs, and perceptions should continue throughout the counseling process as clients' pictures change.

Here are some useful questions to help clients pinpoint what they want:

- If you were the person that you wish you were, what kind of person would you be?
- What would your family be like if your wants and their wants matched?
- What would you be doing if you were living as you want to?
- Do you really want to change your life?
- What is it you want that you don't seem to be getting from life?
- What do you think stops you from making the changes you would like?

This line of questioning sets the stage for applying other procedures in reality therapy. It is an art for counselors to know *what* questions to ask, *how* to ask them, and *when* to ask them.

DIRECTION AND DOING   Reality therapy stresses current behavior and is concerned with past events only insofar as they influence how clients are behaving now. The focus on the present is characterized by the question so often asked by the reality therapist: "What are you doing?" Even though problems may be rooted in the past, clients need to learn how to deal with them in the present by learning better ways of getting what they want. The past may be discussed if doing so will help clients plan for a better tomorrow. The therapist's challenge is to help clients make more need-satisfying choices.

Early in counseling it is essential to discuss with clients the overall direction of their lives, including where they are going and where their behavior is taking them. This exploration is preliminary to the subsequent evaluation of whether it is a desirable direction. The therapist holds a mirror before the client and asks, "What do you see for yourself now and in the future?" It often takes some time for this reflection to become clear to clients so they can verbally express their perceptions (Wubbolding, 1988).

Reality therapy focuses on gaining awareness of and changing current total behavior. To accomplish this, reality therapists focus on questions like these: "What are you doing now?" "What did you actually do this past week?" "What did you want to do differently this past week?" "What stopped you from doing what you say you want to do?" "What will you do tomorrow?"

Listening to clients talk about feelings can be productive, but only if it is linked to what they are doing. When an emergency light on the car dashboard lights up, the driver is alerted that something is wrong and that immediate action is necessary to remedy a problem. In a similar way, when clients talk about problematic feelings, most reality therapists affirm and acknowledge these feelings. Yet, rather than focusing mainly on these feelings, counselors encourage clients to take action by changing what they are doing and thinking. It is easier to change what we are doing and thinking than to change our feelings. According to Glasser (1992), what we are doing is easy to see and impossible to deny; thus, it serves as the proper focus in therapy. Discussions centering on feelings, without strongly relating them to what people are doing, are counterproductive.

EVALUATION   The core of reality therapy, as we have seen, is to ask clients to make the following self-evaluation: "Does your present behavior have a reasonable chance of getting you what you want now, and will it take you in the direction you want to go?" Through skillful questioning, the counselor helps clients evaluate their present behavior and the direction this is taking them. Wubbolding (1988, 2000; Wubbolding & Associates, 1998) suggests questions like these:

- Is what you are doing helping or hurting you?
- Is what you are doing now what you want to be doing?
- Is your behavior working for you?
- Is there a healthy congruence between what you are doing and what you believe?
- Is what you are doing against the rules?

- Is what you want realistic or attainable?
- Does it help you to look at it that way?
- How committed are you to the therapeutic process and to changing your life?
- After you examine what you want carefully, does it appear to be in your best interests and in the best interest of others?

Asking clients to evaluate each component of their total behavior is a major task in reality therapy. It is the counselor's task to get clients to evaluate the quality of their actions and to help them make effective choices. Individuals will not change until they first decide that a change would be more advantageous. Without an honest self-assessment, it is unlikely that clients will change. Thus, reality therapists are relentless in their efforts to help clients conduct explicit self-evaluations of each behavioral component. When therapists ask a depressing client if this behavior is helping in the long run, they introduce the idea of choice to the client. The process of evaluation of the doing, thinking, feeling, and physiological components of total behavior is within the scope of the client's responsibility.

Reality therapists may be directive with certain clients at the beginning of treatment. This is done to help clients recognize that some behaviors are not effective. In working with clients who are in crisis, for example, it is sometimes necessary to suggest straightforwardly what will work and what will not. Other clients, such as alcoholics and children of alcoholics, need direction early in the course of treatment, for they often do not have the thinking behaviors in their control system to be able to make consistent evaluations of when their lives are seriously out of effective control. These clients are likely to have blurred pictures and, at times, to be unaware of what they want or whether their wants are realistic. As they grow and continually interact with the counselor, they learn to make the evaluations with less help from the counselor (Wubbolding, 1988, 2000).

PLANNING AND ACTION   Much of the significant work of the counseling process involves helping clients identify specific ways to fulfill their wants and needs. Once clients determine what they want to change, they are generally ready to explore other possible behaviors and formulate an action plan. The process of creating and carrying out plans enables people to gain effective control over their lives. If the plan does not work, for whatever reason, the counselor and client work together to devise a different plan. The plan gives the client a starting point, a toehold on life, but plans can be modified as needed. Throughout this planning phase, the counselor continually urges the client to be willing to accept the consequences for his or her own choices and actions.

Wubbolding (1988, 1991, 1996, 2000) discusses the central role of planning and commitment. The culmination of the cycle of counseling rests with a plan of action. He uses the acronym SAMIC[3] to capture the essence of a good plan: simple, attainable, measurable, immediate, involved, controlled by the planner, committed to, and continuously done. Wubbolding contends that clients gain more effective control over their lives with plans that have the following characteristics:

- The plan is within the limits of the motivation and capacities of each client. Skillful counselors help clients identify plans that involve greater need-fulfilling payoffs. Clients may be asked, "What plans could you make now that would result in a more satisfying life?"
- Good plans are simple and easy to understand. Although they need to be specific, concrete, and measurable, plans should be flexible and open to revision as clients gain a deeper understanding of the specific behaviors they want to change.
- The plan involves a positive course of action, and it is stated in terms of what the client is willing to do. Even small plans can help clients take significant steps toward their desired changes.
- Counselors encourage clients to develop plans that they can carry out independently of what others do. Plans that are contingent on others lead clients to sense that they are not steering their own ship but are at the mercy of the ocean.
- Effective plans are repetitive and, ideally, are performed daily.
- Plans are carried out as soon as possible. Counselors can ask the question, "What are you willing to do today to begin to change your life?"
- Plans involves process-centered activities. For example, clients may plan to do any of the following: apply for a job, write a letter to a friend, take a yoga class, substitute nutritious food for junk food, devote 2 hours a week to volunteer work, or take a vacation that they have been wanting.
- Before clients carry out their plan, it is a good idea for them to evaluate it with their therapist to determine if it is realistic and attainable and if it relates to what they need and want. After the plan has been carried out in real life, it is useful to evaluate it again and make any revisions that may be necessary.
- To help clients commit themselves to their plan, it is useful for them to firm it up in writing.

Resolutions and plans are empty unless there is a commitment to carry them out. It is up to clients to determine how to take their plans outside the restricted world of therapy and into the everyday world. Effective therapy can be the catalyst that leads to self-directed, responsible living.

Asking clients to determine what they want for themselves, to make a self-evaluation, and to follow through with action plans includes assisting them in determining how intensely they are willing to work to attain the changes they desire. Commitment is not an all-or-nothing matter; it exists in degrees. It is essential that those clients who are reluctant to make a commitment be helped to express and explore their fears of failing. Clients are helped by a therapist who does not easily give up believing in their ability to make better choices, even if they are not always successful in completing their plans.

Reality Therapy Applied to the Case of Stan

The reality therapist is guided by the key concepts of choice theory to identify Stan's behavioral dynamics, to provide a direction for him to work toward, and to teach him about better alternatives for getting what he wants. Stan has chosen a variety of painful symptoms that have not been effective in getting him what he needs—a satisfying relationship.

Stan has been living the life of a victim, blaming others, and looking backward instead of forward. Initially, Stan wants to tell his counselor about the negative aspects of his life, which he does by dwelling on his major symptoms: depression, anxiety, inability to sleep, and other psychosomatic symptoms. The counselor listens, but she also challenges Stan, especially as he concentrates mostly on his misery and his symptoms. Although she has compassion for his suffering and the difficulties he continues to face, the counselor hopes that Stan will come to realize that if he decides to change, he has many options. She operates on the premise that therapy will offer the opportunity to explore with Stan what he can build on—successes, productive times, goals, and hopes for the future.

After creating a relationship with Stan, the therapist shows him that he does not have to be a victim of his past unless he chooses to be, and she assures Stan that he has rehashed his past misery enough. As counseling progresses, Stan learns that even though most of his problems did indeed begin in childhood, there is little he can now do to undo what happened. He learns that all his symptoms and avoidance keep him from getting what he most wants. He eventually realizes that he has little control over changing others but has a great deal of control over what he can do now.

The therapist asks Stan to describe how his life would be different if he had none of his symptoms. She is interested in knowing what he would be doing if he were meeting his needs for belonging, achievement, power, freedom, and fun. She explains to him that he has an ideal picture of what he wants his life to be, yet he does not possess effective behaviors for meeting his needs. The counselor talks to him about all of his basic psychological needs and how this type of therapy will teach him to satisfy them in effective ways. She also explains that his *total behavior* is made up of acting, thinking, feeling, and physiology. Even though he says he

hates feeling anxious most of the time, Stan learns that much of what he is doing and thinking is directly leading to his unwanted feelings and physiological reactions. When Stan complains of feeling depressed much of the time, anxious at night, and overcome by panic attacks, she lets him know that she is more interested in what he is *doing* and *thinking*, because these are the behavioral components that can be directly changed.

The therapist helps Stan come to understand that his *depressing* is the feeling part of his choice. Although he may think he has little control over how he feels, over his bodily sensations, and over his thoughts, the therapist wants Stan to understand that he can begin to take different action, which is likely to change his depressing experience. Stan's therapist frequently asks this question: "Is what you are choosing to do getting you what you want?" She leads Stan to begin to recognize that he has *some* control over his feelings. This is best done after Stan has made some choices about doing something different from what he has been doing. At this point Stan is in a better place to see that the choice to take action has contributed to feeling better, which helps him realize that he has some power to feel good.

Stan tells his counselor about the pictures in his head, a few of which are becoming a counselor, acting confident in meeting people, thinking of himself as a worthwhile person, and enjoying life. Through therapy he makes the evaluation that much of what he is doing is not getting him closer to these pictures or getting him what he wants. After he decides that he is willing to work on himself to be different, the majority of time in the sessions is devoted to making plans and discussing their implementation. Together he and the therapist focus on the specific steps he can take right now to bring about the changes he would like.

Instead of waiting for others to initiate contacts, Stan practices seeking out those people he would like to get to know better. Stan is encouraged to actually do more of the things he wants to do rather than focusing on what he perceives to be his deficits. His therapist strongly encourages him to practice meeting women and talking to them—at stores, on elevators, at meetings, and at church. She suggests that Stan need not

(continued on next page)

have expectations about developing serious relationships, but simply to go out of his way to find opportunities to practice doing what he says he would really like to be able to do. The counselor also suggests that he keep a written record of what he is doing and what actually happened, and to bring this record to his sessions.

As Stan continues to carry out plans in the real world, he gradually begins to experience success. When he does backslide, his counselor does not put him down but helps him do better. Together they develop a new plan that they feel more confident about. The therapist is not willing to give up on Stan even when he does not make significant progress, which is a source of real inspiration for him to keep working on himself.

Stan's therapist will teach him choice theory, and, if he is willing to engage in some reading, she might suggest that he read and reflect on any of the following books: *Choice Theory* (Glasser, 1998), *Counseling With Choice Theory: The New Reality Therapy* (Glasser, 2000), and *A Set of Directions for Putting and Keeping Yourself Together* (Wubbolding & Brickell, 2001). He may bring into his sessions some of what he is learning from his reading, and eventually Stan will be able to take effective control over his own life. The combination of working with a reality therapist, reading, and his willingness to put what he is learning into practice by engaging in new behaviors in the world will assist Stan in replacing ineffective choices with life-affirming choices. Stan will come to increasingly accept that he is the only person who can control his own behavior. He will come to the realization that if he wants a better life he must choose to do things that get him closer to other people. In a period of several months, the combination of reality therapy and learning choice theory is highly likely to substantially change the way Stan chooses to live his life.

Follow-Up: You Continue as Stan's Reality Therapist

Use these questions to help you think about how you would counsel Stan using reality therapy:

- If Stan complains of feeling depressed most of the time and wants you to "cure" him, how might you proceed?
- If Stan persists, telling you that his mood is getting the best of him and that he wants you to work with his physician in getting him on an antidepressant drug, what might you say or do?
- What are some of Stan's basic needs that are not being met? What action plans can you think of to help Stan find better ways of getting what he wants?
- Would you be inclined to do a checklist on alcoholism with Stan? Why or why not? If you determined that he was addicted to alcohol, would you insist that he attend a program such as Alcoholics Anonymous in conjunction with therapy with you? Why or why not?
- In working with Stan as a reality therapist, what interventions might you make to help him explore his total behavior?

 REALITY THERAPY FROM A MULTICULTURAL PERSPECTIVE

Contributions to Multicultural Counseling

The core principles of choice theory/reality therapy have much to offer in the area of multicultural counseling. In cross-cultural therapy it is essential that counselors respect the differences in worldview between themselves and their clients. Counselors demonstrate their respect for the cultural values of their clients by helping them explore how satisfying their current behavior is both to themselves and to others. Once clients make this assessment, they can formulate realistic plans that are consistent with their cultural values. It is a further sign of respect that the counselor refrains from deciding what behavior should be changed. Through skillful questioning on the counselor's part, ethnic minority clients can be helped to determine the degree to which they have acculturated into the dominant society. It is possible for them to find a balance, retaining their ethnic identity and values while integrating some of the values and practices of the dominant group. Again, the counselor does not determine this balance for clients but challenges them to arrive at their own answers. With this focus on acting and thinking rather than on identifying and exploring feelings, many clients are less likely to display resistance to counseling.

Glasser (1998) contends that reality therapy can be applied both individually and in groups to anyone with any psychological problem in any cultural context. We are all members of the same species and have the same genetic structure; therefore, relationships are the problem in all cultures.

Based on the assumption that reality therapy must be modified to fit the cultural context of people other than North Americans, Wubbolding (2000) and Wubbolding and Associates (1998) have expanded the practice of reality therapy to multicultural situations. Wubbolding's experience in conducting reality therapy workshops in Japan, Taiwan, Hong Kong, Singapore, Korea, India, Kuwait, Australia, Columbia, Slovenia, Croatia, Siberia, and countries in Europe has taught him the difficulty of generalizing about other cultures. Growing out of these multicultural experiences, Wubbolding (2000) has adapted the cycle of counseling in working with Japanese clients. He points to some basic language differences between Japanese and Western cultures. North Americans are inclined to say what they mean, to be assertive, and to be clear and direct in asking for what they want. In Japanese culture, assertive language is not appropriate between a child and a parent or between an employee and a supervisor. Ways of communicating are more indirect. Because of these style differences, adaptations such as these are needed to make the practice of reality therapy relevant to Japanese clients:

- The reality therapist's tendency to ask direct questions may need to be softened, with questions being raised more elaborately and indirectly. It may be a mistake to ask individualistic questions built around whether specific behaviors meet the client's need. Confrontation should be done only after carefully considering the context.
- There is no exact Japanese translation for the word "plan," nor is there an exact word for "accountability," yet both of these are key dimensions in the practice of reality therapy.
- In asking clients to make plans and commit to them, Western counselors do not settle for a response of "I'll try." Instead, they tend to push for an explicit pledge to follow through. In Japanese culture, however, the counselor is likely to accept an "I'll try" as a firm commitment.

These are but a few illustrations of ways in which reality therapy might be adapted to non-Western clients. Although this approach assumes that all people have the same basic needs (survival, love and belonging, power, fun, and freedom), the way these needs are expressed depends largely on the cultural context. Reality therapists cannot work in exactly the same manner with all clients. In working with culturally diverse clients, the therapist must allow latitude for a wide range of acceptable behaviors to satisfy these needs. As with other theories and the techniques that flow from them, flexibility is a foremost requirement.

Reality therapy provides clients with tools to make the desired changes. This is especially true during the planning phase, which is so central to the process of reality therapy. The focus is on positive steps that can be taken, not on what cannot be done. Clients identify those problems that are causing them difficulty, and these problems become the targets for change. This type of specificity and the direction that is provided by an effective plan are certainly assets in working with diverse client groups.

Limitations for Multicultural Counseling

One of the shortcomings in working with ethnic minority clients is that this approach may not take fully into account some very real environmental forces that operate against them in their everyday lives. Discrimination and racism are unfortunate realities, and these forces do limit many minority clients in getting what they want from life. If counselors do not accept these environmental restrictions, such clients are likely to feel misunderstood. There is a danger that some reality therapists will too quickly or too forcefully stress the ability of these clients to take charge of their lives.

Another problem with this style of therapy is that some clients are very reluctant to say what they need. Their cultural values and norms may not reinforce them in assertively asking for what they want. In fact, they may be socialized to think more of what is good for the social group than of their individual wants. In working with people with these values, counselors must "soften" reality therapy somewhat. Such clients should not be pushed to assertively declare their wants. If this method is not applied sensitively, these clients are likely to leave therapy. If reality therapy is to be used effectively with clients from other cultures, the procedures must be adapted to the life experiences and values of members from various cultures (Wubbolding, 2000).

Reality therapy should be used artfully and be applied in different ways to a variety of clients. Many of its principles and concepts can be incorporated in a dynamic and personal way in the style of counselors, and there is a basis for integrating these concepts with most of the other therapeutic approaches covered in this book.

 # SUMMARY AND EVALUATION

Summary

The reality therapist functions as a teacher and a model, confronting clients in ways that help them evaluate what they are doing and whether their behavior is fulfilling their basic needs without harming themselves or others. The heart of reality therapy is learning how to make better and more effective choices and gain more effective control. People take charge of their lives rather than being the victims of circumstances beyond their control. Thus, practitioners of reality therapy focus on what clients are *able and willing to do in the present* to change their behavior. Practitioners teach clients how to make significant connections with others. Therapists continue to ask clients to evaluate the effectiveness of what they are choosing to do to determine if better choices are possible.

The practice of reality therapy weaves together two components, the counseling environment and specific procedures that lead to changes in behavior. This therapeutic process enables clients to move in the direction of getting what they want. The goals of reality therapy include behavioral change, better decision making, improved significant relationships, enhanced living, and more effective satisfaction of all the psychological needs.

Contributions of Reality Therapy

Among the advantages of reality therapy are its relatively short-term focus and the fact that it deals with conscious behavioral problems. Insight and awareness are not enough; the client's self-evaluation, a plan of action, and a commitment to following through are the core of the therapeutic process. I like the focus on strongly encouraging clients to engage in self-evaluation, to decide if what they are doing is working or not, and to commit themselves to do what is required to make changes. The existential underpinnings of choice theory are a major strength of this approach. People are not viewed as being hopelessly and helplessly depressed. Instead, people are viewed as doing the best they can, or making the choices they hope will result in fulfilling their needs.

Too often counseling fails because therapists have an agenda for clients. The reality therapist helps clients conduct a searching inner inventory of their own feelings, cognitions, and actions. Once clients decide for themselves that their present behavior is not working, they are then much more likely to consider acquiring a new behavioral repertoire.

Limitations and Criticisms of Reality Therapy

One of the main limitations of reality therapy is that it does not give adequate emphasis to the role of these aspects of the counseling process: the unconscious, the power of the past and the effect of traumatic experiences in early childhood, the therapeutic value of dreams, and the place of transference. Because reality therapy focuses almost exclusively on consciousness, it does not take into account factors such as repressed conflicts and the power of the unconscious in influencing how we think, feel, behave, and choose.

Dealing with dreams is not part of the reality therapist's repertoire. According to Glasser (2000), it is not therapeutically useful to explore dreams.

For him, spending time discussing dreams can be a defense used to avoid talking about one's behavior and, thus, is time wasted. From my perspective, dreams are powerful tools in helping people recognize their internal conflicts. I believe that there is richness in dreams, which can be a shorthand message of clients' central struggles, wants, hopes, and visions of the future. Asking clients to recall, report, share, and relive their dreams in the here-and-now of the therapeutic session can help unblock them and can pave the way for clients to take a different course of action.

Similarly, I have a difficult time accepting Glasser's view of transference as a misleading concept, for I find that clients are able to learn that significant people in their lives have a present influence on how they perceive and react to others. To rule out an exploration of transference that distorts accurate perception of others seems narrow in my view.

Glasser (2003) maintains that the DSM-IV-TR is accurate in describing symptoms, yet he argues that grouping symptoms together and calling them mental disorders is wrong. I share many of Glasser's criticisms of the way the DSM-IV-TR is sometimes used, and I also have trouble with the concept of labeling people. As you will recall, Glasser (2000, 2003) contends that chronic depression and profound psychosis are chosen behaviors. Apart from specific brain pathology, Glasser argues that mental illness is the result of an individual's unsatisfying present relationships or general unhappiness. From my perspective, it is simplistic to view all psychological disorders as behavioral choices. Biochemical and genetic factors are associated with certain forms of behavioral disorders, and I have trouble accepting the notion that all mental illness is chosen behavior. People suffering from chronic depression or schizophrenia are struggling to cope with a real illness. In reality therapy these people may have additional guilt to carry if they accept the premise that they are *choosing* their condition.

Finally, I believe reality therapy is vulnerable to the practitioner who assumes the role of an expert in deciding for others how life should be lived and what constitutes responsible behavior. Therapists who make evaluations for their clients are really imposing their values on them. It is not the therapist's role to evaluate the behavior of clients. However, in cases dealing with child abuse, violence, and substance abuse, there is room for the therapist to confront clients with the harmful ramifications of their behavior. Generally clients need to engage in the process of self-evaluation to determine how well certain behaviors are working and what changes they may want to make. Reality therapists need to monitor the tendency to judge clients' behavior and tell clients how to behave differently. Counselors who are unaware of their own need to give abundant and frequent advice can stunt clients' growth and autonomy by strongly influencing clients to accept their view of reality. If counselors do this, however, they are perverting the basic concepts inherent in reality therapy/choice theory, for the approach calls on clients to make their own evaluation of their behavior.

WHERE TO GO FROM HERE

In the *CD-ROM for Integrative Counseling,* Session 8 ("Behavioral Focus in Counseling"), you will note ways that I attempt to assist Ruth in specifying concrete behaviors that she will target for change. In this session I am drawing heavily from principles of reality therapy in assisting Ruth to develop an action plan to make the changes she desires.

More than 6,000 therapists have completed the training in reality therapy and choice theory offered by the William Glasser Institute. They have been awarded a Certificate of Completion, and many have gone on to become instructors. The training process takes at least 18 months to complete and is offered all over the United States, Canada, and other countries. It consists of a Basic Intensive Week (all weeks are 4 days) and a follow-up Basic Practicum (all practicums are 30 hours), an Advanced Intensive Week, an Advanced Practicum, and a final Certification Week in which trainees demonstrate their skills. Complete information on this program can be obtained directly from the institute.

The William Glasser Institute
William Glasser, M.D., President and Founder
22024 Lassen Street, Suite 118
Chatsworth, CA 91311
Telephone: (818) 700-8000
Toll free: (800) 899-0688
Fax: (818) 700-0555
Email: wginst@wglasser.com
Web site: www.wglasser.com

Center for Reality Therapy
Dr. Robert E. Wubbolding, Director
7672 Montgomery Road #383
Cincinnati, OH 45236
Telephone: (513) 561-1911
Fax: (513) 561-3568
Email: wubsrt@fuse.net
Web site: www.realitytherapywub.com

The *International Journal of Reality Therapy* publishes manuscripts covering both the research and practice of reality therapy and choice theory, as well as many articles applied to education. To subscribe, contact:

Dr. Lawrence Litwack, Editor
International Journal of Reality Therapy
650 Laurel Avenue #402
Highland Park, IL 60035

Telephone: (847) 681-0290
Email: llitwack@aol.com
Web site: www.wglasser.com/internat.htm

InfoTrac College Edition Resources

Reality Therapy   The following key words are listed in such a way as to allow the InfoTrac College Edition search engine to locate a wider range of articles in the online library. The key words should be entered exactly as shown, to include asterisks, "W1," and "AND."

William Glasser	Commitment AND therap*
Reality therapy	Commitment treatment therapy
Choice theory AND Glasser	Self evaluation AND psychol*
Control theory AND Glasser	Autonomy AND psychol*
Commitment AND psychol*	

Recommended Supplementary Readings

Warning: Psychiatry Can Be Hazardous to Your Mental Health (Glasser, 2003) is a provocative look at psychiatric practice and the use of drugs in dealing with the symptoms often labeled as "mental illness." The author proposes an alternative to classifying and pathologizing people.

Counseling With Choice Theory: The New Reality Therapy (Glasser, 2000) represents the author's latest thinking about choice theory and develops the existential theme that we choose all of our total behaviors. Case examples demonstrate how choice theory principles can be applied in helping people establish better relationships.

Reality Therapy for the 21st Century (Wubbolding, 2000) is a comprehensive and practical book that represents major extensions and developments of reality therapy. The practical formulation of the WDEP system of reality therapy is highlighted. Included are multicultural adaptations and summaries of research studies validating the theory and practice of reality therapy.

Case Approach to Counseling and Psychotherapy (Corey, 2005) illustrates how prominent reality therapists Drs. William Glasser and Robert Wubbolding would counsel Ruth from their different perspectives of choice theory and reality therapy.

References and Suggested Readings

AMERICAN PSYCHIATRIC ASSOCIATION. (2000). *Diagnostic and statistical manual of mental disorders, text revision,* (4th ed.). (DSM-IV-TR). Washington, DC: Author.

COREY, G. (2004). *Theory and practice of group counseling* (6th ed.). Pacific Grove, CA: Brooks/Cole.

*COREY, G. (2005). *Case approach to counseling and psychotherapy* (6th ed.). Belmont, CA: Brooks/Cole.

GLASSER, W. (1965). *Reality therapy: A new approach to psychiatry.* New York: Harper & Row.

GLASSER, W. (1992). Reality therapy. *New York State Journal for Counseling and Development, 7*(l), 5–13.

*GLASSER, W. (1998). *Choice theory: A new psychology of personal freedom.* New York: HarperCollins.

* GLASSER, W. (2000). *Counseling with choice theory: The new reality therapy.* New York: HarperCollins.

* GLASSER, W. (2003). *Warning: Psychiatry can be hazardous to your mental health.* New York: HarperCollins.

*WUBBOLDING, R. E. (1988). *Using reality therapy.* New York: Harper & Row (Perennial Library).

*WUBBOLDING, R. E. (1991). *Understanding reality therapy.* New York: Harper & Row (Perennial Library).

WUBBOLDING, R. E. (1996). Reality therapy: Theoretical underpinnings and implementation in practice. *Directions in Mental Health Counseling, 6*(9), 4–16.

*WUBBOLDING, R. E. (2000). *Reality therapy for the 21st century.* Muncie, IN: Accelerated Development (Taylor & Francis).

WUBBOLDING, R. E. (2001). *Reality therapy training* (12th revision). Cincinnati, OH: Center for Reality Therapy.

WUBBOLDING, R. E. (2002). *Cycle of managing, supervising, counseling and coaching (chart)* (13th revision). Cincinnati, OH: Center for Reality Therapy.

WUBBOLDING, R. E., & ASSOCIATES. (1998). Multicultural awareness: Implications for reality therapy and choice theory. *International Journal of Reality Therapy, 17*(2), 4–6.

*WUBBOLDING, R. E., & BRICKELL, J. (2001). *A set of directions for putting and keeping yourself together.* Minneapolis, MN: Educational Media Corporation.

*Books and articles marked with an asterisk are suggested for further study.

Chapter 12

Feminist Therapy

Co-authored by Barbara Herlihy and Gerald Corey

Some Contemporary Feminist Therapists

Feminist therapy does not have a single founder. Rather, it has been a collective effort by many. We have selected a few individuals who have made significant contributions to feminist therapy for inclusion here, recognizing full well that many others equally influential could have appeared in this space. Feminist therapy is truly founded on a theory of inclusion.

JEAN BAKER MILLER, M.D., is a Clinical Professor of Psychiatry at Boston University School of Medicine and Director of the Jean Baker Miller Training Institute at the Stone Center, Wellesley College. She has written *Toward a New Psychology of Women* and coauthored *The Healing Connection: How Women Form Relationships in Therapy and in Life* and *Women's Growth in Connection*. A practicing psychiatrist and psychoanalyst, Miller is a fellow of the American Psychiatric Association, the American College of Psychiatrists, American Orthopsychiatric Association, American Academy of Psychoanalysis, and has been a member of the board of trustees of the last two. In recent decades, Miller has been collaborating with diverse groups of scholars and colleagues to continue development of relational–cultural theory. She has been expanding this theory and exploring new applications to complex issues in psychotherapy and beyond, including issues of diversity, social action, and workplace change.

CAROLYN ZERBE ENNS, PH.D., is Professor of Psychology and an active participant in the Women's Studies program at Cornell College in Mt. Vernon, Iowa. Enns became interested in feminist therapy while she was completing her Ph.D. in Counseling Psychology at the University of California, Santa Barbara. She has devoted much of her work to exploring the diversity of feminist theories that inform the work of feminist therapists. It is Enns's conviction that therapists' feminist theoretical orientations can have a profound impact on the manner in which therapists implement feminist therapy values, and she discusses these themes in her book, *Feminist Theories and Feminist Psychotherapies: Origins, Themes, and Diversity*. As an extension of her commitment to social change, Enns served from 1994 to 1998 as Chair of the American Psychological Association's Division 17 (Counseling Psychology) Committee on Women Task Force on Memories of Childhood Sexual Abuse. She is currently

(continued on next page)

a co-chair of the Task Force to Develop Guidelines for Counseling/Psychotherapy with Women (sponsored by Divisions 17 and 35, Society for the Psychology of Women), which is charged with updating, extending, and revising the guidelines for counseling women that were first developed in 1978. She is also the 2002-2003 chair of the Division 17 Section for the Advancement of Women. Her most recent efforts are directed toward articulating the importance of multicultural feminist therapy, exploring the practice of feminist therapy around the world (especially in Japan), and writing about multicultural feminist pedagogies.

OLIVA M. ESPIN, PH.D., is Professor of Women's Studies at San Diego State University and core faculty at the California School of Professional Psychology, San Diego. She is a pioneer in the theory and practice of feminist therapy with women from different cultural backgrounds and has done extensive research, teaching, and training on multicultural issues in psychology. Espin has published on psychotherapy with Latinas, women immigrants and refugees, the sexuality of Latinas, language in therapy with fluent bilinguals, and training clinicians to work with multicultural populations. A native of Cuba, she did her undergraduate work in psychology at the Universidad de Costa Rica

and her doctorate in Counselor Education and Latin American Studies at the University of Florida. Espin co-edited *Refugee Women and Their Mental Health: Shattered Societies, Shattered Lives* and has written *Latina Healers: Lives of Power and Tradition, Latina Realities: Essays on Healing, Sexuality, and Migration,* and *Women Crossing Boundaries: A Psychology of Immigration and the Transformation of Sexuality,* which is based on a study of women immigrants from all over the world.

LAURA S. BROWN, PH.D., is a founding member of the Feminist Therapy Institute, an organization dedicated to the support of advanced practice in feminist therapy, and a member of the theory workgroup at the National Conference on Education and Training in Feminist Practice. She has written several books considered core to feminist practice in psychotherapy and counseling, and *Subversive Dialogues: Theory in Feminist Therapy* is considered by many to be the foundation book addressing how theory informs practice in feminist therapy. Brown has made particular contributions to thinking about ethics and boundaries, and the complexities of ethical practice in small communities. Her current interests include feminist forensic psychology and the application of feminist principles to treatment of trauma survivors. ■

INTRODUCTION

This chapter provides an alternative perspective to many of the models considered thus far in this book.* As you will see, feminist therapy puts gender and power at the core of the therapeutic process. It is built on the premise that it is essential to consider the social and cultural context that contributes to a person's problems in order to understand that person. My (Jerry Corey's) own training did not include a feminist perspective—or, for that matter, a systemic or multicultural perspective—yet I have become convinced that the feminist perspective offers a unique approach to understanding the roles that both women and men have been socialized to accept. This perspective also has significant implications for the development of counseling theory and for how practitioners intervene with diverse client populations.

A central concept in feminist therapy is the psychological oppression of women and the constraints imposed by the sociopolitical status to which women have been relegated. Our dominant culture reinforces submissive and self-sacrificing behaviors in women. The socialization of women inevitably affects their identity development, self-concept, goals and aspirations, and emotional well-being.

The majority of clients in counseling are women, and the majority of psychotherapy practitioners at the master's level are women. Thus, the need for a theory that evolves from the thinking and experiencing of women seems self-evident. Yet most theories that are traditionally taught—including psychoanalysis, Adlerian therapy, Gestalt therapy, cognitive behavior therapy, reality therapy, and person-centered therapy—were founded by White males from Western (American or European) cultures.

Feminist therapists have challenged the male-oriented assumptions regarding what constitutes a mentally healthy individual and raised some critical questions: Why are women more frequently *diagnosed* with depression than are men in our society? Can theories developed by White males from Western cultures appropriately serve the needs of women clients in counseling? The needs of women of color? Of others who experience marginalization and oppression in our society?

Culture encompasses the sociopolitical reality of people's lives, including how the privileged dominant group (White males) treats those who are different from them. Feminist therapists believe psychotherapy is inextricably bound to culture, and increasingly they are being joined by thoughtful leaders in the field of counseling practice. In their discussion of multicultural counseling, Ivey, D'Andrea, Ivey, and Simek-Morgan (2002) point out that all helping practice

---

*I invited a colleague and friend, Barbara Herlihy, a professor of counselor education at the University of New Orleans, to take the leading role in co-authoring this chapter. We have co-authored three books (Herlihy & Corey, 1992, 1996, 1997), which seems like a natural basis for collaboration on a project that we both consider valuable.

is based on a set of cultural assumptions, and they challenge the contradictions and limitations of the Eurocentric, male construction of the helping process. Ivey and his colleagues believe that understanding and challenging our own personal biases and possible ethnocentric attitudes is a major step toward becoming culturally competent counselors.

Early feminist thought focused on the oppression of women and primarily reflected the views and experiences of largely middle-class, White women. Modern feminism emphasizes an integrated approach that includes an understanding of multiple oppressions, multicultural awareness, and multicultural competence (Beardsley, Morrow, Castillo, & Weitzman, 1998). Today's feminists believe that gender cannot be considered apart from other identity areas such as race, ethnicity, class, and sexual orientation.

The contemporary version of feminist therapy and the multicultural approach to counseling practice have a great deal in common—both of these approaches provide a systemic perspective based on understanding the social context of behavior. Both perspectives are grounded on the assumption that social change is the key to bringing about individual change. This chapter illustrates the common ground that is shared by the feminist and multicultural approaches to clinical practice.

History and Development

Feminist therapy has developed in a grassroots manner, responding to challenges and to the emerging needs of women (Brabeck & Brown, 1997). No single individual can be identified as the founder of this approach, and its history is relatively brief. The beginnings of feminist therapy can be traced to the women's movement of the 1960s, a time when women began uniting their voices to express their dissatisfaction with the limiting and confining nature of traditional female roles. Consciousness-raising groups, in which women came together to share their experiences and perceptions, helped individual women become aware that they were not alone in their views. A sisterhood developed, and some of the services that evolved from women's collective desires to improve society included shelters for battered women, rape crisis centers, and women's health and reproductive health centers.

Consciousness-raising groups had a significant impact on women, but these groups did not aim to change psychotherapy as it was traditionally practiced. Self-help, rather than "professional" help, was considered the most efficacious mode for helping women break free from role constraints and attitudes resulting from their early socialization. Because the therapeutic relationship is hierarchical, with the therapist in the power position, psychotherapy was viewed as a means of maintaining the oppressive status quo. Changes in psychotherapy occurred only when women therapists participated in consciousness-raising groups and were changed by their experiences. They formed feminist therapy groups that operated from the same norms as the consciousness-raising groups, including nonhierarchical structures, equal sharing of resources and power, and empowerment of women that could be achieved by practicing new skills and ways of being in a safe environment.

Feminist principles also began to find their way into the work that many women therapists were doing with their individual clients. Believing that personal counseling was also a legitimate means to effect change, they viewed therapy as a partnership between equals. As therapists became sensitive to the potentially destructive power dynamics in therapy, they began building mutuality into the therapeutic process. They took the stance that therapy needed to move away from reliance on an intrapsychic psychopathology perspective (in which the sources of a woman's unhappiness or mental illness reside within her) to a focus on understanding the pathological forces in the culture that damage and constrain women.

A profusion of research on gender bias emerged in the 1970s, which helped further feminist therapy ideas, and organizations began to foster the development of feminist therapy. Among them were the Association for Women in Psychology (AWP) and various efforts by the American Psychological Association (APA), including the Task Force on Sex Bias and Sex Role Stereotyping (APA, 1975), the APA's Division 35 (Society for the Psychology of Women), and APA's (1979) Division 17 "Principles Concerning the Counseling and Therapy of Women," which specify counselor knowledge, attitudes, and skills essential to effectively address gender issues in the counseling process. The counselor's knowledge base includes being familiar with the biological, psychological, and social issues that influence women and men. In addition, counselors must examine their own personal attitudes about gender bias and sexism to understand the various kinds of oppressions that may affect their clients.

The 1980s were marked by efforts to define feminist therapy as an entity in its own right (Enns, 1993), and individual therapy was the most frequently practiced form of feminist therapy (Kaschak, 1981). Gilligan's (1977, 1982) work on the different voice of women and the morality of care and the work of Miller (1986) and the Stone Center scholars on the self-in-relation model (now called the "relational-cultural" model) of women's development were influential in the development of a feminist personality theory. New theories emerged that honored the relational and cooperative nature of women's experiencing (Enns, 1991, 2000, 2004; Enns & Sinacore, 2001). Feminist therapists began to examine the relationship of feminist theory to traditional psychotherapy systems, and integrations with various existing systems were proposed. These efforts were particularly directed toward development of a feminist psychoanalysis (Chodorow, 1989; Lerner, 1988), feminist family therapy, and feminist career counseling.

By the 1980s feminist group therapy had changed dramatically, becoming more diverse as it focused increasingly on specific problems and issues such as body image, abusive relationships, eating disorders, and incest and sexual abuse (Enns, 1993), and the feminist philosophies that guided the practice of therapy also became more diverse. Enns (1993, 2004; Enns & Sinacore, 2001) identified four enduring feminist philosophies, which are often described as

the "second wave" of feminism: liberal, cultural, radical, and socialist feminism. These philosophies all advocate activism as a goal but have differing
views on the sources of oppression and the most effective methods of effect-
ing changes in society. They are best seen as existing along a continuum rather
than as completely separate philosophical stances. Practitioners interpret the
basic tenets of feminist therapy in different ways depending on the feminist
philosophy they espouse and their theoretical orientation.

Liberal feminists focus on helping individual women overcome the limits
and constraints of their socialization patterns. Liberal feminists argue that
women deserve equality because they have the same capabilities as men.
These feminists tend to believe the differences between women and men will
be less problematic as work and social environments become more bias-free.
For liberal feminists, the major goals of therapy include personal empowerment of individual women, dignity, self-fulfillment, and equality.

Cultural feminists believe oppression stems from society's devaluation of
women's strengths. They emphasize the differences between women and men
and believe the solution to oppression lies in feminization of the culture so
that society becomes more nurturing, intuitive, subjective, cooperative, and
relational. For cultural feminists, the major goal of therapy is social transformation through the infusion of feminine values (such as cooperation, altru-
ism, and connectedness) into the culture.

Radical feminists focus on the oppression of women that is embedded in
patriarchy and seek to change society through activism. Therapy is viewed as a
political enterprise with the goal of transformation of society. Radical feminists
strive to identify and question the many ways in which patriarchy dominates
every area of life including household chores, paid employment, intimate part-
nerships, violence, and parenting. The major goals are to transform gender
relationships, transform societal institutions, and increase women's sexual and
procreative self-determination.

Socialist feminists share with radical feminists the goal of societal change.
Their emphasis differs, however, in that they focus on multiple oppressions
and believe solutions to society's problems must include considerations of
class, race, economics, nationality, and history. Socialist feminists pay close
attention to ways that work, education, and family roles affect their lives. For
socialist feminists, the major goal of therapy is to transform social relationships and institutions.

In recent years, feminist women of color and postmodern feminists have
found classic feminist theories wanting and have offered new theoretical perspectives focused on issues of diversity, the complexity of sexism, and the cen-
trality of social context in understanding gender issues. In 1993 psychologists
who embraced a diversity of feminist perspectives met at the National Conference on Education and Training in Feminist Practice. They reached consensus
on a series of basic themes and premises underlying feminist practice, thus taking a significant step toward integration of a number of feminist perspectives.
This "third wave" of feminism embraces diversity with its inclusion of women

of color, lesbians, and the postmodern and constructivist viewpoints espoused by many in the most recent generation of women. New developments in feminism also include global and international perspectives (Enns & Sinacore, 2001). Let's examine some of the key characteristics associated with each of the third wave feminist approaches. These descriptions are based on Enns and Sinacore's overview of feminist theories.

Postmodern feminists provide a model for critiquing the value of other traditional and feminist approaches, addressing the issue of what constitutes reality and proposing multiple truths as opposed to a single truth. This approach calls attention to the limitation of knowledge and the fallibility of "knowers." Other key themes include the tendencies to engage in ethnocentric thinking, misunderstand reality, and draw incorrect generalizations about human experience. Polarities such as masculine–feminine are deconstructed, which involves an analysis of how such constructs are created.

Women of color feminists believe it is essential that feminist theory be broadened and made more inclusive. Women of color have criticized some White feminists who overgeneralize the experiences of White women to fit the experiences of all women. Women of color point out that they not only have to deal with gender discrimination but with oppression on the basis of race, ethnicity, and class. They challenge feminist theory to include an analysis of multiple oppressions, an assessment of access to privilege and power, and to emphasize activism.

Lesbian feminists share commonalities with many aspects of radical feminism. Both perspectives view women's oppression as related to sexualized images of women. Lesbians who define themselves as feminists sometimes feel excluded by heterosexual feminists who do not understand discrimination based on sexual orientation. Heterosexism fosters the value of male–female relationships as the foundation of society; same-sex relationships are not valued as healthy. Lesbians of color often must deal with multiple forms of discrimination—for being lesbians, women, and persons of color. This perspective calls for feminist theory to include an analysis of multiple identities and their relationship to oppression and to recognize the diversity that exists among lesbians.

Global–international feminists take a worldwide perspective and seek to understand the ways in which racism, sexism, economics, and classism affect women in different countries. Western feminists are challenged to recognize their ethnocentrism and stereotyping of women in different parts of the world. Global feminists assume that each woman lives under unique systems of oppression. Although they respect a range of diversity among women, they see a need to address those cultural differences that directly contribute to women's oppression.

It is clear that there is no single, unified feminist theory. Rather, a variety of feminist theories provide a range of different but overlapping perspectives (Enns & Sinacore, 2001) and try to answer questions such as these: "Why have women and men held unequal power across time and place?" "Historically, why has knowledge been gathered by and for men and often excluded women?" "How can women and men best address these problems and achieve equality?"

Feminist therapists will continue to work to integrate the disparate themes of past decades into a cohesive theory and to define the principles and practices that unify the various approaches to feminist therapy. According to Enns (1993), feminism must "search for balance between appreciating diversity between women, self-discovery, and self-determination while also maintaining some common framework that focuses on the collective transformation of society" (p. 48). As can be readily seen, feminist therapy is continually evolving and maturing.

Given the diversity of philosophies, and the fact that there is no set definition of feminist therapy, just who is a feminist therapist? Many therapists, both male and female, support the ideals of the feminist movement. However, if they do not incorporate feminist methods of therapy in their practice, they are not feminist therapists (Brown, 1992). Feminist therapists believe gender is central to therapeutic practice, that understanding a client's problems requires adopting a sociocultural perspective, and that empowerment of the individual and societal changes are crucial goals in therapy. Feminist therapists realize that ethnicity, sexual orientation, and class also may be more important factors in given situations and across situations for many women (Pam Remer, personal communication, April 15, 2002).

 # KEY CONCEPTS

View of Human Nature

The feminist view of human nature is one fundamental idea that differentiates feminist theory from most other therapeutic models. Many of the traditional theories grew out of a historical period in which social arrangements were assumed to be rooted in one's biologically based gender. Women and men were viewed as possessing different personality characteristics. It was assumed that because of biological gender differences women and men would pursue different directions in life. Worell and Remer (2003) describe six characteristics of traditional theories that reflect outdated assumptions about the role gender plays in behavior:

- An *androcentric theory* uses male-oriented constructs to draw conclusions about human nature.
- *Gendercentric theories* propose two separate paths of development for women and men.
- *Ethnocentric theories* assume that the facts pertaining to human development and interaction are similar across races, cultures, and nations.
- *Heterosexist theories* view a heterosexual orientation as normative and desirable and devalues same-sex relationships.

■ An *intrapsychic orientation* attributes behavior to intrapsychic causes, which often results in blaming the victim.

■ *Determinism* assumes that present personality patterns and behavior are fixed at an early stage of development.

To the degree that traditional theories contain these biased elements, they have clear limitations for women and members of subordinate groups when it comes to counseling.

Worell and Remer (2003) describe the constructs of feminist theory as being gender-fair, flexible–multicultural, interactionist, and life-span-oriented. *Gender-fair theories* explain differences in the behavior of women and men in terms of socialization processes rather than on the basis of our "true" natures. These theories avoid stereotypes in social roles and interpersonal behavior. A *flexible–multicultural theory* uses concepts and strategies that apply equally to both individuals and groups regardless of age, race, culture, gender, ability, class, or sexual orientation. *Interactionist theories* contain concepts specific to the thinking, feeling, and behaving dimensions of human experience and account for contextual and environmental factors. A *life-span perspective* assumes that human development is a lifelong process and that personality patterns and behavioral changes can occur at any time rather than being fixed during early childhood.

Feminist Perspective on Personality Development

Feminist therapists emphasize that societal gender-role expectations profoundly influence a person's identity from the moment of birth and become deeply ingrained in adult personality. Because gender politics are imbedded in the fabric of American society, they influence how we see ourselves as girls and boys and as women and men throughout the course of our lives. "Girls are typically expected to be sweet, sensitive, and docile, while boys are expected to be strong, stoic, and brave" (Prochaska & Norcross, 2003, p. 421).

Chodorow (1978, 1989) has theorized that psychological differences between men and women are due to the fact that women are the primary caretakers who raise the children. The identity of girls is based on a sense of continuity in their relationship with their mothers, whereas boys form their identity by defining themselves as different from their mothers and by developing an identification with their fathers. Thus, girls learn from their mothers to be affiliative and nurturing and to place a high priority on relatedness and caring for others. At the same time, by identifying with mothers who sacrifice their own desires and goals to serve the family, girls reduce their capacity for autonomy and independence. Boys model the aggressive, power-seeking nature of adult males and thus reduce their capacity for the expression of empathy and certain emotions.

Recognizing that theories of human development were based almost exclusively on research with boys and men, Gilligan (1977) undertook a series of studies on women's moral and psychosocial development. As a result of her work,

Gilligan came to believe women's sense of self and morality is based in issues of responsibility for and care of other people and is embedded in a cultural context. She posited that the concepts of connectedness and interdependence—virtually ignored in male-dominated developmental theories—are central to women's development. According to Gilligan (1982), women tend toward relationship, whereas men tend toward separation. In later years Gilligan expanded her work to explore crises faced by girls at adolescence. She asserts that it is difficult for girls to maintain a strong sense of identity and inner "voice" when to do so would be to risk disconnection in a society that does not honor their relational needs and desires. She was concerned that traits such as caring and compassion, which define the "goodness" of women, were seen as a deficit in their moral development and that their nurturing and caretaking roles were devalued in comparison to the values placed on independence and achievement.

Most models of human growth and development emphasize a struggle toward independence and autonomy, but feminists recognize that women are searching for a connectedness with others. In feminist therapy women's relational qualities are seen as strengths and as pathways for healthy growth and development instead of being identified as weaknesses or defects.

The founding scholars of relational-cultural theory have elaborated on the vital role that relationships and connectedness with others play in the lives of women (Jordan et al., 1991; Miller, 1986, 1991; Miller et al., 1999; Miller & Stiver, 1997; Surrey, 1991). These scholars suggest that a woman's sense of identity and self-concept develop in the context of relationships. Surrey (1991), like Chodorow, believes the mutually empathic mother–daughter relationship is a crucial model for other relationships, including therapeutic relationships. As you will see, many of the techniques of feminist therapy foster mutuality, relational capacities, and growth in connection.

Sandra Bem's (1981, 1983, 1993) *gender schema theory* provides another perspective on the development of women. According to Bem (1981), children learn society's view of gender and apply it to themselves. This gender schema is an organized set of mental associations people use to interpret what they see. They learn, for instance, that girls wear makeup and boys do not, that petite girls and tall boys are attractive, and that certain behaviors are desirable for girls to be considered "feminine" and for boys to be considered "masculine." Bem (1983, 1993) argues that gender schema is one of the strongest perceptual sets we use when looking at society and our place within it and that the ingrained gender schemas of American society are extremely limiting for *both* genders.

Kaschak (1992) used the term *engendered lives* to describe her belief that gender is the organizing principle in people's lives. She has studied the role gender plays in shaping the identities of women and men and believes the masculine defines the feminine. For instance, because men pay great attention to women's bodies, women's appearance is given tremendous importance in Western society. Men, as the dominant group, determine the roles that women play. Men are not expected to control their sexual impulses, but women are expected to remain chaste, to have sexually appealing bodies, and to control men's sexual impulses. Because women occupy a subordinate position, they must be able to interpret the needs and behaviors of the dominant group. To that end, women have developed "women's intuition" and have included in their gender schema an internalized belief that women are less important than men. Women's roles include service to others and anticipating the needs of others, thus they may be labeled as passive, dependent, and lacking in initiative.

Although most of the early research focused on women's development, the relational-cultural theory and other feminist views on development have been expanded to include men. Feminist researchers have demonstrated that when all human development is seen through the lens of male gender, important qualities of both women and men are overlooked. Through the work of Gilligan, Miller, and others, we have new models of development to understand women and a new perspective that recognizes that both women and men have been mislabeled and misunderstood.

Feminist therapists remind us that traditional gender stereotypes of women are still prevalent in our cultures. They teach their clients that uncritical acceptance of traditional roles can greatly restrict their range of freedom to define the kind of person they want to be. Today many women and men are resisting being so narrowly defined. Women and men in therapy learn that, if they choose to, they can experience mutual behavioral characteristics such as accepting themselves as being both dependent and independent at different times, being interdependent, giving to others and being open to receiving, thinking and feeling, and being tender and tough. Rather than being cemented to a single behavioral style, women and men who reject traditional roles are saying that they are entitled to express the complex range of characteristics that are appropriate for different situations and that they are open to their vulnerability as human beings.

SUMMARY   Chodorow's (1989) work on identity development, Gilligan's (1977, 1982) research into women's moral and psychosocial development, the relational-cultural theory, gender schema theory, the notion of engendered lives, and the permission to challenge gender stereotypes all have contributed to our understanding of women's development. According to Lerman (1986), all of these approaches view women in a positive light, arise out of women's experience, encompass the diversity and complexity of women's lives, attend to the ways in which diversity influences self-structures, recognize the inextricable connection between internal and external worlds, and acknowledge the political and social oppression of women. Each has made a unique contribution and has had an impact on the practice of feminist therapy. These common characteristics enable practitioners to assess the adequacy of whatever personality theory they use.

Principles of Feminist Psychology

A number of feminist writers have articulated core principles that form the foundation for the practice of feminist therapy. These principles are interrelated and have a great deal of overlap.

1. *The personal is political.* Clients' individual problems have societal and political roots. Feminist therapy aims not only for individual change but for social change. Feminists view their therapy practice as existing not only to help individual clients in their struggles but also as a strategy for advancing a transformation in society. Direct action for social change is part of their responsibility as therapists. It is important that women who engage in the therapy process— clients and therapists alike—recognize that they have suffered from oppression as members of a subordinate group and that they can join with other women to right these wrongs. Identifying external sources of problems often results in anger, which can be harnessed as energy to take action for change. If the environment is a major source of pathology in the lives of women and men, then the toxic aspects of the environment must be changed if individual change is to occur. The goal is to advance a different vision of societal organization that frees both women and men from the constraints imposed by gender-role expectations.

2. *Personal and social identities are interdependent.* Clients can best be understood in the context of their sociocultural environments (Worell & Remer, 2003). Interdependence between personal and social identities is a major vehicle for integrating diversity in feminist therapy. Individuals have membership in interdependent social groups that are structured by cultural norms, and people occupy several different "social locations" such as gender, ethnicity, race, social class, sexual orientation, age, and physical abilities and characteristics within this matrix.

Feminist therapists work to help individuals make changes in their lives, but they are also committed to working toward social change that will liberate all members of society from stereotyping, marginalization, and oppression. Diverse sources of oppression, not simply gender, are identified and interactively explored as a basis for understanding the concerns that clients bring to therapy. Framing clients' issues within a cultural context leads to empowerment, which can be realized only through social change (Worell & Remer, 2003). The ultimate goal is to intervene in ways that produce change in our dysfunctional sociopolitical environment (Remer, Rostosky, & Wright, 2001).

3. *Definitions of distress and "mental illness" are reformulated.* Feminist therapy rejects the "disease model" of mental illness. Instead, feminist therapists consider intrapsychic and interpersonal factors as only partial explanations for the pain that brings people to therapy. External factors are also highly influential. Psychological distress is reframed, not as disease but as a communication about unjust systems. Pain is defined not as evidence of deficit or defect but as evidence of resistance and the skill and will to survive (Worell & Johnson, 1997). Resistance is seen as an indicator that the person is able to remain alive and powerful in the face of oppression (Brown, 1994).

Furthermore, by considering contextual variables, symptoms are reframed as survival strategies. Women's responses to pathological environmental forces are not viewed as symptoms but rather as creative strategies for coping with society's oppression (Worell & Remer, 2003). Finally, Enns (1993) makes the important point that learning to identify sources of pain and to express pain are crucial for the healing process. Enns suggests that learning to directly express this internalized pain (and anger, grief, and sorrow) represents a basic aspect of healing because it enables clients to productively redirect emotions they have introjected, or swallowed.

4. *Feminist therapists use an integrated analysis of oppression.* Gender is an essential consideration in feminist therapy, both in terms of oppression and in terms of differences that may influence one's understanding (Hill & Rothblum, 1996). Feminist therapists recognize that both women and men are affected by being raised in a culture where the sexes are differentially privileged. Men who have learned that vulnerability is a weakness may have difficulty expressing emotions in and outside the therapeutic relationship. Women who have learned to subordinate their own wishes to care for their families may have difficulty identifying and honoring what they want out of therapy.

The therapist has a gender too, and the therapist's perceptions will always be filtered through the lens of her or his own experiences, which may be vastly different from those of the client. Although gender is emphasized, feminist therapists recognize that all forms of oppression profoundly influence beliefs, options, and perceptions, and they are equally committed to working against oppression on the basis of race, ethnicity, class, culture, religious beliefs, affectional or sexual orientation, age, and physical abilities and characteristics. Thus, feminists challenge all forms of oppression, not just oppression of women (Worell & Remer, 2003).

5. *The counseling relationship is egalitarian.* Attention to power is central in feminist therapy, and the therapeutic relationship is egalitarian. Clients are assumed to be experts on themselves (Worell & Remer, 2003), and the voices of the oppressed are acknowledged as authoritative and valuable sources of knowledge (Worell & Johnson, 1997). The therapeutic relationship is a collaborative process in which clients are viewed as active participants in redefining themselves. Finding ways to share power with clients and to demystify therapy is essential because feminist therapists believe all relationships should strive for equality, or better, mutuality (a condition of authentic connection between the client and the therapist). Other elements essential to an egalitarian relationship are therapist self-disclosure when appropriate, therapist authenticity and presence with clients, and clients' informed consent.

6. *Women's perspectives are valued.* Women's perspectives are considered central in understanding their distress. Traditional therapies that operate on androcentric norms compare women to the male norm and find them deviant. Much of psychological theory and research tends to conceptualize women and men in a polarized way, forcing a male–female split in most aspects of human experience (Bem, 1993). Our society has tended to devalue subjective experience in favor of the objective. A goal of feminist therapy is to replace patriarchal "objective truth" with feminist consciousness, which acknowledges a diversity of ways of knowing. Women are encouraged to express their emotions and their intuition and to use their personal experience as a touchstone for determining what is "reality."

Theories of feminist therapy evolve from and reflect lived experiences that emerge from the relationships among the participants. Women's experiences include a number of gender-based phenomena such as rape, sexual assault, sexual harassment, childhood sexual abuse, eating disorders, and domestic violence. Feminist therapists are aware of and attend to these phenomena (Moradi, Fischer, Hill, Jome, & Blum, 2000).

 # THE THERAPEUTIC PROCESS

Therapeutic Goals

Five goals for feminist therapy have been proposed by Enns (2004): equality, balancing independence and interdependence, empowerment, self-nurturance, and valuing diversity. But the ultimate goal of feminist therapy is to create the kind of society where sexism and other forms of discrimination and oppression are no longer a reality (Worell & Remer, 2003). Feminist therapy strives for transformation, for both the individual client and society as a whole.

At the individual level feminist therapists work to help women and men recognize, claim, and embrace their personal power. Through this empowerment, clients are able to free themselves from the constraints of their gender-role socialization and to challenge ongoing institutional oppression. Therapists help clients become interdependent, strong, resilient, and trusting of self and others. Women clients often are helped to rethink their relationship with their body. By examining the devastating effects of unrealistic societal expectations communicated by the media, women can assign less importance to appearance and focus more on pleasing themselves rather than conforming to a societal ideal.

Feminist therapy is a consciously political enterprise. The aim is to replace the current patriarchy with a feminist consciousness, creating a society in which relationships are interdependent, cooperative, and mutually supportive. Feminist therapists work to help women and men alike recognize that how they define themselves and how they relate to others are inevitably influenced by gender-role expectations. Although some steps are being taken to change institutionalized sexism and other forms of oppression, there are still far too many examples of inequity between men and women and between people from dominant and subordinate groups in matters such as promotions and salaries. Thus, transcendence rather than adjustment is the goal.

The full meaning of "the personal is political" is that women learn to free not only themselves but all people from the bonds of oppression and stereotypes. According to Worell and Remer (2003), feminist therapists help clients:

- Become aware of their own gender-role socialization process
- Identify their internalized messages and replace them with more self-enhancing beliefs
- Understand how sexist and oppressive societal beliefs and practices influence them in negative ways

- Acquire skills to bring about change in the environment
- Restructure institutions to rid them of discriminatory practices
- Develop a wide range of behaviors that are freely chosen
- Evaluate the impact of social factors on their lives
- Develop a sense of personal and social power
- Recognize the power of relationships and connectedness
- Trust their own experience and their intuition

Feminist therapists also work toward reinterpreting women's mental health. Their aim is to depathologize women's experiencing and to change society so that women's voices are honored and women's relational qualities are valued. Women's experiences are examined without the bias of patriarchal values, and women's life skills and accomplishments are acknowledged.

Therapist's Function and Role

Feminist therapy rests on a set of philosophical assumptions that can be applied to various theoretical orientations. Any theory can be evaluated against the criteria of being gender-fair, flexible–multicultural, interactionist, and life-span-oriented. The therapist's role and functions will vary to some extent depending on what theory is combined with feminist principles and concepts. In *Case Approach to Counseling and Psychotherapy* (Corey, 2005, chap. 10) five different feminist therapists demonstrate a variety of feminist interventions in their work with Ruth. They also conceptualize the case of Ruth from a feminist therapy perspective.

A therapist of another orientation who incorporates feminist principles and practices is not the same as a feminist therapist. Feminist therapists have integrated feminism into their approach to therapy and into their lives. Their actions and beliefs and their personal and professional lives are congruent. They use gender and power analyses to understand clients and their concerns, and they are committed to monitoring their own biases and distortions, especially the social and cultural dimensions of women's experiences. Feminist therapists are also committed to understanding oppression in all its forms— sexism, racism, heterosexism—and they consider the impact of oppression and discrimination on psychological well-being. They value being emotionally present for their clients, being willing to share themselves during the therapy hour, modeling proactive behaviors, and being committed to their own consciousness-raising process. Finally, although feminist therapists may use techniques and strategies from other theoretical orientations, they are unique in the feminist assumptions they hold.

Feminists share common ground with existential therapists who emphasize therapy as a shared journey—one that is life changing for both client and therapist. Feminist therapists hold many beliefs in common with humanistic or person-centered therapists, trusting in the client's ability to move forward in a positive and constructive manner. They believe the therapeutic relationship should be a nonhierarchical, person-to-person relationship, and they aim to empower clients to live according to their own values and to rely on an internal (rather than external or societal) locus of control in determining what is right for them. Like person-centered therapists, feminist therapists convey their genuineness and strive for mutual empathy between client and therapist.

Unlike person-centered therapists, however, feminist therapists do not see the therapeutic relationship in and of itself as being sufficient to produce change. Insight, introspection, and self-awareness are springboards to action, and feminist therapists work to free women (and men) of roles that have prohibited them from realizing their potential. Therapy must not replicate the societal power imbalance and foster dependency in the client. Rather, therapist and client take active and equal roles, working together to determine goals and procedures. Throughout this process, the therapist is appropriately self-disclosing. The *Feminist Therapy Code of Ethics* (Feminist Therapy Institute, 2000) directly addresses the role and function of self-disclosure and notes the importance of using self-disclosure "with purpose and discretion in the interests of the client" (p. 39).

Client's Experience in Therapy

Clients are active participants in the therapeutic process. Feminist therapists are committed to ensuring that this does not become another arena in which women remain passive and dependent. It is important that clients tell their stories and give voice to their experiencing. Initially, clients may look to the therapist for answers or advice. As the therapist continues to place the responsibility back on clients and to relate to clients more as a person than as an "expert," clients come to trust more in their own power. As clients realize they are really understood, they begin to get in touch with a range of feelings, including anger and other "prohibited" emotions that they may have learned to deny to themselves.

The female therapist may share some of her own struggles with gender-role oppression, and as an analysis of gender-role stereotyping is conducted, the client's consciousness is raised. For example, a female client will come to recognize her unity with other women and to realize that she is not alone. As she becomes more aware of ways she has been limited with respect to the development of her identity, her self-concept, and her goals and aspirations, she will begin to take on new roles. She may negotiate equality in her relationships with others in her life, be more assertive when needed, and identify her own needs and take the actions necessary to meet them. She will move from the safe environment of individual therapy sessions out into the larger support system of women. Perhaps she will join a women's self-help group. She may become an activist and participate in groups that are working to foster social change.

Feminist therapists do not restrict their practice to women clients; they also work with men, couples, families, and children. The experiences of a male client in therapy will in many ways parallel those of the female client just described.

The therapeutic relationship is a partnership, and the client will be the expert in determining what he needs and wants from therapy. He will explore ways in which he has been limited by his gender-role socialization. He may become more aware of how he is constrained in his ability to express a range of emotions, and in the safe environment of the therapeutic sessions he may be able to fully experience such feelings as sadness, tenderness, uncertainty, and empathy. As he transfers these ideas to daily living, he may find that relationships change in his family, his social world, and at work.

The major goal of feminist therapy is empowerment, which involves acquiring a sense of self-acceptance, self-confidence, joy, and authenticity. Worell and Remer (2003) write that feminist therapy clients acquire a whole new way of looking at and responding to their world. They add that the shared journey of empowerment can be both frightening and exciting—for both client and therapist. Clients can expect more than adjustment or simple problem-solving strategies; they need to be prepared for major shifts in their way of viewing the world around them, changes in the way they perceive themselves, and transformed interpersonal relationships.

Relationship Between Therapist and Client

The therapeutic relationship is based on empowerment and egalitarianism. The very structure of the client–therapist relationship models how to identify and use power responsibly. Feminist therapists clearly state their values to reduce the chance of value imposition. This allows clients to make a choice regarding whether or not to work with the therapist.

Although there is an inherent power differential in the therapy relationship, feminist therapists work to equalize the power base in the relationship by employing a number of strategies (Thomas, 1977). First, they are acutely sensitive to ways they might abuse their own power in the relationship, such as by diagnosing unnecessarily, by interpreting or giving advice, by staying aloof behind an "expert" role, or by discounting the impact the power imbalance between therapist and client has on the relationship. Counselor self-disclosure and authenticity tend to reduce the power differential between client and counselor and aid in identifying their common issues as women.

Second, therapists actively focus on the power clients have in the therapeutic relationship. They encourage them to get in touch with their feelings and to honor their experiencing, to become aware of the ways they relinquish power in relationships with others as a result of socialization or as a means for survival, and to take charge of their lives and relationships by making choices that increase the possibility for experiencing mutuality in their relationships.

Third, feminist therapists work to demystify the counseling relationship. They do this by sharing with the client their own perceptions about what is going on in the relationship, by making the client an active partner in determining any diagnosis, and by making use of appropriate self-disclosure. If the therapist suggests a particular technique, she fully explains what its possible effects may be and her rationale for suggesting it, and she fully respects the client's decision to proceed or not to proceed. Some feminist therapists use contracts as a way to make the goals and processes of therapy overt rather than covert and mysterious.

To free women and men of roles that have prohibited them from realizing their potential, an egalitarian counseling relationship is established. The counselor is not the all-knowing expert but rather is a "relational expert," who strives to develop a collaborative relationship in which clients can become experts on themselves. A defining theme of the client–counselor relationship is the inclusion of clients in both the assessment and the treatment process. This commitment to include clients from the initial through the final session helps to keep the therapeutic relationship as egalitarian as possible. Walden (1997) emphasizes the value of educating and empowering clients. When counselors keep their clients uninformed about the nature of the therapeutic process, they deny them the potential for active participation in their therapy. When counselors make decisions about a client *for* the client rather than *with* the client, they rob the client of power in the therapeutic relationship. Collaboration with the client in all aspects of therapy leads to a genuine partnership and empowerment of the client.

 # APPLICATION: THERAPEUTIC TECHNIQUES AND PROCEDURES

The Role of Assessment and Diagnosis

Feminist therapists have been sharply critical of the DSM classification system, and research indicates that gender and race may influence assessment of clients' symptoms (Enns, 2000). To the degree that assessment is influenced by subtle forms of sexism, racism, ethnocentricism, heterosexism, ageism, or classism, it is impossible to arrive at an appropriate assessment or diagnosis. Sources of bias include disregarding or minimizing the effect of environmental factors on behavior; providing different treatments to various groups of individuals who display similar symptoms; inappropriately selecting diagnostic labels due to stereotypical beliefs; and operating from a gender-biased theoretical orientation (Worell & Remer, 2003). Feminist therapists have challenged sexism in diagnostic categories and have proposed alternative classifications that reflect women's experiences.

According to Enns (1993), many feminist therapists do not use diagnostic labels, or they use them reluctantly. Feminist therapists believe diagnostic labels are severely limiting for these reasons: (a) they focus on the individual's symptoms and not the social factors that cause dysfunctional behavior; (b) as part of a system developed mainly by White male psychiatrists, they may represent an instrument of oppression; (c) they (especially the personality disorders) may reinforce gender-role stereotypes and encourage adjustment to the norms of the status quo; (d) they may reflect the inappropriate application of power in the therapeutic relationship; (e) they can lead to an overemphasis on individual solutions rather than social change; and (f) they have the potential to reduce one's respect for clients.

The feminist approach emphasizes the importance of considering the context of women's lives and points out that many symptoms can be understood as coping or survival strategies rather than as evidence of pathology (Worell & Remer, 2003). In keeping with the focus on client empowerment, diagnosis is a shared process in which clients are the experts on the meaning of their distress. Reframing symptoms as coping skills or strategies for survival and shifting the etiology of the problem to the environment avoids "blaming the victim" for her problems. Assessment is viewed as an ongoing process between client and therapist and is connected to treatment interventions (Enns, 2000). In the feminist therapy process, diagnosis of distress becomes secondary to identification and assessment of strengths, skills, and resources (Brown, 2000). Worell and Remer (2003) make the excellent point that although individuals are not to *blame* for personal problems that are largely caused by dysfunctional social environments, they are *responsible* for working toward change.

Sharf (2004) discusses feminist therapy perspectives on certain "mental disorders" identified in the DSM-IV-TR as being particularly common in women: depression, posttraumatic stress disorder, borderline personality disorder, and eating disorders. Using these diagnostic categories may contribute to a victim-blaming stance and dull the therapist's sensitivity to external factors that contribute to a client's symptoms (Enns, 2000). Diagnostic categories used to label individuals who have experienced violence are another area of controversy for feminist therapists. Connecting the personal to the political, they have stressed that many of the symptoms are normal responses to violence. New diagnostic categories—such as "abuse and oppression artifact disorder" (Brown, 1994) and "complex posttraumatic stress disorder" (Herman, 1992)—have been proposed as alternatives that might better describe the wide range of responses to long-term subjugation and abuse.

According to the DSM-IV-TR, depression is twice as common among women (American Psychiatric Association, 2000). Feminist therapists believe women have many more reasons to experience depression than do men, and they often frame depression as a normative experience for women. Women are often financially disadvantaged or dependent, relationally submissive, and strive to please others by anticipating their needs. Thus, depression may result from women's internalized perception, belief, and experience of not being in control of their lives or bodies and feeling less valuable than men. Similarly, with eating disorders feminist therapists focus on messages given by society, and by the mass media in particular, about women's bodies and the importance of being thin. The therapist uses a gender-role analysis to help clients who suffer from anorexia or bulimia examine these societal injunctions and how they have come to accept them. Therapist and client work together on ways to challenge and change these messages. Common threads are an emphasis on gender-role socialization and the power differences between women and men, and attention to societal as opposed to intrapsychic origins of problems.

Feminist therapists do not refuse to use the DSM-IV-TR in this age of managed care and the prevalence of the medical model of mental health, but diagnosis results from a shared dialogue between client and therapist. The therapist is careful to review with the client any implications of assigning a diagnosis so the client can make an informed choice, and discussion focuses on helping the client understand the role of socialization and culture in the etiology of her problems.

An alternative form of assessment preferred by feminist therapists is gender-role analysis, which involves a cooperative exploration by client and therapist of the impact of gender on the client's distress. Santos De Barona and Dutton (1997) stress the importance of incorporating other contextual variables (such as racism and heterosexism) in assessment procedures in ways that are meaningful for the client. Worell and Remer's (2003) focus on the multiple personal and social identities of each client provides a vehicle for this diversity analysis. Clients identify the range of their identities and their awareness of privilege and oppression associated with these identities. Whatever approach to assessment is used, the client is included in each of the stages of the process and participates in shaping the strategies, which build on the client's individual strengths.

Techniques and Strategies

Feminist therapists have developed several techniques, and others have been borrowed from traditional approaches and adapted to the feminist therapy model. Particularly important are consciousness-raising techniques that help women differentiate between what they have been taught is socially acceptable or desirable and what is actually healthy for them. Some of the techniques described by Sharf (2004), Worell and Remer (2003), and Enns (1993) are discussed in this section, using the case example of Susan to illustrate how these techniques might be applied.

> Susan, age 27, comes to therapy stating that she is depressed. She says she "hates herself" for having gained so much weight since she left college, and she is certain she is doomed to be alone for the rest of her life. She says, "I missed my chance. I was popular and attractive when I was in college, but no man would ever look twice at me the way I am now."

EMPOWERMENT   At the heart of feminist strategies is the goal of empowering the client. Susan's therapist will pay careful attention to *informed consent* issues, discussing ways of getting the most from the therapy session, clarifying expectations, identifying goals, and working toward a contract that will guide the therapeutic process. By explaining how therapy works and enlisting Susan as an active partner in the therapeutic venture, the therapy process is demystified and Susan becomes an equal participant. Susan will learn that she is in charge of the direction, length, and procedures of her therapy.

SELF-DISCLOSURE   Feminist therapists use therapeutic self-disclosure to equalize the client–therapist relationship, to normalize women's collective experiences, to empower clients, and to establish informed consent. Appropriate self-disclosure helps to decrease power differentials, is useful for supporting clients, and can be liberating for clients (Enns, 2000). For example, Susan's therapist may disclose her own difficulties in learning to accept that her body is different now, after her pregnancy and childbirth, and that she is not a size 10 either. Susan benefits from this modeling by a woman who does not meet society's standards for thinness but is comfortable with her body and the ways in which it has worked for her, not against her. Self-disclosure shows Susan that the therapist is a real person with her own struggles, and through this common connection Susan begins to understand that the "personal is political."

Self-disclosure is not just sharing information and experiences. It also involves a certain quality of presence the therapist brings to the therapeutic sessions. Effective therapist self-disclosure is grounded in authenticity and a sense of mutuality. The therapist considers how the disclosures may affect the client by using what relational-cultural theorists refer to as "anticipatory empathy." Feminist therapists, like counselors who have other theoretical orientations, are ethically committed to using self-disclosure to enhance the therapeutic process.

The therapist also clearly states her relevant values and beliefs about society to allow Susan to make an informed choice about whether or not to work with this therapist. Susan's therapist explains to her the therapeutic interventions that are likely to be employed. Susan, as an informed consumer, can be involved in evaluating how well these strategies are working and the degree to which her personal goals in therapy are being met.

GENDER-ROLE ANALYSIS   A hallmark of feminist therapy, gender-role analysis explores the impact of gender-role expectations on the client's well-being or distress and draws upon this information to make decisions about future gender-role behaviors (Enns, 2000). The therapist begins by asking Susan to identify messages that she received related to weight and appearance from society, her peers, the media, and her family. Susan remembers that her mother struggled with weight gain and often made remarks to Susan like, "It's a good thing I captured your father while I still had a figure" and "You'll have your choice of men if you stay a perfect size 10." Susan struggles to identify some positive consequences of these messages. She states that she *did* feel attractive through her adolescence and college years and her self-confidence helped her develop a winning personality, make friends, and enjoy social activities. The negative consequences are easier to see and are evident when the therapist asks Susan to repeat the statements she made at the beginning of the session. Together the therapist and Susan decide which messages she wants to change, and they develop and implement a plan for creating those changes.

GENDER-ROLE INTERVENTION   Using this technique the therapist responds to Susan's concern by placing it in the context of society's role expectations for women. The aim is to provide Susan with insight into the ways that social issues are affecting her problem. Susan's therapist responds to her statement with, "Our society really is obsessed with thinness. The media bombards women with the message that they need to be rail-thin to be attractive. The reality is, most women don't look like models and those who try to often end up with eating disorders like anorexia." By placing Susan's concern in the context of societal expectations, the therapist gives Susan insight into how these expectations have affected her psychological condition and have led to her depression. The therapist's statement also paves the way for Susan to think more positively about her unity with other women who are not rail-thin.

POWER ANALYSIS AND POWER INTERVENTION   These techniques are similar to the analysis and intervention with gender roles. The emphasis here, however, is on helping Susan become aware of the power difference between men and women in our society and empowering Susan to take charge of herself and her life. Power analysis includes recognizing different kinds of power that clients possess or to which they have access. In Susan's case the power analysis may focus on helping Susan identify alternate kinds of power she may exercise and to challenge the gender-role messages that prohibit the exercise of that kind of power. The power analysis helps Susan recognize that in this society women often gain power through their association with a powerful male and are perceived as powerless if they do not have a man in their lives. Interventions are aimed at helping Susan learn to appreciate herself as she is, regain her self-confidence based on the personality attributes she possesses, and set goals that will be fulfilling to her and do not depend on whether she "finds a man."

BIBLIOTHERAPY   Nonfiction books, psychology and counseling textbooks, autobiographies, self-help books, educational videos, and films can all be used as bibliotherapy resources. At times, a novel may be extremely therapeutic and provide rich material for discussions in therapy sessions. The therapist describes a number of books that address the consequences of society's obsession with thinness, and Susan selects one to read over the next few weeks. Providing Susan with reading material increases her expertise and decreases the power difference between Susan and her therapist. Reading can supplement what is learned in the therapy sessions, and Susan can enhance her therapy by exploring her reactions to what she is reading. Through well-timed reading assignments, Susan can learn valuable lessons about the influence of gender-role stereotypes, how sexism is promoted, the power differential between women and men, and the effects of gender inequality. She can also learn specific coping skills that she can add to her behavioral repertoire.

ASSERTIVENESS TRAINING

ASSERTIVENESS TRAINING   By teaching and promoting assertive behavior, women become aware of their interpersonal rights, transcend stereotypical gender roles, change negative beliefs, and implement changes in their daily lives. The therapist must consider what is culturally appropriate for each client, and some clients may choose not to behave assertively in certain situations.

Through learning and practicing assertive behaviors and communication, Susan may increase her own power, thus alleviating the depression she feels as a result of having measured herself against societal expectations rather than her own self-evaluations. Susan will learn about some important distinctions between being assertive and being aggressive. She will learn that it is her right to ask for what she wants and needs. The therapist helps Susan to evaluate and anticipate the possible negative consequences of behaving assertively. They talk about the possibility of being viewed as aggressive and how to best deal with this situation. Based on some of the issues that Susan is struggling with, her therapist recommends that she read Mary Crawford's (1995) book, *Talking Difference: On Gender and Language*.

REFRAMING AND RELABELING

REFRAMING AND RELABELING   Like bibliotherapy, therapist self-disclosure, and assertiveness training, reframing is not unique to feminist therapy. However, reframing is applied differently in feminist therapy. Reframing implies a shift from "blaming the victim" to a consideration of social factors in the environment that contribute to a client's problem. In reframing, rather than dwelling on intrapsychic factors, the focus is on examining societal or political dimensions. Thus, Susan may come to understand that her depression is linked to social pressures to have the "ideal body" rather than stemming from some deficiency in her.

Relabeling is an intervention that changes the label or evaluation applied to some behavioral characteristic. Susan can change certain labels she has attached to herself, such as being inadequate or unattractive because she is not thin. She might relabel her depression and concerns about her weight as reactions to externally derived standards of how she should be.

GROUP WORK

GROUP WORK   An important adjunct to individual feminist therapy, group work alone is often the preferred modality for some issues that women experience in our culture. Women's groups, including self-help groups and advocacy groups, help women experience their connectedness and unity with other women. Susan and her therapist will likely discuss the possibility of Susan joining a women's support group or other type of group as a part of the process of terminating individual therapy. By joining a group Susan will have opportunities to discover that she is not alone in her struggles. Other women can provide her with nurturance and support, and Susan will have the chance to be significant to other women as they engage in their healing process.

SOCIAL ACTION   Feminist therapists may suggest to clients that they become involved in activities such as volunteering at a rape crisis center, writing letters to lawmakers, or providing community education about gender issues. Participating in such activities can empower clients and help them see the link between their personal experiences and the sociopolitical context in which they live. Susan might decide to join and participate in organizations that are working to change societal stereotypes about women's bodies. Taking this kind of social action is another way for Susan to feel more empowered.

The Role of Men in Feminist Therapy

Can a man be a feminist therapist? Feminist therapists are divided on this issue. Certainly, men can be nonsexist therapists. We hope that all therapists strive to incorporate awareness of gender bias in their thinking and their practices with clients. It seems to us that men can be pro-feminist therapists when they embrace the principles and incorporate the practices of feminism in their work. This entails being willing to confront sexist behavior in themselves and others, redefining masculinity and femininity according to other than traditional values, working toward establishing egalitarian relationships, and actively supporting women's efforts to create a just society.

Feminist therapy can be an effective method for working with men as clients. Men, as well as women, are oppressed by a patriarchal system and can work for social change (Brown, 1994). Social mandates about masculinity such as restrictive emotionality, overvaluing power and control, the sexualization of emotion, and obsession with achievement can be oppressive to men (Gilbert & Scher, 1999; Pleck, 1995; Pollack, 1995, 1998; Real, 1998).

Feminist therapists routinely work with men, especially with abusive men and in battering groups. According to Ganley (1988), issues that men can deal with productively in feminist therapy include learning how to increase their capacity for intimacy, expressing their emotions and learning self-disclosure, balancing achievement and relationship needs, accepting their vulnerabilities, and creating collaborative relationships at work and with significant others that are not based on a "power-over" model of relating. Some of these themes emerge in the section Feminist Therapy Applied to the Case of Stan.

 # FEMINIST THERAPY FROM A MULTICULTURAL PERSPECTIVE

Contributions to Multicultural Counseling

Of all the theoretical approaches to counseling and psychotherapy in this book, feminist therapy and multicultural perspectives of therapy practice have the most in common. Feminist therapists suggest that multicultural counseling refers to the analysis of social structures affecting mental health, including

(*continued on p. 366*)

Feminist Therapy Applied to the Case of Stan

Stan's fear of women and his gender-role socialization experiences make him an excellent candidate to benefit from feminist therapy. A therapeutic relationship that is egalitarian, with a strong woman who respects and empowers him and does not demean him, will be a new kind of experience for Stan.

Stan has clearly indicated that he is willing and even eager to change. Despite his low self-esteem and negative self-evaluations, Stan is able to identify some positive attributes. These include his determination, his ability to feel his feelings, and his gift for working with children. Stan knows what he wants out of therapy and has clear goals: to stop drinking, to feel better about himself, to relate to women on an equal basis, and to learn to love and trust himself and others. His feminist therapist will build on these strengths.

In the first session Stan's therapist focuses on establishing an egalitarian working relationship to help Stan begin to regain his personal power. Stan may hold the assumption that because his therapist is a woman she will take a dominant role and tell him what he needs to do to accomplish his goals. It is important that the therapeutic relationship does not replicate other relationships Stan has had with women in his life, especially his mother and his ex-wife. The therapist consciously works to demystify the therapeutic process and equalize the relationship, conveying to Stan that he is in charge of the direction his therapy will take. She spends considerable time explaining her view of the therapy process and how it works. She lets Stan know that he is in charge of not only the direction but also the duration of therapy and that she will not abandon him.

A gender-role analysis is conducted to help Stan become aware of the influence of gender-role expectations in the development of his problems. First, Stan is asked to identify gender-role messages he received while growing up from a variety of societal sources including his parents, teachers, the media, church, and peers. In his autobiography Stan has already written about some of the messages his parents gave him, and this provides a natural starting point for his analysis. He remembers his father calling him "dumb" and his mother saying, "Why can't you grow up and be a man?" Stan wrote about his mother "continually harping at" his father and telling Stan that he did many things to hurt her and that she wished she hadn't had him. Stan describes his father as weak, passive, and mousy in relating to his mother and remembers that his father compared him unfavorably with his siblings. Stan internalized these messages, often crying himself to sleep and feeling disgusted with himself.

The therapist asks Stan to identify the self-statements he makes now that are based on these early messages. As they review his writings, Stan sees how societal messages he received about what a man "should" be have been reinforced by those parental messages that have led to Stan's view of himself today. He and the therapist explore how his autobiography illuminates some societal messages he appears to have introjected, or swallowed whole. For instance, he wrote that he feels sexually inadequate and worries that he won't be able to perform. It appears that he has introjected the societal notion that men should always initiate sex, be ready for sex, and be able to achieve and sustain an erection. Stan also sees that he has already identified and written about how he wants to change those messages, as exemplified in his statements that he wants to "feel equal with others" and not "feel apologetic" for his existence and develop a loving relationship with a woman. Stan begins to feel capable and empowered as his therapist acknowledges the important work he has already done, even before he entered therapy.

The therapist follows this gender-role analysis with a gender-role intervention to place Stan's concerns in the context of societal role expectations. She says, "Indeed, it is a burden to try to live up to society's notion of what it means to be a man, always having to be strong and tough. Those aspects of yourself that you would like to value—your ability to feel your feelings, being good with children—are qualities society tends to label as 'feminine.'" Stan replies wistfully, "Yeah, it would be a better world if women could be strong without being seen as domineering and if men could be sensitive and nurturing

(continued on next page)

without being seen as weak." The therapist gently challenges this statement by asking, "Are you sure that's not possible? Have you ever met a woman or a man who was like that?" Stan ponders for a minute and then with some animation describes the college professor who taught his Psychology of Adjustment class. Stan saw her as very accomplished and strong but also as someone who empowered him by encouraging him to find his own voice through writing his autobiography. He also remembers a male counselor at the youth rehabilitation facility where he spent part of his adolescence as a man who was strong as well as sensitive and nurturing.

As the first session draws to a close, the therapist asks Stan to say what he has gotten out of their time together. Stan says that two things stand out for him. First, he is beginning to believe he doesn't need to keep blaming himself. He realizes that many of the messages he has received from his parents and from society about what it means to be a man have been unrealistic and one-dimensional. He acknowledges that he has been limited and constrained by his gender-role socialization. Second, he feels hopeful because there are alternatives to those parental and societal definitions—people he admires have been able to successfully combine "masculine" and "feminine" traits. If they can do it, maybe he can too. The therapist asks Stan whether he chooses to return for another session. When he answers in the affirmative, she gives him W. S. Pollack's (1998) book *Real Boys* and suggests that he read it in a personal way. The therapist explains that this book descriptively captures the gender-role socialization boys are subjected to in this culture.

Stan comes to the second session eager to talk about his bibliotherapy homework assignment. He tells the therapist that he gained some real insights into his own attitudes and beliefs by reading *Real Boys*. What Stan learned from reading this book leads to a further exploration of Stan's relationship with his mother. He becomes tearful as he expresses the terrible bind he felt he was placed in as a child. On one hand he became very angry when she belittled him and told him he was a "mistake." On the other hand he was terrified to express his anger because he so desperately wanted her love and approval. When the therapist asks him about his feel-

ings toward his father, Stan realizes that he is again both angry and afraid. He is angry not only that his father allowed himself to be pushed around by his mother but also that his father didn't seem to value Stan as he was, instead wanting him to be more like his siblings. He says he would like to be closer to his father but is afraid to try.

The therapist asks Stan whether he has been able, as an adult, to express either his anger or his fear to his parents. Stan seems startled at the very idea but says he sure wishes he could tell them how he feels. The therapist then explains to Stan what an empty chair dialogue is like and how he might use it to "talk" to his parents in the safe environment of the therapy session. Stan says he would like to try that but finds it pretty scary. The therapist assures him that he is fully in charge of what he decides to say, he can stop at any time, and that his parents are not really there and can't actually hear him. She adds that this experiment is entirely his decision, and he can try it another time if not now.

Stan decides to go ahead and puts his parents in two empty chairs that are arranged facing him. He sits silently for several minutes, and then turns to the therapist saying, "I keep picturing how my father reacted when my mother went after him. He was just passive, a real mouse. I can be like that, but I don't know how else to be." The therapist suggests that maybe they can have some fun with this experiment instead of making it into a "perfect performance." She asks Stan if he is willing to be a mouse.

Stan says he thinks this will be easy, turns and faces the empty chairs, and begins talking to his "father" in a timid way with a squeaky voice. Tears well up as he says, "You were supposed to teach me how to be a man. But you weren't interested in me, except to compare me with my brother and sister." He turns to his "mother," and in an almost inaudible voice asks, "Why did you keep telling me I was a mistake? I tried so hard to please you, but it was never good enough." Speaking to both of them, he says in a stronger voice, "It wasn't fair!" As he continues to express his feelings, his voice gradually becomes louder and louder. He ends by yelling, "I don't care how miserable your lives were, you had no right to take it out on a helpless child!" He stops, takes a deep breath, and shoves his chair back. Turning to face the therapist, he starts to grin and says, "Wow, I guess I am the mouse that roared!"

The remainder of the session is spent in processing this Gestalt exercise. The therapist helps Stan understand his family from a feminist perspective that does not take his father or mother out of context. For example, the therapist and Stan discuss one possible explanation for his mother's behavior. Stan's mother may have been doing what she believed was best for Stan, trying to encourage masculine behaviors so that he would not suffer societal consequences for not being "manly" enough. His father may have had much the same goal; believing he had failed to be a "strong man," he may have hoped to spare Stan the same kind of failure. Stan finds that he still has mixed feelings toward his parents, but those feelings are different now. He is still angry but finds that his anger is tempered by compassion for how trapped they felt in a life that was not fulfilling to them. He is still afraid of them, but he no longer feels immobilized by his fear.

Understanding his parents' perspective may be Stan's first step on the road toward tolerance, healing, and forgiveness. He finds it helpful to understand their behavior in the context of societal expectations and stereotypes rather than continuing to blame them. The therapist helps Stan to see how our culture tends to hold extreme positions about mothers—that they are either perfect or wicked—and that neither of these extremes is true. As Stan learns to reframe his relationship with his mother, he develops a more realistic picture of her as neither perfect nor wicked. He comes to realize, too, that his father has been oppressed by his own socialization experiences and by an idealistic view of masculinity that he may have felt unable to achieve. Stan notes that he felt powerful when he was doing the empty chairs experiment but that he didn't hurt anyone by doing it. He thinks of the saying, "Are you a man or a mouse?" This provides a springboard for further discussion of societal stereotypes about manliness and how he has been limited by his unquestioning acceptance of them.

Stan continues to work at learning to value the "feminine" parts of himself as well as the "masculine" or strong aspects of the women with whom he is interacting. He also continues to monitor and make changes in his self-talk about what it means to be a man. He is involved in gaining ongoing awareness of these messages that come from current sources such as the media and friends. Since a number of Stan's sessions were devoted to exploring his relationship with his mother, along with his resentment toward her, the therapist suggests another reading assignment—Caplan's (1989) book, *Don't Blame Mother.* The aim of this assignment is to assist Stan in exploring alternatives to blaming his mother for his present problems.

Throughout the therapeutic relationship, Stan and the therapist discuss with immediacy how they are communicating and relating to each other during the sessions. The therapist is self-disclosing and treats Stan as an equal, continually acknowledging that he is the "expert" in knowing and getting what he wants out of life.

Follow-Up: You Continue as Stan's Feminist Therapist

Use these questions to help you think about how you would counsel Stan using a feminist therapy model:

- What unique values do you see in working with Stan from a feminist perspective as opposed to working with Stan from the other therapeutic approaches you've studied thus far?
- If you were to continue working with Stan, what self-statements regarding his view of himself as a man might you focus on and how might you challenge his beliefs?
- In what ways could you integrate cognitive behavior therapy with feminist therapy in Stan's case? What possibilities do you see for integrating Gestalt therapy methods with feminist therapy? What other therapies might you combine with a feminist approach?
- Stan's feminist therapist used bibliotherapy as a form of homework assignment. Would you suggest books for Stan to read? If so, what books do you think would be useful for him? What other homework might you suggest to Stan? What other feminist therapy strategies would you utilize in counseling Stan?

sexism, racism, and other levels of both oppression and privilege (Martinez, Davis, & Dahl, 1999). Likewise, multicultural approaches point to oppression, discrimination, and racism as the source of many of the problems faced by people of color. Feminist counseling centers in Japan, founded by Japanese women for Japanese women, build on Western concepts but add unique therapeutic concepts that are effective within Japanese culture (Matsuyuki, 1998).

The feminist perspective of understanding the use of power in relationships has application for understanding power inequities due to racial and cultural factors as well. The "personal is political" principle has equal value when applied to counseling women and counseling culturally diverse client groups. Neither feminist nor multicultural therapists are willing to settle for adjustment to the status quo. Nor does either approach rest solely on individual change; both demand direct action for social change as a part of the role of therapists. Many of the social action and political strategies that call attention to oppressed groups have equal relevance for women and for ethnic minorities.

It is possible to incorporate the principles of feminist therapy with a multicultural perspective. Comas-Diaz (1987) describes a feminist model that empowers minority women by helping them to:

- Acknowledge the negative effects of sexism and racism
- Identify and deal with their feelings pertaining to their status as ethnic minority women
- View themselves as able to find solutions to their problems
- Understand the interplay between the external environment and their reality
- Integrate ethnic, gender, and racial components into their identity

Both the women's movement and the multicultural movement have called to our attention the negative effects discrimination and oppression have on its targets and also on those doing the discriminating and oppressing. McIntosh (1988, 1998) has described the concept of *White privilege* as an invisible package of unearned assets White people enjoy that are not extended to people of color. Adapting her notion of White privilege to both race and gender, we would like to suggest that *White male heterosexual privilege* is operating in our society. The reality is that racism, sexism, and heterosexism still favor one group of citizens—White heterosexual males—while excluding other groups of citizens from the same opportunities. Therapy should free individuals and increase their range of choices. It is to the credit of both feminist and multicultural therapists that policies have been established to lessen the opportunities for discrimination based on gender, race, culture, sexual orientation, ability, and age.

Culturally competent feminist therapists look for ways to work within the client's culture by exploring consequences and alternatives. They appreciate the complexities involved in changing within one's culture but do not view culture as sacrosanct (Worell & Remer, 2003). It is important to understand and respect diverse cultures, but most cultural contexts have both positive and toxic aspects. Feminist therapists are committed to challenging cultural beliefs and practices that discriminate against, subordinate, and restrict the potential of groups of individuals.

Limitations for Multicultural Counseling

If feminist therapists are not aware of the consequences of certain choices their clients make, they are likely to increase their clients' dissatisfaction with life. Being aware of the cultural context is especially important when feminist therapists work with women from cultures that endorse culturally prescribed roles that keep women in a subservient place or from cultures that are based on patriarchy.

Consider this scenario. You are a feminist therapist working with a Vietnamese woman who is struggling to find a way to be true to her culture and also to follow her own educational and career aspirations. Your client is a student in a helping profession who is being subjected to extreme pressure from her father to return home and take care of her family. Although she wants to complete a degree and eventually help others in the Vietnamese community, she feels a great deal of guilt when she considers "selfishly" pursuing her education when her family at home needs her. If you were counseling this woman, would you challenge her to take care of herself and do what is right for her? Might you try to persuade her to tell her father that she is going to follow her own path? The price may be very high if this woman chooses to go against what is culturally expected of her.

In this complex situation, therapist and client will work together to find a path that enables the client to realize her individualistic goals without ignoring or devaluing her collectivistic cultural values. We see the therapist's job as helping the client balance the potential costs associated with any action she might choose. Indeed, it is likely that this client will experience pain no matter what her choice. The therapist's job is not to take away any of her pain or struggle, nor to choose for her client, but to be present in such a way that the client will truly be empowered to decide for herself. The core value of equality in feminist therapy may limit the effectiveness of the therapist in working with clients from culturally different backgrounds.

 # SUMMARY AND EVALUATION

Summary

The origins of feminist therapy are connected with the women's movement of the 1960s, when women united in vocalizing their dissatisfaction over the restrictive nature of traditional female roles. Feminist therapy largely grew out of the recognition by women that the traditional models of therapy suffer from basic limitations due to the inherent bias of earlier theoreticians. Feminist therapy emphasizes these concepts:

- Viewing problems in a sociopolitical and cultural context rather than on an individual level
- Recognizing that clients know what is best for their lives and are experts on their own lives
- Striving to create a therapeutic relationship that is egalitarian through the process of self-disclosure and informed consent
- Demystifying the therapeutic process by including the client as much as possible in all phases of assessment and treatment, which increases client empowerment
- Viewing the nature of women's experiences from a unique perspective
- Understanding and appreciating the lives and perspectives of diverse women
- Challenging traditional ways of assessing the psychological health of women
- Understanding that individual change will best occur through social change
- Emphasizing the role of the therapist as advocate as well as facilitator of change within the individual
- Encouraging clients to take social action to address oppressive aspects of the environment

Feminist therapy is aimed at both individual and social change. The model is not static but is continually evolving. The major goal is to replace the current patriarchal system with feminist consciousness and thus create a society that values equality in relationships, that stresses interdependence rather than dependence, and that encourages both women and men to define themselves rather than being defined by societal demands.

Instead of being a singular and unified approach to psychotherapy, feminist practice tends to be diverse. As feminist therapy has matured, it has become more self-critical and varied. Emerging diversity perspectives—women of color feminism, lesbian feminism, global feminism, and postmodern perspectives—have led to examining issues of diversity among women and men in new ways.

Each of the eight basic philosophies underlying feminist practice—liberal, cultural, radical, socialist, postmodernist, women of color, lesbian, and global–international—has a different view on the sources of oppression and what is needed to bring about substantial social transformation. Regardless of their particular perspective, feminist therapists share a number of basic assumptions and roles: they engage in appropriate self-disclosure; they make their values and beliefs explicit so that the therapy process is clearly understood; they establish egalitarian roles with clients; they work toward client empowerment; and they emphasize the commonalities among women while honoring their diverse life experiences.

Feminist therapists are committed to actively breaking down the hierarchy of power in the therapeutic relationship through the use of various interventions. Some of these strategies are unique to feminist therapy, such as gender-role analysis and intervention, power analysis and intervention, assuming a stance of advocate in challenging conventional attitudes toward appropriate roles for women, and encouraging clients to take social action. Many other therapeutic strategies are borrowed from various therapy models. A few of these interventions include bibliotherapy, assertiveness training, cognitive restructuring, role playing, psychodramatic techniques, identifying and challenging untested beliefs, and journal writing. Feminist therapy principles and techniques can be applied to a range of therapeutic modalities such as individual therapy, couples counseling, family therapy, group counseling, and community intervention. Regardless of the specific techniques used, the overriding goals are client empowerment and social transformation.

Contributions of Feminist Therapy

One of the major contributions feminists have made to the field of counseling and psychotherapy is paving the way for gender-sensitive practice and an awareness of the impact of the cultural context and multiple oppressions. Therapists with a feminist orientation understand how important it is to become fully aware of typical gender-role messages clients have grown up with, and they are skilled in helping clients identify and challenge these messages (Philpot, Brooks, Lusterman, & Nutt, 1997).

Feminism has done a good deal to make therapists sensitive to the gendered uses of power in relationships. For example, in writing about feminist couples therapy, Rampage (1998) claims that therapists should identify and challenge the distribution of power in relationships where it is unequal and this inequality is preventing the problem from being solved. Doing this often results in empowering women to claim what they want for themselves in their relationships. Examining the power differential in their relationship often helps partners demystify and depathologize the gendered differences between them.

Nichols and Schwartz (2001) credit gender-sensitive therapists with helping families reorganize so that neither the woman nor the man remains stuck in destructive patterns. Family therapists with a feminist orientation assist the family in critically examining and changing the rules and roles that have kept the mother down and the father out. According to Nichols and Schwartz, it is only when therapists look through the lens of gender that they will be able to interrupt the cycle of mother-blaming and will stop looking to mothers to do all the changing.

Feminist therapists have also made important contributions in questioning traditional counseling theories and models of human development, especially the assumptions that these traditional approaches make concerning clients' experiences. Most theories place the cause of problems within individuals rather than with external circumstances and the environment. This has led to holding women and men responsible for their problems and not giving full recognition to social and political realities that create problems for women and men. A key contribution feminists continue to make is reminding all of us that the proper focus of therapy includes working to change oppressive factors in society rather than expecting individuals to merely adapt to expected role behaviors.

Major contributions of the feminist movement are in the areas of ethics in psychology and counseling practice (Brabeck, 2000) and ethical decision making in therapy (Rave & Larsen, 1995). The unified feminist voice called attention to the extent and implications of child abuse, incest, rape, sexual harassment, and domestic violence. It was feminists who pointed out the consequences of failing to recognize and take action in cases where children and women were victims of physical, sexual, and psychological abuse. Feminist therapists work with male clients who are abusive, and increasing numbers of groups composed of male batterers are led or co-led by feminist therapists.

Feminist therapists demanded action in cases of sexual misconduct at a time when male therapists misused the trust placed in them by their female clients. Not too long ago the codes of ethics of all the major professional organizations were silent on the matter of therapist and client sexual liaisons. Now, virtually all of the professional codes of ethics prohibit sexual intimacies with current clients and prohibit sexual relationships between therapists and former clients for a specified time period. Furthermore, many of the professions agree that a sexual relationship cannot later be converted into a therapeutic relationship. Largely due to the efforts and input of women on ethics committees, the existing codes are explicit with respect to sexual harassment and sexual relationships with clients, students, and supervisees (Herlihy & Corey, 1997).

Feminist therapy principles have been applied to supervision, teaching, consultation, ethics, research, and theory building as well as to the practice of psychotherapy. Building community, providing authentic mutual empathic relationships, creating a sense of social awareness, and the emphasis on social change are all significant strengths of this approach.

The principles and techniques of feminist therapy can be incorporated in other therapy models and visa versa. Both feminist and Adlerian therapists are united in viewing the therapeutic relationship as egalitarian. Both feminist and person-centered therapists agree on the importance of therapist authenticity, modeling, and self-disclosure; empowerment is the basic goal of both orientations. When it comes to making choices about one's destiny, existential and feminist therapists are speaking the same language—both emphasize choosing for oneself instead of living a life determined by societal dictates. Both cognitive behavioral therapy and feminist therapy share the importance of the collaborative relationship, learning coping skills, establishing mutually agreed on counseling goals, the value of educating clients about how therapy works, and including clients in evaluating how well the process is working for them.

Although feminist therapists have been critical of psychoanalysis as a sexist orientation, a number of feminist therapists believe psychoanalysis can be an appropriate approach to helping women. Object-relations theory may help clients examine internalized object representations that are based on their relationships with their parents. Therapy might include an examination of unconscious learning about women's roles through the mother–daughter relationship to provide insights into why gender roles are so deeply ingrained and difficult to change.

Gestalt therapy and feminist therapy share the goal of increasing the client's awareness of personal power. A Gestalt-oriented feminist therapist functions as a facilitator of the client's active experimentation with new roles and behaviors. Contemporary Gestalt therapy stresses dialogue between client and therapist. This approach creates a basis for genuine contact and mutuality between client and counselor, and it also establishes the groundwork for contact and experiments that are spontaneous in the moment-to-moment experience of the therapeutic engagement. In many ways the dialogic and collaborative model of Gestalt therapy fits well with the philosophy of a feminist perspective (Enns, 1987, 2004).

Cognitive behavioral therapies and feminist therapy are compatible in that they view the therapeutic relationship as a collaboration and the client as being in charge of setting goals and selecting strategies for change. They both aim to help clients take charge of their own lives. Another commonality of both approaches is the commitment to demystifying therapy. Both the cognitive behavior therapist and the feminist therapist assume a range of information-giving functions and teaching functions so clients can become active partners in the therapy process.

A feminist therapist could employ action-oriented strategies such as assertiveness training and behavioral rehearsal and suggest homework assignments for clients to practice in their everyday lives. The therapist might explore with clients how their beliefs about women's roles and women's experiencing are limiting their choices. Clients would be invited to explore how their gender-role socialization and institutional sexism has resulted in these beliefs. Clients then decide which of these beliefs to change or reconstruct. Three useful sources for further discussion of feminist cognitive behavior therapy are Worell and Remer (2003), Fodor (1988), and Kantrowitz and Ballou (1992).

Therapists of any orientation can infuse feminist-informed practices and techniques into their work if they conduct therapy with a positive attitude toward women, value what is feminine, and are willing to confront patriarchal systems, empower women, and help them find their voice. Additionally, it is important that therapists pay attention to women's and men's development and gender-role socialization, power issues in the therapeutic relationship, and their own gender biases and stereotypes. Therapists need to identify any sources of bias in a given theory and work toward restructuring or eliminating biased aspects.

Feminist therapy suggests that a counseling theory should be gender-fair, flexible–multicultural, interactionist, and life-span-oriented. A feminist therapy approach can contribute to broadening the theoretical base of other therapy models as well as enriching all of our lives by encouraging positive social activism in our communities and throughout the world.

Limitations and Criticisms of Feminist Therapy

Some feminist therapists may become overzealous and in subtle ways impose their values on clients. Although a useful role of feminist therapists is to teach women about options for change, this role should not include persuading clients to move in a specific direction. The therapist's function is to offer a blend of support and challenge to examine what clients have in their lives. It is the clients' responsibility to weigh the potential benefits and risks involved in remaining as they are or changing.

Feminist therapists do not take a neutral stance. They advocate definite change in the social structure, especially in the area of equality, power in relationships, the right to self-determination, freedom to pursue a career outside the home, and the right to an education. This agenda could pose some problems when working with clients who do not share these beliefs. What if a woman chooses to make her primary commitment to her children and decides she does not want to get professionally involved outside the home? What about the woman who realizes she is both financially and emotionally dependent on her husband but does not want to change this aspect of her relationship, or who feels she cannot realistically change her relationship? And how about a woman who recognizes she is sacrificing some of her personal educational or career ambitions for the sake of others? What if a woman clearly recognizes the hierarchy in her family yet does not choose to risk upsetting her husband?

Feminist therapists should challenge clients' unexamined choices, but most contemporary feminists honor clients' choices as long as those choices are indeed informed ones. It is essential that clients understand the impact of gender and cultural factors on their choices. Facilitating informed choice is part of the essence of feminist therapy. Rather than imposing specific directions on clients, feminist therapists are committed to helping clients weigh the costs and benefits of their current life choices. Lenore Walker (1994) raises this issue with regard to working with abused women. Although Walker focuses on the importance of asking questions that challenge women to think through their situations in new ways and of helping women develop "safety plans," she emphasizes how critical it is to understand those factors in a woman's life that often pose difficulties for her in making changes.

Feminist therapists need to be cautious to avoid imposing their values on their clients, even in subtle ways. The critical questions are, "Why is this client seeing me? What does the client want in life? How can I help the client sort her or his values and assist the client in deciding what to do?" The client is ultimately responsible for answering these questions. Worell and Remer (2003) assert that all therapy is a value-laden process. Feminist therapists believe it is important to be clear with clients about values. This is different, however, from imposing values on clients. When therapists are aware of their values and explicitly share these values with clients in an appropriate and timely manner, they reduce the risk of value imposition.

Looking at contextual or environmental factors that contribute to a woman's problems and moving away from exploring the intrapsychic domain can be both a strength and a limitation. Instead of being blamed for her depression, the client is able to come to an understanding of external realities that are indeed oppressive. However, viewing the source of a client's problem in the environment may actually contribute to not taking personal responsibility to act in the face of an unfair world. Therapists must balance an exploration of the outer and inner worlds of the client if the client is to find a way to take action in her own life. Although a woman may not be responsible for creating many of her problems, she will find empowerment by learning what she can do to assume responsibility for changing in the direction she chooses—whether or not certain facets of the environment change. Another choice would be to decide to leave an oppressive environment.

Two other criticisms of feminist therapy deserve a brief mention. There is some disagreement as to whether feminist therapy is a philosophical orientation or a theory. Recent writings and research have begun to clarify this debate (Brown, 1994; Worell & Johnson, 1997). Another criticism is that feminist therapy was developed by White, middle-class, heterosexual women (Brown, 1994). It was not until the late 1980s that developers of feminist theory acknowledged that they had overlooked women of color and assumed that race was not as crucial as gender in understanding oppression. The fact that many women of color preferred to call themselves "womanists" is a testament to their feeling excluded from feminism. Feminist therapy has responded to this criticism and has made progress in being more inclusive (Brown & Root, 1990; Enns & Sinacore, 2001; Worell & Johnson, 1997).

 ## WHERE TO GO FROM HERE

The *CD-ROM for Integrative Counseling* is especially useful as a demonstration of interventions I make with Ruth that illustrate some principles and procedures of feminist therapy. In Session 1 ("Beginning of Counseling"), I ask Ruth about her expectations and initiate the informed consent process. I attempt to engage Ruth as a collaborative partner in the therapeutic venture, and I teach her how counseling works. In Session 2 ("The Therapeutic Relationship"), I focus on our relationship, realizing that Ruth will not make significant progress unless we have a good working relationship. In Session 3 ("Establishing Therapeutic Goals"), I demonstrate how I assist Ruth in formulating clear and personal goals that will guide the course of therapy.

Clearly, Ruth is the expert on her own life and my job is to assist her in attaining the goals we collaboratively identify as a focus of therapy. In Session 4 ("Understanding and Dealing With Diversity"), you can observe some of my interventions in dealing with the differences between us. I am open in exploring with Ruth how any of our differences might affect our therapeutic task. Ruth brings up gender differences, but she also mentions our differences in religion, education, culture, and socialization. Rather than making assumptions about which differences might affect Ruth's work with me, I encourage her to explore the degree to which she feels comfortable with me and trusts me. Such open exploration is essential if therapy is to be effective.

The Jean Baker Miller Training Institute offers workshops, courses, professional training, publications, and ongoing projects that explore applications of the relational-cultural approach and integrate research, psychological theory, and social action. This relational-cultural model is based on the assumption that growth-fostering relationships and disconnections are constructed within specific cultural contexts. For more information, contact:

Jean Baker Miller Training Institute
Stone Center, Wellesley College
106 Central Street
Wellesley, MA 02481
Telephone: (781) 283-3800
Fax: (781) 283-3646
Web site: jbmti.org

The Stone Center Work in Progress Series includes more than 100 papers and books describing various applications of the relational-cultural model. For a list of publications, contact:

Stone Center/ JBM 77 Publications
The Wellesley Centers for Women
Wellesley College
Wellesley, MA 02481
Telephone: (781) 283-2510
Fax: (781) 283-2504
Web site: www.wcwonline.org

The American Psychological Association has two divisions devoted to special interests in women's issues: Division 17 (Counseling Psychology's Section on Women) and Division 35 (Psychology of Women). For further information about these divisions, contact:

American Psychological Association
750 First Street, N.E.
Washington, DC 20002-4242
Telephone: (202) 336-5500 or (800) 374-2721
Fax: (202) 336-5568

Association Web site: http://www.apa.org
Division 17 Web site: http://www.div17.org
Division 35 Web site: http://www.apa.org/divisons/div35

The Association for Women in Psychology (AWP) sponsors an annual conference dealing with feminist contributions to the understanding of life experiences of women. AWP is a scientific and educational feminist organization devoted to reevaluating and reformulating the role that psychology and mental health research generally play in women's lives. For more information about this organization and its annual conference, contact the AWP:

Web site: www.theworks.baka.com/awp

The Psychology of Women Resource List, or POWR online, is co-sponsored by APA Division 35, Society for the Psychology of Women, and the Association for Women in Psychology. This public electronic network facilitates discussion of current topics, research, teaching strategies, and practice issues among people interested in the discipline of psychology of women. Most people with computer access to Bitnet or the Internet can subscribe to POWR-L at no cost. To subscribe, send the command below via e-mail to:

LISTSERV@URIACC (Binet) or LISTSERV@URIACC.URI.EDU
Subscribe POWR-L Your name (Use first and last name)

The University of Kentucky offers a minor specialty area in counseling women and feminist therapy within Counseling Psychology M.S. and Ph.D. programs. For information, contact:

Dr. Pam Remer
University of Kentucky
Department of Educational and Counseling Psychology
251-C Dickey Hall
Lexington, KY 40506-0017
Telephone: (859) 257-4158
Email: Premer@uky.edu
Web site: www.uky.edu/Education/edphead.html

Texas Women's University offers a training program with emphasis in women's issues, gender issues, and family psychology. For information, contact:

Dr. Roberta Nutt
Texas Women's University
Counseling Psychology Program
P. O. Box 425470
Denton, Texas 76204
Telephone: (940) 898-2313
Email: F_Nutt@twu.edu
Web site: www.twu.edu/as/psyphil/cppc

Some other resources pertaining to women's issues include those listed here.

National Organization for Women (NOW)
1000 16th St. NW, Suite 700
Washington, DC 20036
Telephone: (202) 331-0066
Web site: www.now.org

National Women's Health Network
514 10th Street NW, Suite 400
Washington, DC 20004
Telephone: (202) 347-1140
Fax: (202) 347-1168
Web site: www.womenshealthnetwork.org

National Abortion and Reproductive Rights Action League (NARAL)
1156 15th St. NW, Suite 700
Washington, DC 20005
Telephone: (202) 973-3000
Fax: (202) 973-3096
Email: naral-comments@client-mail.com
Web site: http://www.naral.org

Newcomb College Center for Research on Women
20 Caroline Richardson Building
Tulane University
New Orleans, LA 70118-5683
Telephone: (504) 865-5238
Fax: (504) 862-8948
Email: willing@mailhost.tcs.tulane.edu
Web site: http://www.tulane.edu/wc

InfoTrac College Edition Resources

Feminist Therapy   The following key words are listed in such a way as to allow the InfoTrac College Edition search engine to locate a wider range of articles in the online library. The key words should be entered exactly as shown, and include asterisks, "W1," and "AND."

Laura Brown	Relational W1 model
Carol Gilligan	Heterosexism
Jean Baker Miller	Gender W1 schema*
Feminist Therapy	Feminist W1 consciousness
Femin* AND psychol*	Assertiveness training
Stone W1 Center	Bibliotherapy

Recommended Supplementary Readings

Feminist Perspectives in Therapy: Empowering Diverse Women (Worell & Remer, 2003) is an outstanding text that clearly outlines the foundations of Empowerment Feminist Therapy. The book covers a range of topics such as integrating feminist and multicultural perspectives on therapy, changing roles for women, feminist views of counseling practice, feminist transformation of counseling theories, and a feminist approach to assessment and diagnosis. There are also excellent chapters dealing with depression, surviving sexual assault, confronting abuse, choosing a career path, and lesbian and ethnic minority women.

Feminist Theories and Feminist Psychotherapies (Enns, 2004) describes the wide range of feminist theories that inform feminist therapies, including women of color feminism, liberal feminism, radical feminism, cultural feminism, socialist feminism, and postmodern perspectives. The book discusses the manner in which each of these feminisms is likely to influence feminist practice and includes short self-assessment questionnaires designed to help readers clarify their feminist theoretical perspective. A series of chapters discuss the compatibility of various psychotherapy theories with diverse feminist theories.

The Healing Connection: How Women Form Relationships in Therapy and Life (Miller & Stiver, 1997) describes how connections are formed between people and how this leads to strong, healthy individuals. The authors also deal with disconnections between people that lead to anxiety, isolation, and depression.

Women's Growth in Diversity: More Writings From the Stone Center (Jordan, 1997) builds on the foundations laid by *Women's Growth in Connection*. This work offers insights on issues such as sexuality, shame, anger, depression, power relations between women, and women's experiences in therapy.

Shaping the Future of Feminist Psychology: Education, Research, and Practice (Worell & Johnson, 1997) is a valuable resource on feminist perspectives on research, education, and practice. A detailed treatment of topics includes feminist perspectives on assessment, feminist theory and psychological practice, training in feminist therapy, and supervision issues.

Subversive Dialogues: Theory in Feminist Therapy (Brown, 1994) is a significant work that brings feminist theory and therapy together. The author illustrates the application of feminist principles using case examples.

References and Suggested Readings

AMERICAN PSYCHIATRIC ASSOCIATION. (2000). *Diagnostic and statistical manual of mental disorders, text revision* (4th ed.). (DSM-IV-TR). Washington, DC: Author.

AMERICAN PSYCHOLOGICAL ASSOCIATION. (1975). Report on the task force on sex bias and sex role stereotyping in psychotherapeutic practice. *American Psychologist, 30,* 1169–1175.

AMERICAN PSYCHOLOGICAL ASSOCIATION. (1979). (Division 17). Principles concerning the counseling and psychotherapy of women. *The Counseling Psychologist, 8,* 21.

BEARDSLEY, B., MORROW, S. L., CASTILLO, L., & WEITZMAN, L. (1998, March). *Perceptions and behaviors of practicing feminist therapists: Development of the feminist multicultural practice instrument.* Paper presented at the 23rd annual conference of the Association for Women in Psychology, Baltimore.

BEM, S. L. (1981). Gender schema theory: A cognitive account of sex typing. *Psychological Review, 88*, 354–364.

BEM, S. L. (1983). Gender schema theory and its implications for child development. *Signs, 8*, 598–616.

*BEM, S. L. (1993). *The lenses of gender.* New Haven, CT: Yale University Press.

BIAGGIO, M., & HERSEN, M. (2000). *Issues in the psychology of women.* New York: Kluwer.

*BRABECK, M. M. (Ed.). (2000). *Practicing feminist ethics in psychology.* Washington, DC: American Psychological Association.

BRABECK, M., & BROWN, L. (1997). Feminist theory and psychological practice. In J. Worell & N. G. Johnson (Eds.), *Shaping the future of feminist psychology: Education, research, and practice* (pp. 15–35). Washington, DC: American Psychological Association.

BROWN, L. S. (1992). A feminist critique of the personality disorders. In L. S. Brown & M. Ballou (Eds.), *Personality and psychopathology: Feminist reappraisals* (pp. 206–228). New York: Guilford Press.

*BROWN, L. S. (1994). *Subversive dialogues: Theory in feminist therapy.* New York: Basic Books.

BROWN, L. S. (2000). Feminist therapy. In *Handbook of psychological change* (pp. 358–380). Chichester, NY: Wiley.

BROWN, L. S., & ROOT, M. (1990). *Diversity and complexity in feminist therapy.* New York: Hayworth.

*CAPLAN, P. J. (1989). *Don't blame mother.* New York: Harper & Row.

CHODOROW, N. J. (1978). *The reproduction of mothering.* Berkeley: University of California Press.

CHODOROW, N. J. (1989). *Feminism and psychoanalytic theory.* New Haven, CT: Yale University Press.

COMAS-DIAZ, L. (1987). Feminist therapy with mainland Puerto Rican women. *Psychology of Women Quarterly, 11*, 461–474.

COREY, G., & COREY, M. (2002). *I never knew I had a choice* (7th ed.). Pacific Grove, CA: Brooks/Cole.

*CRAWFORD, M. (1995). *Talking difference: On gender and language.* Newbury Park, CA: Sage.

*ENNS, C. Z. (1987). Gestalt therapy and feminist therapy: A proposed integration. *Journal of Counseling and Development, 66*, 93–95.

ENNS, C. Z. (1991). The "new" relationship models of women's identity: A review and critique for counselors. *Journal of Counseling and Development, 69*, 209–217.

*ENNS, C. Z. (1993). Twenty years of feminist counseling and therapy: From naming biases to implementing multifaceted practice. *The Counseling Psychologist, 21*(1), 3–87.

---

*Books and articles marked with an asterisk are suggested for further study.

*ENNS, C. Z. (2000). Gender issues in counseling. In S. D. Brown & R. W. Lent (Eds.), *Handbook of counseling psychology* (3rd ed., pp. 601–638). New York: Wiley.

*ENNS, C. Z. (2004). *Feminist theories and feminist psychotherapies: Origins, themes, and diversity.* 2nd ed. New York: Haworth.

*ENNS, C. Z., & Sinacore, A. L. (2001). Feminist theories. In J. Worell (Ed.), *Encyclopedia of gender* (Vol. 1, pp. 469–480). San Diego, CA: Academic Press.

ESPIN, O. M. (1999). *Women crossing boundaries: A psychology of immigration and the transformation of sexuality.* New York: Routledge.

FEMINIST THERAPY INSTITUTE. (2000). *Feminist therapy code of ethics* (revised, 1999). San Francisco: Feminist Therapy Institute.

FODOR, I. G. (1988). Cognitive behavior therapy: Evaluation of theory and practice for addressing women's issues. In M. A. Dutton-Douglas & L. E. Walker (Eds.), *Feminist psychotherapies: Integration of therapeutic and feminist systems* (pp. 91–117). Norwood, NJ: Ablex.

GANLEY, A. L. (1988). Feminist therapy with male clients. In M. A. Dutton-Douglas & L. E. Walker (Eds.), *Feminist psychotherapies: Integration of therapeutic and feminist systems* (pp. 186–205). Norwood, NJ: Ablex.

GILBERT, L. A., & SCHER, M. (1999). *Gender and sex in counseling and psychotherapy.* Boston: Allyn & Bacon.

GILLIGAN, C. (1977). In a different voice: Women's conception of self and morality. *Harvard Educational Review, 47,* 481–517.

*GILLIGAN, C. (1982). *In a different voice.* Cambridge, MA: Harvard University Press.

HERLIHY, B., & COREY, G. (1992). *Dual relationships in counseling.* Alexandria, VA: American Counseling Association.

HERLIHY, B., & COREY, G. (1996). *ACA ethical standards casebook* (5th ed.). Alexandria, VA: American Counseling Association.

HERLIHY, B., & COREY, G. (1997). *Boundary issues in counseling: Multiple roles and responsibilities.* Alexandria, VA: American Counseling Association.

HERMAN, J. L. (1992). *Trauma and recovery: The aftermath of violence.* New York: Basic Books.

HILL, M., & ROTHBLUM, E. (Eds.). (1996). *Couples therapy: Feminist perspectives.* New York: Haworth Press.

IVEY, A. E., D'ANDREA, M., IVEY, M. B., & SIMEK-MORGAN, L. (2002). *Theories of counseling and psychotherapy: A multicultural perspective* (5th ed.). Boston: Allyn & Bacon.

*JORDAN, J. V. (Ed.). (1997). *Women's growth in diversity: More writings from the Stone Center.* New York: Guilford Press.

*JORDAN, J. V., KAPLAN, A. G., MILLER, J. B., STIVER, I. P., & SURREY, J. L. (Eds.). (1991). *Women's growth in connection: Writings from the Stone Center.* New York: Guilford Press.

KANTROWITZ, R. E., & BALLOU, M. (1992). A feminist critique of cognitive-behavioral therapy. In L. S. Brown & M. Ballou (Eds.), *Personality and psychopathology: Feminist reappraisals* (pp. 70–87). New York: Guilford Press.

KASCHAK, E. (1981). Feminist psychotherapy: The first decade. In S. Cox (Ed.), *Female psychology: The emerging self* (pp. 387–400). New York: St. Martins.

KASCHAK, E. (1992). *Engendered lives.* New York: Basic Books.

LERMAN, H. (1986). From Freud to feminist personality theory: Getting there from here. *Psychology of Women Quarterly, 10,* 1–8.

LERNER, H. G. (1988). *Women in therapy.* New York: Harper & Row.

LOTT, B. (1994). *Women's lives: Themes and variations in gender learning* (2nd ed.). Pacific Grove, CA: Brooks/Cole.

MAHALIK, J. R., VAN ORMER, E. A., & SIMI, N. L. (2000). Ethical issues in using self-disclosure in feminist therapy. In M. M. Brabeck (Ed.), *Practicing feminist ethics in psychology* (pp. 189–202). Washington, DC: American Psychological Association.

MARTINEZ, L. J., DAVIS, K. C., & DAHL, B. (1999). Feminist ethical challenges in supervision: A trainee perspective. *Women & Therapy, 22*(4), 35–54.

MATSUYUKI, M. (1998). Japanese feminist counseling as a political act. *Women and Therapy, 21*(2), 65–77.

MCINTOSH, P. (1988). *White privilege and male privilege: A personal account of coming to see correspondence through work in women's studies* [Working paper #189]. Wellesley, MA: Wellesley College Center for Research on Women.

MCINTOSH, P. (1998). White privilege, color, and crime: A personal account. In C. R. Mann & M. S. Zatz (Eds.), *Images of color, images of crime* (pp. 207–216). Los Angeles, CA: Roxbury.

MILLER, J. B. (1986). *Toward a new psychology of women* (2nd ed.). Boston: Beacon.

MILLER, J. B. (1991). The development of women's sense of self. In J. V. Jordan, A. G. Kaplan, J. B. Miller, I. P. Stiver, & J. L. Surrey (Eds.), *Women's growth in connection* (pp. 11–26). New York: Guilford Press.

MILLER, J. B., JORDON, J., STIVER, I. P., WALKER, M., SURREY, J., & ELDRIDGE, N. S. (1999). *Therapists' authenticity* [Work in progress No. 82]. Wellesley, MA: Stone Center Working Paper Series.

*MILLER, J. B., & STIVER, I. P. (1997). *The healing connection: How women form relationships in therapy and in life.* Boston: Beacon Press.

MORADI, B., FISCHER, A. R., HILL, M. S., JOME, L. M., & BLUM, S. A. (2000). Does "feminist" plus "therapist" equal "feminist therapist?" An empirical investigation of the link between self-labeling and behaviors. *Psychology of Women Quarterly, 24,* 285–296.

MORADI, B., SUBICH, L. M., & PHILLIPS, J. C. (2002). Revisiting feminist identity development theory, research, and practice. *The Counseling Psychologist, 30*(1), 6–43.

NICHOLS, M. P., & SCHWARTZ, R. C. (2001). *Family therapy: Concepts and methods* (5th ed.). Boston: Allyn & Bacon.

*PHILPOT, C. L., BROOKS, G. R., LUSTERMAN, D. D., & NUTT, R. L. (1997). *Bridging separate gender worlds: Why men and women clash and how therapists can bring them together.* Washington, DC: American Psychological Association.

PLECK, J. H. (1995). The gender role strain paradigm: An update. In R. R. Levant & W. S. Pollack (Eds.), *A new psychology of men* (pp. 11–32). New York: Basic Books.

POLLACK, W. S. (1995). No man is an island: Toward a new psychoanalytic psychology of men. In R. F. Levant & W. S. Pollack (Eds.), *A new psychology of men* (pp. 33–67). New York: Basic Books.

*POLLACK, W. S. (1998). *Real boys.* New York: Henry Holt.

PROCHASKA, J. O., & NORCROSS, J. C. (2003). *Systems of psychotherapy: A transtheoretical analysis* (5th ed.). Pacific Grove, CA: Brooks/Cole.

RAMPAGE, C. (1998). Feminist couple therapy. In F. M. Dattilio (Ed.), *Case studies in couple and family therapy: Systemic and cognitive perspectives* (pp. 353–370). New York: Guilford Press.

RAVE, E. J., & LARSEN, C. C. (Eds.). (1995). *Ethical decision making in therapy: Feminist perspectives.* New York: Guilford Press.

*REAL, T. (1998). *I don't want to talk about it: Overcoming the secret legacy of male depression.* New York: Simon & Schuster (Fireside).

REMER, P., ROSTOSKY, S., & WRIGHT, M. (2001). Counseling women from a feminist perspective. In E. R. Welfel & R. E. Ingersoll (Eds.), *Mental health desk reference* (pp. 341–347). New York: Wiley.

SANTOS DE BARONA, M., & DUTTON, M. A. (1997). Feminist perspectives on assessment. In J. Worell & N. G. Johnson (Eds.), *Shaping the future of feminist psychology: Education, research, and practice* (pp. 37–56). Washington, DC: American Psychological Association.

SHARF, R. S. (2004). *Theories of psychotherapy and counseling: Concepts and cases* (3rd ed.). Pacific Grove, CA: Brooks/Cole.

*SURREY, J. L. (1991). The "self-in-relation": A theory of women's development. In J. V. Jordan, A. G. Kaplan, J. B. Miller, I. P. Stiver, & J. L. Surrey (Eds.), *Women's growth in connection* (pp. 51–66). New York: Guilford Press.

THOMAS, S. A. (1977). Theory and practice in feminist therapy. *Social Work, 22,* 447–454.

WALDEN, S. L. (1997). Inclusion of the client perspective in ethical practice. In B. Herlihy & G. Corey, *Boundary issues in counseling: Multiple roles and responsibilities* (pp. 40–47). Alexandria, VA: American Counseling Association.

WALKER, L. (1994). *Abused women and survivor therapy: A practical guide for the psychotherapist.* Washington, DC: American Psychological Association.

*WORELL, J., & JOHNSON, N. G. (Eds.). (1997). *Shaping the future of feminist psychology: Education, research, and practice.* Washington, DC: American Psychological Association.

*WORELL, J., & REMER, P. (2003). *Feminist perspectives in therapy: Empowering diverse women.* New York: Wiley.

Postmodern Approaches

Some Contemporary Founders of Postmodern Therapies

The postmodern approaches do not have a single founder. Rather, they have been a collective effort by many. I have highlighted two co-founders of solution-focused brief therapy and two co-founders of narrative therapy who have had a major impact on the development of these therapeutic approaches.

INSOO KIM BERG is executive director, and co-founder with Steve de Shazer, of the Brief Family Therapy Center in Milwaukee. As a leading theoretician in solution-focused brief therapy (SFBT), she has provided workshops in the United States, Japan, South Korea, Australia, Denmark, England, and Germany. Among her writings are *Family Based Services: A Solution-Focused Approach* (1994), *Working With the Problem Drinker: A Solution-Focused Approach* (Berg & Miller, 1992), and *Interviewing for Solutions* (De Jong & Berg, 2002).

STEVE DE SHAZER is one of the pioneers of solution-focused brief therapy. He is a senior research associate at the Brief Family Therapy Center in Milwaukee and author of several books on SFBT, including *Keys to Solutions in Brief Therapy* (1985), *Clues: Investigating Solutions in Brief Therapy* (1988), *Putting Difference to Work* (1991), and *Words Were Originally Magic* (1994). He has presented workshops, trained, and consulted widely in North America, Europe, Australia, and Asia. He and his colleagues continue to develop the theory and practice of constructing solutions.

(continued on next page)

MICHAEL WHITE is the co-founder, with David Epston, of the narrative therapy movement. He is at the Dulwich Centre in Adelaide, Australia, and his work with families and communities has attracted widespread international interest. He loves being with his family and friends and enjoys swimming, flying a small plane, and bike riding. Among his many books are *Narrative Means to Therapeutic Ends* (White & Epston, 1990), *Reauthoring Lives: Interviews and Essays* (1995), and *Narrative of Therapists' Lives* (1997).

DAVID EPSTON is one of the co-developers of narrative therapy. He is co-director of the Family Therapy Centre in Auckland, New Zealand, and is a writer and teacher in the

field of narrative ideas. He is a constant international traveler, presenting lectures and workshops in Australia, Europe, and North America. Among his professional interests are working with children with life-threatening asthma, establishing support groups for women struggling with anorexia, and engaging disengaged fathers in the parenting of their children. He is a co-author of *Narrative Means to Therapeutic Ends* (White & Epston, 1990) and *Playful Approaches to Serious Problems: Narrative Therapy With Children and Their Families* (Freedman, Epston, & Lobovits, 1997). He is an enthusiastic bike rider and loves relaxing with his wife Anne in a secluded cottage on Waiheke Island. ■

INTRODUCTION TO SOCIAL CONSTRUCTIONISM

Each of the models of counseling and psychotherapy we have studied so far has its own version of "reality." The simultaneous existence of multiple and often conflicting "truths" has led to increasing skepticism in the possibility that a singular, universal truth will one day explain human beings and the systems in which they live. We have entered a postmodern world in which truth and reality are often understood as points of view bounded by history and context rather than as objective, immutable facts.

Modernists believe in objective reality that can be observed and systematically known. They further believe reality exists independent of any attempt to observe it. Modernists believe people seek therapy for a problem when they have deviated too far from some objective norm. For example, clients are depressed when the range of their mood is below a level we would consider normal, everyday sadness—or when that sadness lasts longer than is useful. Clients then label their sadness as abnormal and seek help to return to "normal" behavior.

Postmodernists, in contrast, believe in subjective realities that do not exist independent of observational processes. *Social constructionism* is a therapeutic perspective within a postmodern worldview: it stresses the client's reality without disputing whether it is accurate or rational (Weishaar, 1993). To social constructionists, reality is based on the use of language and is largely a function of the situations in which people live. Realities are socially constructed. A problem exists when people agree there is a problem that needs to be addressed: A person is depressed when he or she adopts a definition of self as depressed. Once a definition of self is adopted, it is hard to recognize behaviors counter to that definition; for example, it is hard for someone who is suffering from depression to acknowledge the value of a periodic good mood in his or her life.

In postmodern thinking, language and the use of language in stories create meaning. There may be as many stories of meaning as there are people to tell the stories, and each of these stories is true for the person telling it. Further, every person involved in a situation has a perspective on the "reality" of that situation. When Kenneth Gergen (1985, 1991, 1999) and others began to emphasize the ways in which people make meaning in social relationships, the field of social constructionism was born. Berger and Luckman (1967) are reputed to be the first to use the term *social constructionism*, and it signaled a shift in emphasis in individual and family systems psychotherapy.

In social constructionism, the therapist disavows the role of expert, preferring a more collaborative or consultative stance. Clients are viewed as experts about their own lives. De Jong and Berg (2002) put this notion about the therapist's task well:

> We do not view ourselves as expert at scientifically assessing client problems and then intervening. Instead, we strive to be expert at exploring clients' frames of reference and identifying those perceptions that clients can use to create more satisfying lives. (p. 19)

Empathy and the collaborative partnership in the therapeutic process are more important than assessment or technique. Narratives and language processes (linguistics) have become the focus for both understanding individuals and helping them construct desired change.

Social constructionist theory is grounded on four key assumptions (Burr, 1995), which form the basis of the difference between postmodernism and traditional psychological perspectives. First, social constructionist theory invites a critical stance toward taken-for-granted knowledge. Social constructionists challenge conventional knowledge that has historically guided our understanding of the world, and they caution us to be suspicious of assumptions of how the world appears to be. Second, social constructionists believe the language and concepts we use to generally understand the world are historically and culturally specific. Knowledge is time- and culture-bound, and our ways of understanding are not necessarily better than other ways. Third, social constructionists assert that knowledge is constructed through social processes. What we consider to be "truth" is a product of daily interactions between people in daily life. Thus, there is not a single or "right" way to live one's life. Fourth, negotiated understandings, or "social constructions," take a wide variety of different forms. Knowledge and social action go together.

Postmodern thought is having an impact on the development of many psychotherapy theories and is influencing contemporary psychotherapeutic practice. For a more detailed treatment of the historical and conceptual foundations of the constructivist psychotherapies, consult Neimeyer and Mahoney (1995).

Historical Glimpse of Social Constructionism

A mere hundred years ago, Freud, Adler, and Jung were part of a major paradigm shift that transformed psychology as well as philosophy, science, medicine, and even the arts. In the 21st century, postmodern constructions of alternative knowledge sources seem to be one of the paradigm shifts most likely to affect the field of psychotherapy. The creation of the self, which so dominated the modernist search for human essence and truth, is being replaced with the concept of socially *storied lives*. Diversity, multiple frameworks, and an integration–collaboration of the knower with the known are all part of this new social movement to enlarge perspectives and options. For some social constructionists the process of "knowing" includes a distrust of the dominant culture positions that permeate families and society today (White & Epston, 1990), and change begins by deconstructing the power of cultural narratives and then proceeds to the co-construction of a new life of meaning. For an example of this method, refer to *Case Approach to Counseling and Psychotherapy* (Corey, 2005, chap. 11) to see how Dr. Jennifer Andrews counsels Ruth from a social constructivist perspective.

There are a number of postmodern perspectives on therapy practice; among the best known are the collaborative language systems approach (Anderson & Goolishian, 1992), solution-focused brief therapy (de Shazer, 1985,

1988, 1991, 1994), solution-oriented therapy (Bertolino & O'Hanlon, 2002; O'Hanlon & Weiner-Davis, 1989), and narrative therapy (White & Epston, 1990). The next section examines the collaborative language systems approach, but the heart of this chapter addresses two of the most significant postmodern approaches: solution-focused brief therapy and narrative therapy.

The Collaborative Language Systems Approach

A relatively unstructured social-constructionist dialogue has been suggested by Harlene Anderson and the late Harold Goolishian (1992) of the Houston Galveston Institute. Rejecting the more therapist-controlled and theory-based interventions of other North American therapeutic approaches, Anderson and Goolishian developed a therapy of *caring* and *being with* the client. Their stance is similar to the person-centered way of being that originated with Carl Rogers. Informed by and contributing to the field of social constructionism, they came to believe human life is constructed in personal and family narratives that maintain both process and meaning in people's lives. These narratives are constructed in social interaction over time. The sociocultural systems in which people live are a product of social interaction, not the other way around. In this sense, therapy is also a system process created in the therapeutic conversations of the client and the listener-facilitator.

When people seek therapy, they are often "stuck" in a dialogic system that has a unique language, meaning, and process related to "the problem." Therapy is another conversational system that becomes therapeutic through its "problem-organizing, problem-dissolving" nature (Anderson & Goolishian, 1992, p. 27). It is therapists' willingness to enter the therapeutic conversation from a "not-knowing" position that facilitates this caring relationship with the client. In the *not-knowing position,* therapists still retain all of the knowledge and personal, experiential capacities they have gained over years of living, but they allow themselves to enter the conversation with curiosity and with an intense interest in discovery. The aim here is to enter a client's world as fully as possible. Clients become the experts who are informing and sharing with the therapist the significant narratives of their lives. The not-knowing position is empathic and is most often characterized by questions that "come from an honest, continuous therapeutic posture of not understanding too quickly" (Anderson, 1993, p. 331).

In this approach the questions the therapist asks are always informed by the answers the client-expert has provided. The therapist enters the session with some sense from referral or intake of what the client wishes to address. The client's answers provide information that stimulates the interest of the therapist, still in a posture of inquiry, and another question proceeds from each answer given. The process is similar to the Socratic method without any preconceived idea about how or in which direction the development of the stories should go. The intent of the conversation is not to confront or challenge the narrative of the client but to facilitate the telling and retelling of the story until opportunities for new meaning and new stories develop: "Telling one's story is a representation of experience; it is constructing history in the present" (Anderson & Goolishian, 1992, p. 37). By staying with the story, the therapist–client conversation evolves into a dialogue of new meaning, constructing new narrative possibilities. The not-knowing position of the therapist has been infused as a key concept of both the solution-focused and the narrative therapeutic approaches.

 # SOLUTION-FOCUSED BRIEF THERAPY

Introduction

Growing out of the strategic therapy orientation at the Mental Research Institute, solution-focused brief therapy (SFBT) shifts the focus from problem solving to a complete focus on solutions. Steve de Shazer (with Insoo Kim Berg) initiated this shift at the Brief Therapy Center in Milwaukee in the late 1970s. Having grown dissatisfied with the constraints of the strategic model, in the 1980s de Shazer collaborated with a number of therapists, including Eve Lipchik, John Walter, Jane Peller, and Michelle Weiner-Davis, who each wrote extensively about solution-focused therapy and started their own solution-focused training institutes. Later Scott Miller joined forces with Insoo Kim Berg (Berg & Miller, 1992; Miller & Berg, 1995), and Weiner-Davis later joined Bill O'Hanlon, who had been trained by Milton Erickson. Together this group of practitioners expanded the foundation originated by de Shazer (Nichols & Schwartz, 2001, 2002).

Key Concepts

Solution-focused brief therapy differs from traditional therapies by eschewing the past in favor of both the present and the future. It is so focused on what is possible that it has little or no interest in gaining an understanding of the problem. De Shazer (1988, 1991) suggests that it is not necessary to know the cause of a problem to solve it and that there is no necessary relationship between problems and their solutions. Gathering information about a problem is not necessary for change to occur. If knowing and understanding problems are unimportant, so is searching for "right" solutions. Any person might consider multiple solutions, and what is right for one person may not be right for others. In solution-focused brief therapy clients choose the goals they wish to accomplish in therapy, and little attention is given to diagnosis, history taking, or exploration of the problem (Bertolino & O'Hanlon, 2002; Gingerich & Eisengart, 2000; O'Hanlon & Weiner-Davis, 1989).

POSITIVE ORIENTATION   Solution-focused brief therapy (SFBT) is grounded on the optimistic assumption that people are healthy and competent and have the ability to construct solutions that can enhance their lives. Regardless of what shape clients are in when they enter therapy, Berg believes clients are competent and that the role of the therapist is to help clients recognize the competencies they possess (as cited in West, Bubenzer, Smith, & Hamm, 1997). The therapeutic process provides a context whereby individuals focus on recovering and creating solutions rather than talking about their problems. O'Hanlon (1994) describes this positive orientation: "grow the solution–life enhancing part of people's lives rather than focus on the pathology–problem parts and amazing changes can happen pretty rapidly" (p. 23).

Because clients often come to therapy in a "problem-oriented" state, even the few solutions they have considered are wrapped in the power of the problem orientation. Clients often have a story that is rooted in a deterministic view that what has happened in their past will certainly shape their future. Solution-focused therapists counter this client presentation with optimistic conversations that highlight their belief in achievable, usable goals that are just around the corner. Therapists can be instrumental in assisting people in making a shift from a fixed problem state to a world with new possibilities. The therapist can encourage and challenge clients to write a different story that can lead to a new ending (O'Hanlon, cited in Bubenzer & West, 1993).

LOOKING FOR WHAT IS WORKING Individuals bring stories to therapy. Some are used to justify their belief that life can't be changed or, worse, that life is moving them further and further away from their goals. Solution-focused brief therapists assist clients in paying attention to the exceptions to their problem patterns (Miller, Hubble, & Duncan, 1996). SFBT focuses on finding out what people are doing that is working and then helps them in applying this knowledge to eliminate problems in the shortest amount of time possible. As O'Hanlon (1999) states: "It encourages people to move out of analyzing the nature of the problem and how it arose and instead to begin to find solutions and take action to solve it" (p. 11).

There are various ways to assist clients in thinking about what has worked for them. De Shazer (1991) prefers to engage clients in conversations that lead to progressive narratives whereby people create situations in which they can make steady gains toward their goals. De Shazer might say, "Tell me about times when you felt a little better and when things were going your way." It is in these stories of life worth living that the power of problems is deconstructed and new solutions are manifest and made possible.

BASIC ASSUMPTIONS GUIDING PRACTICE Walter and Peller (1992, 2000) think of solution-focused therapy as a model that explains how people change and how they can reach their goals. Here are some of their basic assumptions about solution-focused therapy:

■ There are advantages to a positive focus on solutions and on the future. If clients can reorient themselves in the direction of their strengths using solution-talk, there is a good chance therapy can be brief.

- Individuals who come to therapy do have the capability of behaving effectively, even though this effectiveness may be temporarily blocked by negative cognitions. Problem-focused thinking prevents people from recognizing effective ways they have dealt with problems.
- There are exceptions to every problem. By talking about these exceptions, clients can get control over what had seemed to be an insurmountable problem. The climate of these exceptions allows for the possibility of creating solutions.
- Clients often present only one side of themselves. Solution-focused therapists invite clients to examine another side of the story they are presenting.
- Small changes pave the way for larger changes. Any problem is solved one step at a time.
- Clients want to change, have the capacity to change, and are doing their best to make change happen. Therapists should adopt a cooperative stance with clients rather than devising strategies to control resistive patterns.
- Clients can be trusted in their intention to solve their problems. There are no "right" solutions to specific problems that can be applied to all people. Each individual is unique and so, too, is each solution.

Walter and Peller (2000) have moved away from the term *therapy* and refer to what they do as *personal consultation*. They facilitate *conversations* around the preferences and possibilities of their clients to help them create a positive future. By avoiding the stance of the expert, Walter and Peller believe they can be interested, curious, and encouraging in jointly exploring the desires of their clients.

The Therapeutic Process

Bertolino and O'Hanlon (2002) stress the importance of creating collaborative therapeutic relationships and see doing so as necessary for successful therapy. Acknowledging that therapists have expertise in creating a context for change, they stress that clients are the experts on their own lives and often have a good sense of what has or has not worked in the past and, as well, what might work in the future. If clients are involved in the therapeutic process from beginning to end, the chances are increased that therapy will be successful. In short, collaborative and cooperative relationships tend to be more effective than hierarchical relationships in therapy.

Walter and Peller (1992) describe four steps that characterize the process of SFBT: (1) Find out what clients want rather than searching for what they do not want. (2) Do not look for pathology, and do not attempt to reduce clients by giving them a diagnostic label. Instead, look for what clients are doing that is already working and encourage them to continue in that direction. (3) If what clients are doing is not working, then encourage them to experiment with doing something different. (4) Keep therapy brief by approaching each session as if it were the last and only session. Although these steps seem fairly obvious, the collaborative process of the client and therapist constructing solutions is not merely a matter of mastering a few techniques. The solution-focused model requires a philosophical stance of accepting people where they are and assisting them in creating solutions. The attitudes of the therapist are crucial to the effectiveness of the therapeutic process.

De Shazer (1991) believes clients can generally build solutions to their problems without any assessment of the nature of their problems. Given this framework, the structure of solution building differs greatly from traditional approaches to problem solving as can be seen in this brief description of the steps involved (De Jong & Berg, 2002):

1. Clients are given an opportunity to describe their problems. The therapist listens respectfully and carefully as clients answer the therapist's question, "How can I be useful to you?"
2. The therapist works with clients in developing well-formed goals as soon as possible. The question is posed, "What will be different in your life when your problems are solved?"
3. The therapist asks clients about those times when their problems were not present or when the problems were less severe. Clients are assisted in exploring these exceptions, with special emphasis on what they did to make these events happen.
4. At the end of each solution-building conversation, the therapist offers clients summary feedback, provides encouragement, and suggests what clients might observe or do before the next session to further solve their problem.
5. The therapist and clients evaluate the progress being made in reaching satisfactory solutions by using a ratings scale. Clients are also asked what needs to be done before they see their problem as being solved and also what will be their next step.

THERAPEUTIC GOALS   SFBT reflects some basic notions about change, about interaction, and about reaching goals. The solution-focused therapist believes people have the ability to define meaningful personal goals and that they have the resources required to solve their problems. Goals are unique to each client and are constructed by the client to create a richer future (Prochaska & Norcross, 2003). A lack of clarity regarding client preferences, goals, and desired outcomes can result in a rift between therapist and client. Thus, it is essential that the initial stages of therapy address what clients want and what concerns they are willing to explore (Bertolino & O'Hanlon, 2002).

Solution-focused therapists concentrate on small, realistic, achievable changes that may lead to additional positive outcomes. Because success tends to build upon itself, modest goals are viewed as the beginning of change. Solution-focused practitioners join with the language of their clients, using similar words, pacing, and tone. Therapists use questions such as these that presuppose change, posit multiple answers, and remain goal-directed and future-oriented: "What did you do and what has changed since last time?" or "What did you notice that went better?" (Bubenzer & West, 1993).

Walter and Peller (1992) emphasize the importance of assisting clients in creating well-defined goals that are (1) stated in the positive in the client's language, (2) are process or action-oriented, (3) are structured in the here-and-now, (4) are attainable, concrete and specific, and (5) are controlled by the client. However, Walter and Peller (2000) caution against too rigidly imposing an agenda of getting precise goals before clients have a chance to express their concerns. Clients must first feel that their concerns are heard and understood before they can formulate meaningful personal goals. In a therapist's zeal to be solution-focused, it is possible to get lost in the mechanics of therapy and not attend sufficiently to the interpersonal aspects.

In SFBT, there are several forms of goals: changing the viewing of a situation or a frame of reference; changing the doing of the problematic situation; and tapping client strengths and resources (O'Hanlon & Weiner-Davis, 1989). A main goal of SFBT involves helping clients adopt an attitudinal and a language shift from talking about problems to talking about solutions. Clients are encouraged to engage in change- or solution-talk, rather than problem-talk, on the assumption that what we talk about most will be what we produce. Talking about problems will produce ongoing problems. Talk about change will produce change. As soon as individuals learn to speak in terms of what they are able to do competently, what resources and strengths they have, and what they have already done that has worked, they have accomplished the main aim of therapy (Nichols & Schwartz, 2001, 2002).

THERAPIST'S FUNCTIONS AND ROLES   Clients are much more likely to fully participate in the therapeutic process if they perceive themselves as determining the direction and purpose of the conversation (Walter & Peller, 1996). Much of what the therapeutic process is about involves clients' thinking about their future and what they want to be different in their lives. Solution-focused brief therapists adopt a "not knowing" position as a route to putting clients into the position of being the experts about their own lives. Therapists do not assume that they know by virtue of their expert frame of reference the significance of the client's actions and experiences (Anderson & Goolishian, 1992). This model casts the role and functions of a therapist in quite a different light from traditionally oriented therapists who view themselves as experts in assessment and treatment.

Therapists strive to create collaborative relationships because of their belief that doing so opens up a range of possibilities for present and future change (Bertolino & O'Hanlon, 2002). Therapists create a climate of mutual respect, dialogue, inquiry, and affirmation in which clients are free to create, explore, and co-author their evolving stories (Walter & Peller, 1996). The main therapeutic task consists of helping clients imagine how they would like things to be different and what it will take to bring about these changes (Gingerich & Eisengart, 2000). Some of the questions that Walter and Peller (2000, p. 43) find useful are "What do you want from coming here?" "How would that make a difference to you?" and "What might be some signs to you that the changes you want are happening?"

THE THERAPEUTIC RELATIONSHIP   As with any other therapy orientation, the quality of the relationship between therapist and client is a determining factor in the outcomes of SFBT. It is essential to create a sense of trust so clients will return for further sessions and will follow through on homework suggestions (De Jong & Berg, 2002). SFBT is designed to be brief, so the therapist must shift the focus as soon as possible from talking about problems to exploring solutions. Indeed, one way of creating an effective therapeutic partnership is for the therapist to show clients how they can use the strengths and resources they already have to construct solutions.

De Shazer (1988) has described three kinds of relationships that may develop between therapists and their clients:

1. *Customer:* the client and therapist jointly identify a problem and a solution to work toward. The client realizes that to attain his or her goals, personal effort will be required.
2. *Complainant:* the client describes a problem but is not able or willing to assume a role in constructing a solution, believing that a solution is dependent on someone else's actions. In this situation, the client generally expects the therapist to change the other person to whom the client attributes the problem.
3. *Visitor:* the client who comes to therapy because someone else (a spouse, parent, teacher, probation officer) thinks the client has a problem. This client may not agree that he or she has a problem and may be unable to identify anything to explore in therapy.

De Jong and Berg (2002) recommend using caution so that therapists do not box clients into static identities. Rather than categorizing clients, therapists can reflect on the kinds of relationships that are developing between their clients and themselves. For example, clients (complainants) who tend to place the cause of their problems on another person or persons in their lives may be helped by skilled intervention to begin to see their own role in their problems and the necessity for taking active steps in creating solutions. A visitor client may be willing to work with the therapist to create a customer relationship by exploring what the client needs to do to satisfy the other person or "get them off their back." Initially, some clients will feel powerless and overwhelmed by their problems. Even clients who are unable to articulate a problem may change as the result of developing an effective therapeutic alliance. How the therapist responds to different behaviors of clients has a lot to do with bringing about a shift in the relationship. In short, both complainants and visitors have the capacity for becoming customers.

Application: Therapeutic Techniques and Procedures

PRETHERAPY CHANGE   Simply scheduling an appointment often sets positive change in motion. During the initial therapy session, it is common for solution-focused therapists to ask, "What have you done since you called for the appointment that has made a difference in your problem?" (de Shazer, 1985, 1988). By asking about such changes, the therapist can elicit, evoke, and amplify what clients have already done by way of making positive change. These changes cannot be attributed to the therapy process itself, so asking about them tends to encourage clients to rely less on their therapist and more on their own resources to accomplish their treatment goals (Bertolino & O'Hanlon, 2002; McKeel, 1996).

EXCEPTION QUESTIONS   SFBT is based on the notion that there were times in clients' lives when the problems they identify were not problematic. These times are called *exceptions* and represent *news of difference* (Bateson, 1972). Solution-focused therapists ask *exception questions* to direct clients to times when the problem did not exist. Exceptions are those past experiences in a client's life when it would be reasonable to have expected the problem to occur, but somehow it did not (de Shazer, 1985). This exploration reminds clients that problems are not all-powerful and have not existed forever; it also provides a field of opportunity for evoking resources, engaging strengths, and positing possible solutions. The therapist asks clients what has to happen for these exceptions to occur more often. In solution-focused vocabulary, this is called *change-talk* (Andrews & Clark, 1996).

THE MIRACLE QUESTION   Therapy goals are developed by using what de Shazer (1985, 1988) calls the *miracle question*. The therapists asks, "If a miracle happened and the problem you have was solved overnight, how would you know it was solved, and what would be different?" Clients are then encouraged to enact "what would be different" in spite of perceived problems. If a client asserts that she wants to feel more confident and secure, the therapist might say: "Let yourself imagine that you leave the office today and that you are on track to acting more confidently and securely. What will you be *doing* differently?" This process of considering hypothetical solutions reflects O'Hanlon and Weiner-Davis's (1989) belief that changing the *doing* and *viewing* of the perceived problem changes the problem.

De Jong and Berg (2002) identify a number of reasons the miracle question is a useful technique. Asking clients to consider that a miracle takes place opens up a range of future possibilities. Clients are encouraged to allow themselves to dream as a way of identifying the kinds of changes they most want. This question has a future focus in that clients can begin to consider a different kind of life that is not dominated by a particular problem. This intervention shifts the emphasis from both past and current problems toward a more satisfying life in the future.

SCALING QUESTIONS   Solution-focused therapists also use *scaling questions* when change in human experiences are not easily observed, such as feelings, moods, or communication. For example, a woman reporting feelings of panic or anxiety might be asked: "On a scale of zero to 10, with zero being how you felt when you first came to therapy and 10 being how you feel the day after your miracle occurs and your problem is gone, how would you rate your anxiety right now?" Even if the client has only moved away from zero to one, she has improved. How did she do that? What does she need to do to move another number up the scale? Scaling questions enable clients to pay closer attention to what they are doing and how they can take steps that will lead to the changes they desire. This technique can be creatively applied to tap clients' perceptions about a wide range of experiences, including "self-esteem, pre-session change, self-confidence, investment in change, willingness to work hard to bring about desired changes, prioritizing of problems to be solved, perception of hopefulness, and evaluation of progress" (Berg, 1994, pp. 102–103).

FORMULA FIRST SESSION TASK   The formula first session task (FFST) is a form of homework a therapist might give clients to complete between their first and second sessions. The therapist might say: "Between now and the next time we meet, I would like you to observe, so that you can describe to me next time, what happens in your (family, life, marriage, relationship) that you want to continue to have happen" (de Shazer, 1985, p. 137). At the second session, clients can be asked what they observed and what they would like to happen in the future. According to de Shazer, this intervention tends to increase clients' optimism and hope about their situation. Clients generally cooperate with the FFST and report change or improvements since their first session (McKeel, 1996; Walter & Peller, 2000). Bertolino and O'Hanlon (2002) suggest that the FFST intervention be used after clients have had a chance to express their present concerns, views, and stories. It is important that clients feel understood before they are directed to make changes.

THERAPIST FEEDBACK TO CLIENTS   Solution-focused practitioners generally take a break of 5 to 10 minutes toward the end of each session to compose a summary message for clients. During this break therapists formulate feedback that will be given to clients after the break. De Jong and Berg (2002) describe three basic parts to the structure of the summary feedback: compliments, a bridge, and suggesting a task. *Compliments* are genuine affirmations of what clients are already doing that is leading toward effective solutions. These compliments, which are a form of encouragement, create hope and convey the expectation to clients that they can achieve their goals by drawing on their strengths and successes. Second, a *bridge* links the initial compliments to the suggested tasks that will be given. The bridge provides the rationale for the suggestions. The third aspect of feedback consists of *suggesting tasks* to clients, which can be considered as homework. Observational tasks ask clients to simply pay attention to some aspect of their lives. This self-monitoring process helps clients note the differences when things are better, especially what was different about the way they thought, felt, or behaved. Behavioral tasks require that clients actually do something the therapist believes would be useful to them in constructing solutions.

TERMINATING   From the very first solution-focused interview, the therapist is mindful of working toward termination. Once clients are able to construct a satisfactory solution, the therapeutic relationship can be terminated. The initial goal-formation question that a therapist often asks is, "What needs to be different in your life as a result of coming here for you to say that meeting with me was worthwhile?" Another question to get clients thinking is, "When the problem is solved, what will you be doing differently?" Through the use of scaling questions, therapists can assist clients in monitoring their progress and eventually determining when they no longer need to come to therapy (De Jong & Berg, 2002). Prior to ending therapy, therapists assist clients in identifying things they can do to continue the changes they have already made into the future (Bertolino & O'Hanlon, 2002). Clients can also be helped to identify hurdles or perceived barriers that could get in the way of maintaining the changes they have made.

Because this model of therapy is brief, present-centered, and addresses specific complaints, it is very possible that clients will experience other developmental concerns at a later time. Clients can ask for additional sessions whenever they feel a need to get their life back on track or to update their story. Dr. David Clark illustrates assessment and treatment from a solution-focused brief therapy approach in the case of Ruth in *Case Approach to Counseling and Psychotherapy* (Corey, 2005, chap. 11).

 # NARRATIVE THERAPY

Introduction

Of all the social constructionists, Michael White and David Epston (1990) are best known for their use of narrative in therapy. According to White (1992), individuals construct the meaning of life in interpretive stories, which are then treated as "truth." Because of the power of dominant culture narratives, individuals tend to internalize the messages from dominant discourses and form their identity around the positions to live from that these messages offer—even if those positions are not useful to the individual. Like those who identify themselves with feminist therapy, White believes a dominant discourse functions to perpetuate viewpoints, processes, and stories that serve those who benefit from that culture but that may work against the agency and life opportunity of the individual.

Adopting a postmodern, narrative, social constructionist view sheds light on how power, knowledge, and "truth" are negotiated in families and other social and cultural contexts (Freedman & Combs, 1996). Therapy is, in part, a reestablishment of personal agency from the oppression of external problems and the dominant stories of larger systems.

Key Concepts

The key concepts and therapeutic process sections are adapted from several different works, but primarily from these sources: Winslade and Monk (1999),

Monk (1997), Winslade, Crocket, and Monk (1997), McKenzie and Monk (1997), and Freedman and Combs (1996).

FOCUS OF NARRATIVE THERAPY   The narrative approach involves adopting a shift in focus from most traditional theories. Therapists are encouraged to establish a collaborative approach with a special interest in listening to clients' stories; to search for times in clients' lives when they were resourceful (for example, lived alternative stories); to use questions as a way to engage clients and facilitate their exploration; to avoid diagnosing and labeling clients or accepting a totalizing description based on a problem; to assist clients in mapping the influence a problem has had on their lives; and to assist clients in separating themselves from the dominant stories they have internalized so that space can be opened for the creation of alternative life stories (Freedman & Combs, 1996).

THE ROLE OF STORIES   We live our lives by stories we tell about ourselves and that others tell about us. These stories actually shape reality in that they construct and constitute what we see, feel, and do. The stories we live by grow out of conversations in a social and cultural context. Therapy clients do not assume the role of pathologized victims who are leading hopeless and pathetic lives; rather, they emerge as courageous victors who have vivid stories to recount. The stories not only change the person telling the story but also change the therapist who is privileged be a part of this unfolding process (Monk, 1997).

LISTENING WITH AN OPEN MIND   All social constructionist theories place an emphasis on listening to clients without judgment or blame, affirming and valuing them. Lindsley (1994) emphasizes that therapists can encourage their clients to reconsider absolutist judgments by moving toward seeing both "good" and "bad" elements in situations. Narrative therapists make efforts to enable clients to modify painful beliefs, values, and interpretations without imposing their value systems and interpretations. They want to create meaning and new possibilities from the stories clients share rather than out of a preconceived and ultimately imposed theory of importance and value.

Although narrative therapists bring to the therapy venture certain attitudes such as optimism, respectful curiosity and persistence, and a valuing for the client's knowledge, they are able to listen to the problem-saturated story of the client without getting stuck. As narrative therapists listen to the client's story, they stay alert for details that give evidence of the client's competence in taking stands against oppressive problems. Winslade and Monk (1999) capture this notion:

> Persistent questioning and close listening are needed to bring into focus easily discounted or overlooked details of competence or achievement. The counselor needs to maintain a faith that these competencies can be identified, even at times when the client is having difficulty seeing them. (p. 10)

During the narrative conversation, attention is given to avoiding *totalizing language*, which reduces the complexity of the individual by assigning an all-embracing, single description to the essence of the person. Therapists begin to separate the person from the problem in their mind as they listen and respond (Winslade & Monk, 1999).

The narrative perspective focuses on the capacity of humans for creative and imaginative thought. The narrative practitioner never assumes that he or she knows more about the lives of clients than they do. Clients are the primary interpreters of their own experiences. The narrative practitioner views people as active agents who are able to derive meaning out of their experiential world. Thus, the process of change can be facilitated, but not directed, by the therapist.

The Therapeutic Process

This brief overview of the steps in the narrative therapeutic process illustrates the structure of the narrative approach (O'Hanlon, 1994, pp. 25–26):

- Collaborate with the client to come up with a mutually acceptable name for the problem.
- Personify the problem and attribute oppressive intentions and tactics to it.
- Investigate how the problem has been disrupting, dominating, or discouraging to the client.
- Invite the client to see his or her story from a different perspective by offering alternative meanings for events.
- Discover moments when the client wasn't dominated or discouraged by the problem by searching for exceptions to the problem.
- Find historical evidence to bolster a new view of the client as competent enough to have stood up to, defeated, or escaped from the dominance or oppression of the problem. (At this phase the person's identity and life story begin to get rewritten.)
- Ask the client to speculate about what kind of future could be expected from the strong, competent person that is emerging. As the client becomes free of problem-saturated stories of the past, he or she can envision and plan for a less problematic future.
- Find or create an audience for perceiving and supporting the new story. It is not enough to recite a new story. The client needs to live the new story outside of therapy. Because the person's problem initially developed in a social context, it is essential to involve the social environment in supporting the new life story that has emerged in the conversations with the therapist.

Winslade and Monk (1999) stress that narrative conversations do not follow the linear progression described here; it is better to think of these steps in terms of cyclical progression.

THERAPY GOALS   A general goal of narrative therapy is to invite people to describe their experience in new and fresh language. In doing this, they open up new vistas of what is possible. This new language enables clients to develop new meanings for problematic thoughts, feelings, and behaviors (Freedman & Combs, 1996). Narrative therapy almost always includes an awareness of the impact of various aspects of dominant culture on human life. Narrative practitioners seek to enlarge the perspective and focus and facilitate the discovery or creation of new options that are unique to the people they see.

THERAPIST'S FUNCTION AND ROLE   Narrative therapists are active facilitators. The concepts of care, interest, respectful curiosity, openness, empathy, contact, and even fascination are seen as a relational necessity. The not-knowing position, which allows therapists to follow, affirm, and be guided by the stories of their clients, creates participant-observer and process-facilitator roles for the therapist and integrates therapy with a postmodern view of human inquiry.

A main task of the therapist is to help clients construct a preferred story line. The narrative therapist adopts a stance characterized by respectful curiosity and works with clients to explore both the impact of the problem on them and what they are doing to reduce the effects of the problem (Winslade & Monk, 1999). One of the main functions of the therapist is to ask questions of clients and, based on the answers, generate further questions.

White and Epston (1990) start with an exploration of the client in relation to the presenting problem. It is not uncommon for clients to present initial stories in which they and the problem are fused, as if one and the same. White uses questions aimed at separating the problem from the people affected by the problem. This shift in language begins the deconstruction of the original narrative in which the people and the problem were fused; now the problem is objectified as external to them.

Like the solution-focused therapist, the narrative therapist assumes the client is the expert when it comes to what he or she wants in life. The narrative therapist tends to avoid using language that embodies diagnosis, assessment, and intervention. Functions such as diagnosis and assessment often grant priority to the practitioner's "truth" over clients' knowledge about their own lives. The narrative approach gives emphasis to understanding clients' lived experiences and de-emphasizes efforts to predict, interpret, and pathologize. Narrative practitioners are careful not to ascribe the major role of taking initiative in another person's life or usurping the agency (power) of the client in bringing about change (Winslade, Crocket, & Monk, 1997).

THE THERAPEUTIC RELATIONSHIP   Narrative therapists place great importance on the qualities a therapist brings to the therapy venture. Some of these attitudes include optimism and respect, curiosity and persistence, valuing the client's knowledge, and creating a special kind of relationship characterized by a real power-sharing dialogue (Winslade & Monk, 1999). Collaboration, compassion, reflection, and discovery characterize the therapeutic relationship.

If this relationship is to be truly collaborative, the therapist needs to be aware of how power manifests itself in his or her professional practice. This does not mean that the therapist does not have authority as a professional. He or she uses this authority, however, by treating clients as experts in their own lives.

Winslade, Crocket, and Monk (1997) describe this collaboration as co-authoring or sharing authority. Clients function as authors when they have the authority to speak on their own behalf. In the narrative approach, the therapist-as-expert is replaced by the client-as-expert. This notion challenges the stance of the therapist as being an all-wise and all-knowing expert. Winslade, Crocket, and Monk call for the client to become the senior partner in this relationship: "The idea of coauthoring challenges the portrayal of counselors as followers, who must be very cautious about treading on the toes of clients lest some emergent buds of those clients' true inner nature be prevented from flowering" (p. 54).

Clients are often stuck in a pattern of living a problem-saturated story that does not work. The therapist enters this dialogue and asks questions in an effort to elicit the perspectives, resources, and unique experiences of clients. The past is history, but it sometimes provides a foundation for understanding and discovering differences or unique outcomes that will make a difference. It is the present and the future, however, in which life will be lived. The narrative therapist supplies the optimism and sometimes a process, but the client generates what is possible and contributes the movement that actualizes it.

Application: Therapeutic Techniques and Procedures

The effective application of narrative therapy is more dependent on therapists' attitudes or perspectives than on techniques. In the practice of narrative therapy, there is no recipe, no set agenda, and no formula that the therapist can follow to assure positive results (Drewery & Winslade, 1997). When externalizing questions are approached mainly as a technique, the intervention will be shallow, forced, and unlikely to produce significant therapeutic effects (Freedman & Combs, 1996; O'Hanlon, 1994). If counseling is done using a formula approach, clients are likely to feel that things are being done to them and feel left out of the conversation (Monk, 1997).

Narrative therapists are in close agreement with the position of Carl Rogers who stresses the therapist's way of being as opposed to being technique driven. A narrative approach to counseling is more than the application of skills; it is based on the therapist's personal characteristics that create a climate that encourages clients to see their stories from different perspectives. The approach is also an expression of an ethical stance, which is grounded in a philosophical framework. It is from this conceptual framework that practices are applied to assist clients in finding new meanings and new possibilities in their lives (Winslade & Monk, 1999).

QUESTIONS—AND MORE QUESTIONS   The questions narrative therapists ask may seem embedded in a unique conversation, part of a dialogue about earlier dialogues, a discovery of unique events, or an exploration of dominant culture processes and imperatives. Whatever the purpose, the questions are often circular, or relational, and they seek to empower clients in new ways. To use Gregory Bateson's (1972) famous phrase, they are questions in search of a difference that will make a difference. Bateson argued that we learn by comparing one phenomenon with another and discovering what he called "the news of difference."

Narrative therapists use questions as a way to generate experience rather than to gather information. The aim of questioning is to progressively discover or construct the client's experience so that the therapist has a sense of what direction to pursue. Questions are always asked from a position of respect, curiosity, and openness. Therapists ask questions from a not-knowing position, meaning that they do not pose questions that they think they already know the answers to. Monk (1997) describes this stance as follows:

> In contrast to the normative, knowing stance, a narrative way of working invites the counselor to take up the investigative, exploratory, archaeological position. She demonstrates to the client that being a counselor does not imply any privileged access to the truth. The counselor is consistently in the role of seeking understanding of the client's experience. (p. 25)

Therapists using a narrative approach want to take apart, or deconstruct, the discourse that supports a problem's existence. Through the process of asking questions, therapists provide clients with an opportunity to explore various dimensions of their life situations. Doing this helps bring out the unstated cultural assumptions that contribute to the original construction of the problem. The therapist is interested in finding out how the problems first became evident, and how they have affected clients' views of themselves (Monk, 1997). Narrative therapists attempt to engage people in deconstructing problem-saturated stories, identifying preferred directions, and creating alternative stories that support these preferred directions (Freedman & Combs, 1996).

EXTERNALIZATION AND DECONSTRUCTION   Narrative therapists differ from many traditional therapists in believing it is not the person that is the problem, but the problem that is the problem. Living life means relating to problems, not being fused with them. Problems and problem-saturated stories have an impact on people and can dominate living in extremely negative ways. Assumptions about a problem that are uncritically accepted restrict opportunities for both client and therapist to explore new possibilities for change (McKenzie & Monk, 1997). Narrative therapists help clients deconstruct these problematic stories by disassembling the taken-for-granted assumptions that are made about an event, which then opens alternative possibilities for living (Bertolino & O'Hanlon, 2002; Winslade & Monk, 1999).

Externalization is one process for deconstructing the power of a narrative and separating the person from identifying with the problem and sometimes giving it a name. White (1992) proposes an objectification of the problems for which people seek therapy rather than an objectification of the person through assigning a totalizing description such as a personality disorder. When clients view themselves as "being" the problem, they are limited in the ways they can effectively deal with the problem. The impact of this subtle language shift enables clients to experience the problem as being located outside of themselves. Instead of being the problem, the individual has a relationship with the problem. For example, there is quite a difference between labeling someone an alcoholic and indicating that alcohol has invaded his or her life. Separating the problem from the individual facilitates hope and enables clients to take a stand against specific story lines, such as self-blame. By understanding the cultural invitations to blame oneself, clients can deconstruct this story line and generate a more positive, healing story.

Most clients have probably not identified the full effects of a problem story, perhaps because of their fear of being overwhelmed by their difficulties. The method used to separate the person from the problem is referred to as *externalizing conversations*. This method is particularly useful when people have diagnoses and labels that have not been validating or empowering of the change process (Bertolino & O'Hanlon, 2002). Externalizing conversations counteract oppressive, problem-saturated stories, and empower clients to feel competent to handle the problems they face. Two ways of structuring externalizing conversations are (1) to map the influence of the problem in the person's life, or (2) to map the influence of the person's life on the development of the problem (McKenzie & Monk, 1997).

Mapping the influence of the problem on the person generates a great deal of useful information and often results in people feeling less shamed and blamed. People feel listened to and understood when the problem influences are explored in a systematic fashion. When this mapping is done carefully, it lays the foundation for co-authoring a new story line for the client. A common question is, "When did this problem first appear in your life?" The job of the therapist is to assist clients in tracing the problem from when it originated to the present. Therapists put a future twist on the problem by asking, "If the problem were to continue for a month (or any time period), what would this mean for you?" This question can motivate the client to join with the therapist in combating the impact of the problem's effects.

Mapping the effects of the person's life on the development of the problem often results in the client becoming aware that the problem has not completely dominated his or her life. There have been some instances when the client dealt effectively with the problem. This kind of mapping can help the client who is disillusioned by the problem see some hope for a different kind of life. Therapists look for these "sparkling moments" as they engage in externalizing conversations with clients (White & Epston, 1990).

The case of Brandon illustrates an externalizing conversation. Brandon says that he gets angry far too much, especially when he feels that his wife is criticizing him unjustly: "I just flare! I pop off, get upset, fight back. Later, I wish I hadn't, but it's too late. I've messed up again." Although questions about how his anger occurs, complete with specific examples and events, will help chart the influence of the problem, it is really questions like these that *externalize* the problem: "What is the mission of the anger, and how does it recruit you into this mission?" "How does the anger get you, and how does it trick you into letting it become so powerful?" "What does the anger require of you, and what happens to you when you meet its requirements?"

SEARCH FOR UNIQUE OUTCOMES   In the narrative approach, externalizing questions are followed by questions searching for unique outcomes. The therapist talks to the client about moments of choice or success regarding the problem. This is done by selecting for attention any experience that stands apart from the problem story, regardless of how insignificant it might seem to the client. The therapist may ask: "Was there ever a time in which anger wanted to take you over, and you resisted? What was that like for you? How did you do it?" These questions are aimed at highlighting moments when the problem has not occurred or when the problem has been dealt with successfully. Unique outcomes can often be found in the past or the present, but they can also be hypothesized for the future: "What form would standing up against your anger take?" Exploring questions such as these enables clients to see that change is possible. It is within the account of unique outcomes that a gateway is provided for alternative territories of a person's life (White, 1992).

Following the description of a unique event, White (1992) suggests posing questions, both direct and indirect, that lead to more clearly declared narratives:

- What do you think this tells me about what you have wanted for your life and about what you have been trying for in your life?
- How do you think knowing this has affected my view of you as a person?
- Of all those people who have known you, who would be least surprised that you have been able to take this step in challenging the problem's influence in your life?
- What actions might you commit yourself to if you were to more fully embrace this knowledge of who you are? (p. 133)

The development of unique outcome stories into solution stories is facilitated by what Epston and White (1992) call "circulation questions":

- Now that you have reached this point in life, who else should know about it?
- I guess there are a number of people who have an outdated view of who you are as a person. What ideas do you have about updating these views?
- If other people seek therapy for the same reasons you did, can I share with them any of the important discoveries you have made? (p. 23)

These questions are not asked in a barrage-like manner. Questioning is an integral part of the context of the narrative conversation, and each question is sensitively attuned to the responses brought out by the previous question (White, 1992).

McKenzie and Monk (1997) suggest that therapists seek permission from the client before asking a series of questions. By letting a client know that they do not have answers to the questions they raise, therapists are putting the client in control of the therapeutic process. Asking permission of the client to use persistent questioning tends to minimize the risk of inadvertently pressuring the client.

ALTERNATIVE STORIES AND RE-AUTHORING

Constructing new stories goes hand in hand with deconstruction, and the narrative therapist listens for openings to new stories. People can continually and actively re-author their lives, and narrative therapists invite clients to author alternative stories through "unique outcomes" or something not predicted by the problem-saturated story (Freedman & Combs, 1996). The narrative therapist asks for openings: "Have you ever been able to escape the influence of the problem?" The therapist listens for clues to competence in the midst of a problematic story and builds a story of competence around it.

A turning point in the narrative interview comes when clients make the choice of whether to continue to live by a problem-saturated story or create an alternative story (Winslade & Monk, 1999). Through the use of unique possibility questions, the therapist moves the focus into the future. For example: "Given what you have learned about yourself, what is the next step you might take? When you are acting from your preferred identity, what actions will it lead you to do more of?" Such questions encourage people to reflect upon what they have presently achieved and what their next steps might be.

The therapist works with clients collaboratively by helping them construct more coherent and comprehensive stories (Neimeyer, 1993). Whether involved in a free-flowing conversation or engaged in a series of questions in a relatively consistent process, the narrative therapist seeks to elicit new possibilities and embed them in the life narratives and processes of the people they serve. White and Epston's (1990) inquiry into unique events is similar to the exception questions of solution-focused therapists. Both seek to build on the competence already present in the person. The development of alternative stories, or narratives, is an enactment of ultimate hope: Today is the first day of the rest of your life.

DOCUMENTING THE EVIDENCE

Narrative practitioners believe that new stories take hold only when there is an audience to appreciate and support them. Thus, an appreciative audience to new developments is consciously sought out. Gaining an audience for the news that change is taking place needs to occur if alternative stories are to stay alive (Andrews & Clark, 1996).

One technique for consolidating the gains a client makes is by writing letters. Narrative letters written by the therapist record the session and may include an externalizing description of the problem and its influence on the client as well as an account of the client's strengths and abilities identified in a session. The letter highlights the struggle the client has had with the problem and draws distinctions between the problem-saturated story and the developing new and preferred story (McKenzie & Monk, 1997). These letters are frequently mailed to clients between sessions (Andrews, Clark, & Baird, 1997).

Epston has developed a special facility for carrying on therapeutic dialogues between sessions through the use of letters (White & Epston, 1990).

His letters may be long, chronicling the process of the interview and the agreements reached, or short, highlighting a meaning or understanding reached in the session and asking a question that has occurred to him since the end of the previous therapy visit. These letters are also used to encourage clients, noting their strengths and accomplishments in relation to handling problems or noting the meaning of their accomplishments for others in their community. Winslade and Monk (1999) note that letters documenting the changes clients have achieved tend to strengthen the significance of the changes, both for the client and for others in the client's life.

David Nylund, a clinical social worker, uses narrative letters as a basic part of his practice. Nylund describes a conceptual framework he has found useful in structuring letters to his clients (Nylund & Thomas, 1994):

- The introductory paragraph reconnects the client to the previous therapy session.
- Statements summarize the influence the problem has had and is having on the client.
- Questions the therapist thought about after the session may be posed to the client. Questions may pertain to the alternative story that is developing.
- The letter documents unique outcomes or exceptions to the problematic story that emerged during the session. At times, direct quotes of the client are used.

Nylund and Thomas (1994) contend that narrative letters reinforce the importance of carrying what is being learned in the therapy office to everyday life. The message conveyed is that participating fully in the world is more important than being in the therapy office. In an informal survey of the perceptions of the value of narrative letters by past clients, the average worth of a letter was equal to more than three individual sessions. This finding is consistent with McKenzie and Monk's (1997) statement: "Some narrative counselors have suggested that a well-composed letter following a therapy session or preceding another can be equal to about five regular sessions" (p. 113). Narrative letters seem to have a maximum impact in the least number of sessions.

This section, and much of the chapter thus far, addresses therapeutic techniques used by narrative and solution-focused therapists. As you have seen, the emphasis on these approaches is on people's strengths and resources—psychologically, emotionally, socially, and spiritually. The therapeutic process is characterized by collaboration, respect for the client's ability to change, and creating a context that allows for the emergence of new possibilities for living. Refer to *Case Approach to Counseling and Psychotherapy* (Corey, 2005, chap. 11) for a concrete example of a narrative therapist's way of working with many of these techniques as Dr. Gerald Monk counsels Ruth. In the following section, some of the concepts and therapeutic procedures from the solution-focused and narrative approaches are applied to a particular client—Stan.

Postmodern Approaches Applied to the Case of Stan

This therapist operates from an integrative perspective by combining concepts and techniques from the solution-focused and narrative approaches. She believes Stan is the expert on his life and that he has the internal and external resources he needs to make the kind of changes he is seeking. She views her expertise as constructing questions that will assist Stan in discovering more choices and in accomplishing his goals.

As a therapist who functions within the framework of a postmodern orientation, she is philosophically opposed to assessment and diagnosis using the DSM-IV-TR model. It is her belief that such classification promotes an orientation toward inadequacy and personal failure rather than toward solutions and attention to resources and competence. Thus, she does not begin therapy with a formal assessment leading to diagnostic categorizing. She does, however, involve Stan as a collaborator in an ongoing assessment from the beginning to the end of the therapeutic process. Rather than simply ask Stan questions about his history, the therapist engages him in collaborative conversations centering around change, competence, preferences, possibilities, and ideas for making changes in the future.

The therapist begins her work with Stan by inviting him to tell her about the concerns that brought him to therapy and what he expects to accomplish in his sessions. She also provides Stan with a brief orientation of some of the basic ideas that guide her practice and describes her view of counseling as a collaborative partnership in which he is the senior partner. She explains her view of the therapy process and how it works. Stan is somewhat surprised by this because he expected that she was the person with the experience and expertise. He informs her that he has very little confidence in knowing how to proceed with his life, especially since he has "messed up" so often. The therapist notes that he has self-doubts when it comes to assuming the role of senior partner. However, she works to demystify the therapeutic process and establish a collaborative relationship, conveying to Stan that he is in charge of the direction his therapy will take.

Soon after this orientation to how therapy works, the therapist inquires about some specific goals that Stan would like to reach through the therapy sessions. Stan gives clear signs that he is willing and even eager to change. However, he adds that he suffers from low self-esteem. The therapist begins to focus Stan on looking for exceptions to the problem of low self-esteem. She poses an exception question (solution-focused therapy): "What is different about the contexts or times when you have not experienced low self-esteem?" Stan is able to identify some positive characteristics: his courage, his determination, his willingness to try new things in spite of his self-doubts, and his gift for working with children. Stan knows what he wants out of therapy and has clear goals: to achieve his educational goals, to enhance his belief in himself, to relate to women without fear, and to feel more joy instead of sadness and anxiety. The therapist invites Stan to talk more about how he has managed to make the gains he has in spite of struggling with the problem of self-doubt and low self-esteem.

The therapist allows Stan to share his problem-saturated story, but she does not get stuck in this narrative. She invites Stan to think of his problems as external to the core of his selfhood. Even during the early sessions, the therapist encourages Stan to separate his being from his problems by posing questions that externalize his problem.

Stan presents several problems that are of concern to him. The therapist gets him to zero in on one particular problem that he wants to address. Stan says he is depressed a great deal of the time, and he worries that his depression might someday swallow him up. After listening to Stan's fears and concerns, the therapist asks Stan the miracle question (solution-focused technique): "Let's suppose that a miracle were to happen while you are asleep tonight. When you wake up tomorrow, the problems you are mentioning are totally solved. What would be the signs to you that this miracle actually occurred and that your problems were solved? How would your life be different?" With this intervention, the therapist is shifting the focus from talking about problems to talking about solutions. She explains to Stan that much of his therapy will deal with finding both present and future solutions rather than dwelling on past problems. Together they engage in a conversation about the value of change-talk rather than problem-talk.

To a great extent, Stan has linked his identity with his problems, especially depression. He rarely thinks of his problems as being separate from himself. The therapist wants Stan to realize that he personally is not his problem, but instead that the problem is the problem. When the therapist asks Stan to give a name to his problem, he eventually comes up with "Disabling depression!" He then relates how his depression has kept him from functioning the way he would like in many areas of his life. She then uses externalizing questions (narrative technique) as a way to separate Stan from his problem: "How long has depression gotten the best of you?" "Have there been times when you stood up to depression and did not let it win?" "What has depression cost you?" Of course, Stan's therapist briefly explains to him what she is doing by using externalizing language, lest he think this is a strange way to counsel. She talks more about the advantages of engaging in externalizing conversations. She also talks with Stan about the importance of mapping the effects of the problem on his life. This process involves exploring how long the problem has been around, the extent to which the problem has influenced various aspects of his life, and how deeply the problem continues to affect him.

As the sessions progress, there is a collaborative effort aimed at investigating how the problem has been a disrupting, dominating, and discouraging influence. Stan is invited to see his story from a different perspective. The therapist continues talking with Stan about those moments when he has not been dominated or discouraged by depression and anxiety and continues to search for exceptions to these problematic experiences. Stan and his therapist participate in conversations about unique outcomes, or occasions when he has demonstrated courage and persistence in the face of discouraging events. Some of these "sparkling moments" include Stan's accomplishments in college, volunteer work with children, progress in curbing his tendencies to abuse alcohol, willingness to challenge his fears and make new acquaintances, talking back to self-defeating internal messages, accomplishments in securing employment, and his willingness to create a vision of a productive future.

With his therapist's help, Stan accumulates evidence from his past to bolster a new view of himself as competent enough to have escaped from the dominance of problematic feelings. At this phase in his therapy, Stan makes a decision to create an alternative narrative. Several sessions are devoted to re-authoring Stan's story in ways that are lively, creative, and colorful. Along with the process of creating an alternative story, the therapist explores with Stan the possibilities of recruiting an audience who will reinforce his positive changes. His therapist asks, "Who do you know who would be least surprised to hear of your recent changes and what would this person know about you that would lead to him or her not being so surprised?" Stan identifies one of his early teachers who served as a mentor to him and who believed in him when Stan had little belief in himself. Some therapy time is devoted to discussing how new stories take root only when there is an audience to appreciate them.

After five sessions with his therapist, Stan brings up the matter of termination. At the sixth and final session, the therapist introduces scaling questions to ask Stan to rate his degree of improvement on a range of problems they explored in the past weeks. On a scale of zero to 10, Stan ranks how he saw himself before his first session until today on various specific dimensions. They also talked about what Stan wants for his future and what kinds of improvements he will need to make to attain what he wants. The therapist then gives Stan a letter she wrote summarizing what she believes to be some of the positive attributes Stan has demonstrated. In her narrative letter, the therapist compliments Stan for his determination and cooperation and encourages him to circulate the news of the differences he has brought about in his life.

Follow-Up: You Continue as Stan's Postmodern Therapist

Use these questions to help you think about how to counsel Stan from a postmodernist approach:

- Stan's therapist borrowed key concepts and techniques common to both solution-focused and narrative orientations. In your work with Stan, what specific concepts would you borrow

(continued on next page)

from each of these approaches? What techniques would you draw from each of the approaches? What possible advantages do you see, if any, in applying an integration of solution-focused and narrative models in your work with Stan?

- What unique values, if any, do you see in working with Stan from a postmodern perspective as opposed to working with Stan from the other therapeutic approaches you've studied thus far?
- The therapist asked many questions of Stan. List some additional questions you would be

particularly interested in pursuing with Stan.

- In what ways could you integrate SFBT and narrative therapy with feminist therapy in Stan's case? What other therapies might you combine with the postmodern approaches?
- At this point, you are very familiar with the themes in Stan's life. If you were to write a narrative letter that you would then give to Stan, what would you most want to compliment him on? What would you want to talk to him about regarding his future?

POSTMODERN APPROACHES FROM A MULTICULTURAL PERSPECTIVE

Contributions to Multicultural Counseling

Social constructionism is congruent with the philosophy of multiculturalism. One of the problems that culturally diverse clients often experience is the expectation that they should conform their lives to the truths and reality of the dominant society of which they are a part. With the emphasis on multiple realities and the assumption that what is perceived to be a truth is the product of social construction, the postmodern approaches are a good fit with diverse worldviews.

The social constructionist approach to therapy provides clients with a framework to think about their thinking and to determine the impact their stories have on what they do. Clients are encouraged to explore how their realities are being constructed and the consequences that follow from such constructions. Within the framework of their cultural values and worldview, clients can explore their beliefs and provide their own reinterpretations of significant life events. The practitioner with a social constructivist perspective can guide clients in a manner that respects their underlying values. This dimension is especially important in those cases where counselors are from a different cultural background or do not share the same worldview as their clients.

Narrative therapy is grounded in a sociocultural context, which makes this approach especially relevant for counseling culturally diverse clients. Many of the modern approaches that have been discussed in this book are based on the assumption that problems exist within individuals. Some of these traditional models define mental health in terms of dominant cultural values. In contrast, narrative therapists operate on the premise that problems are identified within social, cultural, political, and relational contexts rather than existing within individuals. They are very much concerned with considering issues of gender, ethnicity, race, sexual orientation, and social class in the therapeutic process. Furthermore, the therapy venture gives attention to the socially constructed dialogue and narrative accounts that clients describe.

Narrative therapists concentrate on problem stories that dominate and subjugate at the personal, social, and cultural levels. The sociopolitical conceptualization of problems sheds light on those cultural notions and practices that produce dominant and oppressive narratives. From this orientation, practitioners take apart the cultural assumptions that are a part of a client's problem situation. People are able to come to an understanding of how oppressive social practices have affected them. This awareness can lead to a new perspective on dominant themes of oppression that have been such an integral part of a client's story, and with this cultural awareness new stories can be generated.

In their discussion of the multicultural influences on clients, Bertolino and O'Hanlon (2002) make the point that they do not approach clients with a preconceived notion about their experience. Instead, they learn from their clients about their experiential world. Bertolino and O'Hanlon practice multicultural curiosity by listening respectfully to their clients, who actually become their best teachers. Here are some questions these authors suggest as a way to more fully understand multicultural influences on a client:

- Tell me more about the influence that [some aspect of your culture] has played in your life.
- What can you share with me about your background that will enable me to more fully understand you?
- What challenges have you faced growing up in your culture?
- What, if anything, about your background has been difficult for you?
- How have you been able to draw on strengths and resources from your culture? What resources can you draw from in times of need?

Questions such as these can shed light on specific multicultural influences that have been sources of support or that contributed to a client's problem.

Limitations for Multicultural Counseling

A potential limitation of the postmodern approaches pertains to the "not-knowing stance" the therapist assumes, along with the assumption of the "client-as-expert." Individuals from many different cultural groups tend to elevate the professional as the expert who will offer direction and solutions for the person seeking help. If the therapist is telling the client "I am not really an expert; you are the expert; I trust in your resources for you to find solutions to your problems," then this is likely to engender lack of confidence in the therapist. To avoid this situation, the therapist using a solution-focused or a narrative orientation needs to convey to clients that he or she has expertise in the process of therapy but will not direct clients to engage in behaviors that are contrary to their underlying goals.

SUMMARY AND EVALUATION

Summary

In social constructionist theory the therapist-as-expert is replaced by the client-as-expert. Although clients are viewed as experts on their own lives, they are often stuck in patterns that are not working well for them. Both solution-focused and narrative therapists enter into dialogues in an effort to elicit the perspectives, resources, and unique experiences of their clients. The therapeutic endeavor is a highly collaborative relationship in which the client is the senior partner. The qualities of the therapeutic relationship are at the heart of the effectiveness of both SFBT and narrative therapy. This has resulted in many therapists giving increased attention to creating a collaborative relationship with clients.

The not-knowing position of the therapist has been infused as a key concept of both the solution-focused and narrative therapeutic approaches. The not-knowing position, which allows therapists to follow, affirm, and be guided by the stories of their clients, creates participant-observer and process-facilitator roles for the therapist and integrates therapy with a postmodern perspective of human inquiry.

Both solution-focused brief therapy and narrative therapy are based on the optimistic assumption that people are healthy, competent, resourceful, and possess the ability to construct solutions and alternative stories that can enhance their lives. In SFBT the therapeutic process provides a context whereby individuals focus on creating solutions rather than talking about their problems. Common techniques include the use of miracle questions, exception questions, and scaling questions. In narrative therapy the therapeutic process provides the sociocultural context wherein clients are assisted in separating themselves from their problems and are afforded the opportunity of authoring new stories.

Practitioners with solution-focused or narrative orientations tend to engage clients in conversations that lead to progressive narratives whereby they create situations in which they can make steady gains toward their goals. Therapists often ask clients: "Tell me about times when your life was going the way you wanted it to." These conversations illustrate stories of life worth living. On the basis of these conversations, the power of problems is taken apart (deconstructed) and new directions and solutions are manifest and made possible.

Contributions of Postmodern Approaches

Social constructionism, SFBT, and narrative therapy are making many contributions to the field of psychotherapy. I especially value the optimistic orientation of these postmodern approaches that rest on the assumptions that people are competent and can be trusted to use their resources in creating better solutions and more life-affirming stories. Many postmodern practitioners and writers have found that clients are able to make significant moves toward building more satisfying lives in a relatively short period of time (Bertolino & O'Hanlon, 2002; de Shazer, 1991; De Jong & Berg, 2002; Freedman & Combs, 1996; Miller, Hubble, & Duncan, 1996; O'Hanlon & Weiner-Davis, 1989; Walter & Peller, 1992, 2000; Winslade & Monk, 1999).

I think the nonpathologizing stance characteristic of practitioners with a social constructionist, solution-focused, or narrative orientation is a major contribution to the counseling profession. As you have seen, practitioners with a postmodern orientation do not support a pathology-oriented view of people, take issue with the DSM-IV-TR labeling system, and challenge the notion that the therapist is the expert who applies treatment interventions to a passive client. Rather than dwelling on what is wrong with a person, these approaches view the client as being competent and resourceful. The key question underlying consultative conversations is this: "How can we create a space for dialogue and wonder, where purpose, preferences, and possibilities can emerge and evolve?" (Walter & Peller, 2000, p. xii).

To its credit, solution-focused therapy is a brief approach, of about five sessions, that seems to show promising results (de Shazer, 1991). In de Shazer's summary of two outcome studies at the Brief Family Therapy Center, he reports that 91% of the clients who attended four or more sessions were successful in achieving their treatment goals. Brevity is a main appeal of SFBT in an era of managed care, which places a premium on short-term therapy.

Research from an "empirical generalizable" perspective is somewhat antithetical to the social constructionist approach. Research should always be conducted from the perspective of the client and not from a generalizable or expert external perspective. With this in mind, the question can be raised, "How effective is solution-focused brief therapy?" Regardless of the specific theoretical orientation of the therapist, brief therapy has been shown to be effective for a wide range of clinical problems. Studies that have compared brief therapies with long-term therapies have generally found no difference in outcomes (McKeel, 1996). In a review of current research of SFBT, McKeel concludes that when SFBT techniques have been tested the results are generally favorable. Although only a few studies of SFBT exist, outcome studies generally show that most clients receiving SFBT report accomplishing their treatment goals. Based on process studies of SFBT techniques, McKeel identified these trends:

■ Presuppositional questions get clients to look at what they have done already that has been useful. The therapist asks: "What have you done in the past that worked?" Such questions often result in a client developing a new perspective on his or her situation.
■ Scaling questions are an effective technique for monitoring treatment progress.

- Client–therapist collaboration tends to be associated with treatment success.
- When therapists are able to get clients to engage in solution-talk (instead of problem-talk), clients often report that change occurs (p. 264).

In their review of 15 outcome studies of SFBT, Gingerich and Eisengart (2000) found that 5 studies were well-controlled and all showed positive outcomes. The other 10 studies, which were only moderately controlled, supported a hypothesis of the effectiveness of SFBT. The review of these studies provided preliminary support for the efficacy of SFBT, but methodological flaws did not permit a definitive conclusion.

A major strength of both solution-focused and narrative therapies is the use of questioning, which is the centerpiece of both approaches. Open-ended questions about the client's attitudes, thoughts, feeling, behaviors, and perceptions are one of the main interventions. As we have seen, skilled therapists do not barrage clients with questions; instead, by a combination of respectful listening and appropriate questioning it is possible for clients to make progress. Especially useful are future-oriented questions that challenge clients to think about how they are likely to solve potential problems in the future.

Limitation and Criticisms of Postmodern Approaches

A concern that I have about both solution-focused brief therapy and narrative therapy pertains to the manner in which some therapists may glorify a technique and make it an end in itself. Several writers and practitioners have emphasized that when it comes to effective practice of SFBT or narrative therapy there are no set formulas or recipes to follow (Freedman & Combs, 1996; Monk, Winslade, Crocket, & Epston, 1997; O'Hanlon, 1994; Winslade & Monk, 1999). Monk (1997) makes an excellent point in emphasizing that narrative therapy will vary with each client, since each person is unique. For Monk, narrative conversations are based on a way of being, and if narrative counseling "is seen as a formula or used as a recipe, clients will have the experience of having things done *to* them and feel left out of the conversation" (p. 24).

To effectively practice solution-focused brief therapy, it is essential that therapists be skilled in brief interventions. In a relatively short time practitioners must be able to make assessments, assist clients in formulating specific goals, and effectively use appropriate interventions. Some inexperienced or untrained therapists may be enamored of any number of techniques: the miracle question, scaling questions, the exception question, and externalizing questions. But effective therapy is not simply a matter of pulling out any of these interventions from a bag! The attitudes of the therapist and his or her ability to use questions that are reflective of genuine respectful interest are crucial to the therapeutic process.

McKenzie and Monk (1997) express their concerns over those counselors who attempt to employ narrative ideas in a mechanistic fashion. They caution that a risk in describing a map of a narrative orientation lies in the fact that some beginners will pay more attention to following the map than they will to following the lead of the client. In such situations, McKenzie and Monk are convinced that mechanically using techniques will not be effective. They add that although narrative therapy is based on some simple ideas it is a mistake to assume that the practice is simple. However, this criticism pertains more to certain practitioners than it does to the social constructionist approaches.

McKeel (1996) observes that recent research on the importance of the therapeutic relationship is consistent with the SFBT view that positive treatment outcomes are linked to therapists developing effective and collaborative working relationships with clients. He cautions practitioners that losing sight of the potency of the therapeutic relationship "will only doom SFBT to be remembered as a disembodied set of clever techniques" (p. 265). Some solution-focused therapists now acknowledge the problem of relying too much on a few techniques, and they are placing increased importance on the therapeutic relationship and the overall philosophy of the approach (Nichols & Schwartz, 2001).

In spite of these limitations, the postmodern approaches have much to offer practitioners. Many of the basic ideas and techniques of both solution-focused brief therapy and narrative therapy can be integrated into the other therapeutic orientations addressed in this book. These newer approaches provide a challenge to practitioners, regardless of their theoretical orientation, to critically examine the basic assumptions that guide their practice.

 ## WHERE TO GO FROM HERE

Drs. Jennifer Andrews and David Clark have created a number of videotapes that present solution-focused, narrative, and collaborative language systems therapies. For information about postmodern theory and clinical practice on videotape, consult this Web site: **www.masterswork.com**

If you are interested in keeping up to date with the development in brief therapy, the *Journal of Brief Therapy* is devoted to developments, innovations, and research related to brief therapy with individuals, couples, families, and groups. The articles deal with brief therapy related to all theoretical approaches, but especially to social constructionism, solution-focused therapy, and narrative therapy. For subscription information, contact:

Springer Publishing Company
536 Broadway
New York, NY 10012-3955
Telephone: (212) 431-4370
Fax: (212) 941-7842
Web site: www.springerpub.com

Training in Solution-Focused Therapy Approaches

Center for Solution-Focused Brief Therapy
John Walter and Jane Peller
2320 Thayer Street
Evanston, IL 60201-1412
Telephone: (773) 338-7230
Email: WalterPeller@aol.com

The Brief Family Therapy Center
Insoo Kim Berg and Steve de Shazer
P. O. Box 13736
Milwaukee, WI 53213
Telephone: (414) 302-0650
Fax: (414) 302-0753
Email: Briefftc@aol.com
Web site: www.brief-therapy.org

Bill O'Hanlon, Possibilities
551 Cordova Rd. #715
Santa Fe, NM 87501
Telephone: (800) 381-2374
Fax: (505) 983-2761
Email: PossiBill@aol.com
Web site: http://www.brieftherapy.com

Bob Bertolino, Therapeutic Collaborations
Consultation & Training
P. O. Box 1175
St. Charles, MO 63302
Telephone/Fax: (314) 983-9861
Email: info@tcctinc.com
Web site: www.tcctinc.com

Institute for the Study of Therapeutic Change
Scott Miller
Web site: www.talkingcure.com

Training in Narrative Therapy

Evanston Family Therapy Institute
Jill Freedman and Gene Combs
636 Church Street #901
Evanston, IL 60201

The Family Therapy Centre
David Epston
6 Goring Rd.

Sandringham, Auckland 4
New Zealand

Dulwich Centre
Michael White
345 Carrington St.
Adelaide, South Australia 5000

Counsellor Education Programme
University of Waikato
Private Bag 3105
Hamilton, New Zealand
Web site: www.soe.waikato.ac.nz/counselling

Bay Area Family Therapy Training Associates
J. L. Zimmerman and V. C. Dickerson
21760 Stevens Creek Blvd., Suite 102
Cupertino, CA 95015
Telephone: (408) 257-6881
Fax: (408) 257-0689
Email: baftta@aol.com
Web site: www.baftta.com

The Houston-Galveston Institute
3316 Mount Vernon
Houston, TX 77006
Telephone: (713) 526-8390
Email: harleneanderson@earthlink.net

 ## InfoTrac College Edition Resources

Postmodern Approaches   The following key words are listed in such a way as to
allow the InfoTrac College Edition search engine to locate a wider range of articles in the online library. The key words should be entered exactly as shown,
including asterisks, "W1," and "AND."

Insoo Kim Berg	Solution-focused therapy
Steve de Shazer	Brief psychotherapy
Michael White	Narrative W1 therapy
David Epston	

Recommended Supplementary Readings

Becoming Solution-Focused in Brief Therapy (Walter & Peller, 1992) and *Recreating
Brief Therapy: Preferences and Possibilities* (Walter & Peller, 2000) are clearly written books that contain a great deal of useful information on basic ideas of brief
therapy and ways of implementing solution-focused brief therapy.

Interviewing for Solutions (De Jong & Berg, 2002) is a practical text aimed at teaching and learning solution-focused skills. It is written in a conversational and informal style and contains many examples to solidify learning of skills.

Handbook of Solution-Focused Brief Therapy (Miller, Hubble, & Duncan, 1996) is an edited collection of 28 experts who provide case examples and practical information in delivering solution-focused therapy in a variety of treatment settings.

Collaborative, Competency-Based Counseling and Therapy (Bertolino & O'Hanlon, 2002) is a blend of various postmodern approaches that emphasizes ways therapists can create collaborative relationships with clients that will result in opening new possibilities for living. This book is an update of solution-oriented and possibility therapies.

Narrative Therapy: The Social Construction of Preferred Realities (Freedman & Combs, 1996) is an exceptionally clear explanation of the basic ideas of narrative therapy. The authors emphasize key concepts and the application of specific clinical practices. This is one of the best sources on the theory and practice of narrative therapy.

Narrative Counseling in Schools (Winslade & Monk, 1999) offer a basic and easy-to-read guide to applying concepts and techniques of narrative therapy to school settings.

Narrative Therapy in Practice: The Archaeology of Hope (Monk, Winslade, Crocket, & Epston, 1997) clarifies and translates many of the ideas of Michael White and David Epston. This edited text contains some excellent discourse on how narrative therapy works, the therapeutic relationship, and learning and teaching narrative ideas.

References and Suggested Readings

ANDERSON, H. (1993). On a roller coaster: A collaborative language system approach to therapy. In S. Friedman (Ed.), *The new language of change* (pp. 324–344). New York: Guilford Press.

*ANDERSON, H., & GOOLISHIAN, H. (1992). The client is the expert: A not-knowing approach to therapy. In S. McNamee & K. J. Gergen (Eds.), *Therapy as social construction* (pp. 25–39). Newbury Park, CA: Sage.

ANDREWS, J., & CLARK, D. J. (1996). In the case of a depressed woman: Solution-focused or narrative therapy approaches? *The Family Journal, 4*(3), 243–250.

ANDREWS, J., & CLARK, D. J. (1998). Postmodern ideas and relational conversations in clinical practice. *The Family Journal, 6*(4), 316–322.

ANDREWS, J., CLARK, D. J., & BAIRD, F. (1997). Therapeutic letter writing: Creating relational case notes. *The Family Journal, 5*(2), 149–158.

BATESON, G. (1972). *Steps to an ecology of mind.* New York: Ballantine.

BERG, I. K. (1994). *Family based services: A solution-focused approach.* New York: Norton.

BERG, I. K., & MILLER, S. D. (1992). *Working with the problem drinker: A solution-focused approach.* New York: Norton.

BERGER, P. L., & LUCKMAN, T. (1967). *The social construction of reality: A treatise in the sociology of knowledge.* London: Penguin.

*Books and articles marked with an asterisk are suggested for further study.

*BERTOLINO, B., & O'HANLON, B. (2002). *Collaborative, competency-based counseling and therapy.* Boston: Allyn & Bacon.

*BOHART, A. C., & TALLMAN, K. (1999). *How clients make therapy work: The process of active self-healing.* Washington, DC: American Psychological Association.

BROWN, J. H., & CHRISTENSEN, D. N. (1999). *Family therapy: Theory and practice* (2nd ed.). Pacific Grove, CA: Brooks/Cole.

BUBENZER, D. L., & WEST, J. D. (1993). William Hudson O'Hanlon: On seeking possibilities and solutions in therapy. *The Family Journal: Counseling and Therapy for Couples and Families, 1*(4), 365–379.

BUBENZER, D. L., WEST, J. D., & BOUGHNER, S. R. (1994). Michael White and the narrative perspective in therapy. *The Family Journal: Counseling and Therapy for Couples and Families, 2*(1), 71–83.

BURR, V. (1995). *An introduction to social constructionism.* London: Routledge.

*CADE, B., & O'HANLON, W. H. (1993). *A brief guide to brief therapy.* New York: Norton.

COREY, G. (2005). *Case approach to counseling and psychotherapy* (6th ed.). Belmont, CA: Brooks/Cole.

*DE JONG, P., & BERG, I. K. (2002). *Interviewing for solutions* (2nd ed.). Pacific Grove, CA: Brooks/Cole.

*DE SHAZER, S. (1985). *Keys to solutions in brief therapy.* New York: Norton.

*DE SHAZER, S. (1988). *Clues: Investigating solutions in brief therapy.* New York: Norton.

*DE SHAZER, S. (1991). *Putting difference to work.* New York: Norton.

*DE SHAZER, S. (1994). *Words were originally magic.* New York: Norton.

DREWERY, W., & WINSLADE, J. (1997). The theoretical story of narrative therapy. In G. Monk, J. Winslade, K. Crocket, & D. Epston (Eds.), *Narrative therapy in practice: The archaeology of hope* (pp. 32–52). San Francisco: Jossey-Bass.

EPSTON, D., & WHITE, M. (1992). Consulting your consultants: The documentation of alternative knowledges. In *Experience, contradiction, narrative and imagination: Selected papers of David Epston and Michael White, 1989–1991* (pp. 11–26). Adelaide, South Australia: Dulwich Centre Publications.

*FREEDMAN, J., & COMBS, G. (1996). *Narrative therapy: The social construction of preferred realities.* New York: Norton.

FREEDMAN, J., & COMBS, G. (2002). *Narrative therapy with couples . . . and a whole lot more! A collection of papers and essays and exercises.* Adelaide: South Australia. Dulwich Centre Publishers.

FREEDMAN, J., EPSTON, D., & LOBOVITS, D. (1997). *Playful approaches to serious problems: Narrative therapy with children and their families.* New York: Norton.

GERGEN, K. (1985). The social constructionist movement in modern psychology. *American Psychologist, 40,* 266–275.

GERGEN, K. (1991). *The saturated self.* New York: Basic Books.

GERGEN, K. (1999). *An invitation to social construction.* Thousand Oaks, CA: Sage.

GINGERICH, W. J., & EISENGART, S. (2000). Solution-focused brief therapy: A review of the outcome research. *Family Process, 39*(4), 477–498.

*HUBBLE, M. A., DUNCAN, B. L., & MILLER, S. D. (1999). *The heart and soul of change: What works in therapy*. Washington, DC: American Psychological Association.

LINDSLEY, J. R. (1994). Rationalist therapy in a constructivistic frame. *The Behavior Therapist, 17*(7), 160–162.

McKEEL, A. J. (1996). A clinician's guide to research on solution-focused brief therapy. In S. D. Miller, M. A. Hubble, & B. L. Duncan (Eds.), *Handbook of solution-focused brief therapy* (pp. 251–271). San Francisco: Jossey-Bass.

McKENZIE, W., & MONK, G. (1997). Learning and teaching narrative ideas. In G. Monk, J. Winslade, K. Crocket, & D. Epston (Eds.), *Narrative therapy in practice: The archaeology of hope* (pp. 82–117). San Francisco: Jossey-Bass.

*McNAMEE, S., & GERGEN, K. J. (Eds.). (1992). *Therapy as social construction*. Newbury Park, CA: Sage.

METCALF, L., THOMAS, F. N., DUNCAN, B. L., MILLER, S. D., & HUBBLE, M. A. (1996). What works in solution-focused brief therapy: A qualitative analysis of client and therapist perceptions. In S. D. Miller, M. A. Hubble, & B. L. Duncan (Eds.), *Handbook of solution-focused brief therapy* (pp. 335–349). San Francisco: Jossey-Bass.

MILLER, S. D., & BERG, I. K. (1995). *The miracle method: A radically new approach to problem drinking*. New York: Norton.

*MILLER, S. D., HUBBLE, M. A., & DUNCAN, B. L. (Eds.). (1996). *Handbook of solution-focused brief therapy*. San Francisco: Jossey-Bass.

*MONK, G. (1997). How narrative therapy works. In G. Monk, J. Winslade, K. Crocket, & D. Epston (Eds.), *Narrative therapy in practice: The archaeology of hope* (pp. 3–31). San Francisco: Jossey-Bass.

*MONK, G., WINSLADE, J., CROCKET, K., & EPSTON, D. (Eds.). (1997). *Narrative therapy in practice: The archaeology of hope*. San Francisco: Jossey-Bass.

NEIMEYER, R. A. (1993). An appraisal of constructivist psychotherapies. *Journal of Consulting and Clinical Psychology, 61*(2), 221–234.

*NEIMEYER, R. A., & MAHONEY, M. J. (Eds.) (1995). *Constructivism in psychotherapy*. Washington, DC: American Psychological Association.

*NICHOLS, M. P., & SCHWARTZ, R. C. (2001). *Family therapy: Concepts and methods* (5th ed.). Boston: Allyn & Bacon.

*NICHOLS, M. P., & SCHWARTZ, R. C. (2002). *The essentials of family therapy*. Boston: Allyn & Bacon.

NYLUND, D., & THOMAS, J. (1994). The economics of narrative. *The Family Therapy Networker, 18*(6), 38–39.

*O'HANLON, W. H. (1994). The third wave: The promise of narrative. *The Family Therapy Networker, 18*(6), 19–26, 28–29.

*O'HANLON, W. H. (1999). *Do one thing different*. New York: Harper-Collins.

*O'HANLON, W. H., & WEINER-DAVIS, M. (1989). *In search of solutions: A new direction in psychotherapy*. New York: Norton.

PROCHASKA, J. O., & NORCROSS, J. C. (2003). *Systems of psychotherapy: A transtheoretical analysis* (5th ed.). Pacific Grove, CA: Brooks/Cole.

*WALTER, J. L., & PELLER, J. E. (1992). *Becoming solution-focused in brief therapy.* New York: Brunner/Mazel.

*WALTER, J. L., & PELLER, J. E. (1996). Rethinking our assumptions: Assuming anew in a postmodern world. In S. D. Miller, M. A. Hubble, & B. L. Duncan (Eds.), *Handbook of solution-focused brief therapy* (pp. 9–26). San Francisco: Jossey-Bass.

*WALTER, J. L., & PELLER, J. E. (2000). *Recreating brief therapy: Preferences and possibilities.* New York: Norton.

WEISHAAR, M. E. (1993). *Aaron T. Beck.* London: Sage.

WEST, J. D., BUBENZER, D. L., SMITH, J., & HAMM, T. (1997). Insoo Kim Berg and solution-focused therapy. *The Family Journal: Counseling and Therapy for Couples and Families, 5,* 346–354.

WHITE, M. (1992). Deconstruction and therapy. In *Experience, contradiction, narrative, and imagination: Selected papers of David Epston and Michael White, 1989–1991* (pp. 109–151). Adelaide, South Australia: Dulwich Centre Publications.

WHITE, M. (1995). *Reauthoring lives: Interviews and essays.* Adelaide, South Australia: Dulwich Centre Publications.

WHITE, M. (1997). *Narrative of therapists' lives.* Adelaide, South Australia: Dulwich Centre Publications.

*WHITE, M., & EPSTON, D. (1990). *Narrative means to therapeutic ends.* New York: Norton.

*WINSLADE, J., CROCKET, K., & MONK, G. (1997). The therapeutic relationship. In G. Monk, J. Winslade, K. Crocket, & D. Epston (Eds.), *Narrative therapy in practice: The archaeology of hope* (pp. 53–81), San Francisco: Jossey-Bass.

*WINSLADE, J., & MONK, G. (1999). *Narrative counseling in schools.* Thousand Oaks, CA: Corwin Press (Sage).

*WINSLADE, J., & MONK, G. (2000). *Narrative mediation: A new approach to conflict resolution.* San Francisco: Jossey-Bass.

*WYLIE, M. S. (1994). Panning for gold. *The Family Therapy Networker, 18*(6), 40–48.

* ZIMMERMAN, J. L., & DICKERSON, V. C. (1996). *If problems talked: Narrative therapy in action.* New York: Guilford Press.

Chapter 14

Family Systems Therapy

Co-authored by James Robert Bitter and Gerald Corey

Family systems therapy is represented by a variety of theories and approaches, all of which focus on the relational aspect of human problems. Some of the individuals most closely associated with the origins of these systemic approaches are featured here.

ALFRED ADLER was the first psychologist of the modern era to do family therapy using a systemic approach. He set up more than 30 child guidance clinics in Vienna after World War I and later Rudolf Dreikurs brought this concept to the United States in the form of family education centers. Adler conducted family counseling sessions in an open public forum to educate parents in greater numbers; he believed the problems of any one family are common to all others in the community.

MURRAY BOWEN was one of the original developers of mainstream family therapy. Much of his theory and practice grew out of his work with

schizophrenic individuals in families. He believed families could best be understood when analyzed from a three-generation perspective because patterns of interpersonal relationships connect family members across generations. His major contributions include the core concepts of differentiation of the self and triangulation.

VIRGINIA SATIR developed conjoint family therapy, a human validation process model (an experiential approach) that emphasizes communication and emotional experiencing. Like Bowen, she used an intergenerational model, but she worked to bring family patterns to life in the present through sculpting and family reconstructions. Claiming that techniques were secondary to relationship, she concentrated on the personal relationship between therapist and family to achieve change.

(continued on next page)

CARL WHITAKER is the creator of symbolic-experiential family therapy, a freewheeling, intuitive approach to helping families open channels of interaction. His goal was to facilitate individual autonomy while retaining a sense of belonging in the family. He saw the therapist as an active participant and coach who enters the family process with creativity, putting enough pressure on this process to produce change in the status quo.

SALVADOR MINUCHIN began to develop structural family therapy in the 1960s through his work with delinquent boys from poor families at the Wiltwyck School in New York. Working with colleagues at the Philadelphia Child Guidance Clinic in the 1970s, Minuchin refined the theory and practice of structural family therapy. Focusing on the structure, or organization, of the family, the therapist helps the family modify its stereotyped patterns and redefine relationships among family members. He believed structural changes in families must occur before individual members' symptoms could be reduced or eliminated.

 INTRODUCTION

Although the seeds of a North American family therapy movement were planted in the 1940s, it was during the 1950s that systemic family therapy began to take root (Becvar & Becvar, 2003). During the early years of its evolution, working with families was considered to be a revolutionary approach to treatment. In the 1960s and 1970s, psychodynamic, behavioral, and humanistic approaches (called the first, second, and third force, respectively) dominated counseling and psychotherapy. Today, the various approaches to family systems represent a paradigm shift that we might even call the "fourth force."

JAY HALEY, a prolific writer, has had a significant impact on the development of strategic family therapy. He blends structural family therapy with the concepts of hierarchy, power, and strategic interventions. Strategic family therapy is a pragmatic approach that focuses on solving problems in the present; understanding and insight are neither required nor sought.

CLOÉ MADANES, with Jay Haley, established the Family Institute in Washington, D.C. in the 1970s. Through their combined therapy practice, writings, and training of family therapists, strategic family therapy became the most popular family therapy approach by the 1980s. This is a brief, solution-oriented therapy approach. The problem brought by the family to therapy is treated as "real"— not a symptom of underlying issues—and is solved. Her emphasis is on the caring and emotional aspects of family patterns. ∎

The Family Systems Perspective

Perhaps the most difficult adjustment for counselors and therapists from Western cultures is the adoption of a "systems" perspective. Our personal experience and Western culture often tell us that we are autonomous individuals, capable of free and independent choice. And yet, we are born into families—and most of us live our entire lives attached to one form of family or another. Within these families, we discover who we are; we develop and change; and we give and receive the support we need for survival. We create, maintain, and live by often unspoken rules and routines that we hope will keep the family (and each of its members) functional.

In this sense, a family systems perspective holds that individuals are best understood through assessing the interactions between and among family members. The development and behavior of one family member is inextricably interconnected with others in the family. Symptoms are often viewed as an expression of a set of habits and patterns within a family. It is revolutionary to conclude that the identified client's problem might be a symptom of how the system functions, not just a symptom of the individual's maladjustment, history, and psychosocial development. This perspective is grounded on the assumptions that a client's problematic behavior may (1) serve a function or purpose for the family, (2) be unintentionally maintained by family processes, (3) be a function of the family's inability to operate productively, especially during developmental transitions, or (4) be a symptom of dysfunctional patterns handed down across generations. All these assumptions challenge the more traditional intrapsychic frameworks for conceptualizing human problems and their formation.

The one central principle agreed upon by family therapy practitioners, regardless of their particular approach, is that the client is connected to living systems. Attempts to change are best facilitated by working with and considering the family or relationship as a whole. Therefore, a treatment approach that comprehensively addresses the family as well as the "identified" client is required. Because a family is an interactional unit, it has its own set of unique traits. It is not possible to accurately assess an individual's concern without observing the interaction of the other family members, as well as the broader contexts in which the person and the family live. Studying the internal dynamics of an individual without adequately considering interpersonal dynamics yields an incomplete picture. Because the focus is on interpersonal relationships, Becvar and Becvar (2003) maintain that family therapy is a misnomer and that *relationship therapy* is a more appropriate label.

Family therapy perspectives call for a conceptual shift, for the family is viewed as a functioning unit that is more than the sum of the roles of its various members. The family provides a primary context for understanding how individuals function in relation to others and how they behave. Actions by any individual family member will influence all the others in the family, and their reactions will have a reciprocal effect on the individual. Goldenberg and Goldenberg (2004) point to the need for therapists to view all behavior, including all symptoms expressed by the individual, within the context of the family and society. They add that a systems orientation does not preclude dealing with the dynamics within the individual, but that this approach broadens the traditional emphasis on individual internal dynamics.

Differences Between Systemic and Individual Approaches

There are significant differences between individual therapeutic approaches and systemic approaches. A case may help to illustrate these differences. Ann, age 22, sees a counselor because she is suffering from a depression that has lasted for more than 2 years and has impaired her ability to maintain friendships and work productively. She wants to feel better, but she is pessimistic about her chances. How will a therapist choose to help her?

Both the individual therapist and the systemic therapist are interested in Ann's current living situation and life experiences. Both discover that she is still living at home with her parents, who are in their 60s. They note that she has a very successful older sister, who is a prominent lawyer in the small town in which the two live. The therapists are impressed by Ann's loss of friends who have married and left town over the years while she stayed behind, often lonely and isolated. Finally, both therapists note that Ann's depression affects others as well as herself. It is here, however, that the similarities tend to end:

The individual therapist may:	*The systemic therapist may:*
Focus on obtaining an accurate diagnosis, perhaps using the DSM-IV-TR (APA, 2000)	Explore the system for family process and rules, perhaps using a genogram
Begin therapy with Ann immediately	Invite Ann's mother, father, and sister into therapy with her
Focus on the causes, purposes, and cognitive, emotional, and behavioral processes involved in Ann's depression and coping	Focus on the family relationships within which the continuation of Ann's depression "makes sense"
Be concerned with Ann's individual experiences and perspectives	Be concerned with transgenerational meanings, rules, cultural, and gender perspectives within the system, and even the community and larger systems affecting the family
Intervene in ways designed to help Ann cope	Intervene in ways designed to help change Ann's context

Systemic therapists do not deny the importance of the individual in the family system, but they believe an individual's systemic affiliations and interactions have more power in the person's life than a single therapist could ever hope to have. By working with the whole family—or even community—system, the therapist has a chance to observe how individuals act within the system and participate in maintaining the status quo; how the system influences (and is influenced by) the individual; and what interventions might lead to changes that help the couple, family, or larger system as well as the individual expressing pain.

In Ann's case, her depression may have organic, genetic, or hormonal components. It may also involve cognitive, experiential, or behavioral patterns that interfere with effective coping. Even if her depression can be explained in this manner, however, the systemic therapist is very interested in how her depression affects others in the family and how it influences family process. Her depression may signal both her own pain and the unexpressed pain of the family. Indeed, many family systems approaches would investigate how the depression serves other family members; distracts from problems in the intimate relationships of others; or reflects her need to adjust to family rules, to cultural injunctions, or to processes influenced by gender or family life-cycle development. Rather than losing sight of the individual, family therapists understand the person as specifically embedded in larger systems.

THE DEVELOPMENT OF FAMILY SYSTEMS THERAPY

Family systems theory has evolved throughout the past 50 years, and today therapists creatively employ various perspectives when tailoring therapy to a particular family. Later in the chapter we discuss eight lenses through which family systems therapists view the family. In this section we present a brief historical overview of some of the key figures associated with the development of family systems therapy.

Adlerian Family Therapy

Alfred Adler was the first psychologist of the modern era to do family therapy (Christensen, 1993). His approach was systemic long before systems theory had been applied to psychotherapy. Adler's original conceptualizations can still be found within the principles and practice of other models.

Adler (1927) was the first to notice that the development of children within the family constellation (his phrase for family system) was heavily influenced by birth order. Adler was a phenomenologist, and even though birth order appeared to have some constancy to each position, he believed it was the interpretations children assigned to their birth positions that counted. Adler also noted that all behavior was purposeful—and that children often acted in patterns motivated by a desire to belong, even when these patterns were useless or mistaken.

It was Rudolf Dreikurs (1973), however, who refined Adler's concepts into a typology of mistaken goals and created an organized approach to family therapy. A basic assumption of modern Adlerian family therapy is that both parents and children often become locked in repetitive, negative interactions based on mistaken goals that motivate all parties involved. Although much of Adlerian family therapy is conducted in private sessions, Adlerians also use an educational model to counsel families in public in an open forum in schools, community agencies, and specially designed family education centers.

Multigenerational Family Therapy

Murray Bowen was one of the developers of mainstream family therapy. His family systems theory, which is a theoretical and clinical model that evolved from psychoanalytic principles and practices, is sometimes referred to as multigenerational family therapy. Bowen and his associates implemented an innovative approach to schizophrenia at the National Institute of Mental Health where Bowen actually hospitalized entire families so that the family system could be the focus of therapy.

Bowen's observations led to his interest in patterns across multiple generations. He contended that problems manifested in one's current family will not significantly change until relationship patterns in one's family of origin are understood and directly challenged. His approach operates on the premise that a predictable pattern of interpersonal relationships connects the functioning of family members across generations. According to Kerr and Bowen (1988), the cause of an individual's problems can be understood only by viewing the role of the family as an emotional unit. Within the family unit, unresolved emotional fusion to one's family must be addressed if one hopes to achieve a mature and unique personality. Emotional problems will be transmitted from generation to generation until unresolved emotional attachments are dealt with effectively. Change must occur with other family members and cannot be done by an individual in a counseling room.

One of Bowen's key concepts is *triangulation*, a process in which triads result in a *two-against-one* experience. Bowen assumed that triangulation could easily happen between family members and the therapist, which is why Bowen placed so much emphasis on his trainees becoming aware of their own family-of-origin issues (Kerr & Bowen, 1988).

A major contribution of Bowen's theory is the notion of *differentiation of the self*. Differentiation of the self involves both the psychological separation of intellect and emotion and independence of the self from others. In the process of individuation, individuals acquire a sense of self-identity. This differentiation from the family of origin enables them to accept personal responsibility for their thoughts, feelings, perceptions, and actions.

Human Validation Process Model

At about the same time that Bowen was developing his approach, Virginia Satir began emphasizing family connection. Her therapeutic work had already led her to believe in the value of a strong, nurturing relationship based on interest and fascination with those in her care. She thought of herself as a detective who sought out and listened for the reflections of self-esteem in the communication of her clients. It was while working with an adolescent girl that it occurred to her to ask about her mother. She was surprised by how her client's communication and behavior changed when the mother was present. As she worked out their relationship, it again occurred to her to ask about a father. When he came in, the communication and behavior of both the mother and daughter changed. It was in working through this process that Satir discovered the power of family therapy, the importance of communication and meta-communication in family interaction, and the value of therapeutic validation in the process of change (Satir & Bitter, 2000).

Over her lifetime as a family therapist, Satir gained international fame and developed many innovative interventions. She was highly intuitive and believed spontaneity, creativity, humor, self-disclosure, risk-taking, and personal touch were central to family therapy. In her view, techniques were secondary to the relationship the therapist develops with the family. Her experiential and humanistic approach came to be called the human validation process model, but her early work with families was best known as conjoint family therapy (Satir, 1983).

Experiential Family Therapy

Carl Whitaker was a pioneer in experiential family therapy, sometimes known as the experiential-symbolic approach. Clearly an application of existential therapy to family systems, Whitaker stressed choice, freedom, self-determination, growth, and actualization (Whitaker & Bumberry, 1988). Like Satir and other existential approaches, Whitaker stressed the importance of the relationship between the family and the therapist. Whitaker was clearly more confrontive in his "realness" than was Satir, who was more nurturing. Whitaker's interventions were almost always enacted with co-therapists. Toward the end of his life, he would only see families, and he even tried to get community and work associates of the family to come in.

Whitaker's freewheeling, intuitive approach sought to unmask pretense and create new meaning while liberating family members to be themselves. Whitaker did not propose a set of methods; rather, it is the personal involvement of the therapist with a family that makes a difference. When techniques are employed, they arise from the therapist's intuitive and spontaneous reactions to the present situation and are designed to increase clients' awareness of their inner potential and to open channels of family interaction.

For Whitaker, family therapy was a way for therapists to be actively engaged in their own personal development. Indeed, therapy might actually help the therapist as much as the family. Whitaker did not treat families. Instead, he saw his role as creating with the family a context in which change can occur through a process of reorganization and reintegration (Becvar & Becvar, 2003).

Structural-Strategic Family Therapy

The origins of structural family therapy can be traced to the early 1960s when Salvador Minuchin was conducting therapy, training, and research with delinquent boys from poor families at the Wiltwyck School in New York. Minuchin's (1974) central idea was that an individual's symptoms are best understood from the vantage point of interactional patterns within a family and that structural changes must occur in a family before an individual's symptoms can be reduced or eliminated. The goals of structural family therapy are twofold: (1) reduce symptoms of dysfunction and (2) bring about structural change within the system by modifying the family's transactional rules and developing more appropriate boundaries.

In the late 1960s Jay Haley joined Minuchin at the Philadelphia Child Guidance Clinic. The work of Haley and Minuchin shared so many similarities in goals and process that many clinicians in the 1980s and 1990s would question whether the two models were distinct schools of thought. Indeed, by the late 1970s, structural-strategic approaches were the most used models in family systems therapy. Both models seek to reorganize dysfunctional or problematic structures in the families; boundary setting, unbalancing, reframing, ordeals, and enactments all became part of the family therapeutic process. Neither approach deals much with exploration or interpretation of the past. Rather, it is the job of structural-strategic therapists to join with the family, to block stereotyped interactional patterns, to reorganize family hierarchies or subsystems, and to facilitate the development of more flexible or useful transactions.

The structural and strategic models differ somewhat in how each view family problems: Minuchin (1974) tends to see individual and family difficulties as symptomatic whereas Haley (1976) sees them as "real" problems that need real answers. Both models are directive in nature, and both expect therapists to have a certain level of expertise to bring to the family therapy process.

In 1974, Haley and Cloé Madanes started the Family Therapy Institute of Washington, D.C. For more than 15 years they wrote, developed therapeutic practice, and provided intensive training in strategic family therapy. Their strategic approach views presenting problems as both real and as metaphor for system functioning. Considerable emphasis is given to power, control, and hierarchies in families and in the therapy sessions.

Haley (1984) and Madanes (1981) have been more interested in the practical applications of strategic interventions to ameliorate a family's problems than in formulating a theory of therapy distinct from the structural model. This is especially evident in Madanes's (1990) model for working with families that include a sex offender. Madanes brought a humanistic perspective to strategic therapy by addressing the need to be loved and by emphasizing the nurturing aspects of therapy.

Recent Innovations

In the last decade, feminism, multiculturalism, and postmodern social constructionism have all entered the family therapy field. These models are more collaborative, treating clients—individuals, couples, or families—as experts in their own lives. The eight lenses we present in this chapter would not exist had the field not included these newer postmodern approaches.

Tom Andersen (1987, 1991) practices family therapy in northern Norway, and his approach to family therapy is based on social constructionism. A social psychiatrist, Andersen has both pioneered community-based mental health programs and initiated a "reflecting team" approach to systemic family therapy. When Andersen started to visit the smaller communities in the north, he immediately recognized that "help" would often include work with extended families. Starting in the mid-1970s, he and his colleagues began to study the structural and strategic approaches used in the United States, and they incorporated some of the behind-the-mirror processes Haley had popularized (see Madanes, 1984). One therapist would interview a family in one room while a team of consulting therapists watched through a two-way mirror in another room. The therapy team remained detached from the family, continuing to work behind the observation mirrors. By 1984, Andersen and his colleagues had changed their methods of practice and were becoming more concerned with the interactions between the team and the family and less concerned about interventions.

Andersen (1991) reports that it was a family mired in misery that pulled the therapy team out of the darkness and into the light. One day when the team was getting nowhere with its interventions, a therapist knocked on the door of the interview room and asked the family members if they would like to watch and listen to the team's conversation about the family. When the family agreed, the lights in the observation room were turned on, and the family and their interviewer listened to the team process their session. This was the birth of the *reflecting team,* an approach that has quickly gained wide acceptance in family therapy, and in teaching and supervision of trainees as well.

Over time, an interviewing process that Andersen (1991) calls "dialogues and dialogues about the dialogues" has been developed to facilitate the use of a reflecting team. An initial interview with a family provides an extensive picture of the clients, the therapist, and "the history of the idea of coming for therapy" (pp. 131–133). A second level of dialogue is about the family members' stories of how their family picture and history came to be, and each person in the family may have a different story. A third level of dialogue is about the future: how family members would like the picture of themselves to change and what alternative stories about their lives might be developed.

When the reflecting team responds to the family, the team members are expected to let their imaginations flow, subject only to a respect for the family. Reflections are most often offered as tentative ideas directly connected to the verbal and nonverbal information in the preceding dialogue. The team remains positive in reflecting, reframing stories and parts of stories, looking for alternative stories, and wondering out loud about the possibility and impact of implementing these alternative stories. The family and the initial interviewer listen, and the interviewer monitors family reactions, looking for ways in which the reflecting team may be expanding the family's ideas. The session ends with the initial interviewer seeking the family members' reactions to what they have experienced (Becvar & Becvar, 2003).

This brief discussion of the various systemic viewpoints in family therapy provides a context for understanding the development of family therapy. Table 14-1 outlines the differences in these historical perspectives. For an in-depth treatment of the schools of family therapy, see the recommended readings at the end of the chapter. Dr. Mary Moline demonstrates an integrated approach using the multigenerational and structural-strategic models in the assessment and treatment of Ruth in *Case Approach to Counseling and Psychotherapy* (Corey, 2005, chap. 12).

 # EIGHT LENSES IN FAMILY SYSTEMS THERAPY

This chapter is about learning to think and practice within the multiple perspectives that family systems seem to require. This is no easy task! In 1992, Breunlin, Schwartz, and MacKune-Karrer (1997) introduced the concept of metaframeworks as a means for transcending the various approaches to family therapy, and they identified "six core metaframeworks" (p. 55) that function as therapeutic lenses. Taken together, these lenses provide six different perspectives from which a family system might be assessed and a "blueprint for therapy" (p. 281) developed.

The original six metaframeworks are internal family systems (or individual); sequences (or patterns of interaction); organization (of the system); developmental; multicultural; and gender. To these six lenses, we have added two more that we call the teleological (or goal-orientation) and process metaframeworks. Any or all of these eight lenses may have meaningful applications with a given couple or family. Furthermore, use of any particular lens influences and is influenced by the other seven perspectives, a feature common to all systems theories. The value of this approach is that it allows the therapist to draw on multiple perspectives rather than being locked into a single viewpoint. The lenses can be used for assessment as well as to *tailor* therapeutic interventions to the specific needs of the family (Carlson, Sperry, & Lewis, 1997; Goldenberg & Goldenberg, 2002). These eight lenses provide a foundation for integrating the various models of family systems therapy.

The Individual's Internal Family System

Although Richard Schwartz (1995) is credited with the development of internal family systems, he is not the only therapist to have noticed that there are parts to an individual's personality. Virginia Satir used several avenues to gain access to various parts of the self, including a phenomenological family mapping process, a wheel of influence, and a self-mandala (Satir, Banman, Gerber, & Gamori, 1991). Her most ingenious process was called "the parts party" (p. 175), which involves a psychodramatic integration and transformation of extreme parts. The parts party was especially effective when working with a couple in conflict (Bitter, 1993b). But perhaps the most complete approach to working with parts was developed by Erving Polster (1995), a key figure in Gestalt therapy.

Each of these theorists and practitioners has made contributions to a lens that views the individual as an organismic system, complete with structure, organization, and subsystems. An individual is made up of many parts, or dimensions, to his or her personality. Some of these facets of personality are self-enhancing,

TABLE 14-1 A Comparison of Six Systemic Viewpoints in Family Therapy

	Adlerian Family Therapy	Multi-Generational Family Therapy	Human Validation Process Model	Experiential/ Symbolic Family Therapy	Structural Family Therapy	Strategic Family Therapy
Key figures	Afred Adler Rudolf Dreikurs Oscar Christensen & Manford Sonstegard	Murray Bowen	Virginia Satir	Carl Whitaker	Salvador Minuchin	Jay Haley & Cloé Madanes
Time focus	Present with some reference to the past	Present and past: family of origin; three generations	Here and now	Present	Present and past	Present and Future
Therapy goals	Enable parents as leaders; unlock mistaken goals and interactional patterns in family; promotion of effective parenting	Differentiate the self; change the individual within the context of the system; decrease anxiety	Promote growth, self-esteem, and connection; help family reach congruent communication and interaction	Promote spontaneity, creativity, autonomy, and ability to play	Restructure family organization; change dysfunctional transactional patterns	Eliminate presenting problem; change dysfunctional patterns; interrupt sequence

TABLE 14-1 A Comparison of Six Systemic Viewpoints in Family Therapy (continued)

	Adlerian Family Therapy	Multi-Generational Family Therapy	Human Validation Process Model	Experiential/Symbolic Family Therapy	Structural Family Therapy	Strategic Family Therapy
Role and function of the therapist	Educator; motivational investigator; collaborator	Guide, objective researcher, teacher; monitor of own reactivity	Active facilitator; resource detective; model for congruence	Family coach; challenger; model for change through play	"Friendly uncle"; stage manager; promoter of change in family structure	Active director of change; problem solver
Process of change	Formation of relationship based on mutual respect; investigation of birth order and mistaken goals, re-education	Questions and cognitive processes lead to differentiation and understanding of family of origin	Family is helped to move from status quo through chaos to new possibilities and new integrations	Awareness and seeds of change are planted in therapy confrontations	Therapist joins the family in a leadership role; changes structure; sets boundaries	Change occurs through action-oriented directives and paradoxical interventions
Techniques and innovations	Family constellation; typical day; goal disclosure; natural/logical consequences	Genograms; dealing with family-of-origin issues; detriangulating relationships	Empathy; touch, communication; sculpting; role playing; family-life chronology	Co-therapy; self-disclosure; confrontation; use of self as change agent	Joining & accommodating; unbalancing; tracking; boundary making; enactments	Reframing; directives and paradox; amplifying; pretending; enactments

433

and some are self-destructive. Some of these aspects may be physical, cognitive, emotional, social, or spiritual. Some are used more than others. These parts emanate from our social interactions and developmental experiences. They are often evaluative in nature, declaring something about who we are and what has meaning to us: "all parts, in their nonextreme, natural state, want something positive for the person and desire to play a valuable role in the internal system" (Breunlin et al., 1997, p. 66). It is when parts become polarized and extreme—or needed parts seem inaccessible—that individuals experience internal conflict.

Stan's problems with alcohol are causing him to experience such a conflict, and a therapist might explore with Stan the different parts of himself that draw him toward alcohol and those that help him refrain from drinking. Every theorist-practitioner who works with the concepts of internal parts posits a super-entity that integrates, governs, organizes, and selects essential parts. That entity, known as the *self* or the *person*, is the "whole" of the individual system—that which operates the rest of the parts. Stan is currently struggling with such a reorganization of his internal parts.

The Teleological Lens

Teleology refers to the study of final causes, goals, endpoints, and purposes. The teleological lens enables the family therapist to develop an understanding of what motivates individual behavior, the systemic purposes of symptoms, the goals of triangulation, and the uses of patterned interactions and routines.

Both individuals and families-as-a-whole act purposively. Purposeful actions promote growth and development when they are characterized by reasonable risk, courage, confidence, self-esteem, energy, optimism, hope, and sequences of experience that open even wider possibilities for experience. Alternatively, actions and interactions characterized by retreat, fear, and protection tend to constrain growth and development.

The teleological lens is associated with the Adlerian, Bowenian, structural, and strategic approaches to family therapy. Adlerian family therapists make particular use of this lens. Purposive action and life goals are central to an Adlerian understanding of individual, internal family systems, called lifestyle assessments (see Chapter 5). Adlerians also use Kefir's (1981) *personality priorities* (significance, pleasing, control, and comfort) to understand impasses and goals during couples counseling. Personality priorities are closely related to Satir's (1988) communication stances (blaming, placating, super reasonable, and irrelevant, respectively) and can be understood as the goals of dysfunctional communication (Bitter, 1993b).

In Adlerian family therapy, goal orientation and recognition are central for understanding motivations of parents and children—and for unlocking mistaken interactions (Bitter, Roberts, & Sonstegard, 2002; Christensen, 1993). Dreikurs first delineated four goals of children's misbehavior as a motivational typology for the everyday behaviors of children. These goals are attention getting, power struggle, revenge, and a demonstration of inadequacy (also called an assumed disability). They act as "shorthand [explanations] consistent patterns of misbehavior in children" (Bitter, 1991, p. 210). Dreikurs (1950; Dreikurs & Soltz, 1964) developed a systematic approach to goal recognition based on (a) descriptions of the child's misbehavior, (b) the parents' reactions to the misbehavior, and (c) the child's reaction to the parents' attempts at discipline.

The teleological lens is central to Adlerian family therapy, but it can be used in any model that includes assessment and the generation of meaning as well as for interventions such as *reframing*, or putting what is known into a new, more useful perspective. Family therapists often reframe difficult behaviors by noting the motivation or personal intentions behind the behaviors. Reframing begins by asking these kinds of questions:

- What purpose does this symptom, interaction, or process serve?
- How does the individual's behavior protect the self?
- What are the social consequences of an action or interaction?
- How are the goals of family members at cross-purposes with each other?
- Are the goals of the family at odds with the goals of therapy?

Sequences: Tracking Patterns of Interaction

One of the defining aspects of family life is that it is ordered, and family members tend to interact in sequences that, over time, are repeated in multiple forms. Breunlin and his associates (1997) refer to these patterns as *embedded sequences*, and they occur at multiple levels within the sequencing metaframework.

Level 1 sequences occur between two or more family members who are face-to-face. The *face-to-face sequence* can be diagrammed as follows:

Father confronts → Daughter enacts hurt → Mother rescues
daughter   and helplessness   daughter

Level 2 sequences support the functioning of the family and become accepted as *routines*. These sequences support processes that are typical of the family and tend to be enacted almost daily. Adlerians initiated the idea of asking family members to describe a "typical day" (Bitter et al., 2002), and this information has become increasingly important for family therapists working with many different models. Here is an example of the morning routine for one family:

Father gets up first and wakes oldest daughter.
↓
Oldest daughter gets up, gets dressed, and feeds dog.
↓
Mother gets up and wakes 3-year-old daughter.
↓
Father fixes breakfast for children while mother dresses 3-year-old.
↓
Children eat. Oldest daughter fixes lunches while mother and father dress.
↓
Parents grab bagels. Everyone leaves for school and work.

In this sequence, individual roles support a smooth process for the whole system. If any part of this routine stops or breaks down, the whole system must adjust.

Level 3 sequences have to do with the *ebbs and flows* of life. These much longer sequences often account for family adjustments to outside forces or developmental changes. The classic leaving home sequence is an example for strategic therapists (Haley, 1980):

1. The child, who has distracted the spousal couple from their relational problems for many years, gets ready to leave for college.
2. Anxiety goes up, and when the young person actually leaves, open conflict, threatening divorce, breaks out.
3. The young person becomes symptomatic at school, requiring a return home, and parental conflict seems to disappear.

When Level 1 and 2 sequences effectively resolve difficulties, the ebbs and flows that constitute the processes of family change at Level 3 also tend to find a functional balance.

Level 4 sequences are *transgenerational*. They include sequences that reflect larger system values and rules about culture or gender roles. These sequences are passed from one generation to the next and are intended to provide a sense of continuity to life. In our discussion of the case of Stan later in the chapter, you will see how the use of alcohol has affected the family over at least three generations and has become part of the family culture.

Adaptive sequences require leadership that is balanced, fair, and cooperative. Maladaptive sequences occur when rules are rigid and inflexible, when parts are polarized, and when change is resisted. Family therapy is often about developing more useful sequences at any or all of these four levels.

The Organization Lens

Individuals and families have some organizing process that holds everything together and provides a sense of unity. In family systems, organization is manifest in family rules, routines, rituals, and expected roles (that is, the living structure of the family). In the early years of family therapy, emphasis was given to the concept of the *hierarchy* of the family system, and strategic interventions were designed to establish a more functional hierarchy and to redistribute the power in the system toward more productive ends.

Breunlin and his colleagues (1997) take a more collaborative approach with families and have replaced the idea of hierarchy with the idea of *leadership*. Collaboration is found in mutual or egalitarian relationships between couples, and the function of leadership in the family is to organize the system in clear, useful ways. For each of the parts to grow and develop as well as contribute to the family as a whole, there must be room for involved members in the decision-making processes; reasonable access to family resources; and appropriate responsibility for self and the system as a whole. In general, the leadership of families works best in the hands of adults—people with some maturity and life experience who parent out of choice and a desire to raise the next generation.

To this concept of leadership, Breunlin and his colleagues (1997) add the concept of balance:

> In balanced systems, [the members] cooperate, are willing to sacrifice some of their individual interests for the greater good, care about one another and feel valued by the larger system, and have clear boundaries that allow a balance between belonging and separateness. (p. 136)

Balanced family leadership requires the ability to be firm, but friendly, and to set developmentally appropriate limits while remaining fair, flexible, and encouraging. In balanced families, individuality and connection to the family are both significant: both fit generational, cultural, and developmental needs. As children get older, balanced leadership shifts to more egalitarian, collaborative stances, and family processes tend to be cooperative, consistent, and caring. In effectively led families, children have a sense of safety, room to grow, and the belief that they are valued.

The Developmental Lens

Though the concept of development took hold in psychology in the 1940s, it did not enter the world of family systems therapy until the 1970s. Even then, many family therapists tended to eschew all that they had learned about individual development in favor of a developmental framework that focused on the nuclear family, a model called the "family life cycle." Unlike individual development models that map the stages of life from birth onward, the family life cycle focuses on six significant transitions (Carter & McGoldrick, 1999):

1. A single, young adult leaves home to live a more or less independent life.
2. Individuals marry or become a couple to build a life together.
3. The couple has children and starts a family.
4. The children become adolescents.
5. The parents launch their children into the world and prepare to live a life without children.
6. The family reaches its later years where children may have to care for parents as well as their own children, and the parents prepare for the end of their lives.

Consider the case of Stan as an example of these transitional stages. Stan is currently in Stage 1 of the family life cycle. He is a young man struggling with the transition from living at home to an independent life. His parents are at Stage 5, struggling with issues related to launching Stan into the world. A complicating factor may be worries they have about living together without children.

The family life cycle perspective was an innovation in developmental literature that widened the conceptualization of development and gave it a decidedly systemic focus. It also depathologized many of the family life experiences that brought couples and families into therapy. The first presentations of the family life cycle were focused almost entirely on a two-parent, Caucasian, nuclear family, but today there are developmental models for single-parent families; remarried, blended, or stepfamilies; cross-generational, extended families; lesbian, gay, and bisexual families; families from diverse cultures; poverty and the family life cycle; and the effects of gender (and roles) in the family life cycle (Carter & McGoldrick, 1999).

Breunlin and his associates (1997) propose a developmental lens (metaframework) that reintegrates individual development with developmental perspectives on the family and society. Their model includes "five levels: biological, individual, subsystemic (relational), familial, and societal" (p. 159). Each level affects the other with no requirement of a specific order for growth and development. The focus of therapy is on whether individuals and families are achieving necessary *levels of competence* to facilitate growth and development.

At the societal level, individuals and families often incorporate the values and beliefs of the dominant cultures in which they live (White & Epston, 1990). In the past, values and mores were passed along through contact with extended family, and to some extent, this may still happen in some communities. We are, however, a global community now, and multiple forms of media have a tremendous influence on individual and familial experience (Gergen, 1991). The power of the dominant culture on families is similar to the powerful influence parents have on young children. This power cannot be ignored. The value of examining the family life cycle can be both remedial (explain behavior viewed as dysfunction) and preventative (prepare the system for change), but it is important to remember that every family is also in the process of individual, relational, and societal development. Family therapy serves a valuable function in challenging patriarchy and other forms of dominant culture privilege, bias, or discrimination.

Change is inevitable and, indeed, it *is* life (Satir et al., 1991). In family therapy, growth and development are desired processes. Our belief in development and evolution is optimistic and hopeful. Family therapists address the needs of individuals while simultaneously considering the needs of relationships, the family, and larger systems. In assessing different levels, family therapists look for constraints and seek to remove them so that natural growth and transitions become possible once again (Breunlin et al., 1997).

The Multicultural Lens

Discrimination and oppression shape experiences and symptoms, and these factors are found in all cultures. The *dominant culture* organizes around two immediate goals, both related to power: (a) it reinforces itself and its values and (b) minimizes the power and influence of alternative positions and the people who hold them (Foucault, 1970, 1980). It is from this power base that all discrimination and oppression flow.

In the United States, the dominant power base is male, heterosexual, Caucasian, English-speaking, Eurocentric, Christian, 35–50 years of age, rich, and educated. Historical narratives are filled with phrases like "the divine right of kings," "manifest destiny," or "in the name of progress." They all have to do with *privilege*, which includes the assumption that those who have it are both "normal" and "the norm." Everything else is a deviation from normal. In dominant cultures, there are those with vast amounts of privilege, and those who experience discrimination—who are *marginalized*, oppressed, or left out.

A multicultural lens challenges dominant culture and introduces diversity and complexity into our understanding of the human condition. This lens reframes dominant culture as simply one of many. It seeks not tolerance but an appreciation and valuing of diversity. McGoldrick, Pearce, and Giordano (1996) describe the multiple cultures that comprise Europe and that have "blended" into the dominant culture we call "American." This multiplicity challenges the notion that there is a single Western norm to which all people should aspire. As therapists, we do well to consider that our perspective might be biased and only one of many useful perspectives in understanding reality.

Breunlin and his colleagues (1997) describe both intracultural and intercultural experiences. Intracultural experiences and sequences happen *within* a cultural system. They serve as cultural definitions, give a sense of continuity to community life, and reinforce values and convictions specific to that culture. Intercultural experiences and sequences happen *between* (or even among) cultural systems. They are based on commonalities of experience that may exist across several cultures.

Ten areas of assessment assist family therapists in bringing a multicultural perspective to their work (Breunlin et al., 1997):

- Membership as an immigrant in a dominant society
- Level of economic privilege or poverty
- Level of education and process of learning
- Ethnicity
- Religion
- Gender
- Age
- Race, discrimination, and oppression
- Minority versus majority status
- Regional background

These assessment areas produce phenomenological meaning that may be different for each member of a family as well as for the therapist. Acknowledging areas of "fit" and areas of difference is foundational for most therapeutic processes. In Stan's family, the multigenerational relationships with alcohol may be based in particular cultural expectations about the use and abuse of this substance. An Irish family's values on this issue may differ significantly from those of an Arab family, for example. Family therapists must view each family through the appropriate multicultural lens in their work.

The Gender Lens

The oldest and most pervasive discrimination and oppression in the world is against women in all cultures, and with few exceptions, across the human life span. Feminists have challenged not only the fundamental precepts of family therapy (Luepnitz, 1988) but also the idea that the family, itself, is good for women (Hare-Mustin, 1978). Women still bear the largest responsibility for, and most of the work related to, child rearing, kin-keeping, homemaking, and community involvement. Financially, women tend to earn less than men in comparable positions. Even when women earn significant wages, they often have little or no say in how the family finances are spent. Between a man and a woman, the woman is more likely to sacrifice self for the good of the whole.

As you will recall from Chapter 12 on feminist therapy, the feminist impact on family therapy has led to a reconsideration of many central tenets. Family therapists have increasingly accepted an advocacy stance as part of their therapy. Therapists can no longer ignore their personal influence and their responsibility to challenge unequal status and treatment of women. Power positions, like hierarchy, enmeshment, and unbalancing—catchwords that have been associated with structural-strategic approaches to families for years—are slowly being replaced with ideas about leadership, connection, conversation, and collaboration.

In Stan's case, a consideration of gender might lead the therapist to examine stereotyped roles that Stan has experienced and stills feels he must follow. We might also consider the ways in which male requirements for power and control, emotional restriction, expectations for achievement and success, and general dominance have affected his relationship with women.

The Process Lens

What is happening between people—the process of communication—is essential to experiential models of family therapy. The meaning of any communication is always contained within the metacommunication: *how* we communicate contextualizes *what* we have to say. Process is also about our movement through significant events in life. *Clarity of process* tells us where we are and delineates where we are likely to go. It allows the therapist and the family to examine where they are in the flow of life, the process of change, and the experience of therapy.

To function effectively, couples and families create routines that enable them to meet the needs and demands of everyday life (Satir & Bitter, 2000). As long as these routines generally help and enable people within their living systems, they are maintained as the status quo. When essential routines are interfered with, the result is a disruption that throws a system out of balance. In the face of disruption, families may initially seek to retreat, but they generally fall into a state of chaos. Because chaos is experienced as crisis, family members often want to make huge decisions even though everything seems out of balance. Therapists immediately become one of the family's external resources with a primary responsibility to help individuals reconnect with their internal resources and strengths, which are often not recognized.

Somewhat paradoxically, change is facilitated by staying present and by not trying to change anything at all. Staying with feelings and present experience, finding ways to become grounded and rebalanced, and reconnecting with useful internal parts and external resources help people to develop new possibilities. With support and practice, new possibilities become a new integration—a new routine and, therefore, a new status quo.

When sources of disruption are extreme, such as an affair in a relationship, a divorce, or a death, therapists often are challenged to deal with family members in chaos. For example, when Stan's wife left him, Stan initially felt devastated and totally blamed himself for another failure. Using a process lens, a family therapist would acknowledge Stan's hurt and fear but be open to exploring other feelings Stan may have, such as betrayal, disappointment, and hopelessness. The most direct route to get to these additional concerns is to simply stay focused on what Stan is feeling in the present.

The process of therapy is intimately connected to the process of change. Carl Whitaker (1976, 1989) used to play with both family process and the process of therapy. He did so with a co-therapist present and many years of therapy experience. Like most family therapists, he recognized that systems were more powerful than individuals—and that the family counselor can easily become triangulated or incorporated into the systemic processes of the family.

In a sense, Whitaker became a source of disruption that initiated the family into a new change process. In one session, he suggested that if the woman was depressed someone in the family must want her dead (Whitaker & Bumberry, 1988). This systems intervention goes beyond what the family is initially willing to consider and invites them into a shared responsibility for the welfare of the woman. At the heart of Whitaker's therapy are these very important process questions.

- What is the family doing with its time in therapy?
- What are the family members experiencing, and what am I experiencing with each family member?
- What place does my informed and educated intuition have in this therapeutic process?
- What is my best use of self with this family?
- What is happening right now?

The eight lenses described here are multidimensional and were developed across several models of family therapy. They serve as a basic structure for assessment. To use them effectively, however, the lenses must be integrated into a coherent therapeutic process. The next section clarifies how this might be done.

A MULTILENSED PROCESS OF FAMILY THERAPY

The eight lenses described in the previous section presuppose certain assumptions about families, the therapist, and family therapy. Families are multilayered systems that both affect and are affected by the larger systems in which they are embedded. Families can be described in terms of their individual members and the various roles they play, the relationships between the members, and the sequential patterns of the interactions. In addition, nuclear families in a global community are often part of extended, if distant, families; multiple families make up a community; multiple communities make up both regions and cultures, which in turn constitute nations (or society). The power of these macrosystems to influence family life—especially in the areas of gender and culture—is significant. Given our presuppositions about families and the larger systems in which families are embedded, a multilensed approach to family therapy is essential.

Several forms and structures have been proposed for integrative models of family counseling and therapy (e.g., Carlson, Sperry, & Lewis, 1997; Gladding, 2002; Nichols, 2000; Worden, 2003). The integrative model we have chosen to present here is similar to the "blueprint for therapy" proposed by Breunlin and colleagues (1997, pp. 281–316), but it allows for an enlarged integration of ideas from multiple models of family therapy. Similar to a piece of classical music, the process of family therapy, it seems to us, has movements. These movements can be described as separate experiences embedded in the larger flow of therapy. In this section we describe four general movements, each with different tasks: forming a relationship, conducting an assessment, hypothesizing and sharing meaning, and facilitating change. In rare instances, these four movements might occur within a single session: in most cases, however, each movement requires multiple sessions.

Forming a Relationship

Over the years, family systems therapists have used a wide range of metaphors to describe the role of the therapist and the therapeutic relationship. As you have seen in the two previous chapters, in the last decade, the emergence of feminist and postmodern models in therapy has moved the field of family therapy toward more egalitarian, collaborative, cooperative, co-constructing relationships (see Andersen, 1987, 1991; Anderson, 1993; Anderson & Goolishian, 1992; Epston & White, 1992; Luepnitz, 1988).

The debate Carl Rogers (1980) first introduced to individual therapy in the 1940s has reemerged within family therapy in the form of these questions:

- What expertise does the therapist have in relation to the family, and how should that expertise be used?
- How directive should therapists be in relation to families, and what does that say about uses of power in therapy?

We believe a multilensed approach to family therapy is best supported by a collaborative therapist–client relationship in which mutual respect, caring, empathy, and a genuine interest in others is primary. In addition, we believe directed actions and enactments are most useful when they are a joint venture of both the therapist and the family.

Therapists begin to form a relationship with clients from the moment of first contact. In most cases, we believe therapists should make their own appointments, answer initial questions clients may have, and give clients a sense of what to expect when they come. This is also a time when counselors can let families know their position on whether all members should be present. Some family therapists will work with any of those members of the family who wish to come; others will only see the family if everyone is a part of the therapy session.

From the moment of first face-to-face contact, good therapeutic relationships start with efforts at making contact with each person present (Satir & Bitter, 2000). Whether it is called *joining*, *engagement*, or simple *care and concern*, it is the therapist's responsibility to meet each person with openness and warmth. Generally, a focused interest on each family member helps to reduce the anxiety the family may be feeling.

Therapeutic process and structure are part of the therapist's job description. It is important for family members to introduce themselves and to express their concerns, but the therapist should not focus too tightly on content issues. Understanding family process is almost always facilitated by *how* questions. Questions that begin with *what*, *why*, *where*, or *when* tend to overemphasize content details (Gladding, 2002).

Conducting an Assessment

The eight lenses we have proposed provide structure for conducting family assessments, but other assessment procedures, such as *genograms* (McGoldrick, Gerson, & Shellenberger, 1999), *circular questioning*, or even *formal tests and rating scales* (see, for example, Gottman, 1999), may also be useful.

As the therapist listens to family members describe their hopes for the family, it is often difficult to keep all eight perspectives going at once. Focusing on the meta-issues presented in content is one way to begin to select lenses that will provide meaning for the therapist and the family. For example, suppose Tammy is upsetting the family system by ignoring the curfew her parents have set for her. The therapist might ask: "What will happen if Tammy stays out past curfew and is picked up by the police? Who will be most upset by this?" Here is her father's reply:

> I will probably be the most upset on the outside. I tend to go off before I think, and then I regret it later. On the other hand, her mother may not show it immediately, but her hurt will stay with her longer, and then she will get mad at me for "letting Tammy off the hook."

She will say that Tammy is manipulating me, but I just don't see why we should keep fighting about things. It doesn't do any good. We fight, and Tammy disappears. She wants to run with the big kids, some of whom are in college, over 18, and have no curfew.

The therapist might choose to select any one of these lenses for further inquiry:

Internal Family Systems: Work with anger and guilt parts.

Sequences: Work related to the sequential patterns for resolving conflict and handling problems.

Gender Lens: Work related to the roles of men, women, and female children in families.

Developmental Lens: Work around issues related to Tammy wanting to be older than she is.

In the assessment process, it is helpful to inquire about family perspectives on issues inherent in each of the lenses. We have already noted some questions related to a few of the lenses. Here, are some starting questions for each lens that may be useful in a more detailed assessment.

Internal Family Systems

- What parts do each of you bring to this session?
- What parts do each of you rely on to describe who you really are?
- Sometimes we find the best parts of ourselves almost at war (polarized) with other parts of ourselves. What parts cause internal conflicts in you?
- Do certain parts of you get ignored?
- Does it seem to you that interactions with your (spouse, parents, children) tend to call out certain parts of you more than others?

The Teleological Lens

- What purposes do you seem to have for what you feel (or how you behave)?
- What purpose is served when your children interact with you in the way they do?
- When you think about your intent, does it match the actual outcome?
- What goals do you have for yourself and for other people in the family?

Sequences

- What routines support your daily living?
- Who does what with whom when decisions are made, conflicts are resolved, or problems handled?
- What parts are involved in the most common sequences in the family?
- How does a typical day go?

■ Are there processes, patterns, or sequences that characterize current or past transitions for the family?

The Organization Lens

■ Are the parents effective leaders of the family?
■ How do the children respond to parental leadership?
■ Is the process of leadership balanced or imbalanced?
■ Does it lead to harmony or conflict?
■ Does the family need further education about effective leadership, or are there internal parts that constrain such leadership?

The Developmental Lens

■ Where is each person in the family in relation to personal biological, cognitive, emotional, and social development?
■ Where is the family in the family life cycle, and how are they handling transitions?
■ What relational processes have developed over time, and how have they changed or developed through transitional periods?
■ What developments in larger systems (especially society or the world) are affecting the family?

The Multicultural Lens

■ What cultures are in the family backgrounds of each of the family members?
■ In what culture or region is the family currently living?
■ Is immigration or migration a recent family experience?
■ How do economics, education, ethnicity, religion, race, regional background, gender, and age affect family processes?
■ How is the fit between the therapist and the family with regard to economics, education, ethnicity, religion, gender, age, race, majority/minority status, and regional background?

The Gender Lens

■ What gender role is each member of the family assuming?
■ What effects has patriarchy had on this family and its members?
■ Where are family members in terms of gender development: traditional, gender-aware, polarized, transitional, or balanced?
■ What ideas in relation to gender need to be affirmed or challenged?
■ What effect would role reversals have on the personal parts and relational activities of the family members?
■ What is the impact of your community's beliefs about men and women on the members of your family?
■ What impact will your gender roles have on the preparation of young girls and boys for living in this new century?

The Process Lens

- Are there family members who lack a clear sense of purpose, function out of awareness, have poor contact with others, or lack experiences to support a productive life?
- Where is this family in the process of change?
- What resources (internal or external) need to be accessed?
- What am I, as the therapist, experiencing, and what does it tell me about the relationship and process of therapy?
- Which communication patterns do family members use under stress?

Hypothesizing and Sharing Meaning

To hypothesize is to form a set of ideas about people, systems, and situations that focus meaning in a useful way. In multilensed family therapy, hypothesizing flows from understandings generated by work through the eight lenses discussed previously. Two questions are germane to the form of hypothesizing one chooses to do: (1) How much faith do the therapist and the family have in the ideas they generate? (2) How much of an influence is the therapist willing to be in the lives of people and families?

Family counselors, like individual therapists, cannot avoid influencing the family and its members. The question is: What kind of influence will the therapist bring to the session? Satir and Bitter (2000) suggest that family therapists cannot be in charge of the people but that they need to be in charge of the process; that is, they own the responsibility for how therapy is conducted. Feminists and social constructionists are, perhaps, the most expressive of their concerns about the misuse of power in therapy. They are joined by multiculturalists, person-centered therapists, Adlerians, and existentialists, to name a few, who have also witnessed the often unconscious imposition of "dominant culture" in therapy. In the early days of family therapy, the mostly male therapists often ignored the effects on family life of patriarchy, poverty, racism, cultural discrimination and marginalization, homoprejudice, and other societal problems. At the strategic-structural end of the continuum, therapists were more likely to claim a certain expertise in systems work that allowed them to make direct interventions in the enactment of "needed" changes in the family. To counteract therapeutic abuses and what some perceived to be an ongoing misuse of power in therapy, some narrative therapists adopted a *decentered* position in relation to the family (White, 1997). Like person-centered therapists before them, decentered therapists seek to keep families and family members at the center of the therapeutic process.

It is important for families to be invited into respectful, essentially collaborative dialogues in therapeutic work. The different perspectives discovered in this work tend to coalesce into working hypotheses, and sharing these ideas provides the family with a window into the heart and mind of the therapist as well as themselves. Sharing hypotheses almost immediately invites and invokes feedback from various family members. And it is this feedback that allows the therapist and the family to develop a good fit with each other, which in turn tends to cement a working relationship.

The tentative hypothesizing and sharing process that Dreikurs (1950, 1997) developed is well designed for the kind of collaborative work envisioned here. Dreikurs would use a passionate interest and curiosity to ask questions and gather together the subjective perspectives of family members. And he would honor ideas that individuals brought to their joint understanding. When he had an idea that he wanted to share, he would often seek permission for his disclosure:

1. I have an idea I would like to share with you. Would you be willing to hear it?
2. Could it be that . . .

The value of this way of presenting hypotheses is that it invites families and family members to consider and to engage without giving up their right to discard anything that does not fit. When a suggested idea does not fit, the therapist is then clear about letting it go and letting the family redirect the conversation toward more useful conceptualizations.

Facilitating Change

Facilitating change is what happens when family therapy is viewed as a joint or collaborative process. Techniques are more important to models that see the *therapist-as-expert* and in charge of *making change happen*. Collaborative approaches require *planning*. "Planning can still include what family therapy has called *techniques* or *interventions*, but with the family's participation" (Breunlin et al., 1997, p. 292). Two of the most common forms for facilitation of change are enactments and assignment of tasks. Both of these processes work best when the family co-constructs them with the therapist—or at least accepts the rationale for their use.

Even within the change process, the first seven lenses can be used as a guide for preferred or desired outcomes. In general, internal parts function best when they are balanced (not polarized) and when the individual experiences personal parts as resources. Being able to think is usually more useful than emotional reactivity; being able to feel is better than not feeling; good contact with others is more rewarding than isolation or self-absorption; and taking reasonable risks in the service of growth and development is more beneficial than stagnation or a retreat into fear.

Further, knowing the goals and purposes for our behaviors, feelings, and interactions tends to give us choices about their use. Similarly, understanding the patterns we enact in face-to-face relationships, the ebbs and flows of life, or across generations provides multiple avenues for challenging patterns and the enactment of new possibilities.

Family Therapy Applied to the Case of Stan

In our work with Stan here, we include examples of forming a relationship and joining, reading Stan's genogram, a multilensed assessment, reframing, boundary setting in therapy, and facilitating change. In the rich field of family therapy, there are many useful models and ways to work with families. The processes described here do not represent the *right way* to do family systems therapy; rather, they represent some possible ways to work from a multilensed approach.

At an intake interview, a family therapist meets with Stan to explore his issues and concerns and to learn more about him and his life situation. As they talk, the therapist brings an intense interest and curiosity to the interview and wonders out loud about the familial roots of some of Stan's problems. It does not take much of an inquiry to learn that parts of Stan are still very much engaged with his parents and siblings, no matter how difficult these relationships seem to him. This initial conversation involves the development of a genogram of Stan's family of origin (see Figure 14-1). This map will serve both Stan and the therapist as a guide to the people and the processes that constitute Stan's life.

Stan's genogram is really a family picture, or map, of his family-of-origin system. In this genogram, we learn that Stan's grandparents tend to have fairly long lives. Stan's maternal grandparents are both alive. The shaded lower half of their square and circle indicates that each had some problem with alcohol. In the case of Tom, Stan reports that he was an admitted alcoholic who recommitted himself to Christ and found help through Alcoholics Anonymous. Stan's maternal grandmother always drank a little socially and with her husband, but she never considered herself to have a problem. In her later years, however, she seems to sneak alcohol more and more, and it is a source of distress in her marriage. Stan also knows that Margie drinks a lot, because he has been drinking with his aunt for years. She is the one who gave him his first drink.

Angie, Stan's mother, married Frank Sr. after he had stopped drinking, also with the help of AA. He still goes to meetings. Angie is suspicious of all men around alcohol. She is especially upset with Stan and with Judy's husband, Matt, who "also drinks too

much." The genogram makes it easy to see the pattern of alcohol problems in this family.

The jagged lines ∧∧∧ between Frank Sr. and Angie indicate conflict in the relationship. The three solid lines ═══ between Frank Sr. and Frank Jr., and between Angie and Karl, indicate a very close or even fused relationship. The double lines ═══ between Karl and Stan are used to note a close relationship only. As we will see, Karl actually looks up to Stan in this family. The dotted lines - - - - - between Frank Sr. and Stan and between Frank Jr. and Stan indicate a distant or even disengaged relationship.

Since the family therapist believes that the whole family is involved in Stan's use of alcohol, she spends a good part of the first session exploring with Stan processes for asking his other family members to join him in therapy. Stan may have many difficulties, but at the moment his difficulty with alcohol is the primary focus. Alcohol is a negative part of his life, and as such it has systemic meaning. It may have started out as a symptom of other problems, but now the alcohol is a problem in itself. From a systemic perspective, the questions are "How does this problem affect the family?" and "Is the family using this problem to serve some other purpose?"

In the first therapy session with the family, the therapist's main focus is in forming a relationship with each of the family members, but even here, avenues into various lenses present themselves.

Therapist [to Frank Sr.]: I know this time was an inconvenience for you, but I want you to know how appreciative I am that you came. Can you tell me what it's like for you to be here? [*forming a relationship through joining*]

Frank Sr.: Well, I have to tell you that I don't like it much. [*pause*] Things are a lot different today than they used to be. We didn't have counseling 20 years ago. I had a problem with drinking at one point, but I got over it. I just quit—on my own. That's what Stan needs to do. He just needs to stop.

Therapist: So I'm hearing that life is better for you without alcohol, and you would like Stan's life to be better too. [*reframing*]

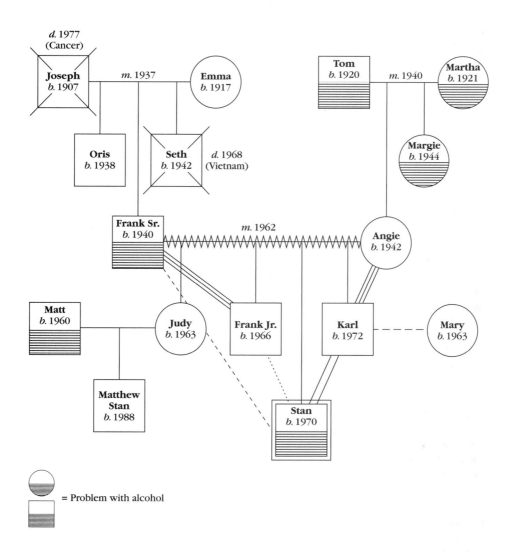

FIGURE 14-1   Three Generation Genogram of Stan's Family

Frank Sr.: Yeah. I'd like his life to be better in a lot of different ways.

Therapist: Angie, what about you? What is it like for you to be here? [*forming a relationship with each member*]

Angie: It's heartbreaking. It's always heartbreaking. He [*referring to Frank Sr.*] makes it sound as if he just summoned up his own personal power and quit drinking through his own strength of character. That's a laugh. I threatened to leave him. That's what really happened. I was ready to get a divorce! And we're Catholic. We don't get divorced. [*possible face-to-face sequence around family stress and coping*]

Therapist: So you've been through this before.

(continued on next page)

Angie: Oh my, yes. My father and mother drank. Dad still does. My sister won't admit it, but she drinks too much. She gets crazy with it. Judy's husband has a problem. I'm surrounded. I get so angry. I wish they would all just die or go away. [*possible trangenerational family sequence: an avenue for exploring values, beliefs, and rules*]

Therapist: So this is something the whole family has been dealing with for a long time.

Angie: Not everyone. I don't drink. Frankie and Judy don't drink. And Karl doesn't seem to have a problem.

Therapist: Is that how the family gets divided: into those who drink and those who don't? [*possible organization lens application*]

Judy: Drinking isn't the only problem we have. It's probably not even the most important.

Therapist: Say more about that.

Judy: Stan has always had it hard. I feel sorry for him. Frankie is clearly Dad's favorite [*Frank Sr. protests, saying he doesn't have favorites*], and things have always come easily for me. And Karl, he gets whatever he wants. He's Mom's favorite. Mom and Dad have fought a lot over the years. None of us have been all that happy, but Stan seems to have gotten the worst of it. [*again, possible sequence and organization lens applications*]

Frank Jr.: As I remember it, Stan gave Dad and Mom a lot to fight about. He was always messing up in one way or another.

Therapist: Frankie, when your father was talking earlier, I sensed he had some disappointment about Stan too, but he also wanted to see things work out better for him. Is that true for you too? [*reframing Frankie's comment, maintaining a focus on new possibilities and new relations that might be developed*]

Frank Jr.: Yes. I would like his life to be better.

The initial part of this counseling session has been devoted to meeting family members, listening intently to the multiple perspectives they present, and reframing Stan's problem into a family desire for a positive outcome. Although there is a long way to go, the seeds of change have already been planted. There is evidence in these early interactions that

Stan's problem has a multigenerational context. If this context is explored, family sequences that support and maintain alcohol as a problem may be identified. It is possible to track these interactions and to work toward more congruent communications. Evolving relational, organizational, developmental sequences might be explored as a means of freeing family members for new possibilities in their life together. Among other possibilities still to be explored are perspectives related to gender and culture. If the therapist were just listening to Stan, only one point of view would be evident. In this family session, multiple perspectives and the entire interactive process become clear in a very short time.

As the family interview proceeds, a number of possibilities are presented for consideration. The therapist considers and may structure therapy around any or all of the following possibilities:

1. Stan's parents have not functioned as a leadership team for a long time, and both their spousal relationship and their parenting have suffered.

2. The adult siblings need a new opportunity to function together without the influence and distractions continually imposed by the parents.

3. Stan has been reduced to a single part (his alcoholic part), and his description and experience of himself needs to be enlarged—both for his own perspective and in the eyes of others.

A new place for Stan in the family, a better way of relating, and an ability to access "lost" parts of his internal system are all critical to winning his battle with alcohol. As therapy continues, it becomes clear that there are really two separate relational–organization hypotheses that must be explored. One is that the spousal relationship has been defined by the problem of alcohol too, and it has not evolved or developed over the years. Two, the transgenerational sequences have targeted Stan and assigned him to a fixed role that he has been expected to play that has blocked development past his middle to late adolescence, the period in which he started drinking.

Follow-Up: You Continue as Stan's Family Therapist

Use these questions to help you think about how you would counsel Stan from a family systems perspective:

- What unique values do you see in working with Stan from a multilensed, systemic perspective as opposed to doing individual therapy?
- What internal parts might Stan re-access as he continues in therapy? What parts of him might be polarized?

- Assuming that Stan was successful in getting at least some of his family members to another session, where would you want to begin? How would you get everyone involved in the sessions?
- What are some specific ways in which you might explore other lenses with this family?
- What hypotheses are you developing, and how might you share them with the family?
- Are there systemic interventions that you might find hopeful in terms of facilitating change?

FAMILY SYSTEMS THERAPY FROM A MULTICULTURAL PERSPECTIVE

Contributions to Multicultural Counseling

One of the contributions of the systemic perspective in working from a multicultural framework is that many ethnic and cultural groups place great value on the extended family. If therapists are working with an individual from a cultural background that gives special value to including grandparents, aunts, and uncles in the treatment, it is easy to see that family approaches have a distinct advantage over individual therapy. Family therapists can do some excellent networking with members of the extended family.

In many ways, family therapists are like systems anthropologists. They approach each family as a unique culture whose particular characteristics must be understood. Like larger cultural systems, families have a unique language that governs behavior, communication, and even how to feel about and experience life. Families have celebrations and rituals that mark transitions, protect them against outside interference, and connect them to their past as well as a projected future.

Just as differentiation means coming to understand our family well enough to be a part of it—to belong—and also to be separate and our own person, understanding cultures allows therapists and families to appreciate diversity and to contextualize family experiences in relation to the larger cultures. Today, family therapists explore the individual culture of the family, the larger cultures to which the family members belong, and the host culture that dominates the family's life. They look for ways in which culture can both inform and modify family work. Interventions are no longer applied universally, regardless of the cultures involved: rather, they are adapted and even designed to join with the cultural systems.

Limitations for Multicultural Counseling

Given the multicultural lens and collaborative approach of family systems therapy, it is difficult to find limitations for multicultural counseling. This model of family therapy embraces attitudes, knowledge, and skills that are essential to a multicultural perspective. Perhaps the major concern for non-Western cultures would be with regard to the balance that this model advocates for the individual versus the collective. The process of differentiation occurs in most cultures, but it takes on a different shape because of cultural norms. For instance, a young person may become separate from her parents yet not move out of the house. When ethnic-minority families immigrate to North America, their children often adapt to a Western concept of differentiation. In such cases, the intergenerational process of therapy is appropriate if the therapist is sensitive to the family of origin's cultural roots. Although a multilensed approach addresses the notion of togetherness and individuality from a balanced perspective, many non-Western cultures would not embrace a theory that valued individuality above loyalty to family in any form. Nor would non-Western cultures have the same conceptualizations of time or even emotions. Therapists, regardless of their model of therapy, must find ways to enter the family's world and honor the traditions that support the family.

 # SUMMARY AND EVALUATION

Summary

Let's first review the themes that unite the many approaches to family therapy, with particular emphasis on the multilensed approach.

BASIC ASSUMPTION   If we hope to work therapeutically with an individual, it is critical to consider him or her within the family system. An individual's problematic behavior grows out of the interactional unit of the family as well as the larger community and societal systems.

FOCUS OF FAMILY THERAPY   Most of the family therapies tend to be brief, because families who seek professional help typically want resolution of some problematic symptom. Changing the system can stimulate change quickly. In addition to being short-term, solution-focused, and action-oriented, family therapy tends to deal with present interactions. The main focus of family therapy is on here-and-now interactions in the family system. One way in which family therapy differs from many individual therapies is its emphasis on how current family relationships contribute to the development and maintenance of symptoms.

ROLE OF GOALS AND VALUES   Specific goals are determined by the practitioner's orientation or by a collaborative process between family and therapist. Global goals include using interventions that enable individuals and the family to change in ways that will reduce their distress. Tied to the question of what goals should guide a therapist's interventions is the question of the therapist's values. Family therapy is grounded on a set of values and theoretical assumptions. Ultimately, every intervention a therapist makes is an expression of a value judgment. It is critical for therapists, regardless of their theoretical orientation, to be aware of their values and monitor how these values influence their practice with families.

HOW FAMILIES CHANGE   An integrative approach to the practice of family therapy includes guiding principles that help the therapist organize goals, interactions, observations, and ways to promote change. Some perspectives of family systems therapy focus on perceptual and cognitive change, others deal mainly with changing feelings, and still other theories emphasize behavioral change. Regardless of the lens that a family therapist operates from, change needs to happen in relationships, not just within the individual.

TECHNIQUES OF FAMILY THERAPY   The intervention strategies therapists employ are best considered in conjunction with their personal characteristics. Goldenberg and Goldenberg (2004) and Nichols and Schwartz (2001) emphasize that techniques are tools for achieving therapeutic goals but that these intervention strategies do not make a family therapist. Personal characteristics such as respect for clients, compassion, empathy, and sensitivity are human qualities that influence the manner in which techniques are delivered. It is also essential to have a rationale for the techniques that are used, with some sense of the expected outcomes. Faced with meeting the demands of clinical practice, practitioners will need to be flexible in selecting intervention strategies. The central consideration is what is in the best interests of the family.

A multilensed approach to family therapy is more complex than models with a singular focus. At least initially, some of the confidence and clarity that might be gained from a single approach may be lost, but in time the flexibility to change directions is an asset. We have presented a structure for therapy that is useful across models. We have integrated a substructure for the use of multiple perspectives (lenses) in assessment, hypothesizing, and facilitating change. And we have described a collaborative process for therapy in which both the family and the therapist share influence according to the needs of the situation. It is our hope that this chapter gives you enough of an introduction to the diverse field of family therapy that you will want to learn more through reading as well as watching the many videotapes currently available.

Contributions of Family Systems Approaches

One of the key contributions of most systemic approaches is that neither the individual nor the family is blamed for a particular dysfunction. The family is empowered through the process of identifying and exploring internal, developmental, and purposeful interactional patterns. At the same time, a systems perspective recognizes that individuals and families are affected by external forces and systems, among them illness, shifting gender patterns, culture, and socioeconomic considerations. If change is to occur in families or with individuals, therapists must be aware of as many systems of influence as possible.

Most of the individual therapies considered in this textbook fail to give a primary focus to the systemic factors in influencing the individual. Family therapy redefines the individual as a system embedded within many other systems, which sheds an entirely different perspective on assessment and treatment. An advantage to this viewpoint is that an individual is not scapegoated as the "bad person" in the family. Rather than blaming either the "identified patient" or a family, the entire family has an opportunity (a) to examine the multiple perspectives and interactional patterns that characterize the unit and (b) to participate in finding solutions.

Limitations and Criticisms of Family Systems Approaches

In the early days of family therapy, therapists all too often got lost in their consideration of the "system." In adopting the language of systems, therapists began to describe and think of families as being made up of "dyads" and "triads"; as being "functional" or "dysfunctional," "stuck" or "unstuck," and "enmeshed" or "disengaged"; and as displaying "positive" and "negative" outcomes and "feedback loops." It was as if the family were a well-oiled machine or perhaps a computer that occasionally broke down. Just as it was easy to fix a machine without an emotional consideration of the parts involved, some therapists approached family systems work with little concern for the individuals as long as the "whole" of the family "functioned" better. Enactments, ordeals, and paradoxical interventions were often "done to" clients—sometimes even without their knowledge (see Haley, 1963, 1976, 1984; Minuchin & Fishman, 1981; Selvini Palazzolli, Boscolo, Cecchin, & Prata, 1978).

Feminists were perhaps the first, but not the only, group to lament the loss of a personal perspective within a systemic framework. As the field moves now toward an integration of individual and systemic frameworks, it is important to reinvest the language of therapy with human emotional terminology that honors the place real people have always held in families.

 WHERE TO GO FROM HERE

To learn more about family systems approaches to therapy, join the International Association of Marital and Family Counselors (IAMFC), a division of the ACA. *The Family Journal* is the official journal of IAMFC, and it aims to advance the theory, research, and practice of counseling with couples and families from a family systems perspective. In addition to other membership benefits, IAMFC members receive a subscription to *The Family Journal*. For more information about this association, contact:

Robert L. Smith, Executive Director, IAMFC
University of Colorado at Denver
Campus Box 106, P. O. Box 173364
Denver, CO 80217-3364

Another option is to join the American Association for Marriage and Family Therapy, which has a student membership category. You must obtain an official application, including the names of at least two Clinical Members from whom the association can request official endorsements. You also need a statement signed by the coordinator or director of a graduate program in marital and family therapy in a regionally accredited educational institution, verifying your current enrollment. Student membership may be held until receipt of a qualifying graduate degree or for a maximum of 5 years. Members receive the *Journal of Marital and Family Therapy*, which is published four times a year, and a subscription to six issues yearly of *The Family Therapy Magazine*. For a copy of the AAMFT Code of Ethics, membership applications, and further information, contact:

American Association for Marriage and Family Therapy
112 South Alfred Street
Alexandria, VA 22314
Telephone: (703) 838-9808
Fax: (703) 838-9805
Web site: http://www.aamft.org

InfoTrac College Edition Resources

Family Systems Therapy   The following key words are listed in such a way as to allow the InfoTrac College Edition search engine to locate a wider range of articles in the online library. The key words should be entered exactly as shown, to include asterisks, "W1," and "AND."

Murray Bowen	Family systems the*
Jay Haley	Family systems theory
Salvador Minuchin	Family systems therapy
Virginia Satir	Family W2 system*
Carl Whitaker	Family W2 dysfunction
Intergenerational W1 approach	Family W2 origin
Strategic family therapy	Genogram*
Family therapy	

Recommended Supplementary Readings

Ethnicity and Family Therapy (McGoldrick, Pearce, & Giordano, 1996) is the seminal work on culture in family therapy. The authors review the importance of cultural considerations in relation to family therapy and provide chapters on the background, research, and therapy issues of more than 15 cultures.

Family Therapy Basics (Worden, 2003) offers practical guidelines for conducting family interviews, emphasizes common clinical problems, and serves as a springboard for clinical and theoretical discussions.

Family Therapy: Concepts and Methods (Nichols & Schwartz, 2001) is an AAMFT-based text that covers seven of the major contemporary family systems models. The final chapter presents an integration of key themes among diverse approaches to family therapy.

Family Therapy: History, Theory, and Practice (Gladding, 2002) is an overview of family therapy models and therapeutic interventions designed for counselors associated with ACA.

Family Therapy: An Overview (Goldenberg & Goldenberg, 2004) provides an excellent basic overview of these contemporary perspectives on family therapy.

Family Therapy: A Systemic Integration (Becvar & Becvar, 2003) provides a clear and comprehensive discussion of the contemporary models of family therapy.

Metaframeworks: Transcending the Models of Family Therapy (Breunlin, Schwartz, & MacKune-Karrer, 1997) is the basis for a multilensed approach for understanding families and the larger system in which they are embedded. A blueprint for integrative family therapy is provided.

The Practice of Family Therapy: Key Elements Across Models (Hanna & Brown, 2004) focuses on the diversity of family therapy and integrates common elements of the field. It also deals with family therapy assessment and treatment skills.

Theories and Strategies of Family Therapy (Carlson & Kjos, 2002) is a comprehensive presentation of family therapy models with chapters written by people who practice what they have demonstrated in the video series entitled *Family Therapy With the Experts* (Carlson & Kjos, 1999).

Family Counseling and Therapy (Horne, 2000) is a comprehensive overview of the major models of family therapy, each written by an expert in the field. The format of the book allows for comparisons among the models.

Effectiveness Research in Marriage and Family Therapy (Sprenkle, 2002) presents chapters written by scholars in the field that support the effectiveness and efficacy of family therapy in areas such as alcohol abuse, marital problems, relationship enhancement, domestic violence, affective disorders, and physical disorders. Also included is a meta-analysis of marriage and family therapy interventions.

References and Suggested Readings

ADLER, A. (1927). *Understanding human nature* (W. B. Wolfe, Trans.). New York: Fawcett.

AMERICAN PSYCHIATRIC ASSOCIATION. (2000). *Diagnostic and statistical manual of mental disorders* (4th ed., text revision). Washington, DC: Author.

ANDERSEN, T. (1987). The reflecting team: Dialogue and metadialogue in clinical work. *Family process, 26*(4), 415–428.

ANDERSEN, T. (1991). The reflecting team: Dialogues and dialogues about the dialogues*. New York: Norton.

ANDERSON, H. (1993). On a roller coaster: A collaborative language system approach to therapy. In S. Friedman (Ed.), *The new language of change* (pp. 324–344). New York: Guilford Press.

*ANDERSON, H., & GOOLISHIAN, H. (1992). The client is the expert: A not-knowing approach to therapy. In S. McNamee & K. J. Gergen (Eds.), *Therapy as social construction* (pp. 25–39). Newbury Park, CA: Sage.

*BECVAR, D. S., & BECVAR, R. J. (2003). *Family therapy: A systemic integration* (5th ed.). Needham Heights, MA: Allyn & Bacon.

BITTER, J. R. (1991). Conscious motivations: An enhancement to Dreikurs' goals of children's misbehavior. *Individual Psychology, 47*(2), 210–221.

BITTER, J. R. (1993a). Communication styles, personality priorities, and social interest: Strategies for helping couples build a life together. *Individual Psychology, 49* (3-4), 330–350.

BITTER, J. R. (1993b). Satir's parts party with couples. In T. S. Nelson & T. S. Trepper (Eds.), *101 interventions in family therapy* (pp. 132–136). New York: Haworth Press.

*BITTER, J. R., ROBERTS, A., & SONSTEGARD, M. A. (2002). Adlerian family therapy. In J. Carlson & D. Kjos (Eds.), *Theories and strategies of family therapy* (pp. 41–79). Boston: Allyn & Bacon.

*BREUNLIN, D. C., SCHWARTZ, R. C., & MACKUNE-KARRER, B. (1997). *Metaframeworks: Transcending the models of family therapy* (Rev. ed.). San Francisco: Jossey-Bass.

CARLSON, J., & KJOS, D. (Producers & Moderators). (1999). *Family therapy with the experts: Instruction, demonstration, discussion* [videotape series]. Boston: Allyn & Bacon.

*CARLSON, J., & KJOS, D. (Eds.). (2002). *Theories and strategies of family therapy*. Boston: Allyn & Bacon.

*CARLSON, J., SPERRY, L., & LEWIS, J. A. (1997). *Family therapy: Ensuring treatment efficacy*. Pacific Grove, CA: Brooks/Cole.

*CARTER, B., & McGOLDRICK, M. (1999). *The expanded family life cycle: Individual, family and social perspectives* (3rd ed.). Needham Heights, MA: Allyn & Bacon.

CHRISTENSEN, O. C. (Ed.). (1993). *Adlerian family counseling* (Rev. ed.). Minneapolis, MN: Educational Media Corp. (Original work published 1983)

COREY, G. (2005). *Case Approach to Counseling and Psychotherapy* (6th ed.). Belmont, CA: Brooks/Cole.

DREIKURS, R. (1950). The immediate purpose of children's misbehavior, its recognition and correction. *Internationale Zeitschrift fur Individual-psychologie, 19*, 70–87.

DREIKURS, R. (1957). Our child guidance clinics in Chicago. *Collected papers of Rudolf Dreikurs*. Eugene, OR: University of Oregon Press.

DREIKURS, R. (1973). Counseling for family adjustment. In R. Dreikurs, *Psychodynamics, psychotherapy, and counseling* (Rev. ed.). Chicago: Alfred Adler Institute. (Original work published 1949)

---

*Books and articles marked with an asterisk are suggested for further study.

DREIKURS, R. (1997). Holistic medicine. *Individual Psychology, 53*(2), 127–205.

*DREIKURS, R., & SOLTZ, V. (1964). *Children: The challenge*. New York: Hawthorn.

EICHLER, M. (1988). *Nonsexist research methods*. London: Allen & Unwin.

EPSTON, D., & WHITE, M. (1992). Consulting your consultants: The documentation of alternative knowledges. In *Experience, contradiction, narrative and imagination: Selected papers of David Epston and Michael White, 1989–1991* (pp. 11–26). Adelaide, South Australia: Dulwich Centre Publications.

FOUCAULT, M. (1970). *The order of things: An archaeology of the human sciences*. New York: Random House.

FOUCAULT, M. (1980). *Power/knowledge: Selected interviews and other writings*. New York: Pantheon Books.

GERGEN, K. J. (1991). *The saturated self: Dilemmas of identity in contemporary life*. New York: Basic Books.

*GLADDING, S. T. (2002). *Family therapy: History, theory, and practice* (3rd ed.). Upper Saddle River, NJ: Merrill/Prentice-Hall.

GOLDENBERG, H., & GOLDENBERG, I. (2002). *Counseling today's families* (4th ed.). Pacific Grove, CA: Brooks/Cole.

*GOLDENBERG, I., & GOLDENBERG, H. (2004). *Family therapy: An overview* (6th ed.). Pacific Grove, CA: Brooks/Cole.

GOTTMAN, J. M. (1999). *The marriage clinic: A scientifically based marital therapy*. New York: Norton.

HALEY, J. (1963). *Strategies of psychotherapy*. New York: Grune & Stratton.

HALEY, J. (1976). *Problem-solving therapy: New strategies for effective family therapy*. San Francisco: Jossey-Bass.

*HALEY, J. (1980). *Leaving home*. New York: McGraw-Hill.

HALEY, J. (1984). *Ordeal therapy*. San Francisco: Jossey-Bass.

*HANNA, S. M., & BROWN, J. H. (2004). *The practice of family therapy: Key elements across models* (3rd ed.). Belmont, CA: Brooks/Cole.

*HARE-MUSTIN, R. T. (1978). A feminist approach to family therapy. *Family Process, 17*(2), 181–194.

*HORNE, A. M. (2000). *Family counseling and therapy* (3rd ed.). Itasca, IL: F.E. Peacock.

KEFIR, N. (1981). Impasse/priority therapy. In R. J. Corsini (Ed.), *Handbook of innovative psychotherapies* (pp. 401–415). New York: Wiley.

*KERR, M. E., & BOWEN, M. (1988). *Family evaluation: An approach based on Bowen theory*. New York: Norton.

*LUEPNITZ, D. A. (1988). *The family interpreted: Feminist theory in clinical practice*. New York: Basic Books.

*MADANES, C. (1981). *Strategic family therapy*. San Francisco: Jossey-Bass.

MADANES, C. (1984). *Behind the one-way mirror*. San Francisco: Jossey-Bass.

MADANES, C. (1990). *Sex, love, and violence: Strategies for transformation*. New York: Norton.

*McGOLDRICK, M., GERSON, R., & SHELLENBERGER, S. (1999). *Genograms: Assessment and intervention* (2nd ed.). New York: Norton.

*McGOLDRICK, M., PEARCE, J. K., & GIORDANO, J. (Eds.). (1996). *Ethnicity and family therapy* (2nd ed.). New York: Guilford Press.

*MINUCHIN, S. (1974). *Families and family therapy.* Cambridge, MA: Harvard University Press.

*MINUCHIN, S., & FISHMAN, H. C. (1981). *Family therapy techniques.* Cambridge, MA: Harvard University Press.

*NICHOLS, M. P., & SCHWARTZ, R. C. (2001). *Family therapy: Concepts and methods* (5th ed.). Boston: Allyn & Bacon.

*NICHOLS, M. P., & SCHWARTZ, R. C. (2002). *The essentials of family therapy.* Boston: Allyn & Bacon.

*NICHOLS, W. C. (2000). Integrative family therapy. In A. Horne (Ed.), *Family counseling and therapy* (3rd ed., pp. 539–564). Itasca, IL: F. E. Peacock.

POLSTER, E. (1995). *A population of selves: A therapeutic exploration of personal diversity.* San Francisco: Jossey-Bass.

ROGERS, C. R. (1980). *A way of being.* Boston: Houghton Mifflin.

*SATIR, V. (1983). *Conjoint family therapy* (3rd ed.). Palo Alto, CA: Science and Behavior Books.

*SATIR, V. (1988). *The new peoplemaking.* Palo Alto, CA: Science and Behavior Books.

*SATIR, V. M., BANMAN, J., GERBER, J., & GAMORI, M. (1991). *The Satir model: Family therapy and beyond.* Palo Alto, CA: Science & Behavior Books.

*SATIR, V. M., & BITTER, J. R. (2000). The therapist and family therapy: Satir's human validation process model. In A. M. Horne (Ed.), *Family counseling and therapy* (3rd ed., pp. 62–101). Itasca, IL: F. E. Peacock.

*SCHWARTZ, R. (1995). *Internal family systems therapy.* New York: Guilford Press.

*SELVINI PALAZZOLI, M., BOSCOLO, L., CECCHIN, F. G., & PRATA, G. (1978). *Paradox and counterparadox.* Northvale, NJ: Aronson.

SPRENKLE, D. H. (Ed.). (2002). *Effectiveness research in marriage and family therapy.* Alexandria, VA: American Association for Marriage and Family Therapy.

WEST, J. D., BUBENZER, D. L., & BITTER, J. R. (Eds.). (1998). *Social construction in couple and family counseling.* Alexandria, VA: ACA/IAMFC.

WHITAKER, C. A. (1976). The hindrance of theory in clinical work. In P. J. Guerin, Jr. (Ed.), *Family therapy: Theory and practice.* New York: Gardner Press.

*WHITAKER, C. A. (1989). *Midnight musings of a family therapist* [M. O. Ryan, Ed.]. New York: Norton.

*WHITAKER, C. A., & BUMBERRY, W. M. (1988). *Dancing with the family: A symbolic-experiential approach.* New York: Brunner/Mazel.

*WHITE, M. (1997). *Narratives of therapists' lives.* Adelaide, South Australia: Dulwich Centre Publications.

*WHITE, M., & EPSTON, D. (1990). *Narrative means to therapeutic ends.* New York: Norton. (Original title *Linguistic means to therapeutic ends*)

*WORDEN, M. (2003). *Family therapy basics* (3rd ed.). Pacific Grove, CA: Brooks/Cole.

PART 3

Integration
and
Application

An Integrative Perspective

INTRODUCTION

This chapter will help you think about areas of convergence and divergence among the 11 therapeutic systems. Although the approaches all have some goals in common, they have many differences when it comes to the best route to achieve these goals. Some therapies call for an active and directive stance on the therapist's part, and others place value on clients being the active agent. Some therapies focus on bringing out *feelings,* whereas others stress identifying *cognitive patterns,* and still others concentrate on actual *behavior.* The key challenge is to find ways to integrate certain features of each of these therapies so that you can work with clients on all three levels of human experience.

The field of psychotherapy is characterized by a diverse range of specialized models. With all this diversity, is there any hope that a practitioner can develop skills in all of the existing techniques? How does a student decide which theories are most relevant to practice? In addressing these questions, it is well to consider the competitive strife and theoretical "cold war" that dominated the field of counseling and psychotherapy for decades. The rivalry among theoretical orientations, dating back to Freud, has been characterized by various practitioners battling over who has the "best" way to bring about personality change. According to Norcross (1986a), the proliferation of therapy systems has been accompanied by a deafening cacophony of rival claims. He pleads for networks of practitioners who are willing to work toward rapprochement and integration.

Since the early 1980s, psychotherapy has been characterized by a rapidly developing movement toward integration. This movement is based on combining the best of differing orientations so that more complete theoretical models can be articulated and more efficient treatments developed (Goldfried & Castonguay, 1992). The Society for the Exploration of Psychotherapy Integration is an international organization that was formed in 1983. Its members are professionals who are working toward development of therapeutic approaches that transcend single theoretical orientations.

In this chapter I consider the advantages of developing an integrative perspective for counseling and deal briefly with some of the potential problems. I also present a framework for helping you begin to integrate concepts and techniques from various approaches. As you read, begin to formulate your personal perspective for counseling. Rather than merely reviewing the basic issues, look for ways to synthesize diverse elements from different theoretical perspectives. As much as possible, be alert to how these systems can function in harmony.

 THE TREND TOWARD PSYCHOTHERAPY INTEGRATION

A large number of therapists identify themselves as "eclectic," and this category covers a broad range of practice. At its worst, eclectic practice consists of haphazardly picking techniques without any overall theoretical rationale. This is known as *syncretism*, wherein the practitioner, lacking in knowledge and skill in selecting interventions, grabs for anything that seems to work, often making no attempt to determine whether the therapeutic procedures are indeed effective. Such a hodgepodge is no better than a narrow and dogmatic orthodoxy. Pulling techniques from many sources without a sound rationale can only result in syncretistic confusion (Lazarus, 1986, 1996b; Lazarus, Beutler, & Norcross, 1992).

Psychotherapy integration is best characterized by attempts to look beyond and across the confines of single-school approaches to see what can be learned from other perspectives. The integrative approach is characterized by openness to various ways of integrating diverse theories and techniques. Three of the most common pathways to this goal are technical eclecticism, theoretical integration, and the common factors approach (Arkowitz, 1997). *Technical eclecticism* tends to focus on differences, chooses from many approaches, and is a collection of techniques. This path calls for using techniques from different schools without necessarily subscribing to the theoretical positions that spawned them. In contrast, *theoretical integration* refers to a conceptual or theoretical creation beyond a mere blending of techniques. This path has the goal of producing a conceptual framework that synthesizes the best of two or more theoretical approaches under the assumption that the outcome will be richer than either theory alone (Norcross & Newman, 1992). The *common factors approach* searches for common elements across different theoretical systems. Despite many differences among the theories, a recognizable core of counseling practice is composed of nonspecific variables common to all therapies. These common factors are thought to be at least as important in accounting for therapeutic outcomes as the unique factors that differentiate one theory from another.

One reason for the trend toward psychotherapy integration is the recognition that no single theory is comprehensive enough to account for the complexities of human behavior, especially when the range of client types and their specific problems are taken into consideration. Because no one theory has a patent on the truth, and because no single set of counseling techniques is always effective in working with diverse client populations, crossing boundaries by developing integrative approaches holds promise for counseling practice (Kelly, 1988, 1991; Lazarus, 1996b).

Practitioners who are open to an integrative perspective will find that several theories play a crucial role in their personal counseling approach. Each theory has its unique contributions and its own domain of expertise. By accepting that each theory has strengths and weaknesses and is, by definition, "different" from the others, practitioners have some basis to begin developing a theory that fits for them. Developing an integrative perspective is a lifelong endeavor that is refined with experience.

The Future of Psychotherapy Orientations: Some Predictions

The 11 systems discussed in this book have evolved in the direction of broadening their theoretical and practical bases, becoming less restrictive in their focus. Thus, many practitioners who claim allegiance to a particular system of therapy are expanding their theoretical outlook and developing a wider range of therapeutic techniques to fit a more diverse population of clients. Arkowitz (1997) views current integrative approaches as an attempt to build a coherent framework for understanding or predicting change and for determining the choices of therapy techniques.

Norcross, Hedges, and Prochaska (2002) and Prochaska and Norcross (2003) developed the Delphi poll to forecast the future of theories of psychotherapy over the next 10 years. The participants in the poll, who were considered experts in the field of psychotherapy, predicted that these theoretical orientations would increase the most: cognitive behavior therapy, culture sensitive multicultural counseling, cognitive therapy (Beck), interpersonal therapy, technical eclecticism, theoretical integration, behavior therapy, family systems therapy, exposure therapies, and solution-focused therapy. Therapeutic approaches that were predicted to decrease the most included classical psychoanalysis, implosive therapy, Jungian therapy, transactional analysis, Adlerian therapy, and the humanistic therapies. The poll also revealed that methods and modalities of therapy are changing:

> [T]he consensus is that psychotherapy will become more directive, psychoeducational, technological, problem-focused, and briefer in the next decade. Concomitantly, relatively unstructured, historically oriented, and long-term approaches are predicted to decrease. . . . Short term is in, and long term on its way out. (Prochaska & Norcross, 2003, p. 545)

In addition, over the next decade short-term therapy, psychoeducational groups for specific disorders, crisis intervention, group therapy, and couples/marital therapy are expected to increase (Norcross et al., 2002).

Integration of Multicultural Issues in Counseling

Because of the increased diversity of client problems and client populations, psychotherapy integration must include cultural factors in the assessment and treatment process. Multiculturalism is a reality that cannot be ignored by practitioners if they hope to meet the needs of their diverse client groups. "A major challenge for the field of psychotherapy will be to discover creative ways to integrate the values and worldviews of multiple cultures within the discourse of efficiency and evidence that currently dominate health care" (Norcross et al., 2002, p. 322).

There is a growing movement toward creating a separate multicultural theory of counseling and therapy (Sue, Ivey, & Pedersen, 1996; Sue & Sue, 2003). However, I believe current theories can and should be expanded to incorporate a multicultural component. As I have consistently pointed out in this book, if contemporary theories do not account for the cultural dimension, they will have limited applicability in working with culturally diverse client populations. Harm can come to clients who are expected to fit all the specifications of a given theory, whether or not the values espoused by the theory are consistent with their own cultural values. Rather than stretching the client to fit the dimensions of a single theory, practitioners must tailor their theory and practice to fit the unique needs of the client. This requirement calls for counselors to possess knowledge of various cultures, be aware of their own cultural heritage, and have skills to assist a wide spectrum of clients in dealing with the realities of their culture.

In your role as a counselor, you need to be able to assess the special needs of clients. Depending on the individual client's ethnicity and culture and on the concerns that bring this person to counseling, you are challenged to develop flexibility in utilizing an array of therapeutic strategies. Some clients will need more direction, and even advice. Others will be very hesitant in talking about themselves in personal ways, especially during the early phase of the counseling process. You need to recognize that what may appear to be resistance is very likely to be the client's response to years of cultural conditioning and respect for certain values and traditions. What the matter comes down to is your familiarity with a variety of theoretical approaches and the ability to employ and adapt your techniques to fit the person-in-the-environment. It is not enough to merely assist your clients in gaining insight, expressing suppressed emotions, or making certain behavioral changes. The challenge is to find practical strategies for adapting the techniques you have developed to enable clients to question the impact their culture continues to have on their lives and to make decisions about what they want to change.

Being an effective counselor involves reflecting on how your own culture influences you and your interventions in your counseling practice. This awareness is critical in becoming more sensitive to the cultural backgrounds of the clients who seek your help. Using an integrative perspective, therapists can encompass social, cultural, spiritual, and political dimensions in their work with clients.

Integration of Spiritual/Religious Issues in Counseling

The field of counseling and psychotherapy has been slow to recognize the need to address spiritual/religious concerns. During the past decade, more attention has been given to this topic, and there has been increasing debate over the role spiritual and religious issues should play in psychotherapy (Younggren, 1993). There is now widespread interest in the topic of spiritual and religious beliefs—both the counselor's and the client's—and how such beliefs might be incorporated in therapeutic relationships (Frame, 2003; Miller, 1999). There is growing empirical evidence that our spiritual values and behaviors can promote physical and psychological well-being (Benson & Stark, 1996; Richards & Bergin, 1997; Richards, Rector, & Tjeltveit, 1999). It is clear that spirituality is an important component for mental health, and its inclusion in counseling practice can enhance the therapeutic process.

Spirituality has been described as that which "connects us to other people, nature, and the source of life. The experience of spirituality is greater than ourselves and helps us transcend and embrace life situations" (Faiver, Ingersoll, O'Brien, & McNally, 2001, p. 2). Whatever one's particular view of spirituality, it is a force that can help the individual make sense of the universe and find a purpose (or purposes) for living. Spirituality and religion are critical sources of strength for many clients—the bedrock for finding meaning in life—and can be a key factor in promoting healing and well-being. Some clients cannot be understood without appreciating the central role of religious or spiritual beliefs and practices. I believe spirituality should be addressed if it is a concern of the client.

For some clients spirituality entails embracing a religion, which can have many different meanings. Other clients value spirituality yet do not have any ties to a formal religion. There are many paths toward fulfilling spiritual needs, and it is not your task as a counselor to prescribe any particular pathway. If clients give an indication that they are concerned about any of their beliefs or practices, this is a useful focal point for exploration. The key here is that you remain finely tuned to clients' stories and to the purpose for which they sought therapy.

COMMON GOALS   In some ways a spiritual/religious perspective and a counseling perspective have similar goals. Both emphasize learning to accept oneself, forgiving others and oneself, admitting one's shortcomings, accepting personal responsibility, letting go of hurts and resentments, dealing with guilt, and learning to let go of self-destructive patterns of thinking, feeling, and acting.

Spiritual/religious values have a major part to play in human life and struggles, which means that exploring these values has a great deal to do with providing solutions for clients' struggles. Because spiritual and therapeutic paths converge in some ways, integration is possible, and dealing with a client's spirituality will often enhance the therapy process. Themes that have healing influences include loving, caring, learning to listen with compassion, challenging clients' basic life assumptions, accepting human imperfection, and going outside of self-oriented interests (social interest). Both religion and counseling help people ponder questions of "Who am I?" and "What is the meaning of my life?" At their best, both counseling and religion are able to foster healing through an exploration of the role of shame and guilt in human behavior, understanding the differences between blame and responsibility, healthy and unhealthy guilt, and the power of sharing deeply human concerns.

IMPLICATIONS FOR ASSESSMENT AND TREATMENT   Traditionally, when clients come to a therapist with a problem, the therapist explores all the factors that contributed to the development of the problem. Even though clients may no longer consider themselves to be religious or spiritual, a background of involvement in religion should be explored as part of clients' history. These beliefs may have been factors in the development of the problem, and thus could be part of the problem.

Some practitioners believe it is essential to understand and respect clients' religious beliefs and to include such beliefs in their assessment and treatment practice (Faiver & O'Brien, 1993; Frame, 2003; Kelly, 1995). Frame (2003) presents many reasons for including spirituality in assessments: understanding clients' worldviews and the contexts in which they live, assisting clients in grappling with questions regarding the purpose of their lives and what they most value, exploring religion and spirituality as client resources, and uncovering religious and spiritual problems. This information will assist the therapist in choosing appropriate interventions.

Faiver and O'Brien (1993) believe the assessment process should include questions pertaining to spiritual and religious issues as they are relevant to clients' presenting problems, questions about the roles religion and spirituality have played or currently play in clients' lives, and questions about how religious and spiritual beliefs might be related to clients' cognitive, affective, and behavioral processes. For example, is guilt an issue? What is the source of guilt, and does it serve any functional purpose? And Kelly (1995) endorses the notion of including items pertaining to general information about clients' spirituality and religion that serve the purposes of (a) obtaining a preliminary indication about the relevance of spirituality and religion for clients, (b) gathering information that the helper might refer to at a later point in the helping process, and (c) indicating to clients that it is acceptable to talk about religious and spiritual concerns.

YOUR ROLE AS A COUNSELOR   Counselors must be prepared to deal with spiritual issues that lie at the very core and essence of the clients' being (Miranti & Burke, 1995). If counselors are to effectively serve diverse clients, it is essential that they pay attention to their training and competence in addressing spiritual and religious concerns their clients bring to therapy. Counselors must understand their own spiritual/religious beliefs if they hope to understand and respect the beliefs of their clients (Faiver et al., 2001). For many clients in crisis, the spiritual domain offers solace, comfort, and is a major sustaining power that keeps them going when all else seems to fail. The guilt, anger, and sadness that clients experience often results from a misinterpretation of the spiritual and religious realm, which can lead to depression and a sense of worthlessness. If counselors are adequately prepared to deal with these concerns, they can assist clients in clearing up their misinterpretations.

Personal beliefs have been shown to directly and indirectly affect the course of therapy (Younggren, 1993). Therapists must be careful not to make decisions for clients but to let clients choose how their own values will guide their behavior. There is always a danger that counselors may inadvertently or purposely impose their own values, in any direction. Therapists must guard against indoctrinating clients with a particular set of spiritual/religious values (Grimm, 1994).

I believe the emphasis on spirituality will continue to be important in counseling practice, and I hope you will prepare yourself to work effectively with clients' spiritual/religious concerns. If you are interested in integrating a spiritual orientation in your counseling style, I recommend Faiver, Ingersoll, O'Brien, and McNally (2001), Faiver and O'Brien (1993), Faiver, O'Brien, and Ingersoll (2000), Frame (2003), Grimm (1994), Hinterkopf (1994, 1998), Miller (1999), Miranti and Burke (1995), Richards and Bergin (1997, 2004), Richards, Rector, Tjeltveit (1999), and Younggren (1993).

The Challenge of Developing an Integrative Perspective

A survey of approaches to counseling and psychotherapy reveals that no common philosophy unifies them. Messer (1986, 1992) concludes that the debate will continue between adherents of a single theoretical system and those who favor moving toward some form of integration. Many of the theories have different basic philosophies and views of human nature (Table 15-1). As the postmodern therapists remind us, our philosophical assumptions are important because they influence which "reality" we perceive, and they direct our attention to the variables that we are "set" to see. A word of caution, then: Beware of subscribing exclusively to any one view of human nature; remain open and selectively incorporate a framework for counseling that is consistent with your own personality and your belief system.

Despite the divergences in the various theories, creative syntheses among some models are possible. For example, an existential orientation does not necessarily preclude using techniques drawn from behavior therapy or from some of the cognitive theories. Each point of view offers a perspective for helping clients in their search for self. I encourage you to study all the major theories, to resist being converted to any single point of view, and to remain open to what you might take from the various orientations as a basis for an integrative perspective that will guide your practice.

In developing a personal integrative perspective, it is important to be alert to the problem of attempting to mix theories with incompatible underlying assumptions. Lazarus (1995) asks: "How is it possible to blend two systems that rest on totally different assumptions about the meaning, origins, development, maintenance, significance, and management of problems?" (p. 156). An advocate of technical eclecticism, Lazarus has consistently emphasized that a blend of different theories is likely to result in confusion. He argues against the notion of theoretical integration. He adds that basic concepts that may seem compatible often are, upon closer scrutiny, quite irreconcilable (see Table 15-2). Although Lazarus is not aware of any instances where blending different theories resulted in a more powerful technique, he points to numerous cases where techniques drawn from different theoretical systems have enriched a practitioner's therapeutic style. Lazarus stresses that psychotherapy integration does not have to rely on a theoretical amalgamation. Clinicians can be technically eclectic in that they can select methods from any discipline without necessarily endorsing any of the theories that spawned them.

By remaining theoretically consistent but technically eclectic, practitioners can spell out precisely the interventions they will employ with various clients, as well as the means by which they will select these procedures. The purpose of technical eclecticism is not to produce another separate school of therapy but to "engender an open system of empirically grounded clinical practice, an interdisciplinary and collaborative cadre of researchers building on each other's work" (Lazarus et al., 1992, p. 17). Lazarus and his colleagues hope that in the future therapists will think and practice eclectically and integratively—but critically.

TABLE 15-1   The Basic Philosophies

Psychoanalytic therapy	Human beings are basically determined by psychic energy and by early experiences. Unconscious motives and conflicts are central in present behavior. Irrational forces are strong; the person is driven by sexual and aggressive impulses. Early development is of critical importance because later personality problems have their roots in repressed childhood conflicts.
Adlerian therapy	Humans are motivated by social interest, by striving toward goals, and by dealing with the tasks of life. Emphasis is on the individual's positive capacities to live in society cooperatively. People have the capacity to interpret, influence, and create events. Each person at an early age creates a unique style of life, which tends to remain relatively constant throughout life.
Existential therapy	The central focus is on the nature of the human condition, which includes a capacity for self-awareness, freedom of choice to decide one's fate, responsibility, anxiety, the search for meaning, being alone and being in relation with others, and facing the reality of death.
Person-centered therapy	The view of humans is positive; we have an inclination toward becoming fully functioning. In the context of the therapeutic relationship, the client experiences feelings that were previously denied to awareness. The client actualizes potential and moves toward increased awareness, spontaneity, trust in self, and inner-directedness.
Gestalt therapy	The person strives for wholeness and integration of thinking, feeling, and behaving. The view is nondeterministic in that the person is viewed as having the capacity to recognize how earlier influences are related to present difficulties. As an experiential approach, it is grounded in the here-and-now and emphasizes personal choice and responsibility.
Behavior therapy	Behavior is the product of learning. We are both the product and the producer of the environment. No set of unifying assumptions about behavior can incorporate all the existing procedures in the behavioral field.
Cognitive behavior therapy	Individuals tend to incorporate faulty thinking, which leads to emotional and behavioral disturbances. Cognitions are the major determinants of how we feel and act. Therapy is primarily oriented toward cognition and behavior, and it stresses the role of thinking, deciding, questioning, doing, and redeciding. This is a psychoeducational model, which emphasizes therapy as a learning process, including acquiring and practicing new skills, learning new ways of thinking, and acquiring more effective ways of coping with problems.

TABLE 15-1   The Basic Philosophies (continued)

Reality therapy	Based on choice theory, this approach assumes that we are by nature social creatures and we need quality relationships to be happy. Psychological problems are the result of our resisting the control by others or of our attempt to control others. Choice theory is an explanation of human nature and how to best achieve satisfying interpersonal relationships.
Feminist therapy	Feminists criticize many traditional theories to the degree that they are based on gender-biased concepts and practices of being: androcentric, gendercentric, ethnocentric, heterosexist, and intrapsychic. The constructs of feminist therapy include being gender-fair, flexible, interactionist, and life-span-oriented.
Postmodern approaches	Based on the premise that there are multiple realities and multiple truths, postmodern therapies reject the idea that reality is external and can be grasped. People create meaning in their lives through conversations with others. The postmodern approaches avoid pathologizing clients, take a dim view of diagnosis, avoid searching for underlying causes of problems, and place a high value on discovering clients' strengths and resources. Rather than endless talking about problems, the focus of therapy is on creating solutions in the present and the future.
Family systems therapy	The family is viewed from an interactive and systemic perspective. Clients are connected to a living system; a change in one part of the system will result in a change in other parts. The family provides the context for understanding how individuals function in relationship to others and how they behave. Treatment is best focused on the family unit. An individual's dysfunctional behavior grows out of the interactional unit of the family and out of larger systems as well.

According to Lazarus (1997a, 1997b), therapists who hope to be effective with a wide range of problems and with different client populations must be flexible and versatile. Therapists should ask these basic questions when devising a treatment program: What works for whom under which particular circumstances? Why are some procedures helpful and others unhelpful? What can be done to ensure long-term success and positive follow-ups? Lazarus believes some clients respond to warm, informal counselors but that others want more formal counselors. Some clients work well with therapists who are quiet and nonforceful, whereas others work best with directive and outgoing therapists. Further, the same client may respond favorably to various therapeutic techniques and styles at different times.

TABLE 15-2   Key Concepts

Psychoanalytic therapy	Normal personality development is based on successful resolution and integration of psychosexual stages of development. Faulty personality development is the result of inadequate resolution of some specific stage. Anxiety is a result of repression of basic conflicts. Unconscious processes are centrally related to current behavior.
Adlerian therapy	Key concepts of this model include the unity of personality, the need to view people from their subjective perspective, and the importance of life goals that give direction to behavior. People are motivated by social interest and by finding goals to give life meaning. Other key concepts are striving for significance and superiority, developing a unique lifestyle, and understanding the family constellation. Therapy is a matter of providing encouragement and assisting clients in changing their cognitive perspective and behavior.
Existential therapy	Essentially an experiential approach to counseling rather than a firm theoretical model, it stresses core human conditions. Normally, personality development is based on the uniqueness of each individual. Sense of self develops from infancy. Focus is on the present and on what one is becoming; that is, the approach has a future orientation. It stresses self-awareness before action.
Person-centered therapy	The client has the potential to become aware of problems and the means to resolve them. Faith is placed in the client's capacity for self-direction. Mental health is a congruence of ideal self and real self. Maladjustment is the result of a discrepancy between what one wants to be and what one is. Focus is on the present moment and on experiencing and expressing feelings.
Gestalt therapy	Emphasis is on the "what" and "how" of experiencing in the here-and-now to help clients accept all aspects of themselves. Key concepts include holism, figure-formation process, awareness, unfinished business and avoidance, contact, and energy.
Behavior therapy	Focus is on overt behavior, precision in specifying goals of treatment, development of specific treatment plans, and objective evaluation of therapy outcomes. Present behavior is given attention. Therapy is based on the principles of learning theory. Normal behavior is learned through reinforcement and imitation. Abnormal behavior is the result of faulty learning.
Cognitive behavior therapy	Although psychological problems may be rooted in childhood, they are perpetuated through reindoctrination in the now. A person's belief system is the primary cause of disorders.

TABLE 15-2   Key Concepts (continued)

	Internal dialogue plays a central role in one's behavior. Clients focus on examining faulty assumptions and misconceptions and on replacing these with effective beliefs.
Reality therapy	The basic focus is on what clients are doing and how to get them to evaluate whether their present actions are working for them. People are mainly motivated to satisfy their needs, especially the need for significant relationships. The approach rejects the medical model, the notion of transference, the unconscious, and dwelling on one's past.
Feminist therapy	Core principles that form the foundation for practice of feminist therapy are that the personal is political, the counseling relationship is egalitarian, women's experiences are honored, definitions of distress and mental illness are reformulated, gender equality is emphasized, and there is a commitment to confronting oppression on any grounds.
Postmodern approaches	Therapy tends to be brief and focuses on the present and the future. The person is not the problem; the problem is the problem. The emphasis is on externalizing the problem and looking for exceptions to the problem. Therapy consists of a collaborative dialogue in which the therapist and the client co-create solutions. By identifying instances when the problem did not exist, clients can create new meanings for themselves and fashion a new life story.
Family systems therapy	Focus is on communication patterns within a family, both verbal and nonverbal. Problems in relationships are likely to be passed on from generation to generation. Symptoms are viewed as ways of communicating with the aim of controlling other family members. Key concepts vary depending on specific orientation but include differentiation, triangles, power coalitions, family-of-origin dynamics, functional versus dysfunctional interaction patterns, and dealing with here-and-now interactions. The present is more important than exploring past experiences.

Lazarus (1996a) mentions the value of a therapist assuming an active role in blending a flexible repertoire of relationship styles with a wide range of techniques as a way to enhance therapeutic outcomes. He maintains that a skilled therapist is able to determine when and when not to be confrontational, when to be directive and when to allow the client to struggle, when to be formal or informal, when to self-disclose or remain anonymous, and when to be gentle or tough. Lazarus asserts that relationships of choice are at least as important as techniques of choice. (For a review of multimodal procedures and their rationale, see Chapter 9.)

One of the challenges you will face as a counselor is to deliver therapeutic services in a brief, comprehensive, effective, and flexible way. Many of the theoretical orientations addressed in this book can be applied to brief forms of therapy. The clinical realities associated with brief therapy imply a flexible, eclectic orientation. Most forms of short-term psychotherapy are active in nature, collaborative in relationship, and eclectic in orientation (Preston, 1998; Prochaska & Norcross, 2003). One of the driving forces of the psychotherapy integration movement has been the increase of brief therapies and the pressures to do more for a variety of client populations within the limitations of 6 to 20 sessions. Prochaska and Norcross make an excellent point in stating that effective brief therapy depends less on the hours counselors put in than on what they put into those hours. The challenge is for eclectic practitioners to learn how to rapidly and systematically identify problems, create a collaborative relationship with clients, and intervene with a range of specific methods. In his excellent book *Brief But Comprehensive Psychotherapy: The Multimodal Way* (1997a), Lazarus shows how to provide short-term comprehensive psychotherapy.

An integrative perspective at its best entails a *systematic integration* of underlying principles and methods common to a range of therapeutic approaches. To develop this kind of integration, you will eventually need to be thoroughly conversant with a number of theories, be open to the idea that these theories can be unified in some ways, and be willing to continually test your hypotheses to determine how well they are working. An integrative perspective is the product of a great deal of study, clinical practice, research, and theorizing.

If you are interested in developing an integrative approach to therapeutic practice, consult some of these resources: Abernethy (1992), Alford and Beck (1997), Arkowitz (1997), Garfield (1992a), Goldfried and Newman (1992), Lazarus (1995, 1996a, 1996b, 1997a, 1997b), Lazarus and Beutler (1993), Lazarus, Beutler, and Norcross (1992), Mikulas (2002), Moursund and Erskine (2004), Norcross (1986a, 1986b), Norcross and Goldfried (1992), Norcross and Newman (1992), Preston (1998), Prochaska and Norcross (2003), and Young (1992).

 ISSUES RELATED TO THE THERAPEUTIC PROCESS

Therapeutic Goals

The goals of counseling are almost as diverse as are the theoretical approaches. Some goals include restructuring the personality, uncovering the unconscious, creating social interest, finding meaning in life, curing an emotional disturbance, examining old decisions and making new ones, developing trust in oneself, becoming more self-actualizing, reducing anxiety, shedding maladaptive behavior and learning adaptive patterns, gaining more effective control of one's life, and re-authoring the story of one's life (Table 15-3). Is there a common denominator in this range of goals?

This diversity can be simplified by considering the degree of generality or specificity of goals. Goals exist on a continuum from specific, concrete, and short term, on one end, to general, global, and long term, on the other. The cognitive behavioral approaches stress the former; the relationship-oriented therapies tend to stress the latter. The goals at opposite ends of the continuum are not necessarily contradictory; it is a matter of how specifically they are defined.

Therapist's Function and Role

In working toward an integrative perspective, we need to address a number of questions about the counselor's behaviors: How do the counselor's functions change depending on the stage of the counseling process? Does the therapist maintain a basic role, or does this role vary in accordance with the characteristics of the client? How does the counselor determine how active and directive to be? How is structuring handled as the course of therapy progresses? What is the optimum balance of responsibility in the client–therapist relationship? When and how much does the counselor self-disclose?

As you saw through your study of the 11 therapeutic approaches, a central issue of each system is the degree to which the therapist exercises control over clients' behavior both during and outside the session. Cognitive behavior therapists and reality therapists, for example, operate within a directive and didactic structure. They frequently suggest homework assignments that are designed to get clients to practice new behavior outside therapy sessions. In contrast, person-centered therapists operate with a much looser and less defined structure. Postmodern therapists view the client as the expert on his or her own life, but often they are directive and active with their questioning.

Structuring depends on the particular client and the specific circumstances he or she brings to the therapy situation. From my perspective, clear structure is most essential during the early phase of counseling. It helps encourage clients to talk about the problems that led them to seek therapy. In a collaborative way, it is useful for both counselor and client to make some initial assessment that can provide a focus for the therapy process. As soon as possible, clients should be given a significant share of the responsibility for deciding on the content of the sessions. From early in the therapy process clients can be empowered if the counselor expects that they will become active participants in the process.

Client's Experience in Therapy

What expectations do clients have as they approach therapy? What are their responsibilities in the process? Is therapy only for the "disturbed"? Can the relatively healthy person benefit from therapy? Are there any commonalities among the grand diversity of clients?

Most clients share some degree of suffering, pain, or at least discontent. There is a discrepancy between how they would like to be and how they are. Some initiate therapy because they hope to cure a specific symptom or set of

TABLE 15-3   Goals of Therapy

Psychoanalytic therapy	To make the unconscious conscious. To reconstruct the basic personality. To assist clients in reliving earlier experiences and working through repressed conflicts. To achieve intellectual and emotional awareness.
Adlerian therapy	To challenge clients' basic premises and life goals. To offer encouragement so individuals can develop socially useful goals. To develop the client's sense of belonging.
Existential therapy	To help people see that they are free and become aware of their possibilities. To challenge them to recognize that they are responsible for events that they formerly thought were happening to them. To identify factors that block freedom.
Person-centered therapy	To provide a safe climate conducive to clients' self-exploration, so that they can recognize blocks to growth and can experience aspects of self that were formerly denied or distorted. To enable them to move toward openness, greater trust in self, willingness to be a process, and increased spontaneity and aliveness.
Gestalt therapy	To assist clients in gaining awareness of moment-to-moment experiencing and to expand the capacity to make choices. Aims not at analysis but at integration.
Behavior therapy	To eliminate maladaptive behaviors and learn more effective behaviors. To focus on factors influencing behavior and find what can be done about problematic behavior. Clients have an active role in setting treatment goals and evaluating how well these goals are being met.
Cognitive behavior therapy	To challenge clients to confront faulty beliefs with contradictory evidence that they gather and evaluate. To help clients seek out their rigid beliefs and minimize them. To become aware of automatic thoughts and to change them.
Reality therapy	To help people become more effective in meeting their needs. To enable clients to get reconnected with the people they have chosen to put into their quality worlds and teach clients choice theory.
Feminist therapy	To bring about transformation both in the individual client and in society. To assist clients in recognizing, claiming, and using their personal power to free themselves from the limitations of gender-role socialization. To confront all forms of institutional policies that discriminate on any basis.
Postmodern approaches	To change the way clients view problems and what they can do about these concerns. To collaboratively establish specific, clear, concrete, realistic, and observable goals leading to

TABLE 15-3 Goals of Therapy (continued)

	increased positive change. To help clients create a self-identity grounded on competence and resourcefulness so they can resolve present and future concerns.
Family systems therapy	To help family members gain awareness of patterns of relationships that are not working well and to create new ways of interacting to relieve their distress.

symptoms: They want to get rid of migraine headaches, free themselves of chronic anxiety attacks, lose weight, or get relief from depression. They may have conflicting feelings and reactions, may struggle with low self-esteem, or may have limited information and skills. Many seek to resolve conflicts with a marital partner. Increasingly, people are entering therapy with existential problems; their complaints are less defined but relate to the experiences of emptiness, meaninglessness in life, boredom, dead personal relationships, anxiety over uncertainty, a lack of intense feelings, and a loss of their sense of self.

The initial expectations of many clients are expert help and a fast result. They often have great hope for major changes in their lives with little effort on their part. As therapy progresses, clients discover that they must be active in the process, selecting their own goals and working toward them, both in the sessions and in daily living. Some clients can benefit from recognizing and expressing pent-up feelings, others will need to examine their beliefs and thoughts, others will most need to begin behaving in different ways, and others will benefit from talking with you about their relationships with the significant people in their lives.

In deciding what interventions are most likely to be helpful, take into account the client's cultural, ethnic, and socioeconomic background. Moreover, the focus of counseling may change with each of these clients at different phases in the counseling process. Although some clients initially feel a need to be listened to and allowed to express deep feelings, they can profit later from examining the thought patterns that are contributing to their psychological pain. And certainly at some point in therapy it is essential that clients translate what they are learning about themselves into concrete action. The client's given situation in the environment provides a framework for selecting interventions that are most appropriate.

Relationship Between Therapist and Client

Most approaches share common ground in accepting the importance of the therapeutic relationship. The existential, person-centered, Gestalt, and post-modern views focus on the personal relationship as the crucial determinant of treatment outcomes. Rational emotive behavior therapy, cognitive behavior therapy, and behavior therapy do not ignore the relationship factor, but they do not give it a place of central importance (Table 15-4).

TABLE 15-4   The Therapeutic Relationship

Psychoanalytic therapy	The analyst remains anonymous, and clients develop projections toward him or her. Focus is on reducing the resistances that develop in working with transference and on establishing more rational control. Clients undergo long-term analysis, engage in free association to uncover conflicts, and gain insight by talking. The analyst makes interpretations to teach clients the meaning of current behavior as it relates to the past.
Adlerian therapy	The emphasis is on joint responsibility, on mutually determining goals, on mutual trust and respect, and on equality. Focus is on identifying, exploring, and disclosing mistaken goals and faulty assumptions within the person's lifestyle.
Existential therapy	The therapist's main tasks are to accurately grasp clients' being-in-the-world and to establish a personal and authentic encounter with them. The immediacy of the client–therapist relationship and the authenticity of the here-and-now encounter are stressed. Both client and therapist can be changed by the encounter.
Person-centered therapy	The relationship is of primary importance. The qualities of the therapist, including genuineness, warmth, accurate empathy, respect, and nonjudgmentalness—and communication of these attitudes to clients—are stressed. Clients use this real relationship with the therapist to help them transfer what they learn to other relationships.
Gestalt therapy	Central importance is given to the I/Thou relationship and the quality of the therapist's presence. The therapist's attitudes and behavior count more than the techniques used. The therapist does not interpret for clients but assists them in developing the means to make their own interpretations. Clients identify and work on unfinished business from the past that interferes with current functioning.
Behavior therapy	The therapist is active and directive and functions as a teacher or trainer in helping clients learn more effective behavior. Clients must be active in the process and experiment with new behaviors. Although a quality client–therapist relationship is not viewed as sufficient to bring about change, it is considered essential for implementing behavioral procedures.
Cognitive behavior therapy	In REBT the therapist functions as a teacher and the client as a student. The therapist is highly directive and teaches clients an A-B-C model of changing their cognitions. In CT the focus is on a collaborative relationship. Using a Socratic dialogue, the therapist assists clients in identifying dysfunctional beliefs and discovering alternative rules for living. The therapist promotes corrective experiences that lead to learning new skills. Clients gain insight into their problems and then must actively practice changing self-defeating thinking and acting.

TABLE 15-4 The Therapeutic Relationship (continued)

Reality therapy	A therapist's main function is to create a good relationship with the client. Therapists are then able to engage clients in an evaluation of all their relationships with respect to what they want and how effective they are in getting this. Therapists find out what clients want, ask what they are choosing to do, invite them to evaluate present behavior, help them make plans for change, and get them to make a commitment. The therapist is a client's advocate, as long as the client is willing to attempt to behave responsibly.
Feminist therapy	The therapeutic relationship is based on empowerment and egalitarianism. Therapists actively break down the hierarchy of power and reduce artificial barriers by engaging in appropriate self-disclosure and teaching clients about the therapy process. Therapists strive to create a collaborative relationship in which clients can become their own expert.
Postmodern approaches	Therapy is a collaborative partnership. Clients are viewed as the experts on their own life. Therapists use questioning dialogue to help clients free themselves from their problem-saturated stories and create new life-affirming stories. Solution-focused therapists assume an active role in guiding the client away from problem-talk and toward solution-talk. Clients are encouraged to explore their strengths and to create solutions that will lead to a richer future. Narrative therapists assist clients in externalizing problems and guide them in challenging self-limiting stories and creating new and more liberating stories.
Family systems therapy	The family therapist functions as a teacher, coach, model, and consultant. The family learns ways to detect and solve problems that are keeping members stuck, and it learns about patterns that have been transmitted from generation to generation. Some approaches focus on the role of therapist as expert; others concentrate on intensifying what is going on in the here-and-now of the family session. All family therapists are concerned with the process of family interaction and teaching patterns of communication.

Counseling is a personal matter that involves a personal relationship, and evidence indicates that honesty, sincerity, acceptance, understanding, and spontaneity are basic ingredients for successful outcomes. Therapists' degree of caring, their interest and ability in helping their clients, and their genuineness influence the relationship. Lazarus (1996b) views the client–therapist relationship as the soil that enables the therapist's techniques to take root. Within the context of a warm, caring, therapeutic relationship, faulty cognitions and maladaptive behaviors can be remedied. To bring about these changes, therapists teach clients a range of coping skills they can use to create solutions to the problems of living.

As you think about developing your personal counseling perspective, give consideration to the issue of the match between client and counselor. I certainly do not advocate changing your personality to fit your perception of what each client is expecting; it is important that you *be yourself* as you meet clients. You also need to consider the reality that you will probably not be able to work effectively with every client. Some clients will work better with counselors who have another type of personal and therapeutic style than yours. Thus, I recommend sensitivity in assessing what your client needs, along with good judgment about the appropriateness of the match between you and a potential client.

Although you do not have to be like your clients or have experienced the same problems to be effective with them, it is critical that you be able to understand their world and respect them. Ask yourself how well prepared you are to counsel clients from a different cultural background. To what degree do you think you can successfully establish a therapeutic relationship with a client of a different race? Ethnic group? Gender? Age? Sexual orientation? Spiritual/religious orientation? Socioeconomic group? Do you see any potential barriers that would make it difficult for you to form a working relationship with certain clients? (This would be a good time to review the discussion of the culturally skilled counselor in Chapter 2 and to consult Tables 15-7 and 15-8, which appear later in this chapter.)

THE PLACE OF TECHNIQUES AND EVALUATION IN COUNSELING

Drawing on Techniques From Various Approaches

Effective therapists incorporate a wide range of procedures into their therapeutic style. Much depends on the purpose of therapy, the setting, the personality and style of the therapist, the qualities of the particular client, and the problems selected for intervention. Regardless of the therapeutic model you may be working with, you must decide *what* techniques, procedures, or intervention methods to use, *when* to use them, and with *which* clients. Take time to review Tables 15-5 and 15-6 on therapeutic techniques and applications of techniques. Pay careful attention to the focus of each type of therapy and how that focus might be useful in your practice.

It is critical to be aware of how clients' cultural backgrounds contribute to their perceptions of their problems. Each of the 11 therapeutic approaches has both strengths and limitations when applied to culturally diverse client populations (Tables 15-7 and 15-8 on pages 485–487). Although it is unwise to stereotype clients because of their cultural heritage, it is useful to assess how the cultural context has a bearing on their concerns. Some techniques are contraindicated because of a client's socialization. Thus, the client's responsiveness (or lack of it) to certain techniques is a critical barometer in judging the effectiveness of these methods.

Effective counseling involves proficiency in a combination of cognitive, affective, and behavioral techniques. Such a combination is necessary to help clients *think* about their beliefs and assumptions, to experience on a *feeling* level their conflicts and struggles, and to translate their insights into *action* programs by behaving in new ways in day-to-day living. Tables 15-9 and 15-10 on pages 488–491 outline the contributions and limitations of the various therapeutic approaches. These tables will help you identify elements from the various approaches that you may want to incorporate in your own counseling perspective.

TABLE 15-5 Techniques of Therapy

Psychoanalytic therapy	The key techniques are interpretation, dream analysis, free association, analysis of resistance, and analysis of transference. All are designed to help clients gain access to their unconscious conflicts, which leads to insight and eventual assimilation of new material by the ego.
Adlerian therapy	Adlerians pay more attention to the subjective experiences of clients than to using techniques. Some techniques include gathering life-history data (family constellation, early recollections, personal priorities), sharing interpretations with clients, offering encouragement, and assisting clients in searching for new possibilities.
Existential therapy	Few techniques flow from this approach, because it stresses understanding first and technique second. The therapist can borrow techniques from other approaches and incorporate them in an existential framework. Diagnosis, testing, and external measurements are not deemed important.
Person-centered therapy	This approach uses few techniques but stresses the attitudes of the therapist. Basic techniques include active listening, reflection of feelings, clarification, and "being there" for the client. This model does not include diagnostic testing, interpretation, taking a case history, or questioning or probing for information.
Gestalt therapy	A wide range of experiments are designed to intensify experiencing and to integrate conflicting feelings. Experiments are co-created by therapist and client through an I/Thou dialogue. Therapists have latitude to invent their own experiments. Formal diagnosis and testing are not a required part of therapy.
Behavior therapy	The main techniques are systematic desensitization, relaxation methods, flooding, eye movement and desensitization reprocessing, reinforcement techniques, modeling, cognitive restructuring, assertion and social skills training, self-management programs, behavioral rehearsal, coaching, and various multimodal therapy techniques. Diagnosis or assessment is done at the outset to determine a treatment plan. Questions concentrate on "what," "how," and "when" (but not "why"). Contracts and homework assignments are also typically used.

(continued on next page)

TABLE 15-5   Techniques of Therapy (continued)

Cognitive behavior therapy	Therapists use a variety of cognitive, emotive, and behavioral techniques; diverse methods are tailored to suit individual clients. This is an active, directive, time-limited, present-centered, structured therapy. Some techniques include engaging in Socratic dialogue, debating irrational beliefs, carrying out homework assignments, gathering data on assumptions one has made, keeping a record of activities, forming alternative interpretations, learning new coping skills, changing one's language and thinking patterns, role playing, imagery, and confronting faulty beliefs.
Reality therapy	This is an active, directive, and didactic therapy. Various techniques may be used to get clients to evaluate what they are presently doing to see if they are willing to change. If clients decide that their present behavior is not effective, they develop a specific plan for change and make a commitment to follow through.
Feminist therapy	Although techniques from traditional approaches are used, feminist practitioners tend to employ consciousness-raising techniques aimed at helping clients recognize the impact of gender-role socialization on their lives. Other techniques frequently used include gender-role analysis and intervention, power analysis and intervention, bibliotherapy, journal writing, therapist self-disclosure, assertiveness training, reframing and relabeling, cognitive restructuring, identifying and challenging untested beliefs, role playing, psychodramatic methods, group work, and social action.
Postmodern approaches	In solution-focused therapy the main technique involves change talk, with emphasis on times in a client's life when the problem was not a problem. Other techniques include creative use of questioning, the miracle question, and scaling questions, which assist clients in developing alternative stories. In narrative therapy, specific techniques include listening to a client's problem-saturated story without getting stuck, externalizing and naming the problem, and discovering clues to competence. Narrative therapists often write letters to clients and assist them in finding an audience that will support their changes and new stories.
Family systems therapy	A variety of techniques may be used, depending on the particular theoretical orientation of the therapist. Techniques include genograms, teaching, asking questions, joining the family, tracking sequences, issuing directives, use of countertransference, family mapping, reframing, restructuring, enactments, and setting boundaries. Techniques may be experiential, cognitive, or behavioral in nature. Most are designed to bring about change in a short time.

TABLE 15-6   Applications of the Approaches

Psychoanalytic therapy	Candidates for analytic therapy include professionals who want to become therapists, people who have had intensive therapy and want to go further, and those who are in pain. Analytic therapy is not recommended for self-centered and impulsive clients or for severely impaired psychotics. Techniques can be applied to individual and group therapy.
Adlerian therapy	Because the approach is based on a growth model, it is applicable to such varied spheres of life as child guidance, parent–child counseling, marital and family therapy, individual counseling with all age groups, correctional and rehabilitation counseling, group counseling, substance abuse programs, and brief counseling. It is ideally suited to preventive care and alleviating a broad range of conditions that interfere with growth.
Existential therapy	This approach is especially suited to people facing a developmental crisis or a transition in life and for those with existential concerns (making choices, dealing with freedom and responsibility, coping with guilt and anxiety, making sense of life, and finding values) or those seeking personal enhancement. Can be applied to both individual and group counseling, and to marital and family therapy, crisis intervention, and community mental health work.
Person-centered therapy	Has wide applicability to individual and group counseling. It is especially well suited for the initial phases of crisis intervention work. Its principles have been applied to marital and family therapy, community programs, administration and management, and human relations training. It is a useful approach for teaching, parent–child relations and for working with groups of people from diverse cultural backgrounds.
Gestalt therapy	Addresses a wide range of problems and populations: crisis intervention, treatment of a range of psychosomatic disorders, marital and family therapy, awareness training of mental health professionals, behavior problems in children, and teaching and learning. It is well suited to both individual and group counseling. The methods are powerful catalysts for opening up feelings and getting clients into contact with their present-centered experience.
Behavior therapy	A pragmatic approach based on empirical validation of results. Enjoys wide applicability to individual, group, marital, and family counseling. Some problems to which the approach is well suited are phobic disorders, depression, sexual disorders, children's behavioral disorders, stuttering, and prevention of cardiovascular disease. Beyond clinical practice, its principles are applied in fields such as pediatrics, stress management, behavioral medicine, education, and geriatrics.

(continued on next page)

TABLE 15-6   Applications of the Approaches (continued)

Cognitive behavior therapy	Has been widely applied to treatment of depression, anxiety, marital problems, stress management, skill training, substance abuse, assertion training, eating disorders, panic attacks, performance anxiety, and social phobia. The approach is especially useful for assisting people in modifying their cognitions. Many self-help approaches utilize its principles. Can be applied to a wide range of client populations with a variety of specific problems.
Reality therapy	Geared to teaching people ways of using choice theory in everyday living to increase effective behaviors. It has been applied to individual counseling with a wide range of clients, group counseling, working with youthful law offenders, and marital and family therapy. In some instances it is well suited to brief therapy and crisis intervention.
Feminist therapy	Principles and techniques can be applied to a range of therapeutic modalities such as individual therapy, relationship counseling, family therapy, group counseling, and community intervention. The approach can be applied to both women and men with the goal of bringing about empowerment.
Postmodern approaches	Solution-focused therapy is well suited for people with adjustment disorders and for problems of anxiety and depression. Narrative therapy is now being used for a broad range of human difficulties including eating disorders, family distress, depression, and relationship concerns. These approaches can be applied to working with children, adolescents, adults, couples, families, and the community in a wide variety of settings.
Family systems therapy	Useful for dealing with marital distress, problems of communicating among family members, power struggles, crisis situations in the family, helping individuals attain their potential, and enhancing the overall functioning of the family.

TABLE 15-7   Contributions to Multicultural Counseling

Psychoanalytic therapy	Its focus on family dynamics is appropriate for working with many minority groups. The therapist's formality appeals to clients who expect professional distance. Notion of ego defense is helpful in understanding inner dynamics and dealing with environmental stresses.
Adlerian therapy	Its focus on social interest, collectivism, pursuing meaning in life, importance of family, goal orientation, and belonging is congruent with many cultures. Focus on person-in-environment allows for cultural factors to be explored.
Existential therapy	Focus is on understanding client's phenomenological world, including cultural background. This approach leads to empowerment

TABLE 15-7   Contributions to Multicultural Counseling (continued)

	in an oppressive society. It can help clients examine their options for change within the context of their cultural realities.
Person-centered therapy	Focus is on breaking cultural barriers and facilitating open dialogue among diverse cultural populations. Main strengths are respect for clients' values, active listening, welcoming of differences, nonjudgmental attitude, understanding, willingness to allow clients to determine what will be explored in sessions, and prizing cultural pluralism.
Gestalt therapy	Its focus on expressing oneself nonverbally is congruent with those cultures that look beyond words for messages. Provides many experiments in working with clients who have cultural injunctions against freely expressing feelings. Can help to overcome language barrier with bilingual clients. Focus on bodily expressions is a subtle way to help clients recognize their conflicts.
Behavior therapy	The focus on behavior, rather than on feelings, is compatible with many cultures. Strengths include a collaborative relationship between counselor and client in working toward mutually agreed-upon goals, continual assessment to determine if the techniques are suited to clients' unique situation, assisting clients in learning practical skills, an educational focus, and stress on self-management strategies.
Cognitive behavior therapy	The collaborative approach offers clients opportunities to express their areas of concern. The psychoeducational dimensions are often useful in exploring cultural conflicts and teaching new behavior. The emphasis on thinking (as opposed to identifying and expressing feelings) is likely to be acceptable to many clients. The focus on teaching and learning tends to avoid the stigma of mental illness. Clients may value active and directive stance of therapist.
Reality therapy	Focus is on members' making their own evaluation of behavior (including how they respond to their culture). Through personal assessment they can determine the degree to which their needs and wants are being satisfied. They can find a balance between retaining their own ethnic identity and integrating some of the values and practices of the dominant society.
Feminist therapy	This approach is not willing to settle for adjustment to the status quo. Both individual change and social transformation are the ultimate goals of therapy. A key contribution is that both the women's movement and the multicultural movement have called attention to the negative impact of discrimination and oppression for both women and men.

(continued on next page)

TABLE 15-7   Contributions to Multicultural Counseling (continued)

Postmodern approaches	The social and cultural context of behavior is stressed. Stories that are being authored in the therapy office need to be anchored into the social world in which the client lives. Therapists do not make assumptions about people and honor each client's unique story and cultural background. Therapists take an active role in challenging social and cultural injustices that lead to oppression of certain groups. Therapy becomes a process of liberation from oppressive cultural values and enables clients to become active agents of their destinies.
Family systems therapy	Many ethnic and cultural groups place value on the role of the extended family. Many family therapies deal with extended family members and with support systems. Networking is a part of the process, which is congruent with the values of many clients. There is a greater chance for individual change if other family members are supportive. This approach offers ways of working toward the health of the family unit and the welfare of each member.

TABLE 15-8   Limitations in Multicultural Counseling

Psychoanalytic therapy	Its focus on insight, intrapsychic dynamics, and long-term treatment is often not valued by clients who prefer to learn coping skills for dealing with pressing daily concerns. Internal focus is often in conflict with cultural values that stress an interpersonal and environmental focus.
Adlerian therapy	This approach's detailed interview about one's family background can conflict with cultures that have injunctions against disclosing family matters. Some clients may view the counselor as an authority who will provide answers to problems, which conflicts with the egalitarian, person-to-person spirit as a way to reduce social distance.
Existential therapy	Values of individuality, freedom, autonomy, and self-realization often conflict with cultural values of collectivism, respect for tradition, deference to authority, and interdependence. Some may be deterred by the absence of specific techniques. Others will expect more focus on surviving in their world.
Person-centered therapy	Some of the core values of this approach may not be congruent with the client's culture. Lack of counselor direction and structure are unacceptable for clients who are seeking help and immediate answers from a knowledgeable professional.
Gestalt therapy	Clients who have been culturally conditioned to be emotionally reserved may not embrace Gestalt experiments. Some may not see how "being aware of present experiencing" will lead to solving their problems.

TABLE 15-8 Limitations in Multicultural Counseling (continued)

Behavior therapy	Counselors need to help clients assess the possible consequences of making behavioral changes. Family members may not value clients' newly acquired assertive style, so clients must be taught how to cope with resistance by others.
Cognitive behavior therapy	Before too quickly attempting to change the beliefs and actions of clients, it is essential for the therapist to understand and respect their world. Some clients may have serious reservations about questioning their basic cultural values and beliefs. Clients could become dependent on the therapist for deciding what are appropriate ways to solve problems. There may be a fine line between being directive and promoting dependence.
Reality therapy	This approach stresses taking charge of one's own life, yet some clients hope to change their external environment. Counselor needs to appreciate the role of discrimination and racism and help clients deal with social and political realities.
Feminist therapy	This model has been criticized for its bias toward the values of White, middle-class, heterosexual women, which are not applicable to many other groups of women. It is based on feminist notions of collaborative relationships, self-determination, and empowerment. Therapists need to assess with their clients the price of making significant personal change, which may result in isolation from extended family as clients assume new roles and make life changes.
Postmodern approaches	Some clients come to therapy wanting to talk about their problems and may be put off by the insistence on talking about exceptions to their problems. Clients may view the therapist as an expert and be reluctant to view themselves as experts. Certain clients may doubt the helpfulness of a therapist who assumes a "know-nothing" position.
Family systems therapy	Family therapy rests on value assumptions that are not congruent with the values of clients from some other cultures. Concepts such as individuation, self-actualization, self-determination, independence, and self-expression may be foreign to some clients. In some cultures, admitting problems within the family is shameful. The value of "keeping problems within the family" may make it difficult to explore conflicts openly.

TABLE 15-9 Contributions of the Approaches

Psychoanalytic therapy	More than any other system, this approach has generated controversy as well as exploration and has stimulated further thinking and development of therapy. It has provided a detailed and comprehensive description of personality structure and

(continued on next page)

TABLE 15-9   Contributions of the Approaches (continued)

	functioning. It has brought into prominence factors such as the unconscious as a determinant of behavior and the role of trauma during the first 6 years of life. It has developed several techniques for tapping the unconscious and shed light on the dynamics of transference and countertransference, resistance, anxiety, and the mechanisms of ego defense.
Adlerian therapy	One of the first approaches to therapy that was humanistic, unified, holistic, and goal-oriented and that put an emphasis on social and psychological factors. A key contribution is the influence that Adlerian concepts have had on other systems and the integration of these concepts into various contemporary therapies.
Existential therapy	Its major contribution is recognition of the need for a subjective approach based on a complete view of the human condition. It calls attention to the need for a philosophical statement on what it means to be a person. Stress on the I/Thou relationship lessens the chances of dehumanizing therapy. It provides a perspective for understanding anxiety, guilt, freedom, death, isolation, and commitment.
Person-centered therapy	Clients take an active stance and assume responsibility for the direction of therapy. This unique approach has been subjected to empirical testing, and as a result both theory and methods have been modified. It is an open system. People without advanced training can benefit by translating the therapeutic conditions to both their personal and professional lives. Basic concepts are straightforward and easy to grasp and apply. It is a foundation for building a trusting relationship, applicable to all therapies.
Gestalt therapy	Main contribution is an emphasis on direct experiencing and doing rather than on merely talking about feelings. It provides a perspective on growth and enhancement, not merely a treatment of disorders. It uses clients' behavior as the basis for making them aware of inner creative potential. The approach to dreams is a unique, creative tool to help clients discover basic conflicts. Therapy is viewed as an existential encounter; it is process-oriented, not technique-oriented. It recognizes nonverbal behavior as a key to understanding.
Behavior therapy	Emphasis is on assessment and evaluation techniques, thus providing a basis for accountable practice. Specific problems are identified, and clients are kept informed about progress toward their goals. The approach has demonstrated effectiveness in many areas of human functioning. The roles of the therapist as reinforcer, model, teacher, and consultant are explicit. The approach has undergone extensive expansion, and research literature abounds. No longer is it a mechanistic approach, for it now makes room for cognitive factors and encourages self-directed programs for behavioral change.

TABLE 15-9   Contributions of the Approaches (continued)

Cognitive behavior therapy	Major contributions include emphasis on a comprehensive and eclectic therapeutic practice; numerous cognitive, emotive, and behavioral techniques; an openness to incorporating techniques from other approaches; and a methodology for challenging and changing faulty thinking. Most forms can be integrated into other mainstream therapies. REBT makes full use of action-oriented homework, listening to tapes, and keeping records of progress. CT is a structured therapy that has a good track record for treating depression and anxiety in a short time.
Reality therapy	Consists of simple and clear concepts that are easily grasped in many helping professions; thus, it can be used by teachers, nurses, ministers, educators, social workers, and counselors. It is a positive approach with an action orientation. Due to the direct methods, it appeals to many clients who are often seen as resistant to therapy. It is a short-term approach that can be applied to a diverse population, and it has been a significant force in challenging the medical model of therapy.
Feminist therapy	Major contributions are paving the way for gender-sensitive practice and bringing attention to the gendered uses of power in relationships. The feminist perspective is responsible for encouraging increasing numbers of women to question gender stereotypes and to reject limited views of what a woman is expected to be. The unified feminist voice brought attention to the extent and implications of child abuse, incest, rape, sexual harassment, and domestic violence. Feminist principles and interventions can be incorporated in other therapy approaches.
Postmodern approaches	The brevity of these approaches tends to fit well with the limitations imposed by a managed care structure. The emphasis on client strengths and competence appeals to clients who want to create solutions and revise their life stories in a positive direction. These approaches are useful in assisting clients to move from a powerless stance to a place of empowerment. Clients are not blamed for their problems but are helped to understand how they might relate in more satisfying ways to such problems. A strength of these approaches is the question format that invites clients to view themselves in new and more effective ways.
Family systems therapy	From a systemic perspective, neither the individual nor the family is blamed for a particular dysfunction. The family is empowered through the process of identifying and exploring interactional patterns. Working with an entire unit provides a new perspective on understanding and working through both individual problems and relationship concerns. By exploring one's family of origin, there are increased opportunities to resolve other relationship conflicts outside of the family.

TABLE 15-10   Limitations of the Approaches

Psychoanalytic therapy	Requires lengthy training for therapists and much time and expense for clients. The model stresses biological and instinctual factors to the neglect of social, cultural, and interpersonal ones. Its methods are not applicable for solving specific daily life problems of clients and are not appropriate for many ethnic and cultural groups. Many clients lack the degree of ego strength needed for regressive and reconstructive therapy. It is inappropriate for the typical counseling setting.
Adlerian therapy	Weak in terms of precision, testability, and empirical validity. Few attempts have been made to validate the basic concepts by scientific methods. Tends to oversimplify some complex human problems and is based heavily on common sense.
Existential therapy	Many basic concepts are fuzzy and ill-defined, making its general framework abstract at times. Lacks a systematic statement of principles and practices of therapy. Has limited applicability to lower functioning and nonverbal clients and to clients in extreme crisis who need direction.
Person-centered therapy	Possible danger from the therapist who remains passive and inactive, limiting responses to reflection. Many clients feel a need for greater direction, more structure, and more techniques. Clients in crisis may need more directive measures. Applied to individual counseling, some cultural groups will expect more counselor activity. The theory needs to be reassessed in light of current knowledge and thought if rigidity is to be avoided.
Gestalt therapy	Techniques lead to intense emotional expression; if these feelings are not explored and if cognitive work is not done, clients are likely to be left unfinished and will not have a sense of integration of their learning. Clients who have difficulty using imagination may not profit from experiments.
Behavior therapy	Major criticisms are that it may change behavior but not feelings; that it ignores the relational factors in therapy; that it does not provide insight; that it ignores historical causes of present behavior; that it involves control and manipulation by the therapist; and that it is limited in its capacity to address certain aspects of the human condition.
Cognitive behavior therapy	Tends to play down emotions, does not focus on exploring the unconscious or underlying conflicts, and sometimes does not give enough weight to client's past. REBT, being a confrontational therapy, might lead to premature termination. CT might be too structured for some clients.
Reality therapy	Discounts the therapeutic value of exploration of the client's past, dreams, the unconscious, early childhood experiences,

TABLE 15-10 Limitations of the Approaches (continued)

	and transference. The approach is limited to less complex problems. It is a problem-solving therapy that tends to discourage exploration of deeper emotional issues. It is vulnerable to practitioners who want to "fix" clients quickly.
Feminist therapy	A possible limitation is the potential for therapists to impose a new set of values on clients—such as striving for equality, power in relationships, defining oneself, freedom to pursue a career outside the home, and the right to an education. Therapists need to keep in mind that clients are their own best experts, which means it is up to them to decide which values to live by.
Postmodern approaches	There is little empirical validation of the effectiveness of therapy outcomes. Some critics contend that these approaches endorse cheerleading and an overly positive perspective. Some are critical of the stance taken by most postmodern therapists regarding assessment and diagnosis, and also react negatively to the "know-nothing" stance of the therapist. Because some of the solution-focused and narrative therapy techniques are relatively easy to learn, practitioners may use these interventions in a mechanical way.
Family systems therapy	Limitations include problems in being able to involve all the members of a family in the therapy. Some family members may be resistant to changing the structure of the system. Therapists' self-knowledge and willingness to work on their own family-of-origin issues is crucial, for the potential for countertransference is high. It is essential that the therapist be well trained, receive quality supervision, and be competent in assessing and treating individuals in a family context.

Evaluating the Effectiveness of Counseling and Therapy

Research in psychotherapy gained little momentum until the 1950s. Since the late 1950s and the early 1960s researchers have mainly addressed the process and outcomes of therapy to gain a clearer understanding of what constitutes therapeutic change and how it comes about (Strupp, 1986; VandenBos, 1986).

The acceleration of public funding for all types of human services programs during the 1960s also stirred a keen interest in evaluation research. In essence, if government funds were to continue to be allocated to human services agencies, the burden of proof rested on researchers and practitioners to demonstrate the effectiveness of psychotherapy by using scientific methods. The central question raised was "Of what value is psychotherapy to the individual and society?" (Strupp, 1986). Mental health providers are still faced with accountability. In the era of managed care, it becomes even more essential for practitioners to demonstrate the degree to which their interventions are both clinically sound and cost-effective.

Does therapy make a significant difference? Are people substantially better after therapy than they were without it? Can therapy actually be more harmful than helpful? A thorough discussion of these questions is beyond the scope of this book, but I will address a few basic issues related to evaluating the effectiveness of counseling. If you are interested in an in-depth review of psychotherapy research, I suggest Garfield (1987, 1992b); Imber and colleagues (1986); Lambert (1992); Lambert and Bergin (1992); Smith, Glass, and Miller (1980); Strupp (1986); Strupp and Howard (1992); and VandenBos (1986).

Evaluating how well psychotherapy works is far from simple. Therapeutic systems are applied by practitioners with unique individual characteristics, and clients themselves have much to do with therapeutic outcomes. If clients choose to engage in activities that are self-destructive, this behavior will cancel out the positive effects of therapy. To add to the problem, effects resulting from unexpected and uncontrollable events in the environment can destroy gains made in psychotherapy. As Garfield (1992b) has pointed out, the basic variables that influence therapy research are extremely difficult to control.

Most of the outcome studies have been done by two divergent groups: (1) the behavior and cognitive therapists, who have based their therapeutic practice on empirical studies, and (2) the person-centered researchers, who have made significant contributions to understanding both process and outcome variables. Most of the other models covered in this book have not produced significant empirical research dealing with how well their therapy works.

By about 1980 a consensus had emerged that psychotherapy was demonstrably more effective than no treatment (VandenBos, 1986). A meta-analysis of psychotherapy outcome literature conducted by Smith and colleagues (1980) concluded that psychotherapy was highly effective. Despite this general support of the value of psychotherapy, hard data of the effects of concepts and procedures of most of the therapeutic approaches is sparse at best. One reason is that one approach's "cure" is another approach's "resistance." In other words, because each approach works toward different outcomes, it is almost impossible to compare them. Despite the wide range of purportedly distinct psychotherapeutic treatments, most reviews of outcome research show little differential effectiveness of the tested psychotherapies (Stiles, Shapiro, & Elliott, 1986). Factors other than scientific data must be considered if we are to determine the validity and usefulness of most of the therapeutic approaches.

Lambert (1992) writes that because of the wide variability of techniques employed by integrative practitioners, it is extremely difficult to assess the effectiveness of standard eclectic approaches. One of Lambert's key points is the lack of clear research evidence to support the therapeutic value of many eclectic practices. He concludes that until empirical investigations are conducted integrative therapists would do well to be more modest in their claims of being superior to the single-school models.

The general question "Does psychotherapy work?" is very difficult to answer meaningfully (Strupp & Howard, 1992). Garfield (1980) argues that psychotherapy is not a clearly defined and uniform process and that there is thus no basis for any objective answer to the question. As VandenBos (1986) concludes, it appears that outcome research aimed at proving the efficacy of therapy should be a thing of the past. He contends that future research should focus on exploring the relative advantages and disadvantages of alternative treatment strategies for clients with different psychological and behavioral problems. Included in this research should be factors such as the relative cost, the length of time necessary to effect change, and the nature and extent of change. Whatever form it takes, research will apparently play an increasingly important role in determining the future of psychotherapy (Strupp, 1986).

A guideline for improving on the global question regarding the effectiveness of therapy is provided by Paul (1967, p. 111): *"What* treatment, by *whom,* is the most effective *for this* individual with *that* specific problem, and under what set of circumstances?" Moreover, practitioners who adhere to the same approach are likely to use techniques in various ways and to relate to clients in diverse fashions, functioning differently with different clients and in different clinical settings. It is clear that greater precision and specificity are needed in research (Stiles et al., 1986). Thus, the question of the effectiveness of psychotherapy must be narrowed to a specific type of therapy and usually narrowed further to a certain technique as well.

 ## SUMMARY

Creating an integrative stance is truly a challenge. Therapists cannot simply pick bits and pieces from theories in a random and fragmented manner. In forming an integrated perspective, it is important to ask: Which theories provide a basis for understanding the *cognitive* dimensions? What about the *feeling* aspects? And how about the *behavioral* dimension? Most of the 11 therapeutic orientations discussed here focus on one of these dimensions of human experience. Although the other dimensions are not necessarily ignored, they are often given short shrift.

Developing an integrated theoretical perspective requires much reading, thinking, and actual counseling experience. Without an accurate, in-depth knowledge of these theories, you cannot formulate a true synthesis. Simply put, you cannot integrate what you do not know (Norcross & Newman, 1992). A central message of this book has been to remain open to each theory, to do further reading, and to reflect on how the key concepts of each approach fit your personality. Building your personalized orientation to counseling, which is based on what you consider to be the best features of several theories, is a long-term venture.

Besides considering your own personality, think about what concepts and techniques work best with a range of clients. It requires knowledge, skill, art, and experience to be able to determine what techniques are suitable for particular problems. It is also an art to know when and how to use a particular therapeutic intervention. Although reflecting on your personal preferences is important, I would hope that you also balance your preferences with scientific evidence. Developing a personal approach to counseling practice does not imply that anything goes. Indeed, in this era of managed care and cost-effectiveness, your personal preferences may not always be the sole determinant of your psychotherapy practice. In counseling clients with certain problems, specific techniques have demonstrated their effectiveness. For instance, behavior therapy, cognitive therapy, interpersonal therapy, and short-term psychodynamic therapy have repeatedly proved successful in treating depression. Although I am not suggesting that you adopt a theory with which you are uncomfortable, ethical practice implies that you employ efficacious procedures in dealing with clients and their problems. You might ask yourself these questions: "Under what circumstances is it appropriate, or ethical, for me to bypass a scientifically proven treatment for a treatment that I personally prefer?"

This is a good time to review what you have learned about counseling theory and practice. Identify a particular theory that you might adopt as a foundation for establishing your counseling perspective. Consider from which therapies you would be most inclined to draw (1) underlying assumptions, (2) major concepts, (3) therapeutic goals, (4) therapeutic relationship, and (5) techniques and procedures. Also, consider the major applications of each of the therapies as well as their basic limitations and major contributions. The charts presented in this chapter are designed to assist you in conceptualizing your view of the counseling process.

Recommended Supplementary Readings

Integrative Psychotherapy: The Art and Science of Relationship (Moursund & Erskine, 2004) is a relationship-focused integrative approach to practice. The book deals with both theoretical foundations and therapeutic interventions.

Handbook of Psychotherapy Integration (Norcross & Goldfried, 1992) is an excellent resource for conceptual and historical perspectives on therapy integration. This edited volume gives a comprehensive overview of the major current approaches, such as theoretical integration and technical eclecticism.

Systematic Treatment Selection: Toward Target Therapeutic Interventions (Beutler & Clarkin, 1990) is a useful source on an integrated approach. The authors describe the ingredients of good therapy and how to maximize their effectiveness by matching clients to both therapists and techniques.

The Art of Integrative Counseling (Corey, 2001) is designed to assist students in developing their own integrative approach to counseling. This book is geared very closely to the CD-ROM described next.

CD-ROM for Integrative Counseling (Corey & Haynes, 2005) illustrates an integrative perspective in working with a hypothetical client, Ruth. This interactive program brings together most of the therapies discussed in this book.

Case Approach to Counseling and Psychotherapy (Corey, 2005) illustrates each of the 11 contemporary theories by applying them to the single case of Ruth. I also demonstrate my integrative approach in counseling Ruth in the final chapter.

References and Suggested Readings

*ABERNETHY, R. (1992). The integration of therapies. In J. S. Rutan (Ed.), *Psychotherapy for the 1990s* (pp. 19–34). New York: Guilford Press.

*ALFORD, B. A., & BECK, A. T. (1997). *The integrative power of cognitive therapy.* New York: Guilford Press.

*ARKOWITZ, H. (1997). Integrative theories of therapy. In P. L. Wachtel & S. B. Messer (Eds.), *Theories of psychotherapy: Origins and evolution* (pp. 227–288). Washington, DC: American Psychological Association.

BENSON, H., with STARK, M. (1996). *Timeless healing: The power and biology of belief.* New York: Scribner.

BEUTLER, L. E. (1983). *Eclectic psychotherapy: A systematic approach.* New York: Pergamon Press.

BEUTLER, L. E., & CLARKIN, J. (1990). *Systematic treatment selection: Toward targeted therapeutic interventions.* New York: Brunner/Mazel.

*COREY, G. (2001). *The art of integrative counseling.* Pacific Grove, CA: Brooks/Cole.

*COREY, G., & HAYNES, R. (2005). *CD-ROM for integrative counseling.* Belmont, CA: Brooks/Cole.

*COREY, G. (2005). *Case approach to counseling and psychotherapy* (6th ed). Belmont, CA: Brooks/Cole.

FAIVER, C. M., INGERSOLL, R. E., O'BRIEN, E., & MCNALLY, C. (2001). *Explorations in counseling and spirituality: Philosophical, practical, and personal reflections.* Pacific Grove, CA: Brooks/Cole.

FAIVER, C. M., & O'BRIEN, E. M. (1993). Assessment of religious beliefs form. *Counseling and Values, 37*(3), 176–178.

FAIVER, C. M., O'BRIEN, E., & INGERSOLL, R. E. (2000). Religion, guilt, and mental health. *Journal of Counseling and Development, 78*(2), 155–161.

FRAME, M. W. (2003). *Integrating religion and spirituality into counseling: A comprehensive approach.* Pacific Grove, CA: Brooks/Cole.

GARFIELD, S. L. (1980). *Psychotherapy: An eclectic approach.* New York: Wiley.

GARFIELD, S. L. (1987). Ethical issues in research on psychotherapy. *Counseling and Values, 31*(2), 115–125.

GARFIELD, S. L. (1992a). Eclectic psychotherapy: A common factors approach. In J. C. Norcross & M. R. Goldfried (Eds.), *Handbook of psychotherapy integration* (pp. 169–201). New York: Basic Books.

GARFIELD, S. L. (1992b). Major issues in psychotherapy research. In D. K. Freedheim (Ed.), *History of psychotherapy: A century of change* (pp. 335–359). Washington, DC: American Psychological Association.

---

*Books and articles marked with an asterisk are recommended for further study.

GOLDFRIED, M. R., & CASTONGUAY, L. G. (1992). The future of psychotherapy integration. *Psychotherapy, 29*(1), 4–10.

*GOLDFRIED, M. R., & NEWMAN, C. (1992). A history of psychotherapy integration. In J. C. Norcross & M. R. Goldfried (Eds.), *Handbook of psychotherapy integration* (pp. 46–93). New York: Basic Books.

GRIMM, D. W. (1994). Therapist spiritual and religious values in psychotherapy. *Counseling and Values, 38*(3), 154–164.

HINTERKOPF, E. (1994). Integrating spiritual experiences in counseling. *Counseling and Values, 38*(3), 165–175.

HINTERKOPF, E. (1998). *Integrating spirituality in counseling: A manual for using the experiential focusing method.* Alexandria, VA: American Counseling Association.

IMBER, S. D., GLANZ, L. M., ELKIN, I., SOTSKY, S. M., BOYER, J. L., & LEBER, W. R. (1986). Ethical issues in psychotherapy research. *American Psychologist, 41*(2), 137–146.

KELLY, E. W. (1995). *Spirituality and religion in counseling and psychotherapy.* Alexandria, VA: American Counseling Association.

LAMBERT, M. J. (1992). Psychotherapy outcome research: Implications for integrative and eclectic therapists. In J. C. Norcross & M. R. Goldfried (Eds.), *Handbook of psychotherapy integration* (pp. 94–129). New York: Basic Books.

LAMBERT, M. J., & BERGIN, A. E. (1992). Achievements and limitations of psychotherapy research. In D. K. Freedheim (Ed.), *History of psychotherapy: A century of change* (pp. 360–390). Washington, DC: American Psychological Association.

LAZARUS, A. A. (1986). Multimodal therapy. In J. C. Norcross (Ed.), *Handbook of eclectic psychotherapy* (pp. 65–93). New York: Brunner/Mazel.

*LAZARUS, A. A. (1989). *The practice of multimodal therapy.* Baltimore: Johns Hopkins University Press.

LAZARUS, A. A. (1992). Multimodal therapy: Technical eclecticism with minimal integration. In J. C. Norcross & M. R. Goldfried (Eds.), *Handbook of psychotherapy integration* (pp. 231–263). New York: Basic Books.

*LAZARUS, A. A. (1995). Different types of eclecticism and integration: Let's be aware of the dangers. *Journal of Psychotherapy Integration, 5*(1), 27–39.

LAZARUS, A. A. (1996a). Some reflections after 40 years of trying to be an effective psychotherapist. *Psychotherapy, 33*(1), 142–145.

*LAZARUS, A. A. (1996b). The utility and futility of combining treatments in psychotherapy. *Clinical Psychology: Science and Practice, 3*(1), 59–68.

*LAZARUS, A. A. (1997a). *Brief but comprehensive psychotherapy: The multimodal way.* New York: Springer.

LAZARUS, A. A. (1997b). Can psychotherapy be brief, focused, solution-oriented, and yet comprehensive? A personal evolutionary perspective. In J. K. Zeig (Ed.), *The evolution of psychotherapy: The third conference* (pp. 83–94). New York: Brunner/Mazel.

*LAZARUS, A. A., & BEUTLER, L. E. (1993). On technical eclecticism. *Journal of Counseling and Development, 71*(4), 381–385.

*LAZARUS, A. A., BEUTLER, L. E., & NORCROSS, J. C. (1992). The future of technical eclecticism. *Psychotherapy, 29*(1), 11–20.

MESSER, S. B. (1986). Eclecticism in psychotherapy: Underlying assumptions, problems, and trade-offs. In J. C. Norcross (Ed.), *Handbook of eclectic psychotherapy* (pp. 379–397). New York: Brunner/Mazel.

MESSER, S. B. (1992). A critical examination of belief structures in integrative and eclectic psychotherapy In J. C. Norcross & M. R. Goldfried (Eds.), *Handbook of psychotherapy integration* (pp. 130–165). New York: Basic Books.

*MIKULAS, W. L. (2002). *The integrative helper: Convergence of Eastern and Western traditions.* Pacific Grove, CA: Brooks/Cole.

*MILLER, W. R. (Ed.). (1999). *Integrating spirituality into treatment: Resources for practitioners.* Washington, DC: American Psychological Association.

MIRANTI, J., & BURKE, M. T. (1995). Spirituality: An integrated component of the counseling process. In M. T. Burke & J. G. Miranti (Eds.), *Counseling: The spiritual dimension* (pp. 1–3). Alexandria, VA: American Counseling Association.

*MOURSUND, J. P., & ERSKINE, R. G. (2004). *Integrative psychotherapy: The art and science of relationship.* Pacific Grove, CA: Brooks/Cole.

NORCROSS, J. C. (1986a). Eclectic psychotherapy: An introduction and overview. In J. C. Norcross (Ed.), *Handbook of eclectic psychotherapy* (pp. 3–24). New York: Brunner/Mazel.

NORCROSS, J. C. (Ed.). (1986b). *Handbook of eclectic psychotherapy.* New York: Brunner/Mazel.

*NORCROSS, J. C., & GOLDFRIED, M. R. (Eds.). (1992). *Handbook of psychotherapy integration.* New York: Basic Books.

NORCROSS, J. C., HEDGES, M., & PROCHASKA, J. O. (2002). The face of 2010: A Delphi poll on the future of psychotherapy. *Professional Psychology: Research and Practice, 33*(3), 316–322.

NORCROSS, J. C., & NEWMAN, C. F. (1992). Psychotherapy integration: Setting the context. In J. C. Norcross & M. R. Goldfried (Eds.), *Handbook of psychotherapy integration* (pp. 3–45). New York: Basic Books.

PAUL, G. L. (1967). Outcome research in psychotherapy. *Journal of Consulting Psychology, 31,* 109–188.

*PRESTON, J. (1998). *Integrative brief therapy: Cognitive, psychodynamic, humanistic and neurobehavioral approaches.* San Luis Obispo, CA: Impact.

*PROCHASKA, J. O., & NORCROSS, J. C. (2003). *Systems of psychotherapy: A transtheoretical analysis* (5th ed.). Pacific Grove, CA: Brooks/Cole.

*RICHARDS, P. S., & BERGIN, A. E. (1997). *A spiritual strategy for counseling and psychotherapy.* Washington, DC: American Psychological Association.

*RICHARDS, P. S., & BERGIN, A. E. (2004). *Casebook for a spiritual strategy in counseling and psychotherapy.* Washington, DC: American Psychological Association.

*RICHARDS, P. S., RECTOR, J. M., & TJELTVEIT, A. C. (1999). Values, spirituality, and psychotherapy. In W. R. Miller (Ed.), *Integrating spirituality into treatment: Resources for practitioners* (pp. 133–160). Washington, DC: American Psychological Association.

SMITH, M. L., GLASS, G. V., & MILLER, T. I. (1980). *The benefits of psychotherapy.* Baltimore: Johns Hopkins University Press.

STILES, W. B., SHAPIRO, D. A., & ELLIOTT, R. (1986). Are all psychotherapies equivalent? *American Psychologist, 41*(2), 165–180.

STRUPP, H. H. (1986). Psychotherapy: Research, practice, and public policy (How to avoid dead ends). *American Psychologist, 41*(2), 120–130.

STRUPP, H. H., & HOWARD, K. I. (1992). A brief history of psychotherapy research. In D. K. Freedheim (Ed.), *History of psychotherapy: A century of change* (pp. 309–334). Washington, DC: American Psychological Association.

SUE, D. W., IVEY, A., & PEDERSEN, P. (1996). *A theory of multicultural counseling and therapy.* Pacific Grove, CA: Brooks/Cole.

*SUE, D. W., & SUE, D. (2003). *Counseling the culturally diverse: Theory and practice* (4th ed.). New York: Wiley.

VANDENBOS, G. R. (1986). Psychotherapy research: A special issue. *American Psychologist, 41*(2), 111–112.

YOUNG, M. E. (1992). *Counseling methods and techniques: An eclectic approach.* New York: Macmillan.

YOUNGGREN, J. N. (1993). Ethical issues in religious psychotherapy. *Register Report, 19*(4), 1–8.

Chapter 16

Case Illustration: An Integrative Approach in Working With Stan

INTRODUCTION

The purpose of this chapter is to bring together in an integrative fashion the 11 approaches you have studied by using a thinking, feeling, and acting model in counseling Stan. At this point I recommend that you review the background material and themes in Stan's life presented in Chapter 1.

Table 16-1 illustrates how I am likely to work with Stan by selecting goals, key concepts, and techniques from the various approaches. As Stan's therapist, I would have a different area of focus when operating under each theoretical orientation. My hope is that you will think concretely about how to blend the concepts and techniques of various theories in a way that makes the most sense to you so that you can move toward developing your own integrative approach.

 WORKING WITH STAN: INTEGRATION OF THERAPIES

In this section, I describe how I would integrate concepts and techniques from the 11 theoretical perspectives in counseling Stan on the levels of *thinking*, *feeling*, and *doing*. I use information presented in Stan's autobiography, and I indicate from what orientations I am borrowing ideas at the various stages of his therapy. As you read, think about interventions you might make with Stan that would be either similar to or different from mine. Questions at the end of the chapter will guide you as you reflect on being Stan's counselor and working with him from your own integrative perspective.

A Place to Begin

I start by giving Stan a chance to say how he feels about coming to the initial session. To begin to understand why Stan has sought therapy, I might explore with him any of these questions:

- "What brings you here? What has been going on in your life recently that gave you the impetus to seek professional help?"
- "What expectations do you have of therapy? of me? What are your hopes, fears, and any reservations? What goals do you have for yourself through therapy?"
- "Could you give me a picture of some significant turning points in your life? Who have been the important people in your life? What significant decisions have you made? What are some of the struggles you've dealt with, and what are some of these issues that are current for you?"
- "What was it like for you to be in your family? How did you view your parents? How did they react to you? What about your early development?" (It would be useful to administer the Adlerian lifestyle questionnaire.)

TABLE 16-1   Major Areas of Focus in Stan's Therapy

Psychoanalytic therapy	My focus is on the ways in which Stan is repeating his early childhood in his present relationships. I am particularly interested in how he brings his experiences with his father into the sessions with me. As it is relevant, I will focus on his feelings for me, because working with transference is one path toward insight. I am interested in his dreams, any resistance that he reveals in the sessions, and other clues to his unconscious processes. One of my main goals is to assist him in bringing to awareness buried memories and experiences, which I assume have a current influence on him.
Adlerian therapy	My focus is on determining what Stan's lifestyle is. In conducting a lifestyle assessment, I will examine his early childhood experiences through his recollections and family constellation. My main interest is in identifying what his goals and priorities in life are. I assume that what he is striving toward is equally as valid as his past dynamics. Therapy will consist of doing a comprehensive assessment, helping him understand his dynamics, and then helping him define new goals and translate them into action.
Existential therapy	My aim is to be as fully present and available for Stan as possible, for I assume that the relationship I am able to establish with him will be the source of our work together. An area that I am likely to concentrate on is how he finds meaning in life and whether spiritual values have been or currently are a part of his life. Although I would not impose any spiritual or religious beliefs during therapy, it is important to let Stan know that we can talk about his beliefs and values if he so chooses. He says he feels anxious a great deal, and this is an avenue to explore. Because Stan mentioned a fear of dying, and even entertained suicide as an option, I will certainly encourage him to explore his thoughts and feelings in these areas. Stan's anxiety and fear of death may be related to his early experiences with religion. I want to find out more about the nature of his fear of death and what keeps him alive, and I will assess the risk of suicide at the outset. We will also explore what quality of life he is striving for. I am interested in how Stan is dealing with freedom and the responsibility that accompanies it. Therapy is a venture that can help him expand his awareness of the way he is in his world, which will give him the potential to make changes.
Person-centered therapy	Because I trust Stan to find his own direction for therapy, I will avoid planning and structuring the sessions. My main focus is on being real, on accepting his feelings and thoughts, and on demonstrating my unconditional positive regard for him. Although Stan is only dimly aware of his feelings at the initial phase of therapy, he will move toward increased clarity as I accept him fully, without conditions and without judgments. If I

TABLE 16-1   Major Areas of Focus in Stan's Therapy (continued)

	can create a climate of openness, trust, caring, understanding, and acceptance, then Stan can use this relationship to move forward and grow.
Gestalt therapy	My focus is on noticing signs of Stan's unfinished business, as evidenced by the ways in which he reaches a stuck point in his therapy. If he has never worked through his feelings of not being accepted, for example, these issues will appear in his therapy. I will ask Stan to bring them into the present by reliving them rather than merely talking about past events. I hope to help him experience his feelings fully, instead of simply gaining insight into his problems or speculating about why he feels the way he does. I'll encourage Stan to pay attention to his moment-by-moment awareness, especially to what he is aware of in his body. We will concentrate on how he is behaving and what he is experiencing. Stan will lead the way in therapy by the concerns he identifies in the present moment. My job is to intervene in ways that will enable Stan to work through places where he is stuck.
Behavior therapy	Initially, I'll conduct a thorough assessment of Stan's current behavior. I'll ask him to monitor what he is doing so that we can create baseline data to evaluate any changes. We will continue our work by collaboratively developing concrete goals to guide our work, and I will draw on a wide range of cognitive and behavioral techniques to help Stan achieve his goals. We may use techniques such as role playing, modeling, coaching, assertion training, carrying out homework assignments, and relaxation methods. I will stress learning new coping skills that Stan can use in everyday situations. He will practice what he learns in therapy sessions in his daily life.
Cognitive behavior therapy	My focus is on how Stan's internal dialogue and thinking processes are affecting his behavior. I will use an active and directive therapeutic style. Therapy will be time-limited, present-centered, and structured. My task is to create a form of collaborative working relationship in which Stan will learn to recognize and change self-defeating beliefs. We will concentrate on the content and process of his thinking by looking for ways to restructure some of his beliefs. Rather than merely telling Stan what faulty beliefs he has, I will emphasize his gathering data and weighing the evidence in support of certain beliefs. By the use of Socratic dialogue, I will assist Stan in detecting his faulty thinking, in learning ways of correcting his distortions, and in substituting more effective self-talk and beliefs. We will be using a wide range of cognitive, emotive, and behavioral techniques to accomplish our goals.

(continued on next page)

TABLE 16-1 Major Areas of Focus in Stan's Therapy (continued)

Reality therapy	Counseling will be guided by the principles of choice theory. First, I will do my best to demonstrate my personal involvement with Stan by listening to his story. The emphasis is on his total behavior, including his doing, thinking, feeling, and physiology. If we concentrate on what he is actually doing and thinking and if change occurs on these levels, I assume Stan will automatically change on the feeling and physiological levels. After he evaluates his present behavior, it is up to him to decide the degree to which it is working for him. We will explore those areas of his behavior that he identifies as not meeting his needs. Much of therapy will consist of creating specific, realistic, and attainable plans. Once Stan agrees to a plan of action, it is essential that he make a commitment to following through with it.
Feminist therapy	Stan comes to therapy with clear goals: to stop drinking, to feel better about himself, to relate to women on an equal basis, and to learn to love and trust himself and others. I build on these strengths. I focus on establishing an egalitarian working relationship to help Stan begin to regain his personal power. I spend considerable time explaining my view of the therapy process and how it works. By demystifying the therapeutic process, I am conveying to Stan that he is in charge of the direction his therapy will take. Our therapy might include a gender-role analysis so that Stan can come to a fuller understanding of the limiting roles he has uncritically accepted.
Postmodern approaches	Operating from the joint perspectives of the solution-focused and narrative approaches, a basic assumption that guides my practice is that Stan is an expert on his life and that I am a consultant who invites and assists Stan in identifying, clarifying, and achieving his goals and preferences. I believe Stan has the internal and external resources he needs to make the kinds of changes he is seeking. One of my tasks is to construct questions that will assist Stan in discovering more choices and in accomplishing his goals, and ultimately, in assisting him in re-authoring the story of his life.
Family systems therapy	Stan has identified a number of strained relationships with his mother, father, and siblings. Ideally, we will have at least one session with all of the members of his family. The focus will be on his gaining greater clarity on how his interpersonal style is largely the result of his interactions with his family of origin. If I work individually with Stan, the emphasis can still be on the many ways in which his current struggles are related to the system of which he is a part. Through our therapy, Stan will learn to recognize the rules that governed his family of origin and the decisions he made about himself. Rather than trying to change the members of his family, we will largely work on discovering what Stan most wants to change about himself in relation to how he interacts with them.

Clarifying the Therapeutic Relationship

I will work with Stan to develop a contract, which involves a discussion of our mutual responsibilities and a clear statement of what he wants from these sessions and what he is willing to do to obtain it. I believe it is important to discuss any factors that might perpetuate a client's dependency on the therapist, so I invite Stan's questions about this therapeutic relationship. One goal is to demystify the therapy process; another is to get some focus for the direction of our sessions.

In establishing the therapeutic relationship, I am influenced by the person-centered, existential, Gestalt, feminist, postmodern, and Adlerian approaches. They do not view therapy as something that the therapist *does* to a passive client. I will apply my knowledge of these therapies to establish a working relationship with Stan that is characterized by mutual trust and respect. I will ask myself these questions: "To what degree am I able to listen to and hear Stan in a nonjudgmental way? Am I able to respect and care for him? Do I have the capacity to enter his subjective world without losing my own identity? Am I able to share with him my own thoughts and reactions as they pertain to our relationship?" This relationship is critical at the initial stages of therapy, but it must be maintained during all stages if therapy is to be effective.

My contract with Stan specifies his rights and responsibilities as a client and my role as his therapist. Expectations are explored, goals are defined, and there is a basis for therapy as a collaborative effort. This emphasis is consistent with Adlerian therapy, the behavior therapies, the cognitive therapies, feminist therapy, the postmodern therapies, and reality therapy. An excellent foundation for building a working partnership is openness by the counselor about the process of therapy. I think it is a mistake to hide behind "professionalism" as a way of keeping distance from the client. Therefore, I begin by being as honest as I can be with Stan as the basis for creating this relationship.

Clarifying the Goals of Therapy

It is not enough simply to ask clients what they hope they will leave with at the conclusion of therapy. Typically, I find that clients are vague, global, and unfocused about what they want. From behavior therapy, cognitive behavior therapy, Adlerian therapy, and reality therapy, I borrow the necessity of getting Stan to be specific in defining his goals. Thus, Stan says: "I want to stop playing all these games with myself and others. I'd hope to stop putting myself down. I want to get rid of the terrible feelings I have. I want to feel OK with myself and begin living." I strive to get more concrete responses: "Let's see if we can narrow down some of these broad goals into terms specific enough that both you and I will know what you're talking about." I might pursue any of the general topics Stan provided by asking further questions such as these:

- "What exactly are these games you talk about?"
- "In what ways do you put yourself down?"

- "What are some of these terrible feelings that bother you?"
- "In what specific ways do you feel that you're not living now?"
- "What would it take for you to begin to feel alive?"

It is essential to work with Stan toward greater precision and clarity. If we merely talk about lofty goals such as self-actualization, I fear we will have directionless sessions. Thus, I focus on concrete language and specific goals that both of us can observe and understand. Once we have identified some goals, Stan can begin to observe his own behavior, both in the sessions and in his daily life. This self-monitoring is a vital step in any effort to bring about change.

My main aim is to encourage Stan to assume responsibility for what he wants to accomplish from the onset of our relationship. A large part of our early work together consists of helping Stan get a clear sense of concrete changes he would most like to make and how he can make them happen. Here are a few interchanges that focus on the process of defining goals that will give direction to Stan's therapy:

Jerry: What would you most hope for, through our work together?

Stan: Well, I know I put myself down all the time. I'd really like to feel better about myself.

Jerry: You put yourself down all of the time? Is what you've just said an example of how you are being hard on yourself right now?

Stan: Well, once in a great while I don't put myself down.

Jerry: If you had what you want in your life today, what would that be like? What would it take for you to feel good about yourself?

Stan: For one thing, I'd have people in my life, and I wouldn't run from intimacy.

Jerry: So this might be an area you'd be willing to explore in your sessions.

Stan: Sure, but I wouldn't know where to begin.

Jerry: I'll be glad to provide suggestions of ways to begin, if I know what you want.

Stan: Well, for sure I'd like to get over my fears of being with people. All my dumb fears really get in my way.

Jerry: I like it that you're willing to challenge your fears. Are you aware that you also just put yourself down again in labeling your fears as dumb?

Stan: It just comes as second nature to me. But I really would like to be able to feel more comfortable when I'm with others.

Jerry: How is it for you to be here with me now?

Stan: It's really not like me to do something like this, but it feels good. At least I'm talking, and I'm saying what's on my mind.

Jerry: It's good to see you give yourself credit for being different in our interchange right now.

This process of formulating goals is not accomplished in a single session. Throughout our time together, I ask Stan to decide time and again what he wants from his therapy and to assess the degree to which our work together is resulting in his meeting his goals. As his therapist, I expect to be active, yet it is important that Stan provide the direction in which he wants to travel on his journey. If Stan has clear, specific, and concrete goals for each therapy session, he will be the one who determines what we explore in our sessions. Once I have a clear sense of the specific ways Stan wants to change how he is thinking, feeling, and acting, I am likely to take an active role in co-creating experiments with Stan that he can do both in the therapy sessions and on his own outside of our sessions.

Identifying Feelings

The person-centered approach stresses that one of the first stages in the therapy process involves identifying, clarifying, and learning how to express feelings. Because of the therapeutic relationship I have built with Stan, I expect him to feel increasingly free to mention feelings that he has kept to himself. In some cases these feelings are out of his awareness. Thus, I encourage Stan to talk about any feelings that are a source of difficulty. Again drawing on the person-centered model, I expect these feelings to be vague and difficult to identify at first.

During the early stages of our sessions, I rely on empathic listening. If I can really hear Stan's verbal and nonverbal messages, some of which may not be fully clear to him, I can respond to him in a way that lets him know that I have some appreciation for what it is like in his world. I need to do more than merely reflect what I hear him saying; I need to share with him my reactions as I listen to him. As I communicate to Stan that he is being deeply understood and accepted for the feelings he has, he has less need to deny or distort his feelings. His capacity for clearly identifying what he is feeling at any moment gradually increases.

There is a great deal of value in letting Stan tell his story in a way he chooses. The way he walks into the office, his gestures, his style of speech, the details he chooses to go into, and what he decides to relate and not to relate— to mention just a few elements—provide me with clues to his world. If I do too much structuring too soon and if I am too directive, I will interfere with his typical style of presenting himself. At this stage I agree with the Adlerians, who stress attending and listening on the counselor's part and who focus on the productive use of silence. Although I am not inclined to promote long silences early in counseling, there is value in not jumping in too soon when silences occur. Instead of coming to the rescue, it is better to explore the meanings of the silence.

Expressing and Exploring Feelings

My belief is that it is my authenticity as a person that encourages Stan to begin to identify and share with me a range of feelings. But I do not believe an open and trusting relationship between us is sufficient to change Stan's personality and behavior. I am convinced that I must also use my knowledge, skills, and experiences.

As a way of helping Stan express and explore his feelings, I draw heavily on Gestalt experiments. Eventually, I ask Stan to avoid merely talking about situations and about feelings. Rather, I encourage him to bring whatever reactions he is having into the present. For instance, if Stan reports feeling tense, I ask him *how* he experiences this tension and *where* it is located in his body. One of the best ways I have found to encourage clients to make contact with their feelings is to ask them to "be that feeling." Thus, if Stan has a knot in his stomach, he can intensify his feeling of tension by "becoming the knot, giving it voice and personality." If I notice that he has moist eyes, I may direct him to "be his tears now." By putting words to his tears, he avoids merely abstractly intellectualizing about all the reasons he is sad or tense. Before he can change his feelings, Stan must allow himself to *fully experience* these feelings. The experiential therapies give me valuable tools for guiding Stan to the expression of his feelings.

Here are some segments of our dialogue in a session where Stan becomes quite aware of what he is feeling as he talks about his relationship with his father:

Jerry: You mentioned that your father often compared you with your brother Frank and your sister Judy. What was that like for you?

Stan: I hated it! He told me that I'd never amount to anything.

Jerry: And when he said that, how did that affect you?

Stan: It made me feel that I could never measure up to all the great things that Judy and Frank were accomplishing. I felt like a failure. [*As he says this, he begins welling up with tears, and his voice changes.*]

Jerry: Stan, what are you experiencing now?

Stan: All of a sudden a wave of sadness is coming over me. I'm getting all choked up. Wow—this is heavy!

Jerry: Stay with what you're feeling in your body. What's going on?

Stan: My chest is tight, like something wants to come out.

Jerry: And what's there?

Stan: I'm feeling very sad and hurt.

Jerry: Would you be willing to try something? I'd like you to talk to me as though I were your father. Are you willing?

Stan: Well, you're not mean the way he was to me, but I can try.

Jerry: How old are you feeling now?

Stan: Oh, about 12 years old—just like when I had to be around him and listen to all the stuff he told me about how useless I was.

Jerry: Let yourself be 12 again, and tell me what it's like for you to be you— speaking to me as your father.

Stan: There was nothing that I could ever do that was good enough for you. No matter how hard I tried, I just couldn't get you to notice me. [*crying*] Why didn't I count, and why did you ignore me?

Jerry: Stan, I'll just let you talk for a while, and I'll listen. So keep on telling me all the things you may be feeling as that 12-year-old now.

Stan: All I ever wanted was to know that I mattered to you. But no matter how hard I tried, all you'd do was put me down. Nothing I ever did was worth anything. All you ever told me was that I could never do anything right. I just wanted you to love me. Why didn't you ever do anything with me? [*Stan stops talking and just cries for a while.*]

Jerry: What's happening with you now?

Stan: I'm just feeling so sad. As if it's hopeless. Nothing I can do will ever get his approval. And that hurts!

Jerry: At 12 it was important for you to get his acceptance and his love. There is still that part in you that wants his love.

Stan: Yeah, and I don't think there's much I can do now to get it.

Jerry: So, tell him more of what that's like.

Stan continues talking to his "father" and recounts some of the ways in which he tried to live up to his expectations. Stan lets him know that no matter what he did there was no way to get the acceptance that Frank and Judy got from him.

Jerry: Having said all that, what are you aware of now?

Stan: I'm feeling kind of embarrassed. I shouldn't have gotten so emotional and worked up over such a dumb thing.

Jerry: You say you're embarrassed. Whom are you aware of?

Stan: Well, right now of you. I'm such a wimp. You're probably thinking that I'm really weak and dumb for letting this get to me.

Jerry: Tell me more about feeling weak and dumb.

Stan expresses that he should be stronger and that he is afraid I'll think he is hopeless. He goes into some detail about putting himself down for what he has just experienced and expressed. I do not too quickly reassure him that he "shouldn't feel that way." Instead, I let him talk, for this is what he so often feels. After expressing many of the ways in which he is feeling embarrassed, he wonders if I still want to work with him. At this point I let him know that I respect his struggle and hope that he can eventually learn to avoid judging himself so harshly. Because this session is coming to an end, I talk with Stan about the value of releasing feelings that he has been carrying around for a long time, suggesting that this work is a good beginning. I am also interested in getting him to do some homework before the next session.

Jerry: Stan, I'd like to suggest that you write a letter to your father . . .

Stan [*interrupting*]: Oh no! I'm not going to give that guy the satisfaction of knowing that I need anything from him!

Jerry: Wait. I was about to say that I hope you'll write him a letter that you don't mail.

Stan: What's the point of a letter that won't be sent?

Jerry: Writing him a letter is an opportunity for further release and to gain some new insights. I hope you'll let yourself write about all the ways you tried to live up to his expectations. Let him know what it felt like to be you when you were around him. Tell him more about you, especially how you felt in not getting those things that you so much wanted.

Stan: OK, I'll do it if you think it might help.

In this session I might have made many different interventions. For the moment, I chose to let him "borrow my eyes" and talk to me as his father while he was 12 years old. I asked him to stay with whatever he was experiencing, paying particular attention to his body and to the emotions that were welling up in him. I see therapeutic value in letting Stan identify and express his feelings. It is premature to suggest problem-solving strategies or to attempt to figure everything out. My intent in offering him the homework assignment of writing a letter was to promote further work during the week. Writing the letter may trigger memories, and he may experience further emotional release. I hope this will help Stan begin thinking about the influence his father had on him then and also now.

At our next session I will ask Stan if he wrote the letter and, if he did, what it was like for him to do so. What was he feeling and thinking as he was writing to his father? How was he affected when he read the letter later? Is there anything that he wants to share with me? The direction of our next session could depend on his response. Again, Stan will provide clues to where we need to go next.

Working With Stan's Past, Present, and Future

DEALING WITH THE PAST   Reality therapy, behavior therapy, and rational emotive behavior therapy do not place much emphasis on the client's history. Their rationale is that early childhood experiences do not necessarily have much to do with the maintenance of present ineffective behavior. My inclination, in contrast, is to give weight to understanding, exploring, and working with Stan's early history and to connect his past with what he is doing today. My view is that themes running through our life can become evident if we come to terms with significant turning points in our childhood. The use of an Adlerian lifestyle questionnaire would indicate some of these themes that originate from Stan's childhood. The psychoanalytic approach, of course, emphasizes uncovering and reexperiencing traumas in early childhood, working through the places where we have become "stuck," and resolving unconscious conflicts.

Although I agree that Stan's childhood experiences were influential in contributing to his present personality (including his ways of thinking, feeling, and behaving), it does not make sense to me to assume that these factors have *determined* him. I favor the Gestalt approach of having Stan bring his "toxic introjects" to the surface by dealing in the here-and-now with people in his life with whom he feels unfinished. This can be accomplished by fantasy exercises and a variety of role-playing techniques. In these ways Stan's past comes intensely to life in the present moment of our sessions.

DEALING WITH THE PRESENT   Being interested in Stan's past does not mean that we get lost in history or that we dwell on reliving traumatic situations. In fact, by paying attention to what is going on in the here-and-now of the counseling session, I get excellent clues to what is unfinished for him in his past. There is no need to go on digging expeditions, because the present is rich with material. He and I can direct attention to his immediate feelings as well as to his thoughts and actions. It seems essential to me that we work with all three dimensions—what he is thinking, what he is actually doing, and how his thoughts and behaviors affect his feeling states. Again, by directing Stan's attention to what is going on with him during our sessions, I can show him how he interacts in his world apart from therapy.

DEALING WITH THE FUTURE   Adlerians are especially interested in where the client is heading. Humans are pulled by goals, strivings, and aspirations. It would help to know what Stan's goals in life are. What are his intentions? What does he want for himself? If he decides that his present behavior is not getting him what he wants, he is in a good position to think ahead about the changes he would like and what he can do *now* to actualize his aspirations. The present-oriented behavioral focus of reality therapy is a good reference point for getting Stan to dream about what he would like to say about his life 5 years hence. Connecting present behavior with future plans is an excellent device for helping Stan formulate a concrete plan of action. He will have to actually *create* his future.

The Thinking Dimension in Therapy

Once Stan has gotten in touch with some intense feelings and perhaps experienced catharsis (release of pent-up feelings), some cognitive work is essential. Stan needs to be able to experience his feelings fully, and he may need to express them in symbolic ways. This may include getting out his anger toward women by hitting a pillow and by saying angry things that he has never allowed himself to say. Eventually Stan needs to begin to make sense of the emotional range of material that is surfacing.

To bring in this cognitive dimension, I focus Stan's attention on messages he incorporated as a child and on the decisions he made. I get him to think about the reason he made certain early decisions. Finally, I challenge Stan to look at these decisions about life, about himself, and about others and to make necessary revisions that can lead him to getting on with his living.

After getting basic information about Stan's life history (by means of the Adlerian lifestyle assessment form), I summarize and interpret it. For example, I find some connections between his present fears of developing intimate relationships and his history of rejection by his siblings and his parents. Thus, I am interested in his family constellation and his early recollections. Rather than working exclusively with his feelings, I want Stan to begin to understand (cognitively) how these early experiences affected him then and how they still influence him today. I concur with the Adlerians in their therapeutic interest in identifying and exploring basic mistakes. Here my emphasis is on having Stan begin to question the conclusions he came to about himself, others, and life. What is his private logic? What are some of his mistaken, self-defeating perceptions that grew out of his family experiences? An Adlerian perspective provides tools for doing some productive cognitive work both in and out of the therapy sessions.

From rational emotive behavior therapy I especially value the emphasis on learning to think rationally. I look for the ways in which Stan contributes to his negative feelings by the process of self-indoctrination with irrational beliefs. I get him to really test the validity of the dire consequences he predicts. I value the stress put on doing hard work in demolishing beliefs that have no validity and replacing them with sound and rational beliefs. I do not think Stan can merely think his way through life or that examining his faulty logic is enough by itself for personality change. But I do see this process as an essential component of therapy.

The cognitive behavioral therapies have a range of cognitive techniques that can help Stan recognize connections between his cognitions and his behaviors. He should also learn about his inner dialogue and the impact it has on his day-to-day behavior. Eventually, our goal is some cognitive restructuring work by which Stan can learn new ways to think, new things to tell himself, and new assumptions about life. This provides a basis for change in his behavior.

I have given Stan a number of homework assignments aimed at helping him identify a range of feelings and thoughts that may be problematic for him. In several of our sessions Stan has talked about messages he picked up about himself through his family. We have explored some specific beliefs he holds about himself, and he is beginning to recognize how his thinking processes are influencing the way he feels and what he is doing. Here are some sample pieces of a session in which we focus on his cognitions.

Jerry: Several times now you've brought up how you're sure you'd be judged critically if you allowed yourself to get close to a woman. Is this a topic you want to explore in more depth?

Stan: For sure. I'm tired of avoiding women, but I'm still too scared of approaching a woman. Part of me wants to meet a woman, and the other part of me wants to run. I'm convinced that if any woman gets to know me, she'll eventually reject me.

Jerry: Really, any woman will reject you? Have you checked out this assumption? How many women have you approached, and how many of them have actually rejected you?

Stan: Well, it's not that bad! They never tell me these things. But in my head I keep telling myself that if they get to know the real me they'll be turned off by my weakness and then they wouldn't want anything to do with me.

Jerry: How about telling me some of the things you tell yourself when you think of meeting a woman? Just let yourself go for a while, listing out loud some of the statements you make to yourself internally. Ready?

Stan: So often I say to myself that I'm not worth knowing. [*pause*]

Jerry: Just rattle off as many of these self-statements as you can. Don't worry about how it sounds. Rehearse out loud some of the familiar self-talk that keeps you from doing what you want.

Stan: What a nerd! Every time you open your mouth, you put your foot in it. Why don't you just shut up and hide in the corner? When you do talk to people, you always freeze up. They're judging you, and if you say much of anything, they'll find out what a jerk you are! You're a complete and utter failure. Anything you try, you fail in. There's not much in you that anybody would find interesting. You're stupid, boring, weak, and a scared kid. Why don't you keep to yourself so that others won't have a chance to reject you?

Stan continues with this list, and I listen. After he seems finished, I tell him how I'm affected by hearing his typical self-talk. I let him know that it saddens me to see how hard he is on himself. Although I like Stan, I don't have the sense that he will emotionally believe that I care about him. I let him know that I respect the way he doesn't run from his fears and that I like his willingness to talk openly about his troubles.

Stan has acquired a wide range of critical internal dialogues that he has practiced for many years. My hope is that he will begin to challenge those thoughts that are unfounded, that he will discover the nature of his faulty thinking, and that eventually he will restructure some of his beliefs. Along this line, I work with him to pinpoint specific beliefs and then do my best to get him to come up with evidence to support or refute them. I am influenced by the constructivist trend in cognitive behavior therapy. Applied to Stan, constructivism holds that his subjective framework and interpretations are far more important than the objective bases that may be at the origin of his faulty beliefs. Thus, rather than imposing my version of what may constitute faulty, irrational, and dysfunctional beliefs on his part, I pursue a line of Socratic questioning whereby I get Stan to evaluate his own thinking processes and his conclusions.

Jerry: Let's take one statement that you've made a number of times: "When I'm with other people, I feel stupid most of the time." What goes on within you when you say this?

Stan: It's like I hear critical voices, almost like people are in my head or are sitting on my shoulder.

Jerry: Name one person who often sits on your shoulder and tells you you're stupid.

Stan: My dad, for one. I hear his voice in my head a lot.

Jerry: Let me be Stan for a moment, and you be your dad, saying to me some of those critical things that you hear him saying inside your head.

Stan: Why are you going to college? Why don't you quit and give your seat to someone who deserves it? You always were a bad student. You're just wasting your time and the taxpayers' money by pretending to be a college student. Do yourself a favor and wake up to the fact that you'll always be a dumb kid.

Jerry: How much truth is there in what you just said as your dad?

Stan: You know, it sounds stupid that I let that old guy convince me that I'm totally stupid.

Jerry: Instead of saying that you're stupid for letting him tell you that you're stupid, can you give yourself credit for being smart enough to come to this realization?

Stan: OK, but he's right that I've failed at most of the things I've tried.

Jerry: Does failing at a task mean that you're right holding to the label of being a failure in life? I'd like to hear you produce the evidence that supports your interpretation of being stupid and of being a failure.

Stan: How about the failure in my marriage? I couldn't make it work, and I was responsible for the divorce. That's a pretty big failure.

Jerry: And were you totally responsible for the divorce? Did your wife have any part in it?

Stan: She always told me that no woman could ever live with me. She convinced me that I couldn't have a satisfying relationship with her or any other woman.

Jerry: Although she could speak for herself, I'm wondering what qualifies her to determine your future with all women. Tell me what study was conducted that proves that Stan is utterly destined to be allergic to all women forever.

Stan: I suppose I just bought into what she told me. After all, if I couldn't live with her, what makes me think I could have a satisfying life with any woman?

At this point, there are many directions in which I could go with Stan to explore the origin of his beliefs and to assess the validity of his interpretations about life situations and his conclusions about his basic worth. In this and other sessions, we explore what cognitive therapists call "cognitive distortions." Here are some of Stan's cognitive distortions:

- *Arbitrary inferences.* Stan makes conclusions without supporting and relevant evidence. He often engages in "catastrophizing," or thinking about the worst possible scenario for a given situation.
- *Overgeneralization.* Stan holds extreme beliefs based on a single incident and applies them inappropriately to other dissimilar events or settings. For instance, because he and his wife divorced, he is convinced he is destined to be a failure with any woman.
- *Personalization.* Stan has a tendency to relate external events to himself, even when there is no basis for making this connection. He relates an incident in which a female classmate did not show up for a lunch date. He agonized over this event and convinced himself that she would have been humiliated to be seen in his presence. He did not consider any other possible explanations for her absence.

- *Labeling and mislabeling.* Stan presents himself in light of his imperfections and mistakes. He allows his past failures to define his total being.
- *Polarized thinking.* Stan frequently engages in thinking and interpreting in all-or-nothing terms. Through this process of dichotomous thinking, he has created self-defeating labels and boxes that keep him restricted.

Over a number of sessions we work on specific beliefs. The aim is for Stan to critically evaluate the evidence for many of his conclusions. My role is to promote corrective experiences that will lead to changes in his thinking. I am striving to create a collaborative relationship, one in which he will discover for himself how to distinguish between functional and dysfunctional beliefs. He can learn this by testing his conclusions.

Doing: Another Essential Component of Therapy

Stan can spend countless hours gathering interesting insights about why he is the way he is. He can learn to express feelings that he kept inside for many years. And he can think about the things he tells himself that lead to defeat. Yet in my view feeling and thinking are not a complete therapy process. *Doing* is a way of bringing these feelings and thoughts together by applying them to real-life situations in various action programs. I am indebted to Adlerian therapy, behavior therapy, reality therapy, rational emotive behavior therapy, and solution-focused brief therapy, all of which give central emphasis to the role of action as a prerequisite for change.

Behavior therapy offers a multitude of techniques for behavioral change. In Stan's case I am especially inclined to work with him in developing self-management programs. For example, Stan complains of often feeling tense and anxious. Daily relaxation procedures are one way Stan can gain more control of his physical and psychological tension. Perhaps by a combination of meditation and relaxation procedures he can get himself centered before he goes to his classes, meets women, or talks to friends. He can also begin to monitor his behavior in everyday situations to gain increased awareness of what he tells himself, what he does, and then how he feels. When Stan gets depressed, he tends to drink to alleviate his symptoms. He can carry a small notebook with him and actually record events that lead up to his feeling depressed (or anxious or hurt). He might also record what he actually did in these situations and what he might have done differently. By paying attention to what he is doing in daily life, he is already beginning to gain more control of his behavior.

This behavioral monitoring can be coupled with both Adlerian and cognitive approaches. My guess is that Stan gets depressed, engages in self-destructive behavior (drinking, for one), and then feels even worse. I work very much on both his behaviors and cognitions and show him how many of his actions are influenced by what he is telling himself. For example, Stan wants to go out and apply for a job but is afraid that he might "mess up" in the interview and not get the job. This is an ideal time to use behavioral rehearsal. Together we work on how he is setting himself up for failure by his self-defeating expectations. True to the spirit of rational emotive behavior therapy, we explore his faulty assumptions that he *must* be perfect and that if he does not get the job, life will be unbearable. There are many opportunities to help Stan see connections between his cognitive processes and his daily behavior. I encourage Stan to begin to behave differently and then look for changes in his feeling states and his thinking.

With this in mind I ask Stan to think of as many ways as possible of actually bringing into his daily living the new learning he is acquiring in our sessions. Practice is essential. Homework assignments (preferably ones that he could give himself) are an excellent way for Stan to become an active agent in his therapy. He must do something himself for change to occur. I hope that he sees that the degree to which he will change is directly proportional to his willingness to get out in life and experiment. I want Stan to learn from his new behavior in life. Thus, each week we discuss his progress toward meeting his goals and review how well he is completing his assignments. If he does not like the way he carried out an assignment, we can use this as an opportunity to talk about how he can adjust his behavior. I am firm about expecting a commitment from him that he have an action plan for change and that he continually look at how well his plan is working.

I am very interested in what Stan is doing and how his thoughts and emotions are affecting this behavior. In the following dialogue, our interchanges deal primarily with Stan learning a more assertive style of behavior with one of his professors. Although this session focuses on Stan's behavior, we are also dealing with what he is thinking and feeling. These three dimensions are interactive.

Jerry: Last week we role-played different ways you could approach a professor with whom you were having difficulty. You learned several assertive skills that you used quite effectively when I assumed the role of the critical professor. Before you left last week, you agreed to set up a time to meet with your professor and let her know how she affects you. When we did the role playing, you were very clear about what you wanted to say and strong in staying with your feelings. Did you carry out your plan?

Stan: The next day I tried to talk to her before class. She said she didn't have time to talk but that we could talk after class.

Jerry: And how did that go?

Stan: After class all I wanted to do was make an appointment with her so that I could talk in private and without feeling hurried. When I tried to make the appointment, she very brusquely said that she had to go to a meeting and that I should see her during her office hours.

Jerry: How did that affect you?

Stan: I was mad. All I wanted to do was make an appointment.

Jerry: Did you go to her office hours?

Stan: I did, that very afternoon. She was 20 minutes late for her office hours, and then a bunch of students were waiting to ask her questions. All I got to do was make an appointment with her in a couple of days.

Jerry: Did that appointment actually take place?

Stan: Yes, but she was 10 minutes late and seemed preoccupied. I had a hard time at the beginning.

Jerry: How so? Tell me more.

Stan: I feel stupid in her class, and I wanted to talk to her about it. When I ask questions, she gets a funny look on her face—as if she's impatient and hopes I'll shut up.

Jerry: Did you check out these assumptions with her?

Stan: Yes I did, and I feel proud of myself. She told me that at times she does get a bit impatient because I seem to need a lot of her time and reassurance. Then I let her know how much I was studying for her class and how serious I was about doing well in my major. It was good for me to challenge my fears, instead of avoiding her because I felt she was judgmental.

Jerry: It's good to hear you give yourself credit for the steps you took. Even though it was tough, you hung in there and said what you wanted to say. Is there anything about this exchange with her that you wish you could have changed?

Stan: For the most part, I was pretty assertive. Generally, I blame people in authority like her for making me feel stupid. I give them a lot of power in judging me. But this time I remembered what we worked on in our session, and I stayed focused on myself rather than telling her what she was doing or not doing.

Jerry: How did that go?

Stan: The more I talked about myself, the less defensive she became. I learned that I don't need to give all my power away and that I can still feel good about myself, even if the other person doesn't change.

Jerry: Great! Did you notice any difference in how you felt in her class after you had this talk?

Stan: For a change, I didn't feel so self-conscious, especially when I asked questions or took part in class discussions. I was not so concerned about what she might think about me.

Jerry: What did your meeting with her teach you about yourself?

Stan: For one thing, I'm learning to check out my assumptions. That frees me up to act much more spontaneously. Also, I learned that I could be clear, direct, and assertive without getting nasty. It was possible for me to take care of myself without being critical of her. Normally, I'd just swallow all my feelings and walk away feeling dumb. This time I could be assertive and was able to let her know that I needed some unhurried time from her.

Practicing assertive behavior is associated with working with the feeling and thinking domains. Had Stan not done as well as he did in engaging his professor, we could have examined what had gone wrong from his vantage point.

We could have continued role-playing various approaches in our sessions, and then with new knowledge and skills and more practice, he could have tried again. If Stan hopes to make the changes he desires, it is essential that he be willing to experiment with new ways of acting, especially outside of the therapy sessions. In a sense, counseling is like a dress rehearsal for living. Stan exhibited courage and determination in carrying out a specific action plan, which is a catalyst for change.

Working Toward Revised Decisions

When Stan has identified and explored both his feelings and his faulty beliefs and thinking processes, it does not mean that therapy is over. Becoming aware of early decisions, including some of his basic mistakes and his self-defeating ideas, is the starting point for change. It is essential that Stan find ways to translate his emotional and cognitive insights into new ways of thinking, feeling, and behaving. Therefore, as much as possible I structure situations in the therapy sessions that will facilitate new decisions on his part on both the emotional and cognitive levels. In encouraging Stan to make these new decisions, I draw on cognitive, emotive, and behavioral techniques. A few techniques I might employ are role playing, fantasy and imagery, assertion training procedures, and behavioral rehearsals. Both reality therapy and Adlerian therapy have a lot to offer on getting clients to decide on a plan of action and then make a commitment to carry out their program for change.

Here are some examples of experiments I suggest for Stan during the therapy sessions and homework assignments. They are geared to helping him apply what he is learning to situations in everyday life.

- I engage in a number of reverse role-playing situations in which I "become" Stan and have Stan assume the role of his mother, father, former wife, sister, older brother, and a professor. Through this process Stan gets a clearer picture of ways in which he allowed others to define him, and he acquires some skills in arguing back to self-defeating voices.
- To help Stan deal with his anxiety, I teach him relaxation methods and encourage him to practice them daily. Stan learns to employ these relaxation strategies in anxiety-arousing situations. I also teach him a range of coping skills, such as assertiveness and disputing irrational beliefs. Stan is able to apply these skills in several life situations.
- Stan agrees to keep a journal in which he records impressions and experiences. After encountering difficult situations, he writes about his reactions, both on a thinking and a feeling level. He also records how he behaved in these situations, how he felt about his actions, and how he might have behaved differently. He also agrees to read a few self-help books in areas that are particularly problematic for him.

- As a homework assignment, I urge Stan to meet with people whom he would typically avoid. For instance, he is highly anxious over his performance in a couple of his classes. He accepts my nudging to make an appointment with each professor to discuss his progress. In one case, a professor takes an increased interest in him, and he does very well in her class. In the other case, the professor is rather abrupt and not too helpful. Stan is able to recognize that this is more the professor's problem than anything he is doing wrong.

- Stan wants to put himself in situations where he can make new friends. We work on a clear plan of action that involves joining a club, going to social events on campus, and asking a woman in his class for a date. Although he is anxious in each of these situations, he follows through with his plans. In our sessions we explore some of his self-talk and actions at these events.

Encouraging Stan to Work With His Family of Origin

After working with Stan for a short time, I suggest that he take the initiative to invite his entire family for a session. My assumption is that many of his problems stem from his family-of-origin experiences and that he is still being affected by these experiences. I think it will be useful to have at least one session with the family so that I can get a better idea of the broader context. The following dialogue illustrates my attempt to introduce this idea to Stan:

Jerry: Our sessions are certainly revealing a good deal of unfinished business with several members of your family. I think it would be useful to bring in as many of them as you can for a session.

Stan: No way! I'm not going to jump in that snake pit.

Jerry: Are you willing to talk with me more about this idea?

Stan: I'll talk, but it won't do any good.

Jerry: What stops you from asking them?

Stan: They already think I'm nutty as a fruitcake, and if they find out I'm seeing a psychologist, that's just one more thing they can throw in my face.

Jerry: You think they'd use this against you?

Stan: Yep. Besides, I can't see how getting my family together is going to help much. My mother and father don't think they have any problems. I don't see them wanting to change much.

Jerry: I wasn't thinking of their changing but more of giving you a chance to say directly some of the things you've said about them in your sessions with me. It might help you gain clarity about how you are with them.

Stan: Maybe, but I'm not ready for that one yet!

Jerry: OK, I can respect that you don't feel ready yet. I hope you'll remain open to this idea, and if you change your mind, let me know.

My rationale for including at least some of Stan's family members is to provide him with a context for understanding how his behavior is being influenced by what he learned as a child. He is a part of this system, and as he changes, it is bound to influence others in his family with whom he has contact. From what he has told me, I am assuming that he has unclear boundaries with his mother that have an impact on his relationships with other women. He is convinced that if he gets close to a woman she will swallow him up. If he can gain a clearer understanding of his relationship with his mother, he may be able to apply some of these insights with other women. In many ways Stan has allowed himself to be intimidated by his father, and he still hears Dad's voice in his head. In much of his present behavior, Stan compares himself unfavorably with others, which is a pattern he established in early childhood with his siblings. If he is able to begin dealing with the members of his family about some of his past and present pain, there is a good chance that he will be able to free himself of emotional barriers that are preventing him from forming those intimate relationships that he says he would like to have in his life. (For a more complete description of working with Stan from a family systems perspective, see Stan's case in Chapter 14.)

The Spiritual Dimension

Although I do not have an agenda to impose religious or spiritual values on Stan, I want to assess the role spirituality plays, if any, in his life currently— and to assess beliefs, attitudes, and practices from his earlier years. When I ask Stan if religion was a factor in his childhood or adolescence, he informs me that his mother was a practicing Lutheran and his father was rather indifferent to religion. His mother made sure that Stan went to church each week. Stan lets me know that mainly what he remembers from his church experiences is feeling a sense of guilt that he was not good enough and that he was always missing the mark of being a decent person. Stan recalls that his attitudes about religion fit in with his low self-esteem. Not only was he not good enough in the eyes of his parents, but he was also not good enough for God. Stan also adds that when he went to college he developed a new interest in spirituality as a result of a course he took in world religion.

Although formal religion does not seem to play a key role for Stan now, he is struggling to find his place in the universe. He reports that he would like to find a spiritual core as this is a missing dimension in his life. Stan also lets me know that he is pleasantly surprised that I am even mentioning religion and spirituality. He was under the impression that counselors would not be too interested in these areas. Stan would like to find meaning in life, and he indicates that he wants to have a clearer sense of the role of spirituality in his life. Upon further discussion of this area, Stan informs me of his intention to bring up his concerns about his spiritual life at a future session.

Working With Stan's Drinking Problem

Although each of the 11 therapeutic approaches address drug and alcohol abuse in different ways, all probably agree that it is imperative at some point in Stan's therapy to confront him on the probability that he is a chemically dependent person. In this section I describe my approach to working with his dependence as well as giving some brief background information on the alcoholic personality and on treatment approaches.

SOME BASIC ASSUMPTIONS
Stan has given me a number of significant clues suggesting that he may be a chemically dependent person. From the information he has provided, it is clear that Stan has many of the personality traits typically found in alcoholics, including low self-concept, anxiety, sexual dysfunctions, underachievement, feelings of social isolation, inability to love himself or to receive love from others, hypersensitivity, impulsivity, dependence, fear of failure, feelings of guilt, self-pity, and suicidal impulses. In addition, he has used drugs and alcohol as a way of blunting anxiety and attempting to control what he perceives as a painful reality. He has switched from drugs to alcohol, which is a common attempt to control the disastrous effects of addiction.

Once our therapeutic relationship is firmly established, I confront Stan (in a caring and concerned manner) on his self-deception that he is doing something positive by not getting loaded with drugs but is merely getting drunk. He needs to see that alcohol *is* a drug, and I want him to make an honest evaluation of his behavior so that he can recognize the degree to which his drinking is interfering in his living. Although Stan resorts to excuses, rationalizations, denials, distortions, and minimizations about his drinking patterns, I provide some information he can use to examine his confused system of beliefs. Johns Hopkins University Hospital in Baltimore has designed a questionnaire that is useful in assessing the preliminary signs of alcohol addiction. A few questions are:

- Have you lost time from work due to drinking?
- Do you drink to escape from worries?
- Do you drink to build up your self-confidence?
- Have you ever felt remorse after drinking?
- Do you drink because you're shy with other people?
- Does drinking cause you to have difficulty sleeping?

From what I already know of Stan, it is likely that he will answer yes to several of these questions if he responded honestly. "Yes" answers to even one or two of these questions indicate enough of a problem to warrant further assessment for chemical dependency.

A SUPPLEMENTARY TREATMENT PROGRAM
Stan eventually recognizes and acknowledges that he does indeed have a problem with alcoholism, and he says he is willing to do something about this problem. I tell him that alcoholism is considered by most substance abuse experts to be a disease in itself, rather than a symptom of another underlying disorder. It is a chronic condition that can be treated, and it is a progressive disorder that eventually results in death

if it is not arrested. It will be helpful for Stan to know that long-term recovery is based on the principle of total abstinence from all drugs and alcohol and that such abstinence is a prerequisite to effective counseling. In addition to his weekly individual therapy sessions with me, I provide Stan with a referral to deal with his chemical dependence.

I encourage Stan to join Alcoholics Anonymous and attend their meetings. The 12-step program of AA has worked very well for many alcoholics. It is not a substitute for therapy, but it can be an ideal supplement. Once Stan understands the nature of his chemical dependence and no longer uses drugs, the chances are greatly increased that we can focus on the other aspects of his life that he sees as problematic and would like to change. In short, it is possible to treat his alcoholism and at the same time carry out a program of individual therapy geared to changing Stan's ways of thinking, feeling, and behaving.

Moving Toward Termination of Therapy

The process I have been describing will probably take months. During this time, I will continue to draw simultaneously on a variety of therapeutic systems in working with Stan's thoughts, feelings, and behaviors. Although I have described these three dimensions separately in the examples, I tend to work in an integrated fashion among the dimensions as well. Eventually this process will lead to a time when Stan can continue what he has learned in therapy without my assistance.

Termination of therapy is as important as the initial phase, for now the challenge is to put into practice what he has learned in the sessions by applying new skills and attitudes to daily social situations. When Stan brings up a desire to "go it alone," we talk about his readiness to end therapy and his reasons for thinking about termination. I also share with him my perceptions of the directions I have seen him take. This is a good time to talk about where he can go from here. Together we spend a few sessions developing an action plan and talking about how he can best maintain his new learning. He may want to join a therapeutic group. He could find support in a variety of social networks. In essence, he can continue to challenge himself by doing things that are difficult for him yet at the same time broaden his range of choices. Stan might take some dancing classes, an activity he has previously avoided out of a fear of failing. Now he can take the risk and be his own therapist, dealing with feelings as they arise in new situations.

In a behavioral spirit, evaluating the process and outcomes of therapy seems essential. This evaluation can take the form of devoting a session or two to discussing Stan's specific changes in therapy. A few questions for focus are: "What stands out the most for you, Stan? What did you learn that you consider the most valuable? How did you learn these lessons? What can you do now to keep practicing new behaviors that work better for you than the old patterns? What will you do if you experience setbacks? How will you handle any regression to old ways or temporary defeats?" With this last question it is helpful for Stan to know that his termination of formal therapy does not mean that he cannot return for a visit or session when he considers it appropriate. Rather than coming for weekly sessions, Stan might well decide to come in at irregular intervals for a "checkup." Of course, he will be the person to decide what new areas to explore in these follow-up sessions.

Encouraging Stan to Join a Therapy Group

As Stan and I talk about termination, he gives me clear indications that he has learned a great deal about himself through individual counseling. Although Stan has been applying his learning to difficult situations that he encounters, I believe he would benefit from a group experience. I suggest that Stan consider joining a 16-week therapy group that will begin in 2 months.

To me, progressing from individual therapy to a group seems useful for a client like Stan. Because many of his problems are interpersonal, a group is an ideal place for him to deal with them. The group will give Stan a context for practicing the very behaviors he says he wants to acquire. Stan wants to feel freer in being himself, to feel easier in approaching people, and to be able to trust people more fully. He realizes that he has made gains in these areas, yet he has some distance to travel. In addition to a group experience, I will be working with Stan in the final phases of his therapy to find some other steps he can take to continue his growth. Together we will make plans for putting him into situations that will foster change. He might take skiing lessons, attend more parties, engage in volunteer work with children, or continue writing in his journal.

Commentary on the Thinking, Feeling, and Doing Perspective

In applying my integrated perspective to Stan, I've dealt separately with the cognitive, affective, and behavioral dimensions of human experience. Although the steps I outline may appear relatively structured and even simple, actually working with clients is more complex and less predictable. If you are practicing from an integrative perspective, it would be a mistake to assume that it is best to always begin working with what clients are thinking (or feeling or doing). Effective counseling begins where the client is, not where a theory indicates a client should be.

Applied to Stan, a person-centered focus takes into account factors such as his cultural background, his presenting problem, what he says he needs and wants at the initial session, and the clues he gives both verbally and nonverbally. I began by exploring his feelings because he teared up as he was talking, and it was evident that he had a need to express feelings that had been bottled up for years. Some clients might leave counseling never to return if I attempted to call attention to their feelings at the initial session. Feelings might be too threatening for them, and in such situations it might be more appropriate to focus on underlying assumptions or thoughts. For others, a proper launching point might be what they are actually doing, with a discussion of how well it is working for them. By paying attention to the client's energy (or blocked energy), therapists have many clues about where to begin. If the client resists, dealing with the resistance in a respectful way could open other doors.

In summary, depending on what clients need at the moment, I may focus initially on what they are thinking and how this is affecting them, or I may focus on how they feel, or I may choose to direct them to pay attention to what they are doing. Because these facets of human experience are interrelated, one route generally leads to exploring the other dimensions. Thus, I frequently ask a client: "What are you aware of now?" or "What are you experiencing now?" If they say "I'm thinking that . . . ," I may follow that path and ask them to say more about what they are thinking. If they say "I'm feeling a tightness in my chest and . . . ," I am likely to ask them to stay with their bodily sensations for a bit longer and see where that leads them. If they say "What I'm doing is . . . ," I generally encourage them to tell me more about how well their actions are serving them. If they say "I'm feeling lonely and frightened . . . ," I may encourage them to stay with their feelings and talk more about what it is like to experience these feelings.

A person-centered focus respects the wisdom within the client and uses it as a lead for where to go next. My guess is that counselors often make the mistake of getting too far ahead of their clients, thinking, "What should I do next?" By staying with our clients and asking them what they want, we do not need to assume too much responsibility by deciding for them the direction in which they should be heading. Instead, we can learn to pay attention to our own reactions to our clients and to our own energy. By doing so we can engage in a therapeutic dance that is exciting for both parties in the relationship.

Follow-Up: You Continue Working With Stan in an Integrative Style

Think about these questions to help you decide how to counsel Stan from your own integrative approach:

- What themes in Stan's life do you find most significant, and how might you draw on these themes during the initial phase of counseling?
- What specific concepts from the various theoretical orientations would you be most inclined to utilize in your work with Stan?
- Identify some key techniques from the various therapies that you are most likely to employ in your therapy with Stan. What are a few cognitive techniques you'd probably use? emotive techniques? behavioral techniques? What are some interventions you would draw from feminist therapy? postmodern therapies? family therapy?
- How might you invent experiments for Stan to carry out both inside and outside the therapy sessions? How are you likely to present these experiments to him?

- As you were reading about the integrative perspective, what ideas did you have about continuing as Stan's counselor?
- Knowing what you do about Stan, what do you imagine it would be like to be his therapist? What problems, if any, might you expect to encounter in your counseling relationship with him?
- What are your thoughts about ways in which you could pay attention to working with Stan from a thinking, feeling, and behaving perspective? What modalities might you emphasize?

 ## WHERE TO GO FROM HERE

At the beginning of the introductory course in counseling, my students typically express two reactions: "How will I ever be able to learn all these theories?" and "How can I make sense out of this mass of knowledge?" By the end of the course, these students are often surprised by how much work they have done *and* by how much they have learned. Although an introductory survey course will not turn students into accomplished counselors, it generally provides the basis for selecting from among the many models to which they are exposed.

At this point you may be able to begin putting the theories together in some meaningful way for yourself. This book will have served its central purpose if it has encouraged you to read further and to expand your knowledge of the theories that most caught your interest. I hope you have made friends with some theories that were unknown to you before and that you have seen something of value that you can use from each of the approaches described. You will not be in a position to conceptualize a completely developed integrative perspective after your first course in counseling theory, but you now have the tools to begin the process of integration. With additional study and practical experience, you will be able to expand and refine your emerging personal philosophy of counseling.

Finally, the book will have been put to good use if it has stimulated and challenged you to think about the ways in which your philosophy of life, your values, your life experiences, and the person you are becoming are vitally related to the caliber of counselor you can become and to the impact you can have on those who establish a relationship with you personally and professionally. This book and your course may have raised questions for you regarding your decision to become a counselor. If this is the case, I encourage you to seek out at least one of your professors to explore these questions.

Now that you have finished this book, I would be very interested in hearing about your experience with it and with your course. The comments readers have sent me over the years have been helpful in revising each edition, and I welcome your feedback. You can write to me in care of Thomson Brooks/Cole, Belmont, California 94002, or you can complete the reaction sheet at the end of the book and mail it to me.

Author Index

Subject Index

TO THE OWNER OF THIS BOOK:

I hope that you have found *Theory and Practice of Counseling and Psychotherapy,* Seventh Edition, useful. So that this book can be improved in a future edition, would you take the time to complete this sheet and return it? Thank you.

School and address:_____

Department:_____

Instructor's name:_____

1. What I like most about this book is:_____

   _____

   _____

2. What I like least about this book is:

   _____

   _____

3. My general reaction to this book is:

   _____

   _____

4. The name of the course in which I used this book is:

   _____

5. Were all of the chapters of the book assigned for you to read?_____

   If not, which ones weren't?_____

6. In the space below, or on a separate sheet of paper, please write specific suggestions for improving this book and anything else you'd care to share about your experience in using this book.

   _____

   _____

   _____

   _____

THOMSON
™
BROOKS/COLE

NO POSTAGE
NECESSARY
IF MAILED
IN THE
UNITED STATES

FOLD HERE

OPTIONAL:

Your name: _____ Date: _____

May we quote you, either in promotion for *Theory and Practice of Counseling and Psychotherapy*, Seventh Edition, or in future publishing ventures?

Yes: _____ No: _____

Sincerely yours,

Gerald Corey